JCDL 2003

Proceedings

2003 Joint Conference on Digital Libraries

May 27-31, 2003

Rice University

Houston, Texas USA

Edited by

Catherine C. Marshall, Geneva Henry, and Lois Delcambre

Sponsored by

IEEE Technical Committee on Digital Libraries (TCDL)

ACM SIGIR

ACM SIGWEB

In cooperation with

The Coalition for Networked Information (CNI)

DELOS

American Society for Information, Science and Technology (ASIST)

Los Alamitos, California

Washington   •   Brussels   •   Tokyo

IEEE Computer Society Order Number PR01939
ACM Order Number 606032
ISBN 0-7695-1939-3
Library of Congress Number 2003104416

Additional copies may be ordered from:

IEEE Computer Society	IEEE Service Center	IEEE Computer Society
Customer Service Center	445 Hoes Lane	Asia/Pacific Office
10662 Los Vaqueros Circle	P.O. Box 1331	Watanabe Bldg., 1-4-2
P.O. Box 3014	Piscataway, NJ 08855-1331	Minami-Aoyama
Los Alamitos, CA 90720-1314	Tel: + 1 732 981 0060	Minato-ku, Tokyo 107-0062
Tel: + 1 800 272 6657	Fax: + 1 732 981 9667	JAPAN
Fax: + 1 714 821 4641	http://shop.ieee.org/store/	Tel: + 81 3 3408 3118
http://computer.org/cspress	customer-service@ieee.org	Fax: + 81 3 3408 3553
csbooks@computer.org		tokyo.ofc@computer.org

ACM Order Department, P.O. Box 11414, New York, NY 10286-1414
Tel: +1-800-342-6626 (USA and Canada); Tel: +1-212-626-0500 (All other countries); Fax: +1-212-944-1318;
acmhelp@acm.org

Individual paper REPRINTS may be ordered at: reprints@computer.org

Editorial production by Danielle Martin

Cover art production by Joe Daigle/Studio Productions

Printed in the United States of America by The Printing House

Table of Contents

2003 Joint Conference on Digital Libraries (JCDL 2003)

Session 1: Opening Keynote

James Boyle, William Neal Reynolds Professor of Law, Duke University Law School

Session 2A: Music and Digital Libraries: From Users to Algorithms

Session Chair: Gary Marchionini, University of North Carolina-Chapel Hill

Session 3A: Automatic Metadata Creation

Session Chair: Erich Neuhold, Fraunhofer IPSI, Germany

Session 4A: Managing Resources and Services

Session Chair: Richard Furuta, Texas A&M University

Session 4B: Information Retrieval and Data Mining

Session Chair: Edie Rasmussen, University of Pittsburgh

Session 5: Minute Madness: Poster/Demo Short Presentations

Session 6A: Knowledge and Representation

Session Chair: Dagobert Soergel, University of Maryland

Session 6B: User Interaction

Session Chair: Ed Fox, Virginia Tech

Session 7A: OAI in Action

Session Chair: Ghalleb Abdulla, Lawrence Livermore National Lab

Session 8A: Multimedia Issues in Digital Libraries

Session Chair: Mike Christel, Carnegie Mellon University

Session 8B: Designing and Accessing Scientific Digital Libraries

Session Chair: Sally Howe, Nat'l Coordination Office for Information Technology R & D

Session 9A: Digital Libraries in the Classroom

Session Chair: Beth Davis-Brown, Library of Congress

Session 9B: Standards, Mark-Up, and Metadata

Session Chair: Herbert Van de Sompel, Los Alamos National Laboratory

Session 10A: Tools for Building Digital Libraries

Session Chair: Michael L. Nelson, Old Dominion University

Session 10B: Correction and Analysis

Session Chair: Ee-Peng Lim, Nanyang Tech. University, Singapore

Demonstrations

Posters

Session 11: Closing Keynote

Tom Moritz, Boeschenstein Director, Library Services, American Museum of Natural History

Workshops

Chairs

Nadia Caidi
Faculty of Information Studies
University of Toronto
Toronto, ON M5S 3G6, Canada
caidi@fis.utoronto.ca

Anita Komlodi
Department of Information Systems
University of Maryland, Baltimore County
Baltimore, MD 21250
komlodi@umbc.edu

Organizers

Javed Mostafa
Information Science & Informatics
Indiana University
Bloomington, IN 47405, USA
jm@indiana.edu

Katy Börner
School of Library and Information Science
Indiana University
Bloomington, IN 47405, USA
katy@indiana.edu

Organizers

Gail M. Hodge
Information International
Associates, Inc.
gailhodge@aol.com

Marcia Lei Zeng
Kent State University
mzeng@kent.edu

Dagobert Soergel
University of Maryland
ds52@umail.umd.edu

Organizer

Simeon Warner
Computing and Information Science
Cornell University
301 College Ave
Ithaca, NY 14850-4623, USA
simeon@cs.cornell.edu
http://www.cs.cornell.edu/people/simeon/

Preface

Welcome to JCDL 2003! This is the third in a series of IEEE-CS/ACM joint conferences on digital library research and development. The joint conference brings together the diversity and range of two well-established digital library conferences, ACM DL and IEEE ADL, to provide a major international forum focusing on digital libraries and associated technical, practical, theoretical, and social issues. A decade of progress from the field's early days is readily apparent in the impressive cross-institutional and interdisciplinary collaborations, as well as in the growing number of digital libraries that represent real collections in everyday use.

Befitting the conference's beautiful venue, Rice University's Shepherd School of Music, the opening paper session is one about music and digital libraries and runs the gamut from ethnography to algorithms. Other sessions tackle the formidable problem of creating metadata and managing digital resources and services. Humanities digital libraries – collections representing cultural heritage and museum artifacts – stand alongside scientific and business digital libraries. As always, education and evaluation are vital parts of the conference program.

This year, there were 216 submissions from 21 countries. From 91 full papers and 77 short papers, the program committee selected 23 full papers and 32 31 short papers for presentation at the conference; these papers have been revised according to the reviewers' thoughtful comments and are included in the proceedings. The full papers were each assigned to 4 reviewers and the short papers to 3. As in past years, we will be awarding the Vannevar Bush Best Paper Award, sponsored by Knowledge Systems and its president Rob Akscyn, to the paper chosen by the program committee as this year's standout from a set of 23 already outstanding papers. Nominees will be announced at the opening session of the conference and the award will be presented at the banquet.

We would like to thank the international program committee for their dedicated (and sometimes heroic) efforts to review the submissions in their areas of expertise, especially given the short review/revision cycle. Special thanks go to those 17 program committee members who traveled to Houston in early March to meet for two days to construct the conference program after deliberating over more than 500 reviews. We would like to thank venue chairs Frank Shipman, David Levy, Rick Furuta, and Lisa Spiro for their extra work in assembling these portions of the program. And we would like to thank members of the conference committee for doing everything it takes to put on a great conference. Special thanks go to Lois Delcambre for her work on the proceedings and to Lisa Spiro and Unmil Karadkar for their on-going work on the website.

We have put together a program that we hope will have something for everyone – practitioners as well as researchers, librarians and social scientists as well as computer scientists, evaluators as well as developers and designers. The papers reflect the wealth of mature research in our community; the short papers and posters give us a tantalizing look at late breaking results; the panels balance the program by exploring controversies and hot topics in our field; and the demos put theory into action. We hope there's something for participants of every stripe. Thanks for contributing to the success of this year's conference!

<table>
<tr><td>**Cathy Marshall**
Program Chair</td><td>**Geneva Henry**
Conference Chair</td></tr>
</table>

Program Committee

Ghaleb Abdulla, Lawrence Livermore National Lab

Marianne Afifi, University of Southern California

Robert M. Akscyn, Knowledge Systems

Robert B. Allen, University of Maryland

Nicholas J. Belkin, Rutgers University

José Borbinha, National Library of Portugal

Christine Borgman, University of California, Los Angeles

Ching-chih Chen, Simmons College

Hsinchun Chen, University of Arizona

Mike Christel, Carnegie Mellon University

Panos Constantopoulos, University of Crete and FORTH

Beth Davis-Brown, Library of Congress

Lois Delcambre, OGI, Oregon Health & Science University

Edward A. Fox, Virginia Tech

Jonathan Furner, University of California, Los Angeles

Richard Furuta, Texas A&M University

Gene Golovchinsky, FX Palo Alto Laboratory

Sally Howe, National Coordination Office for Information Technology R & D

Judith Klavans, Columbia University

Carl Lagoze, CIS, Cornell University

John Leggett, Texas A&M University

David Levy, University of Washington

Ee-Peng Lim, Nanyang Technological University, Singapore

Clifford Lynch, Coalition for Networked Information

Gary Marchionini, University of North Carolina-Chapel Hill

Cathy Marshall, Microsoft

Alexa T. McCray, National Library of Medicine

Cliff McKnight, Loughborough University, UK

Michael L. Nelson, Old Dominion University

Erich Neuhold, Fraunhofer IPSI, Germany

Craig Nevill-Manning, Google

Andreas Paepcke, Stanford University

Carol Peters, ISTI-CNR, Italy

Edie Rasmussen, University of Pittsburgh

Joyce Ray, InstInstitute. of Museum and Library Services

Allen Renear, University of Illinois, Urbana-Champaign

Berthier Ribeiro-Neto, Federal University de Minas Gerais, Brazil

Neil Rowe, US Naval Postgraduate School

Alfredo Sanchez, Universidad de las Americas-Puebla, Mexico

Frank M. Shipman, Texas A&M University

Dagobert Soergel, University of Maryland

Shigeo Sugimoto, University of Tsukuba, Japan

Ingeborg Sølvberg, Norwegian University of Science & Technology

Costantino Thanos, ISTI-CNR, Italy

Helen Tibbo, University of North Carolina-Chapel Hill

Michael Twidale, University of Illinois, Urbana-Champaign

Nancy Van House, University of California, Berkeley

Herbert Van de Sompel, Los Alamos National Laboratory

Stuart Weibel, OCLC Office of Research

Rebecca Wesley, Stanford University

Ian Witten, University of Waikato, New Zealand

Additional Reviewers:

Giuseppe Amato

David Bainbridge

Maria Bruna Baldacci

Donna Bergmark

Holger Brocks

Pavel Calado

Marco Antonio Cristo

Sally Jo Cunningham

David Dubin

Andre Everts

Ingo Frommholz

Zan Huang

Matt Jones

Gary Marsden

Byron Marshall

Dan McDonald

Andreas Meissner

Pasquale Pagano

Jialun Qin

Maria Elena Renda

Rao Shen

Ulrich Thiel

Gang Wang

Yiwen Zhang

Yilu Zhou

Conference Committee

General Chair
Geneva Henry, Executive Director, Digital Library Initiative, Fondren Library, Rice University

Program Chair
Catherine C. Marshall, Microsoft Corporation

Treasurer
Janet Thompson, Rice University

Workshops Chair
Richard Furuta, Texas A&M University

Tutorials Chair
Lisa Spiro, Director, ERC & ETRAC, Fondren Library, Rice University

Panels Chair
David M. Levy, University of Washington

Posters and Demos Chair
Frank M. Shipman, Texas A&M University

Proceedings Chair
Lois Delcambre, OGI, Oregon Health & Science University

Registration Chair
Andrea Martin, Rice University

Local Arrangements Chair
Elvena Mayo, Rice University

Student Volunteers Chair
Brook Wu, New Jersey Institute of Technology

Webmaster
Lisa Spiro, Rice University

Networking Coordinator
Long Pham, Rice University

Publicity
Marianne Afifi, University of Southern California

Steering Committee

Nabil R. Adam, Rutgers University

Nicholas Belkin, Chair, Rutgers University

Ed Fox, Virgina Tech

Richard Furuta, Texas A&M University

Erich J. Neuhold, Fraunhofer-IPSI, Germany

Gary Marchionini, University of North Carolina

Ingeborg Sølvberg, Norwegian University of Science and Technology

Panels

James Boyle, William Neal Reynolds Professor of Law, Duke University Law School

Session 2A: Music and Digital Libraries: From Users to Algorithms

Session Chair: Gary Marchionini, University of North Carolina-Chapel Hill

An Ethnographic Study of Music Information Seeking: Implications for the Design of a Music Digital Library

Sally Jo Cunningham
Department of Computer Science
University of Waikato
Hamilton, New Zealand
64-7-838-4402
sallyjo@cs.waikato.ac.nz

Nina Reeves, Matthew Britland
Department of Multimedia and Computing
University of Gloucestershire
Cheltenham, Gloucestershire, UK
44 1242 54326
nreeves@glos.ac.uk,
matthewbritland@hotmail.com

Abstract

At present, music digital library systems are being developed based on anecdotal evidence of user needs, intuitive feelings for user information seeking behavior, and a priori assumptions of typical usage scenarios. Emphasis has been placed on basic research into music document representation, efficient searching, and audio-based searching, rather than on exploring the music information needs or information behavior of a target user group. This paper focuses on eliciting the 'native' music information strategies employed by people searching for popular music (that is, music sought for recreational or enjoyment purposes rather than to support a 'serious' or scientific exploration of some aspect of music). To this end, we conducted an ethnographic study of the searching/browsing techniques employed by people in the researchers' local communities, as they use two common sources of music: the public library and music stores. We argue that the insights provided by this type of study can inform the development of searching/browsing support for music digital libraries.

1. Introduction

At present, research in the international and interdisciplinary music information retrieval (MIR) community emphasizes the development of basic tools for music retrieval—for example, the creation of 'query by humming' (QBH) interfaces that allow users to build a query by humming or singing remembered phrases of the desired song, or the investigation of efficient indexing techniques for music documents. Music digital libraries as reported in the research literature are largely developed as proof-of-concept demonstrations for a given tool or technique, or are focused around an available set of music documents [8]. Current efforts at studying MIR system usability issues focus on user behavior exhibited in specific MIR systems, for example by examining transaction logs [15]. This type of study can tell us what actions people take on an existing system, but give no insight into their motivations, their degree of success or failure in their search, or the information seeking strategies that users employ. And, of course, these quantitative studies are limited to describing usage of existing systems—there is no understanding gained on what additional search facilities, document media, browsing support, etc. that users might desire.

There is a dearth of *a priori* research on information behavior as regards to music—that is, how given groups of people prefer to locate music, the strategies that they employ for searching or browsing, and the ways that they use music once it is located. While investigations of the music behavior of people with little or no formal background in music are particularly uncommon, preliminary studies provide interesting suggestions for search support in a music retrieval system. In [13], for example, participants asked to describe specific classical pieces rarely used formal (bibliographic) terms, but instead used words describing other features not currently supported by MIR systems (most frequently, the emotional impact of the song). Designers of music digital library systems have typically concentrated on development of sophisticated querying systems; particularly QBH systems designed to support known-item searches [2]. In the absence of a rich understanding of user needs and information behaviors, the MIR community runs the risk of developing systems ill-suited to their eventual users.

Earlier work examines the musical attributes people prefer to use in specifying music queries, based on analysis of queries posted to a Usenet newsgroup [2]. The focus here is on eliciting the searching and browsing strategies that people 'natively' employ when looking for music, to add empirical grounding for design decisions in creating music digital libraries. Our context is the search for music for personal use, as would be the case in a

5

'public' digital library attempting to serve a broad range of users. We do not examine user requirements for digital libraries supporting specialized music information needs, such as those of musicologists, music historians, performers, etc.

This paper presents results from an ethnographic study of user information behavior in the context of two popular sources of music: the public library and music CD shops. Even with the advent of Internet-based music services such as Napster, Kazaa, Morpheus, and other music sharing services, shops and libraries continue to be commonly used by many people when they search for music. Behavior in these physical environments is also more amenable to observation than actions taken in virtual music retrieval systems; in the shops and public libraries we were able to literally step back and gain a broad view of how relatively large numbers of people searched and browsed for music, and how these shoppers interacted with each other.

Our focus on CD shops and the recorded music section of libraries necessarily restricts our investigation to music behavior as regards to the types of musical document available in those locations: namely, recordings (mainly CDs) of albums and single songs. To our participants, 'looking for music' in CD shops primarily means trying to locate a particular album or single (a known item search), or to locate/identify CDs containing music that the participant might enjoy listening to (generally accomplished by browsing, as discussed in Section 4.3). Eliciting details on other types of music information desired by potential MIR system users (for example, song lyrics or musical scores) or the resolution of other types of music problems (for example, the identification of a song title from a remembered fragment of a chorus) must be accomplished in the context of systems that better support delivery of those types of music information (such as the analysis of Usenet music queries in [2]). The strength of the approach presented in this paper is that it allows researchers to examine searching and browsing behavior, to flesh out results from previous studies of music queries (which focus on information needs rather than searching/browsing strategies).

2. Methodology

The data gathering techniques employed in this study are individual semi-structured interviews, focus group sessions, and participant observations set in CD stores and the music sections of public libraries. Since observed information behavior was similar in both the public libraries and in the CD stores, in the discussions below the term 'shopper' will be used to refer to patrons of both types of music sources.

The shopping observations were intended as opportunities to study 'natural' music searching and browsing activities, and as such were conducted as anonymous 'public space' observations—that is, the researcher mingled with groups of music shoppers and unobtrusively took notes on the shoppers' activities. Since different shops may be aimed at different sectors of the public, and demographics of a crowd of shoppers may change depending on day of week and time of day, the sites and times for observations were varied in an attempt to gain a picture of music browsing and searching for as wide a variety of people as possible. At present, approximately fifteen hours of observations have been conducted in eight different music shops and in the music section of two public libraries, in New Zealand and in England.

Our objective was to explore the information seeking practices embodied in music shopping activity, rather than to follow the more common market research tactics of determining predictive factors for purchasing behavior. We therefore focus on how shoppers locate music CDs, rather than the (often fascinating) factors involved in deciding whether or not to purchase the CDs that are located. This approach means that we do not consider the effectiveness of commercial strategies such as aisle displays or sale pricing to encourage 'retrieval' (purchasing) of specific music items.

These anonymous observations are a rich source of 'what' data—the actions that people take—but they are impoverished sources of 'why' and 'how' data (the motivations behind actions, the goals of activities and the strategies employed to reach those goals). A second type of participant observation was performed, in which the researchers accompanied shoppers who agreed to use the think-aloud protocol to describe their actions. Five people have participated in this type of observation.

Interviews and a focus group session were conducted to provide contextual information for behaviors observed in the shopping observations. At present eight adults and one child have been interviewed about their music shopping strategies, their preferred sources for music and information about music, the ways that they typically 'use' music, and social contexts for locating music. Interview participants commented on how they locate music both in physical stores and by using the Internet/World Wide Web. These interviews were semi-structured; participants were encouraged to expand upon the topics raised by the questions (see Appendix). The four-member focus group discussed strategies for locating music both in physical and online CD shops, the types of music metadata or additional information that may be required to confirm interest in a particular CD or song, and recreational aspects of music shopping. Accompanied shoppers, interview participants and members of the focus group were self-selected from acquaintances and members of the university community who were made aware of this study either through advertising for participants or by word of mouth.

Data from all sources was analyzed using a grounded theory approach [9]. With this technique researchers attempt to approach the data without prior assumptions, and to generate theory from the data. Further qualitative studies or quantitative experiments can then test the validity of the emergent theory.

3. Demographics

The ages of interview participants, focus group members, and accompanied 'think-aloud' shoppers ranged from the early 20s to the mid 30s. Additionally, a ten-year-old girl was given a shortened version of the interview questionnaire. Three of the seven interview participants were female; three of the four accompanied shoppers were male; and the four-member focus group was evenly divided into two males and two females.

Given that the participant observations of music CD shops were anonymous, we were unable to accurately assess demographic data for this portion of the study. The shoppers appeared to be drawn from across the spectrum of society, however; ages ranged from very young children to the elderly, and music shopping appeared to be an appealing activity for all ethnic groups.

Interestingly, we observed significant numbers of men shopping for CDs—easily half of the shoppers in most stores were male. This is a relatively unusual situation with most shopping studies, as historically, 'the vast majority of the world's shoppers have been women' [19]. Female domination of shopping, and particularly recreational shopping, has been the case in the Western world for over 300 years. With the development of modern-style malls and department stores in the 19th century the majority of shop assistants were also female (though not, of course, the less-visible store managers). Shops and shopping were feminized to such an extent that the female attendants at the large Marshall Field department store giggled scornfully at the 'Molly Husbands' who accompanied their wives to the store [14]. Music shopping is, in fact, one of the very few shopping activities in the Western world that men engage in to the same extent as women [5], and so music shops are constructed to be relatively gender-neutral places— allowing us to assume that shopping observations are a reasonable source of information of music information behavior for both sexes.

The age range of the shoppers whom we observed appeared to be skewed towards the younger end of society, as might be expected given that people under thirty tend to spend more money on music CDs. CD stores generally target that age group in both the store décor and in the available music selection. For example, one store had a small 'oldies' section where the CDs ranged from Victorian melodies to Benny Goodman to Lou Reed. Older shoppers (those apparently aged sixty or above) appeared to feel less comfortable looking for music in CD stores; they often hesitated in the entranceway and looked momentarily disoriented as they tried to take in the bright lights, the large posters of chart topping musicians, and loud contemporary music. If music information seeking strategies vary by age group— and we have no evidence either way on this question— then the results presented below will be most valid for younger people.

4. Observed music behavior

The following sub-sections describe the searching and browsing strategies displayed by music shoppers and public library patrons. As no difference was detected between music seeking behaviors in the shops and the libraries, for readability's sake the discussion below refers to all observations as being of 'shoppers', no matter the location. The ethnographic methodology is best suited to exploratory studies such as this, where the goal is to create as comprehensive a catalog as possible of music-related information behaviors. Further research is required to determine the relative importance of these strategies, the pre-conditions for employing each strategy, etc.

4.1. Searching and browsing are interleaved

Consider the following pattern of shopping behavior, commonly observed in CD stores:

The shopper enters the store, and is attracted to a colorful display of chart-toppers or sale items near the entranceway. She briefly scans these CDs, perhaps picking one or two up to examine the tracklist on the back. Next, the shopper goes directly to the racks marked Jazz—her favorite type of music. She's looking for a particular CD that a friend has recommended, and she searches for that artist in the alphabetized rack [*searching*]. She finds the CD, reads the tracklist on the back, and then decides to purchase it. There's a sales table nearby marked '50% off' that grabs her attention, and she spends a few minutes looking through the assortment of bargains. Some CDs are piled haphazardly, and she doesn't bother looking through an entire stack; instead, she glances only at the top layer of CDs, picking up the occasional one with a colorful or interesting cover. Some sit spine-up and she flicks through them, but there is no logic to the arrangement and so she loses interest [*browsing*]. As she goes to pay, she stops by the 'Oldies' section—another type of music that she enjoys—and flips through a few of the CDs on display [*browsing*]. That reminds her that she wanted a copy of an old Rolling Stones album, so she goes to the Rs of the Oldies section [*searching*], finds the album, but decides not to buy it at that time. She then walks to the checkout and purchases the Jazz CD.

Specific searching and browsing behaviors are analyzed in Sections 4.2 – 4.8. Here, the interesting point is how casually searching and browsing can be interleaved—that a known-item search can quickly be followed by relatively directionless browsing (for example, trying to find 'something interesting' on the sales table), and that browsing can inspire the formulation of a search (when the shoppers abandons browsing the Oldies to locate a specific CD).

Current music retrieval systems generally strictly differentiate between searching and browsing, forcing users to choose to engage in one or the other (indeed, if they support browsing at all). Moving between the two activities may be awkward or disorienting, making it difficult to maintain a sense of direction of focus. One focus group participant described the ability to browse as a facility supported in shops, but not in the music resources that he consults on the WWW: "You also can't choose random CDs, which I suppose is the advantage of shops as you can just search at random." In the Greenstone-based MELDEX [1] music retrieval system, for example, the browse and search screens are functionally separated—it is not possible, for example, to locate an interesting song and then directly move to browsing a list of other songs in that genre. Clearly, however, music seekers would benefit from an interface that would allow them to move seamlessly between the two information seeking behaviors.

4.2. Known-item searches are conducted

Observations and interviews confirm that people conduct known-item searches for music—that is, they look for a specific music document, basing their search on known features of the document. Features guiding the search were bibliographic (primarily artist/group name,

album name, and song title), indicating the importance of including quality bibliographic data in a music digital library.

As with any search based on bibliographic details, at times people have difficulty in accurately or effectively conducting the search; the shopper might not know, or may not remember correctly, some of the descriptive information for the desired item. One interview participant commented on a frequent frustration of hers with searching for music online: "I have a lot of trouble looking up a song and I don't know who sang it. They really need to come up with a better way for people to look up music if they know a few words of the song."

In this latter case, the interviewee had been attempting to look up a song online; she was unaware of lyric servers, and had certainly never heard of QBH systems (which, at present, are not common). While research articles describing query-by-humming interfaces frequently cite anecdotal evidence that music-seekers "often hum or whistle a phrase of music and ask them [search facilitators] to identify the corresponding musical work" [21], no such behavior was observed. Interview participants professed a reluctance to approach either librarians or music shop workers with queries (sung or spoken); this point is further discussed in Section 4.7.

Intuitively, it seems likely that QBH systems would be popular, but little hard evidence exists to confirm this conjecture. When the idea of a QBH system was described to focus group participants, they were enthusiastic about the possibility of using this type of interface:

> Participant 3: That would be great as half the time I don't know what the song is called or who it was by. However I often know the lyrics or how the tune goes.
>
> Participant 4: Yes I agree, I think lots of people are like that.
>
> Participant 1: It would certainly make searching a lot easier.

Taken together, evidence from observations and the focus groups suggest that while the current incidence of sung queries may not be as common as is suggested in the QBH literature, a QBH interface might be welcomed, as users could avoid the discomfiture involved in singing in the hearing of a shop clerk or a reference librarian.

Once a CD is located, the shopper must confirm that this is indeed the particular music that was desired. As suggested in the scenario presented in Section 4.2, at this point the tracklist on the back of the CD is often consulted. In compilation albums, the shopper may wish to determine whether the original artists perform the songs: one accompanied shopper was concerned that a CD might "be a 'sounds like', not a proper album". More generally, the shopper is attempting to ensure that these are the correct songs: "The titles—are they familiar to me, can I hear the song in my head?"

The ability to listen to song clips would support a more natural way for users to verify that the right song has been located than does forcing them to rely solely on text-based metadata. While an online music retrieval system will presumably have song files available, the user might not wish to take time to download the entire song or album in order to verify that it is the desired item—or a commercial music library might not make the entirety of a song available without payment. Clips may also provide a means for aurally scanning a list of search hits, in much the same way that most search engines return brief extracts from text documents.

4.3. Browsing is a significant activity

The anthropological research literature on shopping draws the distinction between 'shopping for' (searching for specific, required items) and 'shopping around' (non-directed shopping that includes recreational or pleasurable elements) [5]. Music shopping is primarily 'shopping around', and as such frequently incorporates aspects of information browsing into the shopping activity. Browsing involves a semi-structured investigation of an information resource [4]; it is differentiated from searching in that browsing is more exploratory and less directed. Music shoppers browse the contents of a shop or public library mainly by genre; typically music is grouped into broad categories (rap, pop and rock, oldies, etc.) and then further subdivided by artist, and shoppers scan only those categories that appear likely to have music that the shoppers enjoy. The genres do not have to be tightly defined—shoppers are often willing to spend significant amounts of time flipping through a category of interest, and this type of browsing also supports the monitoring strategy (Section 4.5).

Shoppers appreciate stores whose genre categorizations correspond to their personal view of which artists or compilations are 'like' each other. One interview participant mentioned a store in which she particularly enjoyed browsing. When asked what she liked about that store's CD arrangement, she replied that it seemed to fit well with her view of a 'natural' clustering of music:

"The CDs seem to clump into era/genre groups. You'll find Fleetwood Mac and Bruce Springsteen and Carole King all reasonably close to each other. If I go for something from that kind of era, genre, what I call real music as opposed to the candy floss we get now, they're all together, so you might find something new that way. Trance music is together, you can go 'I know that song and that song, they're on the same CD here'. I can bypass the stuff I don't like. I don't like ethnic and classical … and so I can avoid them."

The diffuse boundary between different genres makes problematic the assignment of a single classification to a given work of music. This is a problem that the CD store shares with the physical library, in that a CD is an object that can be displayed in only one location in the store, no matter how many different genres that it might possibly belong to, or no matter how many different genres that individual shoppers may think of it as belonging to: "I have trouble finding things sometimes, sometimes a group or person can fit into more than one category. [Q: Can you give an example?] Pop music can be alternative or easy listening sometimes, or hard rock, or rap, it can be any of those things."

Pachet and Cazaly note that while genre categorization is desirable, the development of a generally acceptable genre classification scheme is not a straightforward process:

'Good' genre groupings appear to be appealing to browsers, although the construction of genre categories and taxonomies is problematic, to say the least. The most extensive genre classification schemes have been constructed by commercial music providers or retailers, and these have been structured to meet the needs of the recording industry. These taxonomies of genres exhibit inconsistencies between each other in naming and definition of genres as well as in scheme structure (depth and organization of the classification tree), and individual schemes include semantic and logical inconsistencies [16].

At this point, we argue that any attempt to support genre browsing should be based on a deep understanding of how the potential users of a MIR system define, perceive, and describe genre. Attempts to correct the perceived inadequacies of commercial genre taxonomies by appealing to 'objective' design principles can lead to classification schemes that may be less usable in practice: for example, the taxonomy developed by [16] includes features that even the authors describe as 'surprising', such as the elimination of Rap as a genre. This situation arose by defining Rap as "more a diction type than an actual stylistic specificity"—a decision which is indeed logically dictated by the construction rules of this particular scheme, but which surely would surprise and confuse the hordes of teenaged males that we observed converging on the Rap sections of CD stores!

Similarly, Fabbri [6] observes that these commercial genre taxonomies frequently fail to clearly differentiate between musical style and genres proper—a confusion which appears to be acceptable to lay users, though not to musicologists. We concur that usability and conformance to user understandings of the music world are paramount: "the point here is classification *per se*, not according to what principles or parameters." [6]

Further, the development of authoritative, completely consistent and logical genre taxonomy may be counter-productive. People generally find it difficult to clearly differentiate one genre from another (the classic example is the diffuse boundary between the Pop and Rock genres) or to infer the (generally implicitly defined) definitions of genres. This latter problem is particularly difficult to overcome when the user is faced with an unfamiliar genre label. For example, is 'Zouk' a different name for a type of music already familiar to the user, an existing type of music that the user has genuinely never encountered before, or an emerging genre? What sort of definition could allow a user to determine which case holds, and to decide whether or not s/he will like this music?

When asked to provide definitions for named genres, people are often unable to express clear rules for constructing example pieces in that genre or to precisely delimit the boundary between proximal genres. As Fabbri notes:

> In our cognitive experience, we recognize types of phenomena according to partial descriptions, to truncated knowledge. Curiously, but truthfully, genre appears to be a less specific concept than style: … we know how to recognize instantly a few genres (even without listening to any music), though we would not be able to give someone else a set of instructions to carry out that recognition. We would rather point at prototypes, at 'best examples', as interpretants of our own, private cognitive type. Genres are more about beliefs and practice than about theory. [6]

Indeed, in describing an enjoyable type of music, the reaction is often to give the genre a label (if possible) and then to name an artist, album, or song that the individual considers to be an exemplar of that genre. For example, one interview participant mentioned exercising to what she called 'gym music', and provided the exemplar of Kylie Minogue's 'Can't Get You Out of My Head'.

People may also develop their own, idiosyncratic categories, such as 'gym music' or 'study music', or group music by its emotional impact ('depressing'). Since the construction of these novel categories involves mentally grouping familiar songs, the individual has at hand examples of songs falling within the novel genre; locating new songs in an idiosyncratic genre could be supported by search tools that allow the user to ask for 'more songs like these'. A next step is to clearly identify the musical facets most useful for characterizing genres—timbre, instrumentation, rhythm, etc—and to develop interfaces for specifying musical query-by-example searches.

Consider, for example, an interview participant describing the type of music that he selected to listen to as he wrote his thesis: "It's sort of like progressive rock music. It wasn't too heavy or violent, doesn't break concentration much, and I think it's good music." The desired works were a selection from (or possibly an idiosyncratically defined sub-genre of) the commonly known genre "progressive rock", with the caveat that the songs do not convey the emotional tone of "heaviness" or "violence", that the songs allow the student to focus on the task at hand rather than attending to the lyrics or melody, and also, perhaps most importantly, that "I think it's good music."

And of course, 'good music' is what people are really looking for. The idiosyncratic nature of what constitutes "good music"—or even simply music itself—cannot be overstated. As one interview participant observed, "To person A, the car goes by and you hear 'boomph, boomph, boomph'. To me, in my humble opinion, they might as well have recorded a milking machine."

4.4. Shopping is often collaborative

Music shopping is often not a solitary task—people frequently entered the CD shops in groups, and proceeded to work together (to a greater or lesser extent) in browsing and searching the store. The observed group sizes ranged from two to seven people, and varied greatly in their composition: one or more parents with children; romantic couples; groups of teenaged males or females; mixed gender groups of university-aged students; several sets of couples; and so forth.

Group shopping is not generally the task-oriented, directional shopping associated with 'shopping for', unless the shoppers are, for example, all searching for a gift for someone else. Instead, group music shopping is usually 'shopping around', a relatively directionless activity that allows the shoppers to spend time together and to affirm their relationships by demonstrating their knowledge of each others' tastes, styles, and interests [17].

The majority of the groups of shoppers observed during the participant observation study did not appear to have made the trip to the mall or shopping area with the sole purpose of shopping together for music. Instead, usually they appeared to take in the CD stores as a side trip on a larger shopping excursion; the group might, for example, 'drift' into a CD shop for a few minutes as they walk down the street together, then drift out and continue down the road. Interviews supported the collegial, unplanned nature of much music shopping: "Yeah, if I'm going to town I'll normally go with my flatmate. I don't normally go out just to look around [that is, make a special trip solely to visit a CD store]. If I'm walking around a mall I might go in [to a CD store]." This participant further noted that browsing in a shop has "more to do with having the time than motivation." Another interviewee emphasized the place that shopping, and particularly music shopping, plays in maintaining relationships among her circle of friends: "I go shopping with friends occasionally, if the friend is there and there's nothing else to do. I go with whoever is around, male or female."

If musical preferences are often highly individual and strongly felt, then surely demonstrating an understanding of another's musical likes and dislikes indicates a bond with that person, and sharing those tastes confirms a still stronger tie. This sort of bonding can occur even in relatively casual relationships. For example, one of the authors displayed an interest in a particular CD on an accompanied shopping trip; the shopper then immediately added to his browsing a search for things that might interest her, with his understanding of her tastes based on the artist that she identified, and the era and genre associated with the artist. Ties between two people can be demonstrated through music shopping even if only one person is present. Shopping for a CD to be given as a gift for an absent friend or relative clearly demonstrates both a bond and an understanding of that person's interests; one interview participant, whose musical interests are both arcane and specialized, noted that "if you collect anything, as soon as people know, they bring things to you."

Romantic couples provided the most striking example of the use of collaborative music browsing to affirm or strengthen a relationship. These pairs wander arm in arm through the store; when one picks up a CD, the other holds it as well, and they read the tracklist together and discuss the CD before returning it to the rack and moving along to the next item of mutual interest. For these shoppers, browsing the CD stores appeared to be a courtship ritual, as their identical tastes and opinions affirm their 'couplehood'.

It will be difficult for a virtual digital library to match the rich collaborative browsing environment afforded by the physical CD store. In stores, friends can impulsively decide to indulge in music shopping, quickly share 'finds' with each other both orally and visually (by holding up a CD or passing it from one person to another), and just as casually end the excursion. Synchronizing collaborative sessions online may be a more bothersome task than simply zipping into a store as friends stroll down a street—although facilities such as instant messaging or chat rooms may provide promising ways to add spontaneity to collaborative exploration of digital libraries.

More formally constituted online 'interest communities', as described in [12], may also provide online meeting places for music digital library users. In this case, on online resource dedicated to a particular artist (John Prine) included an online chat room in which Prine devotees discussed the artist and his music. These communities require careful nurturing and constant monitoring, however, to maintain focus in the online discussions and to preserve an open, social atmosphere.

Interview and focus group participants also expressed an appreciation of more impersonal venues for feedback from other people, specifically mentioning chart sales, reviews (written by both fans and professional reviewers), and online lists of CDs purchased by other shoppers. The most useful information gives insight into the preferences and recommendations of others. Relative sales rankings give broad impressions of what is currently 'hot': "The chart section is always a good place to look as it shows what other people have bought." Some interviewees and focus group participants valued indications of other peoples' purchasing patterns, such as Amazon's 'customers who bought this title also bought' listings:

Q: Does that make you want to buy the other CDs more?

Participant 4: It certainly makes it more of a possibility, as I may have similar tastes to those people.

Opinions on the usefulness of reviews were mixed. No interview participant reported regularly reading professionally written music reviews; one stated that that is something "real fans" do, and none of these participants strongly identified with any single musical genre to the extent of becoming a 'fan'. Shoppers occasionally glanced at the reviews of CDs on display near listening posts, but very few were observed reading them with any degree of thoroughness—users of the listening posts generally preferred to gaze around the store rather than to focus on written material. Reviews written by non-professionals were more favorably received. One interview participant preferred these to formal reviews, as the other music lovers tended to describe CDs using the same sort of terms and attributes that he himself would employ. Three of the four focus group participants found reviews by other customers or music fans to be useful:

Q: Do online reviews help you choose music?

Participants 4, 3, 2: Definitely.

Participant 4: If someone has said they are good, it would definitely influence me to buy them and vice versa. As if they are a reviewer they must know what they are talking about.

Participant 1: I disagree it doesn't really make a difference to me, I like to make up my own mind. Everyone has their own opinion on what is good or bad.

On balance, it would appear that facilities providing support for users to annotate music documents with ratings and reviews could be useful in a music digital library.

4.5. The 'Journal Run' strategy is useful

As shoppers browse, they may identify a section of the store that appears likely to contain an item of interest. Desultory, seemingly random flipping of a few scattered stacks of CDs quickly switches to methodical examination of each CD in the area; typically, the shopper works row by row, rack by rack, flicking through to expose the covers to view the album title and artist. These shoppers are adopting the 'extraction' information seeking strategy, commonly known in academia as the 'journal run': they are systematically working through a particular group of CDs in order to identify material of interest, much as researchers engaged in a literature search may examine a series of issues from a journal one by one in hopes of locating a useful research article. [4].

Shoppers appreciate displays in which the CD spines or covers are easily viewable, and the CDs are alphabetically ordered. A common complaint of accompanied shoppers was that the sales CDs tended to be haphazardly stacked: "Unfortunately they're not in alphabetical order, so I have to go through the whole damn thing." One accompanied shopper explained that she likes the display racks in a particular store because the labels on the sections are labeled with group names, not just letters of the alphabet.

Other information on the CD cover or spine may be quickly consulted. In Section 4.7, we discuss cover art in detail, and in Section 4.2 we describe the examination of back-cover tracklists by shoppers. Other less formal bits of information may be useful in focusing interest in a CD:

Participant 3: Yes sometimes say if it has limited edition on the front or a warning it may attract me.

Participant 4: Also if it says it has a free poster inside and things like that it may encourage me to buy it.

At times, however, more details are required to make an informed decision about a potential purchase than is available on the cover, and the shopper may wish to consult the CD's liner notes. Frustratingly, this is often not possible: a focus group participant complained that, "Sometimes I want to look inside the CD cover but most of the shops seal them so you cannot open them up." What sort of information are these shoppers hoping to find? Anything that can help them to ensure that they have correctly identified this CD, and that can assist them in deciding whether or not they will enjoy this collection of songs: "The lyrics…do they have the words to the song. Anything biographical about the artist, what was inspirational to him, when it was written, where it was recorded."

As with any information resource, is not possible to determine *a priori* what particular items of information/data are likely to appeal to users, or to predict all possible uses to which the music may be put. A musicologist's information needs in a music digital library, for example, are likely to differ dramatically from those of a mother seeking good children's songs to play on a long car journey. A collection developer can only attempt to present all types of data available about the collection contents. As one focus group participant emphatically responded, "Basically the more information the better." An alphabetic sorting for browsing, based on artist, appears essential. One interview participant pointed out the potential usefulness of sorting by release date, either as a secondary or primary sort, as music lovers may have a good 'feel' for when various CDs were released.

4.6. Keeping up to date

The stock for sale in a music store changes constantly—new CDs are released, old music is re-released, CDs sell out and more copies are brought in. Shoppers keep up to date on the music available for sale through the *monitoring* information seeking strategy [4]:

they peruse the store displays just to stay current on the locally obtainable offerings.

At present it can be surprisingly difficult to effectively pursue the monitoring strategy in a CD store, unless one is concerned only with top-selling works:

Participant 1: It would help when shopping for someone or even if you were shopping for yourself if the shops had release dates up, so you knew when things came out.

Participant 2: They do I think, but it is usually very limited to popular releases.

It can also be difficult to determine whether a given CD has not yet been released, been released and not yet reached this store, or was stocked by the store but sold out. An accompanied shopper searched in vain for a Norah Jones CD under the 'Jones' label in three different genres, only to learn from the sales clerk that it had sold out: "Shouldn't there have been a sign up in the Jones', saying Sold Out, when I was jonesing back there?"

It is trite to note at this point that the music world is exceptionally diverse, and that the popular music scene is highly eventful. Monitoring of all current music activity is hardly possible solely through the auspices of a single digital library; the focus must be on providing links to outside music information resources—current event descriptions, music reviews, chart lists, etc. Monitoring support for the contents of a given music digital library should be more straightforward to provide—for example, through "what's new in this collection" summaries that could be subdivided by genre as well as date (so that the user does not have to scan every section of the library to find music that is of interest).

4.7. Music shopping is surprisingly visual

Originally album covers featured simple designs, with color usage limited by printing techniques and graphics limited to relatively simple drawn or stenciled images. New printing technologies introduced after World War II allowed black and white photographs (and later color images) to be reproduced cheaply and with good definition. These technological changes allowed album producers to enhance the attractiveness of their offerings. Some record companies quickly developed distinctive cover appearances; for example, Blue Note used blue motifs on nearly all of the albums produced under that label. Musical genres also came to be represented with distinctive cover styles and cover images; frequently the images were associated with the individual musicians or the popular associations with that type of music. For example, in the late '40s and 1950s the unsmiling photographs of Blues artists allowed those albums to easily be distinguished from Swing albums, which invariably featured widely grinning, exuberant band members. The general effect of Blues albums also often reflected the melancholy, erotic, and risqué nature of the music itself [20].

Today's music shoppers can generally recognize the cover style of music genres that they enjoy, and cover appearance plays a part in browsing and searching for music. Although one interview participant discounted the idea that cover styles can be reliably distinguished ("I don't think you can read too much into that"), others quite clearly used the cover art to gain clues about how the music would be likely to sound: one shopper, confused by an unfamiliar cover style, held the CD up to one of the authors and asked, 'What would this sound like?' Some interviewees felt that they were able to use a CD's appearance to make quite sophisticated inferences about the music that it is likely to contain:

[Question: *Can you recognize different artists or types of music by the CD cover art?*] " Within reason. Some people slap a weird cover on something, but mostly you can tell whether something is heavy metal or soft rock or pop. Trance music all has the same type of cover: a weird computer generated shape with a list of artists down the front. Expensive trance music comes in a cardboard box that takes 10 minutes to dismantle it to find out what's on the CD. The coolest ever cover is [garbled], they put out a cover with all clear plastic overlays with body parts on the CD cover, there's no writing on it. You can't tell from the CD or CD cover what the hell is on the CD, you might put it in mistaking it for a medical database."

This interviewee goes on to add that it is not always straightforward to deduce genre from the CD cover art: "Some people do gratuitous things with CD covers just to confuse you." Another participant noted that some motifs or styles may be common to more than one genre representation, even though the genres themselves may be quite different: during an accompanied shopping excursion she picked up a CD with a picture of a castle and 'lots of greenery', but quickly returned it to the rack, noting that: "Covers with old world style catch my attention, they might be Celtic music—this isn't, it's U2!"

The images on CD covers are used by shoppers in a variety of ways: to speed searches through a large stack of CDs, as the shopper quickly flicks through the stack searching for a desired CD; to scan distant stacks for interesting images; to provide guidance on the genre of music by an unfamiliar artist; and to quickly indicate to wandering companions when an interesting CD has been located (by holding up the CD for the companion to see).

Some browsers deliberately focus on cover art as a way of quickly identifying a given CD: when one shopper was asked why he was intently looking at a CD that he was not going to purchase on that particular shopping excursion, he responded that he wanted "to remember what it looks like, to make it easier to recognize if I haven't seen it before" (that is, in future browsing he will know whether or not he has previously considered this particular CD).

CD cover art provides a useful communication tool for collaborative browsing during group shopping excursions: in one observation of two shoppers, the pair held up a CD to ask, "have you seen this?" three times in thirty minutes. Later as the two left the store Shopper 1 wanted to ask questions about a CD that Shopper 2 had recommended, but Shopper 1 couldn't remember the CD's title. When Shopper 1 described it as, "the one that looks like a paint sample", Shopper 2 immediately recognized which CD that Shopper 1 wanted to discuss.

Individual CD covers can be highly memorable, and as such can be useful in locating older, familiar music. One participant explained that when he was younger he didn't know much about music, but "I used to go through the albums at the public library as a kid, now sometimes I see a CD with a cover from an album [I saw] as a kid, and now they're old, and cheaper. Sometimes I buy an album I saw as a kid..." This selection is made because the cover art jogs memories of the music that he listened to years before. The covers of new, high sales CDs are often also familiar; this participant noted that for contemporary music, 'often I know what the album looks like from the TV ads.'

As mentioned in Section 3, music shopping and browsing is an activity that people of all ages participate in. Young children were frequently observed browsing through the CD shops and the public library CD section, of course often accompanied by an adult or older sibling. The children tended to browse independently of their 'minders', and to have musical tastes that ranged far beyond the small Children's Music section of the stores. Children appear to browse almost entirely by recognition of CD covers—and even the very young are sometimes able to recognize relatively large numbers of contemporary artists and current chart-topping CDs. One observation highlighted this point:

> Girl, age 4, comes rushing into the store, straight to the Top Ten rack closest to entry. Her 3-year-old niece is close behind. The 4-year-old immediately grabs a CD and tells the 3-year-old they want it. The 3-year-old points to two other

CDs they want. The 4-year-old takes the CD back to the entry, where Mother (who is also grandmother of the 3-year-old) is entering the store: 'Mum! I want this!' She pulls Mother into the store and over to the Top Ten rack. The 3-year-old, 'And this one!' They are very excited. The Mother and I are laughing; I ask whether they actually know what the CDs are. Yes, they do! Mother demonstrates by asking them who the artist is for the CDs they've chosen and for other CDs. The Shrek [animated movie soundtrack] CD is easy to identify, but the girls know them all. Mother: 'Nelly Furtado, I didn't even know about this one, they told me about her.' The kids know the CDs by cover image. Mother confirms that the girls definitely can't read.

The relatively small size of the CD in relation to LP vinyl albums is one limiting factor in the use of CD cover art in browsing. One participant notes that, "The 'CDs don't cut it, the album cover is better, there's something about that [the vinyl album] size.' However, despite their small size, the covers may be immediately recognizable from a distance: "I'll quite often spot something across the store and go ooh ooh ooh."

CD shops exploit cover art to draw shoppers into the store, by presenting racks of current chart-topping CDs in the entranceway. It is striking to watch people walk briskly up to a store, slow as they scan the entranceway rack, then stop to examine a particular CD. A quick glance inside the store is often rewarded by the sight of another interesting CD display, and the shopper makes a brief, unplanned foray into the shop to browse. As noted above, in some cases the shopper's eye is caught by a cover that is already familiar; in other cases, a distinctive cover may pique a shopper's interest enough to pick up the CD to learn more about it: one shopper, for example, explained that she pulled a particular CD from a large rack for close examination because "This is a cool cover, picturesque".

The utility of the CD cover images lie in their familiarity (from advertising and from sightings in previous shopping trips), and in the existence of design conventions for different genres; it is important, then, that any images used in a music digital library be similarly recognizable and well-known to users. Images could be used as thumbnails accompanying search hits or browsing displays, to support fast scanning for items or genres of interest.

4.8. Sales staff may be intimidating

The sales staff of a CD store provide services analogous to those provided by reference librarians in a physical library: they help the shopper to locate items that are proving difficult to find. Customers are sometimes reluctant to approach sales staff with more general questions about the availability or location of CDs, however. This phenomenon has also been noted in physical libraries, where patrons may be reluctant to approach reference staff; for example, Maori [native New Zealand] students find it particularly difficult to ask questions of the library staff. In this case, the students are intimidated by their perception of the relative differences in status, age, race, and extent of the sense of 'belonging' to the library environment [3].

In both the library and the CD store, this reluctance to ask for help appears to be grounded in what Goffman terms "impression management"—an avoidance of situations that the shopper feels may cause embarrassment, by making the shopper appear cheap, foolish, or ill-informed [10]. In this situation, embarrassment may occur because the shopper may be exposed as being ignorant relative to the presumed expertise of the staff member, or because the shopper may be expressing an interest in music considered unfashionable or of inferior quality. One interviewee was particularly scathing about how she disliked having to "put up with pretentious a-holes behind the counter who if you ask [for a particular album] say 'I don't know if you're cool enough to talk to'".

Although some members of the focus groups mentioned the sales staff as an obvious first step for locating an CD or genre of interest if they could not be quickly spotted in the store, evidence emerged from the participant observations that many shoppers appeared diffident about approaching the sales counters: the shoppers would come near the clerks, retreat, then return to ask their question. An interview participant confirmed that for her, asking the staff for help was a last resort: "If I really, really want it I will, otherwise I don't. It depends on how mean looking they are."

Impression management also influences the willingness of shoppers to ask CD store staff to play a particular CD on one of the store 'listening posts' (stations set up with a CD player and a headset). While shoppers sometimes wish to listen to samples from a CD before making a purchasing decision, many dislike asking to listen to the song in-store (one shopper commented, "I hate making a fuss"). In the stores where our observations took place, the posts that play shopper-selected music are generally very close to the sales counter, and so listening at these posts effectively puts the shopper on display to the rest of the store and in close proximity to the queue of purchasers—a location that may feel awkward and uncomfortable.

Additionally, the price of a CD may affect the shopper's willingness to listen it in-store. One shopper commented that "I feel guilty not buying it if I listen to it", and so listening to a new release might lead to an expensive purchase. This shopper felt that listening to a bargain bin CD held even greater potential for embarrassment, as he felt that he would appear cheap if he then decided not to buy it—or that he would look foolish even if he made the purchase, because he had to listen to an inexpensive CD to decide whether or not to buy it. Instead, he usually bases these purchase decisions on liner notes and inferences on style and genre based on the cover art: "I have bought a lot of stuff [from the bargain bin] on a punt, [thinking] 'I should like this'."

The presence of sound clips for many of the CDs available at Amazon.com was noted by two interviewees as a welcome alternative to CD store listening posts: "If I ever do feel like finding out how the songs on an album sound, I go over to Amazon and listen to the sound clips they have." The anonymity in previewing music afforded by a music digital library would probably prove welcome.

Many shops contain additional listening posts that play only featured CDs, although the listener can switch between tracks. These may be more or less useful to a shopper in browsing or making a purchase decision, depending on whether or not the shopper happens to be interested in the type of music currently installed on the posts; one focus group participant dismissed the selections at this type of post: "The listening posts in [Store X] and similar shops are usually rubbish, they very rarely have what you want." Observations indicate that other shoppers may find the store selections appealing, as they listen at the posts for times ranging from a few seconds to nearly 20 minutes. Pairs of shoppers may trade a headset back and forth as they discuss a song—particularly teenaged girls or romantic couples. The posts see particularly heavy use by one group of shoppers: those in their early teens or younger, who often flit from post to post until they find a song that they particularly enjoy. The 10-year-old interviewee commented that, "Since I'm only 10 and can't afford to buy, usually what I'll do is put the headphones on and press replay about 50 times."

5. Summary

This study suggests that findings from studies of music information behavior, as displayed in setting such as music stores and public libraries, can be used to inform the design of useful and usable music digital libraries. We have identified behaviors that are not well supported by current MIR systems, for example the 'journal run' strategy. Some of these potentially useful features could be easily incorporated into existing MIR software—such as the suggested ability to sort search results by release date. Perhaps one explanation for the absence of these technically simple features is that many MIR systems have been developed in academia are developed as proof of concept prototypes, with the focus on demonstrating the effectiveness or potential of advanced features such as QBH.

Support for some music information behaviors may be achieved by borrowing from related techniques supporting exploration of textual or visual documents. For example, consider the comment of the focus group participant who critiqued the relative difficulty of browsing in MIR systems ("You also can't choose random CDs, which I suppose is the advantage of shops as you can just search at random"; Section 4.1). Serendipitous browsing of this sort should of course be easier in an MIR system than in the shops—for example, by borrowing from the visual arts the idea of a 'collage machine' [11] that successively displays a series of documents, in this case perhaps CD covers, accompanied by snippets of songs from each album as it is briefly given prominence in the shifting collage. Given the difficulties of developing and applying taxonomy of musical genres, perhaps genre browsing could be better supported by automatic clustering based on similarities of sound or rhythm (for example, using self-organizing map displays originally intended for clustering text documents [18]).

Still other identified behaviors will be less straightforward to support with MIR software. How, for example, could real time collaborative browsing be implemented with the same speed of interaction and sense of immediacy as is achieved when friends flick through CD racks together? Web chat facilities such as those described in the online music community in [12] will remain a poor substitute for face-to-face interactions.

One shortcoming of this type of study is that basing design recommendations for future software on current information handling practices may unnecessarily limit possible interface innovations. The appeal or usability of specific interface designs cannot accurately be predicted by our work, and the development of truly novel or ground-breaking information exploration applications is likely to require developers to imagine new information designs and uses rather than to simply support existing information behavior. In some cases, it may not be possible to evaluate the potential usefulness or effectiveness of a new interface without testing a prototype on potential users. Fernstrom and Maidin, for example, report success in creating a browsing system for musicologists that supported an information need that the potential users had not anticipated:

When showing a musicologist a *sonic browser* prototype, he expressed great surprise, *'I've never seen a collection this way before"* … This is a very important comment as he had been working for a couple of years re-cataloging the collection, from index cards to database, via desktop publishing tools to its final form—a paper based product, ready to print. Still, in paper or data base format, one cannot get a visual spatial overview of, for example, '*here* are the jigs and *there* are the reels'. [original emphasis] [7]

Our work can best be used to suggest information needs that must be filled in a music retrieval system targeted at the general public—for example, the need to support effective browsing by genre or to permit users to browse/search collaboratively.

6. References

[1] Bainbridge, D., Nevill-Manning, C.G., Witten, I.H., and Smith, L.A., "Towards a digital library of popular music", in *Proceedings of the Fourth ACM Conference on Digital Libraries* (Berkeley, CA, USA, 1999), pp. 161-169.

[2] Downie, J.S., and Cunningham, S.J., "Toward a theory of music information retrieval queries: system design implications", in *Proceedings of the Third International Conference on Music Information Retrieval* (ISMIR) (Paris, France, 2002), pp. 299-300.

[3] Duncker, Elke, "Cross-cultural usability of the library metaphor", in *Proceedings of the 2nd ACM/IEEE-CS Joint Conference on Digital Libraries* (Portland, OR, USA, 2002), pp. 223-230.

[4] Ellis, D. "A behavioural approach to information retrieval design", *Journal of Documentation* 46 (1989), pp. 313-338.

[5] Falk, P., and Campbell, C., "Introduction", in *The Shopping Experience* (P. Falk and C. Campbell, eds.), Sage Publications, New York, 1997.

[6] Fabbri, Franco, "Browsing music spaces: categories and the musical mind", presented at the 3rd Triennial British Musicological Societies' Conference (Guildford, UK, 1991), available at http://www.theblackbook.net/acad/others /fabbri990717.pdf.

[7] Fernstrom, Mikael, and O Maidin, Donncha, "Computer-supported browsing for MIR", in *Proceedings of the 2nd International Symposium on Music Information Retrieval* (Bloomington, IN, USA, 2001), pp. 9-10.

[8] Futrelle, Joe, and Downie, J. Stephen, "Interdisciplinary Communities and Research Issues in Music Information Retrieval", in *Proceedings of the Third International Conference on Music Information Retrieval* (ISMIR) (Paris, France, 2002), pp. 215-221.

[9] Glaser, B., and Strauss, A., *The Discovery of Grounded Theory: Strategies for Qualitative Research* (1967), Chicago.

[10] Goffman, Erving, *The Presentation of Self in Everyday Life* (1959), Anchor Press, New York, NY. As referenced in Prus, 1993.

[11] Kerne, Andruid, "CollageMachine: An Interactive Agent of Web Recombination", *Leonardo* 3/5 (November 2000), pp. 347-350.

[12] Kibby, Marjorie D., "Home on the page: a virtual place of music community", *Popular Music* 19/1 (2000), pp. 91-100.

[13] Kim, Ja-Young and Belkin, Nicholas J., "Categories of music description and search terms and phrases used by non-music experts", in Michael Fingerhut (Editor) *Proceedings of the Third International Conference on Music Information Retrieval: ISMIR* (Paris, France, October 2002), pp. 209-214.

[14] Lancaster, B., *The Department Store: A Social History*, Leicester University Press, Leicester, UK, 1995.

[15] McPherson, J.R. and Bainbridge, D., "Usage of the MELDEX Digital Music Library", in *Proceedings of the International Symposium on Music Information Retrieval* (Bloomington, IN, USA, 2001), pp. 19-20.

[16] Pachet, Francois, and Cazaly, Daniel, "A taxonomy of musical genres", in *Proceedings of the Content-Based Multimedia Information Access Conference (RIAO)* (Paris, France, April 2000), vol. 2, pp. 1238-1245.

[17] Prus, Robert, "Shopping with companions: Images, influences and interpersonal dilemmas", *Qualitative Sociology* 16(2) (1993), pp. 87-110.

[18] Rauber, Andreas, Pampalk, Elias, and Merkl, Dieter, "Using psycho-acoustic models and self-organizing maps to create a hierarchical structuring of music by sound similarity", in Michael Fingerhut (Editor) *Proceedings of the International Symposium on Music Information Retrieval* (Paris, France, October 2002), pp. 71-80.

[19] Reekie, G., *Temptations, Sex, Selling and the Department Store*, Allen and Unwin, Sydney, Australia, 1993.

[20] Ruffins, F.D., "Reflecting on ethnic imagery in the landscape of commerce, 1945-1975", in *Getting and spending: European and American consumer societies in the Twentieth Century* (Susan Strasser, Charles McGovern, and Matthias Judt, eds.), Cambridge University Press, Cambridge, 1998.

[21] Smith, L, and Medina, R., "Discovering themes by exact pattern matching", in *Proceedings of the International Symposium on Music Information Retrieval* (2001), Bloomington, IN, USA, pp. 31-32.

Appendix: Interview questions

1. What kinds of music do you like to listen to?
2. How many CDs, cassettes, mp3s, etc. do you own?
3. How do you usually acquire music? (For example, shopping (store, online, mail order), downloading mp3s, …)
4. Do you ever get music from the public library?
5. Do you ever listen to the radio?
6. Do you ever watch music videos?
7. Do you particularly notice the music/CD ads on TV?
8. Are there any music magazines, websites, etc. that you read?
9. Can you recognize different artists or types of music by the CD cover art?
10. Do you go to music/CD stores to browse, rather than to purchase a particular item?
11. Is there any particular store that you prefer? Why?
12. Talk me through a typical visit to your favorite store.
13. Do you ever use the 'listening post' or ask to listen to a CD?
14. How comfortable do you feel asking the people at the counter for help or to listen to a CD?
15. Do you every listen to sound clips online, for example at Amazon, to see how a particular album sounds?
16. Do you ever go shopping with friends?
17. Do you give music (for example a CD) as a gift? Receive music as a gift?
18. When do you listen to music? Do you listen to different types of music at different times?

Content-based Indexing of Musical Scores

Richard A. Medina
NM Highlands University
richspider@cs.nmhu.edu

Lloyd A. Smith
SW Missouri State University
lloydsmith@smsu.edu

Deborah R. Wagner
NM Highlands University
dwagner@nmhu.edu

Abstract

This paper describes a method of automatically creating a content-based index of musical scores. The goal is to capture the themes, or motifs, that appear in the music. The method was tested by building an index of 25 orchestral movements from the classical music literature. For every movement, the system captured the primary theme, or a variation of the primary theme. In addition, it captured 13 of 28 secondary themes. The resulting index was 14% of the size of the database. A further reduction of 2% is possible; however, this discards secondary themes. A listening experiment using five orchestral movements showed that people can reliably recognize secondary themes after listening to a piece of music–therefore, it may be necessary to retain secondary themes in a score index.

1. Introduction

Content-based music information retrieval (MIR) enables people to locate and retrieve music based on its musical characteristics, rather than on metadata such as composer and title. The potential utility of such systems is attested to by music librarians, who report that library patrons often hum or whistle a phrase of music and ask them to identify and locate a score or recording of the corresponding musical work [7, 10].

1.1. Score-based Music Information Retrieval

Score-based MIR systems operate by accepting a musical query (such as a string of notes) from the user and searching a database of musical scores for a pattern closely matching the query. The returned music may be in any form – an audio recording, a midi file, a score, or metadata such as synopses, critiques, or historical notes, but the query is processed against a collection of musical scores. The search is typically carried out by exhaustively matching the query against the database. This has been successful in such systems as Meldex [7], which incorporates a database of 10,000 folk tunes. However, exhaustive search is not likely to scale well to large collections such as thousands of symphonies or other major works.

The scaling problem is two-fold. First, as stated above, the search is carried out over the entire database and, therefore, grows in relation to the size of the database. Second, inaccuracies may be introduced into the search in several ways: the user may not correctly remember the musical pattern he or she is trying to recreate, the user may not correctly play, whistle or hum the musical pattern, the musical pattern may be inaccurately captured by the system (especially if it is transcribed from audio input), the database may have coding mistakes in it (especially if it is created by optical music recognition), the user may know a different variant than the one represented in the database (especially in the case of folk music), or the notation in the database may not match the user's performance concept (especially in the case of popular or jazz music). For all these reasons, it is necessary to carry out the search using an algorithm that finds "degrees of match" [9]. Such approximate search algorithms are much slower than those that look for an exact match of the query.

1.2. Content-based Indexing in MIR

Downie and Nelson [4] introduced the use of a content-based index in music information retrieval. While their index (based on the same folk tune collection used by Meldex) included all notes in the database, a more selective index can be used to reduce the amount of data that is searched.

In classical music, the natural unit for indexing is the theme. A theme is a melody that the composer uses as a starting point for musical development. A piece of music may have several themes; by definition, themes will repeat and may be slightly changed ("variations") by the composer on repetition. Using an index that incorporates musical themes can reduce the search on a collection of classical major works. Furthermore, themes are the musical phrases that a listener is most likely to remember, so such an index focuses the search on the data most likely to match a query.

1.3. Automatic Theme Discovery

Theme indices, such as Barlow and Morgenstern's *A Dictionary of Musical* Themes [2] are well known in the music literature. These compilations are useful for linking themes to their musical works, but they suffer from two major drawbacks. First, they are created manually – the author (or authors) of such an index must either listen carefully to each piece of music to be represented, or must comb the literature for analysis by musicologists. Therefore, the index takes a great deal of time and effort to build. Second, a printed index is frozen in time – any music written after publication of the index must wait to be included in a later edition.

Automatic theme discovery systems attempt to overcome the problems of manual compilation. Because themes are, by definition, musical sequences that are repeated and developed by the composer, these systems operate by finding repeating patterns in music. Liu, et al. [6], for example, search for small repeating melodic sequences, joining them into longer ones. The Melodic Motive Extractor (MME) algorithm, developed by Meek and Birmingham [8], also assembles long repeating patterns from shorter ones. MME then prunes the set of candidate themes using features such as duration, length, and position of first occurrence in the music.

This paper describes our method for building an index of musical scores. Like the theme discovery algorithms described above, our method is based on finding repeating melodic sequences, with the goal of capturing the themes of major works in the resulting index. Unlike those systems, ours starts by locating the longest repeating sequences, then deleting substrings of longer patterns. The method was tested by implementing it in software and building an index of 25 orchestral movements from the Baroque, Classical and Romantic periods. Section 2 describes the indexing algorithm and its implementation, while section 3 describes the evaluation experiment. Section 4 presents the results of the experiment, and section 5 discusses those results. Section 6 describes and discusses a

listening experiment carried out in order to better interpret the results. Section 7 presents conclusions and ideas for further work.

2. An Algorithm For Building A Musical Score Index

This section describes a computational method for building an index from a collection of musical scores. The initial step is to extract a list of repeating melodic patterns from a composition. The strategy is then to isolate the patterns most likely to be themes by removing those determined to be trivial, or that are represented in other patterns. The general procedure is as follows.

1. Find repeating patterns of length equal to or greater than the threshold.
   a. Ignore patterns that contain only one pitch.
   b. Ignore patterns that contain only two alternating pitches.
2. Remove all duplicate patterns.
3. Remove patterns that are substrings of longer patterns.
4. Remove variations of patterns that are already captured.

The method is organized in two phases – *extraction* and *pruning*. The first phase (step 1, above) generates a list of repeating patterns within a musical work, while the second phase (steps 2 through 4) consists of a series of pruning stages in which the list is iteratively reduced to its final form. The result is a melodic pattern list for the input musical score. Combining the lists for all the scores produces an index to the collection.

2.1. Pattern Extraction

The first step is to assemble a list of repeating melodic sequences. Discovering these sequences is essentially a search for self-similarity in a musical work. Because of this, a self-similarity matrix is used as a structure for extracting repeating patterns.

The self-similarity matrix is an n x n bit matrix, where n is the number of notes in the musical work. The matrix indicates where each note exactly matches another note in the music. Comparison is based on the interval and duration properties of each note. Intervals are used to make the analysis independent of key. Matched notes are denoted with a *1* (one) in the matrix, while a *0* denotes non-matching notes. Because every note matches itself, the main diagonal is all ones. Descending diagonal ones that are off the main diagonal indicate repeating patterns.

The algorithm for creating the self-similarity matrix is illustrated below.

1. Let S be a sequence of intervals of length n
2. Let M be a two dimensional matrix of size n x n
3. Let $i \leftarrow 0$
4. For each S_i such that $i < n$, let $j \leftarrow 0$
   4.1. For each S_j such that $j < n$
        If $S_i = S_j$ then $M_{ij} \leftarrow 1$
        Else $M_{ij} \leftarrow 0$

Figure 1 shows the self-similarity matrix for *Fugue No. 7*, from *The Well Tempered Klavier*, by J.S. Bach [1]. For easier reading, the zeros have been replaced by spaces, and 1's are represented by dots. The long line of dots is the main diagonal. Because the halves of the matrix on either side of the main diagonal are mirror images of one another, it is only necessary to compute and scan half the matrix in searching for repeating patterns.

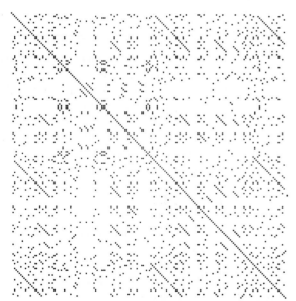

Figure 1. Self-similarity matrix for Fugue No. 7, by J. S. Bach

It is presumed that a theme is a melodically interesting phrase with at least some degree of entropy among pitches. Based on this heuristic, the algorithm

does not retain patterns that demonstrate little or no melodic variation.

Determining whether a pattern contains a single pitch involves parsing the pattern and noting the lack of any change in pitch. In the intervallic representation this is a pattern containing all zeros.

Trills are indicated by a single interval that alternates in opposite directions. For our purposes, trills include tympani parts, for example, that contain long patterns of alternating perfect fifths, such as the pattern 7 -7 7 -7 7 -7 7.

Repeating patterns extracted using the self-similarity matrix are assembled in a list for further processing. For example, the well-known theme from Beethoven's *Symphony No. 5* appears first in measure 1; it repeats later in the score and is entered into the pattern list.

2.2. Pruning

The list created from the self-similarity matrix contains all patterns of musical intervals that occur more than once in the musical score. The goal of the pruning phase is to reduce the list into a small set of patterns that contain the themes associated with that score. This is done by eliminating patterns that are: 1) exact duplicates of other previously occurring patterns, 2) substrings of longer patterns, or 3) variations of other patterns.

During processing of the matrix, every repeated pattern is recorded individually. If a pattern repeats more than once, there will be a duplicate or duplicates in the pattern list. A duplicate is a pattern that exactly matches another pattern in content and in length (number of intervals). Starting with the first pattern, each pattern is matched against subsequent patterns in the list. When an exact match is found, the duplicate is replaced by a timestamp giving the location (in the score) of the first occurrence of the sequence.

Once the end of the list has been reached, the list is sorted by earliest occurrence, as determined by the timestamps. This applies a chronological structure to the list that stresses factors such as when a melody is first introduced into a composition. In subsequent pruning phases, this is useful for determining the importance of a melody in relation to others in the list.

The removal of substring patterns entails a process much like the one used to remove duplicates; however, in this stage, a match between two patterns is found by determining if one pattern is a proper substring of the other. If a match is found, the smaller pattern is recorded as a substring of the longer pattern and removed.

Removing substrings does not discard melodic information – the string still appears in the index as part of a longer sequence. With the exception of trills and single note sequences, the index still contains every repeated melodic sequence originally extracted from the self-similarity matrix.

The next goal of the procedure is to remove variations of melodic sequences already found. These variations are identified as containing partial substrings of longer patterns. The procedure matches substrings of length greater than or equal to a threshold. The underlying premise is that, because a theme index will be searched using approximate pattern matching [7], it is unnecessary to keep theme variations.

Proper substring matching may not give an accurate measure of similarity among patterns that vary by a few notes. For example, the list in Table 1 contains 9 patterns extracted from the self-similarity matrix for Bach's Fugue No. 7. It is clear that patterns F and R share a common substring. The previous stage would not consider these patterns similar because the shorter pattern, R, does not appear in its entirety in F. Figure 2 illustrates the close proximity between the two patterns.

Table 1. Sequences from Fugue No. 7

Pattern ID	Intervals
P	-3 -2 2 -4 5 -1 1 4 -2 -1 -4 10 -1 -2 -2 7 -3 -4 -2 9 -3 -6 -
O	-4 10 -1 -2 -2 7 -3 -4 -2 9 -3 -6 -1 8 -12
Q	-1 -2 -2 -3 2 1 2 0 -2 2 2 1 -3 -7 10 –1
F	-1 -2 2 -4 5 -1 1 4 -2 -3 -4 10 -1 -2 -2 7 –3
H	2 0 -2 2 2 1 -3 –7 10 -1 3 -3 -4 5 0 –3
C	-1 -2 -2 -1 1 2 2 0 -2 2 2 1 -3 -7 10 –1
K	0 -3 -4 -2 9 -3 –6 -1 3 5
D	8 -5 -3 1 7 -4 -3 -3 8 -5 -3 1 7 -3 –4
R	0 -1 -2 2 -4 5 -1 1 4 -2 -3 -4 10 -1 –2

Pattern R is a proper substring of F, if its first interval is ignored while comparing the two. In order to capture this partial similarity, variation removal looks for significant parts of patterns that match. This also captures the instance when two partially similar patterns only differ by their surrounding background material.

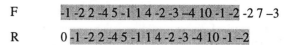

F   -1 -2 2 -4 5 -1 1 4 -2 -3 -4 10 -1 -2 -2 7 –3

R   0 -1 -2 2 -4 5 -1 1 4 -2 -3 -4 10 -1 –2

Figure 2. Two closely related patterns

Each pair of strings is matched to see which ones may be considered variations of others. Through experimentation, the value chosen as a significant match length was 10, or half the length of the shorter of the two strings being matched, whichever is greater. Applying this rule to the set of patterns in Table 1 results in removal of pattern R. The algorithm for variation removal is illustrated below.

1. Let P be a list of k patterns, $P_0 \ldots P_{k-1}$
2. For each P_i such that $i < k$, i initialized to 0
   2.1. Let $j \leftarrow i + 1$
   2.2. For each P_j such that $j < k$, and $P_i > P_j$
   2.3. Let l be the length of P_j divided by two
      2.3.1. If l is less than 10, $l \leftarrow 10$
      2.3.2. If Pj exactly matches a substring of P_i of length w, $w >= l$
         2.3.2.1. Remove P_j from P

This step takes most of the computational time during the pruning process. The key to this stage is the fact that the longer pattern of the two partial matches is retained, and the shorter one removed. It does, however, remove some melodic information. The assumption is that by repeatedly retaining the longer pattern, we are casting a wider net through the list and stand a better chance at retaining the themes of the composition.

3. Evaluation

The purpose of the index-building algorithm is to provide a computational method for extracting important melodic patterns from a musical score. This section describes an experiment designed to evaluate its effectiveness.

3.1. Test Data

The data set for this experiment was a corpus comprised of 25 classical orchestral scores. The reason for using these works is that they represent large, multifaceted musical compositions that consistently adhere to principles of theme usage. Forming a theme index from them is a practical application of an automated score indexing system.

Each musical score used in the experiment was digitally encoded as an ASCII text file. All the pieces were drawn from the MuseData virtual score collection, assembled at the Center for Computing Assisted Research in the Humanities (CCARH) [3]. The MuseData collection was used because of its open format [5] and its high quality of encoding.

The data set consisted of 6 movements from 4 concerti and 19 movements from 14 symphonies. Composers represented in the test data set include Bach, Mozart, Haydn, and Beethoven. The entire test collection represented approximately 6,000 measures and 225,000 notes. On average, each composition contained 241 measures and 9000 notes.

3.2. Experimental Procedure

To implement the algorithm, a Java application was created that accepts a MuseData file as input. The program parses each input file and translates it to a sequence of music nodes. A music node is a compound data structure that specifies a pitch (name and octave), duration, interval (relative to the previous note), and a timestamp relative to the musical score (instrument:measure:beat). Multi-voice compositions are flattened by consecutively stringing together the nodes from each part. A three-part fugue, for example, is converted to a single voice by concatenating the middle part to the upper part, then concatenating the lower part to the end of the middle part. The assumption is that themes are melodic sequences that appear within one voice – our algorithm will not find an occurrence of a theme that is split among different instruments. Timing information, however, is preserved – so a theme that occurs at the beginning of the second part will be located at the beginning of the composition, rather than one third of the way through.

Subsequently, each composition is treated as a single string of nodes. The output is a file containing melodic sequences extracted by the algorithm. Other intermediary output was also recorded in order to observe the behavior of the system after key stages had completed.

To verify whether a theme was successfully captured in the index, the primary and secondary themes for the entire data set were manually transcribed from Barlow and Morgenstern's Dictionary of Musical Themes [2] into an intervallic format. These transcribed themes were then compared against the score index.

4. Results

Two criteria for evaluating the performance of the algorithm are the successful extraction of themes and reduction of the data that must be searched relative to the size of the entire collection.

4.1. Theme Discovery

The first objective of the score-indexing algorithm is to extract the themes of the musical work. A theme may appear in the index as a standalone sequence, or may appear as a substring of a longer sequence.

The index building algorithm successfully captures the primary theme in 23 of the 25 musical works in the data set, a 92% discovery rate. The two instances where the theme is not found are due to the fact that the theme, as listed by Barlow and Morgenstern [2], does not repeat. In both of these cases the theme is introduced once at the beginning of the composition and is slightly varied thereafter. These variations do repeat and are captured in the index.

For many of the orchestral works in the data set, Barlow and Morgenstern list secondary themes. There were 19 works containing second themes; the algorithm found 9. Additionally, it found 3 of the 7 third themes, and 1 of 2 fourth themes.

Figure 3 shows the performance of the algorithm on capturing themes from the musical works in the test data collection.

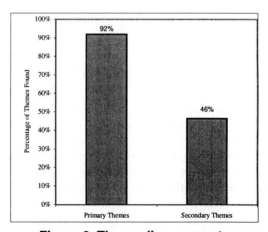

Figure 3. Theme discovery rate

4.2. Index Size

The second goal of the algorithm was to reduce the amount of searchable data in the test collection. This is essentially a measure of compression. The size of the index is calculated for the entire data set and recorded after various pruning stages in the algorithm.

Table 2 shows the number of notes stored in the index during the processing stages. Before pruning, the index is larger than the collection because of the large number of duplicate patterns. The pruning process reduces the note count significantly.

Table 2. Size of index during processing

Procedure Stage	No. Notes
Size of collection	225,897
Index before pruning	647,407
Duplicates removed	116,666
Substrings removed	73,036
Variations removed	31,569

Figure 4 shows the index size, as a percentage of the entire collection, at the various processing stages. The first pruning operation – removal of duplicate patterns – has the largest effect, removing 82% of the original index. The final index is 14% of the size of the collection.

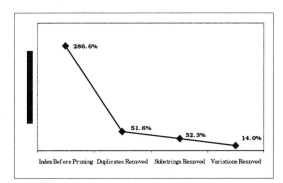

Figure 4. Index size, relative to collection

Table 3 shows the average number of patterns for each score at various stages in the processing. Before pruning, the index holds, on average, 1513 entries for each musical score (if trills and single note patterns are included in the index, that number balloons to 19,307 entries for each score). The final index holds, on average, 65 patterns for each musical score in the collection, making for a total of 1324 entries in the

overall index. The sequences average 20 notes in length.

Table 3. Average no. of patterns for each score at various stages of processing

Procedure Stage	Avg. # Patterns per Score
Index before pruning	1,513
Duplicates removed	247
Substrings removed	143
Variations removed	65

5. Discussion

The index building algorithm successfully captured all primary themes that repeat at least once, and produced an index 14% of the size of the collection. This discussion focuses on the performance of the algorithm on capturing primary and secondary themes, and on further reducing the size of the index.

5.1. Theme Discovery

A theme that does not repeat exactly will not be extracted using the approach taken in this investigation. In 2 of the 25 compositions processed, the primary theme was not found because it did not repeat. In both cases, however, a variation of the primary theme was captured. Figure 5 shows the theme from Mozart's *Symphony No. 41, "Jupiter," 3rd movement*, as listed by Barlow and Morgenstern, followed by the variation that was captured by the algorithm; figure 6 shows the interval representations of the same theme and variation (rests are removed from the interval representation).

Figure 5. Theme and variation from the Mozart's *Jupiter* Symphony, 3rd movement

-1 -1 -1 -2 -2 -1 1 4 -2 7 -2 -1 -1 -1 -2 -2 2
-1 -1 -1 -2 -2   9   -1 -1 -1 -2 -2

Figure 6. Interval representation of theme and variation from Mozart's *Jupiter* symphony

The variation matches the theme for the first 5 intervals, and 5 of the last 6 intervals are the same. The difference occurs in the middle, where the variation makes a single jump of a major sixth, while the theme ascends a major sixth in a more roundabout way.

The index also retains a variation, rather than the theme, in Beethoven's *Violin Concerto, Op. 61, 1st movement*. In this case the variation exactly matches the last 10 intervals of the theme. Figure 7 shows the musical notation for the theme and variation; figure 8 shows the interval representation. It is clear, looking at figure 7, that the theme and variation match exactly, starting with measure 3 of the theme and measure 2 of the variation.

Figure 7. Theme and variation from Beethoven's *Violin Concerto Op. 6, 1st Movement*

2 -2 -2 -1 -2 -2 -1 1 2 3 -1 5 -2
-1 -2 -2 -1 1 2 3 -1 5 -2

Figure 8. Interval representation for theme and variation from Beethoven's *Violin Concerto Op. 6, 1st movement*

These examples illustrate that, although a primary theme may not repeat exactly, some variation of it is likely to repeat and be represented in the index.

The algorithm was less successful at finding secondary themes. We believe the reason for this is that secondary themes, by definition, appear later in the music than primary themes; therefore, the composer has less time to develop them. While two secondary themes found by the algorithm occurred in the first 10% of their respective scores, most made their first appearances later – some as late as a third of the way through the score. Furthermore, because secondary themes are usually less important in the overall musical context, they are less likely than primary themes to receive the prominence accorded by exact repetition.

5.2. Reducing the Size of the Index

The primary themes, in these works, occur near the beginning of their musical scores – all of them are within the first 17% of the score, as determined by measure number. The majority (80%) of them begin within the first two measures of the composition. Because the index building algorithm lists sequences in order of their first occurrence in the score, the primary theme of a given score typically appears near the beginning of the index for that score – consistently within the first 10% of sequences listed. Over 80% of the primary themes are within the first 5% of the indexed sequences for that score. Figure 9 shows the distribution of the first appearances among primary themes. The horizontal axis represents each of the 23 primary themes found, sorted by their position of first occurrence in the score.

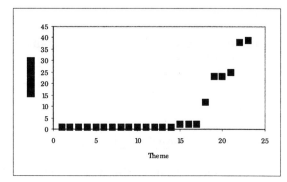

Figure 9. First appearance of primary themes by measure number.

These results are similar to those of Meek and Birmingham [8], who found that *position* was their most highly weighted feature for finding primary themes.

The observation that primary themes occur early in the music leads to the following heuristic for reducing the size of the index:

For any given musical score, discard all sequences not in the top 10% of the index for that score.

In our data set, this heuristic retains all primary themes that were found, and one of the two primary theme variations, and results in an index approximately 2% of the collection size. It does, however, remove all but two secondary themes.

6. Are Secondary Themes Needed?

While the heuristic discussed above is attractive from the standpoint of index size reduction, it produces an index that can be expected to represent only primary themes. This is suitable, if we expect users to use only primary themes in forming musical queries.

In order to determine whether it is necessary to retain secondary themes, we would like to analyze musical queries that users have submitted to a classical music database over a long period of time. However, we do not have access to that data (indeed, it is unlikely that such data exists), so we carried out a listening experiment to get some indication of how well people can be expected to remember secondary themes after listening to a piece of classical music. The assumption is that, if people can't remember secondary themes shortly after listening to a piece of music, then they will not be able to use them in formulating queries.

6.1. Listening Experiment

Participants listened to 5 orchestral movements, played from compact disc on a stereo sound system. After each movement, participants listened to 5 themes played on a piano. One of the themes was the primary theme for that movement, as listed by the Barlow and Morgenstern theme dictionary [2]. The remaining 4 themes were any secondary themes listed in the theme dictionary, and other themes randomly chosen from those listed by the same composer. The order of play for the five themes was randomly set. For example, in the first trial, participants listened to the first movement from Beethoven's *Symphony No. 9*. They then listened to the first theme from the fourth movement of *Beethoven's Piano Sonata No. 1 (Op. 2, No. 1)*, the second theme from the first movement of *Symphony No. 9*, the first theme from the first movement of *Symphony No. 9*, the third theme from the first movement of Beethoven's *Symphony No. 4*, and, finally the third theme from the first movement of *Symphony No. 9*. Each theme was played twice on the piano.

For each theme, listeners were asked to indicate (by circling Yes or No) whether the theme played on the piano occurred in the symphonic movement they had just listened to.

Each trial was carried out on a separate day. The 5 movements used were: Beethoven, *Symphony No. 9, movement 1*, Bach, *Brandenburg Concerto No. 2, movement 1*, Mendelssohn, *Symphony No. 4, movement 1*, Mozart, *Symphony No. 40, movement 1*, and Tchaikovsky, *Symphony No. 6, movement 4*.

6.2. Participants

Participants in the experiment were 28 students (16 women and 12 men) in a music appreciation class at New Mexico Highlands University. The class was comprised of a cross section of students, ranging in academic level from freshman (first year) to senior (fourth year). 22 of the students had some musical background in singing or playing an instrument; 6 had no formal musical background. Two were music majors.

Participation was optional; students were told their participation, or lack thereof, would not affect their grades. Not all participants took part in all trials – the number of listeners in the 5 trials ranged from 20 to 23.

6.3. Results and Discussion

Table 4 shows the number of listeners correctly identifying primary and secondary themes as being present in the orchestral movement they listened to, and extraneous themes as not being present in the movement. Statistical significance was evaluated using a chi-squared test; all results are significant at well below the 1% level.

Table 4. Results of listening test

	Correct	Incorrect
Primary themes	60	4
Secondary themes	67	18
Extraneous Themes	189	61

The results show that, for the Baroque, Classical, and Romantic music used in this test, listeners recognized primary themes more accurately than secondary themes. However, it is clear that people can reliably recognize secondary themes, as well.

What we have tested here is, of course, recognition, rather than memory. The fact that people can reliably recognize secondary themes, shortly after listening to a piece of music, does not necessarily mean they remember them well enough to recreate them. We believe it may well be that users will consistently use primary themes in forming musical queries to a classical music database. However, given these results, it is plausible that users may base some queries on secondary themes. Therefore, at this point, we choose to take the conservative approach and retain secondary themes in the musical score index.

7. Conclusion

This paper has described a method for building an index of musical scores. Such an index can reduce the amount of searching necessary for processing a user query against a collection of classical musical scores.

The method is very effective for capturing primary themes; in an experiment using 25 symphonic movements, an implementation of the algorithm captured 23 of the 25 primary themes, and captured variations of the remaining 2 themes. We consider capturing a theme variation a success, because we expect the index to be searched using an approximate matching algorithm [7]. Approximate search is necessary because it is impossible to predict what variation of a theme (possibly caused by errors) a user will enter as a retrieval query.

Our algorithm is less successful at capturing secondary themes, finding 13 of the 28 secondary themes listed for the indexed movements by a well-known theme dictionary [2]. We believe the relatively poor performance on secondary themes is caused by the fact that, because secondary themes appear later in the score, the composer has less time to develop them, and is therefore less likely to repeat them exactly as they first appear. Our method relies on extracting exact repetitions of musical patterns, so it will not find patterns that repeat only in variations.

In our index building experiment, the resulting index was 14% of the size of the collection. A heuristic that discards all patterns not appearing early in the score reduces the index to 2% of the collection size, but this removes secondary themes. A listening experiment, using 5 orchestral movements, showed that people can reliably recognize secondary themes from music they have just listened to. Therefore, it is plausible that users might base some queries on secondary themes, so it may be necessary to retain secondary themes in the index.

Our current goal is to extend the number and style of musical works in our index, to ensure that our results hold up over a wider variety of music. At this point, we are still focusing on classical music; it is clear that the thematic base of most styles of classical music provides a solid basis for indexing, although we are unsure what to expect when analyzing modern styles such as minimalist compositions. A further goal is to build indices of popular music. It is not clear whether a popular music index will capture anything meaningful in terms of user queries, but song "hooks" may provide such a base.

The algorithm itself may be further developed in several ways. First, it may be possible to reduce the size of the index by better identification of variations within the index itself, the goal being to keep only one variation of any melodic sequence in the index.

Second, we would like to improve the algorithm's performance on finding secondary themes. This will likely involve some use of approximate matching in the algorithm itself. Reliable location of secondary themes will be useful for musicological applications, even if the eventual decision is to build indices, for music information retrieval, intended to capture only primary themes.

Finally, we would like to definitively answer the question of whether it is necessary to keep secondary themes in a music retrieval index. This will require more focused user studies than we have carried out to this point.

8. References

[1] Bach, J.S. Prelude and Fugue in Eb Major, The Well-Tempered Klavier, Book 1, Bach-Gesellschaft Edition. MuseData virtual scores. http://www.ccarh.org.

[2] Barlow, H., and Morgenstern, S. A Dictionary of Musical Themes. Crown Publishers, NY, 1948.

[3] CCARH: Center for Computer Assisted Research in the Humanities. MuseData virtual scores. http://www.ccarh.org.

[4] Downie, J. S., and Nelson, M. Evaluation of a simple and effective music information retrieval method. Proc. ACM SIGIR 2000, 73-80, 2000.

[5] Hewlett, W. MuseData: Multipurpose representation. In E. Selfridge-Field (ed.), Beyond MIDI: The Handbook of Musical Codes, 402-445, MIT Press, Cambridge, MA, 1997.

[6] Liu, C.C., Hsu, J.L., and Chen, A.L.P. Efficient theme and non-trivial repeating pattern discovering in music databases. Proc. IEEE Intl. Conf. on Data Engineering, 14-21, 1999.

[7] McNab, R.J., Smith, L.A., Witten, I.H., and Henderson, C.L. Tune retrieval in the multimedia library. Multimedia Tools and Applications 10, 113-132, 2000.

[8] Meek, C. and Birmingham, W. Thematic Extractor. Proc. ISMIR 2001, 119-128, 2001.

[9] Mongeau, M., and Sankoff, D. Comparison of musical sequences. Computers and the Humanities 24, 161-175, 1990.

[10] Salosaari, P., and Jarvlin, K. MUSIR – A retrieval model for music. Tech Report RN-1998-1, University of Tampere, 1998.

Structural Analysis of Musical Signals for Indexing and Thumbnailing

Wei Chai   Barry Vercoe

MIT Media Laboratory

{chaiwei, bv}@media.mit.edu

Abstract

A musical piece typically has a repetitive structure. Analysis of this structure will be useful for music segmentation, indexing and thumbnailing. This paper presents an algorithm that can automatically analyze the repetitive structure of musical signals. First, the algorithm detects the repetitions of each segment of fixed length in a piece using dynamic programming. Second, the algorithm summarizes this repetition information and infers the structure based on heuristic rules. The performance of the approach is demonstrated visually using figures for qualitative evaluation, and by two structural similarity measures for quantitative evaluation. Based on the structural analysis result, this paper also proposes a method for music thumbnailing. The preliminary results obtained using a corpus of Beatles' songs show that automatic structural analysis and thumbnailing of music are possible.

1. Introduction

A musical piece typically has a repetitive structure. For example, a song may have a structure of ABA, indicating a three-part compositional form in which the second section contrasts with the first section, and the third section is a restatement of the first. Methods for automatically detecting the repetitive structure of a musical piece from acoustical signals is valuable for information retrieval systems and digital libraries; for example, the result can be used for indexing the musical content or for music thumbnailing.

There has been some recent research on this topic. Dannenberg and Hu presented a method to automatically detect the repetitive structure of musical signals [6]. The process consists of searching for similar segments in a musical piece, forming clusters of similar segments, and explaining the musical structure in terms of these clusters. Three representations were investigated: monophonic pitch estimation, chroma representation, and polyphonic transcription followed by harmonic analysis. Although the promise of this method was demonstrated in several examples, there was no quantitative evaluation of the method in their paper.

Two topics closely related to structural analysis of music have also been investigated. One is *music thumbnailing* (or *music summarization*), which aims at finding the most representative part (normally assumed to be the most repeated section) of a song. Some research on music thumbnailing deals with symbolic musical data (e.g., MIDI files and scores) [10]. There have also been studies on thumbnailing of musical signals. Logan and Chu attempted to use a clustering technique or Hidden Markov Models to find key phrases of songs. Mel Cepstral features were used to characterize each song [11].

The other related topic is *music segmentation*. Most previous research in this area attempted to segment musical pieces by detecting the locations where a significant change of statistical properties occurs [1]. This method is more appropriate for segmenting different local events rather than segmenting the semantic components of the global structure.

Additionally, Foote proposed a representation called a *similarity matrix* for visualizing and analyzing the structure of audio, including symbolic music, acoustic musical signals or more general audio [7][8]. One attempt using this representation was to locate points of significant change in music (e.g., score analysis) or audio (e.g., speech/music segmentation) [8]. Bartsch and Wakefield used the similarity matrix and chroma-based features for music thumbnailing [4]. A variation of the similarity matrix was also proposed for music thumbnailing [12].

This paper describes research into automatic identification of the repetitive structure of musical pieces from acoustic signals. Specifically, an algorithm is presented that will output structural information, including both the form (e.g., AABABA) and the boundaries indicating the beginning and the end of each section. It is assumed that no prior knowledge about musical forms or the length of each section is provided, and the restatement of a section may have variations. This assumption requires both robustness and efficiency of the algorithm.

Two novel structural similarity measures are also proposed in this paper to quantitatively evaluate the performance of the algorithm, in addition to the qualitative evaluation presented by figures.

The remainder of this paper is organized as follows. Section 2 illustrates the structural analysis approach. Section 3 presents the experimental results. Section 4 explains how the structural analysis result can be used for music thumbnailing. Section 5 gives conclusions and proposes future work.

2. Approach

This section illustrates the structural analysis method, which follows five steps and is also illustrated in Figure 1:

1) Segment the signal into frames and compute the feature of each frame;
2) Segment the feature sequence into overlapped segments of fixed length and compute the repetition property of each segment using dynamic programming;
3) Detect the repetitions of each segment by finding the local minima in the dynamic programming result;
4) Merge consecutive segments that have the same repetitive property into sections and generate pairs of similar sections;
5) Segment and label the repetitive structure.

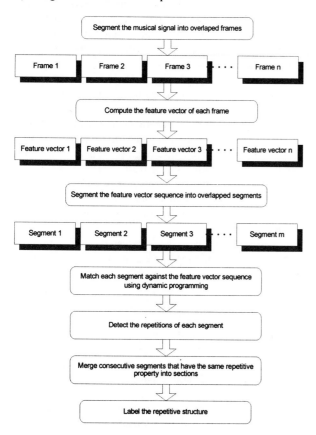

Figure 1. Overview of the approach.

The following five sections explain each step in detail. All the parameter configurations are tuned based on the experimental corpus, which is described in Section 3.

2.1. Feature extraction

The algorithm first segments the signal into overlapped frames (e.g., 1024-sample window length with 512-sample overlap) and computes the feature of each frame.

Two representations are investigated in this paper. One is the pitch representation, which uses autocorrelation [13] to estimate the main frequency component of each frame. Although all the test data in the experiment are polyphonic, it turns out that, for musical signals with a leading vocal, this feature can still capture much information. The other representation explored is the spectral representation, i.e., FFT magnitude coefficients.

The distance between two pitch features v_1 and v_2 is defined as

$$d_p(v_1, v_2) = \frac{|v_1 - v_2|}{normalization\ factor} \quad (1)$$

The distance between two spectral features $\vec{v}_1$ and $\vec{v}_2$ is defined as

$$d_f(\vec{v}_1, \vec{v}_2) = 0.5 - 0.5 \cdot \frac{\vec{v}_1 \bullet \vec{v}_2}{|\vec{v}_1| \| \vec{v}_2 |} \quad (2)$$

In both cases, a distance value ranges between 0 and 1.

2.1. Pattern matching

After computing the feature vector v_j (one-dimensional vector for the pitch representation and N-dimensional vector for the spectral representation) for each frame, the algorithm segments the feature vector sequence $V[1,n] = \{v_j \mid j = 1,...,n\}$ (n is the number of frames) into overlapped segments of fixed length l (e.g., 200 consecutive vectors with 150 vectors overlap). Since previous research has shown that dynamic programming is effective for music pattern matching [9][14], here dynamic programming is used to match each segment (i.e., $s_i = V[j, j+l-1]$) with the feature vector sequence starting from this segment (i.e., $V[j,n]$). The dynamic programming algorithm will fill in a matrix M_i (i.e., the dynamic programming matrix of the ith segment) as shown in Figure 2 based on Equation 3.

$$M[p,q] = \min \begin{cases} M[p-1,q]+e & (p \geq 1) \\ M[p,q-1]+e & (q \geq 1) \\ M[p-1,q-1]+c & (p,q \geq 1) \\ 0 & o.w. \end{cases} \quad (3)$$

where e is the insertion or deletion cost, c is the distance between the two corresponding feature vectors, which has been defined in Section 2.1. The last row of matrix M_i is defined as function $d_i[r]$ (shown as the shaded area in Figure 2). In addition, the trace-back step of dynamic programming determines the actual alignments (i.e., the locations in $V[j,n]$ matching the beginning of s_i) that result in $d_i[r]$. The trace-back result is denoted as $t_i[r]$.

	$\leq$	$V_{(j+1)}$	$V_{(j+2)}$	$\vdots$	$\vdots$	$\vdots$	$\vdots$	$\vdots$	$\leq$
	0	0	0	0	...	...	...	...	...	0
v_j	e								
$V_{(j+1)}$	2e								
...	...								
...	...								
$V_{(j+l-1)}$	le								

Figure 2. Dynamic programming matrix M_i.

This step is the most time consuming one in the structural analysis algorithm; its time complexity is $O(n^2)$.

2.3. Repetition detection

This step of the algorithm detects the repetition of each segment. To achieve this, the algorithm detects the local minima in the function $d_i[r]$ for each i, because normally a repetition of segment i will correspond to a local minimum in this function.

There are four predefined parameters in the algorithm of detecting the local minima: the width parameter w, the distance parameter d, the height parameter h, and the shape parameter p. To detect local minima of $d_i[r]$, the algorithm slides the window of width w over $d_i[r]$. Assume the index of the minimum within the window is r_0 with value $d_i[r_0]$, the index of the maximum within the window but left to r_0 is r_1 (i.e., $r_1 < r_0$) with value $d_i[r_1]$, and the index of the maximum within the window but right to r_0 is r_2 (i.e., $r_2 > r_0$) with value $d_i[r_2]$. If

(1) $d_i[r_1] - d_i[r_0] > h$ $\ and\ $ $d_i[r_2] - d_i[r_0] > h$ (i.e., the local minimum is deep enough); and

(2) $\dfrac{d_i[r_1] - d_i[r_0]}{r_1 - r_0} > p$ $\ or\ $ $\dfrac{d_i[r_2] - d_i[r_0]}{r_2 - r_0} > p$ (i.e., the local minimum is sharp enough); and

(3) No two repetitions are closer than d, the algorithm adds the minimum into the detected repetition set. In our experiment, we set $w=400$, $d=5$, and $p=0.1$. Figure 3 shows the repetition detection result of one segment in the song *Yesterday*.

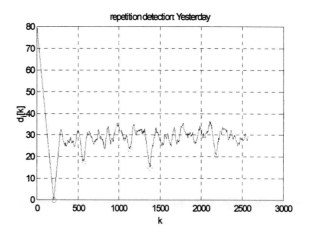

Figure 3. One-segment repetition detection result of *Yesterday*. The local minima indicated by circles correspond to detected repetitions of the segment.

The repetitions detected may have add or drop errors, meaning a repetition is falsely detected or missed. For example, in Figure 3, the first, the second, the fourth and the fifth detected local minima correspond to the four restatements of the same melodic segment in the song ("... here to stay ...", "... over me ...", "... hide away ...", "... hide away ..."). However, there is an add error occurring at the third detected local minimum. The number of add errors and that of the drop errors are balanced by the predefined parameter h; whenever the local minimum is deeper than height h, the algorithm reports a detection of repetition. Thus, when h increases, there are more drop errors but fewer add errors, and vise versa. For balancing between these two kinds of errors, the algorithm searches within a range for the best value of h (e.g., decreasing from 10 to 5 with step -1 for the pitch representation, and decreasing from 12 to 8 with step -1 for the spectral representation), so that the number of detected repetitions of the whole song is reasonable (e.g., *# detected repetitions / n ≈ 2*).

For each detected minimum $d_i[r^*]$ for $s_i = V[j, j+l-1]$, let $k^* = t_i[r^*]$; thus, it is detected that the segment starting at v_j is repeated at v_{j+k^*}. Please note that by the nature of dynamic programming, the matching part may not be of length l due to the variations in the repetition.

29

2.4. Segment merging

The algorithm merges consecutive segments that have the same repetitive property into sections and generates pairs of similar sections in this step.

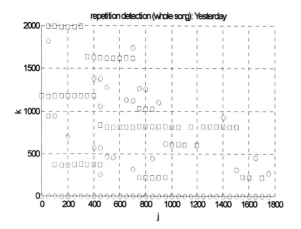

Figure 4. Whole-song repetition detection result of *Yesterday*. A circle or a square at location (j, k) indicates that the segment starting at v_j is detected to repeat at v_{j+k}.

Figure 4 shows the repetition detection result of the song *Yesterday* after this step. In this figure, a circle or a square at (j, k) corresponds to a repetition detected in the last step (i.e., the segment starting at v_j is repeated at v_{j+k}). Since typically one musical phrase consists of multiple segments, based on the configurations in previous steps, if one segment in a phrase is repeated by a shift of k, all the segments in this phrase are repeated by shifts roughly equal to k. This phenomenon can be seen from Figure 4, where the squares have the horizontal patterns indicating consecutive segments have roughly the same shifts.

By detecting these horizontal patterns (denoted by squares in Figure 4) and discarding other detected repetitions (denoted by circles in Figure 4) obtained from the third step, the effects of add/drop errors are further reduced.

The output of this step is a set of merged sections in terms of tuples $< j_1, j_2, shift >$, indicating that the segment starting at v_{j_1} and ending at v_{j_2} repeats roughly from $v_{j_1+shift}$ to $v_{j_2+shift}$. Each tuple corresponds to one horizontal pattern in the whole-song repetition detection result. For example, the tuple corresponding to the left-bottom horizontal pattern in Figure 4 is <100, 450, 370>. Since the shifts of repetitions may not be exactly the same for segments in the merged section, the shift of the whole section is the average value.

2.5. Structure labeling

Based on the tuples obtained from the fourth step, the last step of the algorithm segments the whole piece into sections and labels each section according to the repetitive relation (i.e., gives each section a symbol such as "A", "B", etc.). Thus, this step will output the structural information, including both the form (e.g., AABABA) and the boundaries indicating the beginning and the end of each section.

To solve conflicts that might occur, the rule for labeling is always labeling the most frequently repeated section first. Specifically, the algorithm finds the most frequently repeated section based on the first two columns in the tuples, and labels it and its shifted versions as section A. Then the algorithm deletes the tuples already labeled, repeats the same procedure for the remaining tuples, and labels sections produced in each step as B, C, D and so on. If conflicts occur (e.g., a later labeled section has overlap with the previous labeled sections), the previous labeled sections will always remain intact and the current section will be truncated.

3. Experiment and evaluation

This section presents the experimental results and evaluations of the structural analysis approach.

3.1. Data set

The experimental corpus consists of the 26 Beatles' songs in the two CDs *The Beatles* (1962-1966). All these songs have clear repetitive structures and leading vocal. The data were mixed to 8-bit mono and down-sampled to 11kHz.

3.2. Measures of structural similarity

Figure 5. Comparison of the computed structure (above) using the pitch representation and the ideal structure (below) of *Yesterday*. Sections in the same color indicate restatements of the section. Sections in the lightest grey correspond to the sections with no repetition.

To qualitatively evaluate the results, figures as shown in Figure 5 are used to compare the structure obtained from the algorithm with the ideal structure obtained by manually labeling the repetition. This paper also proposes two measures of structural similarity to quantitatively evaluate the result. Both of the measures need to be as small as possible, ideally equal to zero.

Measure 1 (structural measure) is defined as the edit distance between the strings representing different forms. For the example in Figure 5, the distance between the ideal structure AABABA and the computed structure AABBABA is 1, indicating one insertion. Here how the algorithm labels each section is not important as long as the repetitive relation is the same; thus, this ideal structure is deemed as equivalent (0-distance) to structure BBABAB, or structure AACACA.

Measure 2 (boundary measure) is mainly used to evaluate how accurate the boundaries of each section are. It is defined as

$$BM = (1 - r)/s \qquad (4)$$

where r is the ratio of the length of parts where both structures have the same labeling to the whole length, and s is the number of the repetitive sections in the ideal structure.

3.3. Results

Figure 6 and Figure 7 show the structural and boundary measures of the experimental results using both the pitch representation and the spectral representation. In Figure 7, the baseline results corresponding to labeling the whole song as a single section are also plotted for a comparison.

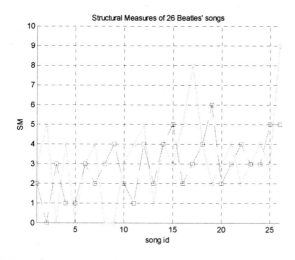

Figure 6. Structural measures of the 26 Beatles' songs. The solid line with circle markers corresponds to the pitch representation results. The dashed line with square markers corresponds to the spectral representation results.

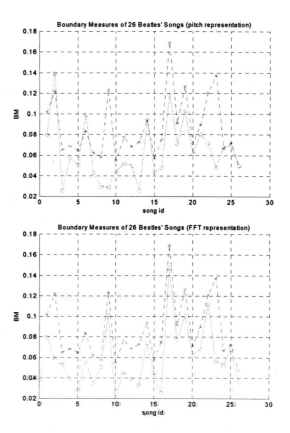

Figure 7. Boundary measures of the 26 Beatles' songs. The solid lines with circle markers correspond to the computed results (above: pitch representation; below: spectral representation). The dotted lines with x markers correspond to the baseline.

It is easily seen from the above figures that the performance of the third, the eighth and the ninth song using the pitch representation are the best (the structural measures are 0 and the boundary measures are low). For example, the result of the third song *From me to you* using the pitch representation is shown in Figure 8.

Figure 8. Comparison of the computed structure (above) using the pitch representation and the ideal structure (below) of *From me to you*.

The one of the worst performance is the seventeenth song *Day tripper* using the pitch representation, whose result is shown in Figure 9.

Figure 9. Comparison of the computed structure (above) using the pitch representation and the ideal structure (below) of *Day tripper*.

Some interesting results also occur. For example, for the twelfth song *Ticket to ride*, although the computed structure using the spectral representation is different from the ideal structure as shown in Figure 10, it also looks reasonable by seeing section A in the computed structure as the combination of section A and section B in the ideal structure.

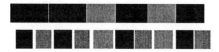

Figure 10. Comparison of the computed structure (above) using the spectral representation and the ideal structure (below) of *Ticket to ride*.

3.4. Discussions

The experimental result shows that, by either the pitch representation or the spectral representation, the performance of 15 out of 26 songs have structural measures less than or equal to 2 (Figure 6) and the results of all the songs have boundary measures better than the baseline (Figure 11). This demonstrates the promise of the method.

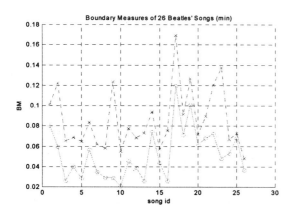

Figure 11. Boundary measures of the 26 Beatles' songs. The solid line with circle markers corresponds to the best computed result for each song using either the pitch representation or the spectral representation. The dotted line with x markers corresponds to the baseline.

The result does not show one representation is significantly superior to the other. However, for each song, the result of one representation is often better than the result of the other. This indicates that the representation does play an important role in performance and investigating other feature representations might help improve the accuracy of the algorithm.

One can notice that, even for the song with the best performance, the computed boundaries of each section were slightly shifted from the ideal boundaries. This was mainly caused by the inaccuracy of the approximate pattern matching. To tackle this problem, other musical features (e.g., chord progressions, change in dynamics, etc.) can be used to detect local events so as to locate the boundaries accurately. In fact, this problem suggests that computing only the repetitive relation might not be sufficient for finding the semantic structure. "The position of phrase boundaries in tonal melodies relates to a number of interacting musical factors. The most obvious determinants of musical phrases are the standard chord progressions known as cadence. Other factors include 'surface features' such as relatively large interval leaps, change in dynamics, and micropauses ('grouping preference rules'), and repeated musical patterns in terms of harmony, rhythm and melodic contour." [3]

4. Music thumbnailing via structural analysis

The problem of music thumbnailing aims at finding the most representative part of a song, which can be used for music browsing and searching. It would be helpful if the song has been segmented into semantically meaningful sections before summarization, because, although what makes a part of a song most memorable is not clear, this part often appears at particular locations within the structure, e.g., the beginning or the end part of each section.

For example, among the 26 Beatles' songs, 6 songs have the song titles in the first sentence of a section; 9 songs have them in the last sentence of a section; and 10 songs have them in both the first and the last sentences of a section. For many pop/rock songs, titles are contained in the "hook" sentences. This information is very useful for music thumbnailing: once we have the structure of a song, a straightforward strategy is to choose the beginning or the end part of the most repeated section as the summary of the music. For example, if ten-second summaries are wanted, Table 1 shows the performance of this strategy based on the criteria proposed by Logan and Chu [11]. The four columns in Table 1 indicate the percentage of summaries that contain a vocal portion, contain the song's title, are the beginning of a section, and are the beginning of a phrase. The algorithm first find the most repeated sections, take the first section among these and truncate the beginning ten seconds of it as the summary of the song. The thumbnailing result using this method highly depends on the accuracy of the structural analysis result. For example, the summary of the song *From me to you* using the pitch representation is "If there's anything that you want; If there's anything I can do; Just call…"; the summary of the song *Yesterday* using the pitch representation is "Yesterday, all my troubles seemed so far away; Now it looks as though…". Both of the summaries start right at the beginning of the most repetitive section. However, the summary of song *Day tripper* using the pitch representation does not contain any vocal portion due to the poor structural analysis result of this song.

Table 1: Thumbnailing results of the 26 Beatles' songs

	Vocal	Title	Beginning of a section	Beginning of a phrase
Pitch	85%	23%	50%	58%
FFT	88%	35%	46%	58%

5. Conclusions and future work

This paper presents an algorithm for automatically analyzing the repetitive structure of music from acoustic signals. Preliminary results were evaluated both qualitatively and quantitatively, which demonstrate the promise of the proposed method. To improve the accuracy, more representations need to be investigated. The possibility of generalizing this method to other music genres should also be explored.

Additionally, inferring the hierarchical repetitive structures of music and identifying the functionality of each section within the structure would be a more complicated yet interesting topic.

Music segmentation, thumbnailing and structural analysis are three coupled problems. Discovery of effective methods for solving any one of the three problems will benefit the other two. Furthermore, the solution to any of them depends on the study of humans' perception of music, for example, what makes part of music sounds like a complete phrase and what makes it memorable or distinguishable. Human experiments are always necessary for exploring such questions.

Finally, while most previous research on music digital libraries was based on symbolic representations of music (e.g., MIDI, scores), this paper attempts to address the structural analysis problem of acoustic musical data. We believe that current automatic music transcription techniques are still far from robust and efficient, and thus analyzing acoustic musical data directly without transcription is of great application value for indexing the digital music repository, segmenting music at transitions, and summarizing the thumbnails of music, all of which will benefit the users' browsing and searching in a music digital library.

6. References

[1] J.J. Aucouturier and M. Sandler. "Segmentation of Musical Signals using Hidden Markov Models," *In Proc. AES 110th Convention*, May 2001.

[2] J.J. Aucouturier and M. Sandler. "Using Long-Term Structure to Retrieve Music: Representation and Matching," *In Proc. International Symposium on Music Information Retrieval*, Bloomington, IN, 2001.

[3] M. Balaban, K. Ebcioglu, and O. Laske, Understanding Music with AI: Perspectives on Music Cognition, Cambridge: MIT Press; Menlo Park: AAAI Press, 1992.

[4] M.A. Bartsch and G.H. Wakefield, "To Catch a Chorus: Using Chroma-based Representations for Audio Thumbnailing," *In Proc. Workshop on Applications of Signal Processing to Audio and Acoustics*, 2001.

[5] W.P. Birmingham, R.B. Dannenberg, G.H. Wakefield, M. Bartsch, D. Bykowski, D. Mazzoni, C. Meek, M. Mellody, and W. Rand, "MUSART: Music Retrieval via Aural Queries," *In Proc. International Symposium on Music Information Retrieval*, Bloomington, IN, 2001.

[6] R.B. Dannenberg and N. Hu, "Pattern Discovery Techniques for Music Audio," *In Proc. International Conference on Music Information Retrieval*, October 2002.

[7] J. Foote, "Visualizing Music and Audio using Self-Similarity," *In Proc. ACM Multimedia Conference*, Orlando, FL, pp. 77-80, 1999.

[8] J. Foote, "Automatic Audio Segmentation using a Measure of Audio Novelty." *In Proc. of IEEE International Conference on Multimedia and Expo*, vol. I, pp. 452-455, 2000.

[9] J. Foote, "ARTHUR: Retrieving Orchestral Music by Long-Term Structure," *In Proc. International Symposium on Music Information Retrieval*, October 2000.

[10] J.L. Hsu, C.C. Liu, and L.P. Chen, "Discovering Nontrivial Repeating Patterns in Music Data," *IEEE Transactions on Multimedia*, Vol. 3, No. 3, pp. 311-325, September 2001.

[11] B. Logan and S. Chu, "Music Summarization using Key Phrases," *In Proc. International Conference on Acoustics, Speech and Signal Processing*, 2000.

[12] G. Peeters, A. L. Burthe and X. Rodet, "Toward Automatic Music Audio Summary Generation from Signal Analysis,"

In Proc. International Conference on Music Information Retrieval, October 2002.

[13] C. Roads, The Computer Music Tutorial, MIT Press, 1996.

[14] C. Yang, "Music Database Retrieval Based on Spectral Similarity," *In Proc. International Symposium on Music Information Retrieval*, 2001.

Session 3A: Automatic Metadata Creation

Session Chair: Erich Neuhold, Fraunhofer IPSI, Germany

Automatic Document Metadata Extraction using Support Vector Machines

Hui Han[1] C. Lee Giles[1,2] Eren Manavoglu[1] Hongyuan Zha[1]
[1]Department of Computer Science and Engineering [2]The School of Information Sciences and Technology
The Pennsylvania State University University Park, PA, 16802
{hhan,zha,manavogl}@cse.psu.edu giles@ist.psu.edu

Zhenyue Zhang
Department of Mathematics, Zhejiang University
Yu-Quan Campus, Hangzhou 310027, P.R. China
zyzhang@math.zju.edu.cn

Edward A. Fox
Department of Computer Science, Virginia Polytechnic Institute and State University
660 McBryde Hall, M/C 0106, Blacksburg, VA 24061
fox@vt.edu

Abstract

Automatic metadata generation provides scalability and usability for digital libraries and their collections. Machine learning methods offer robust and adaptable automatic metadata extraction. We describe a Support Vector Machine classification-based method for metadata extraction from header part of research papers and show that it outperforms other machine learning methods on the same task. The method first classifies each line of the header into one or more of 15 classes. An iterative convergence procedure is then used to improve the line classification by using the predicted class labels of its neighbor lines in the previous round. Further metadata extraction is done by seeking the best chunk boundaries of each line. We found that discovery and use of the structural patterns of the data and domain based word clustering can improve the metadata extraction performance. An appropriate feature normalization also greatly improves the classification performance. Our metadata extraction method was originally designed to improve the metadata extraction quality of the digital libraries Citeseer[17] and EbizSearch[24]. We believe it can be generalized to other digital libraries.

1 Introduction and related work

Interoperability is crucial to the effective use of Digital Libraries (DL) [19, 23]. The Open Archive Initiatives Protocols for Metadata Harvesting (OAI-PMH) is critical for the process, facilitating the discovery of content stored in distributed archives [7, 18]. The digital library CITIDEL (Computing and Information Technology Interactive Digital Educational Library), part of NSDL (National Science Digital Library), uses OAI-PMH to harvest metadata from all applicable repositories and provides integrated access and links across related collections [14]. Support for the Dublin Core (DC) metadata standard [31] is a requirement for OAI-PMH compliant archives, while other metadata formats optionally can be transmitted.

However, providing metadata is the responsibility of each data provider with the quality of the metadata a significant problem. Many data providers [13, 4] have had significant harvesting problems with XML syntax and encoding issues, even leading to unavailability of service [18]. In fact, some digital libraries have no metadata to harvest (some search engines have little or no metadata), or metadata that is not OAI compliant, e.g., CiteSeer [17]. Non-compliant metadata must be either automatically wrapped to work with the OAI protocol, or manually encoded. Building tools for automatic document metadata extraction and representation will therefore significantly improve the amount of metadata available, the quality of metadata extracted, and the efficiency and speed of the metadata extraction process.

Several methods have been used for automatic metadata extraction; regular expressions, rule-based parsers, and machine learning are the most popular of these. In general machine learning methods are robust and adaptable and, theoretically, can be used on any document set. Generating the labeled training data is the rather expensive price that has to be paid for learning systems. Although regular expressions and rule-based systems do not require any training and are straightforward to implement, their dependence on the application domain and the need for an expert to set the rules or regular expressions causes these methods to have limited use. Machine learning techniques for information extraction include symbolic learning, inductive logic programming, grammar induction, Support Vector Machines, Hidden Markov models, and statistical methods. Hidden Markov models (HMMs) are the most widely used generative learning method for representing and extracting information from sequential data. However, HMMs are based on the assumption that features of the model they represent are not independent from each other. Thus, HMMs have difficulty exploiting regularities of a semi-structured real system. Maximum entropy based Markov models [20] and conditional random fields [16] have been introduced to deal with the problem of independent features.

Recent work by Chieu [5] suggests that the information extraction task also can be addressed as a classification problem. Encouraged by their success in handling high dimensional feature spaces for classification problems [12, 9], we investigate Support Vector Machines (SVMs) for metadata extraction. Related work includes Kudoh et al using the SVM method for chunk identification, Mcnamee et al using a SVM for named entity extraction [22, 15, 29], and Pasula et al using relational probability models to solve identity uncertainty problems [10].

This paper discusses a machine learning method for automatic metadata extraction. The reported extraction results are based on experiments conducted on research papers. Most of the directly indexable information (e.g., authors' names, affiliations, addresses, and the title of the paper) are gathered in the header of a research paper. The header [27] consists of all the words from the beginning of the paper up to either the first section, usually the introduction, or to the end of the first page, whichever occurs first. In the experimental results section we illustrate the dominance of the introduced SVM-based metadata extraction algorithm over the well-known HMM based systems [27]. We also introduce a method for extracting individual names from the list of authors within the same framework and present a new document metadata extraction method using SVM classification, combining chunk identification. A new feature extraction method and an iterative line classification process using contextual information also are presented.

The remainder of the paper is organized as follows: section 2 describes the problem and dataset; section 3 presents our metadata extraction method, together with the cross validation results on 500 training headers; section 4 presents the experiment result of our metadata extraction algorithm on the test dataset; section 5 discusses the aspects to be improved and planned future work.

2 Problem definition and dataset

The Dublin Core has been widely used as a metadata standard and defines 15 elements for resource description: Title, Creator, Subject, Description, Contributor, Publisher, Date, Type, Format, Identifier, Source, Relation, References, Is Referenced By, Language, Rights and Coverage. However, this is only a basic set of metadata elements and is used by OAI-PMH for "minimal" interoperability. Extending document metadata through information on both authors (such as affiliation, address, and email), and documents (such as publication number and thesis type), would provide greater representation power. It also would help in building unified services for heterogeneous digital libraries, while at the same time enabling sophisticated querying of the databases and facilitating construction of the semantic web [3]. Seymore et al defined 15 different tags for the document header [27] to populate the Cora search engine [21], 4 of which are the same as those in the Dublin Core. Two of the remaining tags, introduction and end of page, are functional rather than informative, indicating the end of the header. Leaving out the functional tags, we adopt their format as extended metatags for research papers. We further propose to define affiliation as part of the address, instead of an exclusive tag. Table 1 is a short explanation of the extended metatags and the mapping to Dublin Core metadata elements.

Figure 1 is an example of meta-tagged document header. Document metadata extraction also can be viewed as labeling the text with the corresponding metatags. Each metatag corresponds to a class. Lines 22 and 25 are multi-class lines containing chunks of information from multiple classes. We define a chunk of information as consecutive words that belong to the same class. Line 22 and 25 contain the chunks of 5 classes: email, web, affiliation, address, and note. All the other lines contain information belonging to one class only and are therefore called single-class lines.

We use the labeled dataset provided by Seymore et al [27] to test our method of metadata extraction. The dataset contains 935 headers of computer science research papers, with 500 of those belonging to the training set and the remaining 435 headers belonging to the test set. The training set includes a total of 10025 lines and 23557 word tokens whereas there are 8904 lines and 20308 word tokens in the test set. These headers are text files converted from the pdf and ps files. Each line ends with a carriage return and the line break marks $+L+$ are provided by the dataset for identification.

The document headers are semi-structured. We observe that among total 10025 lines from 500 training headers, the majority (9775 lines, 97.51%) are single-class lines and only 250 (2.49%) lines are multi-class lines. Even after removing the abstract section which is mostly single-class

Table 1. Extended metatags and their mapping to Dublin Core metadata elements

Extended Metatag	DC Element	Explanation
Title	Title	Title of the paper
Author	Creator	The name(s) of the author(s) of the document
Affiliation		Author's affiliation
Address		Author's address
Note		Phrases about acknowledgment, copyright, notices, and citations
Email		Author's email address
Date		Publication date
Abstract Introduction	Description	An account of the content Introduction part in the paper
Phone		Author's phone number
Keyword	Subject	The topic of the content of the document
Web		URL of Author's webpage of the document
Degree		Language associated with thesis degree
Pubnum		Publication number of the document
Page		The end of the page

1:<title> Stochastic Interaction and Linear Logic +L+ </title>
2:<author> Patrick D. Lincoln John C. Mitchell Andre Scedrov +L+ </author>
3: Abstract +L+
4:We present stochastic interactive semantics for prepositional linear +L+
...
22:<email>   jcm@cs.stanford.edu   </email>   <web> http://theory.stanford.edu/people/jcm/home.html </web> <affiliation> Department of Computer Science, Stanford University, </affiliation> <address> Stanford, CA 94305.</address> <note> Supported in part +L+
23:by an NSF PYI Award, matching funds from Digital Equipment Corporation, the Pow-ell Foundation, and Xerox Corporation; and the Wallace F. and Lucille M. Davis Faculty +L+
24:Scholarship. +L+ </note>
25:<email>   andre@cis.upenn.edu   </email> <web>http://www.cis.upenn.edu/~andre   </web>   <affiliation> Department of Mathematics, University of Pennsylvania, </affiliation> <address> Philadelphia, PA 19104-6395. </address> <note> Partially supported by +L+
26:NSF Grants CCR-91-02753 and CCR-94-00907 and by ONR Grant N00014-92-J-1916. Sce-drov is an American Mathematical Society Centennial Research Fellow. +L+ </note>

Figure 1. Example 1 labeled document header and metadata. Each line starts with the line number.

lines, multi-class lines still account for only 4.98% of all lines. Classifying each line into one or more classes thus appears to be more efficient for meta-tagging than classifying each word. Table 2 lists the class distributions of the lines from the 500 training headers.

The predicted tags for previous and next lines are also good indicators of the class(es) to which a line belongs. For instance, an abstract has consecutive lines uninterrupted by lines of other classes, and title lines usually come before author lines. Making use of such contextual information among lines we feel will increase the line classification performance.

We propose a third algorithm for processing the lines predicted to contain chunks of information from multiple classes. Since each chunk has consecutive words, we consider extracting metadata from the multi-class lines as the problem of seeking the optimal chunk boundaries. Recognition of individual author names within multi-author lines can also be considered as the problem of seeking the right chunk boundary, in this case between the author names. For example, does the line "Chungki Lee James E. Burns" refer to two authors "Chungki Lee" and "James E. Burns," two authors "Chungki Lee James" and "E. Burns," or one author "Chungki Lee James E. Burns"?

Based on the structural patterns of the document headers,

we decompose the metadata extraction problem into two sub-problems – (1) line classification and (2) chunk identification of multi-class and multi-author lines. Accurate line classification is a critical step, since it directly affects the performance of the chunk identification module.

3 Metadata Extraction Algorithm

This section describes two important aspects of our work, SVM classification and feature extraction. The metadata extraction algorithm is discussed in detail, together with the corresponding ten-fold cross-validation result on the 500 training headers. Performance is evaluated using accuracy, precision, recall, and F measure.

3.1 Support Vector Machine Classification

Support Vector Machine is well known for its generalization performance and ability in handling high dimension data. Consider a two class classification problem. Let $\{(x_1, y_1), ... ,(x_N, y_N)\}$ be a two-class training dataset, with x_i a training feature vector and their labels $y_i \subset (-1, +1)$. The

Table 2. Class distribution among 10025 total lines from 500 training header

Class No.	Class Name	Number of Lines	Percentage
1	Title	832	8.3%
2	Author	724	7.2%
3	Affiliation	1065	10.6%
4	Address	629	6.3%
5	Note	526	5.2%
6	Email	336	3.4%
7	Date	182	1.8%
8	Abstract	5007	50.0%
9	Introduction	326	3.3%
10	Phone	61	0.6%
11	Keyword	142	1.4%
12	Web	38	0.4%
13	Degree	169	1.7%
14	Pubnum	116	1.1%
15	Page	166	1.7%

SVM attempts to find an optimal separating hyperplane to maximally separate two classes of training samples. The corresponding decision function is called a classifier. The kernel function of an SVM is written as $K(x_a, x_b)$ and it can be an inner product, Gaussian, polynomial, or any other function that obeys Mercer's condition [30, 6].

We choose the Gaussian kernel for the SVM and base our experiment on the software SVM_light [11]. We set the parameter gamma (-g), the spread of the Gaussian kernel as 0.1, and all other parameters set by SVM_light. We extend the SVM to multi-class classifiers in the "One class versus all others" approach, i.e., one class is positive and the remaining classes are negative.

3.2 Feature Extraction

Most of the previous work on information extraction uses word-specific feature representations [27, 15, 29]. Recent research on the topic suggests that line-specific features also could be useful [20].

We make use of both **word** and **line**-specific features to represent our data. Each line is represented by a set of word and line-specific features.

We design a rule-based, context-dependent word clustering method explained below for word-specific feature generation, with the rules extracted from various domain databases and text orthographic properties of words (e.g. capitalization) [26]. Word clustering methods group similar words and use the cluster as a feature. Distributional clustering methods have shown significant dimensionality reduction and accuracy improvement in text classification

[2, 28, 8]. While distributional clustering needs to use labeled training data, our rule-based method relies on the prior knowledge embedded in domain databases.

We collect the following databases to gather apriori knowledge of the domain:

- Standard on-line dictionary of Linux system
- Bob Baldwin's collection of 8441 first names and 19613 last names
- Chinese last names
- USA state names and Canada province names
- USA city names
- Country names from the World Fact Book [1], and
- Month names and their abbreviations

We also construct domain databases, i.e., word lists from training data for classes: affiliation, address, degree, pubnum, note, abstract, keyword, introduction, and phone. Words and bigrams that appear frequently in the lines of each class mentioned are selected to enter these word lists. Frequency thresholding is used to define the list size [32]. The abstract class word list contains one word "abstract" and the affiliation class list contains words shown in Table 3.

We then cluster words and bigrams based on their membership in the domain databases and their text orthographic properties. The words and bigrams in the same cluster are represented by a common feature, which we call word-specific feature. For example, an author line *"Chungki Lee James E. Burns"* is represented as *"Cap1NonDictWord: :MayName: :MayName: :SingleCap: :MayName:"*, after word clustering.

Such word clustering shows significant improvement in our experiment of classifying lines (details will be given in another paper). A reason is that the word cluster statistics give a more robust estimate than the original sparse word statistics [2, 28].

We define the weight of a word-specific feature as the number of times this feature appears in the sample (line).

The following is the list of line-specific features we believe to be useful for line classification. In particular, feature ClinePos is found to be very important in correct classification of title lines.

CsenLen Number of the words the line contains.

ClinePos The position of the line, i.e., line number.

CDictWordNumPer The percentage of the dictionary words in the line.

CNonDictWordNumPer The percentage of the non-dictionary words in the line.

CCap1DictWordNumPer The percentage of the dictionary words with first letter capitalized in the line.

CCap1NonDictWordNumPer The percentage of the non-dict words with first letter capitalized in the line.

CdigitNumPer The percentage of the numbers in the line.

We also have a feature for representing the percentage of the class-specific words in a line. CaffiNumPer is the percentage of the affiliation words in the line and CaddrNumPer, CdateNumPer, CdegreeNumPer, CphoneNumPer, CpubNumPer, CnoteNumPer, and CpageNumPer are the percentage of the address words, date words, degree words, phone words, publication number words, note words, and page number words, respectively. We assign weight to the line-specific features according to their definition.

Table 3. Affiliation Class Word List

DF Value	Word	DF Value	Word
325	University	37	Laboratory
221	Department	34	Technology
111	Univ	33	Dept
77	Institute	27	Systems
47	Research	26	School
39	Sciences	26	Center

However, our experiments show that SVM doesn't handle well the case when different features have very different ranges of values. For example, the feature "CsenLen" could have a weight of 40, while the line-specific feature **CdictWordNumPer** weight is over the range [0, 1]. Features with large scale may dominate the features with small weight. Therefore, we use the $\|X\|_\infty$ to normalize the feature weight and increase the classification performance as shown in the next section.

3.3 Line Classification Algorithms

The following is a two-step algorithm for classifying text lines into a single class or multiple classes. The two components are independent line classification followed by contextual line classification.

3.3.1 Independent line classification

In the first step, feature vectors are generated based on the feature extraction methodology described in the previous section. After removing the features with data frequency values < 3, we get feature vectors with 1100 dimensions on average for ten-fold cross validation. A feature vector is labeled as class C if the corresponding line contains words belonging to class C. Training feature vector set for class C is generated by collecting all the feature vectors with label C as positive samples and all the rest as negative; the same procedure applies to all classes. Note that a feature vector could have multiple labels and thus can belong to multiple training feature vector sets. 15 classifiers are then trained

Table 4. Word-specific feature set

Feature	Explanation
:email:	using regular expression match
:url:	using regular expression match
:singleCap:	a capital letter like M or M.
:postcode:	such as PA, MI
:abstract:	abstract
:keyword:	key word, key words, keyword, keywords
:intro:	introduction
:phone:	tel, fax, telephone
:month:	a word in the month list
:prep:	at, in, of
:degree:	a word or bigram in the degree domain word list
:pubnum:	a word or bigram in the publication number domain word list
:notenum:	a word or bigram in the note domain word list
:affi:	a word or bigram in the affiliation domain word list
:addr:	a word or bigram in the address domain word list
:city:	a word or bigram in the city name list
:state:	a word or bigram in the state name list
:country:	a word or bigram in the country name list
:mayName:	a word in one of the 3 name lists
:Cap1DictWord:	a dictionary word with first letter capitalized
:DictWord:	small case dictionary word
:NonDictWord:	small case non dictionary word
:Dig[3]:	a number of three digits

The word-specific feature considers text orthographic properties, e.g., BU-cs-93 is converted to :CapWord2-LowerWord2-Digs2:

on the 15 labeled feature vector sets. Test lines are classified into one or more classes if their feature vectors are scored positive by the corresponding classifier. This process is called independent line classification (also shown in Figure 2), since each line is classified independently.

Table 5 lists the ten-fold cross-validation results on the training dataset for the independent line classification algorithm. Figure 3 shows the F measure of independent line classification before and after normalization using ten-fold cross-validation on 500 training headers. Due to space limitations, we are not able to report our results for precision, recall, and accuracy. The effect of normalization is a significant improvement in performance. Normalization is especially important in identifying the rare classes, such as class 5 (note), 11 (keywords), and 12 (web). Consider class 5 "note" as an example, the positive note samples occupy 5.3% (53 out of 1001.5 averaged for each fold of ten-fold cross validation) of all test samples. Without normalization,

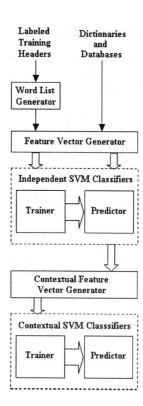

Figure 2. Overview of Line Classification Training Module.

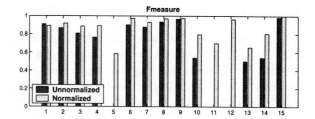

Figure 3. F measure of the independent line classification before and after normalization. X axis - class number; Y axis - F measure.

the note classifier classifies all testing samples into non-"note" classes. Thus, the recall for class 5 "note" is zero and the precision is infinite. Normalization appears to increase the importance of features in the class "note", which then enhances "note" samples for the "note" classifier.

3.3.2 Iterative contextual line classification

The second step makes use of the sequential information among lines discussed in section 2 to improve the classification of each line. We encode the class labels of N lines before and after the current line L as binary features and concatenate them to the feature vector of line L formed in step one, independent line classification. A contextual line classifier for each metatag is then trained based on these labeled feature vectors with additional contextual information. Line feature vectors for testing are extended the same way. Their neighbor lines' class labels are those predicted by the independent line classifier. Test lines are then reclassified into one or more classes by the contextual line classifiers. This contextual line classification is repeated such that in each iteration, the feature vector of each line is extended by incorporating the neighbor lines' class label informa-

tion predicted in the previous iteration. The procedure converges when the percentage of lines with new class labels is lower than a threshold. The threshold value is set to 0.7% in our experiments, and N is chosen to be 5. Ramshaw et al show the positive effect of a similar iterative algorithm on transformation-based learning for rule-selection [25].

The contextual information we use for line classification is encoded by the binary features P_{ij} if the previous ith closest line belongs to class j and N_{ij} if the next ith closest line belongs to class j, with $i \in (1..5)$ and $j \in (1..15)$. We found that choosing P_{ij} and N_{ij} to be 0.5/0, instead of 1/0 achieves better line classification performance, based on the experiment on the training dataset. This is because the line feature values are already normalized into the range [0, 1]. Choosing the midpoint of this range as the weight for up to 150 ($15*10$) contextual features is a type of normalization and is found to be more effective.

Figure 4 shows the performance evaluated by the F measure in each round of the iterative contextual line classification. As expected, the performance is stabilized within the first 10 iterations. It also shows that the first two rounds are responsible for most of the performance improvement. This behavior suggests two iteration steps can be used instead of waiting for absolute convergence. Table 6 lists the results achieved for each of the 15 classes when the iterative procedure converges. The small sample sizes of the class – degree, note, phone, keyword, and publication number – as shown in Table 6 may account for their poor classification performance. Seymore et al report the same phenomenon on the class – degree, note and publication number – using HMM model [27].

3.4 Extract metadata from multi-class lines

After classifying each line into one or more classes, we now extract metadata from each multi-class line based on the predicted class labels for this line. As discussed the metadata extraction task from multi-class lines is turned into the chunk identification task. Chunk identification of

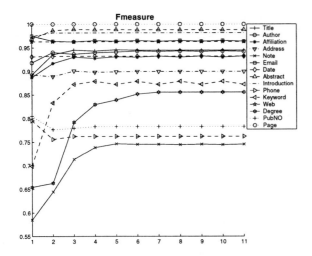

Figure 4. F measure in each round of the iterative contextual line classification. X axis - iteration round; Y axis - F measure.

Table 5. Independent line classification performance.

Class Name	Precision	Recall	F measure	Accuracy
Title	89.6%	88.9%	89.3%	98.2%
Author	94.2%	89.6%	91.8%	98.8%
Affiliation	93.8%	84.2%	88.7%	97.7%
Address	93.9%	85.1%	89.3%	98.8%
Note	82.3%	45.4%	58.5%	96.6%
Email	97.6%	97.4%	97.5%	99.8%
Date	97.2%	89.4%	93.1%	99.8%
Abstract	96.1%	97.7%	96.9%	96.9%
Introduction	98.8%	96.0%	97.4%	99.8%
Phone	93.8%	69.1%	79.5%	99.8%
Keyword	95.2%	55.2%	69.9%	99.3%
Web	100%	92.8%	96.3%	99.9%
Degree	86.0%	52.8%	65.4%	98.9%
Pubnum	91.7%	71.8%	80.5%	99.6%
Page	100.0%	100.0%	100.0%	100.0%

an N-class line is analogous to finding $N-1$ chunk boundaries in the line. Punctuation marks and spaces between words are candidate chunk boundaries.

Table 7 shows that 86% of the multi-class lines in training data are two-class lines. We search for the optimal chunk boundary which yields the maximum difference between the two chunks. Independent line classifiers are applied to calculate the difference between chunks.

Every punctuation mark and space can be a candidate chunk boundary for two-class lines. We consider only punctuation marks as candidates if two or more punctuation marks are used in the line; otherwise we try each punctuation mark and space. Assuming that each class has only one chunk in the line, two-class chunk identification is to find the optimal chunk boundary.

"The Ohio State University, Columbus, OH 43210-1277" is an example of two-class line of affiliation and address. Each comma is a candidate chunk boundary.

We call the affiliation classifier as classifier 1 and the address classifier as classifier 2. The classifiers we use here are the SVM line classifiers trained by single-class lines of the training dataset. We consider each chunk as a short line.

Definitions:

P_1 the classification score of chunk P by classifier 1;

P_2 the classification score of chunk P by classifier 2;

N_1 the classification score of chunk N by classifier 1;

N_2 the classification score of chunk N by classifier 2;

$P_{12} = P_1 - P_2; N_{21} = N_2 - N_1;$

$PN_1 = P_1 - N_1; PN_2 = P_2 - N_2;$

We choose the optimal chunk boundary as the punctuation mark or space yielding the maximal $P_{12} * N_{21}$. Chunk P is classified into class 1 if $PN_1 > 0$, and (1) $PN_1 * PN_2 < 0$ or (2) $PN_1 * PN_2 > 0$ and $\|PN_1\| = max(\|PN_1\|, \|PN_2\|)$, class 2 otherwise.

This two-class chunk identification algorithm results in an accuracy of 75.5% (160 out of 212 two-class lines from training samples). Accuracy here is defined as the percentage of the lines whose chunk boundaries are correctly predicted versus the total number of two-class lines. (This is the lower boundary of the accuracy.)

Many N-class ($N > 2$) chunk identification tasks may be simplified to two-class chunk identification tasks. For instance, using the positions of email and URL in the line, we may simplify the three-class chunk identification tasks as two-class chunk identification tasks. The position of the email address in the following three-class line *"International Computer Science Institute, Berkeley, CA 94704. email: aberer@icsi.berkeley.edu. Supported by Schweizerische Gesellschaft zur Forderung der Informatik und ihrer Anwendungen"* is a natural chunk boundary between the other two classes.

We are exploring more general multi-class chunk identification techniques.

3.5 Recognize authors in the multi-author lines

We consider the author lines with less than 4 words as *single-author lines* and the author lines with 4 or more words as *multi-author lines*. We further define a multi-author line where the authors are separated by spaces only

Table 6. Performance (%) of contextual line classification iteration algorithm when converges and the F measure increase than that of the independent line classification

Class Name	Precision	Recall	F measure (Increase)	Accuracy
Title	93.9	95.0	94.5(5.2)	99.1
Author	97.3	91.4	94.2(2.4)	99.2
Affiliation	96.4	90.3	93.3(4.5)	98.6
Address	93.6	86.7	90.0(0.71)	98.8
Note	86.4	65.6	74.6(16.0)	97.6
Email	98.9	94.0	96.4(-1.1)	99.8
Date	97.2	89.5	93.2(0.1)	99.8
Abstract	98.5	99.2	98.8(1.9)	98.8
Introduction	100.0	96.4	98.2(0.8)	99.9
Phone	98.3	62.3	76.2(-3.3)	99.7
Keyword	96.7	79.5	87.2(17.3)	99.7
Web	100.0	92.8	96.3(0.0)	99.9
Degree	91.4	80.5	85.6(20.1)	99.3
Pubnum	97.3	65.5	78.3(-2.2)	99.6
Page	100.0	100.0	100.0(0.0)	100.0

Table 7. The distribution of the multi-class lines in 500 training headers

N-Class	Number of Lines	Percentage
2	212	84.8%
3	33	13.2%
4	4	1.6%
5	1	0.4%

as *space-separated multi-author line*. Similarly, a multi-author line where the authors are separated by punctuation marks is defined as *punctuation-separated multi-author line*.

We extract a total of 326 multi-author lines from the training dataset as the dataset for our experiment on recognizing authors from the multi-author lines. Among the 326 multi-author lines, 227(69.6%) lines are punctuation-separated and 99(30.4%) are space-separated. Based on the different characteristics punctuation-separated multi-author lines and space-separated multi-author lines possess, we choose the following different strategies for either case.

3.5.1 Chunk identification in punctuation-separated multi-author lines

As we discussed before, to recognize each name from the multi-author lines is to identify chunk boundaries between

author names. It is obvious that the spaces and punctuation marks between words are the candidate chunk boundaries. The problem now becomes classifying each space or punctuation mark as chunk boundary or not. We consider only the punctuation mark in the line as the candidate chunk boundary if there are two or more punctuation marks in the line; otherwise, we examine each space and punctuation mark. The dictionary word "and" is considered as a punctuation mark. The spaces next to a punctuation mark are ignored.

We design the feature vector for each space and punctuation mark using both the raw features of the punctuation mark itself such as "," or "&", and the contextual features listed in Table 8. We also convert each word of the line into a 5-tuple $< FN, LN, L, FC, D >$. Each element of the 5-tuple is defined as follows.

FN: 1 if the word is in the first name list, 0 otherwise.

LN: 1 if the word is in the last name list, 0 otherwise.

L: 1, 2 or 0, indicates the word is of one letter, two letters, or more than two letters, respectively.

FC: 1 if the word is capitalized, 0 otherwise.

D: 1 if the word is a dictionary word, 0 otherwise.

We use the attributes defined in the above tuple to represent the contextual feature (8) in Table 8 in the converted format. The motivation is that if the closest word to a punctuation mark appears only on the first name list, or only on the last name list, it helps to classify if this punctuation mark is the right chunk boundary. For example, if "Leonidas Fegaras, David Maier" satisfies this pattern "[10010(First name)] [01011(Last name)], [10011(First name)] [00010(Last name)]", it will be reasonable to classify the comma as the right chunk boundary. However, the big overlap between the first name list and the last name list makes such feature representation of each word ineffective.

We find from the stepwise feature selection that the dominating features in classifying chunk boundary are the punctuation marks themselves. Therefore in implementation, we design simple heuristic rules to make use of the punctuation marks to extract each name from the punctuation-separated multi-author line.

Table 9 lists the chunk identification performance on punctuation-separated multi-author lines. The evaluation is based on the percentage of punctuation marks classified correctly.

3.5.2 Chunk identification in space-separated multi-author lines

Space-separated multi-author lines do not have any explicit information for chunk boundary recognition, unlike punctuation-separated lines. The valid patterns for author

Table 8. Contextual features for each candidate chunk boundary in punctuation-separated multi-author line

No.	Feature
1	The number of total punctuation marks of the same kind in the line
2	The position of this punctuation mark
3	The number of words before this punctuation mark
4	The number of words after this punctuation mark
5	The number of words between the previous and the current punctuation mark
6	The number of words between the current and the next punctuation mark
7	The ratio of the number of words before and after this punctuation mark
8	The previous and next 5 words in converted feature representation

Table 9. Chunk boundary identification performance of punctuation-separated multi-author lines

Accuracy	Precision	Recall	F measure
93.31	82.38	96.65	88.95

Table 10. The valid patterns of a name. "F"- Full Name; "F^{-}" - Full Name with hyphen, e.g., Jon-hey; "I" - Name Initial; "s" - lower case word

Pattern Class	Patterns
1	$(F\|F^-)F, (F\|F^-)(F\|F^-)F$ $(F\|F^-)(F\|F^-)(F\|F^-)F$ e.g., Yu-Chee Tseng
2	$(F\|F^-)IF, (F\|F^-)IIF, (F\|F^-)IIIF$ e.g., Dhabaleswar K. Panda
3	IF, IIF e.g., C. L. Giles
4	$I(F\|F^-)F$
5	$(F\|F^-)ssF$ e.g., Th.P. van der Weide

names are the source of information in this case. [Mary(Full Name)] [Y.(Name Initial)], for instance, cannot be a valid name.

The algorithm for extracting names from space-separated multi-author lines has four steps. Step 1, generate all potential name sequences for the space-separated multi-author lines based on the valid patterns of names that we define in Table 10. Step 2, design the feature vector for each potential name sequence. We manually label each potential name sequence as 1 or -1 by checking each name in this sequence from the web. Step 3, train a SVM name sequence classifier by the labeled training samples. Step 4, if the test space-separated multi-author line has only one potential name sequence, it is the predicted name sequence. Otherwise, classify each of its potential name sequences. The name sequence with the highest score is predicted as the correct name sequence.

For example, the line "Alan Fekete David Gupta Victor Luchangco Nancy Lynch Alex Shvartsman" has three potential name sequences (Figure 5). We generate three reasonable sequences, with each name separated by ⋄. The "1" and "-1" in front of each name sequence identifies the sequence as a positive sample or a negative sample. The number at the beginning of each sequence is the classifica-

tion score. The first sequence achieves the highest score and is predicted correctly.

The feature vector designed for each name sequence is based on the following features. Let us assume L is a line that contains M names, n_1, n_2 through n_M. For name n_i ($1 \leq i \leq M$) that has N_k words, we define the following five features.

$Form_{i,j}$ the form of the jth word of n_i, $Form_{i,j} \in \{F, F^-, I, s, o\}$. "$o$" - others.

$Pos_{i,j}$ the position of the jth word of n_i in the line.

$FN_{i,j}$ is equal to 1 if the jth word of n_i is only in the first name list, 0 otherwise.

$LN_{i,j}$ is equal to 1 if the jth word of n_i is only in the last name list, 0 otherwise.

$NonDic_{i,j}$ is equal to 1 if the jth word of n_i is a non-dictionary word, 0 otherwise.

The feature $Form_{i,j}$ has non-numerical values such as "F", "I" or "s". We enumerate each of these name patterns and assign these values as the weights of the corresponding features.

We generated all the potential name sequences expanded from the 99 space-separated name sequences as the name sequence dataset. We achieve a classification accuracy of 90.9% for ten-fold cross validation. Since we pick the potential sequence with the highest score for each unknown name sequence, the accuracy is the ratio of the correct predictions to the total number of name sequences, which is 99 in this case.

Using SVM supervised learning to classify name sequences helps find the implicit regularities that could have been missed by the manual inspection. A regularity discovered from the training data is: hyphenated names such as Jon-hey are not likely to be the last name.

Classification Score	Class label	Potential name sequences
1.6398636	1	Alan Fekete ◇ David Gupta ◇ Victor Luchangco ◇ Nancy Lynch ◇ Alex Shvartsman
0.8996393	-1	Alan Fekete ◇ David Gupta ◇ Victor Luchangco Nancy ◇ Lynch Alex Shvartsman
0.0061073704	-1	Alan Fekete ◇ David Gupta Victor ◇ Luchangco Nancy ◇ Lynch Alex Shvartsman

Figure 5. Example of potential name sequences

4 Experimental results

Performance is evaluated by precision, recall, F measure, and accuracy as described below.

Overall evaluation: The overall word classification accuracy for the header is the percentage of the header words that are tagged with the words' true labels.

Class-specific evaluation: We define A as the number of true positive samples predicted as positive, B as the number of true positive samples predicted as negative, C as the number of true negative samples predicted as positive and D as the number of true negative samples predicted as negative. The sample may refer to the line in the line classification task and refer to the word when evaluating the final metadata extraction performance.

$$Precision = \frac{A}{A+C} \quad Recall = \frac{A}{A+B}$$

$$Accuracy = \frac{A+D}{A+B+C+D}$$

$$Fmeasure = \frac{2 Precision * Recall}{Precision + Recall}$$

We apply the metadata extraction method discussed earlier, with the parameters chosen from ten-fold cross-validation on 500 training headers and 435 test headers. Our method achieves an overall accuracy of 92.9%, better than 90.1% reported by Seymore et al. Table 11 compares our method with the HMM method of multi-state L+D model from Seymore et al on the classification performance for each class, except two functional classes "introduction" and "end of page". However, we are unable to obtain the class-specific accuracy method used by Seymore et al at the time we submit this paper. Therefore, we also list class-specific precision and recall for more effective evaluation.

We present below the Example 2 document header with its true labels (Figure 6) and predicted labels (Figure 7) by our metadata extraction algorithm. We also present the labels (Figure 8) our algorithm predicted for the Example 1 header shown in Figure 1 of section 2. The bold fonts indicate the predicted labels different from the true labels. Both examples show the good performance of our algorithm on labeling the single-class lines, and recognizing the individual authors from the multi-author lines. Line 6 in Figure 7 and line 22 in Figure 8 also show the good performance of our two-class chunk identification algorithm. The only dif-

Table 11. Comparison on the performance(%) of metadata extraction using HMM and SVM evaluated based on words. A **- Accuracy;** P **- Precision and** R **- Recall**

Class	HMM(A)	SVM(A)	SVM(P)	SVM(R)
Title	98.3	98.9	94.1	99.1
Author	93.2	99.3	96.1	98.4
Affiliation	89.4	98.1	92.2	95.4
Address	84.1	99.1	94.9	94.5
Note	84.6	95.5	88.9	75.5
Email	86.9	99.6	90.8	92.7
Date	93.0	99.7	84.0	97.5
Abstract	98.4	97.5	91.1	96.6
Phone	94.9	99.9	93.8	91.0
Keyword	98.5	99.2	96.9	81.5
Web	41.7	99.9	79.5	96.9
Degree	81.2	99.5	80.5	62.2
Pubnum	64.2	99.9	92.2	86.3

ference between our algorithm's predictions and the original labels is line 7. Although we count this as a false prediction (in our evaluation), the original label for this line "note" can be argued itself. The line contains two email addresses. Therefore it could be labeled as email just as well. This kind of uncertainty of labels is rare, though. Figure 8 shows the direct impact the line classification has on the chunk identification performance. Wrongly classifying the five-class line 22 in Figure 8 as the four-class line, causes the further incorrect chunk identification. Wrongly classifying the five-class line 25 as a single class line "note", also disables the further chunk identification algorithm. A reason that line 25 is wrongly classified as single-class line, is because our contextual line classification algorithm in Section 3.3.2 over weighs the contextual information of the "note" text from line 22 to line 26.

5 Discussion and future work

This paper describes a classification-based method using Support Vector Machines (SVM) for metadata extraction. These initial results achieve nominally better results than Hidden Markov Model based methods. This occurs

1:<title> THE CORAL USER MANUAL +L+

2:A Tutorial Introduction to CORAL +L+ </title>

3:<author> Raghu Ramakrishnan Praveen Seshadri Divesh Srivastava +L+ </author>

4:<author> S. Sudarshan +L+ </author>

5:<affiliation> Computer Sciences Department, +L+

6:University of Wisconsin-Madison,</affiliation><address> WI 53706, U.S.A. +L+ </address>

7:<note>The authors' e-mail addresses are fraghu,divesh, praveeng@cs.wisc.edu; sudarsha@research.att.com.+L+</note>

Figure 6. Example 2 document header with the true labels.

1: chunk(1) - <title> - THE CORAL USER MANUAL

2: chunk(1) - <title> - A Tutorial Introduction to CORAL

3: chunk(1) - <author> - Raghu Ramakrishnan

chunk(2) - <author> - Praveen Seshadri

chunk(3) - <author> - Divesh Srivastava

4: chunk(1) - <author> - S. Sudarshan

5: chunk(1) - <affiliation> - Computer Sciences Department,

6: chunk(1) - <affiliation> - University of Wisconsin-Madison

chunk(2) - <address> - WI 53706, U.S.A.

7: chunk(1) - <email> - The authors' e-mail addresses are fraghu,divesh,praveeng@cs.wisc.edu; sudarsha@research.att.com.

Figure 7. Example 2 document header labeled by SVM metadata extraction algorithm.

1:chunk(1) - <title> - Stochastic Interaction and Linear Logic

2:chunk(1) - <author> - Patrick D. Lincoln

chunk(2) - <author> - John C. Mitchell

chunk(3) - <author> - Andre Scedrov

3:chunk(1) - - Abstract

4:chunk(1) - - We present stochastic interactive semantics for propositional linear

...

22:chunk(1) - <note> - jcm@cs.stanford.edu

chunk(2) - <web> - http://theory.stanford.edu/people/jcm/home.html)

chunk(3) - <affiliation> - Department of Computer Science, Stanford University

chunk(4) - <address> - Stanford, CA 94305. **Supported in part**

23:chunk(1) - <note> - by an NSF PYI Award , matching funds from Digital Equipment Corporation, the Pow-ell Foundation, and Xerox Corporation; and the Wallace F. and Lucille M. Dav is Faculty

24:chunk(1) - <note> - Scholarship.

25:chunk(1) - <note> - andre@cis.upenn.edu

http://www.cis.upenn.edu/~andre Department of Mathematics, University of Pennsylvania, Philadelphia, PA 19104-6395. **Partially supported by**

26:chunk(1) - <note> - NSF Grants CCR-91-02 753 and CCR-94-00907 and by ONR Grant N0001 4-92-J-1916. Scedrov is an American Mathematical Society Centennial Research Fellow.

Figure 8. Example 1 document header labeled by SVM metadata extraction algorithm.

because we use apriori information of the structural pattern of the data, feature extraction based on domain specific databases, an appropriate normalization technique, and an iterative correction procedure. In addition, the method we propose for extracting individual names from a list of author names has good performance. We believe that our results indicate a promising classification-based method for information extraction.

There are some aspects of our method that could still be improved. The line classification performance limits the further multi-class line chunk identification performance as shown in Figure 8. We will add the functionality to correct the errors caused by the line classification algorithm. Some chunks such as an integrated name may be broken into two lines occasionally. In this case, the multi-class chunk algorithm may make the incorrect decision. We will combine some of the consecutive lines of the same class to minimize the corresponding errors. Currently we assume each line has only one chunk for each class. This is not appropriate even though it is rare for a class to have multiple chunks of the same class in one line. It is worthwhile to explore more general multi-class chunk identification techniques.

In addition to extracting the taggable metadata from the header part of the research papers, we will apply text summarization techniques, such as Zha's [33], to extract the implicit metadata subject and description. This will have the potential for generating a hierarchical metadata representation of the document. We also will intend to develop a robust and accurate wrapper for bibliographies and to define and extract metatags for metadata as well as for equations and figures.

6 Acknowledgments

We acknowledge Cheng Li and Guangyu Chen for useful comments on the first draft of the paper. We acknowledge the valuable comments from reviewers. We would like to acknowledge the support from NSF NSDL 0121679, partial support from the Special Funds for Major State Basic Research Projects of China (project G1999032800), and partial support from Lockheed-Martin.

References

[1] The world factbook. *http://www.cia.gov/cia/publications/factbook/*, 2002.

[2] L. D. Baker and A. K. McCallum. Distributional clustering of words for text classification. In W. B. Croft, A. Moffat, C. J. van Rijsbergen, R. Wilkinson, and J. Zobel, editors, *Proc. of SIGIR-98*, pages 96–103, 1998.

[3] T. Berners-Lee, J. Hendler, and O. Lassila. The semantic web. *Scientific American*, 2001.

[4] T. Brody. Celestial - Open Archives Gateway. *http://celestial.eprints.org/*, 2002.

[5] H. L. Chieu and H. T. Ng. A maximum entropy approach to information extraction from semi-structured and free text. In *Proc. 18th National Conference on Artificial Intelligence (AAAI 2002)*, pages 786–791, 2002.

[6] N. Cristianini and J. Shawe-Taylor. *An Introduction to Support Vector Machines and Other Kernel-Based Learning Methods*. Cambridge University Press, 2000.

[7] H. de Sompel and C. Lagoze. The Open Archives Initiative Protocol for Metadata Harvesting, January 2001.

[8] I. Dhillon, S. Manella, and R. Kumar. A divisive information theoretic feature clustering for text classification. *Machine Learning Research (JMLR)*, 2002.

[9] S. Dumais, J. Platt, D. Heckerman, and M. Sahami. Inductive learning algorithms and representations for text categorization. In *Proc. 7th International Conference on Information and Knowledge Management*, pages 148–155, November 1998.

[10] H.Pasula, B.Marthi, B.Milch, S.Russell, and I.Shpitser. Identity uncertainty and citation matching. In *Proc. of the Advances in Neural Information Processing Systems (NIPS)*, 2002.

[11] T. Joachims. Making large-scale Support Vector Machine learning practical. In B. Scholkopf, C. Burges, and A. Smola, editors, *Advances in Kernel Methods: Support Vector Machines*. MIT Press, Cambridge, MA, 1998.

[12] T. Joachims. A statistical learning model of text classification with Support Vector Machines. In W. B. Croft, D. J. Harper, D. H. Kraft, and J. Zobel, editors, *Proc. SIGIR-01, 24th ACM International Conference on Research and Development in Information Retrieval*, pages 128–136, 2001.

[13] A. Kent. OAI Harvester Crawling Status. *http://www.mds.rmit.edu.au/~ajk/oai/interop/summary.htm*, 2001.

[14] D. Knox. CITIDEL: Making resources available. In *Proc. 7th Annual Conference on Innovation and Technology in Computer Science Education*, pages 225–225, 2002.

[15] T. Kudoh and Y. Matsumoto. Use of support vector learning for chunk identification. In *Proc. of CoNLL-2000 and LLL-2000*, 2000.

[16] J. Lafferty, A. McCallum, and F. Pereira. Conditional random fields: Probabilistic models for segmenting and labeling sequence data. In *Proc. 18th International Conf. on Machine Learning*, pages 282–289, 2001.

[17] S. Lawrence, C. L. Giles, and K. Bollacker. Digital Libraries and Autonomous Citation Indexing. *IEEE Computer*, 32(6):67–71, 1999.

[18] X. Liu. Federating heterogeneous Digital Libraries by metadata harvesting. *Ph.D. Dissertation, Old Dominion University*, December 2002.

[19] C. C. Marshall. Making metadata: A study of metadata creation for a mixed physical-digital collection. In *Proc. 3rd ACM International Conference on Digital Libraries*, pages 162–171, June 1998.

[20] A. McCallum, D. Freitag, and F. Pereira. Maximum entropy Markov models for information extraction and segmentation. In *Proc. 17th International Conf. on Machine Learning*, pages 591–598, 2000.

[21] A. McCallum, K. Nigam, J. Rennie, and K. Seymore. Automating the construction of internet portals with machine learning. *Information Retrieval Journal Volume 3*, pages 127–163, 2000.

[22] P. Mcnamee and J. Mayfield. Entity extraction without language-specific resources. In D. Roth and A. van den Bosch, editors, *Proc. of CoNLL-2002*, pages 183–186, 2002.

[23] A. Paepcke, C.-C. K. Chang, H. Garcia-Molina, and T. Winograd. Interoperability for Digital Libraries worldwide. *Communications of the ACM*, 41(4):33–43, 1998.

[24] Y. Petinot, P. B. Teregowda, H. Han, C. L. Giles, S. Lawrence, A. Rangaswamy, and N. Pal. eBizSearch: An OAI-Compliant Digital Library for eBusiness. In *Proc. the ACM/IEEE Joint Conference on Digital Libraries (JCDL)*, 2003. In this proceeding.

[25] L. Ramshaw and M. Marcus. Text chunking using transformation-based learning. In D. Yarovsky and K. Church, editors, *Proc. 3rd Workshop on Very Large Corpora*, pages 82–94, 1995.

[26] P. Schone and D. Jurafsky. Knowlege-free induction of inflectional morphologies. In *Proc. of the North American chapter of the Association for Computational Linguistics (NAACL-2001)*, 2001.

[27] K. Seymore, A. McCallum, and R. Rosenfeld. Learning hidden Markov model structure for information extraction. In *Proc. of AAAI 99 Workshop on Machine Learning for Information Extraction*, pages 37–42, 1999.

[28] N. Slonim and N. Tishby. The power of word clusters for text classification. In *Proc. 23rd European Colloquium on Information Retrieval Research (ECIR)*, 2001.

[29] K. Takeuchi and N. Collier. Use of Support Vector Machines in extended named entity. In D. Roth and A. van den Bosch, editors, *Proc. 6th Conference on Natural Language Learning (CoNLL-2002)*, 2002.

[30] V. Vapnik. *Statistical Learning Theory*. Springer Verlag, New York, 1998.

[31] S. Weibel. The Dublin Core: A simple content description format for electronic resources. *NFAIS Newsletter*, 40(7):117–119, 1999.

[32] Y. Yang and J. O. Pedersen. A comparative study on feature selection in text categorization. In D. H. Fisher, editor, *Proc. ICML-97, 14th International Conference on Machine Learning*, pages 412–420, 1997.

[33] H. Zha. Generic summarization and keyphrase extraction using mutual reinforcement principle and sentence clustering. In *Proc. 25th Annual International ACM SIGIR Conference on Research and Development in Information Retrieval*, pages 113–120, August 11-15 2002.

Bibliographic Attribute Extraction from Erroneous References Based on a Statistical Model

Atsuhiro Takasu

National Institute of Informatics

2-1-2 Hitotsubashi, Chiyoda-ku

Tokyo 101-8430, Japan

takasu@nii.ac.jp

Abstract

In this paper, we propose a method for extracting bibliographic attributes from reference strings captured using Optical Character Recognition (OCR) and an extended hidden Markov model. Bibliographic attribute extraction can be used in two ways. One is reference parsing in which attribute values are extracted from OCR-processed references for bibliographic matching. The other is reference alignment in which attribute values are aligned to the bibliographic record to enrich the vocabulary of the bibliographic database. In this paper, we first propose a statistical model for attribute extraction that represents both the syntactical structure of references and OCR error patterns. Then, we perform experiments using bibliographic references obtained from scanned images of papers in journals and transactions and show that useful attribute values are extracted from OCR-processed references. We also show that the proposed model has advantages in reducing the cost of preparing training data, a critical problem in rule-based systems.

1. Introduction

Recently, many digital libraries have been constructed and published. Some of them are open to the public, such as CiteSeer [5, 11, 12], while others are in-house libraries and provide information to registered users only. With regard to information capture, libraries that are open to the public tend to gather information from authors directly via Internet crawling and postings from users. As a result, a wide range of documents is gathered, and the quality of the documents is diverse. On the other hand, in-house libraries tend to gather documents systematically based on some policy, like traditional libraries. As a result, comprehensive collections of documents are gathered and the quality of the documents is controlled. For users, both types of digital libraries are valuable information resources, and we want to use these digital libraries in an integrated way. To meet this requirement, the federated digital library (FDL) is an adequate form where local digital libraries (LDL) have autonomous activities and are loosely connected. In an FDL, users first access the index to find LDLs having the required documents, then they access the LDL directly. Therefore, constructing a shared index that contains metadata for all documents in LDLs participating in an FDL is a key problem in developing an FDL.

The fundamental entities in the shared index are article, author, institute, publisher, LDL and FDL; and entries have attributes such as author's name, article/book title, publisher, title of journal, just like catalog databases in traditional libraries. The relationships between article references are also important for document retrieval using referencing information like SiteCeer [5, 11, 12]. Because LDLs gather documents autonomously, there may be discrepancies in data formats (e.g., PostScript, PDF, XML), media (e.g., text, image), data schemas (e.g., relational database schema, DTD for XML) and conventions for attribute value representation (e.g., abbreviation of journal titles, initials of author's name). When constructing a shared index, these discrepancies must be resolved.

A shared index is constructed by the following processes:

Schema design of the shared index:
Designing a global schema is generally very difficult. Fortunately, the library and information science community has a long history and rich experience in designing and maintaining schemas of bibliographic information, and there are global schemas such as the Dublin Core Metadata [1].

Schema transformation:
Usually, each LDL has its own metadata; however, its schema may be different from the schema of the shared in-

---

[1] http://dublincore.org/

dex. Therefore, schema transformation is required to construct a shared index from the metadata in the LDLs. For example, XSLT provides a tool for schema transformation. The metadata from an LDL often lacks information required for the shared index. In this case, information extraction from documents is also required. For example, references in articles are often not included in metadata. Furthermore, references are often represented as a single string without being separated into bibliographic attribute values. In this case, parsing is required to extract bibliographic attributes from the string.

Metadata matching:

Because a document may be contained in several LDLs, bibliographic entities appearing in each LDL must be identified and assigned the same ID. Bibliographic matching has been studied extensively in the library and information science community. Its main use is to detect and remove duplicate records in bibliographic databases [6, 7, 1, 15].

Universal ID assignment:

A universal ID must be assigned to bibliographic entities in the shared index. The Digital Object Identifier (DOI) [2] aims to assign IDs to objects in the Internet; and CrossRef, the central source for reference linking [3], provides an identification scheme for documents. These frameworks are applicable to the shared index.

Despite many studies, we still require more advanced methods of schema transformation and metadata matching for FDLs, because of the various discrepancies. Schema discrepancies make the following three types of bibliographic matching necessary.

Record–record matching:

This type of matching algorithm is used when both schemas of the shared index and LDL metadata represent bibliographic entities at the same granularity. Merging two bibliographic databases is a typical problem to which this type of matching is applied.

Record–string matching:

This type of matching algorithm is used when one of the metadata sources represents entities with a single string. Matching of a bibliographic record and references in articles is a typical problem to which this matching is applied[8].

String–string matching:

This algorithm is used when both metadata sources represent entities with single strings. Matching of references is a typical problem to which this matching is applied.

Another concern is the correctness of the string. Metadata in an LDL usually consists of a bibliographic database, and its records consist of clean strings, although they may include typing errors. However, the metadata may sometimes be extracted from document images using document

[2]http://www.doi.org/
[3]http://www.crossref.org

image analysis and Optical Character Recognition (OCR) when the LDL contains documents as images. In such cases, the metadata may contain recognition errors. As a result, metadata represents attributes of entities with two types of strings: *clean strings* and *erroneous strings*. Matching algorithms for duplicated record detection [6, 7, 1, 15] are categorized as record–record matching of clean strings; however, they are not suitable for other types of matching. CiteSeer's bibliographic matching is categorized into string–string and record–string matching of clean strings.

Matching of recognized bibliographic strings is much more difficult in the presence of OCR errors. We have been studying record–string bibliographic matching of erroneous strings [17], where we matched records consisting of clean strings with reference strings extracted from scanned document images. An OCR error model representing error patterns of OCR is a key requirement for matching data consisting of erroneous strings. We developed a statistical OCR error model and used it to measure similarities of strings obtained by OCR [18]. In the previous study [17], we converted a bibliographic record into a string and measured the similarity of the converted string and the erroneous reference string using the statistical OCR error model. In this paper, we propose two methods for extracting bibliographic attributes from erroneous strings of references based on the OCR error model. We also propose an efficient scheme for obtaining training rules for bibliographic attribute extraction.

In section 2, we first overview our bibliographic matching system and previous work. Then, in section 3, we discuss a statistical model for a method of extracting bibliographic attributes from strings of references, and we propose an efficient training scheme. Section 4 gives experimental results for the method using scanned academic articles published by Japanese societies, and section 5 presents the conclusions of the study.

2. Previous Work

We have been developing a shared index system that connects a bibliographic database and references in scanned images of academic articles. In this system, document page layout analysis is first applied to a scanned document image, to extract reference areas from the page images. The document image analysis community has developed several methods for page layout analysis [20, 14, 3]. OCR is then applied to produce bibliographic strings. During this phase, we obtain strings that may contain recognition errors. Bibliographic string analysis is applied to these erroneous strings for bibliographic matching and extraction of bibliographic attribute values. Figure 1 depicts these steps of bibliographic matching and bibliographic attribute extraction from scanned references. The results of bibliographic

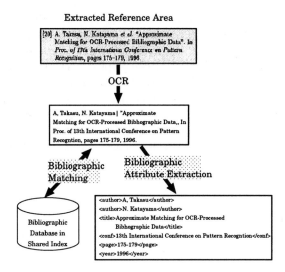

Figure 1. Outline of bibliographic reference analysis

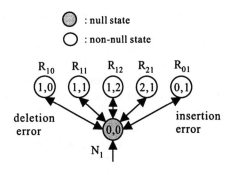

Figure 2. An example of a DVHMM

matching are stored in the shared index as reference relationships, whereas the results of bibliographic attribute extraction are added to the bibliographic database as variations of attribute values.

When using text obtained by document image analysis, OCR error handling is a key requirement for bibliographic matching and bibliographic attribute extraction. We proposed a statistical model called the Dual and Variable-length output Hidden Markov Model (DVHMM), which can represent the recognizer's error patterns probabilistically, and we developed a parameter estimation algorithm for it [18].

Recognition errors in OCR are usually categorized into substitution, deletion, insertion and framing errors [10]. A substitution error means that one character is incorrectly recognized as another character. This type of error happens very frequently. A deletion error means that one character is deleted, and an insertion error means that one character is inserted. A framing error means that a sequence of characters is incorrectly recognized as another sequence of characters. For example, "fi" may be recognized incorrectly as "h".

Several OCR error models have been proposed. The most typical OCR error model is the confusion matrix, which maps a character c to a set of characters that an OCR may incorrectly recognize as c. For each entry in the confusion matrix, we can assign the probability that an OCR will recognize the character incorrectly [9]. However, the confusion matrix and its probabilistic companion cannot handle framing errors. Li and Lopresti proposed an OCR error model in which error patterns were categorized from the viewpoint of string lengths [13]. In this model, a pair (i, j)

of original and recognized string lengths is used as an OCR error pattern, and a weight, or a penalty for incorrect recognition, is assigned to each pattern to calculate the similarity of two strings by dynamic programming matching. This model can represent insertion, deletion and framing errors as well as substitution errors. However, to apply the model to a matching problem, we must determine the weights for every pattern. Furthermore, the weight is the same if an error pattern is the same.

A DVHMM categorizes OCR errors from the viewpoint of output string length, similar to Li and Lopresti's model, and uses a Hidden Markov Model (HMM):

- to define the weights in a more detailed manner, and

- to calculate the weights systematically.

A DVHMM is a form of HMM. Instead of producing a string, it produces a pair of strings, one representing the original string and the other representing the corresponding recognized string. States of the DVHMM correspond to recognition error patterns from the viewpoint of output string length, and they are characterized by the pair of lengths of the original and recognized output strings. For example, a pair $(2, 1)$ of output string lengths means that an OCR recognizes two consecutive characters as one unit and transforms it to a single character. As an output symbol, the state corresponding to a pair (i, j) produces a pair of original and recognized strings with lengths i and j, respectively. States are categorized into two groups:

- *non-null* states, which produce a pair of original and recognized strings, and

- *null* states, which produce no output, but control state transitions.

A state $(1, 0)$ means that the length of the original (resp. recognized) output string is 1 (resp. 0), i.e., a deletion error, whereas a state $(0, 1)$ corresponds to an insertion error. A state (1, 1) corresponds to either a substitution error or a correct recognition.

Figure 2 shows an example of a DVHMM that represents five OCR error patterns, i.e., (1, 0), (0, 1), (1, 1), (2, 1) and (1, 2). In this example, a null state N_1 works as a pivot and has transitions to all non-null states with certain probabilities. R_{10} and R_{01} stand for deletion and insertion errors, respectively. R_{21} and R_{12} stand for framing errors. In figure 2, both transition probabilities and output symbols are omitted because of space restrictions. Suppose the alphabet is {a,b}. Then, for example, the state R_{21} has eight possible output symbols

| (aa,a):0.35 | (aa,b):0.05 | (ab,a):0.10 | (ab,b):0.10 |
| (ba,a):0.05 | (ba,b):0.05 | (bb,a):0.05 | (bb,b):0.25 |

where the real numbers attached to pairs of strings show the output probabilities.

The DVHMM defines the joint probability distribution of a pair of original and recognized strings.

[Example 1]   Suppose that a string "ab" is recognized as "a". Then, the DVHMM in figure 2 produces the pair of strings (ab, a) by one of the following six sequences of state transitions.

$$N_1 R_{10} N_1 R_{10} N_1 R_{01} \quad N_1 R_{10} N_1 R_{11}$$
$$N_1 R_{10} N_1 R_{01} N_1 R_{10} \quad N_1 R_{11} N_1 R_{10}$$
$$N_1 R_{01} N_1 R_{10} N_1 R_{10} \quad N_1 R_{21}$$

Because the probability that the DVHMM produces a pair of strings with a sequence of state transitions is calculated by multiplying the corresponding state transition probabilities and output probabilities, the joint probability of (ab, a) is obtained by summing the probabilities of all six sequences of transitions.

A sequence of state transitions determines an alignment of two strings. For example, the state transition $N_1 R_{11} N_1 R_{10}$ in Example 1 determines the following alignment:

$$
\begin{array}{c|c}
a & b \\
a &
\end{array}
$$

where the first character "a" of the original string is mapped to "a", and the last character "b" of the original string is deleted. On the other hand, the state transition $N_1 R_{10} N_1 R_{11}$ in Example 1 determines the following alignment:

$$
\begin{array}{c|c}
a & b \\
  & a
\end{array}
$$

where the first character "a" of the original string is deleted, and the last character "b" of the original string is mapped to "a".

Before defining the DVHMM formally, we define the notation used in the following discussion. Generally, an uppercase letter denotes a set, a boldface letter denotes a sequence or a string, and Greek and calligraphic letters denote functions. For a set S, S^l denotes the set of sequences of length l consisting of elements in S. $|S|$ denotes the cardinality of the set S. For a sequence $\mathbf{x}$, $|\mathbf{x}|$ denotes its length, $\mathbf{x}[i]$ denotes its ith component, and $\mathbf{x}[i:j]$ denotes the partial sequence starting at the i-th character and ending at the j-th character of $\mathbf{x}$.

A DVHMM is denoted as a four-tuple $M \equiv (A, Q, T, O)$:

- The set A is an alphabet. Although we use the same alphabet for both original and recognized characters, we could use different alphabets.

- The set Q comprises non-null states Q_x and null states Q_0, i.e., $Q = Q_x \cup Q_0$. Q_0 contains a starting state, while Q_x consists of states corresponding to the pairs of lengths. Each non-null state q produces pairs of strings $\{(\mathbf{a}, \mathbf{b}) | \mathbf{a} \in A^a, \mathbf{b} \in A^b\}$, where a and b are the lengths of the original and the recognized strings of q.

- A probability $\tau(q, r) \in T$ is the transition probability from state q to state r.

- A probability $o(q, \mathbf{a}, \mathbf{b}) \in O$ is the output probability that a state q produces $\mathbf{a}$ and $\mathbf{b}$ as the original and recognized string, respectively.

In a DVHMM, we use a starting state (N_1 in figure 2) instead of an initial probability distribution, i.e., any sequence of state transitions commences at the starting state with a probability of 1.0.

DVHMMs differ from ordinary HMMs in the following two respects:

- A DVHMM produces a pair of strings as output, and

- the length of the output symbols differs depending on the states.

We proposed a method for bibliographic matching [17] (see figure 1). In this study we generated a reference string T from a record in the database by concatenating the attribute values. Then, for a given reference string S obtained by OCR, we calculated the joint probability $P(T, S | M)$ based on the DVHMM M with its parameters learned from training data consisting of pairs of original strings and the corresponding OCR-processed strings. The joint probability was used as the similarity of a record in the database to a reference obtained by OCR. We solved bibliographic matching by finding the record with the highest joint probability with the reference obtained by OCR.

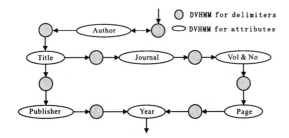

Figure 3. Syntactical Structure of Bibliographic References

3. Bibliographic Attribute Extraction

3.1. Problem Definition

There are two types of bibliographic attribute extraction. One is *reference parsing*, which extracts bibliographic attributes from a reference string obtained via OCR from a document page image. In this case, the reference may contain several OCR recognition errors such as the following string:

[**String 1**] OCR-ed Reference:
A, Takasu, N. Karayama| "Approximate Matching for OCR-Processed Bibhographic Data,, In Proc. of 13th ICPR, pp. 175–179, 1996.

where the underlined strings are incorrectly recognized strings. The reference parsing decomposes the string into substrings and assigns attributes to the decomposed substrings to produce the following tagged string:

[**String 2**] Segmented OCR-ed Reference :
<author>A, Takasu</author> <del>, </del>
<author>N. Karayama</author> <del>|"</del>
<title>Approximate Matching for OCR-Processed
  Bibhographic Data</title> <del>,, In Proc. of </del>
<conf>13th ICPR</conf><del>, pp.</del>
<page>175–179</page><del>, </del>
<year>1996</year><del>.</del>

where a tag <del> stands for delimiters.

The second type of bibliographic attribute extraction is *reference alignment*, which aligns corresponding attributes between a pair of reference strings. Suppose that String 1 and the following reference string composed from a record in a bibliographic database are given:

[**String 3**] Reference Generated from Database :
Atsuhiro Takasu †Norio Katayama †Keizo Oyama ‡Approximate Matching for OCR-Processed Bibliographic

Data §Proceedings of 13th International Conference on Pattern Recognition ¶175–179 †1996

where † is used to separate authors, ‡ separates author and article titles, etc. The reference alignment produces the following pairs of attributes.

[**String 4**] Aligned Pair of Reference :
<author><str1>A, Takasu</str1>
  <str3>Atsuhiro Takasu</str3></author>
<author><str11>N. Karayama</str11>
  <str3>Norio Katayama</str3></author>
<author>
  <str3>Keizo Oyama</str3></author>
<title><str11>Approximate Matching ...</str11>
  <str3>Approximate Matching ...</str3></title>
<conf><str11>13th ICPR</str11>
  <str3>13th International ...</str3></conf>
<page><str11>175–179</str11>
  <str3>175–179</str3></page>
<year><str11>1996</str11>
  <str3>1997</str3></year>

In this example, tags <str1> and <str3> stand for the attributes from String 1 and String 3, respectively.

In our previous work [17], we measured the similarity of the strings in the forms String 1 and String 3 as the joint probability that the DVHMM produces the given pair, and applied it to bibliographic matching. In that study and later experiments, we found that higher matching accuracy was obtained by varying the weights of string similarities of attributes. For example, journal/conference title, pages and published year are important attributes for matching. By assigning higher weights to the similarities of those attributes, higher matching accuracy was obtained. To vary the weights of similarities of attributes, they must be extracted from the reference string. This leads us to study the bibliographic attribute extraction problem.

As shown in the example of String 4, bibliographic attributes are represented in various ways. For example, conference names are often abbreviated, while initials are often used in authors' names. By accumulating the variation of entity strings, a shared index has a rich vocabulary for attribute values, and consequently, the matching accuracy will be improved. Reference alignment is used to extract entities from the references and to accumulate them in the shared index. Bibliographic attribute extraction is used in these problems. This is another motivation for this study.

Only a few studies [2, 16] have addressed bibliographic attribute extraction from erroneous strings. In these studies, heuristic rules were used to extract bibliographic attributes from scanned cataloging cards. However, it is hard to learn heuristic rules from training data, and consequently, they

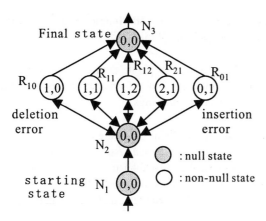

Figure 4. Component DVHMM for Attributes

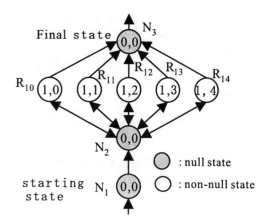

Figure 5. Component DVHMM for Delimiters

increase the cost of rule construction and maintenance. In this paper, we propose well-formulated rules and an efficient rule learning scheme.

3.2. Statistical Model for Attribute Extraction

A DVHMM as described in section 2 has the nature of an HMM and can represent syntactical structures in the class of regular grammars. In this section, we construct a statistical model for attribute extraction from erroneous references. It is a combination of OCR error models and syntactical structure represented by the DVHMM, using the following steps:

1. construct a syntactical structure of bibliographic strings consisting of bibliographic attributes and delimiters,

2. replace each attribute component with a DVHMM that produces a pair comprising the attribute values and the recognized string, and

3. replace each delimiter using a DVHMM in the same way as for a bibliographic attribute.

We call a DVHMM for bibliographic attributes and delimiters a *component DVHMM* whereas we call a DVHMM composed of component DVHMMs a *global DVHMM*.

Bibliographic components are located in a specific order, separated by delimiters in references. The form of the reference may differ depending on the type of article referenced. For example, a reference to an article in a journal may be represented with a regular expression

author(, author)* : "title", journal, vol, no, page, year,

whereas a reference to a book may be represented with

author(, author)* : "title", publisher, year.

This syntactical variety of references is represented using an *or* operator in the regular expression. Figure 3 depicts an example of a finite automaton for references to both an article in a journal and a book. Notice that each regular expression has an equivalent automaton. Possible patterns of references are enumerated manually and combined into a finite automaton.

In bibliographic attribute extraction, delimiters play an important role in segmenting reference strings into attributes. As shown in figure 3, a DVHMM for delimiters is invoked between all bibliographic attributes.

OCR error models are constructed for each attribute using a DVHMM similar to that in figure 2. To handle various errors, let us consider a DVHMM consisting of non-null states that correspond to pairs of output string lengths up to a maximum number m.

$$\{(i, i + 1), (i + 1, i) \mid 0 \leq i < m\} \cup \{(1, 1)\}$$

Figure 4 is a DVHMM for $m = 2$. In this figure, N_1 and N_3 stand for the starting and final states of this bibliographic attribute, respectively. A pair of strings produced with the state transition from N_1 to N_3 is treated as the value of the bibliographic attribute. Generally, a larger m enables more precise modeling of OCR errors. However, the number of parameters for the output probability distribution is $O(|Q| \times |A|^{2m})$ where Q and A, respectively, stand for a set of states and the alphabet, so we cannot estimate the parameters accurately for large m from a limited quantity of training data. This problem becomes serious, particularly for languages using a large set of characters, such as Chinese and Japanese. Therefore, we must find appropriate values for m depending on the language used.

A DVHMM for a delimiter is similar to that for a bibliographic attribute. Various types of delimiters are used in references. For example, the "volume" and "number" of a journal reference may be described as "Vol. 24, No. 3" in some references, and "24(3)" in others. In the former case,

54

the delimiter for "number" is ", No.", whereas in the latter case it is "(". To handle the variation of these delimiters, we use states

$$\{(1, i) \mid 0 \leq i < m\}$$

where m is large enough to express delimiters, including their incorrect recognition. We separate bibliographic attributes in the original strings with a special character that does not appear in the alphabet as shown in String 3. Therefore, the length of the original string is fixed at one. Furthermore, the original string of output symbols is fixed to the special character. Figure 5 depicts a DVHMM for a delimiter for $m = 5$.

To embed component DVHMMs into the automaton representing the syntactical structure of a bibliographic string, the incoming arcs of a bibliographic attribute in the automaton are connected to the starting state of the corresponding DVHMM (N_1 in figures 4 and 5), and the outgoing arcs are started from the final state of the corresponding DVHMM (N_3 in figures 4 and 5).

The reference alignment problem is solved by a DVHMM obtained in the following way. For a given recognized bibliographic string $\mathbf{y}$ such as String 1 and a string $\mathbf{x}$ composed from a record in the bibliographic database such as String 3, let us consider the state transition $\mathbf{q}$ that maximizes the probability that the DVHMM produces the pair $(\mathbf{x}, \mathbf{y})$. Note that a state transition producing a pair $(\mathbf{x}, \mathbf{y})$ separates and aligns them into $(\mathbf{x}_1, \mathbf{y}_1), (\mathbf{x}_2, \mathbf{y}_2)$, $\cdots, (\mathbf{x}_l, \mathbf{y}_l)$. Then, the state transition $\mathbf{q}$ determines the most likely alignment of the pair $(\mathbf{x}, \mathbf{y})$ of reference strings. Because a DVHMM contains information about the syntactical structure of a bibliographic string, the most likely sequence of state transitions can be decomposed into fragments that correspond to the bibliographic attributes, such as author's name and article title. For a bibliographic attribute, let the corresponding fragment of the sequence be $\mathbf{q}[i:j]$ where $\mathbf{q}[i]$ is the starting state (e.g., N_1 in figures 4 and 5) and $\mathbf{q}[j]$ is the final state (e.g., N_3 in figures 4 and 5). Then the substring $\mathbf{y}_i \mathbf{y}_{i+1} \cdots \mathbf{y}_j$ is the most likely portion of the given recognized string in the bibliographic attribute, and the substring $\mathbf{x}_i \mathbf{x}_{i+1} \cdots \mathbf{x}_j$ is the most likely portion of the original string.

Formally, for a pair $(\mathbf{x}, \mathbf{y})$ of strings and a DVHMM M, the reference alignment is defined as

$$\operatorname*{argmax}_{\mathbf{q} \in Q^*} P(\mathbf{x}, \mathbf{y}, \mathbf{q} \mid M) \qquad (1)$$

where Q^* stands for a set of state transitions of any length and $P(\mathbf{x}, \mathbf{y}, \mathbf{q}|M)$ stands for the probability that a DVHMM M produces the pair $(\mathbf{x}, \mathbf{y})$ of strings with the state transition $\mathbf{q}$.

On the other hand, the reference parsing problem can be solved by an ordinary hidden Markov Model (HMM) that has the same graphical structure as the DVHMM in figure 3, but produces single strings at each state instead of pairs of strings. The HMM for the reference parsing problem can be derived from the DVHMM for reference alignment by grouping the output symbols based on the recognized strings. For each state q in the DVHMM, let O be a set of output pairs of strings and let $B \equiv \{\mathbf{b}_1, \mathbf{b}_2, \cdots, \mathbf{b}_n\}$ be a set of recognized strings in O. Then O is grouped into $O_1, O_2, \cdots, O_n$ where O_i is a subset of O such that the recognized symbol of an output symbol of O_i is $\mathbf{b}_i$. The set of output strings of the HMM derived from the DVHMM is B where the output probability of $\mathbf{b}_i$ is the sum of the output probabilities $\sum_{(\mathbf{a}, \mathbf{b}) \in O_i} o(q, \mathbf{a}, \mathbf{b})$.

For example, the output symbols of the state R_{21} in figure 2 are obtained in the following steps. First, the output symbols are grouped into two groups $\{(aa,a):0.35, (ab,a):0.10, (ba,a):0.05, (bb,a):0.05\}$ and $\{(aa,b):0.05, (ab,b):0.10, (ba,b):0.05, (bb,b):0.25\}$. Then, the output probability in each group is obtained as the sum of output probabilities in the group. Finally, two output symbols a:0.55 and b:45 are derived. The reference parsing is defined as

$$\operatorname*{argmax}_{\mathbf{q} \in Q^*} P(\mathbf{y}, \mathbf{q} \mid M') \qquad (2)$$

where M' is the HMM derived from DVHMM.

3.3. DVHMM Training

Because the global DVHMM is a DVHMM, it can be trained from a pair of original and recognized reference strings. Parameters of the DVHMM can be estimated from two types of training data. The first type is an aligned pair of original and recognized strings in which corresponding attributes and delimiters are aligned, such as String 4. In this case, the parameters of each component DVHMM can be estimated from the corresponding pair of strings. For example, the component DVHMM for the bibliographic attribute "page" is trained with the pair (175–179, 175–179) extracted from String 4 and the DVHMM for the delimiter of author and title is trained from (‡, -"). Therefore, accurate parameter estimation is expected.

The other type of training data is a non-aligned pair of original and recognized strings such as String 1 and String 3. The original reference string is automatically constructed from the record of the bibliographic database where bibliographic attributes are separated by delimiters without ambiguity. Therefore, the corresponding part of the original reference is used to train the DVHMM. However, there is no segmentation for recognized sequences, therefore the whole recognized reference is used to train the DVHMM. For example, the component DVHMM for "page" is trained with (175–179, String 1) whereas the DVHMM for a delimiter between author and title is trained from (‡, String 1). Therefore, parameter estimation is expected to be less accurate.

We proposed an efficient DVHMM training algorithm [18]. This algorithm iteratively modifies the parameters of the DVHMM using the training data according to the expectation maximization technique. In this iterative process, similar pairs of substrings in the training data become dominant in parameter modification. For example, the original string for the component DVHMM for "page" is "175–179" in String 3 whereas the recognized reference in String 1 contains the substring "175–179". Because this part is the same as the original string, the training algorithm weights this pair heavily in parameter modification. As a result, parameters are estimated in a similar way as for aligned training data.

The preparation of aligned training data such as String 4 is labor-intensive, because the recognized reference string must be segmented manually. On the other hand, for non-aligned training data, the original reference is constructed from a database record automatically, and a recognized reference is also obtained automatically by OCR. It is therefore sufficient to find the corresponding record from the database. Therefore, large training data sets can be prepared with less cost.

An ordinary HMM can be applied to the reference parsing problem. However, to construct an HMM that has the graphical structure of figure 3, a large amount of segmented training data such as String 2 is required. Preparing this training data requires almost the same labor cost as for the DVHMM. Therefore, it is more efficient to train the DVHMM with non-aligned training data then convert it into an HMM by the method described in the previous section. The acquisition of DVHMM parameters from non-aligned training data is very efficient as a rule learning scheme. We show the effectiveness of this learning scheme experimentally in the next section.

4. Experimental Results

4.1. Experiment Setting

We performed experiments on extracting bibliographic attributes from OCR-processed references. In these experiments, we used two sets of data:

- bibliographic strings obtained from scanned document images, and

- a bibliographic database.

Bibliographic strings were obtained from scanned images of papers in journals and transactions published in 1995 by three major Japanese academic societies, all on the subject of computer science. Most of these were written in Japanese. A total of 1,575 references was used in the experiments. To obtain bibliographic strings, we first applied page layout analysis to scanned reference pages to extract reference image areas, then we corrected the extracted areas manually, and finally we applied a commercial OCR reader (Toshiba Co.'s ExpressReader 70J) to each reference area of the papers as shown in figure 1.

We used a set of bibliographic databases that were compiled and are stored at the National Institute of Informatics [4]. These bibliographic databases contained a total of 2,121,707 bibliographic records of books and academic articles. Most of them are written in Japanese.

In these experiments, we first trained the DVHMM using two kinds of training data, i.e., aligned training data such as String 4 and non-aligned training data such as pairs of String 1 and String 3. Then, we performed two bibliographic attribute extractions: reference alignment and reference parsing using DVHMMs trained with aligned and non-aligned training data. In total, four experiments were performed. Instead of a DVHMM, an HMM was used for reference parsing from aligned training data, because it was sufficient for this problem. The following table summarizes the model used in this experiment.

Problem	Training Data Type	
	Aligned	non-aligned
Alignment	DVHMM	DVHMM
Parsing	HMM	DVHMM

In this experiment, we considered an attribute to be correctly extracted only when both the start and the end positions of the attribute value in the reference string were correctly detected. For the bibliographic attributes: author's name (represented with "Author" in graphs), article title ("Title"), journal title or conference name ("Journal"), volume and number ("VolNo"), page ("Page"), published year ("Year") and publisher's name ("Publisher"), accuracy was measured as

$$\frac{\text{\# correctly extracted attributes}}{\text{\# attributes appearing in test sets}}.$$

In the experiment, fivefold cross validation was applied. We first divided the 1,575 pairs of recognized bibliographic strings and corresponding records in the bibliographic database into five groups. We then estimated the parameters of the DVHMMs as described in section 3 using four groups of bibliographic data. Finally, we extracted bibliographic attributes from recognized bibliographic strings in the remaining group. This experiment was repeated five times for each combination of training and test data and the average accuracy was calculated.

4.2. Accuracy of Attribute Extraction

Figure 6 shows the average accuracies of reference alignment using the DVHMMs trained with aligned training

---

[4]http://www.nii.ac.jp

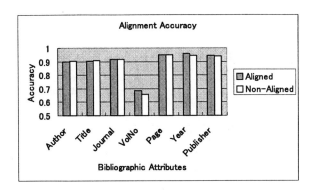

Figure 6. Accuracy of Reference Alignment based on DVHMM

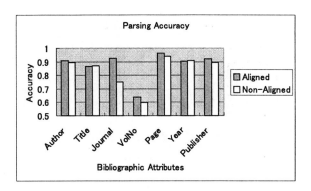

Figure 7. Accuracy of Reference Parsing based on DVHMM

data (labeled with "Aligned" in the graph) and non-aligned training data (labeled with "Non-Aligned"), while figure 7 shows the average accuracies of reference parsing using the HMM trained with aligned training data and the DVHMM trained with non-aligned training data. We obtained more than 90% accuracy in reference alignment except for volume and number and about 90% in reference parsing.

Overall, higher accuracy was achieved in the reference alignment problem than in the reference parsing problem. In the alignment problem, the reference generated from the bibliographic record guides the state transitions of the DVHMM. The effect of guidance from the bibliographic record seems to appear in the difference of accuracies.

In both the alignment and parsing problems, the DVHMM trained with non-aligned training data achieved accuracy similar to one trained with aligned training data for many attributes. Although the difference in accuracy of reference parsing for "journal" is still large, this indicates that non-aligned training data is useful for the attribute extraction problem. This enables the cost of the model training process to be greatly reduced.

Considering each attribute, the accuracy of "volume" and "number" is very low. It should also be noted that the reference parsing accuracy for "journal" is reduced when the DVHMM is trained with non-aligned training data compared with the values from aligned training data. We will discuss these phenomena in section 4.4 by analyzing error patterns.

In this experiment we did not apply any normalizing procedure such as converting capital letters to lower case letters. Heuristic pre- and post-processing will improve the accuracy.

4.3. Training Data Size and Accuracy

To investigate the effect of training data size, we measured the accuracy with respect to the size of the training set. In this experiment, we trained DVHMMs using one, two or three groups of training data as well as the four groups in the fivefold cross validation. The numbers of references used in these experiments are thus 323, 646, 969 and 1,292. Figure 8 depicts the average accuracies of reference alignment from non-aligned training data with respect to training set sizes. For some attributes such as "pages" and "year", the accuracies do not change with respect to the training sizes, whereas the accuracies increase with the training size for other attributes such as "author" and "article title".

Algorithmic learning theory indicates that the empirical accuracy, i.e., accuracy for the training data, decreases as the training data increases, and the generalization accuracy, i.e., accuracy for the test data, increases as the training data increases. These two accuracies converge to the optimal accuracy for very large training data sets (e.g., [4]).

Figure 9 depicts the empirical and generalized accuracies of two bibliographic attributes, "article title" and "page", with respect to the training data size. These two attributes show typical patterns in this experiment. For "article title", the empirical accuracy (labeled with "title-train" in the graph) is very high for any training data size. This means that the DVHMM has sufficient expressive power to represent the article title. On the other hand, the generalized accuracy (labeled with "title-test") increases as the training data size increases. This phenomenon means that the DVHMM overfits to the training data, and the accuracy for "article title" continues to increase as the training data size increases. Because a DVHMM can be trained with non-aligned training data, we can increase the amount of training data with small cost. Therefore, a DVHMM is a suitable model, especially for attributes requiring large training data

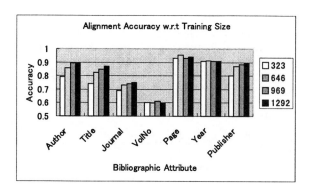

Figure 8. Accuracy of alignment with respect to training data size

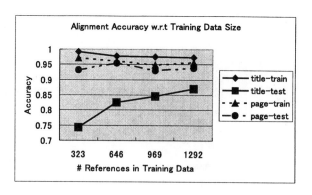

Figure 9. Empirical and generalized accuracy with respect to training data size

sets such as "title", owing to the DVHMM's efficient learning scheme.

For "page", both empirical and generalized accuracies (labeled with "page-train" and "page-test", respectively) are almost the same with respect to the training data size. This phenomenon means that both accuracies have converged to the optimal accuracy. Therefore, the accuracy is not expected to change even if the amount of training data increases. Because "page" mainly consists of digits and a hyphen, a small amount of training is sufficient to train the DVHMM for the page field. On the other hand, the title consists of many characters, especially in oriental languages with large character sets, so a larger amount of training data results in a larger increase in the accuracy of the DVHMM.

On the whole, the accuracies of some attributes are expected to be improved by increasing the amount of training data, and DVHMMs have the preferred characteristic of being able to learn from non-aligned training data, which significantly reduces the cost of preparing large training data sets.

4.4. Error Analysis

We analyzed the errors in reference alignment and parsing and categorized the errors into the following five groups. Figure 10 shows the ratios of error types of each attribute as well as the accuracy of reference parsing from non-aligned training data, which is the lowest accuracy of the four types of experiments.

One-Character Shifted:
The extracted attribute value has one character more or less. For example, suppose a DVHMM extracts "A, Takas" as the first author's name from String 1 in section 3, then it is categorized into this group, because the last character 'u' of the correct value "A, Takasu" is dropped. Similarly "A, Takasu," is also categorized into this group because of the

additional comma. This type of error is referred to as "one-char" in figure 10.

Prefix Detected:
Only the initial part of the attribute value is correctly detected. For example, suppose a DVHMM extracts "175–" as the "page" in String 1, then it is categorized into this group. This type of error is referred to as "prefix" in figure 10.

Suffix Detected:
Only the last part of the attribute value is correctly detected. For example, suppose a DVHMM extracts "–179" as the "page" in String 1, then it is categorized into this group. This type of error is referred to as "suffix" in figure 10.

Overlapped:
The extracted attribute value is overlapped with the correct string. For example, suppose a DVHMM extracts "179,1996" as "page" of String 1, then it is categorized into this group. This type of error is referred to as "overlap" in figure 10.

Others:
These are errors that are not categorized into any of the above four groups. This type of error is referred to as "error" in figure 10.

An error may be categorized into multiple types. For example, some one-character shifted errors are also categorized as prefix-detected errors. Therefore, when categorizing errors, we assign the error pattern in the order:

one-character, prefix, suffix, overlap, error.

If the error is categorized into a certain group, we do not attempt judgment for later groups. For example, if an error is a one-character shifted error, then it is categorized into the one-character shifted class, even if it is also in the prefix detected class.

As shown in figures 6 and 7, the accuracy of "journal name" in reference parsing is low when the DVHMM pa-

58

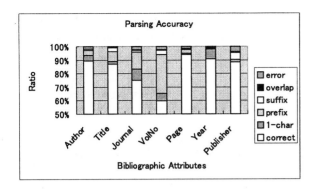

Figure 10. Error patterns for the reference parsing problem

rameters are learned from non-aligned training data. The accuracy of "volume" and "number" in both reference alignment and parsing are also low. This result seems to be caused mainly by the variety of volume and number formats, especially in conference papers. Volume and number are usually separated by a comma, and this delimiter sometimes appears within a string of attribute values. Furthermore, OCR frequently recognizes these characters incorrectly. As shown in the graph in figure 10, the DVHMM detects the start positions of the volume and number with high probability; however, it often fails to detect the end position of this attribute. Note the proportion of prefix errors in the graph of figure 10.

Similar trends are observed for "journal name". Journal names are often abbreviated, and characters such as periods and parentheses are often added. Because these characters are also used for delimiters, it is hard to detect the end positions of attribute values in the reference strings.

Extraction errors are inevitable and we must consider how to utilize the extracted attribute values containing errors. As described in section 3, we have considered using the extracted attribute values to improve the bibliographic matching accuracy and to enrich the vocabulary of the shared index.

For the former purpose, we plan to apply weighted similarity measures where

- first the string similarities of the attribute values are measured,

- then, the similarities of the reference strings are calculated by adding the weighted similarities of each pair of attribute values.

To handle extraction errors in measuring attribute similarity, time warping techniques will be effective. Because the location of the attribute value in the reference string is almost detected in the case of character-shifted, prefix-detected, suffix-detected and overlapped errors, we will be able to find a superstring of the extracted attribute value that may contain the correct attribute value. The time warping technique can then calculate the similarity of attribute values included in the superstring with the attribute value in bibliographic database.

To obtain weights for attributes, a classification technique such as Support Vector Machines (SVMs) [19] can be applied. The similarities of attribute values comprise a feature vector with dimension equal to the number of attributes. Let us consider the decision problem of determining whether a feature vector obtained from attribute similarities indicates that the reference strings represent the same book/article or not. Then, this two-class classification problem can be solved using SVMs, and weights can be obtained by the learning algorithm for SVMs. If this utilization scheme of extracted attribute values is effective, errors other than *others* can be utilized in the bibliographic matching phase, and the proposed attribute extraction method has sufficient performance to construct the shared index.

5. Conclusion

This paper proposes a method for extracting bibliographic attributes from OCR-processed reference strings using an extended HMM called a DVHMM. A DVHMM has the ability to align a pair of strings as well as parse a string. Using these abilities, this paper proposes methods for two problems of bibliographic attribute extraction: reference alignment and reference parsing. Because the DVHMM can be trained using non-aligned pairs of training data, it has advantages in reducing the cost of preparing training data, a critical problem in rule-based systems.

We performed experiments on extraction accuracies of the proposed methods and showed that a DVHMM trained with non-aligned training data has performance similar to one trained with aligned training data. The accuracies differ depending on the attributes and some of them are not high enough. However, we showed that some types of errors can possibly be utilized in the bibliographic matching phase.

From algorithmic learning theory, accuracy for some attributes is expected to be improved by using more training data. We plan to prepare larger training data sets and confirm this experimentally.

We plan to apply the proposed attribute extraction method to bibliographic matching problems. In studying this problem, we will check how many attribute extraction errors are recovered by approximate string matching techniques.

A second future project concerns language. In our experiment, we used articles written in Japanese. The proposed method is applicable to references in any language.

However, parameters of the DVHMM such as the graphical structure of the component DVHMMs should be tuned. For example, because Japanese characters have very similar sizes in printed documents, substitution errors tend to occur in the OCR process, whereas the proportion of framing errors may increase in English text. We plan to conduct experiments on the articles written in languages other than Japanese.

References

[1] F. H. Ayres, J. A. W. Huggill, and E. J. Yannakoudakis. The universal standard bibligraphic code (usbc): its use for clearing, merging and controlling large databases. *Program - Automated Library and Information Systems*, 22(2):117–132, 1988.

[2] A. Belaid, J. C. Anigbogu, and Y. Chenevoy. Qualitative Analysis of Low-Level Logical Structures. In *Proc. of International Conference on Electronic Publishing*, pages 435–446, 1994.

[3] H. Bunke and P.S.P. Wang, editors. *Handbook of Character Recoginition and Document Image Analysis*. World Scientific, 1997.

[4] D. Devroye, L. Gyorfi, and G. Lugosi. *"A Probabilistic Theory of Pattern Recognition"*. Springer, 1996.

[5] C. L. Giles, K. D. Bollacker, and S. Lawrence. CiteSeer: An Automatic Citation Indexing System. In *Proc. of International Conference on Digital Libraries*, pages 89–98, 1998.

[6] P. Goyal. An investigation of different string coding methods. *Journal of the American Society for Information Science*, 35(4):248–252, 1984.

[7] P. Goyal. Duplicate record identification in bibiliographic databases. *Information Systems*, 12(3):239–242, 1987.

[8] S. Hitchcock, L. Carr, S. Harris, J.M.N. Hey, and W. Hall. Citatition linking: Improving access to online journal. In *Proc. of Second ACM Conference on Digital Libraries(DL97)*, pages 115–122, 1997.

[9] S. Kahan, T. Pavlidis, and H. S. Baird. On the recognition of printed characters of any font and size. *IEEE Trans. on Pattern Analysis and Machine Intelligence*, 9(2):274–288, March 1987.

[10] Karen Kukich. *"Techniques for Automtically Correcting Words in Text"*. *ACM Computing Surveys*, 24(4):377–439, 1992.

[11] S. Lawrence, C. L. Giles, and K. D. Bollacker. Digital libraries and autonmous citation indexing. *IEEE Computer*, 32(6):67–71, June 1999.

[12] S. Lawrence, C.L. Giles, and K. D. Bollacker. Autonomous citation matching. In *Proc. of Third International Conference on Autonomous Agents*, 1999.

[13] Y. Li, D. Lopresti, and A. Tomkins. "Validation of Document Image Defect Models for Optical Character Recognition". In *Proc. of 3rd Annual Symposium on Document Analysis and Information Retrieval*, pages 137–150, 1994.

[14] G. Nagy, S. Seth, and M Viswanathan. A prototype document image analysis for technical journals. *IEEE Computer*, 25(7):10–22, July 1992.

[15] T. O'Neill, E., A. Rogers, S., and M. Oskins, W. Characteristics of duplicate records in OCLC's online union catalog. *Library Resources & Technical Services*, 37(1):59–71, 1992.

[16] F. Parmentier and A. Belaid. "Bibliography References Validation Using Emergent Architecture". In *Proc. of IAPR International Conference on Document Analysis and Recognition*, pages 532–535, 1995.

[17] A. Takasu. "Statistical Analysis of Bibliographic Strings for Constructing an Integrated Document Space". In *Proc. of European Conference on Research and Advanced Technology for Digital Libraries (ECDL02)*, pages 75–90, 2002.

[18] A. Takasu and K. Aihara. "DVHMM: Variable Length Text Recognition Error Model". In *Proc. of Internationa Conference on Pattern Recognition (ICPR02)*, Vol.III, pages 110–114, 2002.

[19] Vladimir N. Vapnik. *"Statistical Learning Theory"*. John Wiley & Sons, 1998.

[20] K. Y. Wong, R. G. Casey, and F. M. Wahl. "Document Analysis System". *IBM journal Research and Development*, 26(6):647–656, 1982.

Automated Semantic Annotation and Retrieval Based on Sharable Ontology and Case-based Learning Techniques

Von-Wun Soo, Chen-Yu Lee, Chung-Cheng Li, Shu Lei Chen and Ching-chih Chen*

Department of Computer Science, National Tsing Hua University, HsinChu, 30043, Taiwan
*Graduate School of Library and Information Science, Simmons College, Boston, MA 02115, USA
{soo;leoli}@cs.nthu.edu.tw; {g916711; g916723}@oz.nthu.edu.tw; chen@simmons.edu

Abstract

Effective information retrieval (IR) using domain knowledge and semantics is one of the major challenges in IR. In this paper we propose a framework that can facilitate image retrieval based on a sharable domain ontology and thesaurus. In particular, case-based learning (CBL) using a natural language phrase parser is proposed to convert a natural language query into resource description framework (RDF) format, a semantic-web standard of metadata description that supports machine readable semantic representation. This same parser also is extended to perform semantic annotation on the descriptive metadata of images and convert metadata automatically into the same RDF representation. The retrieval of images then can be conducted by matching the semantic and structural descriptions of the user query with those of the annotated descriptive metadata of images. We tested in our problem domain by retrieving the historical and cultural images taken from Dr. Ching-chih Chen's "First Emperor of China" CD-ROM [25] as part of our productive international digital library collaboration. We have constructed and implemented the domain ontology, a Mandarin Chinese thesaurus, as well as the similarity match and retrieval algorithms in order to test our proposed framework. Our experiments have shown the feasibility and usability of these approaches.

1. Introduction

Image retrieval research has been on-going for sometime. Two major paradigms are: Text-based metadata image retrieval and content-based image retrieval [1-5]. Text-based approaches, based on the keyword match of the text metadata description of images with the text queries, are usually relatively simple and easy to use but have their limitations when retrieving images that require subtle query expressions or domain knowledge. Content-based approaches, on the other hand, usually retrieve relevant images based on similar features of color, texture, shape, and spatial relations among image contexts. They often require advanced image processing and pattern recognition techniques. The low retrieval precision and difficulty to formulate an exact feature query are the major drawbacks of this second approach. To overcome these drawbacks, semantic-sensitive content-based image retrieval techniques have been introduced [5]. In this paper, we focus on the text-based image retrieval paradigm. Traditional text-based information retrieval systems or search engines usually are based on keyword matching techniques [6-10]. Although widely used nowadays, they usually suffer from the so called "too many or nothing" problem for various reasons. One common reason is that the users might not have complete domain knowledge and often cannot specify appropriate and exact keywords for a valid query. The other is that the target documents are expressed in terms of plain-text format that is hard for the search engine to parse; thus it is difficult to understand the semantics of the documents during the retrieval process.

To address these problems, we propose the semantic annotation approach. In other words, we annotate documents to be retrieved with semantic tags that are defined and derived from a set of domain concepts or schemes called domain ontology and thesaurus so that the information retrieval can be conducted to some extent at the abstract "semantic" level instead of at the purely syntactic keyword matching level. However, this often leads to one or more of four major difficulties:

1) Different annotators or domain experts might use a different ontology and so end up with different annotation results,

2) Converting a user natural language query into semantic schema requires one to have a significant amount of domain knowledge for syntactic grammar analysis on the query language,

3) The manual annotation of a large amount of descriptive metadata of images is a laborious task, and

4) Matching a query instance with each annotated image description can be extremely inefficient and tedious particularly when the size of the images is large.

Our previous work [11] proposed a conceptual framework to remedy the first problem mentioned above. It adopted the sharable ontology concept of the semantic web [12] that enables the sharing of the domain knowledge on the web with a standard and uniform representation. WWW consortium (W3C) has recommended several specifications and standards for web ontology languages based on XML (Extensible Markup Language) such as RDF/RDFS (Resource Description Framework/Schema) [13-20], DAML+OIL [21] and OWL [22,23], etc. These languages provide a well-defined set of relational terms essential for building domain concepts, and for serving as a website resource to be referred and shared by other domain ontology resources in terms of name spaces. RDF, a web standard for expressing metadata based on XML, provides interoperability among different platforms and allows knowledge exchange in machine-readable format on the Web. It represents semantic relations as an information resource in terms of a triple of Subject/Resource, Predicate/Property, and Object/Literal. For example: a sentence, "A general wears an armor," can be described as a triple {General, Wear, Armor} where "General", "Wear", and "Armor" correspond to the Subject, Predicate and Object respectively in the RDF schema. By allowing domain ontology and thesauri to be shared by the annotators (content provider) and the users (content consumer), we have designed intelligent software agents [9-11,24] to retrieve images by matching the user's query descriptions with the image descriptions using the same domain ontology expressed in terms of RDF instances and RDF schemas. Since the software agents use the same domain ontology and thesaurus as those used by the original annotators to interpret the annotations during the retrieval of images, it is more likely that we can avoid the mismatch problems of keywords and domain concepts. When compared with the traditional keyword match methods, we have found that the use of this method has enhanced both the recall and precision of image retrieval. Yet, this method has relied heavily on manual annotation of images using a visualization tool and a rough natural language parser to convert metadata descriptions of images and the query phrases into RDF-based annotated image descriptions and query schema respectively.

In order to overcome the other three difficulties mentioned above, we have further proposed a case-based learning approach and a conceptual clustering algorithm, to address specifically the following three main questions:

1)   How to automatically convert a natural language query phrase into a RDF one?

2)   How to perform automatic semantic annotation using the textual metadata descriptions of images and thus automatically convert them into RDF instances?

3)   How to design a fast similarity matching method to match a query instance with a huge number of images in the image base in terms of RDF descriptions?

We have designed an automatic annotation technique using case-based learning to address the first and second issues and implement a conceptual clustering method to deal with the third one. Our test-bed images are the historical images of the terracotta soldiers taken from Prof.

Ching-chih Chen's "First Emperor of China" CD-ROM [25]. She also has provided the simplified version of the metadata descriptions of these images. Before the experiments, we have translated these metadata descriptions together with additional verbal ones into Mandarin Chinese texts and then conducted automatic semantic annotations on these texts with the aid of a Chinese thesaurus and a domain ontology.

We shall provide a brief overview of our system in Section 2; and describe the case-based learning for a natural language query parser in Section 3, automatic semantic annotation approaches in Section 4, the automatic indexing and structural matching for semantic image retrieval in Section 5, and the experimental results in Section 6.   We shall present our conclusions and discuss our potential future work in the final Section 7.

2. System overview

Our overall image retrieval system based on sharable ontology is illustrated in Figure 1. This sharable ontology, expressed in terms of RDF schema together with a sharable thesaurus, provides an aid to convert a user query into a sequence of semantic codes.   The user's natural language (NL) query, parsed by a case-based NL query parser, is converted into a RDF query instance. On the right hand side of Figure 1, the images are first fed into an automatic annotation system that converts the NL

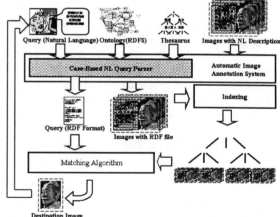

Figure 1. Sharable Ontology Image Retrieval System descriptions of images into image RDF instances. They are then classified into clusters for later retrieval by automatic indexing based on the RDF triple descriptions of the images. A matching algorithm then matches the RDF query instance with the indexed image clusters and finds the most similar image in terms of RDF descriptions.

For the Mandarin Chinese Thesaurus we have augmented it with domain specific lexical items including the names of historical figures, articles, locations, countries, etc for the terracotta soldiers in Qin dynasty. The total size of the thesaurus is now more than 70,000 terms that is organized in a semantic hierarchy. These terms basically are common ones. For the purpose of this project, we have added some proper names into our thesaurus, including 225 names of ancient Chinese kings and heroes, and 178 historical locations although they are seldom used in the image retrieval domain. The hierarchy is divided into 4 levels with the first level the most abstracted layer consisting of words, such as Person, Article, Action, etc. and the fourth level consisting of the synonyms of words. There are 12 categories/concept words in the 1st level, 94 in the 2nd, and 1428 in the 3rd. For example, a word "general" coded as "AE1004" can be separated into four sub-codes as "A", "E", "10", and "04". Here "A" is the code for "Person", "AE" stands for "Career" of a person, "AE10" associates with the "Ranks in Military", and "AE1004" means a specific rank of a military officer such as "general" or "commander". We also have developed a domain ontology specifically for describing historical images [26]. This domain ontology, in contrast to the thesaurus, defines domain concepts and schemas in terms of classes and properties. Currently there are 6 classes and 99 properties for the terracotta soldier domain that define the objects and relations among the objects and data.

3. Case-based learning for implementing a natural language query parser

A full-fledged NL parser for Mandarin Chinese needs a full set of grammar and semantic domain models. It needs also to assign thematic roles of constituents correctly in the parser tree in order to enable the conversion of the user's query into a proper corresponding RDF instance. This is not an easy task. Case-based learning [26-28] is suitable for learning regularities where domain expert rules are difficult to express or acquire. Our hypothesis is that if we could have a case base created by collecting a set of query phrases with their corresponding RDF instances that have been correctly converted, then by looking for a similar query phrase in the case base, a new query phrase can be converted into a similar corresponding RDF instance. Thus, a case-based query parser consists of four functional modules: 1) a Pre-processor module, 2) a Similarity matching module, 3) a Prediction module and 4) a Memory update module. The process and dataflow of our prototype of the Case-based learning NL query parser is shown in Figure 2.

3.1. The pre-processor module

With the aid of a thesaurus, a natural language query phrase is segmented into words. In other words, the query phrase can be divided into several meaningful word

segments that are attached with semantic codes provided by the thesaurus. For example, a specific phrase, "*A Qin Dynasty general wore an armor*" can be converted into four segments -- "Qin Dynasty" "a general", "wear", and "an armor". The thesaurus will assign a semantic code for each word segment; thus "a general" will be assigned a semantic code "AE1004." With the aid of the ontology, the subject in this case is a "person", and the RDF triple expression is {"person", "status", "general"}. The rest of the RDF triples created are: {"person", "wear", "armor"}, {"person", "period", "Qin Dynasty"}. In this case, the "person" is common among all RDF triple expressions. The domain ontology about a "person" in terms of an RDF schema has the "status", "wear", that is a *person* and "period" attributes that have been constructed at the ontology implementation stage.

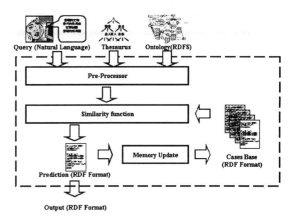

Figure 2. The CBL Natural Language Query Parser

3.2. The similarity module

This module conducts the similarity match between a code sequence of a new incoming query and the code sequences of old query phrases in the case base. When we compare two similarity match algorithms -- a Most Common Subsequence Algorithm (MCS) and a Multiple Layer Recursive Matching (MLRM) algorithm, we found that the MLRM is more effective. We further elaborate on this in the following sections.

3.2.1. The MCS algorithm

In the MCS algorithm, the inputs are two semantic code sequences: a query code sequence (QCS) with word length n and a case code sequence (CCS) with word length m that are denoted as:
QCS = $\{C_0, C_1,..., C_n\}$ and CCS = $\{C_0', C_1',..., C_m'\}$
where C_i , C_j' are the semantic codes of word i in QCS and word j in CCS, respectively.

The MCS algorithm, described in Algorithm 1, uses the

similarity scoring function to find a case code sequence (CCS) that is the most common between this sequence and the query code sequence (QCS). Two codes are considered as a match if their similarity is greater than a certain defined threshold. We define a similarity function Code_S (C_i, C_j') to calculate the abstract similarity between the semantic codes C_i and C_j' in the thesaurus. In our Chinese thesaurus the semantic codes currently have four semantic levels as already stated. For example, for semantic codes "AE0205", it belongs to four semantic categories -- "A", "AE", "AE02", and "AE0205" -- from general to specific. Therefore two codes "AE0205" and "AE0304" are considered as the similar semantic codes if the threshold is set at 3 or 4 since they both have similar Level 1, "A" and Level 2, "AE", but are not considered as similar if the threshold is set at 1 or 2. However, semantic codes "BE0204" and "AE0204" are not matchable because at the semantic category at Level 1, "A" and "B" are different. Likewise, in Algorithm 1 we also use a similarity function Seq_S(QCS, CCS) to calculate the similarity scores between two code sequences QCS and CCS based on accumulation of individual pair of code comparisons.

```
MCS(QCS[C₀, C₁,…, Cₙ], CCS [C₀', C₁',…, Cₘ'], e)
{
   A= 0, B= 0;
   While (A ≦ n and B ≦ m)
   {
      For (i from A to n )
         For (j from B to m )
            If (Code_S (Cᵢ, Cⱼ') > e)
            {
               Seq_S(QCS ,CCS) += Code_S (Cᵢ, Cⱼ');
               A = i + 1; B = j + 1;  Break to While;
            }
   }
   return Seq_S(QCS ,CCS);
}
```

Algorithm 1. The MCS algorithm

MCS is sensitive to the threshold. Yet, it is not easy to select a proper threshold. By decreasing the threshold, MCS might match with a high similarity code while miss the exact match code that follows. For example, as shown in Figure 3, the dotted line indicates that a matching pair with similarity greater than the threshold (the general matches with a solider) is detected before an exact match (a general matches with a commander) that is indicated by a solid line. On the other hand, if we increase the threshold too much, it might miss a pair that is a real match in the domain but cannot simply pass the threshold. It also causes the case-based learning parser to be rigid and unable to cope with various new queries that might match with an old case.

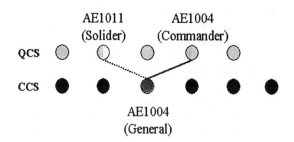

Figure 3. Two mismatch problems in MCS algorithm

3.2.2. The MLRM algorithm

The MLRM algorithm is described in Algorithm 2.

```
MLRM (QCS[C₀, C₁,…, Cₙ], CCS [C₀', C₁',…, Cₘ'], eₖ)
{
   If (either QCS or CCS is empty or no more higher layer)
      return 0;
   A= 0, B= 0;
   While (A ≦ n and B ≦ m)
   {
      For (i from A to n)
         For (j from B to m)
            If (Code_S (Cᵢ, Cⱼ') > eₖ)
            {
               Seq_S(QCS ,CCS) += Code_S (Cᵢ, Cⱼ') * Weightₖ;
               Seq_S(QCS ,CCS) += MLRM (QCS[Cₐ,…, Cᵢ₋₁],
                  CCS[C_B',…, Cⱼ₋₁'], eₖ₊₁);
               A = i +1; B= j+1;  Break to While;
            }
   }
            Seq_S(QCS ,CCS) += MLRM (QCS[Cₐ,…, Cₙ],
                  CCS[C_B,…, Cₘ'], eₖ₊₁)
   return Seq_S(QCS ,CCS);
}
```

Algorithm 2. The MLRM algorithm

Like MCS, MLRM accepts the same input QCS and CCS sequences, but the similarity match is recursively computed at multiple layers with different thresholds (e_k) and similarity weights (Weight$_k$). MLRM attempts to find a node pair from QCS and CCS that has the highest match (with initial threshold e_1 at layer 1). The highest match pair essentially divides the sequences into two subsequences. And then MLRM continues the match process until one of the subsequences becomes empty by recursively matching each subsequence with a lower threshold at the next layer. The thresholds and weights at each layer are empirically and heuristically determined to reflect the relative importance of the similarity match between two code sequences. We tentatively set the thresholds e_1, e_2, e_3 and e_4 as 4, 3, 2, 1 at each layer respectively because we wish to control the semantic code in QCS to match all four semantic levels. The determination of the similarity weights at each layer is also very intuitive. What we hope is to have the effect that each weight assigned at a lower layer should be higher than that at the higher layers while the weight sum at any two higher layers should be greater than the weight at a lower layer. As a result, this process will result in the decrease of the relative importance of any single similarity match, and will guarantee that the relative importance of any two similarity matches at higher layers is greater than that of a single similarity match at a lower layer. It also implies that the setup of the weight at each layer should satisfy mathematically: for all i, $w_k > w_{k+j}$ and $w_i < w_{i+j} + w_{i+k}$ where $j \geq 1$ and $k \geq 1$. Accordingly, we tentatively set the weights w_1, w_2, w_3, and w_4 as 10, 9, 8, and 7 respectively in the experiment.

Figure 4 illustrates MLRM with an example. At Step 0, a pair of nodes is found (connected with a dark line) and divides the sequence into two subsequences. Each subsequence is recursively processed by MLRM as indicated in Step 1. In Step 1, two additional similarity pairs are found and they are further divided into finer subsequences to be processed recursively at Step 2. MLRM stops when no more similarity pairs can be found or no more nodes are left in the subsequences.

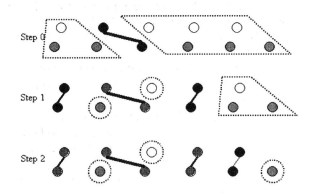

Figure 4. An example of recursive matching in MLRM

3.3. The prediction module

After finding the most similar case by the similarity match algorithm, a predicted RDF instance with descriptors associated with semantic codes provided by the thesaurus and ontology can be generated. For example: If a new query, "A chancellor wore a uniform" is most similar to the old query, "A Qin-dynasty general wore an armor" in the case base (the RDF description of the old query is {Person, Status, General}, {Person, Wear, Armor}, {Person, Period, Qin-dynasty}), the prediction module finds the match for this associated pair -- (Chancellor, General), (wear, wear) and (uniform, armor) among the words in the two queries. It then allows the roles -- {subject, predicate object} -- of the words in RDF triple schema in the old query to be taken by the corresponding words in the new query. Thus, "chancellor" adopts the status of "person" (expressed as {Person, Status, Chancellor}), "uniform" adopts "object" and "wear" adopts "predicate". The new query is predicted as {Person, Wear, Uniform} in an RDF triple.

3.4. The memory update module

When the system converts a NL query into its corresponding RDF instance, the user can add it as a new case to the case base or modify it if the result is not correct. Thus, it becomes a new entry in the case base.

4. Automatic semantic annotation on descriptive metadata of images

It is generally difficult for intelligent software agents to retrieve images based on the NL descriptive metadata of all images because of the inefficiency in parsing and analyzing the NL sentences during the retrieval process. One compromise is to conduct the semantic annotation on the descriptive metadata in advance. The idea of semantic annotation is to assign domain concepts in terms of semantic tags that are well defined in the domain ontology and thesauri to the word segments or phrases in the descriptive metadata so that it could facilitate the retrieval of the images based on the semantic tags. Yet, it is simply too laborious to manually conduct this kind of semantic annotation. Thus, the first essential step is to automate this process in order to facilitate the generation of annotated descriptive results in accordance with the RDF standards.

The descriptive metadata of each image may consist of several sentences, and each sentence may include several phrases. Since the case-based learning query parser can convert the query phrase into an RDF description, we can easily separate a sentence into several phrases and then pass the phrase to the case-based learning query parser to be converted into RDF descriptions one by one. All RDF descriptions can then be combined together at the end. This automatic semantic annotation system is illustrated in Figure 5. It consists of three major modules -- a separation module, a case-based NL parser, and a combination module. We shall elaborate on these modules in the following sections.

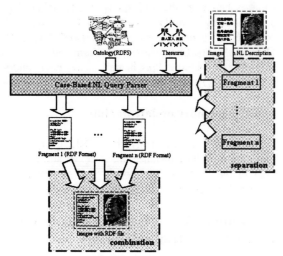

Figure 5. Automatic annotation of metadata descriptions of images

4.1. The separation module

The separation module as shown in Figure 5 separates a sentence description into phrase fragments by punctuations, verbs, or some stop words. For instance, a simple description of a certain image is given as "A tall soldier in a silver armor holds a sharp sword. A leather saddle is on the white horse." This description consists of two simple sentences and can be separated into five fragments as "A tall soldier", "in a silver armor", "holds a sharp sword", "A white horse" and "a leather saddle." It is possible that the semantic links between the phrases might be missing after the separation. In this example since the "soldier" from the first phrase fragment is the subject, it covers the following fragment without a subject ("soldier"). So the phrase fragment becomes "A tall soldier", "soldier holds a sharp sword" and "soldier in a silver armor". In the second sentence, "horse" is the subject of the first phrase; therefore it becomes the subject of the last phrase fragment as "horse with a leather saddle".

Example: A description of Figure 6 could be as "金黃色的兵馬俑, 身分是將軍, 頭戴著頭盔, 身穿著盔甲, 有濃密的眉毛, 表情威武。" (translated to be "*A golden yellow colored terracotta soldier, his status is a general, wearing a helmet on his head, wearing armor, has thick eyebrow, with brave expression*")

The separation module separates the full description into several phrase fragments (PF's) as follow:
PF 1 "金黃色的兵馬俑" (*A golden-yellow colored terracotta soldier*)
PF 2 "身分是將軍" (*The status is a general*)
PF 3 "頭戴著頭盔" (*wear a helmet on his head*)
PF 4 "身穿著盔甲" (*wear armor*)

PF 5 "有濃密的眉毛" (*has thick eyebrows*)
PF 6 "表情威武" (*with brave expression*)

Figure 6. The general in armor

PFs 1-2 are phrases that have a "subject" (terracotta solider and general), and PFs 3-6 are those without a "subject". But in the nearest phrase PF2, a "person" is the "subject" in an ontology schema "a person whose status is a general", so the separation module assigns "*person*" as the "subject" to those phrase fragments following the subject. Thus, PFs 3-6 are modified as follows:
PF 3 "頭戴著頭盔的人" (*the person wears a helmet on his head*)
PF 4 "身穿著盔甲的人" (*the person wears armor*)
PF 5 "有濃密的眉毛的人" (*the person has thick eyebrows*)
PF 6 "表情威武的人" (*the person has brave expression*)

After the processing of the separation module, the automatic semantic annotation system requests the CBL NL query parser to convert PFs 1-6 one by one to corresponding RDF descriptions one of which (PF 1) is shown in Figure 7.

```
金黃色的兵馬俑.rdf - 記事本
檔案(F)  編輯(E)  格式(O)  說明(H)
<?xml version='1.0'?>
<RDF xmlns='http://www.w3.org/1999/02/22-rdf-sy
     xmlns:P='http://home.kimo.com.tw/cadip_jac

<Description about='金黃色的兵馬俑'>
 <p:包含物件為 rdf:resource='#bag'/>
</Description>

<P:物品 rdf:ID='物品1'>
 <p:顏色>金黃</p:顏色>
</P:物品>

<rdf:Bag rdf:ID='bag'>
 <rdf:li rdf:resource='#物品1'/>
</rdf:Bag>
</RDF>
```

Figure 7. The RDF instance for the phrase "A golden-yellow colored terracotta soldier"

4.2. The combination module

Since all phrase fragments are expressed in RDF format using the same domain ontology and thesaurus, the combination module can easily combine all fragments of RDF descriptions back into complete RDF instances. Using the same example in Section 4.1, the RDF instances of all phrase fragments are constructed. The combination module merges these RDF instances from PFs 1 to 6. The PF 1 is determined as belonging to a description of a piece of "Article/Items" (defined a priori in our domain ontology in terms of RDFS), and PFs 2-6 as belonging to the descriptions of a "Person" by the CBL NL query parser. This means that the descriptions consist of one article and one person. The combination module treats PF 1 as a single Subject/Resource (Article1) description, and merges PFs 2-6 into another single Subject/Resource (Person1) description. The PFs 2-6 are merged as:

```
<p:人 rdf:ID='人 1'>
  <p:身分>將軍</p:身分>
  <p:身體.穿著>盔甲</p:身體.穿著>
  <p:頭.盔飾>頭盔</p:頭.盔飾>
  <p:頭.臉部.眉毛>濃密</p:頭.臉部.眉毛>
  <p:頭.臉部.表情>威武</p:頭.臉部.表情>
</p:人>
```

The prefix "p:" is a name space pointer to the resource file of our domain ontology where the conceptual terms and schemas are defined. The English version of the above RDF description is:

```
<p:person rdf:ID='person1'>
<p:status>general</p:status>
<p:body.wear>armor</p:body.wear>
<p:head.wear>helmet</p:head.wear>
<p:head.face.expression>brave</p:head.face.expression>
<p:head.face.eyebrows> thick</p: head.face.eyebrows >
</p:person>
```

After combining the two resource descriptions (Article1 and Person1) into one description, the final RDF description is shown in Figure 8.

5. Automatic indexing and structural matching

To retrieve an image from a large image base by description matching from a query can be very time consuming and inefficient if the images are not properly indexed. Since each image has been described in terms of semantic RDF descriptions, we use an automatic indexing

algorithm by grouping images according to their triple descriptions.

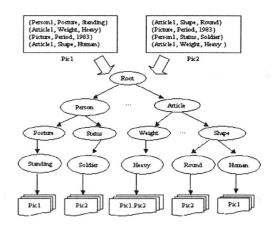

Figure 8. The full description of a RDF instance after combining the phrase fragments

The indexes are formed according to the triples (subject; predicate; object). This indexing technique is somewhat similar to the concept of inverse indexing. However, it is conducted on the conceptual structure level (e.g., a RDF triple structure) rather than on the keyword level. Figure 9 shows a simplified example of two images as the result of the automatic indexing based on the triples.

Figure 9. Automatic Indexing based on RDF triples

After the indexing scheme is formed, a simple structural matching algorithm is used to match between the query description and image descriptions in terms of RDF triples. It first splits the RDF query instance into a set of triples, using a scoring function to weigh the matching of each triple against the indexes of the RDF triples of descriptive metadata of images. It computes the best match image by finding the one with the largest number of triples matched with the query. The major advantage of using this algorithm is the relative ease of matching the image description with the user query and the fast speed in doing it. In other words, the tasks of having to compare the query instance with all image instances one by one is greatly simplified while the computational complexity in time is constant.

6. Experimentation and analysis

6.1. Results of similarity match in CBL

Our case base consists of 100 NL query phrases with corresponding correct RDF descriptions. Five staff members developed the queries of the selected 50 images and manually converted these queries to RDF descriptions. We then used the statistical cross-validation leave-one-out method to compare the performances between the MCS and MLRM algorithms.

We first randomly divided 100 NL query phrases into 10 groups. We used 9 of the 10 groups of these query phrases as the training set and used the last (one) group as the test set. Using the similarity matching algorithms (MCS and MLRM), the test set is used to compare the accuracy of the case-based learning query parsers. The testing experiments were repeated 10 times using 10 different test sets. These experimental results are shown in Figure 10.

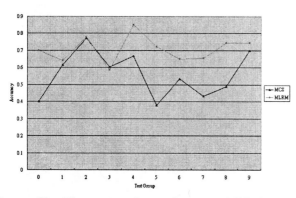

Figure 10. The comparison of cross validation experiments of MCS and MLRM

The accuracy was calculated by using the following formula:

Accuracy = Score of correctness of triples predicted /Total score of all triples to be correctly annotated

The correctness of a triple is scored as 1, 2, or 3 depending on the number of entries in the triple that are correctly predicted. In other word, if all three entries in a triple are predicted all correctly, it is scored as 3.

The experimental results show that the average accuracy of MCS is 0.559 with a variance of 0.0179 while the MLRM is 0.707 with a variance of 0.0059. Thus, we conclude that on the average MLRM significantly outperformed MCS.

6.2. Results of automatic semantic annotation

We further constructed 20 full descriptions (by 4 different persons) of images in NL in order to evaluate the performance of the automatic annotation system. Each description contains about 3 to 7 phrases, and the number of training cases for the CBL NL parser is 100. We calculated the accuracy of the automated semantic annotation according to the following formula:

Annotation accuracy = Score of correctness of annotated triples / Total score of all triples to be correctly annotated

The "total score of all triples to be correctly annotated" is computed from the final correctly generated RDF instance, while the "score of correctness of annotated triples" is computed from the triples that have been correctly generated by the automated annotation method. Figure 11 shows the annotation accuracy for each description. The average accuracy of annotation is 0.6 that is indicated as a horizontal line at the 0.6 accuracy level, while the performance of each individual automated semantic annotation varied, from the worst case at 0.3 for the fifth description, to the best case of perfect annotation at the 6th and 20th descriptions.

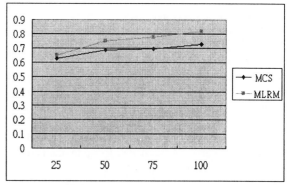

Figure 11. The accuracy of automatic semantic annotation

The automatic annotation module described above has two major potential weaknesses that may decrease the accuracy of annotation: 1) It is based on a CBL NL parser, so the performance of this parser could affect the results of the separation module. 2) Combining RDF instances is a complex task; therefore, our assumption that each description can only describe one instance for each subject is not adequate. For example, the descriptive metadata of a picture of 5 weapons would be treated by the system as that all "weapons" (subject) are of the same kind, thus all properties of these 5 weapons would be merged together. This is clearly not correct if these weapons are not of the same kind.

Despite the imperfect result of the CBL NL parser in this experiment due to the l number of available cases, it is worth noting that most subjects can be assigned even if the separation module did not do so.

6.3. Image retrieval results based on ontology

In this experiment, we selected 30 queries at random, and tested them on 49 images that were manually annotated into RDF instances. We then compared the results of image retrieval by using keyword-based and ontology-based retrieval methods. The keyword-based retrieval methods retrieved images with exact keywords specified both in the queries and the retrieved image descriptions. On the other hand, the ontology-based image retrieval converted the queries to RDF instances and retrieved the images based on the structural match described above.

Of the 30 queries, 14 valid ones did not yield any retrieved images in both methods because no images among the 49 tested met the query criteria. The precision versus recall of image retrieval based on the average of the remaining 16 queries is shown in Figure 12.

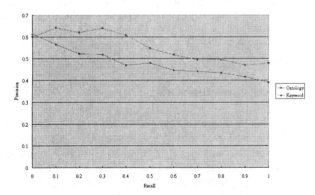

Figure 12. The precision-recall curves of the keyword-based retrieval vs. the ontology-based retrieval

From Figure 12, we observed that the ontology-based retrieval has an advantage over the keyword-based one in terms of precision at the same level of recall. In fact, the 11-point average precisions are 0.55 and 0.48 for the ontology-based retrieval and the keyword-based retrieval, respectively. The average precision gap is 7 %.

To demonstrate further the difference in retrieval accuracy between the keyword-based and the ontology-based methods, and how the ontology-based methods has an advantage over the keyword-based one, two cases are illustrated in the following:

Case 1: The first case used the query – "作戰的士兵" (*"Solider at combat"*) and has yielded significantly different results between the two retrieval methods. This query needs domain ontology information about a *"person"* whose status is *"soldier"* and is in the state of *"combat"*. In the keyword–based retrieval, the relationship between *"combat"* and *"person"* cannot be established together. Yet it can be considered with the aid of the domain ontology. Figure 13 shows the result of the keyword-based retrieval method (5 images in the first row, ranked from left to right according to their match score) vs. the ontology-based retrieval method (5 images in the second row). Clearly, the first image on the left (an inner view of combat carriage) and the second image (another inner view of combat carriage) of the first row should be regarded as mismatches. Thus, results shown on the second row using the ontology-based method had much better retrieval results than those of the keyword-based method.

Figure 13. The images retrieved using the query, "Solider at combat", by using the keyword-based retrieval method (1st row) vs. the ontology-based retrieval method (2nd row), respectively

Case 2: The second case used the query – "左手臂朝左的士兵" (*"The soldier with his left hand directing toward left as viewed by the annotator"*). Again, we have found significantly different retrieval results between the two methods. The query requires to have the ontology describing a person whose status is a soldier and whose left hand directs toward the left. The keyword-based retrieval method cannot establish such a relationship. It can only match the keywords "左手臂" (*left hand*), "朝左" (*directing toward left*), "士兵" (*soldier*) with images, when the metadata descriptions of these images mention those keywords. Figure 14 shows the results of both retrieval methods.

Figure 14. The images retrieved using the query, "The soldiers whose left hand directs toward left" by using the keyword-based retrieval method (1st row) vs. the ontology-based retrieval method (2nd row) respectively

The keyword-based retrieval found 5 images shown in the 1st row, with the first image on the left receiving the highest score. The ontology-based retrieval found 5 images shown in the 2nd row. The correct images retrieved are the 1st and 2nd images from the left of the second row (using the ontology-based retrieval) while the keyword-based method resulted in finding the correct images in the 1st and the 4th positions of the first row. This means that the ontology-based retrieval has yielded more accurate search results, because it ranked more accurately on the relation of the "left hand" and "toward left" as well as the status of person as a "soldier".

7. Conclusions and future work

In this work, we have established a framework for facilitating image retrieval using domain ontology. Building on the assumptions that if the descriptive metadata of the image resources were annotated before retrieval and both information resource descriptions and user queries could be converted into semantic web RDF (resource descriptive framework) format with the aid of a sharable domain ontology and thesaurus, then the information resources can be matched or retrieved to some extent with the user query at an abstract and semantic level. This paper contributes the methodologies for automating the query conversion, the semantic annotation, and the retrieval processes using case-based learning techniques. We have developed two similarity comparison algorithms -- MCS and MLRM -- over the NL phrases that can facilitate the retrieval mechanism for finding a most similar case from the case base. The results indicated that the MLRM performed better than the MCS algorithm. We also have extended the techniques of using a case-based learning phrase parser to address the problem of automatic semantic annotation of descriptive metadata of images. For dealing with large-scale structural matching, we have developed methods for automatic indexing for the RDF instances. The experiments described in this paper have shown the feasibility of automating the semantic annotation of the descriptive metadata of images and automatic conversion of user queries into RDF instances using case-based learning techniques.

While the research results reported here have extended our earlier work as reported in 2001 [11], there are potentials for much more future research including those listed in the following:

1)   The influences of ontology expressions on the performance of retrieval cannot be ignored. It affects the semantic interpretations of query instances, cases of CBL, as well as descriptive metadata of images. A finer ontology representation will enhance the performance. However, precise domain ontology construction is a tedious task that requires commitments of both domain experts and ontology engineers. Conducting logical inferences on the domain ontology can augment the performance further. In OWLIR [29], they showed by conducting additional logical inferences on the campus event ontology and OWLIR could increase the precision of information extraction by almost 20% against a RDF triple matching method.

2)   Although our automatic semantic annotation can handle simple sentences and phrases well, yet it is not as accurate for complex sentences. Ways to enable annotators to write down descriptive metadata of images in terms of NL sentences rather than RDF structures should be further explored.

3)   Merging ontology with more than one RDF instance is a complex but interesting problem. It can be required in many other domains and needs further investigation. How to resolve inconsistencies among many ontological instances is also a real challenge.

8. Acknowledgments

This research is supported in part by the MOE Program for Promoting Academic Excellence of Universities under grant number 89-E-FA04-1-4, and the IDLP project of NSC of Taiwan and is in collaboration with the US NSF/IDLP CMNet project led by Prof. Ching-chih Chen of Simmons College of USA under NSF grant number NSF/IIS-9905833.

9. References

[1] Arnold W.M. Smeulders, "Content-Base Image Retrieval at the End of the Early Years", *IEEE Transactions on pattern analysis and machine intelligence*, Vol. 22, No. 12, December, 2000.

[2] Qasim Iqbal and J.K. Aggarwal, "Image Retrieval via Isotropic and Anisotropic Mapping", *in IAPR Workshop on Pattern Recognition in information system*, Setubal, Portugal, pp. 34-49, July 6-8, 2001.

[3] "Blobworld Image retrieval using regions", Digital Library Project, University of California, Berkeley, http://elib.cs.berkeley.edu/photos/blobworld/.

[4] Wolfgang Muller and Henning Muller, "MRML: A Communication Protocol for Content-Based Image Retrieval", *Tech. Rep.* 01.01, University of Geneva, 2001.

[5] Ching-chih Chen, and James Z. Wang, "Large-scale Emperor Digital Library and Semantics-sensitive Region-based Retrieval", *Proceeding of the International Conference on Digital Library -- IT Opportunities and Challenges in the New Millennium*, National Library of China, Beijing, China, pp. 454-462, July 9-11, 2002.

[6] "The Text REtrieval Conference (TREC), co-sponsored by the National Institute of Standards and Technology (NIST) and the Defense Advanced Research Projects Agency (DARPA)", http://trec.nist.gov/.

[7] Gerard Salton, The SMART Retrieval System--Experiments in Automatic Document Processing. Prentice-Hall, Englewood Cliffs, NJ, 1971.

[8] Gerard Salton and Christopher Buckley, "Term-weighting Approaches in Automatic Text Retrieval. " *Information Processing and Management*, Vol. 24(5), pp.513--523, 1998.

[9] Jyi-Shane Liu, Von-Wun Soo, Chia-Ning Chiang, Chen-Yu Lee and Chun-Yu Lin, "Gaz-Guide: Agent-Mediated Information Retrieval for Official Gazettes," *In AI Lecture Note Series, Springer , in Proc. of PRIMA*, pp. 154-167, 2001.

[10] Von-Wun Soo, Jyi-Shane Liu and Chia-Ning Chiang, "Exploiting Contextual Knowledge for Information Retrieval in a Multiagent-based Digital Library Service System", *NIT 2001, Beijing. Global Digital Library Development in the New Millennium: Fertile Ground for Distributed Cross-Disciplinary Collaboration. Ed. by Ching-chih Chen. Beijing: Tsinghua University Press*, pp. 299-306, 2001.

[11] Von-Wun Soo, Chen-Yu Lee, Chao-Chun Yeh and Ching-chih Chen, "Using Sharable Ontology to Retrieve Historical Images", *in Proc. of ACM/IEEE International Joint Conference of Digital Library*, pp.197-198, 2002.

[12] James Hendler, Tim Berners-Lee, and Eric Miller, "Integrating Applications on the Semantic Web," Journal of the Institute of Electrical Engineers of Japan, Vol 122(10), October, 2002, pp. 676-680, http://www.w3.org/2001/sw/.

[13] "Resource Description Framework (RDF) Model and Syntax Specification W3C Recommendation 22, February, 1999", http://www.w3.org/RDF/.

[14] Boris Motik and Vlado Glavinic, "Enabling Agent Architecture through an RDF Query and Inference Engine", *10th Mediterranean Electro-technical Conference,* MeleCon, 2000.

[15] Stephen Cranefield, "Networked Knowledge Representation and Exchange using UML and RDF", *Journal of Digital Information*, Vol.1, Issue 8, 2001.

[16] Stefan Decker, Frank Van Harmelen and Jeen Broekstra, "The semantic Web - on the respective Role of XML and RDF", http://www.ontoknowledge.org/.

[17] B. Amann and I. Fundulaki, "Integrating Ontologies and Thesauri to Build RDF Schemas", *Third European Conference ECDL'99*, Paris, France, Springer Verlag, pp. 234-253, September, 1999.

[18] Stefan Decker and Sergey Melnik, "The Semantic Web: The Roles of XML and RDF", *IEEE Internet Computing*, Vol. 4(5), pp. 63-74, October 2000.

[19] Steffen Staaba and Michael Erdmann, "An Extensible Approach for Modeling Ontologies in RDF(S)", *in Proc. of ECDL Workshop on the Semantic Web*, pp.11-22, 2000.

[20] Natalya F. Noy, Micheal Sintek and Stefan Decker, "Creating Semantic Web Contents with Protege-2000", *IEEE Intelligent Systems*, Vol.16 (2), pp.60-71, 2001.

[21] "The DARPA Agent Markup Language Homepage", http://www.daml.org/.

[22] Michael K. Smith, and Deborah McGuinness, "Web Ontology Language (OWL) Guide Version 1.0", http://www.w3.org/TR/owl-guide/.

[23] Peter F. Patel-Schneider, and Patrick Hayes, "Web Ontology Language (OWL) Abstract Syntax and Semantics", http://www.w3.org/TR/owl-semantics/.

[24] Yi-Jia Chen and Von-Wun Soo, "Ontology-based Information Gathering Agents", *in Proc. of Web Intelligence*, pp.423-427, 2001.

[25] Ching-chih Chen, "The First Emperor of China", CD-ROM, Voyager, 1991.

[26] David W. Aha. "Case-based Learning Algorithms", *in Proceedings of the DARPA Case--Based Reasoning Workshop*, Morgan Kaufmann, pp. 147-158. 1991.

[27] C. Cardie, "Using Decision Trees to Improve Case-Based Learning", *in Proc.of the Tenth International Conference on Machine Learning*, Morgan Kaufmann, pp. 25-32, 1993.

[28] Kirsti Racine and Qiang Yang. "Maintaining Unstructured Case Bases", *In Proc. of the 2nd International Conference on Case-Based Reasoning (ICCBR)*, SpringerVerlag, pp. 553-564, 1997.

[29] Urvi Shah, Tim Finin, Anupam Joshi, R. Scott Cost and James Mayfield, "Information Retrieval on the Semantic Web", *in Proc. of Conference on Information and Knowledge Management,* Nov 4-9, 2002, McLean, VA., pp. 461-468.

Session 4A: Managing Resources and Services

Session Chair: Richard Furuta, Texas A&M University

Towards a Cultural Heritage Digital Library

Gregory Crane
Tufts University
Perseus Project
Medford, MA 02155 USA
gcrane@perseus.tufts.edu

Clifford Wulfman
Tufts University
Perseus Project
Medford, MA 02155 USA
cwulfman@perseus.tufts.edu

Abstract

This paper surveys research areas relevant to cultural heritage digital libraries. The emerging National Science Digital Library promises to establish the foundation on which those of us beyond the scientific and engineering community will likely build. This paper thus articulates the particular issues that we have encountered in developing cultural heritage collections. We provide a broad overview of audiences, collections, and services.

1. Introduction

The efforts of the Perseus Project are based on a strong and somewhat polemical premise: namely, that digital libraries promise new methods by means of which new audiences can ask new questions about new ideas they would never otherwise have been able to explore. While we are based in a university and are products of US higher education, we see the peer-to-peer interactions between professional colleagues [56, 9, 71] and indeed the formal instruction of 18–22 year old students [50, 74] as instruments for a broader purpose. In one recent survey of 1,500 people, "two fifths ... reported that they pursue a hobby or collection related to the past, and they spoke of those pursuits with words like 'love' and 'passion'" [58]. Tens of millions of Americans visited history museums last year; in the broadcast world, twenty million Americans watched Ken Burns' *Civil War* series [72], while the History Channel and high-end series such as WGBH's *American Experience* have devoted audiences. This passion for history springs from sources as diverse as the hobbyist's light-hearted fascination with 19th-century railroads and the African-American student's searing encounter with the horrors of slavery.

We see in digital libraries an environment in which the barriers between academia and broader historical discourse about the past may be broken down. The Americans surveyed above reported feeling "unconnected to the past in history classrooms because they don't recognize themselves in the version of the past represented there" [60, 59]. Academic historians, by contrast, express frustration with popular histories (see, for example, the debate around Burns' *Civil War* [72, 10, 4]). Digital libraries can reinforce existing structures, providing ever more specialized data to scholarly elites and ever more "edutainment" to society at large. But they can also, if so designed, expose the specialists to the challenges of a far wider and more truly diverse audience than any we encounter in the academy, while providing the authors, producers, and harried developers of websites for popular audiences with a much richer foundation on which to build.

We have approached this broad challenge from a much more modest background. Most of us in our group are trained as classicists, and the Perseus Project concentrated on Greco-Roman antiquity for its first ten years of work (1986-1996). Several factors, however, inspired us to expand beyond our own initial field. First, we had brought the Greco-Roman collections to a reasonable level of maturity. Second, we realized that, unlike biology or physics, classics was not large enough to sustain its own specialized digital library infrastructure. Classical languages raise serious challenges in digital library design; nevertheless, the largest humanities communities in the United States work primarily with English and a few major modern languages. It became clear that, to ensure that our particular needs were not left out of consideration, we needed to share infrastructure with humanists in other disciplines and define our common needs and objectives. The same logic has drawn us into the NSDL and led to an NSDL services project for reading support [13]. Third, a classical digital library is a strategic resource, since Western education and culture stressed classical models and Latin remained a major vehicle of scientific, literary and cultural publication through the eighteenth century. No one can understand the intricacies and subtle needs for all the numerous domains within the humanities, but an ability to handle Latin in particular, multilingual documents in general, and a range of visual materials gave us the tools to undertake a range of projects.

We could not, of course, create a digital library for all of cultural heritage — such a project would be vast and would have to be global in scope. Our Greco-Roman work provided a start for far more areas of Western culture than we could ever hope to explore. We have chosen a number of areas in which to develop additional collections; our decisions have reflected difficult cost/benefit tradeoffs and have been controversial. The issues are particular to our work but they also reflect general issues that arise when a project shifts its focus. We offer the following tradeoffs because they affect many projects as they struggle with their identity.

Perceived Neglect of the Core Collection vs. the Need to Generalize. Many in our classics audience have expressed resentment at our non-classical work and, indeed, the classics collections seem to many to have paid an opportunity cost, as much of our effort has turned elsewhere. In fact, had we not broadened the scope of our approach, we would have even fewer resources to devote to classics, either directly or indirectly (through general development). Furthermore, the NSDL services grant that is about to begin is based on the automatic linking work that we developed for classics. By stressing the general issues of automatic linking, we have identified a service from classics as a general resource that will serve a vastly larger community. As a result, we are able both to improve the automatic linking service for all users and to embed services widely used by our classicist and humanities users within the much larger NSDL community. This service is now, in our view, more sustainable in the long run.

There is also a general developmental principle at work. Few would argue that we should not share infrastructure, but many of us still resist such sharing in practice. Digital library projects like ours, in small, specialized areas of the humanities, must aggressively pursue ways to adapt general solutions that may not at first seem suited to our particular needs [46]. Such projects often give up on general solutions too soon, developing their own DTDs, for example, instead of using those of the Text Encoding Initiative, or creating special purpose software, thus solving short-term problems but creating very difficult problems of support over time. We have seen short-term success kill many projects over the past two decades.

Exploring New Domains vs. the Rigors of Disciplinarity. In developing new collections outside of classics, we initially followed our trained instincts and sought leadership from experts in the fields. In working closely with several well-defined expert groups, however, we found the weight of established practice and tradition to be restrictive. We have shifted instead to seeking advice rather than direction from experts in the field and to offering advice to collection-development projects rather than working under them.

We developed a London collection after making our own

assessments and seeking constructive advice. We were able to build a collection that would, we hoped, stimulate ideas about new kinds of intellectual work rather than simply enhance existing research agendas. Such a strategy is risky, since it reflects a vision of what might be useful, and such visions, if they are at all interesting, will often not be productive. Such a strategy is also very hard to fund in a peer-reviewed environment, precisely because it follows unconventional paths. The Fund for the Improvement of Post-Secondary Education, the IMLS National Leadership Grants, and NSF ITR program are specific attempts to address the challenges of supporting innovative work. The Berger Family Fund for Technology Transfer at Tufts allowed us to establish the London collection.

Our forays into areas such as the history and topography of London, the history of mechanics, early-modern English literature, and others have provoked a range of responses. While interest and excitement are gratifying, the most useful responses have often been the most critical and even hostile. Tangible collections and services provoke concrete discussions based on what does and does not appeal to real users. Digital collections are capital resources that not only retain their value, but can improve over time (e.g., by expanding or by acquiring new metadata or tagging). If the base materials are of sufficient interest, data entry adequate, and document structures solid, publicly accessible collections can attract additional labor and drive debate forward. By intruding into domains beyond classics, we have been able to stimulate thought and debate that would not otherwise have taken place.

Using vs. Creating Digital Collections. It is essential that at least some digital library researchers have an opportunity to build and design collections from the ground up. Like the alphabet soup of evaluation forums for language technologies (e.g., TREC, CLEF, ACE, DUC, etc.), most DL research projects work with third-party collections. While prudent, this strategy is sometimes restrictive: researchers can add metadata to documents, but the documents themselves cannot be modified. Because we are interested in how document form and digital library service influence one another, we need to be able to vary the functionality of our collections by modifying every component, including data acquisition, markup, and delivery. Thus while some of our work uses third-party collections, we also have invested substantial labor in creating testbeds of our own, for which we are responsible but which have few if any restrictions. We now have reasonably large, fairly heterogeneous document sets with which we can take risks, without horrifying living authors or even electronic editors of public-domain materials.

The goal of the Perseus Project has been to provide a set of instruments — collections and services — with which we can study new types of use. The remainder of this paper describes some very preliminary findings and points towards the research agenda that will guide us in the final years of our DLI–2-sponsored research. That agenda focuses on answering two basic questions: first, how do digital libraries support various communities as they work now? Second (and far more challenging), how do digital libraries open up new forms of work and, indeed, potentially create new audiences for new ideas?

The latter question is particularly important, because digital libraries have the potential to so alter user expectations that components designed as long-term infrastructure become obsolete. Consider the following scenario: a group of scholars sets to work on a completely new lexicon for a well-studied language, the first in centuries. No one doubts that the existing lexicographic tools would benefit from being replaced. The project manages to acquire five to ten person-years of labor and creates a lexicon, with beautifully composed new entries. The working environment makes good use of existing computational linguistic tools to track collocations and exploit machine-readable versions of the old lexicon. The project delivers its predicted results, and the community of students and scholars working on this language has a far more up-to-date tool.

How valuable such a new lexicon would be in five to ten years, however, is not clear. Scholars already read source texts in digital libraries that provide a variety of lexical tools, such as automatically generated links from inflected forms to dictionary entries, morphologically sophisticated searching and analysis tools, and other resources that reduce scholarly dependence upon lexica [20, 68]. We do not know how a new lexicon might aid students learning to read the language, as most student problems center on the relatively simple tasks of finding proper definitions and understanding syntax. Thus while a new lexicon would clearly constitute an advance, the field might have been far better served had it spent its costly time and labor on building a treebank: a database of annotated parses of the most heavily read texts in the corpus [48, 49, 11]. A treebank would provide students for the first time with consistent syntactic information about millions of words, potentially a far greater advance than improved lexicon entries. The treebank would also provide a training set for context-free grammars that could be run over tens of millions of words in the remaining corpus, thus providing new research opportunities. The treebank might even answer more scholarly questions about word usage than general lexicographic articles. If this were so, lexicographers might find themselves becoming not archivists creating fixed textual descriptions, but computational linguists producing dynamic lexical databases. In our view, such a transformation would be salutary, for the servants of inquiry — lexicographers and librarians, traditional and digital — should help inquirers answer the questions we pose now and in the future,

rather than serving the needs of an earlier century.

2. Audiences

We have assembled two datasets with which to analyze the needs of the audiences for the collections we have mounted. The Web has clearly allowed new intellectual communities to form, and many intellectual resources formerly available only onsite in special collections are now receiving substantial electronic use (e.g. [12, 44, 53, 37]). The 315 million page-accesses we have tracked since 1996 are a useful diachronic dataset that we are beginning to use to track the evolution of user behavior, while the thousands of email messages to webmaster@perseus.tufts.edu trace the reactions of a patron group (albeit a self-selecting one). We have invested substantial staff time in answering as many messages as possible, and this practice has yielded dialogues with a number of users from varying backgrounds.

The bulk of the current Perseus traffic (84%) is concentrated on the established classical collections. This is unsurprising: we have spent fifteen years developing these collections and accompanying services, while developers — including faculty creating syllabi and non-academic web developers — have spent years creating links into the classical digital library. The remaining 16% of the traffic is, however, non-trivial — 1.2 million page accesses in a month of 8 million — and will provide a reasonable basis on which to study some aspects of user behavior.

It is difficult to identify the audience reached by an open site like the Perseus Digital Library. Clearly, those interested in classical antiquity represent a subset of those with a passion for the past. Nevertheless, the audience for Greco-Roman Perseus has consistently surprised us with its sheer size: 6.7 million pages on classical antiquity in a typical month of 8 million aggregate pages. Even more surprising (and gratifying to a classical philologist), approximately 10% of those pages were Greek and Latin source texts in the original, dictionary entries, morphological analyses and other tools that support reading Latin and Greek.

Counting domain extensions is a notoriously problematic instrument for estimating audience composition. Few Perseus hits, for example, come from the .edu domain, but many students access the Internet from accounts with third-party Internet Service Providers, thereby masking the fact that they are pursuing traditional coursework by new electronic means. Nevertheless, the fluctuations of *.edu usage suggests that the number of non-academic users is substantial and, indeed, predominant.

The two dates in Figure 1 reflect very different sections of the academic year. Mid-November is a peak period of student and traditional academic use. Most US universities are, however, on intercession in the first week of January. The percentage of *.edu use declines by only a factor of

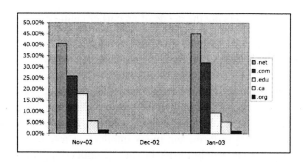

Figure 1. Sample domains for traffic on November 14, 2002 and January 8, 2003.

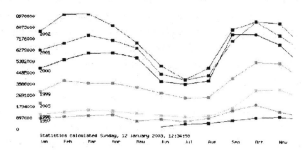

Figure 2. Monthly traffic from mid-1996 through the end of 2002.

two. This suggests the possibility that a large percentage of our student traffic comes from third party ISPs and does not show up in the *.edu aggregates. Basic "signal intelligence" may provide a better view of where our traffic lies.

Tracking web usage, we have been able to identify gross patterns (see Figure 2): October–November and February–March are the times of peak academic activity. Other patterns emerge as well: note that September 2001 marks the first time when traffic declined for a given month over the previous year. Activity rebounded in October 2001, and it is tempting to hypothesize a "September 11" effect, when academic users were distracted from their expected behavior. Serious system problems emerged in the late summer and fall of 2002. The traffic for October 2002 and 2001 were almost identical. Growth resumed in November and December, as system performance improved, but this improvement lagged beyond what we might otherwise have expected: for the first time, fall totals declined from those of the preceding spring. While the exponential growth in usage clearly cannot continue, this decline probably reflects lingering changes in behavior in response to earlier slow and unreliable system performance.

The variance in usage over the course of the year shows the extent to which the academic calendar influences usage. Traffic varies by a factor of two between peak academic months and July (which is consistently the month of lightest usage). By comparing the number of students enrolled in courses during the summer and those in the traditional academic year, we will probably be able to form a reasonable estimate of the size of our academic audience. Even when this audience is factored out, the non-traditional users will, we expect, remain substantial — far larger than we had expected, given the content and design of the site: even 25% of the July audience would suggest that 1 million pages were sent to individuals beyond academia. Certainly our webmaster correspondence demonstrates the qualitative breadth of the user base. Web log analysis suggests a substantial quantitative base as well.

Counting which documents users read most frequently is an obvious technique. Nevertheless, while the technique may be obvious, the significance of the results will vary from field to field. If we assume for now that the Perseus Digital Library reaches a representative selection of those reading classical texts, we have the best data ever on who is doing what. Classical texts are capital resources on which scholars have lavished centuries of effort. A complex network of commentaries, specialized grammars, and studies exists (although most of this network remains sequestered in print libraries with limited clienteles). We can now see what people are reading and from this begin to understand our audience.

The raw statistics above are only the starting point in a more detailed analysis, which will consider the information needs for each of these audiences. The digital library provides the field of classics with a new instrument to see what we are doing and to explore what new information resources might be most useful.

3. Services

To provide the services we felt best addressed the needs of our audience, our project found it necessary to create a full-fledged digital library system. Much of our work consisted of adapting general tools to the particular requirements of our collections. Thus, we wanted to be able to perform morphologically aware information retrieval [e.g., search for *fero* (Latin, "to carry") and retrieve *tuli* ("I carried")] with search engines that had no hooks for morphological analysis [16]. Thus we created surrogate files in which we substitute inflected forms for dictionary entries (e.g., *tuli* maps to *fero*): when users enter queries, we expand them by substituting the inflected forms for the dictionary entries and search for those. The principle was to integrate standard tools into a working system with as little effort as possible.

The rise of robust digital repositories such as Fedora [57] (which the Tufts library system is adopting) and DSpace [69], the Open Archive Initiative (OAI), document-oriented XML searching engines such as HyRex [33, 1, 35, 36, 34,

Table 1. Most commonly viewed primary sources in December 2002. Note the prominence of Marlowe's *Faustus* (which suggests a class project). the Cicero probably reflects high school Latin readership. Monthly totals for individual primary sources fluctuate far more than for the core reference works.

Perseus Document	No. Hits
Aeschylus, *Agamemnon*	5050
Marlowe, *The Tragicall History of D. Faustus* (A text)	4635
Euripides, *Medea*	4543
Vergil, *Aeneid*	3549
Sophocles, *Antigone*	3477
Cicero, *Against Catiline*	3375

Table 2. Five most commonly viewed texts in December 2002. All five are reference works connected to primary texts by an automatic linking service. Dictionary usage suggests that Perseus users spend as much time reading classical Greek as Latin.

Perseus Document	No. Hits
Perseus Encyclopedia	71,784
Charlton T. Lewis, *A Latin Dictionary*	49,347
Henry George Liddell, *A Greek-English Lexicon*	49,258
Thomas R. Martin, *An Overview of Classical Greek History from Homer to Alexander*	44,278
Harry Thurston Peck, *Harpers Dictionary of Classical Antiquities*	20,546

1], and the emerging services component of the National Science Digital Library have, among other things, allowed us to rethink the way that we manage our collections. We have already begun to expose our metadata over the OAI and to integrate OAI services into our own system [66]. We will shift our data object to the Tufts Fedora repository and translate the services we need into Fedora. Nevertheless, even as a new generation of digital library infrastructures emerges, there are still services, some particular to cultural heritage digital libraries, that we must still either maintain or develop.

Most of the services described below reflect different forms of information harvesting. We plan to use the OAI to make as many categories of data available as possible: thus, third-party repositories should be able to harvest not only titles and authors but head words from dictionaries and encyclopedias, automatically mined people, places, and dates and any other extracted information that third parties would find useful.

The following list enumerates some of the most basic services that we identified. The emerging challenge for digital libraries seems to be multisource, customized summarization: a DL system should be able to determine what supporting information a particular user would require to understand a particular piece of information [34]. Most of the services that we describe below are building blocks for such a system. We have chosen, however, to concentrate on those services that we have either implemented or have funding to develop. We do not emphasize those services already under development in the NSDL but concentrate on issues that particularly characterize the needs of cultural heritage digital libraries.

Document Chunking and Navigation Services. Publishers can pressure authors to follow regular style sheets, thus vastly simplifying the infrastructure required to man-

age these documents, but cultural heritage documents are structured in a variety of ways, and overlapping hierarchies are common. Thus an edition of Thucydides' *History of the Peloponnesian War* may be structured into traditional books, chapters, and sections, units suitable for some readers but not for others who may wish to extract Thucydides' speeches, which can begin or end mid-unit. Some modern scholarly documents have extremely complex structures: the New Variorum Shakespeare series contains two kinds of annotation, a range of narrative essays, and small libraries of source materials, which can themselves be documents of considerable complexity. Providing a reasonable default method of paging through such documents while preserving the flexibility for alternate schemes is often messy and requires systems to look beyond the elegance of BNF formats such as XML.

XML Server. At present, most digital libraries tightly couple back-end and front-end, but XML facilitates the separation of content from display. The Perseus Document Management system has for several years worked by extracting well-formed fragments of XML from documents and databases. The task is not always straightforward: extracting lines 21–38 from the scene of a play can be difficult, since line 21 might appear in the middle of a speech that was itself nested deeply in a complex textual hierarchy. Converting this document management system into an independent XML fragment server will allow third parties to add services and new front-ends to the data that we collect.

Visualization Tools. These are crucial, but since we and others have published on their importance in previous digital library conferences, we simply allude to them in passing: [44, 53, 37, 64, 63, 65].

Citation Linking. Automatic citation linking has made immense progress [41], but for humanists, locating the document is only a first step. Humanists cite points and (if we are diligent) spans within a document; sometimes these points and spans designate pages or other coarse units, but at other times we use very precise forms of reference (e.g., Homer's *Odyssey*, Book 9, line 312). In some cases these citations may contain text anchors (Vergil Aen. 1.1: "arma ... cano"), which may need to be expanded (e.g, "arma virumque cano"). Some works (lexica, for example) may vary the word order or even the words themselves, thus requiring fuzzier matching algorithms. Some citation schemes have remained unchanged for centuries. But others remain in flux (each new edition of Shakespeare, for example, has a tendency to introduce new reference schemes, thus causing tremendous problems for citation systems). Adding to the complexity of automated citation linking, humanists often cite passages using languages or spelling conventions different from those in the original sources. At the very least, software supporting pre-nineteenth century scholarship must be able to match original spelling against modernized forms.

Quotation Identification and Source Tracking (not implemented in Perseus). A corollary to the citation-linking problem is that of identifying quotations. Many documents in the humanities contain quotations from earlier sources: almost half of the initial ten million words in the London collection was quoted text. Most of these quotes have no precise references; many do not even mention precise authors. A DL system needs to be able to search quickly and automatically for likely quotation sources. Such a system should also scan for unquoted sources (for which plagiarism detection services provide a technical model [76]).

Named-Entity Identification and Analysis of "Encyclopedic Data." People, places, and things may have bored history students for millennia, but they remain key components of historical documents. Perseus scans for dates and place-names in all full text documents [65, 28, 29]. The service is limited to English at present (in part because we have English translations for the vast majority of source texts), but it enables us to provide automatically generated (and hence scalable) timelines and maps to help users assess the contents of collections, detect events [45, 5, 64, 63], and ultimately search by time and place (e.g., "documents relevant to Worcester County, Mass. in the 1840s"). We have also begun to track personal names, monetary sums, and other readily identifiable entities.

Named-entity identification is notoriously domain specific [39, 40, 38]. Even such apparently universal entities as people, places, and things can vary widely from culture to culture. Western audiences in 2001, for example, learned that Afghans often have only a single name; Greco-Roman

texts do not, of course, use modern year numbers or even easily followed month/day schemes. Digital library systems need to be able to apply different information extraction routines to different collections.

We have begun to see work on integrating information extraction into digital libraries (e.g. [8, 30, 51]), but this task has barely begun. Much named-entity work depends upon heuristics written in application-specific formats: very little work has gone into making such core information portable, much less in creating sharable digital libraries of named-entity heuristics. Just as cultural-heritage scholars have traditionally spent years preparing editions for publication, so corpus editors will spend years developing gazetteers, heuristics, and training sets for large corpora, and they will need to be able to exchange and build on one another's efforts over many years [27, 62].

Semantic Services. A cultural heritage digital library system should automatically integrate new texts, lexica, grammars, treebanks, and other resources into linguistic services that are constantly updated. We have implemented such services for collocations of Greek and Latin words [61, 67]; a mature DL system would harvest new documents to enhance cross-language information retrieval, machine translation, automatic summarization, and other services.

Authority-List Editors (not yet implemented but under development as an NSDL service under [13]). Information-extraction systems can recognize that "Mark Twain" and "Twain" in close proximity are both personal names and probably refer to the same person. But we need tools that connect both references to a general authority list, one that can also help information-extraction systems recognize that "Mark Twain" and "Samuel Clemens" are both instantiations of "Clemens, Samuel, 1835–1910." Likewise, on a semantic level, we need to be able to express the fact that "bank" in a particular document is a financial institution, not the edge of a river, and to connect this instance to a definition in a third-party dictionary. Such an authority-list editor should be able to predict the most likely meaning in the case of multiple instances.

Runtime Automatic Linking. Some texts will have complex pre-established markup associated with them, but we also need to be able to identify and add informative links to key words and phrases on the fly. Such automatic linking has been part of the Perseus system for more than ten years [16, 15, 17, 18, 23, 19], but this feature will be expanded and refined to become a service within the NSDL under [13].

Automatic Evaluation Services. Evaluating digital libraries in general [47], and language technology services in particular, is difficult [35, 73, 2, 42, 31], but because digital libraries contain many knowledge resources, such as encyclopedias, indices, and lexica that include manually verified data, digital library systems should be able to mine their

Table 3. Precision, recall, and F-measures (calculated here as $2 \times precision \times recall / precision + recall$**) for identification of personal names in a series of Civil War books. The DL system automatically calculates these by comparing the output of the named-entity tagger with the contents of online indices.**

Work	Precision	Recall	F-Measure
blcw01[a]	0.877	0.904	0.890
blcw02	0.885	0.908	0.896
blcw03	0.871	0.872	0.871
blcw04	0.894	0.878	0.886
phcw01[b]	0.812	0.937	0.870
phcw02	0.578	0.941	0.716
phcw03	0.609	0.940	0.739
phcw04	0.660	0.895	0.760
phcw05	0.591	0.944	0.727
phcw06	0.801	0.943	0.866
phcw07	0.789	0.935	0.856
phcw08	0.795	0.945	0.864
phcw09	0.848	0.931	0.888
phcw10	0.982	0.949	0.965
rebrec.diary[c]	0.698	0.929	0.797

[a]*Battles and Leaders of the Civil War*[43]
[b]*Photographic History of the Civil War*[52]
[c]Diary sections of the multivolume *Rebellion Record*[54]

manual resources to refine their automated services.

Automated comparisons between information extraction and manual indices reveal interesting differences between human practice and machine performance: humans are better at interpreting indirect references — "the South's best hope" as a reference to Robert E. Lee, for example — but our information extraction services had much better recall than the manual indices. The precision, recall and F-measure numbers listed in Table 3 thus generally underestimate the performance of information extraction routines. Nevertheless, while the numbers may be questionable as absolute measures, the automated measures seem likely to gauge performance between comparable information extraction systems. Much work needs to be done in developing DL services that mine such pre-existing manual data to track new service performance.

4. Collections

The Perseus Digital Library comprises third-party collections and those we have created for experimental purposes. While the Perseus Digital Library includes non-textual materials that are both well understood (color images and their accompanying metadata) and experimental (collections of GIS and 3D materials), we focus here on texts. Where we have the rights to do so, we will make these collections accessible as testbeds to those conducting research in language technologies and digital libraries. All Perseus data is scheduled to become part of the Tufts University Fedora repository [57], which will provide a long-term source on which third party researchers and developers can rely.

At the moment, we have seven substantial collections. Two of these are from third parties; the other five were developed partly or entirely by Perseus.

Each of these collections allows us to experiment with a different domain, a different cluster of audiences, and a different set of research challenges. The London collection, for example, allows us to study problems and opportunities of a geospatially oriented DL with a small geographic focus and centuries of activity. The US Civil War collection, by contrast, is geographically dispersed but temporally compact. Both collections have substantial popular audiences and thus offer greater opportunities for outreach than the Greco-Roman materials. The Early Modern English collection taps into a scholarly infrastructure that superficially resembles that developed for classics, but students of early modern culture in general and Shakespeare in particular have expectations that differ from each other and from classics. Where much of our effort has focused on extracting people, places, dates and other encyclopedic data, the history of mechanics collection has a very different orientation, one which has forced us to consider how to track and analyze formulas, technical language, and broader mental models. The American Memory collections allow us to compare our work with mainstream US collection development, while the Duke Databank of Documentary Papyri is a core resource for an intense, highly organized subdiscipline of classical research.

The eclectic set of collections thus forces us to confront a wide range of challenges, not the least of which is the management of heterogeneous materials. We built the Perseus Digital Library precisely to explore these difficulties, and the major theme of our future work will be designing services that work with diverse collections and audiences.

Elsewhere we have discussed the process of bootstrapping digital collections: to achieve integrated systems in which documents interact not only with users but with each other [70], we place particular emphasis on dictionaries, encyclopedias, handbooks, and other reference materials [28, 29, 24, 25, 21, 22, 26]. While we can work with documents in a variety of formats (including free text, HTML, PDF, and RTF), we continue to explore how structured markup and digital library services co-evolve. Our services, current and envisioned, shape the structure of doc-

Table 4. Size of Perseus's major collections in millions of words.

Collection	Size
Classics	50
US Civil War and other 19th-Century Materials	41
Selected American Memory Collections[a]	38
History of Mechanics[b]	15
London Collection[c]	13
Early Modern English	7.3
Duke Data Bank of Documentary Papyri[d]	4

[a]Derived from collections developed by the Library of Congress
[b]Developed jointly by Perseus and the Archimedes Project at Harvard
[c]Developed jointly by Perseus and the Digital Collections and Archives division of the Tisch Library at Tufts.
[d]Perseus's web interface to the DDBDP developed at Duke University

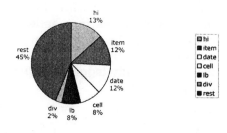

Figure 3. American Memory Collections (selected).

uments, while document structure enables services. Every markup tag is both an interpretation and an investment. In the digital library context, each tag represents a statement by the collection designer that some digital library service either exists or will exist to exploit it. By creating documents and services, we have been able to see in many concrete ways how the two interact.

Consider the markup of quotations, for example. Most projects leave quotations unmarked, but our use of the TEI quote tag forces us to make certain that each quotation is well-formed. Because quotation marks are a major source of typographical error in both transcriptions and original sources, ensuring well-formedness, even with the assistance of reasonable software tools, is labor-intensive and thus expensive. But identifiable quotations are a valuable asset, for they can be used to discover or verify citations and cross-references, both explicit and implicit, across multiple collections. The quote tag thus represents an investment for a service that we have not yet implemented but can easily envision.[1]

We have devoted substantial effort to developing automatic markup engines to support digital library services. Figures 3, 4, 5, and 6 show the density and frequency of markup in four very different collections, and provide some sense of how TEI-conformant collections in a single digital library may differ.

Counting tags is, of course, problematic. Markup quickly clogs files, and information extraction systems have inspired work on more tractable standoff markup schemes [30, 51, 3, 6, 7, 14]. Ten years ago, when the first classical

---

[1]It also constitutes a bet that the cost of well-formed quotations will be less than that of correcting for the problems that arise when we try to extract quotations from texts with unverified quotation marks. Some of our recent research suggests we may lose this bet.

Perseus CD ROMs were produced, we were already using draft TEI guidelines but were generating at least one linguistic tag of standoff markup for each of the million words of Greek [17, 55]. Today we scan for possible place names in all collections that have no explicit geographic tags and store these in standoff markup: the number of tags associated with the American Memory texts is thus already much larger than those encoded in the files. Nevertheless, the figures provide overviews of how each collection differs and at what sorts of services and audiences each is aimed. Note that all three Perseus collections thus have roughly five times as many tags per word as the American Memory collections; the automatically generated tags, however, are not manually checked and thus contain many inaccuracies [65].

4.1. American Memory Collections on California, Chesapeake Bay, and the Upper Midwest

These collections provide textbook examples of well-executed level 4 TEI markup, which focuses on encoding the structural elements of a text [32]. The <hi> tag simply encodes that the source text was in italics and puts off the task of determining where the italics indicates book titles, foreign language quotes, etc. The <cell> tags indicate parts of tables and reflect page layout. Ultimately, tables need to be analyzed, since most table rows are, in fact, nascent database records. Note, however, the large number of <date> tags — these tagged dates allow us to determine the temporal coverage of individual documents within the American Memory collections and are an extremely valuable addition. They represent a judicious cost/benefit judgment, expanding judiciously beyond level 4 markup.

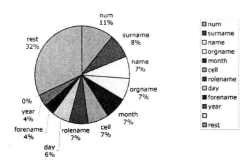

Figure 4. Perseus Civil War and Nineteenth Century US Collections.

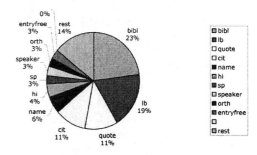

Figure 6. Perseus Early Modern English Collection.

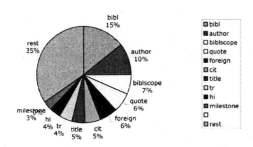

Figure 5. Perseus Classical Collections.

4.2. Perseus Civil War and Nineteenth Century US Collections

All of the ten most common tags are automatically generated. The <num> tag simply brackets every floating number (though the tagger does do a good job of mapping "21" and "twenty-one" etc. to the same quantity). Bracketing tags such as <datestruct> and <persname> have been ignored so as not to count tags twice. The personal name and date routines were fairly general. Most of the <orgname> tags represent regiments and other military units and required domain specific routines. Most of the <name> tags are qualified with the attribute type=place. Thus, we have located more than 1.5 million possible surnames, places, and organizations in the 41-million-word collection.

4.3. Perseus Classical Collections

Two monumental research lexica form core resources for the classical collections. The 1.1 million <bibl> tags represent more than a million point-to-point links. The 400,000 <cit> tags, along with 100,000 annotation tags

(not numerous enough to make the top 10) indicate that we have 500,000 passages where we can associate particular text spans and citations (thus providing data for the 3 dimensional citation links described above). The 250,000 <milestone> tags indicate anchors for citation/chunking schemes that lay outside the dominant XML hierarchies of the texts. While the density of tags is high (15 tags for every 100 words), the classical texts have less automatic internal markup than the Civil War collection. Hence the semantically vacuous <hi> tag, an artifact of the data-entry process signaling text that remains to be disambiguated, is in the top ten.

4.4. Early Modern English Collection

The early modern collection is particularly heterogeneous, including the plays of Marlowe and Shakespeare, as well as substantial prose works such as Holinshed's *Chronicles* and Hakluyt's *Voyages*[75]. Most of the tags in the early modern texts were added either by the data entry firm or by semi-automated post-processing. Nevertheless, the density of tags is high, reflecting the labor costs of production. The Shakespeare community is accustomed to highly finished, manually produced reference works and has proven the most demanding of all of our audiences. The <sp> and <speaker> tags reflect the prominence of dramatic works in the corpus. Three on-line Shakespeare lexica also account for most of the top ten tags.

5. Conclusions

We have provided an overview of the three core topics of our research: how networked digital libraries serve established audiences but also reach new ones; what services cultural heritage digital libraries need to support; and what document structures provide the basis for these services. Like the NSDL, cultural heritage digital libraries have a broad, "K to gray" audience. But cultural heritage digital libraries play a particularly important role for students of the humanities, because the digital library is the humanist's laboratory, its resources the scholar's primary data. In such a laboratory, supports for reading — translingual services for translation and analysis, for example, or sophisticated summarization and information-retrieval tools — are especially important, and our clear focus on reading support has allowed us to begin contributing to the NSDL as well [13]. Because cultural heritage collections do not become obsolete but instead become more valuable as the past recedes, humanists have spent generations (and, in some cases, millennia) creating knowledge bases of paper. We have begun to extend and transform these knowledge bases by digitizing them, mining them, and using them as the common ground on which to build diverse communities of users with a shared passion for the past. Perseus's combinations of audiences, services, and collections, while still unfinished, are now both objects for analysis and instruments for new collaborations.

6. Acknowledgments

A grant from the Digital Library Initiative Phase 2 (NSF IIS-9817484), with particular backing in our case from the National Endowment for the Humanities, provided the primary support for this work.

7. Additional Authors

Lisa Cerrato, Anne Mahoney, Thomas Milbank, David Mimno, and Christopher York at the Perseus Project; Jeffrey Rydberg-Cox at University of Missouri at Kansas City; David Smith at Johns Hopkins University.

References

[1] M. Abolhassani, N. Fuhr, N. Gövert, and K. Großjohann. HyREX: Hypermedia retrieval engine for XML. Technical report, University of Dortmund, 2002.

[2] ACE evaluation plan version 06, August 12 2002.

[3] P. Anand, D. Anderson, J. Burger, J. Griffith, M. Light, S. Ardis, and A. Morgan. Qanda and the Catalyst architecture. In E. M. Voorhees and D. K. Harman, editors, *The Tenth Text REtrieval Conference (TREC 2001)*, page 5, Gaithersburg, MD, 2001. Department of Commerce, National Institute of Standards and Technology.

[4] D. Aucoin. Fast forward into the past: What do we learn when TV becomes our history teacher?, November 2, 1997 1997.

[5] M. Q. W. Baldonado and T. Winograd. Hi-Cites: Dynamically created citations with active highlighting. In *Conference Proceedings on Human Factors in Computing Systems*, pages 408–415. ACM Press, 1998.

[6] S. Bird and M. Liberman. A formal framework for linguistic annotation. *Speech Communication*, 33(1,2):23–60, 2001.

[7] S. Bird, K. Maeda, X. Ma, H. Lee, B. Randall, and S. Zayat. TableTrans, MultiTrans, InterTrans and TreeTrans: Diverse tools built on the Annotation Graph Toolkit. In *Proceedings of the Third International Conference on Language Resources and Evaluation, European Language Resources Association*, Paris, 2002.

[8] K. Bontcheva, D. Maynard, H. Cunningham, and H. Saggion. Using human language technology for automatic annotation and indexing of digital library content. In *6th European Conference on Research and Advanced Technology for Digital Libraries (ECDL 2002)*, pages 626–625, Rome, 2002.

[9] W. S. Brockman, L. Neumann, C. L. Palmer, and T. J. Tidline. Scholarly work in the humanities and the evolving information environment. Technical report, Digital Library Federation and the Council on Library and Information Resources, December 2001.

[10] K. Burns, D. G. McCullough, G. C. Ward, R. Burns, F. Films, and P. Video. The Civil War, 1989.

[11] F.-D. Chiou, D. Chiang, and M. Palmer. Facilitating treebank annotation using a statistical parser. In *HLT2001*, San Diego, 2001.

[12] G. S. Choudhury. Strike up the score: Deriving searchable and playable digital formats from sheet music. *D-Lib Magazine*, 7(2), 2001.

[13] G. Colati. Managing authority lists for customized linking and visualization: A service for the National STEM Digital Library, 2002.

[14] S. Cotton and S. Bird. An integrated framework for treebanks and multilayer annotations. In *Third International Conference on Language Resources and Evaluation. European Language Resources Association*, page 8, Paris, 2002.

[15] G. Crane. Redefining the book: Some preliminary problems. *Academic Computing*, 2(5), February 1988.

[16] G. Crane. Generating and parsing classical Greek. *Literary and Linguistic Computing*, 6(4):243–245, 1991.

[17] G. Crane, editor. *Perseus 1.0: Interactive Sources and Studies on Ancient Greek Culture*. Yale University Press, New Haven, CT, 1992.

[18] G. Crane. What is Perseus? What is it not? Comments on the Bryn Mawr review of Perseus 1.0. *BMCR*, 3(6):497–502, 1992.

[19] G. Crane. Building a digital library: The Perseus Project as a case study in the humanities. In *Proceedings of the 1st ACM International Conference on Digital Libraries*, pages 3–10, 1996.

[20] G. Crane. New technologies for reading: The lexicon and the digital library. *Classical World*, pages 471–501, 1998.

[21] G. Crane. Designing documents to enhance the performance of digital libraries: Time, space, people and a digital library of London. *D-Lib Magazine*, 6(7/8), July/August 2000.

[22] G. Crane. Extending a digital library: Beginning a Roman Perseus. *New England Classical Journal*, 27(3):140–160, 2000.

[23] G. Crane. The Perseus Project: An evolving digital library, 2000.

[24] G. Crane. Cultural heritage digital libraries: Needs and components. In M. Agosti and C. Thanos, editors, *European Conference on Digital Libraries (ECDL)*, pages 626–637, Rome, 2002. Springer.

[25] G. Crane. In a digital world, no book is an island: Designing electronic primary sources and reference works for the humanities. In L. Breure and A. Dillon, editors, *Creation, Use and Deployment of Digital Information*, page forthcoming. Lawrence Earlbaum Associates, 2002.

[26] G. Crane, B. Fuchs, A. C. Smith, and C. E. Wulfman. The symbiosis between content and technology in the Perseus Digital Library. *Culture Interactive*, 2, 2000.

[27] G. Crane and J. A. Rydberg-Cox. New technology and new roles: the need for "corpus editors". In *Proceedings of the 5th ACM Conference on Digital Libraries*, pages 252–253, San Antonio, TX, June 2000.

[28] G. Crane, D. A. Smith, and C. E. Wulfman. Building a hypertextual digital library in the humanities: A case study on London. In *Proceedings of the First ACM+IEEE Joint Conference on Digital Libraries*, pages 426–434, Roanoke, VA, 24-28 June 2001.

[29] G. R. Crane, R. F. Chavez, A. Mahoney, T. L. Milbank, J. A. Rydberg-Cox, D. A. Smith, and C. E. Wulfman. Drudgery and deep thought: Designing a digital library for the humanities. *Communications of the Association for Computing Machinery*, 44(5):35–40, 2001.

[30] H. Cunningham, D. Maynard, K. Bontcheva, V. Tablan, C. Ursu, and M. Dimitrov. Developing language processing components with GATE (a user guide). Technical report, The University of Sheffield, 2002.

[31] M. Dabbadie, A. Hartley, M. King, K. J. Miller, W. M. E. Hadi, A. Popescu-Belis, F. Reeder, and M. Vanni. A hands-on study of the reliability and coherence of evaluation metrics. In *Machine translation evaluation workshop: LREC 2002: Third International Conference on Language Resources and Evaluation*, pages 8–6, Las Palmas, Canary Islands, 2002.

[32] L. Friedland, N. Kushigian, C. Powell, D. Seaman, N. Smith, and P. Willett. *TEI Text Encoding in Libraries: Draft Guidelines for Best Encoding Practices*, 30 July 1999.

[33] N. Fuhr and K. Großjohann. XIRQL: A query language for information retrieval in XML. In B. Croft, D. Harper, D. Kraft, and J. Zobel, editors, *Proceedings of the 24th Annual International Conference on Research and Development in Information Retrieval*, pages 172–180. ACM, New York, 2001.

[34] N. Fuhr, C.-P. Klas, A. Schaefer, and P. Mutchske. Daffodil: An integrated desktop for supporting high-level search activities in federated digital libraries. In M. Agosti and C. Thanos, editors, *European Conference on Digital Libraries (ECDL)*, Rome, 2002. Springer.

[35] N. Fuhr, M. Lalmas, and G. Kazai. INEX: Initiative for the evaluation of XML retrieval, 2002.

[36] N. Fuhr and G. Weikum. Classification and intelligent search on information in XML. *IEEE Data Engineering Bulletin*, 25(1):51–58, 2002.

[37] R. Furuta, S. S. Kalasapur, R. Kochumman, E. Urbina, and R. Vivancos-Perez. The Cervantes Project: Steps to a customizable and interlinked on-line electronic variorum edition supporting scholarship. In P. Constantinopoulos and I. T. Solveborg, editors, *European Conference on Digital Libraries (ECDL 2001)*, pages 71–82, Darmstadt, Germany, 2001. Springer.

[38] R. Gaizauskas, P. Herring, M. Oakes, M. Beaulieu, P. Willett, H. Fowkes, and A. Jonsson. Intelligent access to text: Integrating information extraction technology into text browsers. In *Proceedings of HLT*, San Diego, CA, 2001.

[39] S. Hattunen and Satoshi. Diversity of scenarios in information extraction. In *LREC 2002: Third International Conference on Language Resources and Evaluation*, page 4, Las Palmas, Canary Islands, Spain, 2002.

[40] L. Hirschman, K. Concepcion, L. Damianos, D. Day, J. Delmore, J. G. L. Ferro, J. Henderson, J. Kurtz, I. Mani, S. Mardis, T. McEntee, K. Miller, B. Nunam, J. Ponte, F. Reeder, B. Wellner, G. Wilson, and A. Yeh. Integrated feasibility experiment for bio-security: IFE-bio, a TIDES demonstration. In *HLT2001*, San Diego, CA, 2001.

[41] S. Hitchcock, D. Bergmark, T. Brody, C. Gutteridge, L. Carr, W. Hall, C. Lagoze, and S. Harnad. Open citation linking: The way forward. *D-Lib Magazine*, 8(10), 2002.

[42] E. Hovy, M. King, and A. Popescu-Belis. An introduction to MT evaluation. In *Machine Translation Evaluation Workshop: LREC 2002: Third International Conference on Language Resources and Evaluation*, pages 1–7, Las Palmas, Canary Islands, 2002.

[43] R. U. Johnson, C. C. Buel, C. Company, and M. L. C. B. University). *Battles and Leaders of the Civil War; Being for the Most Part Contributions by Union and Confederate Officers: based upon "The Century War Series" edited by Robert Underwood Johnson and Clarence Clough Buel*. Century Co., New-York, 1887. Includes index. Brown University Library copy (LINC): J000647: 32 v. in 4.

[44] R. Kochumman, C. Monroy, R. Furuta, A. Goenka, E. Urbina, and E. Melgoza. Towards an electronic variorum edition of Cervantes' *Don Quixote*: Visualizations that support preparation. In *JCDL 2002: Proceedings of the second ACM/IEEE-CS Joint Conference on Digital Libraries*, pages 199–200, Portland, OR, 2002.

[45] R. R. Larson. Geographic information retrieval and spatial browsing. In L. C. Smith and M. Gluck, editors, *Geographic Information Systems and Libraries: Patrons, Maps, and Spatial Information*, pages 81–123, April 1995.

[46] A. Mahoney, J. A. Rydberg-Cox, D. A. Smith, and C. E. Wulfman. Generalizing the Perseus XML document manager. In *Linguistic Exploration: Workshop on Web-based Language Documentation and Description*, Philadelpha, December 2000.

[47] G. Marchionini. Evaluting digital libraries: A longitudinal and multi-faceted view. *Library Trends*, 49(2):304–333, 2001.

[48] M. Marcus, G. Kim, M. A. Marcinkiewicz, R. MacIntyre, A. Bies, M. Ferguson, K. Katz, and B. Schasberger. The Penn Treebank: Annotating predicate argument structure. In *ARPA '94*, 1994.

[49] M. P. Marcus, B. Santorini, and M. A. Marcinkiewicz. Building a large annotated corpus of English: The Penn Treebank. *Computational Linguistics*, 19(2):313–330, 1993.

[50] C. C. Marshall and C. Ruotolo. Reading-in-the-small: a study of reading on small form factor devices. In *JCDL*

2002: Proceedings of the Second ACM/IEEE-CS Joint Conference on Digital Libraries, pages 56–64, Portland, OR, 2002.

[51] D. Maynard, H. Cunningham, K. Bontcheva, and M. Dimitrov. Adapting a robust multi-genre NE system for automatic content extraction. In *Tenth International Conference on Artificial Intelligence: Methodology, Systems, Applications*, 2002.

[52] F. T. Miller and R. S. Lanier. *The Photographic History of the Civil War.* Review of Reviews, New York, 1911.

[53] C. Monroy, R. Kochumman, R. Furuta, E. Urbina, E. Melgoza, and A. Goenka. Visualization of variants in textual collations to analyze the evolution of literary works in the Cervantes Project. In *6th European Conference on Research and Advanced Technology for Digital Libraries (ECDL 2002)*, pages 638–653, Rome, 2002.

[54] F. Moore and M. L. C. B. University). *The Rebellion Record: a Diary of American Events.* G. P. Putnam D. Van Nostrand, New York,, 1861.

[55] E. Mylonas, G. Crane, K. Morrell, and N. Smith. The Perseus Project: Data in the electronic age. In *Computing and the Classics*, page forthcoming. University of Arizona Press, Tucson, 1991.

[56] C. Palmer and L. Neuman. The research work of interdisciplinary humanities and scholars: Exploration and translation. *Library Quarterly*, 72(1):85–117, 2002.

[57] S. Payette and T. Staples. The Mellon Fedora project: Digital library architecture meets XML and web services. In M. Agosti and C. Thanos, editors, *Research and Advanced Technology for Digital Libraries*, number 2458 in Lecture Notes in Computer Science, pages 406–421. Springer-Verlag, Berlin and Heidelberg, 2002.

[58] R. Rosenzweig. Everyone a historian — afterthoughts to the presence of the past, 2002.

[59] R. Rosenzweig and D. P. Thelen. *The Presence of the Past: Popular Uses of History in American Life.* Columbia University Press, New York, 1998. Roy Rosenzweig and David Thelen. 24 cm.

[60] R. Rosenzweig and D. P. Thelen. The presence of the past: Popular uses of history in American life – supplementary web site, 1998.

[61] J. A. Rydberg-Cox. Word co-occurrence and lexical acquisition in Ancient Greek texts. *Literary and Linguistic Computing*, 15(2):121–129, 2000.

[62] J. A. Rydberg-Cox, A. Mahoney, and G. Crane. Document quality indicators and corpus editions. In *Proceedings of the First ACM + IEEE Joint Conference on Digital Libraries*, pages 435–436, Roanoke, VA, 24-28 June 2001.

[63] D. A. Smith. Detecting and browsing events in unstructured text. In *Proceedings of the 25th Annual ACM SIGIR Conference*, pages 73–80, Tampere, Finland, August 2002.

[64] D. A. Smith. Detecting events with date and place information in unstructured text. In *Proceedings of the 2nd ACM+IEEE Joint Conference on Digital Libraries*, pages 191–196, Portland, OR, July 2002.

[65] D. A. Smith and G. Crane. Disambiguating geographic names in a historical digital library. In *Proceedings of ECDL*, pages 127–136, Darmstadt, 4-9 September 2001.

[66] D. A. Smith, A. Mahoney, and G. Crane. Integrating harvesting into digital library content. In *Proceedings of the 2nd ACM+IEEE Joint Conference on Digital Libraries*, pages 183–184, Portland, OR, July 2002.

[67] D. A. Smith, A. Mahoney, and J. A. Rydberg-Cox. Management of XML documents in an integrated digital library. In *Proceedings of Extreme Markup Languages 2000*, pages 219–224, Montreal, August 2000.

[68] D. A. Smith, J. A. Rydberg-Cox, and G. R. Crane. The Perseus Project: A digital library for the humanities. *Literary and Linguistic Computing*, 15(1):15–25, 2000.

[69] M. Smith. DSpace: an institutional repository from the MIT Libraries and Hewlett Packard Laboratories. In M. Agosti and C. Thanos, editors, *European Conference on Digital Libraries (ECDL)*, pages 543–549, Rome, 2002. Springer.

[70] D. Soergel. A framework for digital library research: Broadening the vision. *D-Lib Magazine*, 8(12), 2002.

[71] H. R. Tibbo. Primarily history: Historians and the search for primary source materials. In *JCDL 2002: Proceedings of the Second ACM/IEEE-CS Joint Conference on Digital Libraries*, pages 1–10, Portland, OR, 2002.

[72] R. B. Toplin. *Ken Burns's The Civil War: the Historian's Response.* Oxford University Press, New York, 1996.

[73] E. M. Voorhees. Overview of TREC 2001. In *TREC 2001*, Gaithersburg, MD 20899, 2001. NIST.

[74] J. L. Wolfe. Effects of annotations on student readers and writers. In *Proceedings of the Eleventh ACM Conference on Hypertext and Hypermedia*, pages 19–26, San Antonio, TX USA, 2000. ACM Press.

[75] C. E. Wulfman. The Perseus Garner: Early Modern resources in the digital age. *Colleg Literature*, forthcoming, 2004.

[76] A. Zaslavsky, A. Bia, and K. Monostori. Using copy-detection and text comparison algorithms for cross-referencing multiple editions of literary works. In P. Constantinopoulos and I. T. Solveborg, editors, *European Conference on Digital Libraries (ECDL 2001)*, pages 103–114, Darmstadt, Germany, 2001. Springer.

The DSpace Institutional Digital Repository System: Current Functionality

Robert Tansley, Mick Bass, David Stuve

Hewlett-Packard Laboratories
One Cambridge Center
Cambridge, MA 02142

{robert.tansley, mick.bass, david.stuve}

@hp.com

Margret Branschofsky, Daniel Chudnov,
Greg McClellan, MacKenzie Smith

MIT Libraries
77 Massachusetts Ave
Cambridge, MA 02139

{branschofsky, dchud, gam, kenzie}

@mit.edu

Abstract

In this paper we describe DSpace™, an open source system that acts as a repository for digital research and educational material produced by an organization or institution. DSpace was developed during two years' collaboration between the Hewlett-Packard Company and MIT Libraries. The development team worked closely with MIT Libraries staff and early adopter faculty members to produce a 'breadth-first' system, providing all of the basic features required by a digital repository service. As well as functioning as a live service, DSpace is intended as a base for extending repository functionality, particularly to address long-term preservation concerns. We describe the functionality of the current DSpace system, and briefly describe its technical architecture. We conclude with some remarks about the future development and operation of the DSpace system.

Categories and Subject Descriptors

H.3.7 [**Digital Libraries**]: Collection; Standards; User issues; Dissemination; Systems issues

General Terms

Management, Design, Standardization

Keywords

Digital library, preservation, institutional repository, open archives

1. Introduction

As more and more research and educational material is 'born digital', institutions and organizations are increasingly realizing the need for a stable place in which such material may be stored and accessed long-term. The Massachusetts Institute of Technology is a perfect example of an organization with this need. Much of the material produced by faculty, such as datasets, experimental results and rich media data as well as more conventional document-based material (e.g. articles and reports), is housed on an individual's hard drive or department Web server. Such material is often lost forever as faculty and departments change over time [10].

Providing services for the long-term stewardship of digital material seems a natural extension of the role of MIT Libraries. Although systems such as document management systems exist in this area, many are commercial and proprietary. Both of these factors raise the barrier for long-term preservation, since the hosting institution is reliant on the survival and affordability of the vendor. Since no existing system was a good fit, Hewlett-Packard and MIT Libraries collaborated over two years to create the DSpace digital repository platform [18]. DSpace provides the basic functionality required to operate an institutional digital repository, and is intended to serve as a base for future development to address long-term preservation and access issues. On November 4, 2002, the system was launched as a live service hosted by MIT Libraries, and the source code made publicly available according to the terms of the BSD open source license [15], with the intention of encouraging the formation of an open source community around DSpace. Initial developments in this area have been very promising.

This paper describes the various functional aspects of the DSpace system, followed by a brief overview of the architecture of the system. The paper concludes with some remarks about future plans for the DSpace system.

2. Related Work

DSpace draws on a wealth of previous research and development in the area of digital library systems. Though not a full implementation, the DSpace architecture has roots in Kahn and Wilensky's Framework for Distributed Digital Object Services [9], as well as Arms et al.'s work on digital library architecture [1], [2]. DSpace does not yet support complex dissemination of objects, but future releases will build on existing work on Lagoze et al.'s FEDORA architecture [16], and the prototype implementation of FEDORA at the University of Virginia [19].

Another important piece of work that DSpace draws on is the Consultative Committee for Space Data Systems' Reference Model for an Open Archival Information System (OAIS) [4]. This paper makes use of the concepts and terms defined in that work.

The EPrints system developed at the University of Southampton [6] has many similar features to DSpace, but is optimized to provide access to author-deposited, document-style material, while DSpace provides a platform to begin work on long-term preservation strategies for digital material, including documents and other material used in scholarly research. DSpace's submission user interface in particular draws on experience gained from the design and use of EPrints' submission user interface. Interoperability with EPrints is of course desirable, and can currently be achieved in part through use of the OAI Protocol for Metadata Harvesting (OAI-PMH) [14] to provide a cross-archive access service.

The Greenstone software from New Zealand Digital Library Project at the University of Waikato [7] is another open source digital library tool that has a focus on publishing.

CERN have developed the CERN Document Server Software (CDSware) [3] that is another preprint server.

Commercial document management systems offer some of the required functionality but do not really suit the aim of long-term preservation of the material, partly due to their proprietary nature.

3. Functional Overview

DSpace is designed to operate as a centralized, institutional service. Different *communities* within the institution such as labs, centers, schools or departments can have their own separate areas within the system. Members of these communities deposit content directly via a Web user interface designed to make this depositing as simple as possible. Alternatively the system features a batch item importer for the bulk loading of content.

Each community may also appoint people as 'gatekeepers', who may review and edit submissions before their inclusion in the main repository. The DSpace system then indexes the metadata submitted with the digital item and makes it available according to the access privileges determined by the community.

In order to provide a workable service in the available time, DSpace was developed 'breadth-first'. In other words, each of the basic requirements of an institutional digital repository system was addressed in a relatively simple manner, so that functionality can evolve with the service already in production.

The functional aspects of DSpace can be summarized as follows:

- A **data model** for basic organization of data is defined

- **Metadata** of various types is stored by the system

- The system stores information about users of the system. Some users might not be humans but other computerized systems; hence we call users **e-people**

- While much of the effort is concerned with easing access to an institution's digital material, simply allowing full public access is not always acceptable. Additionally functions such as depositing and reviewing must be restricted to appropriate individuals. Hence the system includes an **authorization** function

- The system must be able to accept incoming material, a process called **ingesting** [4]

- Some communities may require that material or accompanying metadata entering the archive be checked or augmented by designated individuals. This process is called **workflow**

- In order that material in the archive may be cited and accessed using information in a citation, the CNRI **Handle system** [8] is used to assign globally unique, persistent identifiers to archived objects ('items').

- End users should be able to explore and discover the contents of the repository. To this end, DSpace must offer **search** and **browse** functions

- To further increase the possibilities for discovering material in DSpace, metadata is exposed via the **Open Archives Initiative Protocol for Metadata Harvesting (OAI-PMH)** [4]

- It should be possible to notify end users of the system when new content of interest to them appears in the archive, rather than requiring them to repeatedly access DSpace to check this. DSpace offers an automatic e-mail alerting service called **subscription**

- A **Web user interface** provides access to the above functionality

The following sections discuss each of these functional aspects in detail.

3.1 Data Model

The way data is organized in DSpace is intended to reflect the structure of the organization using the DSpace system. This is depicted in Figure 1. Table 1 shows examples of each type of object.

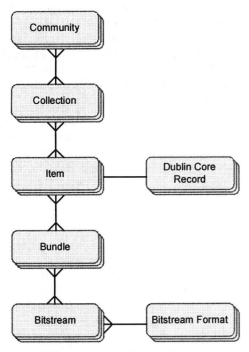

Figure 1: Data Model Diagram

Each DSpace site is divided into *communities*; these typically correspond to a laboratory, research center or department. Communities contain *collections*, which is a grouping of related content. Each collection is composed of *items*, which are the basic archival elements of the archive. Items are further subdivided into *bundles* of *bitstreams*. Bitstreams are, as the name suggests, streams of bits, usually ordinary computer files. Bitstreams that are somehow closely related are organized into bundles, for example HTML files and images that compose a single HTML document.

Object Type	Example Instance
Community	Laboratory for Computer Science; Oceanographic Research Centre
Collection	LCS Technical Reports; ORC Statistical Data Sets
Item	A technical report; a data set with accompanying description; a video recording of a lecture
Bundle	A group of HTML and image bitstreams making up an HTML document
Bitstream	A single HTML file; a single image file; a source code file
Bitstream Format	Microsoft Word version 6.0; JPEG encoded image format

Table 1: Example DSpace Objects

The data model supports multiple inclusion at all levels; that is, an item may belong to more than one collection, and a collection may be in more than one community[1].

Each item has one qualified Dublin Core metadata record. Other metadata might be stored in an item as a serialized bitstream, but we store Dublin Core for every item for interoperability and ease of discovery. The Dublin Core may be entered by end-users as they submit content, or it might be derived from other metadata as part of an ingest process.

In an ideal world, nothing entering a DSpace system should ever be removed; however, practical and legal factors sometimes necessitate this. Items can be removed from DSpace in one of two ways: They may be 'withdrawn', which means they remain in the archive but are completely hidden from view. In this case, if an end-

---

[1] It should be noted that software has not yet been extensively tested to create or deal with such circumstances. This will be a requirement for MIT in the near future so forthcoming updates will address this.

user attempts to access the withdrawn item, they are presented with a 'tombstone' that indicates the item has been removed. For whatever reason, an item may also be 'expunged' if necessary, in which case all traces of it are removed from the archive.

3.1.1 Bitstream Formats. Each bitstream is associated with one Bitstream Format. Because preservation services are an important aspect of the DSpace service, it is important to capture the specific formats of files that users submit. In DSpace, a bitstream format is a unique and consistent way to refer to a particular file format. An integral part of a bitstream format is an either implicit or explicit notion of how material in that format can be interpreted. For example, the interpretation for bitstreams encoded in the JPEG standard for still image compression is defined explicitly in the Standard ISO/IEC 10918-1. The interpretation of bitstreams in Microsoft Word 2000 format is defined implicitly, through reference to the Microsoft Word 2000 application. Bitstream formats can be more specific than MIME types or file suffixes. For example, application/ms-word and .doc span multiple versions of the Microsoft Word application, each of which produces bitstreams with presumably different semantics.

Supported	The format is recognized, and the hosting institution is confident it can make bitstreams of this format useable in the future, using whatever combination of techniques (such as migration, emulation, etc.) is appropriate given the context of need.
Known	The format is recognized, and the hosting institution will promise to preserve the bitstream as-is, and allow it to be retrieved. The hosting institution will attempt to obtain enough information to enable the format to be upgraded to the 'supported' level.
Unsupported	The format is unrecognized, but the hosting institution will undertake to preserve the bitstream as-is and allow it to be retrieved.

Table 2: Bitstream Format Support Levels

Each bitstream format additionally has a *support level*, indicating how well the hosting institution is likely to be able to preserve content in the format in the future. There are three possible support levels that bitstream formats may be assigned by the hosting institution. The host institution should determine the exact meaning of each support level, after careful consideration of costs

and requirements. MIT Libraries' interpretation is shown in Table 2.

3.2 Metadata

Broadly speaking, DSpace holds three sorts of metadata about archived content: Descriptive, administrative and structural metadata.

3.2.1 Descriptive Metadata. Each *Item* has one qualified Dublin Core metadata record. MIT Libraries, and the default configuration shipped with the open source use a derivation of the Library Application Profile set of elements and qualifiers [5]. Institutions with other requirements can easily change this, as DSpace maintains a *registry* of elements and qualifiers, though the system's search functionality and submission UI would not be updated automatically in the present version of the system.

Other descriptive metadata about items, for example MARC records, may be held in serialized bitstreams. *Communities* and *collections* have some simple descriptive metadata (a name, and some descriptive prose), held in the DBMS.

3.2.2 Administrative Metadata. This includes preservation metadata, provenance and authorization policy data. Most of this is held within DSpace's relational DBMS schema. Provenance metadata (prose) is stored in Dublin Core records. Additionally, some other administrative metadata (for example, bitstream byte sizes and MIME types) is replicated in Dublin Core records so that it is easily accessible outside of DSpace, for example via the OAI protocol.

3.2.3 Structural Metadata. This includes information about how to present an item, or bitstreams within an item, to an end-user, and the relationships between constituent parts of the item. As an example, consider a thesis consisting of a number of TIFF images, each depicting a single page of the thesis. Structural metadata would include the fact that each image is a single page, and the ordering of the TIFF images/pages. Structural metadata in DSpace is currently fairly basic; within an item, bitstreams can be arranged into separate bundles as described above. Additional structural metadata can be stored in serialized bitstreams, but DSpace does not currently natively understand this. This will be a very active area of future development of DSpace.

3.3 E-people

Many of DSpace's features such as document discovery and retrieval can be used anonymously, but users must be authenticated to perform functions such as submission, email notification ('subscriptions') or administration. Users are also grouped for easier administration. DSpace calls users *e-people*, since some users may be machines rather than actual people.

DSpace holds the following information about each e-person:

- E-mail address

- First and last names

- Authentication information, such as an encrypted password

- A list of collections for which the e-person wishes to be notified of new items

- Whether the e-person 'self-registered' with the system; that is, whether the system created the e-person record automatically as a result of the end-user independently registering with the system, as opposed to the e-person record being generated from the institutions personnel database, for example.

E-people can be members of 'groups' to make administrator's lives easier when manipulating authorization policies.

READ	The action of knowing of an object's existence, and viewing any metadata associated with it
WRITE	Modifying the metadata associated with an object. This does not include the ability to delete
ADD	The action of adding an object (e.g. an item) to a container (e.g. a collection). In order to submit an item to a collection, an end-user must have ADD permission on that collection
REMOVE	The action of removing an object from a container
WORKFLOW	May participate in a workflow associated with a collection; for example, permission to reject a particular submission from entering the collection

Table 3: Possible Actions in DSpace

3.4 Authorization

DSpace has a flexible authorization system. In order for a user to perform an action on an object, they must have permission; DSpace operates a 'default deny' policy. Permissions do not 'commute'; for example, if an e-person has READ permission on an item, they might not necessarily have READ permission on the bundles and bitstreams in that item.

The actions that the authorization system understands are shown in Table 3. Note that there is no 'DELETE' action. In order to 'delete' an object (e.g. an item) from the archive, one must have REMOVE permission on all objects (in this case, collection) that contain it. The 'orphaned' item is automatically deleted.

Policies can apply to individual e-people or groups of e-people. Additionally they can apply to the 'anonymous' group, which means that anyone can perform the action described by the policy.

3.5 Ingest Process and Workflow

Figure 2 is a simple illustration of the current ingesting process in DSpace. The batch item importer is an application that turns an external Submission Information Package (SIP) [4] (an XML metadata document with some content files) into an "in progress submission" object. The Web submission UI is similarly used by an end-user to assemble an "in progress submission" object.

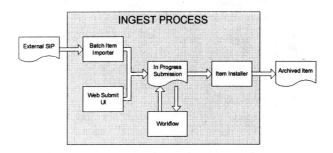

Figure 2: DSpace Ingest Process

Depending on the policy of the collection to which the submission is targeted, a workflow process may be started. This typically allows one or more human reviewers or 'gatekeepers' to check over the submission and ensure it is suitable for inclusion in the collection. Workflows are defined when the collection is first established, set up by the system administrator, and apply to every item submitted to that collection.

When the batch item importer or Web Submit UI completes the InProgressSubmission object, and invokes the next stage of ingest (be that workflow or item installation), a provenance message is added to the Dublin Core which includes the filenames and checksums of the content of the submission. Likewise, each time a workflow changes state (e.g. a reviewer accepts the submission), a similar provenance statement is added. This allows us to track how the item has changed since a user submitted it. (The History subsystem is also invoked, but provenance is easier for us to access at the moment.)

Once any workflow process is successfully and positively completed, the InProgressSubmission object is consumed by an "item installer", that converts the in progress submission into a fully blown archived item in DSpace. The item installer:

- Assigns an accession date
- Adds a "date.available" value to the Dublin Core metadata record of the item
- Adds an issue date if none already present
- Adds a provenance message (including bitstream checksums)
- Assigns a Handle persistent identifier
- Adds the item to the target collection, and adds appropriate authorization policies
- Adds the new item to the search and browse indices
- (Soon) creates and archives an OAIS Archival Information Package, represented in a standard, open format such as METS [12].

3.5.1 Workflow Steps. A collection's workflow can have up to three steps. Each collection may have an associated e-person group for performing each step; if no group is associated with a certain step, that step is skipped. If a collection has no e-person groups associated with any step, submissions to that collection are installed straight into the main archive.

In other words, the sequence is this: The collection receives a submission. If the collection has a group assigned for workflow step 1, that step is invoked, and the group is notified. Otherwise, workflow step 1 is skipped. Likewise, workflow steps 2 and 3 are performed if and only if the collection has a group assigned to those steps.

When a step is invoked, the task of performing that workflow step is put in the 'task pool' of the associated group. One member of that group takes the task from the pool, and it is then removed from the task pool, to avoid

the situation where several people in the group may be performing the same task without realizing it.

The member of the group who has taken the task from the pool may then perform one of three actions, shown in Table 4.

If a submission is rejected, the reason (entered by the workflow participant) is e-mailed to the submitter, and it is returned to the submitter's workspace. The submitter can then make any necessary modifications and re-submit, whereupon the process starts again.

If a submission is 'accepted', it is passed to the next step in the workflow. If there are no more workflow steps with associated groups, the submission is installed in the main archive.

One last possibility is that a workflow can be 'aborted' by a DSpace site administrator. This is accomplished using the administration section of the Web UI.

Workflow Step	Possible actions
1	Can accept submission for inclusion, or reject submission.
2	Can edit metadata provided by the user with the submission, but cannot change the submitted files. Can accept submission for inclusion, or reject submission.
3	Can edit metadata provided by the user with the submission, but cannot change the submitted files. Must then commit to archive; may not reject submission.

Table 4: Possible Workflow Steps in DSpace

3.6 Handles

Researchers require a stable point of reference for their works. The simple evolution from sharing of citations to emailing of URLs broke when Web users learned that sites can disappear or be reconfigured without notice, and that their bookmark files containing critical links to research results could not be trusted long term. To help solve this problem, a core DSpace feature is the creation of persistent identifier for every item, collection and community stored in DSpace. To persist identifiers, DSpace requires a storage- and location-independent mechanism for creating and maintaining identifiers. DSpace uses the CNRI Handle System for creating these identifiers [8]. The rest of this section assumes a basic familiarity with the Handle system.

DSpace uses Handles primarily as a means of assigning globally unique identifiers to objects. Each site running DSpace needs to obtain a Handle 'prefix' from CNRI, so we know that if we create identifiers with that prefix, they will not clash with identifiers created elsewhere.

Presently, Handles are assigned to communities, collections, and items. Bundles and bitstreams are not assigned Handles, since over time, the way in which an item is encoded as bits may change, in order to allow access with future technologies and devices. Older versions may be moved to off-line storage as a new standard becomes de facto. Since it is usually the *item* that is being cited, rather than the particular bit encoding, it only makes sense to persistently identify and allow access to the item, and allow users to access the appropriate bit encoding from there.

The Handle system also features a global resolution infrastructure; that is, an end-user can enter a Handle into any service (e.g. Web page) that can resolve Handles, and the end-user will be directed to the object (in the case of DSpace, community, collection or item) identified by that Handle. In order to take advantage of this feature of the Handle system, a DSpace site must also run a 'Handle server' that can accept and resolve incoming resolution requests. All the code for this is included in the DSpace source code bundle.

Handles can be written in two forms:

```
hdl:1721.123/4567
http://hdl.handle.net/1721.123/4567
```

The above represent the same Handle. The first is possibly more convenient to use only as an identifier; however, by using the second form, any Web browser becomes capable of resolving Handles by means of a proxy server run by CNRI. An end-user need only access this form of the Handle as they would any other URL. It is possible to enable some browsers to resolve the first form of Handle as if they were standard URLs using CNRI's Handle Resolver plug-in, but since the first form can always be simply derived from the second, DSpace displays Handles in the second form, so that it is more useful for end-users.

It is important to note that DSpace uses the CNRI Handle infrastructure only at the 'site' level. For example, in the above example, the DSpace site has been assigned the prefix '1721.123'. It is still the responsibility of the DSpace site to maintain the association between a full Handle (including the '4567' local part) and the community, collection or item in question. This is done internally with a database table.

3.7 Search and Browse

DSpace allows end-users to discover content in a number of ways, including:

- Via external reference, such as a Handle
- Searching for one or more keywords
- Browsing though title, date and author indices

Search is an essential component of discovery in DSpace. Users' expectations from Web search engines are quite high, so a goal for DSpace is to supply as many search features as possible. DSpace's indexing and search module has a very simple API which allows for indexing new content, regenerating the index, and performing searches on the entire corpus, a community, or collection. Behind the API is the Java freeware search engine Lucene. Lucene gives us fielded searching, stop words, stemming, and the ability to incrementally add new indexed content without regenerating the entire index.

Another important mechanism for discovery in DSpace is the browse. This is the process whereby the user views a particular index, such as the title index, and navigates around it in search of interesting items. The browse subsystem provides a simple API for achieving this by allowing a caller to specify an index, and a subsection of that index. The browse subsystem then discloses the portion of the index of interest. Indices that may be browsed are item title, item issue date and authors. Additionally, the browse can be limited to items within a particular collection or community.

3.8 OAI Support

The Open Archives Initiative has developed a Protocol for Metadata Harvesting (OAI-PMH) [14]. This allows sites to programmatically retrieve or 'harvest' the metadata from several sources, and offer services using that metadata, such as indexing or linking services. Such a service could allow users to access information from a large number of sites that are collated in a central catalog.

DSpace exposes the Dublin Core metadata for items that are publicly (anonymously) accessible. Additionally, the community and collection structure is also exposed via OAI-PMH's 'sets' mechanism. OCLC's open source OAICat framework is used to provide this functionality [13].

DSpace's OAI-PMH service exposes deletion information for withdrawn items.

While OAICat supports resumption tokens, DSpace does not, simply because of time and resource constraints on the development effort. The need for flow control in the harvesting will increase as the amount of content in DSpace archives increases, so a future release will include resumption token support.

3.9 Subscriptions

As noted above, end-users (e-people) may 'subscribe' to collections through the Web user interface in order to be alerted when new items are added to those collections. Each day, end-users who are subscribed to one or more collections will receive an e-mail giving brief details of all new items that appeared in any of those collections the previous day. If no new items appeared in any of the subscribed collections, no e-mail is sent. Users can unsubscribe themselves at any time.

3.10 History

While provenance information in the form of prose is very useful, it is not easily programmatically manipulated. The History system captures a time-based record of significant changes in DSpace, in a manner suitable for later 'refactoring' or repurposing.

Currently, the History subsystem is explicitly invoked when significant events occur (e.g., DSpace accepts an item into the archive). The History subsystem then creates RDF data [20] describing the current state of the object. The RDF data is modelled using the ABC Model [11], an ontology for describing temporal-based data, and stored in the file system. Some simple indices for unwinding the data are available.

3.11 Web User Interface

Built on Java Servlet and JavaServer Page technology, DSpace's Web user interface allows end-users to access DSpace via their Web browsers. The user interface consists of the following:

- On-line help
- Community and collection home pages, configurable by individual communities. Recent arrivals in the collection are displayed, as well as convenient subscribing and depositing controls
- Searching and browsing
- Item pages, which display the basic metadata associated with an item. The full Dublin Core and bitstreams contained in an item may be accessed from this page (subject to authorization). DSpace does not yet have a sophisticated dissemination

mechanism; we are investigating relevant work such as FEDORA [16] to address this. Figure 3 shows an example item display page

Figure 3: Item Display Page

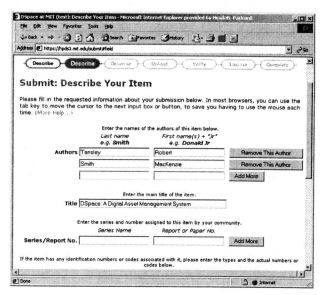

Figure 4: Deposit Interface Screen

- 'My DSpace', where authorized users can deposit material, perform any workflow tasks they have been assigned, and manage their automatic e-mail alert subscriptions. Figure 4 shows an example of the depositing interface

- Administration section, consisting of pages intended for use by central administrators. Presently, this part of the Web UI is very basic so users of the administration subsystem need to know what they are doing! In the future, as this subsystem is improved, it will be possible to pass more responsibility for administration to individual communities as the administration UI becomes more developed.

Although the entire system is designed to be easy to modify to suit an institution's needs, the Web UI has been designed to be particularly so:

- Since JavaServer Pages are mostly HTML with small pieces of Java embedded code, they are easy to modify without touching the business logic code in the Servlets.

- Institutions are also likely to have existing electronic authentication infrastructure. By implementing a Java interface and altering a configuration parameter, DSpace can be made to use this local authentication infrastructure. DSpace is shipped with a simple e-mail address/password authentication module, and the MIT implementation, which understands X509 certificates.

4. System Architecture

The main code of DSpace is implemented in Java, and runs on any UNIX-like system such as Linux or HP-UX. It makes use of several third-party open source systems:

- PostgreSQL, an open source relational database system

- Jakarta Tomcat Java Servlet container

- Apache HTTPD server, for optional SSL and X509 certificate support

Alternative tools may be used in place of these; for example Tomcat may be replaced with Caucho's 'Resin' application server. In order to minimize the barrier to adoption, however, by default DSpace makes use of an entirely free, open source tool stack.

The main DSpace system is organized into three layers, each of which consists of a number of components. Figure 5 depicts this.

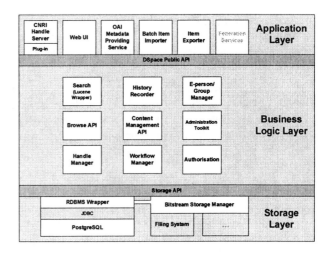

Figure 5: DSpace System Architecture

The storage layer is responsible for physical storage of metadata and content. It consists of a 'wrapper' around JDBC for database access, and a simple bitstream storage and retrieval API called the bitstream storage manager. Presently, the bitstream storage manager is very lightweight and simply stores bitstreams in a file system. This can easily be modified, and will shortly be extended to cover multiple file systems to enable larger volumes of content to be stored.

The business logic layer deals with managing the content of the archive, users of the archive (e-people), authorization, and workflow.

The application layer contains components that communicate with the world outside of the individual DSpace installation, for example the Web user interface and the Open Archives Initiative protocol for metadata harvesting service.

Each layer only invokes the layer below it; the application layer may not use the storage layer directly, for example. Each component in the storage and business logic layers has a defined public API. The union of the APIs of those components is referred to as the Storage API (in the case of the storage layer) and the DSpace Public API (in the case of the business logic layer). These APIs are in-process Java classes, objects and methods. These could be exposed as Web services via a suitable component in the application layer.

Since each component has a clearly defined API, they may be modified and replaced individually, without requiring extensive modification of the rest of the system.

It is important to note that each layer is trusted. Although the logic for authorizing actions is in the business logic layer, the system relies on individual applications in the application layer to authenticate e-people correctly and securely. If a 'hostile' or insecure application were allowed to invoke the Public API directly, it could very easily perform actions as any e-person in the system.

The reason for this design choice is that authentication methods will vary widely between different applications, so it makes sense to leave the logic and responsibility for that in those applications.

5. Conclusions and Future Work

DSpace has been a 'breadth-first' attempt to start addressing a growing and unfulfilled need of academic institutions and other organizations. MIT Libraries has been running DSpace as a live service at MIT for several months, and several other institutions have successfully installed and started to run DSpace. MIT Libraries remain committed to maintaining the DSpace service and software.

Naturally, DSpace does not currently address all of the issues of long-term preservation and access of digital material; however it serves as a useful basis for developing and deploying solutions to those issues. Already, an open source community is forming around DSpace. This exciting development bodes well for the future development and impact of DSpace. In addition, two further pieces of work are already under way to enhance the DSpace system.

Starting with seven other research institutions (Cambridge University in the UK, the University of Toronto in Canada, and Columbia University, Cornell University, Ohio State University, and the Universities of Rochester and Washington in the USA) MIT is establishing a federation of DSpace partners to explore the issues around deploying the DSpace service at different locales. Much of this work will involve exploring organizational issues, as well as maintaining and enhancing the functionality of the DSpace code base.

Hewlett-Packard Laboratories, the World-Wide Web Consortium and MIT are also collaborating in another project called SIMILE [17]. The SIMILE work involves exploring the use of RDF and Semantic Web techniques to address two problems. The first is how to achieve interoperability among diverse metadata schemas, and the digital works to which they are applied. The second problem is to do with individuals interacting with DSpace: Given this diverse metadata, how does DSpace allow individual users to find and organize information relevant to them?

The success of the DSpace work to date, combined with the strong interest in the digital library community and the exciting new work being undertaken, give us great confidence in our ability to contribute to the fields of the preservation and management of digital research and education material, and the field of open access to such material.

6. Acknowledgments

We would like to thank the following for their previous contribution to the DSpace work: Mary Barton, Peter Breton, Peter Carmichael, Bill Cattey, Eric Celeste, Joyce Ng and Julie Harford Walker. We would also like to thank the staff at MIT Libraries and the members of our early adopter communities for their valuable input.

7. References

[1] Arms, William Y.: Key Concepts in the Architecture of the Digital Library, *D-Lib Magazine*, July 1995. http://www.dlib.org/dlib/July95/07arms.html

[2] Arms, William Y., Blanchi, Christophe, and Overly, Edward A.: An Architecture for Information in Digital Libraries, *D-Lib Magazine*, February 1997. http://www.dlib.org/dlib/february97/cnri/02arms1.html

[3] CERN Document Server Software (CDSware). http://cdsware.cern.ch/

[4] Consultative Committee for Space Data Systems, Reference Model for an Open Archival Information System (OAIS), CCSDS 650.0-R-2, Red Book, Issue 2, July 2001. http://ccsds.org/documents/pdf/CCSDS-650.0-R-2.pdf

[5] Dublin Core Library Application Profile. http://dublincore.org/documents/2002/09/24/library-application-profile/

[6] GNU EPrints Software. http://software.eprints.org/

[7] The Greenstone Digital Library Software http://www.greenstone.org/

[8] Handle System Overview. http://www.ietf.org/internet-drafts/draft-sun-handle-system-10.txt

[9] Kahn, Robert and Wilensky, Robert: A Framework for Distributed Digital Object Services, May 1995. http://www.cnri.reston.va.us/home/cstr/arch/k-w.html

[10] Koehler, Wallace: Web Page Change and Persistence-A Four-Year Longitudinal Study. In *Journal of the American Society for Information Science and Technology* 53, 2 (December 2001) 162—180.

[11] Lagoze, C. and Hunter, J. "The ABC Ontology and Model", in *Proceedings of the International Conference on Dublin Core and Metadata Applications 2001,* Tokyo, 2001, 160-176.

[12] Metadata Encoding and Transmission Standard (METS). http://www.loc.gov/standards/mets/

[13] OCLC Research OAICat Open Source Project. http://www.oclc.org/research/software/oai/cat.shtm

[14] Open Archives Initiative. http://www.openarchives.org/

[15] Open Source BSD License. Available at http://www.opensource.org/licenses/bsd-license.php

[16] Payette, Sandra and Lagoze, Carl: Flexible and Extensible Digital Object and Repository Architecture, in Christos Nikolau and Constantine Stephanidis, eds., *Research and Advanced Technologies for Digital Libraries: Proceedings of the Second European Conference, ECDL '98, Heraklion, Crete, Greece, September 21-23, 1998, G. Goos, J. Hartmanis, and J. van Leeuwen, eds., Lecture Notes in Computer Science, 1513 (Berlin: Springer, 1998)*

http://www.cs.cornell.edu/payette/papers/ECDL98/FEDORA.html

[17] SIMILE: Semantic Interoperability of Metadata and Information in unLike Environments. http://web.mit.edu//simile/

[18] Smith, MacKenzie, Barton, Mary, Bass, Mick, Branschofsky, Margret, MacClellan, Greg, Stuve, David, Tansley, Robert and Walker, Julie H: DSpace: An Open Source Dynamic Digital Repository. *D-Lib Magazine* 9, 1 (January 2003). http://www.dlib.org/dlib/january03/smith/01smith.html

[19] Staples, Thornton and Wayland, Ross: Virginia Dons FEDORA: A Prototype for a Digital Object Repository. *D-Lib Magazine* 6, 7/8 *(*July/August 2000). http://www.dlib.org/dlib/july00/staples/07staples.html

[20] W3C Resource Description Framework (RDF). http://www.w3.org/RDF/

Metis: Lightweight, Flexible, and Web-based Workflow Services for Digital Libraries

Kenneth M. Anderson
CU Boulder
kena@cs.colorado.edu

Aaron Andersen
NCAR
aaron@ucar.edu

Neet Wadhwani
CU Boulder
wadhwani@cs.colorado.edu

Laura M. Bartolo
Kent State University
lbartolo@kent.edu

Abstract

The Metis project is developing workflow technology designed for use in digital libraries by avoiding the assumptions made by traditional workflow systems. In particular, digital libraries have highly distributed sets of stakeholders who nevertheless must work together to perform shared activities. Hence, traditional assumptions that all members of a workflow belong to the same organization, work in the same fashion, or have access to similar computing platforms are invalid. The Metis approach makes use of event-based workflows to support the distributed nature of digital library workflow and employs techniques to make the resulting technology lightweight, flexible, and integrated with the Web. This paper describes the conceptual framework behind the Metis approach as well as a prototype which implements the framework. The prototype represents a "proof-of-concept" of the Metis framework and approach as we show how it can both model and execute a peer review workflow drawn from a "real-world" digital library. After describing related work, the paper concludes with a discussion of future research opportunities in the area of digital library workflow and outlines how Metis is being deployed to a small set of digital libraries for additional evaluation.

1. Introduction

Digital libraries face significant challenges beyond providing traditional library services. One key challenge involves supporting the collaborative work of a digital library's stakeholders. In particular, it is challenging to coordinate the actions of these stakeholders as they work together to accomplish an interrelated activity. The difficulty lies in the fact that the stakeholders involved with digital libraries cover a wide spectrum, from publishing vendors and copyright clearance centers, digital reference desk staff and reference clients, to resource providers and reviewers. All of these activities, digital rights management, digital reference services, and digital collection building, are highly distributed, time-sensitive, and complicated events. In addition the groups interacting with the digital libraries in these areas are independent agents who do not share necessarily the similar working styles, goals, or computing platforms with the libraries. In each instance, whether it be a digital rights librarian securing digital rights for copyrighted materials, or a digital reference staff resolving a query for a reference client, or a collection provider processing submitted digital resources for quality content control, the digital library must initiate, track, and complete its responsibilities based upon responses from these independent, outside stakeholders. Traditional libraries have always had difficulty managing the many and diverse "irons in the fire" that comprise their daily work. As the Web continues to evolve and grow, these types of problems will only magnify for digital libraries.

Complicating matters, a particular activity—such as reviewing new materials for inclusion in the digital library—may involve a different subset of stakeholders each time it is initiated. For instance, a digital library specializing in literature, may send materials for 19th century literature to university A, while materials for 18th century literature are reviewed by university B. Thus, the same activity (reviewing new materials) involves university A in one instance and university B in another. Further complicating matters is that for each activity, each stakeholder may have a different set of steps they use to complete the activity. Thus, the review process used by university A can be quite different from university B's review process. These examples lend insight into why it is so difficult to effectively coordinate the activities among stakeholders of a digital library: Each instance of a digital library activity is a highly specialized process. This specialization makes it particularly complex to track and compare the progress of activities. Consider the following example: Two instances of the "review new materials" process may both be at the same step in the process, but one may complete its review much more rapidly than the other based on the performance of the responsible organizations.

In software development, coordinating a group's activities traditionally has been accomplished using software process environments or workflow systems [1, 4]. Workflow technology holds great promise to help digital libraries overcome the problems identified above. However, many traditional approaches to this technology make assumptions about their users that are inappropriate within the digital library context. For instance, some workflow systems assume that all users work for a single organization or, even worse, assume that all users are members of the same team within a single organization [7]. Other workflow systems are only slightly better in that they can support multiple users across multiple groups, but once again make the assumption that all users work for the same organization [6]. These assumptions make certain aspects of the workflow problem easier to manage. For instance, members of the same organization often have access to similar computing platforms, and problems such as "who owns the process" are minimized, often because responsibility is dictated by organizational structure. However, these assumptions are simply invalid in the digital library context, where stakeholders come from different organizations (or have no affiliations at all, e.g. a student or customer of the digital library) and are distributed both in space and time.

Our research via the Metis project addresses the gaps between traditional workflow technology and the needs of digital libraries. We have identified three characteristics for workflow systems that we believe are essential to addressing the unique properties of the digital library domain. In particular, a digital library workflow system must be:

Lightweight: Lightweight workflow technology should have a low entry barrier to use, support multiple computing platforms, and provide a level of autonomy to the organizations that adopt it. This latter requirement implies the need for a modular, or component-based, solution so that organizations can adopt only those parts of the workflow system that they need and are not required to change drastically their existing software to make use of workflow services.

Flexible: Workflow technology needs to conform to the organizations and individuals that use it and not the other way around. As such, workflow technology needs to be flexible and customizable. As discussed in Section 2, we address this issue by basing our workflow abstractions on events.

Web-based: The World Wide Web [5] has had tremendous impact in deploying information technology pervasively across multiple organizations. Indeed, with over 35 million web servers detected in the December 2002 Netcraft Survey (up from 3.1 million in September 1998 [2]), it is becoming possible to assume that individuals in most organizations have access to Web browsers, if not Web servers.[1] As such, workflow technology needs to be accessible via

Web-based services and it must be possible to share and execute workflows between multiple organizations via the Web. We provide details on how we achieve these characteristics in Sections 2 and 3.

In order to evaluate our techniques and technology, we have modeled workflows from three "real-world" digital libraries using the concepts described in Section 2 below. The first digital library is the Web Portal of the Scientific Computing Division (SCD) of the National Center for Atmospheric Research (NCAR). This portal provides access to SCD's formidable computing environment, and manages the collaborative creation and archiving of scientific documents and resources. Our second digital library partner is the JESSE electronic journal, associated with the Digital Library for Earth System Education, which is a digital library that is dedicated to the collection and distribution of materials that facilitate learning about the Earth system at all educational levels. Our third digital library partner is the GREEN Digital Library (GREEN DL), which is a collaboration of materials scientists from the National Institute of Standards and Technology, MIT, and other universities partnered with information scientists at Kent State University. The primary goal of the collaboration is to build a collection of authoritative digital resources integrating education and research in the area of Green's functions.[2] With the completion of the first prototype of the Metis workflow system in December 2002 (discussed below in Section 3), we are deploying Metis to our partner digital libraries for additional evaluation and feedback.

The rest of this paper is organized as follows. Next, we describe the conceptual framework that defines our approach to providing workflow services to digital libraries. Then, in Section 3, we describe the Metis prototype that implements our conceptual framework. In Section 4, we describe a review process used by one of our partner digital libraries and demonstrate how the Metis prototype can be used to implement and manage that activity. Finally, we discuss related work in Section 5 and then conclude with a discussion of our future research plans.

2. Metis Framework

The conceptual framework of Metis is designed to address the unique workflow requirements of the digital library domain. The key contribution of this framework is that it rejects the dominant task-based paradigm of traditional workflow systems and adopts the use of *events* to specify the steps of a workflow. Event-based workflows directly address some of the problems encountered by task-based workflow systems in distributed settings. First, event notification systems (see Section 5.1) can be deployed

---

[1] <http://www.netcraft.com/survey/>

[2] <http://appling.kent.edu/NSDLGreen/>

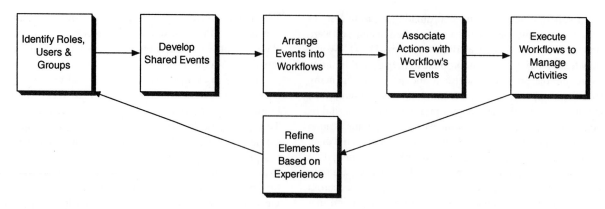

Figure 1. Metis Framework Workflow. Use of the Metis framework is an iterative process of defining the elements of a workflow, executing the workflow, and refining it as experience is gained.

across multiple organizations with ease, and, with the rise of systems like Siena [9], can route events across these organizations in a timely manner, even across wide-area networks. Second, activities are specified in terms of domain-specific events. This approach is an intuitive way to construct workflows since it closely matches what people already do when coordinating their activities, e.g. "I'll wait until I receive that phone call from Dan before proceeding on this task." Third, event-based workflows are more flexible than task-based workflows since they do not force stakeholders to do activities in a particular order. One major problem with traditional workflow technology is that some systems attempt to "enact" or "enforce" a particular workflow even going so far as to make it impossible for a user to work on task B unless they have first completed task A. Users rebel against such systems [22], and will take their work "offline," outside of the system's control, to get work done. Event-based workflows allow users to work on tasks in any order, but may require that they "announce" the completion of task A (via an event) before they "announce" the completion of task B even if they actually completed the tasks in reverse order. Finally, event-based workflows allow multiple organizations to participate in the same activity, enable alternative organizations to be responsible for the same step of an activity, and support different sub-steps (such as the completion of a review activity) being associated with different instances of the same step (e.g., `reviewSubmission`) in a workflow.

Thus, event-based workflows avoid the problems of task-based workflows by inverting the task-based paradigm and allowing each group of stakeholders to specify the tasks they will perform in response to a shared group of events. Returning to the example in Section 1, university A and university B can specify different tasks to be performed in response to a `reviewAssigned` event. As long as each uni-

versity promises to complete their workflows by generating a `reviewComplete` event, the two universities and the editor of the digital library can work independently, synching their work activities upon the receipt of a community-derived set of shared events. Event-based workflows also allow stakeholders to specify their interests in particular types of events. (Event filtering and distribution services are provided by event notification systems, see Section 5.1.) Thus, university A can specify that they are interested only in receiving `submissionReceived` events for submissions that are related to 19th century literature.

In addition to events and workflows, the framework contains elements to support the specification of a wide range of stakeholders as well as the ability to help with the partial automation of tasks related to particular events in a workflow. The elements of the Metis framework include:

Event: An event is a named set of typed attribute-value pairs. Event names belong to a global namespace and must be unique. Each event defines a separate namespace for the names of its attributes and thus different events may contain attributes having the same name. Each attribute has an associated type that constrains the legal set of values for the attribute. Example types include string and numeric types as well as dates, URLs, etc. Furthermore, attributes can be specified as key, meaning that once this attribute receives a value in a particular instance of a workflow, it will retain the same value in all subsequent events that contain the same key attribute. We provide motivation for key attributes in Section 2.1 and an example of their use in Section 4.

Workflow: A workflow is a named arrangement of events, where the arrangement specifies the "legal" order in which events can be received for the activity managed by the workflow. Events can be arranged sequentially (Event B follows Event A), iteratively (the workflow loops over Event A and Event B until Event C is received), and conditionally (after Event A is received, either Event B or Event C will be received, but not both). Workflows can thus be seen as a type of regular expression that can be applied to a trace of event notifications to determine if the event trace satisfies the constraints of the workflow.

Action: Each event in a workflow can have a set of associated actions that will be performed by the workflow system when the event is received at run-time. An action has full access to an event's attributes and can thus aid users in partially automating tasks that must be performed when an event is received. For instance, if an event contains a URL, one action can download the document referenced by the URL to a pre-defined location, while a second action sends an email message to a Metis user to inform him or her of the event and the name and location of the retrieved document.

User: A user represents an entity that can send or receive the events of a workflow. Each user has an associated profile that stores information about them (such as their email address, first and last names, etc.) This information is available to actions, such that actions can route event information to users, or perform tasks on their behalf.

Role: A role is an abstraction mechanism that allows a participant of a workflow to be specified without requiring that the same user be responsible for the same task each time a workflow is run. Thus, it is possible to specify that when a submission is received by a digital library that an email message is sent to the `editor-in-chief` rather than to a particular Metis user. As such, a mechanism must be provided that allows roles to be statically or dynamically bound to particular Metis users or groups. In addition, a mechanism must be provided that allows an action to retrieve the user or group bound to a particular role.

Group: A group is a collection of users and roles. Groups can be used by actions to perform tasks for multiple users at once, without having to specify the same action for each user individually. Thus, an action can specify that an email notification of an event be sent to an entire group as opposed to a single role or user.

2.1. Framework Discussion

In this section, we provide more detail and insight into the elements of the framework and expand on some of the possible interactions between them. With the concepts above, the stakeholders of a digital library can organize themselves into users and groups that play specific roles in their shared activities. Each shared activity can be defined as a set of events arranged in a particular fashion, with actions associated with each event such that the appropriate stakeholders are notified as the state of the activity evolves (see Fig. 1.)

These concepts impose a set of requirements on any system that attempts to implement the framework:

1. It must provide a mechanism for creating and editing event definitions.

2. It must provide a mechanism for creating and editing workflow definitions.

3. It must provide a mechanism for associating actions with the events contained in workflows and it must provide a mechanism for carrying out the actions at run-time.

4. It must provide a mechanism for creating and editing a registry of users, groups, and roles. It must also provide a mechanism for statically and dynamically binding users and groups to roles.

In addition, our goals of producing lightweight, Web-based technology impose additional requirements on a system implementing the Metis framework:

1. It must make use of an event notification system to distribute events to stakeholders. (The benefits provided by this technology are discussed in Section 5.1.)

2. The workflow system must present a low entry barrier to use such that it can be deployed across a wide variety of computing environments. As discussed above, this requirement is necessary since the computing environments of a digital library's stakeholders can vary widely.

3. It should be possible to create, edit, activate and monitor workflows via a Web browser or via a Web-based application program interface (API).[3]

Before we present the Metis prototype that meets these requirements, we return to the concept of `key attributes`. The Metis framework must support the activation of the same workflow multiple times. For instance, if a digital library has defined a workflow to manage their peer review process, then Metis will need to have one instance of this workflow activated for each submission under review. Since each instance of the workflow shares the same set of events, a problem arises when an event notification is received, i.e., which instance of the workflow should receive the event? The problem is simple when the workflows are at different stages of the process, since they are each waiting for a different event. But, if all instances of the workflow are waiting for the same event, then a mechanism is required that can distinguish to which workflow instance the event belongs.

Key attributes provide this mechanism in the Metis framework. Early in the review process, the submission

---

[3]XML-RPC (<http://www.xmlrpc.com/>) and SOAP (<http://www.w3.org/TR/SOAP/>) are examples of protocols that provide APIs for Web-based services.

should be assigned a unique identifier and each event subsequent to the id being created should contain a key attribute that stores this id. Once a key attribute has been assigned a value for a particular workflow instance, then all subsequent events which contain the same key attribute must have that same value. The key attribute and its value become part of the filter that is used to register the subsequent events with the event notification system. Thus the workflow for submission 1 is not just interested in `reviewSubmitted` events but rather is interested in `reviewSubmitted` events whose `id` attribute has a value of 1. Key attributes allow Metis to take advantage of the powerful event filtering capabilities of modern event notification systems and allows implementors of the Metis framework to focus their efforts on workflow services not event distribution and routing.

3. Metis Prototype

We have developed a prototype that implements the Metis framework and meets the requirements listed in Section 2. The architecture of the prototype is shown in Fig. 2. The prototype is implemented as a set of Java servlets (hosted by the Tomcat servlet engine) layered on top of the Siena event notification system [9].[4] When accessed via a Web browser, the servlets provide a user interface to Metis workflow services including the ability to create and edit events and workflows, associate actions with workflow events, activate workflows, publish events, and monitor the status of active workflows. The servlets also provide an XML-RPC interface such that workflows can be activated and monitored programmatically. Additionally, the XML-RPC API also allows events to be published programmatically. This is useful when, for instance, you want a software agent to publish an event for an active workflow when some condition has been met.

This architecture goes a long way in meeting our requirements of producing a workflow system that is lightweight, flexible, and integrated with the Web. The use of Java servlets helps to keep the entry barrier to use low since there are freely available servlet engine, such as Tomcat, for those users concerned with cost. (High-end commercial servlet engines exist for those users concerned with scalability and performance.) The use of servlets deeply integrates Metis with the Web, since servlets are designed to ease the construction of Web applications. Each servlet can be accessed via a Web browser and generates a user interface using "vanilla" HTML.[5] As mentioned above, some of the servlets also provide an XML-RPC interface to their services. XML-RPC requests piggyback on top of the HTTP

requests already handled by the servlet engine, so no additional configuration is required by a Metis administrator to activate the XML-RPC interface after deployment. The use of Java addresses cross-platform issues allowing Metis to be deployed on a variety of computer architectures and operating system platforms. Indeed, each of the four Metis developers made use of different computing platforms during the development of the prototype, including MacOS, Win32, Solaris, and Linux, with no problems. In the same vein, Siena is freely available and is also implemented in Java, allowing it to be deployed on the same platforms as Metis. Finally, Metis also keeps the entry barrier to use low by not requiring the use of a database. Instead, as discussed below, Metis stores event, workflow, action, user, group, and role definitions in a set of XML files. Java-based tools to create and parse XML files are freely available.[6]

The Metis prototype consists of the following servlets:

User Registry: The user registry provides a user interface to create and edit users, groups, and roles. Each user is required to have a name, e-mail address, metis login, and metis password. Additional information, such as the user's affiliation, is stored in a user profile. Metis ships with a standard user profile (including affiliation, first name, and last name) and Metis administrators can add additional fields to the profile, as needed. As mentioned previously, user information is stored in a set of XML files managed by the registry.[7] Groups are named sets of users and roles and the user registry provides an interface for editing a group's members statically. The user registry also provides an interface for creating roles and, optionally, an interface for statically binding a user or group to a role. Dynamic binding of roles during workflow execution is handled by the execution engine, as is discussed below.

Event Editor: The event editor provides a user interface for creating, editing, and deleting event definitions. This servlet allows users to edit event names and to add or remove any number of typed attributes. The prototype currently supports attributes of type string, integer, float, date, and URL. The editor also allows users to specify default values for each attribute. The default value of an attribute is automatically supplied by Metis whenever a user fails to supply a value for the attribute at the time the event is published.

Workflow Editor: The workflow editor provides a user interface for creating, editing, and deleting workflow definitions. Workflows are represented using a tree structure that can consist of the following node types: Workflow, Sequence, Fork, Branch, Loop, and Event. Each node in the tree can have any number of children of any type with the

---

[4] <http://jakarta.apache.org/tomcat/>

[5] By "vanilla," we refer to HTML conforming to either the HTML 4.01 Transitional specification or the XHTML 1.0 Transitional specification with no use of stylesheets, Javascript, or applets.

[6] <http://xml.apache.org/>

[7] Examples of Metis XML files for storing events, workflows, users, groups, and roles are available at the Metis website: <http://www-serl.cs.colorado.edu/metis/>.

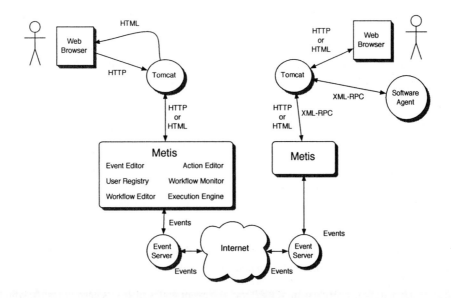

Figure 2. The architecture of the Metis prototype. Metis supports multiple users and software agents. Distribution of events across multiple sites is handled by the event notification layer.

following exceptions: No node can have a child whose type is Workflow. (This means that nodes of type Workflow occur only at the root of the tree.) Fork nodes may only have children whose type is Branch. Fork nodes also have an associated type, one of or, and, or xor. The meanings associated with these types are discussed below. Event nodes may not have children. (As such, Event nodes form the leaves of the workflow's tree structure.) Instead, each Event node holds a reference to one of the events created by the event editor. The workflow editor presents the tree structure using a combined HTML table/form construct and automatically enforces the constraints just listed.

Action Editor: After a workflow has been defined, the action editor is used to associate actions with each of its Event nodes. This process is known as "instantiating" a workflow, and the execution engine (described next) only executes instantiated workflows. A separate editor is used for adding actions to a workflow to reduce the complexity of the workflow editor. Actions are implemented using the Ant build management system developed by the Apache Jakarta project.[8] Similar to our other implementation choices, Ant is a freely available, widely used, open source, Java application. Ant is not typically used as a scripting mechanism. Instead, it is primarily used to compile and deploy Java programs. However, Ant comes with a comprehensive set of "tasks" that can automate the creation of directories, the archiving/extraction of sets of files, sending email, and the storing/retrieving of files on remote servers. Rather than im-

plement yet another scripting language, Metis actions simply piggyback on top of Ant tasks.

As such, the Action editor provides an interface for associating Ant tasks with a workflow's Event nodes as well as an interface for entering the parameters required by each task. For instance, the RetrieveURL task requires a URL parameter. Since the value of some parameters are not known at design-time, the action editor allows a user to specify that the value for a parameter is to be taken from the value of an attribute of the associated event at run-time. For example, if a submissionReceived event contains an attribute of type URL, then the action editor can specify that the URL contained in this attribute at run-time should be passed as the value of the URL parameter of the RetrieveURL task. This mechanism is used to support the dynamic binding of roles at run-time, since we have developed actions that can, for instance, retrieve an e-mail address from an event's attributes, find the Metis user associated with that address, and bind them to a specified role. The actual binding is handled by the execution engine via its bindRole API method. Finally, the action editor provides an interface to associate users, groups, and roles with actions. Thus it is possible to retrieve a URL for a particular Metis user or to specify that an e-mail message be sent to a particular Metis group.

Execution Engine: The execution engine is responsible for managing instances of workflows at run-time. In particular, it provides an API for activating and deactivating workflows, retrieving the status of active workflows, and dynamically binding users and groups to roles within active

---

[8] <http://jakarta.apache.org/ant/>

103

workflows. Roles are bound on a per instance basis rather than a per workflow basis. This choice makes sense when you consider the standard roles of a peer review process: Each instantiation of a peer review process may have different people playing the roles of author, editor, and reviewer. All roles are resolved dynamically with a query to the execution engine. If a dynamic binding does not exist, then the execution engine will check to see if the role is statically bound.

Executing a workflow involves a depth-first traversal of the workflow's tree structure looking for Event nodes. When an event node is reached, the execution engine subscribes to its associated event and waits for delivery of that event by the event notification system. Loop nodes allow certain sequences of events to repeat until an "exit event" is received, at which point, traversal continues in a depth-first manner with the Loop node's sibling. Fork nodes enable a degree of parallelism in Metis workflows. Fork nodes have special traversal semantics based on their type. An *and* Fork node requires that all events found in all of its branches must be delivered by the event notification system in the order specified by each branch before traversal can move on to the Fork node's sibling. An *or* Fork node specifies that all of the events of at least one of its branches must be received before traversal can move on to the Fork node's sibling. Events for each of the branches are allowed to come in but, unlike an *and* Fork node, as soon as one of the branches is completed, the traversal moves on. Finally, an *xor* Fork node is similar to a `switch` or `case` statement from programming languages such that events for only one of the branches will be executed. In this situation, the execution engine registers for the first event found in each branch. As soon as one of these events is delivered, the execution engine unregisters the events from the other branches and only accepts other events from the "selected branch". We provide examples of using Fork nodes in Section 4.

The execution engine is responsible for invoking Ant to execute an event's actions once the event has been delivered by the event notification system. Since Ant receives instructions from an XML file called `build.xml`, action execution is a three step process of creating a temporary directory to store the `build.xml` file, asking the event's associated actions to generate the `build.xml` file in the temporary directory, and invoking Ant on the generated XML file to perform the requested actions. The execution engine monitors the tasks for completion and routes any generated error messages to a log file. Once a received event's actions have been executed, the execution engine unregisters that event, traverses the workflow tree to find the next Event node, and then registers interest in that event with the event notification system.

Finally, the execution engine is responsible for saving the state of a completed workflow (regardless of whether the workflow was halted prematurely or completed normally). Again, this persistent information is stored in an XML file. Its structure is similar to the XML file used to store instantiated workflow descriptions but it also records the values that were associated with each event received at run-time. This allows these workflows to be viewed by users at a later time, perhaps because they are trying to understand how to evolve a workflow based on its past performance.

Workflow Monitor: The workflow monitor has three responsibilities. It allows users to activate and deactivate workflows by passing these requests to the execution engine using the execution engine's API. It allows users to monitor the current status of a workflow. Furthermore, it provides a user interface enabling users to publish events to active workflows. The event publishing interface is integrated into the status display of active workflows. When an active workflow is displayed, a user can select any of the event nodes to see its current status, which is also indicated through the use of color. If the user selects an Event node for which an event has been received, then the user is presented with the values of that event's attributes. If the user selects an Event node that has not yet been reached by the execution engine's traversal, then they are presented with a display of that event's attributes along with the default values (if any) of those attributes. Finally, if the user selects an Event node for an event to which the execution engine is actively subscribed, then they are presented with a user interface for filling out the values of the event and submitting it to the event notification system. When the event is published, the event notification system will deliver the event to the execution engine and it will be processed as described above.

We now evaluate the capabilities of this prototype by presenting a detailed example of how a "real world" review process is modeled by the Metis framework and managed by the prototype.

4. Proof Of Concept

In order to initially evaluate the feasibility of the Metis framework and approach, we solicited a non-trivial peer review process from the GREEN DL and implemented the workflow. In this section, we present an outline of the process and describe how we implemented it using Metis. We view this evaluation as a "proof-of-concept" of the Metis approach to digital library workflow services. As this type of evaluation is insufficient in determining "real-world" utility, we are in the process of deploying Metis to our digital library partners for additional evaluation and feedback. We describe these nascent efforts in Section 6.

The peer review process provided by our digital library partner is as follows. The digital library can receive submissions for one of four topic areas. For each topic area, there is a committee of four editors. Users upload submissions via a Web-based form. An administrator for the digital library processes the submission. The submission is then sent to the relevant committee and the editors decide which committee member will handle the submission. The selected editor finds a set of three reviewers and gives each one a deadline for completing their review. If the deadline expires for a reviewer, the editor sends them a reminder and sets a new deadline. Once all reviews have been received, the editor determines the status of the paper and informs the author. If the paper was accepted, the administrator moves the paper to its final home in the collection. Our digital library partner imposed an additional constraint that the administrator be notified of all events for all active reviews, even though the administrator's work is situated at the beginning and end of the process.

We began the process of modeling this workflow (which is actually two workflows!) by creating a user account for each of the sixteen editors and an additional user account for the administrator. We created four groups for each of the topic areas and assigned the editors to their respective groups. We created roles for the administrator, the committee, the author, the editor, and one for each reviewer. The administrator role was statically bound, all other roles are dynamically bound.

We defined eleven events to support the two workflows.[9] The first workflow, created for the administrator, consisted of two events. The first event, submissionReceived, contained attributes for a document id, topic area, author contact information, document title, authors, keywords, and a URL. The values for all of the attributes, except the document id, are entered by the author in the digital library's Web-based submission form. The document id, which is a key attribute, is assigned by the script that processes the submission form. All subsequent events that contain an attribute for the document id will contain the same value for the life of these two workflows. The administrator's workflow has three actions for the submissionReceived event. The first action sends an e-mail containing the values of all the event's parameters to the administrator (a statically bound role) to indicate that a new review process has started. The second action downloads the document into a "unreviewed" directory within the digital library. The third action dynamically binds one of the four groups to the committee role, based on the value of the topic area attribute. This sets up an action for the second event, submissionProcessed, which sends an e-mail notification to the committee. Note, this event is published by

the administrator using the Metis workflow monitor, once the submission has been processed and is ready for review. This event finishes the workflow for the administrator.

The second workflow supports the activity of the committee, editor, and the reviewers. It begins with the same two events that occurred in the administrator workflow. The actions for the first event perform a variety of tasks including creating a user account for the author based on the author's contact information and dynamically binding this newly created user to the author role. It also sends a "heads-up" message to the appropriate committee (dynamically bound based on the topic area attribute). The action for the second event sends a message to the committee letting them know that the submission is ready for review. The committee takes a look at the paper using the digital library and assigns an action editor to manage its review. They publish an actionEditorAssigned event to dynamically bind the selected committee member to the editor role. The editor receives an e-mail reminding him or her of the selection. In addition, for this event and all subsequent events, an action was added to send an e-mail notification of the event to the administrator to meet the additional requirement imposed by our digital library partner.

The editor assigns three reviewers, publishing a reviewerAssigned event each time. (These events are handled by a loop node consisting of a single reviewer-Assigned event.) An *and* Fork node is used to manage the process of waiting for a review from each reviewer. Each branch of the *and* Fork node, consists of an *or* Fork node with two branches: One branch consists of a loop comprised of two events, deadlineAssigned and deadlineExpired, followed by a cancelReview event. The second branch consists of a single event, reviewReceived. The action for the deadlineAssigned event sets a timer in the execution engine. When the timer expires, it publishes the deadlineExpired event. (The exact event published by an expired timer is configured via the action editor.) This event sends a message to the editor who then contacts the reviewer for the review. At any point, either the reviewer can submit the review (causing the reviewReceived event to be published) or the editor can cancel the review process for this reviewer by publishing the cancelReview event. Either of these events cause the *or* Fork node to complete.

Once all three *or* Fork nodes are complete, the *and* Fork node is complete and the process moves on to notifying the author of the status of the review. This part of the process is managed by an *xor* Fork node since the paper will have one of three results: reject, accept, or revise-and-resubmit. The editor publishes the appropriate review-Result event (which causes a formatted letter to be sent to the author containing the results and the reviewer comments) and then the remaining events in the selected branch

---

[9]Due to space constraints, we will not present details of all eleven events. The XML files that were created to support this peer review process are available from the Metis website: <http://www-serl.cs.colorado.edu/metis/>.

handle finalizing the review process. Rejected papers are moved to a section of the digital library clearly identified as material not accepted by the editorial board. Rejected papers are deleted from the digital library if the author does not want their unaccepted manuscript posted or if material is found to be inaccurate. Accepted papers are moved (by the administrator) to a holding area while final revisions are made, and revise-and-resubmit papers are archived so the reviewers of the revision can access the original paper once the new version has been submitted.

This non-trivial review process demonstrates a proof-of-concept of the Metis approach. A highly distributed set of stakeholders are able to coordinate their actions using the workflow system to synchronize their activities and to handle the mundane tasks of sending notification email and keeping track of review deadlines. The framework's workflow constructs are able to express non-trivial event patterns that include both looping and parallelism and the prototype provides actions that performed a wide range of functions that include the dynamic binding of roles, sending email, and tracking deadlines. While additional evaluation is needed before Metis is ready for production environments, this proof-of-concept has convinced our partners to deploy Metis internally to determine how its services can be used to meet their workflow needs.

5. Related Work

In this section, we briefly review related work in the areas of event notification and workflow management.

5.1. Event Notification

Metis builds on top of the services provided by event notification technology while remaining independent of any particular event notification system; indeed it would be straightforward to migrate the Metis prototype from its current choice, Siena [9], to any other event notification system. Siena was chosen because it specializes in distributing events across wide-area networks.

Event notification, in general, is based on the concepts of events, producers/consumers of events, and event subscriptions/notifications. Typically, an event is a set of attribute/value pairs. Producers publish events to an event server which routes these events to consumers based on their subscriptions. One benefit of this arrangement is that producers are completely unaware of the location of interested consumers and are thus not dependent on these consumers in any way. Likewise consumers are unaware and independent of producers. This arrangement can lead to significant benefits. For instance, the C2 architectural style makes use of these characteristics to provide substrate independence in software architectures [23]. Other advantages

include:

- Producers and consumers focus only on events meaningful to them. They have no need to understand the entire event space being managed by the event system.

- Event systems make efficient use of a network. When an event is produced, only those consumers who subscribed to the event are notified.

- If several event servers are used, the routing of events can be further optimized. Here, an event is only sent to an event server if it has clients that are interested in that event. This facilitates the use of an event notification system across a wide-area network.

- The publish/subscribe model enables dynamic service discovery. For instance, a consumer can publish an event requesting a specific service. If there is a producer that provides the service, it will notify the consumer, and the consumer can subscribe to it.

Event notification systems were first employed to support tool integration in software development environments. One of the first systems to employ this approach in a local-area network setting was Field [21]. Tool integration via events was also a part of Hewlett Packard's SoftBench environment [8]. In recent years, event notification systems have been extended to explore issues related to wide-area networks [9] and project awareness [11, 12, 20]. We selected Siena [9] for use in the Metis prototype due to its ability to support Internet-scale event notification, which is ideal for coordinating the actions of the stakeholders of a digital library, and the fact that both its client and server packages have Java implementations, which supports our goal of producing lightweight workflow technology.

5.2. Workflow Management Systems

Workflow management systems are tools for storage and manipulation of process models that facilitate the completion of some task, such as the development of a software system or the processing of a travel authorization form. These process models act as artifacts for the coordinated activity. Such artifacts can represent, to a limited degree, the procedures and rules that mediate an effort, as well as some aspects of the division of work. This representation is typically limited to the most abstract and restricted sequence of independent work steps. Workflow systems typically do not venture into more complex forms of interaction. However, the results of these more complex interactions can be incorporated to a certain extent via the transformations of artifacts performed by users as a result of decisions made outside the scope of a workflow system proper, e.g., as a result of conversations held over lunch [4]. There are three interaction paradigms used in workflow systems:

Task-oriented: This interaction style involves the use of agendas. Agendas manage lists of relevant tasks for each user, as, e.g., in SPADE-1 [3].

Document-oriented: Interaction is achieved in these systems via documents and document services. In Merlin [15], for instance, a work context graphically displays the relevant documents associated with each user role.

Goal-oriented: Interaction in this paradigm is centered around a list of goals to be accomplished. In Marvel, for instance, these goals represent currently active rules that can be applied to the state of the process [16].

In each of these paradigms, events play a secondary role. Thus, a novel aspect of Metis is to examine the capabilities enabled by making events first-class citizens in workflow technology. Additionally, while various workflow systems have integrated with the Web—for instance, Endeavors [6] and OzWeb [17]—few, if any, have as a goal to make the entry barrier to use of the workflow system as low as possible. Thus, another novel aspect of Metis is to discover the right balance of techniques and technologies to create a truly lightweight workflow system; one that can be deployed in the computing environments of a wide spectrum of digital library stakeholders.

There is a considerable body of research on the subject of distributed workflow systems. An excellent survey of such work can be found in Bolcer and Taylor's "Advanced Workflow Management Technologies" [7]. Bolcer and Taylor identify key limitations of existing workflow systems such as fixed user models, heavyweight requirements (e.g. all-or-nothing buy-in) and "hard-wired" control policies. These limitations are the primary reasons that current workflow technology is inappropriate for the digital library domain.

Bolcer and Taylor go on to provide an extensive list of issues (spanning more than 30 pages of discussion) that need to be addressed by new research in workflow technology and present an argument that no single system comes close to addressing these issues in a comprehensive manner. Some of the issues listed resonate with the issues we identified above: support for multiple stakeholders, low entry barrier to use, and accessibility. Metis has addressed these issues with a minimal technical platform that can be widely deployed on multiple platforms with event-based workflows that can be specified and shared using XML.

Other issues identified by Bolcer and Taylor fall outside the scope of Metis such as the need for data agents, which are small programs that perform tasks for users, or fault tolerance, where a workflow system can handle interruptions in workflows based on user errors, corrupted data, etc. In Metis, actions take the place of data agents although their scope is more limited than the features outlined for data agents by Bolcer and Taylor. Furthermore, we de-

cided against an agent-based design for Metis in order to achieve our low entry barrier requirement. With respect to fault tolerance, our event-based approach avoids some of the traditional problems associated with fault tolerance in workflow systems. In particular, Metis does not try to control or manage the artifacts that are associated with a workflow, and hence Metis cannot directly corrupt their contents or inadvertently delete them. Furthermore, fault tolerance can be built into Metis workflows with events that represent "errors." Actions associated with these events can be used to deactivate an existing workflow (through the use of the Metis Execution API) while simultaneously activating a new workflow to handle the associated error. This support for fault tolerance is admittedly simple but it has the effect of keeping the design of the Metis prototype simple while not preventing the creation of additional support for fault tolerance in future versions of the Metis architecture.

In addition to these high-level issues, we need to compare and contrast Metis to several distributed workflow systems that have been described in the literature:

Milos [19] is a system for providing software process support over the Internet. Similar to Metis, users employ Web applets to access workflows (specified using Microsoft Project) that are stored on centralized servers. Our approach differs in that our workflow is specified using events and our architecture has better support for managing workflows across distributed sites.

Endeavors [6] is a support system for distributed execution of workflow processes. Endeavors is an advanced workflow system with deep integration with the Web, support for agents, and support for providing access to workflows on hand-held devices. While Endeavors is powerful, we believe that a more lightweight approach to workflow technology stands a better chance of success in the digital library domain. Endeavors can specify and support many of the workflows of digital libraries but it is unlikely that all of the stakeholders of a digital library will be able to purchase and install Endeavors on their computing platforms, nor will the stakeholders likely be interested in learning the complex process formalisms and notations that Endeavors supports. Metis offers an alternative that allows stakeholders to specify their participation in workflows by specifying interest in events, e.g. "Let me know when a new paper has arrived. I'll take a look at it, and assign it to a reviewer". Note, that the arguments made here also apply to more well-known commercial workflow systems such as Lotus Notes/Domino and IBM FlowMark.

OzWeb [17] is a web-based system that supports multiple users grouped in multiple teams. OzWeb provides a framework that supports the storage and retrieval of information in a centralized database with support for notifications of process-related events to team members via the Internet. Serendipity [14] is a process modeling and enactment environment that supports collaborative modeling as well as execution of software processes. Change notifications are sent using an event-handling mechanism. With these systems, events are used to notify users of the progress of workflows, however workflows are still modeled in some other formalism. Our approach contrasts to these systems in that events occupy a more prominent place in our design. Our workflows are completely specified using events; events do not simply signify progress, they are the only means by which a workflow can be activated and completed. While other notations will have stronger support for tool integration, we can achieve basic tool integration (e.g. launch tool X when event Y occurs) while keeping entry barrier requirements to a minimum.

Eve [13], while not a complete workflow system, is a middleware system that can be used to execute workflow definitions. Eve takes an event-based approach to support distributed heterogeneous workflows, utilizing event-condition-action rules [10] to specify workflow constraints and behavior. This provides a tight coupling between events and actions. Eve is the only other known approach that we have identified that uses events as first class citizens in workflows. Beyond this similarity, there are distinct differences with Metis. In particular, Metis is not specifically tied to a particular event notification system, while Eve tightly integrates event handling with a construct called event detectors. Our approach uses XML-based trees to define workflows, in contrast to the rule-based approach utilized by Eve. We believe Metis takes a novel approach with regard to actions by making use of Ant to provide a comprehensive and extensible set of tasks to Metis users. Additionally, our approach makes use of the Web to provide a complete workflow solution from workflow construction to workflow execution, while Eve focuses only on workflow execution. Thus, Eve is analogous to the Metis execution engine; similar to Eve, Metis provides an API such that software agents can access its workflow execution services.

Finally, within the digital library community, there is surprisingly little reference to work on automating digital library workflows, despite the fact that many papers identify it as a core need. What work there is, such as the collaboration services of the Alexandria Digital Library[10] or the information services of the Aurora architecture [18], appears to be specific to a particular digital library. Metis is different in that it is designed to be a modular component that can be integrated into any existing digital library.

6. Conclusions

Metis provides a lightweight, flexible, and Web-based approach to digital library workflow services. Event-based

workflows provide Metis with flexibility since stakeholders can partition work around a set of shared events and avoid having to reconcile different working styles or standards. Furthermore, the use of Ant to implement Metis actions provides flexibility via access to a wide range of powerful functionality while providing an extensible mechanism for implementing new actions specific to a particular digital library. Metis is lightweight since it builds on widely-deployed technology such as open source servlet engines and easily-installed event notification systems and handles cross-platform issues by providing a Java implementation of the Metis framework. Additionally, Metis is Web-based by choosing to implement the core services as servlets, enabling distributed access to its workflow services. Human users can access these services via a Web browser while software agents can make use of an XML-RPC interface.

Having developed a core set of workflow services for digital libraries, our future plans involve extensively testing the current prototype in "real-world" settings. We have recently deployed Metis to support the reviewing needs of the GREEN DL and will be deploying Metis shortly to our other digital library partners. Similar to the GREEN DL, the JESSE electronic journal is interested in using Metis to manage its peer review process. JESSE's situation is slightly different from the GREEN DL in that JESSE already makes use of a software system, D3E, to handle a large part of its review process. As such, our work with JESSE will involve integrating Metis with D3E such that Metis can automate the non-D3E portions of JESSE's review process. NCAR's SCD web portal will make use of Metis to manage the workflow for reviewing applications to make use of SCD's computing resources. In addition, Metis will also be used to manage workflows that involve the periodic acquisition of data from NCAR affiliates (such as retrieving the latest set of observational readings from weather stations and other remote sensors). We intend to closely monitor the feedback from our partner digital libraries to improve the quality of the Metis distribution. Our goal is to make Metis as useful "out-of-the-box" as possible. This goal, while practical, is important, both in terms of meeting the needs of our users but also in facilitating adoption of our workflow services.

Our future research plans for Metis involve addressing the issues of security and metadata. Currently, the Metis prototype does not provide support for security, except for a simple password-based login system provided by Tomcat. Before Metis can move beyond its current experimental settings into production environments, its support for security must be greatly expanded. This includes evolving the Metis API such that Metis can integrate with a digital library's existing security system, adding access control lists to constrain the operations that users and roles can perform, and wrapping the event notification system to ensure that only

---

[10] <http://www.alexandria.ucsb.edu/>

authenticated users can publish events.

With respect to metadata, we believe that Metis can be used to automatically generate digital library metadata. For instance, it should be possible for Metis to handle workflows that step students through a digital library's collection. As a student performs the workflow, Metis can update metadata records that track the student's progress.

Both of these issues will require new research to ensure that we balance the tradeoffs of achieving the desired functionality while retaining the characteristics that allow Metis to provide useful workflow services to digital libraries.

7 Acknowledgments

This material is based upon work sponsored by the NSF under Award Number DUE-0121460.

References

[1] V. Ambriola, R. Conradi, and A. Fuggetta. Assessing process-centered software engineering environments. *ACM Transactions on Software Engineering and Methodology*, 6(3):283–328, 1997.

[2] K. M. Anderson. Issues of data scalability in open hypermedia systems. *The New Review of Hypermedia and Multimedia*, 5:151–178, 1999.

[3] S. Bandinelli, E. Di Nitto, and A. Fuggetta. Supporting cooperation in the spade-1 environment. *IEEE Transactions on Software Engineering*, 22(12), 1996.

[4] P. Barthelmess and K. M. Anderson. A view of software development environments based on activity theory. *Computer-Supported Cooperative Work: The Journal of Collaborative Computing*, 11(1-2):13–37, 2002.

[5] T. Berners-Lee. Www: Past, present, and future. *IEEE Computer*, 29(10):69–77, 1996.

[6] G. A. Bolcer and R. N. Taylor. Endeavors: A process system integration infrastructure. In *Proceedings of the 4th International Software Process Workshop*, pages 76–85, December 1996.

[7] G. A. Bolcer and R. N. Taylor. Advanced workflow management technologies. *Software Process: Improvement and Practice*, 4(3):125–171, 1998.

[8] M. R. Cagan. The hp softbench environment: An architecture for a new generation of software tools. *Hewlett-Packard Journal*, 41(3):36–47, 1990.

[9] A. Carzaniga, D. S. Rosenblum, and A. L. Wolf. Design and evaluation of a wide-area event notification service. *ACM Transactions on Computer Systems*, 9(3):332–383, 2001.

[10] F. Casati, S. Ceri, B. Pernici, and G. Pozzi. Deriving active rules for workflow management. In *Proceedings of the 7th DEXA*, 1996. Zurich, Switzerland.

[11] G. Fitzpatrick, T. Mansfield, S. Kaplan, D. Arnold, T. Phelps, and B. Segall. Augmenting the workaday world with elvin. In *Proceedings of the 6th European Conference on Computer Supported Cooperative Work*, pages 431–450, 1999.

[12] L. Fuchs. Area: A cross-application notification service for groupware. In *Proceedings of the 6th European Conference on Computer Supported Cooperative Work*, pages 61–80, 1999.

[13] A. Geppert and D. Tombros. Event-based distributed workflow execution with eve. In *Proceedings of the 1998 IFIP International Conference on Distributed Systems Platforms and Open Distributed Processing Middleware*, 1998.

[14] J. C. Grundy and J. G. Hosking. Serendipity: Integrated environment support for process modelling, enactment, and work coordination. *Automated Software Engineering: Special Issue on Process Technology*, 5(1):27–60, 1998.

[15] G. Junkerman, B. Peuschel, W. Schäfer, and S. Wolf. Merlin: Supporting cooperation in software development through a knowlege-based environment. In A. Finkelstein, J. Kramer, and B. Nuseibeh, editors, *Software Process Modelling and Technology*, pages 103–130. Research Studies Press Ltd., 1994.

[16] G. E. Kaiser, N. Barghouti, and M. Sokolsky. Preliminary experience with process modeling in the marvel software development environment kernel. In *Proceedings of the 23rd Annual Hawaii International Conference on System Sciences, Volume II-Software Track*, pages 131–140, 1990.

[17] G. E. Kaiser, S. Dossick, W. Jiang, and J. J. Yang. An architecture for www-based hypercode environments. In *Proceedings of the 19th International Conference on Software Engineering*, pages 3–13, 1997.

[18] M. Marazakis, D. Papadakis, and C. Nikolaou. The aurora architecture for developing networkcentric applications by dynamic composition of services, 1997. Technical Report, FORTH-ICS/TR-213, Institute of Computer Science, Foundation for Research and Technology.

[19] F. Maurer, G. Succi, H. Holz, B. Kötting, S. Goldmann, and B. Dellen. Software process support over the internet. In *Proceedings of the 1999 International Conference on Software Engineering*, pages 642–645, 1999. Los Angeles, CA, USA. May 16-22, 1999.

[20] W. Prinz. Nessie: An awareness environment for cooperative settings. In *Proceedings of the 6th European Conference on Computer Supported Cooperative Work*, pages 391–410, 1999.

[21] S. P. Reiss. Connecting tools using message passing in the field environment. *IEEE Software*, 7(4):57–66, 1990.

[22] L. A. Suchman. *Plans and Situated Actions: The Problem of Human-Computer Communication*. Cambridge University Press, 1987. New York.

[23] R. N. Taylor, N. Medvidovic, K. M. Anderson, E. J. Whitehead Jr., J. E. Robbins, K. A. Nies, P. Oreizy, and D. L. Dubrow. A component- and message-based architectural style for gui software. *IEEE Transactions on Software Engineering*, 22(6):390–406, 1996.

Session 4B: Information Retrieval and Data Mining

Session Chair: Edie Rasmussen, University of Pittsburgh

Protein Association Discovery in Biomedical Literature

Yueyu Fu, Javed Mostafa, and Kazuhiro Seki
Laboratory of Applied Informatics Research, Indiana University, Bloomington
E-mail: {yufu, jm, kseki}@indiana.edu

Abstract

Protein association discovery can directly contribute toward developing protein pathways; hence it is a significant problem in bioinformatics. LUCAS (Library of User-Oriented Concepts for Access Services) was designed to automatically extract and determine associations among proteins from biomedical literature. Such a tool has notable potential to automate database construction in biomedicine, instead of relying on experts' analysis. This paper reports on the mechanisms for automatically generating clusters of proteins. A formal evaluation of the system, based on a subset of 2000 MEDLINE titles and abstracts, has been conducted against Swiss-Prot database in which the associations among concepts are entered by experts manually.

1. Introduction

There is a huge corpus of biomedical literature available electronically, e.g. the MEDLINE database. The complex medical concept relations in this literature are highly valuable. Unfortunately, there are few comprehensive sources of information on biomedicine that explicitly capture and record such associations.

Researchers have spent much effort developing systems to automatically mine biomedical literature [3, 5, 7, 9]. Early efforts applied Natural language processing (NLP) techniques. More recent efforts concentrate on combining NLP techniques with statistical techniques developed in IR.

In this paper, we discuss a project aimed at automated database construction in biomedicine. LUCAS was developed to automatically discover associations among proteins from biomedical literature. Various strategies, both linguistic and statistical were used in the information extraction and retrieval process.

2. Discovery algorithms

2.1. Protein discovery

Protein names are detected in two steps: protein name fragment detection and name boundary expansion of the detected fragments. In the former step, protein name fragments are detected by hand-crafted rules based on surface clues, which include Arabic numerals, Roman numerals and alphabets, and some suffixes and words peculiar to protein names (e.g., -in, -ase, and factor). As some protein names are compound nouns (e.g., parathyroid hormone-related protein), protein name boundaries of the detected fragments are expanded to recognize full protein names. Then, a protein name dictionary that does not include proteins covered in the rule set is applied to detect additional protein [6]. Finally, $tf \cdot idf$ weight [8] is computed for each unique protein found in individual documents and a list of proteins are extracted based on two user selected parameters, namely rank/document and document frequency of proteins.

2.2. Utilizing latent semantic information

To improve the performance of the protein association discovery (described in the next section), we wanted to enhance the information in the protein-doc matrix. A process known as Latent Semantic Analysis (LSA)[1, 2], to reduce the rank of the matrix, has been shown to enhance document vectors by using latent semantic structure in the vectors to help eliminate noise and deal with co-occurrence of proteins. The protein-doc matrix produced using $tf \cdot idf$ is rank reduced according to singular value decomposition. The resulting vectors help to make the implicit latent semantic information in the protein-doc matrix explicit.

2.3. Protein Association Discovery

Protein association discovery mainly consists of: an unsupervised cluster learning stage and a vector classification stage. During the learning stage, initial cluster hypotheses [$C^1, \ldots, C^k$] are generated from a representative sample of protein vectors [$S^1, \ldots, S^N$]. Each cluster C^i is then represented by its centroid, Z^i. During the classification stage, an incoming protein V^i is classified into a particular class C^k using the learned centroids from the first stage.

A heuristic unsupervised clustering algorithm, called the Maximin-Distance algorithm [10], is used to determine the centroids. In this iterative algorithm, at each stage, a protein vector is selected that has the least similarity with the existing centroids. The similarity of this protein vector with the existing set of centroids, in turn, is the maximum of its similarities over all centroids. The selected point is then added as a new centroid if and only if its similarity with the existing set of centroids is less than an implementation-specified threshold parameter. This process is continued until no new centroids can be identified. During classification each new protein vector is classified to one of the centroids that has the largest similarity with the protein. We refer the reader to [4] for further details.

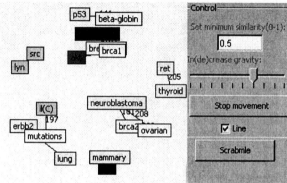

Figure 1. LUCAS interface displaying concept visualization

3. Experiments

An interactive web-based association discovery system called LUCAS was implemented (see Figure 1) to aid biomedical researchers to identify useful links among key concepts. Experiments were conducted to see how well our system could be used to discover relationships among proteins from biomedical literature. The test set was 2000 MEDLINE titles and abstracts from the GENIA corpus3 containing human annotated protein names (www-tsujii.is.s.u-tokyo.ac.jp/GENIA). 75.5% of the proteins in this corpus were detected accurately. Clusters were generated from this set using the methodology outlined above.

The particular rank to select when LSA is used to improve information discovery depends on the domain and the corpus (i.e., it is an empirical problem). Hence, we conducted a series of experiments to examine the impact of varying the LSA rank on cluster overlap. Two proteins are said to overlap if they co-occur in an entry (record) in the Swiss-Prot protein database. The average largest overlap in all the clusters returned from the Maximin clustering was computed. However, since varying parameters in our experiments also varies the number and sizes of clusters, it is not enough to measure only the average size of the overlap. A very large cluster could produce a large overlap, but also contain many

proteins that are not related. To account for this, the key result we were interested in is the average ratio of the largest overlap to cluster size across all clusters for a given test. A ratio of 1.0 would mean that all of the proteins in each cluster are related according to the protein database. The best overlap ratio as shown in Figure 2 was 0.82 when rank equaled 5. Another larger experiment, which contained 247 protein names, produced a similar trend of the curve in the larger experiment. The best result was 0.90 when rank equaled 10. As seen in the plot with increasing rank more "noise' is reintroduced in the protein-doc matrix and hence overlap drops.

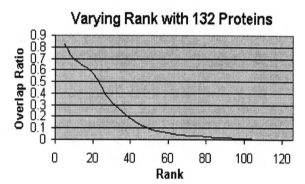

Figure 2. Impact of varying LSA rank on associations

4. Conclusions

In this paper, we investigated the effectiveness of the implemented algorithms in identifying protein association. A general finding was that the implemented algorithms are stable, robust, and are capable of providing useful results. A more specific finding was that LSA can yield successful results for extracting relevant associations among proteins with appropriate selection of parameter value.

5. Acknowledgement

This research was partially supported by a NSF ITR grant #9817572.

6. References

[1] Berry, M., Dumais, S., and Letsche, T. "Computational methods for intelligent information access". *In Proceedings of Supercomputing '95*, San Diego, CA, 1995.

[2] Deerwester, S., Dumais, S. T., Furnas, G. W., Landauer, T. K., and Harshman, R. "Indexing by latent semantic analysis". *Journal of the American Society for Information Science*, 1990, 41:391–407.

[3] Eriksson, G., Franzen, K., Olsson, F., Asker, L., and Liden, P. "Exploiting syntax when detecting protein names in text". *In Proceedings of Workshop on Natural Language Processing in Biomedical Applications*, 2002.

[4] Fu, Y., Bauer, T., Mostafa, J., Palakal, M., & Mukhopadhyay, S. "Concept extraction and association from cancer literature". *In Proceedings of the fourth international workshop on Web information and data management of ACM CIKM*, 2002, 100-103.

[5] Fukuda, K., Tsunoda, T., Tamura, A., and Takagi, T. "Toward information extraction: identifying protein names from biological papers". *In Pac Symp Biocomput*, 1998, 707–18.

[6] Kazuhiro, S., and Mostafa, J. "An approach to protein name extraction using heuristics and a dictionary". Laboratory of Applied Information Research Tech Report 2003-2. Indiana University, Bloomington, IN, USA, 2003.

[7] Rindflesch, T., Rajan, J., and Hunter, L. "Extracting molecular binding relationships from biomedical text". *In Proceedings of the 6th Applied Natural Language Processing Conference*, 2000, 188–195.

[8] Salton, G. *Introduction to modern information retrieval*. McGraw-Hill, New York, 1983.

[9] Thomas, J., Milward, D., Ouzounis, C., Pulman, S., and Carroll, M. "Automatic extraction of protein interactions from scientific abstracts". *In Pac Symp Biocomput*, 2000, 541–52.

[10] Tou, J. T. and Gonzalez, R. C. *Pattern Recognition Principles*. Addision-Wcslcy, 1974.

Genescene: Biomedical Text And Data Mining

Gondy Leroy[1], Hsinchun Chen[1], Jesse D. Martinez[2], Shauna Eggers[1], Ryan R. Falsey[2],
Kerri L. Kislin[2], Zan Huang[1], Jiexun Li[1], Jie Xu[1], Daniel M. McDonald[1], Gavin Ng[1]
Management Information Systems[1], Arizona Cancer Center[2]
The University of Arizona
gleroy@eller.arizona.edu; hchen@eller.arizona.edu; jmartinez@azcc.arizona.edu;
seggers@email.arizona.edu; rfalsey@u.arizona.edu; kkislin@u.arizona.edu;
zhuang@eller.arizona.edu; jiexun@eller.arizona.edu; jxu@eller.arizona.edu;
dmm@eller.arizona.edu; tgavinng@ai.bpa.arizona.edu

Abstract

To access the content of digital texts efficiently, it is necessary to provide more sophisticated access than keyword based searching. Genescene provides biomedical researchers with research findings and background relations automatically extracted from text and experimental data. These provide a more detailed overview of the information available. The extracted relations were evaluated by qualified researchers and are precise. A qualitative ongoing evaluation of the current online interface indicates that this method to search the literature is more useful and efficient than keyword based searching.

1. Introduction

The Internet has increased the availability of and access to publications, leading in many cases to information overload. In biomedicine, this effect has been accelerated by an increase in publications and datasets due to the decoding of the human genome. Every 11 years, the number of researchers doubles [6] and Medline, the main resource of research literature, has been growing with more than 10,000 abstracts per week since 2002 [5]. In addition, large amounts of gene expression data involving expression measurements of thousands of genes, are available from microarray experiments. Gene expression patterns embedded in the data can potentially lead to the discovery of unknown genetic relations.

The information overload problem for both literature and data analysis calls for solutions that can largely automate these processes. Genescene, a toolkit developed for biomedicine, will provide more adequate access to text and data. It will allow researchers to view the findings extracted from Medline abstracts, and compare them with findings from microarray experiments.

2. Related Work

To access the content of documents, natural language processing (NLP) is required. Existing techniques range from simple pattern matching to full parsers. In biomedicine, many NLP approaches start from a list with specific gene names or verbs and extract the surrounding text as relations [2; 7; 8]. The best among these achieve high precision but low recall since few relations are extracted. More general co-occurrence based approaches assume that phrases, e.g., genes, are related when they appear together in a text [3]. This approach extracts more relations but they are less precise. Both methods ignore negation.

3. Genescene

Genescene combines relations between entities in text extracted by a rule-based parser and a corpus-based co-occurrence analysis technique. It will also extract regulatory relations from microarray data and combine these with the relations extracted from text.

3.1. Rule-based findings

The rule-based parser, successfully tested with a small prototype [4], is based on closed-class words which provide a generic structure for the relations. Cascaded finite state automata (FSA), built around prepositions and basic sentence elements, identify the structures. Each FSA incorporates negation, an important element ignored by others, and also captures relations based on conjunctions. For example, from the sentence "Thus hsp90 does not inhibit receptor function solely by… ," the relation "NOT: hsp90 – inhibit – receptor function" is extracted.

3.2. Corpus-based background

The corpus-based background relations represent the knowledge in the entire domain and form the background for the rule-based relations. These corpus-based relations are formed by a co-occurrence-based algorithm tested earlier in an information retrieval context [1]. They represent relations between noun phrases that hold true for the entire collection.

3.3. Ontologies

Three ontologies, the Gene Ontology (GO), the Human Genome (HUGO) Nomenclature, and the Unified Medical Language System (UMLS), are used to better integrate the relations. A term can receive multiple semantic tags based on its being in the ontologies.

3.4. Regulatory relations from data

Regulatory relations are extracted from microarray data using data mining techniques such as Bayesian networks and association rule mining. Incorporating these regulatory relations into Genescene will help researchers compare experimental discovery with previous knowledge from literature. Unexpected gene associations can be identified to guide further literature search or new experimental design.

3.5. Online Access

Users can currently access Genescene's text mining demo (http://ai.bpa.arizona.edu/go/genescene). Keywords are used to retrieve relations found in the Medline abstracts and users can choose the type of relation they want to see. A list of relations is then shown for the search, ordered by the type and number of elements in the relation. The number of abstracts containing the relations is also shown. Clicking on a relation retrieves the list of associated abstracts. The relations and search terms are highlighted in the abstract text.

4. Case study

The extracted relations and online interface are being evaluated with quantitative and qualitative studies.

4.1. Genescene relations

Two researchers evaluated the rule- and corpus-based relations from p53-related abstracts. The rule-based relations were 95% correct and the corpus-based relations were 60% correct. Limiting the corpus-based relations to those that had entities with ontology tags increased their correctness to 78%. Most terms and relations were considered relevant, especially when part of an ontology.

4.2. Genescene content

Encouraged by the excellent evaluation results, three collections with biomedical abstracts were added to Genescene. Different research groups requested the collections. Table 1 provides an overview. The P53 collection contains all abstracts available in Medline (up to and including summer 2002) with the keyword "p53" in the title or abstract. The AP1 collection is similarly based on the keywords: ap1, ap-1, jnk, erk, jun, fos, and p38. The yeast collection is based on the keyword "yeast." Hundreds of thousands of relations are available for each collection. In each, more than half of the terms received a tag from an ontology. The UMLS provided more than 50% of the terms with a tag. Slightly more than 1% of the terms received a GO-tag. HUGO provided the least tags, except for the yeast collection where 1.4% of the terms received a HUGO tag.

Table 1. Overview of Genescene's content

Topic:	P53	AP1	Yeast
Abstracts:	23,234	30,820	56,246
Rule-B. Relations:	270,008	387,666	560,165
Corpus-B. Relations:	5,023,103	6,526,454	7,736,647
Terms w. UMLS tag:	57%	54%	51%
Terms w. HUGO tag:	0.6%	0.9%	1.4%
Terms w. GO tag:	1.1%	1.1%	1.1%
Any ontology tag:	58%	55%	52%

4.3. Genescene interface

The ordering of the relations was very much liked. Researchers felt the most important relations, e.g., conclusions, were presented first. They also liked the highlighting of relations and keywords in the original abstracts. However, currently only one keyword or phrase can be used to search a collection. A multiple-keyword search should be added and the speed of partial match queries for background relations should be improved.

5. Future Directions

In the future, we will integrate both the rule- and corpus-based relations in an interactive graphical map display. Later, visual text mining will become possible. For example, users will be able to search for specific time ranges in the publications or for specific organism. Furthermore, findings from text will be incorporated into microarray data mining results to improve the algorithmic performance and vice versa microarray findings will lead to automatic literature searches.

6. Acknowledgements

Genescene is supported by the grant: NIH/NLM, 1 R33 LM07299-01, 2002-2005, "Genescene: a Toolkit for Gene Pathway Analysis." We thank the National Library of Medicine, the Gene Ontology Consortium, and the Hugo Nomenclature Committee for making the ontologies available to researchers.

7. References

[1]   Chen, H. and Lynch, K. J. Automatic Construction of Networks of Concepts Characterizing Document Databases. *IEEE Transactions on Systems, Man and Cybernetics*, 22, 5 (1992), 885-902.

[2]   Friedman, C., Kra, P., Yu, H., Krauthammer, M. and Rzhetsky, A. GENIES: a natural-language processing system for the extraction of molecular pathways from journal articles. *Bioinformatics*, 17, Suppl. 1 (2001), S74-S82.

[3]   Jenssen, T.-K., Laegreid, A., Komorowski, J. and Hovig, E. A literature network of human genes for high-throughput analysis of gene expression. *Nature Genetics*, 28, (2001), 21-28.

[4]   Leroy, G. and Chen, H. Filling Preposition-based Templates to Capture Information from Medical Abstracts. Paper presented at the *Pacific Symposium on Biocomputing*, (2002), 350-361.

[5]   National-Library-of-Medicine, Fact Sheet - Medline. National   Library   of   Medicine: http://www.nlm.nih.gov/pubs/factsheets/medline.html

[6]   Perutz, M. F. Will biomedicine outgrow support? *Nature*, 399, (1999), 299-301.

[7]   Pustejovsky, J., Castaño, J., Zhang, J., Kotecki, M. and Cochran, B. Robust Relational Parsing Over Biomedical Literature: Extracting Inhibit Relations. Paper presented at the *Pacific Symposium on Biocomputing* (2002), 362-373.

[8]   Thomas, J., Milward, D., Ouzounis, C., Pulman, S. and Carroll, M. Automatic Extraction of Protein Interactions from Scientific Abstracts. Paper presented at the *Pacific Symposium on Biocomputing* (2000), 538-549.

Taxonomies for Automated Question Triage in Digital Reference

Jeffrey Pomerantz
School of Information Studies
Syracuse University
jppomera@syr.edu

R. David Lankes
Information Institute of Syracuse
Syracuse University
rdlankes@ericir.syr.edu

Abstract

This study identifies (1) several taxonomies of questions at different levels of linguistic analysis, according to which questions received by digital reference services are classified, and (2) a simple categorization of triage recipients. The utility of these taxonomies and categorizations of triage recipients is discussed as the basis for systems for automating triage and other steps in the digital reference process.

1. Introduction

The growth in the past decade of both the infrastructure and the number of users of the Internet has enabled a corresponding growth in the number of users of digital reference services on the Internet. This increase in the use of digital reference services has led to increases in the number of questions received by these services, thus putting a strain on the human intermediaries employed therein. The ability of a digital reference service to scale up to handle an increasingly large number of questions, and the quality of the answers provided, is directly affected by the amount of automation employed by that service: the more processes that are automated, the more of the human intermediaries' time and effort can be dedicated to tasks that cannot yet be automated. There is, now more than ever, an increased and immediate need for automation in digital reference services.

2. Identification of question taxonomies

Four question taxonomies were identified through an extensive review of the literature from several fields that deal with questions: desk and digital reference, question answering, linguistics, speech act theory, and discourse analysis [5]. These taxonomies are as follows:

1. Wh- words: The grammatical root word of a question.
2. Subjects of questions: The topic or subject of a question.
3. The functions of expected answers to questions: An indication of the information need underlying the question.
4. The forms of expected answers to questions: An indication of the format of the information requested by the question.

These four taxonomies correspond to the top four levels of linguistic analysis: Syntactic, Semantic, Discourse, and Pragmatic, respectively.

These taxonomies are not necessarily the *only* ones that may exist at each of these four levels of analysis. Indeed, several well-developed classification schemes exist that classify entities according to subject: the Dewey Decimal Classification, the Library of Congress Subject Headings, and the ERIC Thesaurus, to name only a few. There may be equally large numbers of taxonomies at the other levels of linguistic analysis. This study has identified one taxonomy per level, but future work may identify more taxonomies at each level.

3. Question triage

Work is currently being conducted by the Information Institute of Syracuse (iis.syr.edu), the Center for Intelligent Information Retrieval (ciir.cs.umass.edu), and the Wondir Foundation (www.wondir.org) to develop taxonomies representing questions requiring human intermediation and those best handled automatically. The first step in developing these taxonomies was the identification of the four taxonomies discussed above.

The first step in determining which types of questions require human intermediation and which are best handled automatically was the identification of the range of triage actions performed in digital reference services. Triage is the assignment of a question received by a digital reference service to a reference or subject expert 'answerer' [6]. Observation of the performance of triage by digital reference triagers in services affiliated with academic, public, and special libraries, and in AskA services (entirely online services, unaffiliated with any physical library [3]) has determined that a question may be triaged (1) *within* a service (when a question is received by a service, a triager assigns it to a specific expert within that service) or (2) *between* services (if a question is received by a service that for whatever reason it cannot or will not answer, the triager forwards that question to a different service) [5]. Individual services employ answerers to whom questions may be triaged, and may be members of consortia of services that swap questions amongst themselves. As there is such a wide range of recipients to which different services may triage questions, with little overlap, this simple division of triage into internal or external serves as a first step in categorizing triage recipients.

All questions received by digital reference services fall within the "taxonomy space" defined by the three taxonomies discussed above. The "cells" in this taxonomy space formed by the "intersections" of classes along these three dimensions provide a finely-grained means for identifying question types. Some specific question types (cells) were found to have 100% correlation with triage recipients – that is, 100% of the questions of a specific type were triaged either internally or externally to the service that received it. Some example question types for which there was perfect correlation with triage recipients are shown in Table 1. The classes in the Cell column are listed in order of the four taxonomies discussed above, minus the taxonomy of Subjects.

Table 1. Some perfect correlations

Cell	Triage recipient	Example question
How Explanation Factual	Internal	"How does quinine work?"
What-selection Coverage Citation list	External	"Need documentation on schools associated with zoos."

It is these question types for which perfect correlations exist that may be utilized as the basis for designing and building a system to automate the triage process. When a question is received by a service, it would be automatically classified, and a triage action recommended based on that classification. A model of such a system is represented in Figure 1.

The existence of these perfect correlations between certain question types and the triage action taken upon them is an indication that there could similarly be correlations between certain question types and the actions taken in other processes in digital reference.

4. Discussion

It is reasonable to assume that some processes in digital reference may be entirely automated in the near future. The process of tracking received questions for trends, for example, may be automated through the use of data mining or bibliomining techniques [4]. It seems less likely, however, that the triage and answer formulation processes will be fully automated any time soon, as these processes require a great deal of human judgment. Arms [1], often a strong advocate of automation, provides an excellent example of why such processes are difficult to automate. He asks:

> "How would we create a computer system to answer questions such as, 'Why was the space station a bad idea?' … Even with the most advanced parallel computers, nothing on the horizon approaches human judgment in understanding such subtleties."

Arms' example question is a straw man, as Pomerantz [5] has shown that questions requiring value judgments are a small percentage of questions received by digital reference services. Arms' point, however, is a sound one: some questions are not now and may never be amenable to automated answering. Tasks that involve routines and regular actions are amenable to automation, while tasks that require human judgment are not, or at least are only partially amenable to automation. The difficult task is in determining, for tasks of this latter type, where the appropriate balance is between automation and human intermediation. To determine this, more studies are required of such tasks in different environments and contexts, to discover what routines exist in the actions performed by human intermediaries.

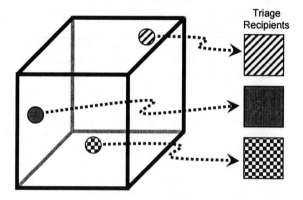

Figure 1. Taxonomy space as a model for automated triage

The NIST Roadmap document [2] provides a vision of the direction in which question answering (QA) research and development should take over a five year span. Part of this vision involves a need for question taxonomies as the basis for any future theory of QA, and the identification of "criteria along which question taxonomies should be formed" (p. 7). The level of complexity and ambiguity of digital reference questions, and the degree of contextual understanding required to answer them, provides a useful benchmark for future QA systems to aim for, if they wish to be able to answer realistic questions.

The most complex or ambiguous questions, or those requiring a great deal of contextual understanding to answer them, are likely to be those that require human intermediation, at least for the immediate future, as QA systems develop and improve. The more processes that are automated, however, the more of human intermediaries' time and effort can be dedicated to tasks that cannot yet be automated, such as formulating answers to such complex or ambiguous questions. Thus, the development of question taxonomies, and criteria for determining the appropriate triage recipient for a question – human or automated – pushes forward work in both QA and digital reference.

5. Acknowledgement

This material is based upon work supported by the National Science Foundation under Grant No. 0121525.

6. References

[1] Arms, W. Y. (2000). Automated Digital Libraries: How Effectively Can Computers Be Used for the Skilled Tasks of Professional Librarianship? *D-Lib Magazine, 6*(7/8). http://www.dlib.org/dlib/july00/arms/07arms.html.

[2] Burger, J., et al. (2001). *Issues, Tasks and Program Structures to Roadmap Research in Question & Answering (Q&A)*: National Institute of Standards and Technology. http://www-nlpir.nist.gov/projects/duc/papers/qa.Roadmap-paper_v2.doc.

[3] Lankes, R. D. (1998). *Building & Maintaining Internet Information Services: K-12 Digital Reference Services*. Syracuse, NY: ERIC Clearinghouse on Information & Technology.

[4] Nicholson, S., & Stanton, J. (in press). Gaining Strategic Advantage through Bibliomining: Data Mining for Management Decisions in Corporate, Special, Digital, and Traditional Libraries. In H. Nemati & C. Barko (Eds.), *Organizational Data Mining: Leveraging Enterprise Data Resources for Optimal Performance*. Hershey, PA: Idea Group Publishing.

[5] Pomerantz, J. (2003). *Question Taxonomies for Digital Reference.* Unpublished doctoral dissertation, Syracuse University, Syracuse, NY.

[6] Virtual Reference Desk Project. (1998, September 29). Virtual Reference Desk AskA Software: Decision Points and Scenarios. http://www.vrd.org/Tech/AskA-sw.PDF.

Topic Detection and Interest Tracking in a Dynamic Online News Source

Andrew J. Kurtz and Javed Mostafa
Laboratory for Applied Informatics Research
Indiana University, Bloomington
http://lair.indiana.edu/research/newssifter
ajkurtz@indiana.edu, jm@indiana.edu

Abstract

Digital libraries in the news domain may contain frequently updated data. Providing personalized access to such dynamic resources is an important goal. In this paper, we investigate the area of filtering online dynamic news sources based on personal profiles. We experimented with an intelligent news–sifting system that tracks topic development in a dynamic online news source. Vocabulary discovery and clustering are used to expose current news topics. User interest profiles, generated from explicit and implicit feedback are used to customize the news retrieval system's interface.

1. Introduction

With the volume of online news available today, it is difficult to manually sort through the hundreds of daily news articles to find articles related to specific topics. It would be valuable to have an automated system, which would sift through the mounds of news and display the articles that match an individual's interests. Such a system would need to identify topics within the articles, group them into clusters, and present the articles sorted based on the user's interest.

Some advances have been made in filtering, but previous research has generally been in areas that deal with relatively static document sets[4]. Little research has been done in the area of filtering online dynamic news sources based on personal profiles. Some previous research includes Watters and Wang[5] who discuss a system that extracts features from news articles such as date, location, and organization and uses those features to calculate the similarity among articles. SCISOR[3] is a system that analyses news articles to extract the concept of the article. Based on the extracted concepts the articles are summarized and grouped together for use in answering user questions presented to the system.

In addition to filtering news articles into categories, we want to present the articles to the users in a way that focuses their attention on the articles that match their interest. Explicit interest indicators may be used which typically require the user to interrupt their activity and select their interest in a particular topic. This mode is not desirable as it disrupts the news reading process. A better option would be to use implicit interest indicators that are used to gather the users' interest on topics without interrupting the task they are completing. Claypool, et. al.[2] shows that using implicit interest indicators are as accurate in tracking a user's interests as using explicit interest indicators. Explicit interest indicators are a good way for the user to provide their initial interests and implicit interest indicators are good for tracking the user's interest over time.

2. System Design and Methodology

We developed an intelligent news-sifting interface to track topics in a dynamic online news source. Vocabulary discovery and clustering is used to expose current news topics that develop over time. User interest profiles, utilizing both explicit and implicit feedback, track the user's interest and are used to customize the news retrieval system's interface. More information on the algorithms used can be found in Mostafa, et. al.[4]. In this paper, we concentrate on experiments to analyze the impact of key components on system performance.

The system uses an existing online news feed service, called ClariNews[1] that is distributed through USNET newsgroups. We gathered news articles from 384 ClariNews newsgroups that are organized into 25 general interest channels such as "business" and "technology". The update frequency of the channels range between 3 and 300 messages a day. For this paper, we concentrated on the "business" channel that receives an average of 34 messages per day.

We selected three periods covering two weeks to track. All of the articles for the business channel were collected during a total of six weeks. Topic detection and topic clustering were performed on the set of articles. The clusters were analyzed based the number of terms articles were classified into the clusters and the classification was analyzed to see if well-separated clusters were generated.

The evaluation of the interest profile associated with the channels was performed by modeling two types of users. One user was focused on reading one particular news channel for all of the sessions and the second user changed reading habits by switching news channels part way through the sessions. The aim was to see how the interest profiles adapt to each type of user.

3. Results and Analysis

Vocabulary discovery and clustering were performed using components of the SIFTER system[4]. A ranking of tokens based on the tf.idf weights of the tokens was created then the terms in the top R ranks, that appear in at least D documents, were selected. The terms were then clustered using a cosine similarity measure with similarity values below the threshold value Theta being clustered together. The settings of R and D control the number of terms selected and the setting of Theta effects the number of clusters produced. Table 1 shows the cluster results for two settings of R and D and two settings of Theta.

Table 1. Cluster results

	R=20, D=4		R=12, D=2	
	Theta=0.75	Theta=0.50	Theta=0.75	Theta=0.50
Number of Terms				
1/3/03	21	21	65	65
1/17/03	16	16	45	45
1/31/03	13	13	48	48
Period Mean	16.7	16.7	52.7	52.7
Number of Clusters				
1/3/03	7	8	16	28
1/17/03	8	9	15	22
1/31/03	6	8	14	22
Period Mean	7.000	8.333	15.000	24.000
Mean Cluster Distance				
1/3/03	0.974	0.952	0.977	0.957
1/17/03	0.948	0.951	0.964	0.938
1/31/03	0.956	0.911	0.989	0.956
Period Mean	0.959	0.938	0.977	0.950
Mean Cluster Homogeneity				
1/3/03	0.322	0.288	0.429	0.304
1/17/03	0.281	0.259	0.398	0.302
1/31/03	0.316	0.269	0.402	0.256
Period Mean	0.306	0.272	0.410	0.287
Mean Documents Per Cluster				
1/3/03	61.1	54.3	28.8	17.5
1/17/03	80.6	72.5	45.3	31.5
1/31/03	61.9	48.1	28.9	18.8
Period Mean	67.9	58.3	34.3	22.6

discovered and the number of clusters that resulted. The

Providing a larger number of clusters is an advantage to the user since the documents will be separated into more specific topics supporting a higher resolution view of the documents. As we altered R and D to increase the terms selected, thus increasing the number of clusters, the performance of the clustering algorithm did not degrade as observed in the distances between the clusters and the homogeneity of clusters. The results show that we can increase resolution while maintaining performance. In addition, we observed, for both settings of R and D, that increasing the number of clusters improves cluster homogeneity.

The documents were well distributed across the clusters and as the number of clusters increased the mean number of documents in each cluster decreased showing that the new clusters were being created in balance with the document topics.

Documents that did not contain any of the vocabulary terms were classified into a null cluster. As the number of clusters increased the number of documents in the null cluster decreased dramatically, from a mean of 100 (R=20, D=4, Theta=.75) to a mean of 27 (R=12, D=2, Theta=.5), demonstrating that the new clusters were finding new topics within the document set.

User interest levels in the topic channels were modeled using one user with constant on one channel and the second user changing channels part way through. Building profiles according to interest in the channels provides a coarse grain interest profile of the user. A screen shot of the client application can be seen in Figure 1.

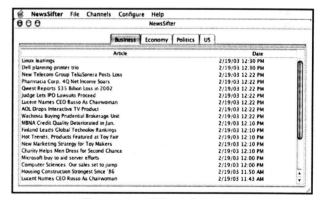

Figure 1. Client interface

Both users initially selected four channels A, B, C, and D and they explicitly set their interest level for each of the channels during the first session at 0.9, 0.8, 0.7, and 0.6 respectively. The level of interest in the four channels was tracked over eight sessions. The interest was tracked using implicit interest indicators.

Figure 2 shows how the interest levels change for a user who monitors and interacts with channel A. The interest level for channel A constantly increases while the interest levels for the other channels constantly decrease.

Figure 3 shows how the interest levels change for a user who focuses on channel A initially then begins to also look at channel B from session five onwards. The change in interest can be seen from the change in the level of channel B as it switches from a downward trend to an upward trend.

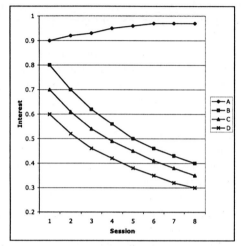

Figure 2. Constant user interest results

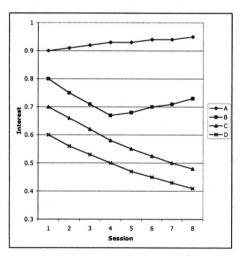

Figure 3. Changing user interest results

As can be seen, the implicit interest indicators used by the system learns a user's interest over time and strengthens the interest level. In addition, the system reacts to a user's change in interest and is able to adapt to the new interest.

4. Conclusion and Future Work

The results described in this paper, show that it is possible to detect topics within a dynamic news source and to track user interest over time. Topic detection and clustering identify the current news topics and a combination of explicit and implicit interest indicators allows the system to track the user's interest with minimal user interruption.

Future work will include adding a second level of interest tracking for the topics within each channel, providing a fine grain interest profile. In addition we will be performing user testing of the system to evaluate performance of the interest tracking based on real users and to evaluate the user interface of the client application.

5. References

[1] ClariNet. http://www.clarinet.com

[2] Claypool, M., Le, P., Wased, M., & Brown, D. (2001). Implicit Interest Indicators. International Conference on Intelligent User Interfaces, 33-40.

[3] Endres-Niggemeyer, B. (1998). SCISOR. In Summarizing Information (pp. 319-327). Berlin: Springer-Verlag.

[4] Mostafa, J., Quiroga, L. M., & Palakal, M. (1998). Filtering Medical Documents Using Automated and Human Classification Methods. JASIS, 49(14), 1304-1318.

[5] Watters, C., & Wang, H. (2000). Rating News Documents for Similarity. JASIS, 51(9), 793-804.

Methods for Precise Named Entity Matching in Digital Collections

Peter T. Davis
Columbia University
450 C.S. Building
New York, NY 10027
ptd7@cs.columbia.edu

David K. Elson
Columbia University
450 C.S. Building
New York, NY 10027
delson@cs.columbia.edu

Judith L. Klavans
Columbia University
508 Butler Library
New York, NY 10027
klavans@cs.columbia.edu

Abstract

In this paper, we describe an interactive system, built within the context of CLiMB project, which permits a user to locate the occurrences of named entities within a given text. The named entity tool was developed to identify references to a single art object (e.g. a particular building) with high precision in text related to images of that object in a digital collection. We start with an authoritative list of art objects, and seek to match variants of these named entities in related text. Our approach is to "decay" entities into progressively more general variants while retaining high precision. As variants become more general, and thus more ambiguous, we propose methods to disambiguate intermediate results. Our results will be used to select records into which automatically generated metadata will be loaded.

1. Computational Linguistics and Metadata

CLiMB (Computational Linguistics for Metadata Building,[1] funded by the Mellon Foundation) is an interdisciplinary project that aims to improve access to scholarly digital image collections by extracting descriptive metadata about images from related texts. With the large volume of image collections now being scanned, it is prohibitively expensive for specialized image catalogers to manually assign robust metadata to every image. By analyzing scholarly texts and associating their contents to related images, CLiMB tools will explore the potential to identify descriptive metadata which can be used to enrich catalog records. To test the process, these records will be mounted in a standard retrieval platform, where users will search for images related to particular keywords generated by CLiMB.

Although the current CLiMB project is aimed at text associated with the information in image collections, our techniques and tools are applicable to texts of many types, not just those associated with images. The application to images is one of the ways to experiment with using computational linguistic techniques to enrich catalog records. Since we are testing with text associated with images, we have designed a narrow testbed with which to measure success. If our techniques prove useful, then they should be applicable to a wide range of text types, and to languages other than English.

2. The Role of Named Entities

In traditional image search platforms, the name of an art object generally serves as the key to a record. These object names tend to be complex, with a series of variants, all of them listed in catalog records to improve user search. The process of automatically associating blocks of prose from scholarly publications with image catalog records requires the identification of these art objects. Because images are discretely grouped into records about specific art objects (the domain of CLiMB's focus), we must be able to confidently identify which sections of a text are "about" which art objects. Each collection might choose a different type of entity as the art object. For example, of the three collections selected for the CLiMB project, each has a different type of object to be identified: for a collection of architectural drawings, the object is a project name for the architects; for a collection of images on South Asian temples, the object is a geographic location of the temple site; for a collection of images of paper gods from China, the art object is the name of the god or gods depicted[2].

A given art object is identified with a set of related named entities, which we call Art Object Identifiers (AO-ID's). An AO-ID can be given *a priori* to CLiMB tools by authority lists such as those from which image catalogers draw. Typically, AO-IDs are complex, with variations, which are often not very obvious. This results in their being difficult to find automatically in a text (see, for example, Table 1, row

---

[1] http://www.columbia.edu/cu/cria/climb

[2] http://www.columbia.edu/cu/cria/climb/collections.html

1). Similarly, for one of the paper gods in the Chinese paper gods collection, there are over 25 variants for most god names, many of which are translations, different transliterations, or different dialects.

One of the collections with which we are developing CLiMB tools is from the American architects Charles and Henry Greene[3]. In this case, the authority list of AO-IDs is a complete list of projects built by the Greene brothers. The image collection consists of architectural drawings and photographs of the finished projects, many of which are private houses. Each image is cataloged in a record that is assigned to a particular AO-ID from the project list as the key to that record. Before passages in text can be mined for metadata, they must be classified as being "about" the record's images. A high precision for this step is crucial, since all further processing depends on the association of metadata with the AO-ID that it describes. Thus, in the precision/recall trade-off, we have opted for precision. (See [10] for a user evaluation of index terms, comparing the value of precision vs. recall.)

The most obvious way to identify a passage as relating to a particular AO-ID is simply to look for the frequency of occurrences of that AO-ID. However, this method by itself is problematic: it is highly unlikely that an AO-ID supplied either by a user or by an authority list will appear verbatim in the text. Table 1, row 1 shows the official AO-ID for the William R. Thorsen House project which does not appear at all in the major scholarly text on the Greene brothers [2]. Thus, a method for finding AO-ID variants is needed.

3. Case Study: Named Entities in Text

Early research in computing and the humanities showed that the frequency of mention of a given term in a section of a text is a straighforward method of identifying segments of text about that term. This applies not only to the use of named entities in identifying meaningful segments, but also to common nouns. Indeed, this principle underlies the term frequency and inverse document frequency relationship (tf*idf) measure popularized by [9].

Within the CLiMB project, we have explored in depth the use of named entities within [2], where different Greene & Greene projects are discussed in succession. We have started with this particular author as representative of the texts that will be processed within the project. A paragraph with a high frequency of mentions of a particular project tends to signify the beginning of a discussion of that project. The challenge of identifying such matches to the authority term is well known in the library[1] and computer science[8] communities, since a project can be known by many different variants. The house that the Greenes de-

[3]http://gamblehouse.usc.edu/architects/index.html

Table 1. Frequency of AO-ID variants in chapter 5 of *Greene & Greene* (approximately 11,500 words)

Project name variant	Occurrences
William R. Thorsen House (Berkeley, Calif)	0
William R. Thorsen House (Calif)	0
William R. Thorsen House	1
William Thorsen House	0
Thorsen House	7
The House	65

signed for William Thorsen, for example, is sometimes referred to as *the Thorsen house* and *the William R. Thorsen house.* Most commonly, a referential term, e.g *the house*, is used in context. By contrast, the AO-ID provided by catalogers is given as a complete, unambiguous *William R. Thorsen House (Berkeley, Calif)* which does not appear at all in the text itself. Thus, the identification of both variants and referents is required to automatically link full terms to the AO-ID to which they refer. We are exploring two techniques in the identification of AO-IDs. One is the use of a named entity finder operating directly on texts. The other, reported in this paper, is on the use of authoritative lists, either via user input or from a given list of precompiled AO-IDs.

4. Using Decay to Locate Variants and Referents

We have built a tool which takes as input a user provided art object name, and a given text over which to search. Building on the role of heads and modifiers [10], we repeatedly "decay" the AO-ID by sequentially removing modifiers, causing it to become more general. We then locate occurrences of the term's variants among the noun phrases in the a text (using tools such as LTChunk from the University of Edinburgh[5]). We observe that the frequency of a variant in chapter 5 of *Greene & Greene* generally increases with the state of its decay (see Table 1). Once we remove all the modifiers, we add the determiner *the* to the head to ensure that all the occurrences are mentions of specific houses.

Our initial results showed that in chapter 5 of [2], 22 noun phrases directly refer to the Thorsen house. Of those, 19 are decayed variants of the original AO-ID. The remaining three, *the Thorsens' Berkeley residence, the project*, and *the Berkeley residence*, may be obtainable through further semantic manipulation of the original AO-ID. Precision, however, is crucial; though none of the other variants of the Thorsen AO-ID match to an unrelated noun phrase, *the house* appears 65 times, of which only 12 are in reference to

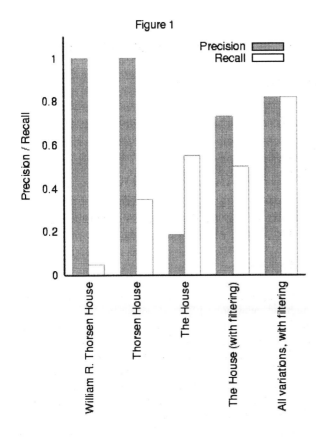

Figure 1

occur at all, while *the house* is too ambiguous. Results are best when combining the accurate forms with seed-based filtering on the ambiguous form.

While our results are encouraging for identifying references to the Thorsen house, there remain challenges in developing this technique into an automatic tool for heterogeneous texts. For example, it took manual intervention to know which AO-ID variant was sufficiently precise but maximally frequent to use as a seed for disambiguating the more general variant.

In future work, we will test these techniques over additional texts and explore ways to incorporate additional authority lists. Our goal is to identify and label named entities, using as much *a priori* information as possible, with the ability to fall back to sensible guessing when no authoritative information is available.

References

[1] M. Baca (ed). Introduction to art image access: issues, tools standards, strategies. Los Angeles: Getty Research Institute, 2002.

[2] E. Bosley, Greene & Greene, Phaidon Press, 2000.

[3] M. Collins, A New Statistical Parser Based on Bigram Lexical Dependencies, Proceedings of the 34th Meeting of the ACL, Santa Cruz, 1996.

[4] J. Cowie, W. Lehnert, Information Extraction, Communications of the ACM, 39 (1), 1996.

[5] S. Finch, A. Mikheev: A Workbench for Finding Structure in Texts, Proceedings of the Fifth Conference of Applied Natural Language Processing (ANLP), Washington D.C., 1997.

[6] S. Lappin and H. Leass. 1994. An Algorithm for Pronominal Anaphora Resolution. *Computational Linguistics*, 20(4):535-562.

[7] MUC-7 - Proceedings of the 7th Message Understanding Conference. http://www.muc.saic.com, 1998.

[8] V. Ng, C. Cardie, Improving Machine Learning Approaches to Coreference Resolution, Proceedings of the 40th Meeting of the ACL, Philadelphia, PA, 2002.

[9] G. Salton, ed. 1971. The SMART Retrieval System: Experiments in Automatic Document Processing. Prentice Hall: Englewood Cliffs, NJ.

[10] N. Wacholder, D. K. Evans, and J. L. Klavans, Automatic identification and organization of index terms for interactive browsing. ACM/IEEE Joint Conference on Digital Libraries (JCDL) 2001.

the Thorsen house (see Fig. 1). Because the 7 occurrences of *Thorsen House* are accurate, it is reasonable to hypothesize that appearances of *the house* near those occurrences are more likely to be coreferents to the AO-ID than those that do not. To test this hypothesis, we modified our algorithm to use high-precision, low-recall matches as seeds for correctly matching more ambiguous terms nearby[6]. Extrapolating the decay technique to all 253 AO-IDs in the project list, there are 27 such seeds, including the 7 occurrences of *Thorsen House* and analogous ones for 8 other projects. An occurrence of *the house*, then, is assigned to refer to the project whose seed occurs most recently.

Of the 15 occurrences of *the house* linked to the Thorsen project by this technique, 11 are linked accurately. When these results are combined with those of the seed matches, both a precision and recall of .82 are achieved for identifying references to the Thorsen house in the chapter. Despite being below 90%, this precision is high considering the difficulty of the problem. For example, in the MUC-7 coreference task, the the highest average F_1 was 61.8%, which is below our F_1 of 82% [7]. In future work, we aim for above 90% precision, which is a benchmark for precision proposed by [4].

Figure 1 shows the precision and recall of variants and referents in correctly identifying mentions of the Thorsen house in Chapter 5 of [2]. The more specific variants do not

An Application of Multiple Viewpoints to Content-Based Image Retrieval

James C. French   A. C. Chapin   Worthy N. Martin
Department of Computer Science
University of Virginia
Charlottesville, VA
01-434-982-2213
{french,acc2a,wnm}@cs.virginia.edu

Abstract

Content-based image retrieval uses features that can be extracted from the images themselves. Using more than one representation of the images in a collection can improve the results presented to a user without changing the underlying feature extraction or search technologies. We present an example of this "multiple viewpoint" approach, multiple image channels, and discuss its advantages for an image-seeking user. This approach has also been shown to dramatically improve retrieval effectiveness in content-based image retrieval systems[3].

1. Introduction

Content-based image retrieval (CBIR) systems[5] search collections of images based on features that can be extracted from the image files themselves without manual descriptive or indexing labor from humans. Identifying such features and methods of extracting them are open areas of research. Using multiple image representations, we have been able to improve the results of existing image retrieval systems without developing any such new methods.

Identifying the most useful distinguishing features of images for searching, especially in cases where the image retrieval task is fairly general and not well specified, is difficult, as is extracting these features from the images in a heterogeneous collection. Frequently a query to an image retrieval system will go unanswered or poorly answered even when there are appropriate images in the collection because while the query seems to the user to communicate the information need, the features actually being used by the system to judge relevance do not quite match the user's expectations.

By performing some simple transformations on query and image collection, we can improve the likelihood of such appropriate but obscured images being found without changing the underlying feature abstraction or retrieval technologies. We have built a system with three additional image representations, or *channels*, beyond the native representation used by the underlying CBIR technology. In this system we perform searches on each

channel, and merge the results to obtain an improved result.

2. Context

Multiple channels are an application of the idea of multiple viewpoints[2], an approach to information retrieval that takes advantage of having more than one set of relevance judgments to improve search results, all unified under a common interface. Each viewpoint embodies a set of relevance judgments, possibly using different representations and search technologies, and the results of consulting each viewpoint for documents (e.g. images, text articles, library book records, etc.) are merged to create a single result in which the weaknesses of each viewpoint may be mitigated by the contributions of the others.

We consider CBIR systems that are queried "by example," that is, an image is given as the query and the system's task is to find other images "like" the query. What it means for one image to be "like" another depends on the representations and the method of comparing representations to determine relevance – that is, on the viewpoint. By using several viewpoints, we increase the likelihood that the elements of the query that the user is interested in will be among those considered in choosing results. Our approach is analogous to the work of Belkin et al. [1] and Shaw and Fox [4], and others in text retrieval.

3. Image Channels and Merging

Conventional single channel CBIR systems represent a collection of images by descriptive vectors in a high-dimensional feature space with features such as color, shape, and texture drawn from analysis of the images. We extend this by creating several additional representations of the images (both the query, and those in the collection, and using some or all of these in our multiple channel approach to retrieval. Each single channel uses the same feature extraction techniques and search strategy (we use an existing CBIR technology, treating it as a black box) and the results of all the

128

Figure 1. First 40 results of Basic CBIR approach.

Figure 2. First 10 results of all four channels.

Figure 3. First 40 results of merging grayscale (B+ and B-) channels.

channels are combined to create the multiple channel result.

Whenever more than one search is used together, we must have some way to combine the results sensibly. Merging results can be very difficult, if heterogeneous searches are in use; in our case, since we are using the same CBIR technology for all channels, ranking and similarity measures for the results are comparable. In the results of our experiments in multiple-channel CBIR, we have used a simple similarity-based merge of the top k results of each channel to create a merged result.

However, in presenting the results to a user in an interactive image search, we may choose to present the top k results of each search, in parallel (see Figure 2).

4. Multiple Channels Applied

Our retrieval example employs a basic CBIR technology, using three color and four texture features, which we treat as a black box. The image collection is 3400 images drawn from 34 categories of the COREL image collection. Our ground truth is based on a labeling of salient foreground and background objects in these images, as described in [3]. We use four channels, the original images, their negatives, their grayscale images, and the negative of the grayscale images; each of these, searched using the basic CBIR technology, constitutes a different viewpoint on the collection.

Here we give a single (but characteristic) example of how multiple channels can improve on single-channel searching. The query image is a rose, and we will call the result images relevant if they contain roses. Figure 1 shows the query image and the first forty results given by the single-channel approach. (Since our query image is drawn from the image collection, the first result of the basic IR system is always the query itself.) Figure 2 shows, instead, the first ten results of each of the four channels, in parallel. The line labeled C+ is the results from the original representation, C- those from the negative channel, B+ those from the grayscale channel, and B- from the negative grayscale channel.

The single-channel approach finds only one rose (other than the query) in its first forty results, and this is at rank 25. A user looking at the first ten or twenty results of the conventional CBIR approach (Figure 1) might be convinced there are no roses in the image collection at all.

This is due to a mismatch in expectations between the user and the system. The user is trying to communicate that the information need is for roses, but the CBIR technology emphasizes the color, and other elements, rather than those the user intends (a different CBIR technology might emphasize different characteristics, but would be subject to the same mismatching). This is the equivalent of a vocabulary mismatch in text-based information retrieval.

The four channel result, shown in Figure 2, shows the user the first ten results of interpreting the query according to four different viewpoints on the same collection. Here there are three roses, two of which are found by both grayscale (B+) and negative grayscale (B-), one of which is the first result in each of those cases.

In presenting the results to the user in parallel, the system gives the user some idea of how the query image is related to the results in the four viewpoints. Thus, a user could observe that the chosen query image effectively communicates characteristics of the information need (roses) in the grayscale cases, but is not so effective in communicating distinguishing characteristics in the color cases. Also, in cases where there is some overlap between the results of different viewpoints this manner of presenting the results allows the user to see how an image may be judged more relevant under one viewpoint than another.

Suppose that the system also gives the user the option of choosing from which viewpoints to see results. Using only the results from the two grayscale channels produces seven roses in the top 40 images of the merged grayscale channels, B+ and B-, as shown in Figure 3.

Alternatively, the system could keep the multiple channels transparent to the user and instead of the four channel display, provide only a single merged result. The top 40 merged results across all four channels for the query above includes all three roses found in the four-channel top-ten. We have investigated this approach thoroughly in [3] and found that we can improve retrieval effectiveness by 22% on average using the merged output.

The choice between making the viewpoints explicit or simply giving the user their merged result depends on an image retrieval system's intended use. If users are most interested in efficient single-step searching, then the merged result is more appropriate; however if the user is willing to spend more time and thought on choosing which viewpoint(s) to use, then showing results of different viewpoints explicitly may be useful. Further, making the viewpoints explicit is appropriate for a class of users who will work extensively with the system, and are aided by knowing what is available and how to take advantages of the different interpretations of a query available through the channels

Another way in which a user may take advantage of information about the viewpoints in use is to choose a new query based on observations of the relation between the query image and the results in each viewpoint. A user observing how results from the color channels seem related more by broad areas of color than by details of texture might decide that the white rose is not an effective query to the color channel viewpoints because so many other kinds of images have a profusion of white around a dark center; however, few landscapes or wild animals exhibit an abundance of bright pink, so a pink rose may be a better query for the color channels. Choosing a new query may also be done automatically and sent to all channels. Such feedback approaches can enhance search effectiveness.

5. Conclusions

We have described a simple strategy for improving the effectiveness of CBIR systems by simply indexing several transformations of the underlying data. The cost per channel is simply another index and is, therefore, modest. The approach lends itself to a variety of interface approaches from multi-channel browsing interfaces to more efficient merged output streams.

6. Acknowledgement

This work sponsored in part by NASA grant NAG5-12025 and by the National Science Foundation. The opinions expressed here are those of the authors, not the sponsors.

7. References

[1] Belkin, N., Kantor, P., Cool, C. and Quatrain, R. Combining Evidence for Information Retrieval in *Proceedings of Trec-2* (March 1994), 35-44.

[2] French, J. C., Chapin, A. C., Martin, W. N., Multiple Viewpoints as an Approach to Digital Library Interfaces. *Workshop on Document Search Interface Design and Intelligent Access in Large-scale Collections*, July 2002.

[3] French, J. C., Watson, J.V.S., Jin, X and Martin, W. N. Using Multiple Image Representations to Improve the Quality of Content-Based Image Retrieval. Technical Report CS-2003-10, Dept. of Computer Science, Univ. of Virginia, March, 2003.

[4] Shaw, J. and Fox, E. Combination of Multiple Searches in *Proceedings of TREC-3* (April 1995) 105-108.

[5] Yoshitaka, A., and Ichikawa, T. A Survey on Content-Based Retrieval for Multimedia Databases, *IEEE Transactions on Knowledge and Data Engineering*, 11(1), 81-93.

Session 5: Minute Madness: Poster/Demo Short Presentations

Session 6A: Knowledge and Representation

Session Chair: Dagobert Soergel, University of Maryland

Convergence of Knowledge Management and E-Learning: the GetSmart Experience

Byron Marshall, Yiwen Zhang,
Hsinchun Chen, Ann Lally
*Department of Management
Information Systems.
The University of Arizona*
byronm@eller.arizona.edu

Rao Shen, Edward Fox
*Department of Computer
Science
Virginia Polytechnic and State
University*
rshen@vt.edu

Lillian N. Cassel
*Department of Computing
Sciences
Villanova University*
Lillian.cassel@villanova.edu

Abstract

The National Science Digital Library (NSDL), launched in December 2002, is emerging as a center of innovation in digital libraries as applied to education. As a part of this extensive project, the GetSmart system was created to apply knowledge management techniques in a learning environment. The design of the system is based on an analysis of learning theory and the information search process. Its key notion is the integration of search tools and curriculum support with concept mapping. More than 100 students at the University of Arizona and Virginia Tech used the system in the fall of 2002. A database of more than one thousand student-prepared concept maps has been collected with more than forty thousand relationships expressed in semantic, graphical, node-link representations. Preliminary analysis of the collected data is revealing interesting knowledge representation patterns.

1. Introduction

The National Science Foundation (NSF) through the National Science Digital Library (NSDL -- www.nsdl.org) intends to create a place where students and educators will find exceptional science education resources. Exemplary resources and services have been and continue to be developed and interconnected to meet this goal. The NSDL is built on a solid base of digital library technology research. While accessing quality resources and employing good technology are important, a learning tool should be also be crafted to support knowledge construction.

According to one definition, "digital library" is not merely equivalent to a digitized collection with information management tools, but also involves a series of activities that brings together collections, services, and people in support of the full life cycle of creation, dissemination, use, and preservation of data, information, and knowledge [20]. GetSmart was developed as an integration of knowledge management (KM) and digital library techniques shaped by constructivist learning theory.

2. Literature review

In this section, we present a few learning models which describe a learner-centered information search process and identify concept mapping as a helpful learning technique. Several types of E-Learning tools are characterized in light of that information search process. We finish with a review of knowledge management ideas which are applicable to the learning process as implemented in the GetSmart system.

2.1. Learning theory

Several learning models were considered as GetSmart was designed and developed. In contrast with logical positivism, which emphasizes observed truths and quantitative data, the constructivist model of learning centers on the learner's knowledge construction. Based on the constructivist model of learning, concept mapping has been identified as an effective learning tool. The GetSmart system encourages meaningful learning by supporting the information search process based on a constructivist outlook.

Ausubel created a learning theory model and evaluated the elements of the teaching-learning environment [1]. He used the term "meaningful learning" and provided significant theoretical support for constructivism. Rote learning is contrasted with meaningful learning and reception learning is contrasted with autonomous discovery learning. In rote learning, facts such as multiplication tables are presented to the learner in a final form and internalized. In autonomous learning, information must be discovered before it can be meaningfully incorporated into the student's cognitive structure. Ausubel outlined and analyzed various learning factors. His work pointed to the need for new approaches to learning. Many of these ideas are embodied in the constructivist model which emphasizes three main ideas [6]. Firstly, there is no single "correct" representation of knowledge. Secondly, people learn through active exploration when exploration uncovers inconsistency between experience and current understanding. Finally, learning occurs within a social context.

The constructivist model has been used to support concept mapping as a learning technique and is used to describe a six-stage information search process. Novak and Gowin synthesized key ideas from Ausubel's work and applied them to concept maps [17]. Having learners construct concept maps moves away from a fact-focused teaching event towards a meaningful learning experience focused on the relationships between knowledge elements as understood by the learner. Novak points out that concept mapping supports meaningful learning, which is different from the rote learning found in most school situations. Kuhlthau applies a constructivist approach to information-age learning environments, identifying six stages in the information search process: initiation, selection, exploration, formulation, collection and presentation [14,13].

2.2. E-Learning tools

In this section we review three types of e-learning tools: curriculum tools, digital library tools and knowledge representation tools. Recalling Kuhlthau's six-stage information search process, we could generally say that each type of tool emphasizes different parts of the process. Curriculum tools provide a systematic and standard environment to support classroom learning; their functions are particularly helpful in the initiation and selection stages. Digital library tools facilitate effective and efficient access to resources to support exploration and collection while knowledge representation tools focus on formulation and representation.

2.2.1. Curriculum tools. Curriculum tools are widely used in high school and college education. Materials are selected and organized to facilitate class activities. Additional tools, such as discussion forums and online quizzes, are integrated to support collaboration and evaluation. A typical commercial curriculum tool includes 3 integrated parts: instructional tools, administration tools, and student tools. Instructional tools include curriculum design and online quizzes with automated grading. Administration tools include file management,

authentication, and authorization. Student tool functions include:

- Browsing class material: readings, assignments, projects, other resources
- Collaboration and sharing: asynchronous and synchronous bulletin boards and discussion forums
- Learning progress scheduling and tracking: assignment reminders and submission, personal calendars, and activity logs
- Self-testing and evaluation: tests designed by instructors to evaluate student performance

WebCT and Blackboard are the most popular commercial curriculum tools. A review comparing these two tools suggests that BlackBoard's flexible content management and group work support [2] make it more suitable for independent and collaborative learning. WebCT's tighter structure and fully embedded support tools make it more appropriate for guided, less independent learning. In general, these tools are tailored more to support class activities than independent research or self-study.

2.2.2. Digital library. While curriculum tools support class functions, digital library tools focus on locating resources. These functions support the exploration and collection phases of information search. Digital library tools help users find the right information amidst a huge amount of digital material. Digital library features usually include search, browsing, and discovering special collections or exhibits. Search and browsing are used to locate resources and explore related topics. Special collections or exhibits contain organized materials representing a unique treasure for interested users.

The NSDL is a digital library of exemplary resource collections and services, organized in support of science education at all levels. Starting with a partnership of NSDL-funded projects, NSDL is emerging as a center of innovation in digital libraries as applied to education, and a community center for groups focused on digital-library-enabled science education. The NSDL includes more than one hundred projects, each with a different focus. Project activities include exemplary collection creation, service development, and core integration. NSDL collections cover a wide range of topics including astronomy, biology, economics, mathematics, and technology. In December 2002 the NSDL core-integration team connected many of these collections in a combined search interface.

In addition to the NSDL, other digital library research continues to address learner needs. For example, the University of Michigan Digital Library (UMDL) project is a learner-oriented initiative. One recent UMDL study recognized that even well-intentioned, kid-oriented search engines have difficulties related to learning support because they: (1) return too many hits; (2) provide no place to store results; and (3) provide no thesaurus [21]. Many well-designed digital libraries address these issues. One example is CITIDEL (www.citidel.org) which records user search activity.

2.2.3. Knowledge representation – concept maps.
Another type of learning tool helps learners visually review, capture, or develop knowledge. Curriculum tools rely primarily on a text-based, syllabus approach to describing course content. This approach often fails to delineate the relationship of concepts and skills covered in one course to those covered in another. It also fails to show the knowledge base that a learner will have acquired at the end of his/her course of study. A visualization tool can engage both learners and instructors in an active learning process when they construct spatial-semantic displays of the knowledge, concepts, and skills that the learner possesses and acquires [19]. Concept mapping is one such knowledge visualization tool. Concept maps represent concepts and relationships as node-link diagrams.

Concept maps and other forms of spatial-semantic displays have "evolved as an alternative to traditional linear presentations of information, and as the basis of effective learning strategies" [5]. Chmielewski and Dansereau found that training participants in knowledge mapping helps those people process text even when a mapping strategy is not explicitly used. Literature evaluating the usefulness of spatial-semantic displays shows them to be effective in cooperative interactions, as study aids, as substitutes for traditional text, and for updating and editing knowledge.

CMap and WebMap are two popular concept-mapping tools which have been documented in a number of publications. CMap was developed by the IHMC (Institute of Human and Machine Cognition) at the University of West Florida. Users can share concept maps through the Internet using CMap's synchronous communication component [11]. IHMC researchers also combine CMap with case-based reasoning to support knowledge access, reuse, and capture [3]. WebMap was developed at the Knowledge Science Institute at the University of Calgary [9]. Gaines & Shaw proposed that concept maps be regarded as basic components of any hypermedia system, complementing text and images with formal and semi-formal active diagrams. They have investigated a number of concept mapping applications including education, artificial intelligence, active documents, hypermedia indexing and concurrent engineering [10].

Vocabulary overlap and link naming impact the construction and use of concept maps to represent knowledge. Research suggests that different people choose the same word to represent the same object less than twenty percent of the time [8]. Some concept mapping research uses closed lists of concepts [16]. Most of the current concept mapping tools allow users to choose their own concept and link names [18]. However, the benefit of using a closed link system, in which users select from a list of link names, has been discussed in the literature on knowledge representation, learning evaluation, and critical thinking [12, 15]. There is a growing consensus among researchers that links should be named, modifiable, directional, and represented by canonical sets.

2.3. The knowledge management process

In some ways, educational systems are like knowledge management (KM) systems; both involve the creation of useful knowledge from information or data found in available resources. Knowledge management is a "system and managerial approach to collecting, processing and organizing enterprise-specific knowledge assets" [4]. Accenture views knowledge management functions as a six-step process: (1) acquire, (2) create, (3) synthesize, (4) share, (5) use to achieve organizational goals, and (6) establish an environment conducive to knowledge sharing. Ernst and Young promotes a 4-phase KM approach: (1) knowledge generation, (2) knowledge representation, (3) knowledge codification, and (4) knowledge application. Not surprisingly, there are some similarities between Kuhlthau's information search process and these KM models.

Both top-down and bottom-up approaches are used in KM systems. For example, search engines are often characterized as either directories or indexes. Directory-based portals such as Yahoo are developed top-down by people who manually categorize information into a pre-defined structure. A user navigates the structure to identify relevant resources. In contrast, indexed-based portals like Google fetch and index the words found in documents on the web. This bottom-up approach tends to let the documents speak for themselves.

3. The GetSmart system

The GetSmart system was built based on a model of how communities and individuals create and share knowledge. Several design goals were identified and a system was developed; digital library tools are integrated with concept mapping and classroom support tools to produce an environment where students can construct representations of the knowledge they acquire. From a KM perspective, GetSmart is a system for the generation, codification and representation of knowledge or, in Accenture's nomenclature, a system to acquire, create, synthesize, and share knowledge. The system design includes both top-down and bottom–up elements.

3.1. Knowledge development in GetSmart

GetSmart is organized to help individuals, groups, and communities develop knowledge. Curriculum tools provide a context for individual and group learning. As users construct concept maps they explore available information and then synthesize selected ideas into personal knowledge representations. This implements the "learn by exploring" constructivist idea. When group maps are created, several users collaborate, clarifying concepts and relationships and fitting them together. The search and curriculum functions access repositories of community knowledge. These repositories tend to be more formal and to use established vocabulary. The search tools help knowledge travel as information to the user/learners. As information is transferred to the individual it becomes enriched, expanded, and synthesized into new or unique contexts. These processes are viewed as information flowing from experts and repositories to individuals and groups. When a body of maps has been created, the information flow could be reversed. Map searching and merging tools would help capture and share individual knowledge representations in a community context. Much of the future work envisioned for GetSmart would support this process. This two-way flow embodies the top-down / bottom–up character of the knowledge management process.

3.2. Architecture and System Description

In this section, we present the architectural design of GetSmart discussing the major components and technical issues. GetSmart was designed to meet several goals:
- Educational Goals
  - support effective learning strategies
  - ease system deployment and training
  - support student evaluation
- Digital Library Design Goals
  - provide content from a flexible platform
  - integrate search and map drawing
  - support access to external resources
  - support generation of new knowledge from external resources

3.2.1. Platform requirements. The GetSmart system is browser-based so that learners can access it from a typical university computer lab. JSP and Java Servlet technologies are used in the middleware and run on a web server. Messages are passed between client and server in an XML format to enhance modularity and support future interfaces for concept map sharing. Much of the program logic for message parsing and authentication is written into stored procedures in the database. GetSmart uses Microsoft SQL Server 8.0. The map drawing tool is a java applet developed using Java 1.4.

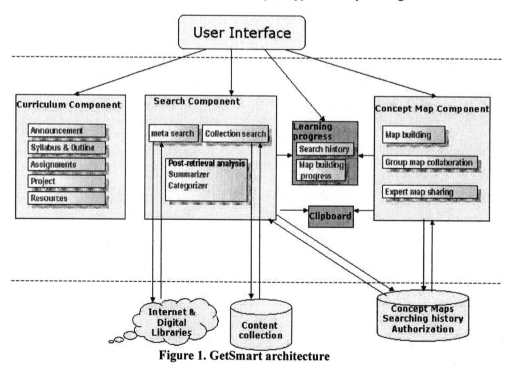

Figure 1. GetSmart architecture

138

3.2.2 Major components. The GetSmart user interface consists of four major components (1) curriculum, (2) search, (3) concept map, and (4) learning progress. These components are represented in Figure 1. The concept map data, user authorizations, and search histories are stored in a database. Another database contains the course resources collection index. Figure 2 shows the user interface. The navigation bar at the top of the interface allows users to switch among the system components -- "Class Info", "Concept Maps", "Search", and "Learning Progress". In addition a row of index-tab buttons highlight available functions for the main window.

The Curriculum Component: A curriculum component provides access to official class information including announcements, the syllabus, a course outline, assignment information, project information, and class resources. These categories are similar to categories used in WebCT and BlackBoard.

The Search Component: The searching component is based on a metasearch framework and supports queries and post-retrieval analysis. Metasearch modules handle query requests and results for several existing search portals.

The first searchable resource listed is labeled "Class Resources". An index was built in advance including instructor-selected material. The selected resources were fetched and indexed. A metasearch module for this collection works with GetSmart's metasearch interface allowing a single search to select results from both the instructor-identified, highly-relevant sources and from outside sources.

Metasearch modules have been created to access a short list of other search engines and digital libraries. Users can select the search engines they want to use for each of their queries. Currently, Altavista, eBizPort, CITIDEL and ACM Digital Library have been implemented as targets for metasearch. Altavista was selected as a general search engine to provide GetSmart a global searching scope. ebizPort is a business and IT information portal. Two digital library portals related to the fall courses were selected. CITIDEL is a part of the NSDL and aims to serve the computing education community. CITIDEL accesses more than one hundred thousand unique resources from member collections. The ACM Digital Library references documents published by the ACM, including journals, conference proceedings, and forums. These resources are not hosted by the GetSmart system; instead, GetSmart accesses the individual search interfaces of the selected portals and compiles the results.

Users can select the resources they want to access and choose the number of results to be listed on each result page. Figure 3 presents several screen shots of query and analysis results. Query results are displayed in a results

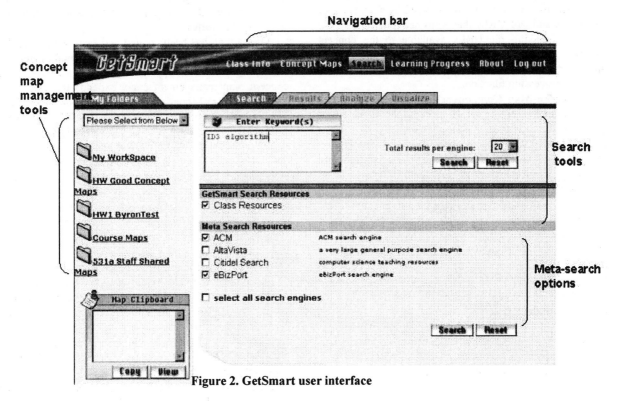

Figure 2. GetSmart user interface

139

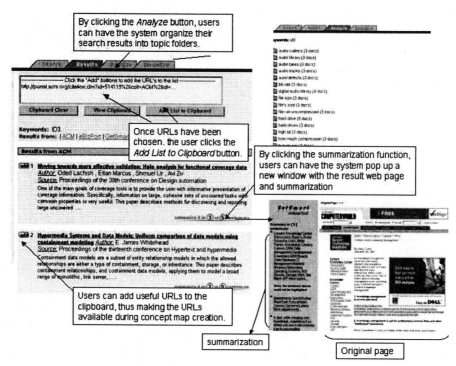

Figure 3. Results page with analysis functions

page with controls to initiate post-retrieval analysis functions. The query results are grouped by source. Users can select and add URLs they consider important to the clipboard, making the URLs available to the concept mapping applet. Each returned page can be summarized and a set of results can be categorized using the post-retrieval processing functions.

The Concept Map Component: The concept mapping component consists of a set of concept map management functions and a concept map building applet.

The concept map management panel is displayed on the left hand side of the interface. Concept maps are organized into folders; users can create different folders to organize the concept maps. Expert and group concept maps are authorized by the system administrator, are displayed in the same folder structure, and are identified with special icons. Three types of concept map operations can be performed using the commands in the pull-down menu.

(1) folder operations: create, delete, and rename a folder
(2) map operations: create, delete, and rename a map
(3) advanced map operations:

- "Turn in a map" submits maps to the instructor.
- "Print a map" requests generation of a web page showing a map image, and a listing of nodes, links and attached resources.

- "Import/export a map" allows XML representations of a concept map to be imported or exported.

After a map has been created and assigned to a folder using the management tools, it is updated using the concept map building applet. Clicking on a folder in the concept map management panel expands the display to list the titles of concept maps stored in the folder. Clicking on the title of a concept map activates a new Java applet window like the one shown in Figure 4.

The applet has three windows. The bigger window on the right is the main window used for graphical manipulation of the concept map elements. Small icons on the nodes indicate resources have been associated with the node. These resources include URLs, notes, or other maps. Users can click pull-down menu options to "Save", "Print", or "Turn In" a map. The procedure for adding links and nodes to a map is depicted in Figure 5. It also shows how resources can be associated with nodes.

The upper left window is the map resource window. It displays all the concept map elements hierarchically. The lower left window is the clipboard window. The map clipboard allows users to paste notes from other sources for inclusion in the concept map. The client side security restrictions may require the use of this feature if direct copy and paste is restricted for applets.

When several users are authorized to update a concept map, additional functions are needed. All authorized users

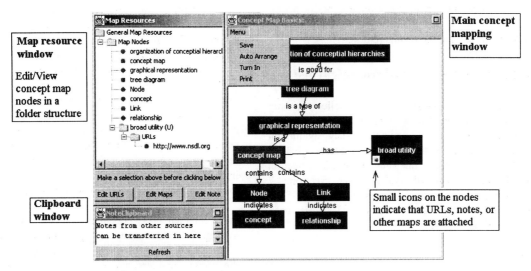

Figure 4. Concept map building applet

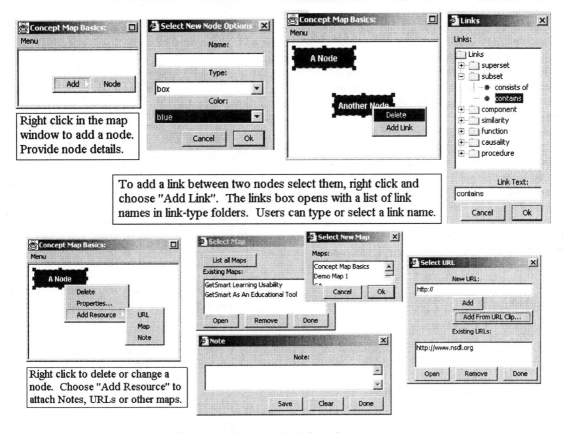

Figure 5. Node and link functions

can view a map at any time. Users with ownership authority for a map can lock the map for update, but only one user can lock the map at any given time.

The Learning Progress Component: The learning progress component allows users to review their concept map and search history. Users can view mapping activity such as the last action performed, when a map was turned

141

in, the number of maps created, and the number of nodes, links, and resources. Search history shows the last 10 searches performed and the results returned.

4. Preliminary results and lessons learned

Although a rich data set has been collected, only preliminary evaluation of the data has been accomplished. Some usage statistics are available. Early evaluation suggests interesting possibilities for a study of how different students represent the same information. Section 4.1 briefly describes overall system usage. Section 4.2 reviews experiences using GetSmart at the U of A. Section 4.3 documents a study done at Virginia Tech using the GetSmart system.

4.1. System usage

The GetSmart system was used at the University of Arizona and at Virginia Tech in graduate-level courses in the fall of 2002. Dr. Edward Fox taught "Information Storage and Retrieval" (CS5604) at Virginia Tech with 60 students creating and accessing concept maps. Dr. Hsinchun Chen taught "Data Structures and Algorithms" (MIS531A) to 54 management information students at the University of Arizona. Students at both universities prepared a series of concept maps. The MIS531A students each created 3 sets of maps as homework assignments and worked in groups to map the main points of their group presentations. The CS5604 students, singly and in groups, created concept maps of the material in each chapter covered in the course. These maps were presented and reviewed during class meetings.

When homework assignments were due the system was accessed twenty four hours a day by students as they completed their assignments. Table 1 lists some overall usage statistics.

Table 1. Overall usage: MIS531A and CS5604

114	Student Users
4,000 +	User Sessions
1,400 +	Homework and Presentation Maps
600 +	Searches Performed
50 +	Group Maps
40,000 +	Relationships Mapped

4.2. U of A concept mapping experiences

Students were assigned to create concept maps covering material presented over several weeks of classes. Maps were scored for "coverage", "correctness", and "creative connections". Approximately 15 key concepts were identified for each assignment. Each map was checked for

the inclusion of those concepts. Students were encouraged to specify relationships specifically. The number of unique link names was used as a proxy for correctness. The maps were reviewed for inclusion of cross-links between hierarchical sections of each map, and for the number of attached resources. Only a moderate level of accomplishment was required to achieve an "A" grade, for example, any recognized expression of approximately three quarters of the concepts was given full credit. Students were given remediation for any difficulties they encountered including extra time and/or compensatory credit if they experienced any difficulties with the system.

Five groups of students in MIS531A created shared maps for their class presentations. We found that on the average 2, and as many as 5, of the 6 students in each group saved changes to each group map. Almost all of the group members opened each of the maps multiple times.

All 54 students in Arizona completed all three of the homework mapping assignments even though they accounted for a total of only five percent of the final class grade. It seems that the system was reasonably usable and the group maps were prepared with some collaboration. Table 2 shows selected map characteristics for the three U of A homework assignments (HW1, HW2, and HW3). While the experiences depicted in Table 2 represent light analysis rather than experimental results, the figures suggest that, over time, students created more complex maps and added information to the maps in less time.

Table 2. MIS531A homework map characteristics

	Maps	Nodes Per Map	Edges Per Map	Elements Per Minute
HW1	2.9	16.9	18.6	0.35
HW2	5.4	22.3	23.8	0.51
HW3	5.2	27.0	27.9	0.75

4.2.1. Map characteristics. A preliminary analysis of the characteristics of the concept maps created is leading to some interesting observations on how users represent their knowledge.

Visual elements: Color and arrangement of nodes in student maps demonstrated a variety of representational schemes. Most of the users used 3-5 colors in each map. Some students used color to indicate the clusters of concepts while others used it to highlight hierarchical relationships. Closely related concepts were usually drawn close to each other. More general concepts tended to be in upper or central sections of the map, while more specific concepts were usually found in the lower or peripheral positions.

Concept vocabulary: For key concepts in one set of maps, we found that sixty percent of the students used the same word or phrase to represent the same concept. This calculation was made after allowing for spelling variances, abbreviations, and compound names. For example, a time complexity of O(n2) was represented 13 different ways and the concept "bubble sort" was found in maps with an abbreviation (bs), several formats (like "bubblesort", "bubble sorting" and "bubble algorithm"), and 4 different misspellings. On the average each concept was represented by eight different words or phrases. This is a much higher level of vocabulary overlap than was found in [8]. However, the maps charted a focused topic, and the material was taken from lecture notes.

Link names: Link names are one important way concept map creators express their knowledge of conceptual relationships. The GetSmart interface suggests a set of categorized link names but the user can override them and enter any words they choose. Our users chose the system provided names less than one-third of the time. A preliminary set of heuristics was used to group the student-entered names into semantically-similar categories based on cue words or phrases in the link names. Some preliminary work has been done to categorize these links further into a short list of abstract link types. Examples of these link types include hierarchical, componential, comparative and procedural.

Our initial analysis of the links in the map collection found the following patterns:

(1) 39,000 analyzed links contained more than 5,300 distinct link names. These links could be clustered into 120 semantically similar categories.

(2) More than half of the links indicate hierarchical or componential relationships although the link-type distribution varies between topics. For example, a higher percentage of hierarchical and componential links were used in topics covered in class lectures based on well-defined concepts. A higher percentage of other link types was found in maps covering material learned by reading course materials or maps generated from open-ended material.

4.3. Results from Virginia Tech

This section reports on a study of GetSmart use at Virginia Tech. In January 2003 we began running GetSmart servers at Virginia Tech for two sections of our spring class "Multimedia, Hyertext, and Information Access" (CS4624), but earlier, in 2002 all use of GetSmart was hosted at the University of Arizona.

4.3.1. GetSmart use and study design.
In the graduate class "Information Storage and Retrieval" (CS5604) in the fall of 2002, each student prepared a number of concept maps. Some were to help with documenting their group term projects, but most were related to the textbook

"Modern Information Retrieval". Each student completed a concept map, using GetSmart from home, for each chapter assigned. Instead of listening to a lecture on each of these chapters, students spent a full period discussing and presenting group-produced concept maps. To make this logistically feasible, the class met in two sections, each with about 30 students. Each section had two meetings per week, one in a classroom with an overhead projector and screen, and one in a computer lab where any student display could be shared across the room. This allowed comparison of concept maps drawn by hand using color pens and transparencies, versus maps created in the lab using GetSmart.

When students met to discuss a textbook chapter, each had previously prepared and submitted for grading their individual map. This ensured that they stayed on schedule and kept current with the reading schedule. Then, in class, they joined with 3-5 others to discuss their maps and to prepare a group map. During the first half of the course all of the group maps covered the entire chapter. During the second half of the semester, the chapter was divided into 3-4 parts, and two groups focused on each of the parts, so that a more detailed map could be constructed.

Each group presented its map to the class as a whole to receive comments and suggestions from classmates and the instructor. This helped the group members identify misconceptions and reinforce understanding.

Another class requirement was for each student, sometime during the semester, to pass (with a score of 80% or higher) an automatically graded online quiz on each chapter in the textbook. If their first attempt was unsuccessful, they were encouraged to study more, and then to take a second version of the quiz. Since mastery was the objective, a third attempt was allowed. More than 90% of the students preferred to prepare a concept map using GetSmart before taking a quiz. The average number of times that students took to pass a quiz in fall 2002 was 1.25. In the same class a year earlier, before GetSmart was developed, the average number of times that students took to pass a quiz was 1.55. That is, without the GetSmart assignments, students took more quizzes to master a chapter.

4.3.2. Analysis.
Our first analysis was a survey, at mid-term. The original data file (www.csc.villanova.edu /~cassel/vtsurveyresults/midtermoriginal.data) is available online. Most of the students thought GetSmart was well designed and helpful, though there were complaints about access to and use of GetSmart (which had its first test in August 2002).

Our second analysis was a comparison of quiz grades, contrasting students in the fall 2002 with those who took the same course in fall 2001. Results are summarized in Figure 6. Our hypothesis, that the mean quiz score in fall

2002 is significantly greater than that in fall 2001, is accepted (using a t test with α=0.25).

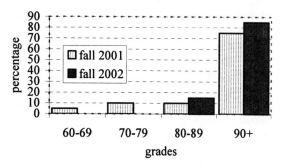

Figure 6. Quiz grades in course CS5604

Our third analysis compared the group maps created by GetSmart with the ones created manually. We found that maps created with GetSmart contain more cross-links. Since cross-links may reflect deeper thought regarding relationships among key concepts, we found this result encouraging. We think GetSmart enables much easier production and modification of concept maps while the pen and transparency approach required more time and effort when drawing and revising maps.

Our fourth analysis concerned concept maps created to support term project work. Project group members shared a folder in GetSmart, which allowed collaboration. To facilitate the project evaluation, students were required to present project maps in the final project demo. Study of the students' project maps suggests that some groups that performed better in collaborative concept mapping produced some remarkably good concept maps and were highly successful in their term projects.

Our fifth analysis compared concept maps developed for project documentation with those developed to aid learning about the chapters. We found that the latter shared more common characteristics regarding structure, while the former had different types of hierarchical structures. Some project maps documented the division of responsibility among group members. Some highlighted the succession of tasks carried out over the course of the project. Further, more URLs and notes were attached to the concept nodes in project maps than to those in chapter maps.

Our final analysis dealt with characteristics of maps related to the textbook chapters. We compared maps created by individuals with maps created by groups (see Table 3). We also compared maps created early in the semester regarding the whole chapter, with maps created later in the semester regarding only a part of the chapter. Our hypothesis that the average number of nodes and links in a group map are significantly greater than those in an individual map is accepted by statistical analysis (t

test with α=0.01). We also noted some qualitative differences, suggesting that maps improved over the course of the semester. Early in the term, key concepts in the introduction and in most of the section titles of a chapter appeared in almost every student's map. Later in the term, students expressed concepts more in their own terms, apparently thinking more deeply about ideas and relationships.

Table 3. Concept map characteristics

	Nodes per Map	Links per Map
Individual	22-23	23-24
Group	29-30	31-32

5. Discussion

Most of the features of the CMap, WebMap, and GetSmart mapping tools are comparable. GetSmart has some features which distinguish it from the others: a familiar right-click interface to access many of its functions, integrated search tools, a browser-based architecture, and a folder-view listing of each node's properties. CMap uses undirected links; GetSmart uses one-directional links; and WebMap allows single-directional and bi-directional links. WebMap implements a scripting function to support the transfer of information from WebMap concept maps to KRS, a knowledge representation system. GetSmart uses an XML format for import, export, and internal communication. CMap and GetSmart export maps as images. Unlike the others, CMap has an embedded synchronous chat function. GetSmart allows several users to share a map while WebMap allows users to make alternative versions of other users' maps. WebMap records a node type for each node, e.g., "Report", "Picture", "Movie", and "Document." The visual representation (color, font, and shape) of each node is controlled by user-editable node type definitions. GetSmart and CMap allow users to change the color of the individual nodes and associate resources with those nodes. GetSmart supports notes, maps, and URLs as resources; CMap allows maps, URLs, images, movies, sounds, and text resources. In WebMap each resource is represented by its own node. Overall, the CMap interface is more mature than the GetSmart interface, but the GetSmart system implements features which are promising as part of an integrated learning environment.

The initial implementation of the GetSmart system meets many of our educational design goals. Our first goal was to support effective learning strategies. Effective learning strategies are supported by the integration of curriculum tools, search tools, and concept mapping.

Combining concept mapping and search technologies is intended to leverage the cognitive benefits of concept mapping in a digital library context. The curriculum component supports the initiation and selection stages of the information search process. The search functions support exploration and collection of information, and the concept mapping tool aims to help students formulate and present the information.

Our second goal was to ease system deployment and training. Because GetSmart is browser-based no specialized software is needed on a client machine. Messages passed in XML over HTTP connections allow for the development of additional interfaces to the backend processes.

The vocabulary and link analysis we are undertaking might lead to automated map scoring techniques that will help the system meet our third goal of supporting student evaluation.

Our digital library design goals also have been largely addressed. The modular, web-based implementation is reasonably flexible. The system ties together searching and mapping functions; however, the search tool was not extensively used (4,000 user sessions with only 600 searches run). Perhaps this is because class activities emphasized map drawing. User input suggests that students are familiar with their favorite search tool and did not see a need to use our search interface. The extensible metasearch framework nicely supports our goal to support access to external resources.

Our last goal was to support the generation of new knowledge from external resources. The GetSmart system supports information flow from outside sources to users in the provision of expert concept maps and in the connection to various search portals. The concept mapping interface can facilitate a precise and compact representation of acquired knowledge. We expect that analysis of the student-created maps will lead to procedures and algorithms for the evaluation, merging, and searching of information captured in concept maps.

Well designed digital libraries, with special services tailored to support teaching and learning, especially supporting visual learning, may help students to clarify their thinking, and to process, organize, and prioritize new information. Experience in MIS531a and a study of the use of GetSmart in the CS5604 course showed that concept maps may be of benefit in both individual and collaborative settings.

6. Future directions

Based on our success, we have extended GetSmart to make it XTM compliant as well as OAI-PMH compliant. We have also developed a standalone version. We hope to make GetSmart more portable by configuring it into an ODL [7] component.

The data collected includes at least 10 individual topic areas. Fifty or more students mapped each topic. This data should provide interesting insights into how students choose to represent acquired knowledge in concept maps. Vocabulary overlap will be analyzed and compared between groups of maps to help in the development of map merging algorithms. Several link alternatives will be explored including closed lists of links, hybrid interfaces where the user can specify a name but must also specify a type, and algorithmic categorization of the link names entered by students. Algorithms to compare maps to expert maps will be proposed to help in the scoring of maps and as a way of developing our knowledge development model.

7. Acknowledgements

We would like to thank the NSF for supporting this project. NSF National STEM Education Digital Library: "Intelligent Collection Services for and about Educators and Students: Logging, Spidering, Analysis and Visualization" Award No. DUE-0121741, Program 7444. September, 2001-August 2003. We also would like to thank the GetSmart team and the other members of the Artificial Intelligence Lab at the University of Arizona who developed modules used in this system, especially Benjamin Smith, Chun Q. Yin, and Steven Trush.

8. References

[1] D. P. Ausubel, Educational Psychology: A cognitive view. New York: Rinehart and Winston, 1968.

[2] S. Bayne and J. Cook, "WebCT vs BlackBoard? An Evaluation of Two Virtual Learning Environments", http://www.ltss.bris.ac.uk/interact21/in21p04.htm,

[3] A. J. Canas, D. B. Leake, and D. C. Wilson, "Managing, Mapping and Manipulating Conceptual Knowledge: Exploring the Synergies of Knowledge Management & Case-Based Reasoning," presented at AAAI Workshop on Exploring Synergies of Knowledge Management and Case-based Reasoning, Menlo Park, CA, 1999.

[4] H. Chen, "Knowledge Management Systems: A Text Mining Approach", http://ai.bpa.arizona.edu/go/download/chenKMSi.pdf, 2001

[5] T. L. Chmielewski and D. F. Dansereau, "Enhancing the recall of text: Knowledge mapping training promotes implicit transfer," Journal of Educational Psychology, vol. 90, pp. 407-413, 1998.

[6] B. Dalgarno, "Interpretations of constructivism and consequences for computer assisted learning," British Journal of Educational Technology, vol. 32, pp. 183-94, 2001.

[7] Edward A. Fox, Hussein Suleman, Ming Luo: Building Digital Libraries Made Easy: Toward Open Digital Libraries. ICADL 2002: 14-24

[8] G. W. Furnas, T. K. Landauer, L. M. Gomez, and S. T. Dumais, "The Vocabulary Problem in Human-System Communication," Communications of the ACM, vol. 30, pp. 964-971, 1987.

[9] B. R. Gaines, "Class Library Implementation of an Open Architecture Knowledge Support System," International Journal of Human-Computer Studies, vol. 41, pp. 59-107, 1995.

[10] B. R. Gaines and M. L. G. Shaw, "Concept Maps as Hypermedia Components," International Journal of Human-Computer Studies, vol. 43, pp. 323-361, 1995.

[11] S. Hamilton, "Thinking Outside the Box at the IHMC," IEEE Computer Magazine, vol 34, pp. 61-71, 2001.

[12] H. E. Herl and et. al., "Reliability and validity of a computer-based knowledge mapping system to measure content understanding," Computers in Human Behavior, 1999.

[13] C. Kuhlthau, "Inside the Search Process: Information Seeking from the User's Perspective," Journal of the American Society for Information Science, vol. 42, pp. 361-371, 1991.

[14] C. Kuhlthau, "Learning in Digital Libraries: An Information Search Process Approach," Library Trends, vol. 45, pp. 708, 17p, 1997.

[15] J. G. Lambiotte, D. F. Dansereau, D. R. Cross, and S. B. Reynolds, "Multi-relational semantic maps," Educational Psychology Review, vol. 1, pp. 331-367, 1989.

[16] J. R. McClure, B. Sonak, and H. K. Suen, "Concept Map Assessment of Classroom Learning: Reliability, Validity and Logistical Practicality," Journal of Research in Science Teaching, vol. 36, pp. 475-492, 1999.

[17] J. Novak and D. B. Gowin, Learning How To Learn. Cambridge, UK: Cambridge University Press, 1984.

[18] J. M. Oughton and W. M. Reed, "The influence of learner differences on the construction of hypermedia concepts: a case study," Computers in Human Behavior, vol. 15, pp. 11-15, 1999.

[19] A. Saad and A.-R. M. Zaghloul, "A Knowledge Visualization Tool for Teaching and Learning Computer Engineering Knowledge, Concepts, and Skills," presented at 32nd ASEE/IEEE Frontiers in Education Conference, Boston, MA, 2002.

[20] N. Seamans and G. McMillan, "Digital Library Definition for DLI2", scholar.lib.vt.edu/DLI12/defineDL.html June 5, 1998

[21] E. Soloway, C. Norris, P. Blumfield, B. Fishman, J. Krajcik, and R. Marx, "K-12 and the Internet," Communications of the ACM, vol. 43, pp. 19-23, 2000.

Acquisition, Representation, Query and Analysis of Spatial Data: A Demonstration 3D Digital Library

Jeremy Rowe
Partnership for Research in Spatial Modeling/Information Technology
Arizona State University
Tempe, Arizona 85287-0101
480-965-8622
jeremy.rowe@asu.edu

Anshuman Razdan
Partnership for Research in Spatial Modeling
Arizona State University
Tempe, Arizona 85287-5906
480-965-5368
razdan@asu.edu

Arleyn Simon
Associate Professor Research
Department of Anthropology
Arizona State University
Tempe, Arizona 85287-2402
480-965-6957
arleyn.simon@asu.edu

Abstract

The increasing power of techniques to model complex geometry and extract meaning from 3D information create complex data that must be described, stored, and displayed to be useful to researchers. Responding to the limitations of two-dimensional (2D) data representations perceived by discipline scientists, the Partnership for Research in Spatial Modeling (PRISM) project at Arizona State University (ASU) developed modeling and analytic tools that raise the level of abstraction and add semantic value to 3D data. The goals are to improve scientific communication, and to assist in generating new knowledge, particularly for natural objects whose asymmetry limit study using 2D representations. The tools simplify analysis of surface and volume using curvature and topology to help researchers understand and interact with 3D data. The tools produced automatically extract information about features and regions of interest to researchers, calculate quantifiable, replicable metric data, and generate metadata about the object being studied. To help researchers interact with the information, the project developed prototype interactive, sketch-based interfaces that permit researchers to remotely search, identify and interact with the detailed, highly accurate 3D models of the objects. The results support comparative analysis of contextual and spatial information, and extend research about asymmetric man-made and natural objects.

Categories and Subject Descriptors

H.3.7 Digital Libraries – Collections, Standards, Systems Issues

General Terms

Measurement, Documentation, Standardization.

Keywords

Digital Library, Geometric Modeling, Image Databases, Information Visualization, Physically Based Modeling, Scientific Visualization, Shape Recognition, WWW Applications.

1. Introduction

The increasing power of computing, techniques to model complex geometry and compare to identify similarities has created powerful new capabilities to analyze and interact with data representing three-dimensional (3D) objects. The techniques to model and extract meaning from 3D information create complex data that must be described, stored, and displayed to be useful to researchers. Responding to the limitations of two-dimensional (2D) data representations perceived by affiliated discipline scientists, the Partnership for Research in Spatial Modeling (PRISM) project at Arizona State University (ASU) developed modeling and analytic tools that raise the level of abstraction and add semantic value to 3D data. The goals have been to improve scientific communication, and to assist in generating new knowledge, particularly for natural objects whose asymmetry limit study using 2D representations. The project sought to develop techniques to model and derive metric measures that permit research and analysis beyond that possible by merely viewing dimensional representations of the objects such as QuickTime VR.

The tools developed by the project team simplify analysis of surface and volume using curvature and topology to help researchers understand and interact with 3D data. The tools produced automatically extract information about features and regions of interest to researchers, calculate quantifiable, replicable metric data, and generate metadata about the object being studied. To make this information useful to researchers, the project developed prototype interactive, sketch-based interfaces that permit researchers to remotely search, identify and interact with the detailed, highly accurate 3D models of the objects. The results support comparative analysis of contextual and spatial information, and extend research about asymmetric man-made and natural objects.

2. Background and Purpose

Digital libraries are in the midst of a rapid and significant evolution. In less than two decades, the scope and complexity of digital collections have blossomed from the CR-ROM and videodiscs of the first American Memory project to the myriad offerings available via the Internet.

Similarly, scientific tools have evolved dramatically from observation, two-dimensional measurements, and statistical computation to include complex three-dimensional models and visualizations even in traditionally low technology disciplines such as anthropology.

Digital libraries today offer text, graphics, images and increasingly video, sound, animation, and sophisticated visual displays. Some now display three-dimensional objects, and permit the user to rotate and view an image of the original object in their browser window using QuickTime, plug-ins, or custom applications. A few examples include:

- Forma Urbis Romae project at Stanford (PHP, MySQL and QSplat 3D viewer) [8]

- University of Texas Digimorph - CAT scan derived surface models of biological specimens displayed using QuickTime [4]

This paper presents an overview of the development and application of powerful tools for geometric visualization and analysis used to create a 3D Digital library to capture, analyze, query, and display three-dimensional data by the Partnership for Research in Stereo Modeling (PRISM), an interdisciplinary research team at Arizona State University. Components of the processes include:

1. Metadata Schema and Organizational Structure

2. 3D data Acquisition - Scanning

3. Feature Extraction

4. Region Identification

5. Query Interface

6. Evaluation

As objects become more complex in terms of variety of shape and changes in curvature, it becomes more difficult to quantify and analyze. By developing mathematical techniques to represent the shape and curvature, accurate models of the surface of 3D objects such as ceramic vessels, bones, or lithics can be created. Figure 1 shows an example of a polygonal mesh model of a ceramic vessel surface with base, body, and neck regions identified. Such surface models and sophisticated mathematical tools developed by the PRISM team provide the ability to analyze, identify, and compare the objects that they represent. The accuracy of the measurements derived from the 3D models created equal or exceed those possible using traditional 2D tools such as calipers and rulers. In addition, measurements such as height, width, maximum height or width, surface area, or volume can be easily, consistently and accurately calculated, even for asymmetric natural objects.

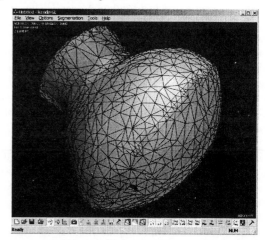

Figure 1. 3D model of Hohokam ceramic vessel.

Use of 3D data also makes possible new measures based on topology and global or local changes in curvature that define the shape of the original object. The project built an interdisciplinary team of discipline and computer scientists, and technologists to guide an interactive development processes. The discipline scientists initially posed research questions, and then the computer scientists developed tools and spatial modeling techniques to address them. Using mathematical models and surface and volume information, many new and powerful analytic tools become available to spatially analyze objects. For example, boundaries between surfaces can be objectively identified, small local areas of changes in curvature identified and compared, and accurate, replicable measurements calculated automatically. In addition, the focus on 3D geometric comparison of shape and curvature permits identification of similar objects without the need for alignment of within a reference grid for comparison.

Once meaning has been linked to the changes in topology, shape, or curvature by the domain scientists a "feature" is defined. The modeling process provides an objective method to calculate physical measurements, and to identify boundaries and local areas of interest to researchers by the changes that are associated with the feature. Figure 2 shows examples of transition points that are of interest to ceramic researchers, and that were the focus of interdisciplinary discussion to determine common vocabulary, and focus on common definitions for these shared terms - a significant effort in projects such as this as tools and processes begin to bridge disciplines.

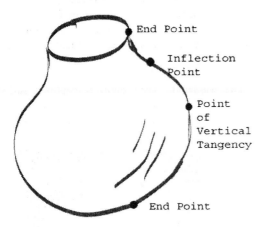

Figure 2. Components of interest for Ceramic Vessel.

Once identified, each feature can be described by its size, position, shape or curvature. Examples of features that can be extracted from the model data include the maximum diameter or height of a ceramic vessel.

Features can also be components of interest to the researcher that are mathematically abstract, such as the base or neck of a vessel, keel of a ship, boundaries of the joint surfaces on a bone or spindles that form in the nucleus of a cell during meiosis. Often the tools developed to identify features and regions also provide additional capabilities that raise new research questions within the disciplines. These tools needed become new design challenges for the computer scientists, fostering a new cycle of tool development. For example, ceramic analysts have found tools that identify mathematically defined features found on the vertical profile curve of a vessel such as end points, points of vertical tangency, inflection points and corner points as features extremely helpful in analyzing vessel shape and style.

In addition to the tangible research benefit the tools and techniques provide, a significant result of this process has been "cross-pollination" that has occurred as graduate students and faculty from different disciplines gravitate to

a given project and explore application of tools and techniques to other discipline research.

A summary of data acquisition and analysis processes begins with initial laser scanning to acquire the 3D data that represents the object. Mathematical modeling is then applied to identify features and regions of interest to the domain scientists. Software tools developed by the project team generate analytic data about the original object, automatically assign metadata about spatial characteristics, and populate the database.

A visual query process was developed to permit researchers to interact with the data using both contextual (text and numeric descriptive data) and spatial (shape and topological attribute) data. A sketch-based interface was developed that permits users to input both context and sketches to visually describe the object to initiate the search. Several text and spatial matching algorithms are used to identify and rank order objects within the database that math the search criteria.

Initial development of the digital collections focused on Classic Period (A. D. 1250 – 1450) prehistoric Hohokam ceramic vessels from central Arizona housed at the Archeological Research Institute at ASU. Additional development has involved bone shape and surface, lithic tools, brain structures and DNA structures in fertilized mouse egg cells. Research has extended to other disciplines with interest in spatial analysis including cloud formation, wind erosion, and facial recognition.

3. Methods

3.1 Metadata Schema and Organizational Structure

One of the greatest challenges in an interdisciplinary research effort is coordinating expectations among team members, and developing communication processes that bridge conceptual, strategic, and linguistic differences across the disciplines.

An iterative process was developed to share research questions, tools and intellectual approaches across disciplines at project meetings. The results were a gradual bonding of researchers, development of a shared vocabulary, and substantial interaction about potential research issues and approaches. These efforts provided a foundation for the initial modeling and analysis, and for developing the metadata structure needed to organize data for storage, analysis, and query.

A schema is an information class hierarchy that defines a shared vocabulary and a structure for documents described by that vocabulary. Use of a common schema for all project data regardless of location offers the potential to link and search across all of the databases that share the common schema. Dublin Core [5] and Council for Preservation of Archeological Records (COPAR) [3] metadata structures were used as foundations for schema development for this project. Extensible Markup Language (XML) tags were used to describe the contextual and spatial data elements, and for query and display of data.

A conceptual goal of the metadata component of the project was to develop an extensible schema structure that could accommodate adding new types of objects as the project continued to evolve. An object class was defined as the master class document type definition (DTD) for each item in the digital library database. For the 3DK digital library project, all of the additional descriptive data about each object was defined and organized as contextual or spatial classes.

Contextual types define text and metric information about the object. This context class includes subclasses for metadata associated with objects as they are acquired, processed, and archived such as type, item name, catalog number, collection, provenance, etc. At this phase of the project these fields were primarily determined by existing descriptive data elements, though efforts were made to design a schema structure that would accommodate adding new object types as necessary. To date, several iterations to refine the schema model to function effectively across object types have been completed.

Spatial data types define the 3D attributes of the object, including raw data, thumbnails, models, and calculated or derived data about the topology, shape, and composition of the object. Use of common descriptive components and geometric elements as new object types are added will permit shared use of the modeling and analysis tools across classes of objects. The project goal is to develop standards for description and organization that permit automated cataloging and population of data as objects are scanned and processed for entry into the database.

Due to familiarity and availability of resources, an SQL database was used to store the contextual and spatial data. Fields were assigned to each data element and large spatial data files were stored as hyperlinks. Generally accepted data formats such as binary, PLY, HTML, and XML have been used to make data accessible and simplify migration and access to the data over time.

3.2 Scanning and 3D Data Acquisition

Three-dimensional data about objects can be obtained from many sources. Laser scanners can capture surface data for 3D objects ranging in size from a few millimeters to large buildings and bridges. Figure 3 show the "trail" of the laser scanner across the surface of the vessel. Scanning laser microscopes create three-dimensional data by stacking or "sandwiching" thin two-dimensional slices of data.

CAT scanners and MRI also capture 2D images or "slices" of a 3D object. Each of these devices has the capacity to capture internal data about the objects in addition to the surface outline in each slice. The 2D image slices can be stacked to assemble a 3D volumetric model of the object. These techniques are used to create three-dimensional models of objects such as human bodies, artifacts, and manufactured objects. Improvements in the resolution, portability, and cost are making three-dimensional data capture devices and the data that they produce obtainable by many researchers.

The PRISM Digital Library project uses two Cyberware scanners, the M15 and 3030 to scan ceramic vessels, bones, and other objects up to roughly a 30" maximum dimension. The object is scanned by a laser, which captures spatial data (x, y, z) values for each point. The object is then rotated, and scanned again to capture additional data. This process is repeated until sufficient scans are obtained to combine to create a point cloud model to document the surface.

The Model 15 laser digitizer captures surface data points less than 300 microns (0.3mm) apart, producing high-density triangular meshes with an average resolution of over 1000 points per cm2.

Figure 3. Laser scanning surface of ceramic vessel.

Figure 4. Point cloud of ceramic vessel combined from multiple scans.

150

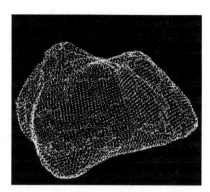

Figure 5. Point Cloud of scanned trapezium bone surface by Matt Tocheri.

The digitized data generated by the scanner is composed of thousands of (x, y, z) coordinates that describe a point cloud that represents the surface of the object scanned. Further analysis requires generating a surface model from the point cloud.

The simplest method to generate a surface that approximates the original smooth continuous object from the thousands of points collected during scanning is to join adjacent data points to form a triangle mesh. Figure 5 shows a point cloud assembled from several scans of a trapezium. The triangle mesh models the object surface, describing the 3D object with both geometry and topology [9], [1]. The geometry describes how the various points are distributed in space while the topology describes the relationships between the points as they are connected in space to form the surface.

It is possible to take several snap shots around the object and "stitch" them together to create a displayable object using techniques such as QuickTime (QTVR). However, the QTVR representation is only a collection of 2D images, which can be presented to emulate a 3D view, and permit user controlled zoom or rotation of the display. Though the image appears to be 3D, there are significant differences between the QTVR display and an actual 3D representation of the object. The geometry and topology conveyed in a true 3D representation offer the capacity to derive measurements such as volume, surface area, diameters, height, or distances between points.

Modeling techniques are needed to create an actual measurable surface that represents the original object. In addition to the triangle meshes, PRISM software can represent these surfaces as Non-Uniform Rational B-spline (NURB) or subdivision surfaces [2], [21], [6], [7]. NURB representation provides the capability to assess curvature distribution in complex objects such as identification of the joint surfaces from scanned data of a bone.

The accurate model of the object that results from this process provides the data and conceptual framework needed for objective, replicable analysis of surface and volume attributes of the objects under study.

3.3 Feature Extraction

Once the geometric structure has been obtained, the next step is to identify features and regions of interest to the discipline researchers. Ceramicists look for shape, symmetry, and curvature, cellular biologists look for structure of bio-molecular machines inside a cell, forensic anthropologists look at shape, and surface comparisons. A number of 3D modeling and analytic algorithms have been combined, and new techniques developed to segment the geometric structure into regions, and to identify meaningful features.

PRISM researchers developed a watershed-based hybrid feature extraction and segmentation scheme to work with the triangular meshes [12], [20]. The algorithm automatically segments the surface into regions of similarity based on curvature. The areas identified can then be merged with adjacent similar regions, or split into smaller meaningful segments based on threshold values that have been defined by researchers. The nontrivial challenge has been to translate these aspects important to the discipline scientists into mathematically definable terms. For example, the transition between a vessel neck and body can be described mathematically as an inflection point, and the maximum width of a vessel by diameter.

Interaction within the project team has resulted in crosswalks of definitions that help translate terms and permit mapping mathematical concepts onto features meaningful to the discipline scientists. The use of 3D data permits accurate identification of maximum and minimum measurements and calculation of complex metric and descriptive data that are extremely difficult to obtain using 2D representations, linear measurements, and traditional measuring tools, particularly for naturally asymmetric or man made objects such as ceramics.

3.4 Region Identification

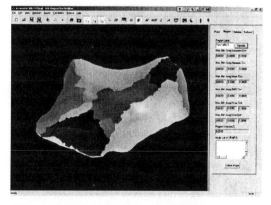

Figure 6. Region editor applied to trapezium data model by Matthew Tocheri.

The second program developed is Region Editor that calculates more complex information about the object and its component features such as total object volume, absolute object symmetry, the area of surfaces identified, and the average angle at which surfaces intersect. Several of these measures are extremely difficult to determine accurately using traditional techniques, particularly for asymmetrical objects.

Figure 6 shows the region-editing program applied to the surface model of the trapezium. The Region Editor also permits researchers to add contextual information such as technical data about the scan, image processing that has been used, provenance, or collection to the 3D data. The final action of the Region Editor is to create the metadata or XML file associated with the 3D data for archiving.

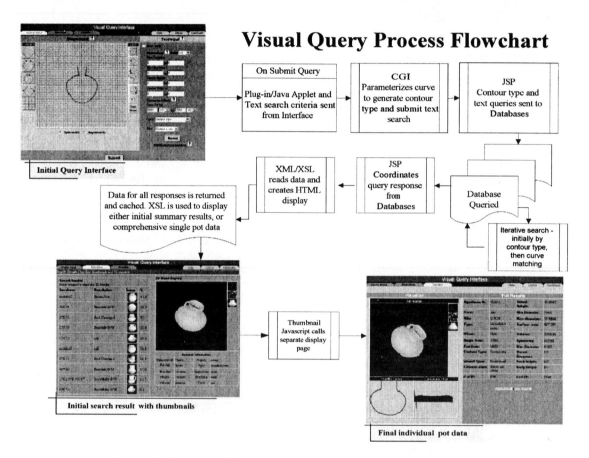

Figure 7. Diagram of Visual Query Interface and Search Process.

3.5 Interface

From the perspective of interface, a primary design problem was how to accept input for both contextual and spatial searches. An interdisciplinary "visual query interface" team guided research into interface design, identification of desired capabilities, development of the interface, and ongoing revision based on evaluation data. Figure 7 shows the schematic of the PRISM interface and its underlying processes.

The PRISM team chose to design separate contextual and spatial input areas in the interface screen. Textual data

was input or selected from pull down menus to query existing descriptive catalogs or databases. Search criteria include metadata such as name, type or number of the item, collection, or other catalog information about the object. This input area also permits the user to limit search by provenance by limiting the search to a specific collection, or by measurements such as height, width, or maximum or minimum diameter.

The most interesting interface design challenge was accommodating the input to query spatial data and to identify matching 3D shapes [25], [17], [22]. To mirror the 2D profiles of the ceramic vessels familiar to anthropologists, the initial interface model used an interactive vessel profile to define the spatial search component. A gridded area presents a sample of a profile curve selected from the menu, or permits the researcher to draw a profile to be searched. Using the mouse and tool palette, the user can interactively create or manipulate the shape until it represents the desired vessel.

Initially developed as a Netscape plug-in, the sketch interface has been converted into a Java applet to support multiple browsers and platforms. Figure 8 shows the initial interface input screen. After descriptive information about context and shape has been entered, the query is submitted. The descriptive and spatial information are separated and the multiple database queries are coordinated by project software. The contextual component of the query is handled as a conventional text and numeric database search. The spatial search uses a variety of size, shape, and curve matching algorithms developed by the project team to identify and locate similarities within the databases.

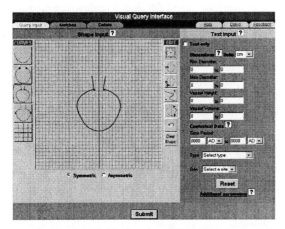

Figure 8. Prototype profile-based visual query interface for searching ceramic vessels.

During search and analysis of potential matches, intelligent filtering techniques are used limit the search pool. Initially simple text, metric, or gross spatial classification criteria are used to identify possible matches from the database and reduce the search domain. As the search progresses, increasingly more complex algorithms are applied t o the shrinking pool of potential matches. The goal is to minimize computational load and search time while accurately identifying all objects that match the search criteria.

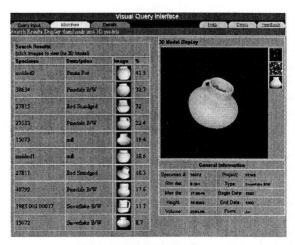

Figure 9. Interface screen with ranked search results.

Another algorithm ranks the query results by descriptive and spatial similarity to the query image. Query response information is presented sequentially over several screens, each providing an additional level of information about the selected objects. Figure 9 shows the first result screen, which displays thumbnail images and brief descriptions of the top search results. Also presented is a large 3D display of the top search result, along with more detailed descriptive and calculated information. The 3D model can be displayed as a point cloud, wire frame, or full shaded surface representation at the discretion of the researcher. Using the mouse, the model can be rotated and viewed from any angle. Selecting a thumbnail of another search result from the cue of search results will replace its model in the 3D display window.

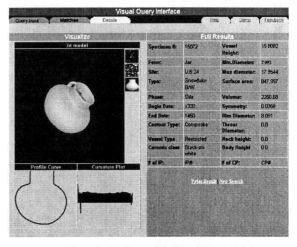

Figure 10. Interface screen with expanded search results.

If more detailed descriptive information is desired, a third window that displays the 3D model, and two additional analytic tools - a profile curve and curvature plot, and additional descriptive data about the object (see Figure 10). A fourth window can be selected to provide access to the complete descriptive and calculated data available.

Significant effort has been given to adapting the interface design to accommodate the differences in contextual data and analytic tools between different classes of objects. The object type metadata can be used to select the customized search template with fields for the contextual and spatial data appropriate for the object.

The visual query interface team developed training materials to guide new users and evaluation instruments to obtain formative guidance from users.

3.6 Evaluation

Several techniques were used to evaluate and guide the development of the project. In addition to general meetings and team building activities, process mapping and interviews of project team members provided qualitative and quantitative input to help build communication among researchers in the team. This iterative process has extended throughout the project.

Initial evaluation input regarding interface components and design were obtained from the roughly 25 project team members. The current version of the interface was used and assessed by the entire group at general and visual query interface team meetings throughout its development. The designs were critiqued, limitations identified, additional capabilities desired described, development challenges identified, and component work delegated to project teams.

Several evaluation sessions were held to obtain input from a representative sample of potential users, including faculty and student researchers in anthropology and ceramics research. After initial orientation, research problems were posed to the evaluation groups, and users used the interface to locate individual target objects by context, shape or size. Users were encouraged to explore the 150 ceramic vessels in the test database and comment on the clarity, scope, and ease of use of the interface. A revision cycle followed each evaluation. Follow up evaluation sessions with larger samples are currently being planned.

4. Findings

The spatial and volume modeling and analytic tools developed by the project team permit discipline researchers to quantify and accurately replicate measurements of complex 3D objects. The feature and region recognition capabilities assist in visualizing complex, abstract concepts of interests to discipline researchers.

The iterative design process and team interaction evolved and worked well, particularly as the project scope and development focused in the second year of the project. The regular interdisciplinary interaction among the faculty and students was essential in developing comprehensive metadata schema, and provided positive, constant pressure to extend the project design requirements.

The challenges involved in developing the conceptual models to extend textual and metric contextual data and develop metadata for surface modeling were significant, but were exceeded by those that arose as volume data was addressed. As the tools and techniques developed for volume data became available, several new capabilities became available to extend analysis of surface models. The growth of capabilities that resulted from this iterative process would have been virtually impossible in traditional research that focused on a single discipline.

The conceptual model developed to describe data using object class with subordinate context and spatial characteristics worked well to guide development of both analytic tools, and the query interface. The ability for users to simultaneously query by context and shape was essential, and provided significant challenges for both computer scientists and interface designers. Initial development of the sketch-based 2D profile model for the spatial query laid the foundation for the even more complex development of the full 3D input modeling for query input that is currently underway.

The capabilities and standards of virtually every technological component of the project were in flux during the course of the project. A few examples include:

- Portable scanners evolved considerably in terms of accuracy, rivaling the larger fixed scanners by the midpoint of the project.

- Metadata and XML capabilities and standards were evolving dramatically. Schema development tools and strategies became more powerful.

- Initial SQL search capabilities began to be augmented by SOAP and XML search capabilities.

- The reliability of distributed servers, databases, and networked access tools has evolved significantly since the start of the project.

- Java development permitted replacement of Netscape plug-ins to simplify configuration and ease cross platform access, and evolution of Java 3D has provided significant new opportunities for development of a full 3D query interface.

5. Discussion

One of the pleasant surprises during this project has been the ease of extending the modeling and analytic tools developed for one specific discipline to other research domains and the interactive growth of the tools for surface and volume modeling and analysis. The improvements that have resulted from the iterative process of identifying a domain research question, developing an application tool, deployment, analysis of potential applications across other research domains, and identification of new research questions has generated significant process in developing modeling and analytic tools applicable to 3D data.

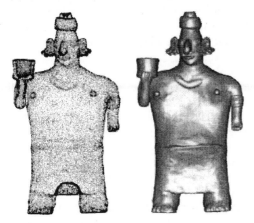

Figure 11. Views of a Mesoamerican figurine. Point cloud data at left, fitted surface at right by David Van Alfen. Artifact from ASU Anthropology collections (87-1686).

As 3D data acquisition tools become more affordable and readily available, the amount of 3D data that must be described, stored and displayed will grow dramatically. Accommodating this huge data management challenge will require development of standards and tools to begin to analyze and add meaning to the data.

The tools have begun to have an impact on the disciplines associated with the project. The archaeological analysis of Hohokam and Salado ceramic vessels has focused on morphology and typology. Analysis traditionally used 2D representations and visual analysis to manually classify and compare objects. The ability to quantitatively represent the vessels and to capture the asymmetry that has been lost in the 2D profile curves traditionally used to represent each vessel in catalogs has significantly expanded the ability to identify and compare vessels within the collection. Figure 11 shows an example of a model of a complex ceramic artifact.

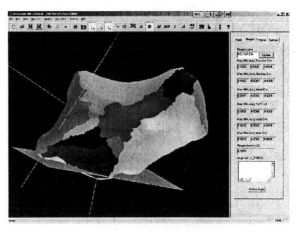

Figure 12. Plane indicating angle of joint surface of trapezium data.

Figure 12 shows an example of an analytic tool applied to the trapezium to show regions of curvature, and planes representing joint surfaces. Anthropologists have had an interest in comparisons of the angles of the joint surfaces to predict tool-handling ability, but have been limited by the lack of precision of tools previously available. The surfaces are highly irregular and the traditional tool has been a protractor, which has limited the precision of measurements made. The analytic tools developed by the PRISM team have permitted the paleoanthropologists associated with the project, Mary Marzke and Matt Tocheri, to accurately compare the joint angles of fossil hominids, such as Homo habilis and Australopithecus afarensis with modern humans, chimps, and gorillas.

Several efforts are underway by the PRISM team, or are planned to further extend the capabilities of the tools developed, and their application to domain research. In terms of infrastructure, the move from custom plug-ins to Java will simplify deployment.

The project team is exploring alternatives to the SQL database currently used, such as object-oriented databases. Another effort to improve searching is a pilot XML search protocol developed by the National Science Foundation Biological Databases and Informatics project at Arizona State University (BDI) research project in conjunction with the ASU Long Term Ecological Research (LTER) Metadata Committee and the Knowledge Network for Biocomplexity (KNB) Project at the National Center for Environmental Analysis and Synthesis (NCEAS). The "Xanthoria" metadata query system Developed by this project team uses SOAP (Simple Object Access Protocol) to send XML query requests and responses, and supports simultaneous web-based querying of distributed, structurally different metadata repositories.

The spatial analytic tools continue to develop as improvements are made in the feature extraction and region editing applications and more powerful techniques are developed compare curvature, identify matches and rank search results. Key to these efforts is the expanding partnerships with other research areas with their own unique modeling and visualization needs. Included to date are more complex anatomical data from CAT scanners and MRI, cloud formation pattern recognition, geological erosion, and identification of targets within complex, noisy environmental data.

Interface design continues to evolve. The project is evaluating models developed for 3D query and display by other projects including:

- Shape Retrieval and Analysis Group Search Engine for 3D models using Takeo Igarashi's Teddy 3D sketch interface at Princeton [18],

- National Center for Biotechnology Information (NCBI) Cn3D Genetic viewer [13],

- CAD searching tools such as the National Design

- Repository at Drexel [15], and CAD Geometric Search Engine at Sandia National Laboratories [26],

- Ogden Search Engine for Polygonal Models by Motofumi T. Suzuki at the National Institute of Multimedia Education, Japan [29].

Projects such as the 3D search engine at Princeton represents significant strides in identifying objects by shape from large collections on the web. The Princeton project uses a technique of statistically representing the 3D object and comparing these representations as a key to determine similarity [16], [17]. A spherical harmonics technique is used to map the 3D object within a series of concentric spheres, then to generate a series of histograms representing averaged object data within the sphere. These histograms are then compared to identify similar objects. They also store several 2 D projects of the3D object. Similar techniques have been used to query databases of solid models of manufactured parts in the SHAPE repository project at Drexel [15].

To permit rapid comparison of large numbers of objects during searching, the user can enter wither 2D sketches, or use Teddy to input a 3D shape to search. Rapid comparisons of the 2D data are less computationally intensive, and can be followed by comparison of the 3D data, and of textual information such as titles, to further refine the search.

These techniques permit rapid identification of generally similar shapes, such as a cigar and submarine, and support iterations to refine the search to locate specific objects within the data pool. Limitations of this approach include reliance on summarized data within the areas analyzed to create the histograms from the 2D or 3D

object representations. These techniques do not work well to recognize subtle variations that appear similar when summarized as a histogram, an tend to initially return relatively large numbers of responses only similar in gross shape, such as an airplane, man standing with arms spread, and a letter "t". When refining the search to reduce the number of matches the reliance on user supplied text titles with limited authority control over terms used or accuracy of cataloging often retains many unrelated objects.

Though these summarization techniques provide a powerful tool for identifying grossly similar shapes, they have difficulty accurately locating only relevant, closely related objects, or finding a specific individual object within a collection. Such processes also provide little support for subsequent interaction or analysis of the object once located.

The techniques developed by the PRISM team permit accurate comparison of the local morphology of discrete local details of features that comprise the object. Discipline scientists have defined the features of interest, and relevant measures of interest for research. The data pre-processing automatically extracts features and intelligently segments meaningful regions, such as the rim, base, neck, and body of ceramic vessels, from the 3D point cloud representation of the object. Relevant descriptive semantic and geometric information about the features and regions of interest are then identified, extracted, and calculated in an automated cataloging process that generates object metadata.

Techniques such as comparisons of b-spline curves and subdivision are used to compare relevant measures (such as surface area or curvature), relationships among features (such as angles between surfaces, rations of regions of interest), support shape matching during queries, and interaction with the data once identified (using tools such as standard metric measures, discriminate analysis, cluster analysis, etc.).

The development of a realistic 3D interface models that permit the researcher to sculpt the query in 3D space is progressing, as are additional analytic tools such as planar overlays to visualize and objectively compare joint surfaces of bones. Techniques to bookmark searches to permit replication and simplify comparison of objects within the databases are also being explored. A complex variation of bookmarks involves providing a replicable trail for researchers using the region editor and additional analytic tools such as the planar overlay to interact with the data and create their own interpretive models. Creating storage techniques for these derived, researcher defined or modeled data, and managing "version control" to permit replication and deconstruction of the analysis is another challenge.

User evaluation of the current interface layout, color palette and design continues using both surface and volume model data. In addition to initially developing specific bone or ceramic vessel interfaces for the different research domains, the project is working to identify commonalities and conventions to develop a unified interface model. This common design appears to be possible in initial query interface screens, with differentiation of interface display occurring as objects are identified, search results are returned, and researchers drill down into object data that may vary across disciplines.

In summary, the PRISM tools and techniques support acquisition, interpretation, and interaction with 3D data about objects at a level of documentation and measurement accuracy that permits represents an entirely new capability of 3D data query and analysis. The binary and derived data describing 3D artifacts offers an accurate, objective set of metrics and descriptors that can be immediately exchanged, re-analyzed, and submitted for comparative analysis within large databases. The system supports research for those without physical access to valuable artifacts, from remote locations, and for objects being repatriated, such as Native American funerary objects. As scanning and acquisition costs continue to fall, these techniques have the potential to augment and extend research capabilities for virtually any field utilizing 3D data.

6. Conclusions

Development of the current model 3D digital library has been an interesting exercise in interdisciplinary project development. Translation between disciplines has taken time and effort. Even when common vocabulary is used, the discipline specific definitions and nuances can vary significantly.

The spatial modeling tools developed to identify features and extract regions of interest have proven valuable additions to research in the partnering disciplines. The initial challenges have focused on data acquisition, and development and display of models.
Initial digital library efforts to display images of surface models using QuickTime and plug-ins have significantly expanded research and science education as complex natural objects become approachable through such visualization. Adding modeling and analytic tools based on surface and volume that permit objective quantification and analysis of 3D data has the potential to further extend research in virtually every discipline studying 3D objects.

As 3D data and the tools for visualization and analysis become more available, there is an increasing need for intuitive interfaces to provide gateways to the data. Researchers bring different strategies and approaches, and learning styles differ widely across potential users of 3D data. Visual literacy and the sophistication of users also vary dramatically among users.

Standards are needed for data description, storage, interchange, and searching. Understanding of this complex multidimensional data will be essential as records managers begin to interact with collections of 3D data, and as it begins to reach archives. Conventions for display and organizing research tools are essential to effective preservation and access.

Evaluation and continued research into learning styles, communication preferences, and visual communication and display are needed to guide interface design. Clearly, development of simple, elegant, easy to use interfaces to accommodate the range of tools and user preferences for spatial data and modeling will be a significant challenge now and in the future.

7. Acknowledgements

This work was supported in part by the National Science Foundation (grant IIS-9980166) and funding from the Vice Provost for Research and Economic Development at Arizona State University. The authors would like to thank all of the collaborators that make up the Partnership for Research in Spatial Modeling (PRISM) team, particularly Anshuman Razdan, Gerald Farin, Daniel Collins, Peter McCartney, Matthew Tocheri, Mary Zhu, Mark Henderson, Arleyn Simon, Mary Marzke, Myung Soo Bae, Matt Tocheri, David Van Alfen and David Capco. For more information on the 3D Knowledge project visit http://3dk.asu.edu.

8. References

[1] A. Amresh, G. Farin A. Razdan, Adaptive Subdivision Schemes for Triangular Meshes, will appear in "Hierarchical and Geometric Methods in Scientific Visualization", edited by G. Farin, H. Hagen, B. Hamann, Springer-Verlag, 2002 (in print).

[2] F. Bernadini, Mittleman, J., Rushmeier, H. Silva, C., Taubin, G. The Ball-Pivoting Algorithm for Surface Reconstruction, IEEE Transactions on Visualization and Computer Graphics, Vol. 5, No. 4, October/December 1999.

[3] Council for Preservation of Archeological Records (COPAR) http://copar.asu.edu/

[4] Digital Morphology project at the University of Texas http://www.digimorph.org/

[5] Dublin Core Metadata Initiative http://dublincore.org/documents/2000/07/11/dcmes-qualifiers/

[6] G. Farin "Curves and Surfaces for CAGD", 5th ed., Morgan-Kaufmann, 2001

[7] G. Farin: History of Curves and Surfaces in CAGD. In: Handbook of CAGD, G. Farin, M.S. Kim, J. Hoschek (eds), Elsevier, 2002.

[8] Forma Urbis Romae project at Stanford http://formaurbis.stanford.edu/docs/FURproject.html

[9] B. Hamann, B. Jean, A. Razdan. CAGD Techniques in the Control of Surface Grid Generation. In: Thompson, J.F., Weatherill, N.P., Soni, B.K. (eds.), Handbook of Grid Generation, CRC Press, Inc., Boca Raton, Fla. pp 29.1-26, 1997.

[10] Knowledge Network for Biocomplexity http://knb.ecoinformatics.org/

[11] Long Term Ecological Research project at Arizona State University http://caplter.asu.edu/

[12] A. Mangan and R. Whitaker. Partitioning 3D Surface Meshes Using Watershed Segmentation. IEEE Transactions on Visualization and Computer Graphics. Vol.5, No. 4, Oct-Dec 1999.

[13] National Center for Biotechnology Information (NCBI) Cn3D Genetic viewer http://www.ncbi.nlm.nih.gov/Structure/CN3D/cn3d.shtml

[14] National Center for Environmental Analysis and Synthesis http://cochise.asu.edu/bdi/Subjects/Xanthoria/index.htm

[15] National Design Repository, Drexel University http://edge.mcs.drexel.edu/repository/frameset.html

[16] R. Osada, T. Funkhouser, B. Chazelle, and David Dobkin, Shape Distributions, to appear in ACM Transactions on Graphics, 2001.

[17] R. Osada, T. Funkhouser, B. Chazelle, and D. Dobkin, Matching 3D Models with Shape Distributions, Shape Modeling International, Genova, Italy, May 2001.

[18] Princeton 3D Models Search Engine using Takeo Igarashi's Teddy 3D sketch interface – http://www.cs.princeton.edu/gfx/proj/shape

[19] Partnership for Research in Spatial Modeling at Arizona State University http://3DK.ASU.EDU

[20] A. Razdan and Myung Soo Bae, A Hybrid Approach to Feature Segmentation, in preparation.

[21] A. Razdan, B. Steinberg, G. Farin. From Digitized Data to NURB Surface Meshes Proceedings of the International Conference of Rapid Prototyping and Manufacturing, pp 749-754, Beijing, China,1998.

[22] A. Razdan, D. Liu, M. Bae, M. Zhu, G. Farin, A. Simon, M. Henderson. Using Geometric Modeling for Archiving and Searching 3D Archaeological Vessels. CISST 2001 June 25- 28, 2001, Las Vegas.

[23] J. Rowe, Developing a 3D Digital Library for Spatial Data: Issues Identified and Description of Prototype, RLG DigiNews October 2002, http://www.rlg.org/preserv/diginews/diginews6-5.html#feature1

[25] H. Sakurai and D. Gossard, Shape Feature Recognition from 3D Solid Models. In ASME Computers in Engineering, San Francisco, 1988.

[26] Sandia National Laboratories CAD Geometric Search Engine http://www.sandia.gov/isrc/Working_with_Us/Organization_Chart/IS_Principles/Geometric_Search_Engine/geometric_search_engine.html

[27] U. Schurmans, A. Razdan, A. Simon, P. McCartney, M. Marzke, D. Van Alfen, G. Jones, J. Rowe, G. Farin, D. Collins, M. Zhu, D. Liu, and M. Bae, "Advances in Geometric Modeling and Feature Extraction on Pots, Rocks and Bones for Representation and Query via the Internet," proceedings Computer Applications in Archaeology (CAA), 2001.

[28] A. Simon, D. Van Alfen, A. Razdan, G. Farin, M. Bae, and J. Rowe, "3D Modeling for Analysis and Archiving of Ceramic Vessel Morphology: A Case Study from the American Southwest," Proceedings of the 33rd International Symposium on Archaeometry. Geoarchaeological and Bioarchaeological Studies, Vrije Universiteit, Amsterdam, 2002.

[29] Suzuki, Motofumi T., National Institute of Multimedia Education, Japan, Ogden Search Engine for Polygonal Models http://www.nime.ac.jp/~motofumi/Ogden/

[30] Utrecht University 3D Shape Retrieval Engine http://www.cs.uu.nl/centers/give/imaging/3Drecog/3Dmatching.html

Leveraging a Common Representation for Personalized Search and Summarization in a Medical Digital Library

Kathleen R. McKeown   Noemie Elhadad   Vasileios Hatzivassiloglou

Department of Computer Science
Columbia University
New York, NY 10027, USA
E-mail: {kathy,noemie,vh}@cs.columbia.edu

Abstract

Despite the large amount of online medical literature, it can be difficult for clinicians to find relevant information at the point of patient care. In this paper, we present techniques to personalize the results of search, making use of the online patient record as a sophisticated, pre-existing user model. Our work in PERSIVAL, a medical digital library, includes methods for re-ranking the results of search to prioritize those that better match the patient record. It also generates summaries of the re-ranked results which highlight information that is relevant to the patient under the physician's care. We focus on the use of a common representation for the articles returned by search and the patient record which facilitates both the re-ranking and the summarization tasks. This common approach to both tasks has a strong positive effect on the ability to personalize information.

1. Introduction

The medical field publishes a high volume of research articles every year and many of these are now available online. While increased availability of online literature suggests that it should be easier to access information, in practice online searches often provide users with more information than needed, much of it irrelevant. This may be caused in part by the fact that often search queries contain only a few words [16]; users are notoriously tight-lipped when providing clues about what they are interested in. If information about the end user could be taken into account when searching and presenting results, a system would be able to better filter results to improve relevance. In this paper, we present methods to re-rank search engine results based on user-specific knowledge, highlighting information in which the user is more likely to be interested through

automated generation of a personalized summary of the re-ranked search results.

Our research on personalized search and summarization is part of PERSIVAL (PErsonalized Retrieval and Summarization over Images, Video and Language) [11], a medical digital library. For physicians, experienced or in training, PERSIVAL will provide access to literature that is clinically relevant to the patient under their care at the point of patient care. In this scenario, the patient record can provide information about articles that are likely to interest the healthcare specialist. This information includes the medical history, laboratory results, procedures performed and diagnoses, which can be used to pinpoint articles that can provide the physician with the latest results relevant to the patient under care. Similarly, the patient record can also be used to determine which information *inside* the articles is likely to be of interest and to highlight it as part of the summary of search results.

We use a unified approach to re-ranking of search results and personalized summarization, using the same representation and basic tools to determine relevance to a patient. We do this by constructing an *article profile* containing a set of terms and values extracted from the article describing the patient study population (e.g., "high blood pressure", "ejection fraction of 30%", "congestive heart failure"). We also construct a *patient profile* by extracting terms and associated values from the patient record. Article relevance is determined by "matching" the article profile against the patient profile, with higher rankings given to articles with a better match. Summary content is determined by matching article sentences against the patient profile, retaining sentences that match well as potential summary content.

Profiling and matching are the basic primitives from which re-ranking and personalized summarization are built. Re-ranking enriches this process using additional features associated with terms that can help determine when an article is a good fit. For example, we might expect that the

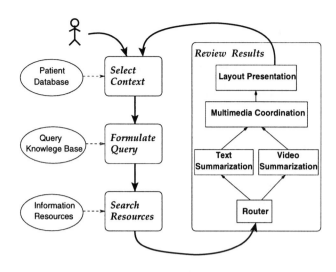

Figure 1. PERSIVAL system architecture with focus on the summarization modules.

semantic category of a term (e.g., *disease* vs. *body part*) would influence how important it is to the match as might the article section in which a term occurs (e.g., "Methods" vs. "Related Work").

Summarization further tailors the information presented to the user by identifying specialized pieces of information within the article, and keeping only those specialized pieces that match the patient's background and current status. User feasibility studies at the early stage of the project [12] indicate that physicians are interested in getting information primarily from technical articles such as clinical studies; further, the information should be tailored to the specific patient at the point of care, and presented in summary form whenever possible. These three desiderata have motivated our approach to personalized summarization. First, an automatic classifier of the relevant articles is needed to filter out articles that were not determined to be of interest (e.g., letters to the editor, case studies); we have built such a classifier for clinical studies, which represent a major portion of the technical articles published in medical journals. Second, the summarizer satisfies the other two user needs: Starting from clinical studies, it selects the sentences that report results using information extraction techniques, and matches them to the patient's profile to keep only the results relevant to that specific patient. However, even including just the results that matched would produce a lengthy and repetitive summary, since we are extracting facts from multiple relevant articles. Instead, we merge matching sentence pieces across articles, identifying repetitions and contradictions and grouping information in a coherent way.

This two-pronged approach of re-ranking results at the article level and then selecting and merging pieces of information across articles to satisfy specific information needs contrasts with current search practice, both in general search engines and in search mechanisms employed in the medical domain. Search engines will retrieve all relevant articles for a given query, and present them as entire documents to the user. In contrast, PERSIVAL utilizes re-ranking to prioritize documents that match the current patient, not just the query, and summarization to only display the most pertinent information.

In the following sections, we first overview the PERSIVAL architecture. We then turn to the themes of this work, personalization and the unified representation and approach to re-ranking and summarization. Following that, we discuss the three major components of the system: article classification, re-ranking, and summarization. We close by showing how the unified approach yields more personalized results than would either approach alone.

2. PERSIVAL: Personalized Access to Medical Literature

PERSIVAL is designed to provide personalized access to a distributed digital library of multimedia medical literature. It is an interdisciplinary project that involves researchers in computer science, electrical engineering, medical informatics and library and information science.

A key feature of PERSIVAL is the user's ability to ask questions and receive related literature within the context of patient information. PERSIVAL links to the large online patient record database available at the New York Presbyterian Hospital, which serves as part of the user model [1, 6]. As shown in Figure 1, interaction with PERSIVAL begins with access to a specific patient record. From the context of the patient record, the user may decide to access the online literature and pose a question. The Query Formulation module helps a user to formulate a good question related to the patient information within the context [13]. The query, along with related patient information, is then sent to the search engine, which allows access to distributed online textual resources [4] as well as a library of digital echocardiograms. The results of the text search are re-ranked by matching the articles returned against the patient record, scoring those articles which discuss results related to the patient's case as more relevant [17]. A textual summarizer [3] and a video summarizer [2] each generate a summary of the relevant results and a multimedia coordination component produces explicit links between the two. The resulting multimedia summary and search results are presented to the user by a sophisticated layout component [10].

160

Figure 2. The PERSIVAL user model, its dimensions and their possible values.

3. Personalization and a Scenario

Digital libraries often serve a wide spectrum of users, varying in level of expertise, interaction goals, and context of question. In the medical setting, users can range from naïve lay consumers, to educated non-specialists, to medical students in training to specialized clinicians.

The user model in PERSIVAL is designed to capture these differences in information need and access strategies between lay people and physicians. Based on our user population analysis done in accordance with the guidelines in [9], we represent three basic dimensions in the user model: (1) the domain expertise of the end user (physician versus layperson); (2) for input, the identity of the patient being treated (a patient of the physician, or the patient end user himself); (3) for output, the user's access task (browsing, searching, or getting a briefing). The attributes and their possible values in our implemented user model are shown in Figure 2. In practice, some dimensions are more salient than others depending on the type of user. When information is needed at the point of patient care, clinicians will prefer just one access task (get briefing), while lay people will tend to look for information for themselves (self).

In this paper, we limit ourselves to physicians and physicians in training (i.e., residents and interns) as end users. As domain experts, physicians are highly knowledgeable about their field of practice; they need access to the latest findings published in the medical literature to keep abreast of new developments in the field. Providing patient-specific information can have enormous benefits, particularly when supporting evidence-based practices [14]; physicians often search for clinical studies with a specific patient they are treating in mind. Thus, to provide relevant information, it is critical for PERSIVAL to take information from the patient record into account.

We use the online patient records at New York Presbyterian Hospital (NYPH) [1] to provide this aspect of the user model. Note that while the physician might be able to provide this information as part of an extended query (e.g., providing background of illness), it would considerably lengthen the time of interaction and if the system can take advantage of the fact that it is already available, there is no need for this additional user input. A patient record for any single patient consists of many individual reports,

Discharge Summary Note — 2000/03/18 15:00

ADMITTED: 02/04/2000

DISCHARGED: 03/16/2000

ATTENDING PHYSICIAN: ZZZZZ, ZZZZZ

NAME: XXXXX, XXXXX

MRN: 4444444

PRINCIPAL REHABILITATION DIAGNOSIS:
Coronary artery disease

ASSOCIATED DIAGNOSIS:
Coronary artery disease Status post myocardial infarction Status post coronary artery bypass grafting Hypertension Diabetes Peripheral vascular disease Sacral Decubitus Bilateral heel ulcers

HISTORY OF PRESENT ILLNESS:
This is a 44 year old female past medical history of coronary artery disease, status post myocardial infarction in 1983, status post CABG in 1989, diabetes for 11 years, hypertension, peripheral vascular disease. The patient was admitted to New York Presbyterian Hospital on 12/03/99 with a worsening CHF and for evaluation for heart transplant. The patient was not a candidate for a heart transplant secondary to peripheral vascular disease.
Her hospital course was complicated by atrial fibrillation requiring cardioversion on 01/03/00. Respiratory decompression following tracheostomy and tracheostomy was closed on 02/10/00. The patient also evaluated for change in mental status and diagnosed as a toxic metabolic encephalopathy with resolution.
The patient was transferred to 7 Hudson North on 01/22/00 followed by psychiatric evaluation for depression, treated with Celexa. The patient also developed acute renal failure requiring hemodialysis three times a week.
[...]

Figure 3. Part of the discharge summary for Patient A.

collected during a visit to the hospital. For some patients, this can be up to several hundred reports. While some of the reports are in tabular format, and thus similar to a database entry, many of the reports are textual (e.g., they may be the result of dictation) and thus require natural language processing in order to be useful for further processing.

As an example, consider the case of Patient A, an anonymized, true case drawn from the online clinical database. She comes to the hospital because of shortness of breath and chest pain. She already has a patient record online, and the discharge summary from the last visit in-

Table 1. Extract from the profile for Patient A.

Term	UMLS Concept ID	Semantic Type	Positive/Negative	Report
hemodynamics	C0019010	Organ or Tissue Function	+	Cath Lab
conduit	C0441247	Medical Device	+	Cath Lab
aorta	C0003483	Body Part or Organ Component	+	Cath Lab
artery	C0003842	Body Part or Organ Component	+	Cath Lab
peripheral vascular disease	C0085096	Disease or Syndrome	+	Cath Lab
diagnosis	C0011900	Diagnostic Procedure	+	Discharge
ischemic cardiomyopathy	C0349782	Disease or Syndrome	+	Discharge
diabetes	C0011847	Disease or Syndrome	+	Discharge
atrial fibrillation	C0004238	Finding	+	Discharge
cardioversion	C0013778	Therapeutic Procedure	+	Discharge

dicates to the examining physician that she has a history of coronary artery disease, diabetes, hypertension, smoking, and atrial fibrillation. Figure 3 shows an extract from the latest discharge summary; an additional 840 words are present in the full discharge summary. Patient A has a total of 125 reports in her record (110 lab and microbiology reports, 9 cardiology and radiology reports, and 6 admit/discharge summaries). Now, her left ventricular ejection fraction is 35%, which indicates that there is a chance of recurrent atrial fibrillation. Given these pieces of information, the physician wants to know what is the best treatment for recurrent atrial fibrillation. In the remainder of the paper, we will use Patient A and this physician question to show how personalization works.

4. Common Methods and Representations

PERSIVAL's user model is made accessible to all components and thus, personalization for re-ranking and summarization is based on identical information. In addition to the user model, re-ranking and summarization both use the same set of primitives for processing the patient record and the articles under consideration. Personalization is carried out by first producing the article and patient record profiles and then matching either the entire article (for re-ranking), or sentences within the article (for summarization) against the patient record.

A key element of our approach is to base relevance decisions on important medical terms rather than all words, as search engines typically do. Both the patient and article profiles consist of the set of all medical terms found in the documents. To build the profile, we use an efficient finite state grammar to extract terms (e.g., "left ventricular ejection fraction"), along with associated values (e.g., "low" or "35%"), that describe the patient study population. The grammar defines terms as noun phrases which are encoded as finite patterns over adjectives, quantifiers,

determiners, and nouns. Conjunction between terms is removed and the two separate terms are generated. Negation is also noted. We filter the non-medical terms by consulting a medical term database, the Unified Medical Language System (UMLS) [7]. UMLS assigns to each string an internal identifier (Concept Unique Identifier, or CUI). For each CUI, UMLS also returns a *semantic type*, an indicator of the broad semantic class where the concept belongs (e.g., disease, symptom, demographic, time, etc.). We remove all terms with semantic types associated with general concepts (e.g., time, persons, and hospital and administrative terms). Acronyms are expanded to the full medical term using a list of 2,011 acronyms in the cardiology domain collected from the Internet. Finally, values associated with terms are identified by a subpart of our finite state grammar which looks for three kinds of context: (a) linking verbs (*is, seems, appears, . . .*) in all types of tense and voice combinations; (b) *of*-constructions ("blood pressure of 90 mm Hg"); or (c) direct comparison operators (e.g., "blood pressure greater than 100 mm Hg").

The resulting profile is thus a list of terms with the associated CUI and semantic type for each term. Table 1 shows a portion of the profile that is constructed for Patient A from a catheterization laboratory report and the discharge summary. The UMLS links terms that refer to the same concept by assigning them the same CUI. For instance, "atrial fibrillation", "auricular fibrillation" and "A-Fib" all share CUI C0004238.

Determining relevance of an article or sentence to the patient record is based on a primitive match function. Matching takes two terms, each possibly with associated values, and matches the CUIs of the terms and their values. This means that two terms match if they are synonymous, whether or not they use exactly the same form. This primitive matching is then extended in various ways by re-ranking and summarization, as discussed below. For example, note that many of the terms shown in Table 1 would not be indicative of a match because they don't refer to disease or treatment (e.g., "diagnosis," or "conduit"). Further extensions deal in part with weighting to place more stress on the more important terms.

As an example, PERSIVAL finds many matching terms given the journal article "Patient Characteristics and Underlying Heart Disease as Predictors of Recurrent Atrial Fibrillation After Internal and External Cardioversion in Patients Treated with Oral Sotalol" from the *American Heart Journal*, which our physician informants indicated is a good article when treating Patient A. Terms such as "atrial fibrillation," "cardioversion," and "coronary artery disease" occur in both patient and article profiles, indicating the overlap in diseases and methods (cardioversion is a method used to treat atrial fibrillation).

We now turn to categorization, re-ranking and summarization, showing how they use the article and patient profiles and embed the basic match primitive in their operation. When possible, we use the scenario presented here to illustrate our approach.

5. Categorization

Our user studies revealed that clinical studies are of more importance to physicians than many other article types. During search, our distributed search component accesses different databases depending on whether the user is a lay person or a physician. In the case of a physician, the search is performed on technical article collections, which include medical research publications. However, there are several possible types of technical medical publications, ranging from the very general (clinical trials and review articles) to more specific (case reports) to miscellaneous publications (such as letters to the editors).

We implemented a categorizer which automatically detects the type of an article. From our local collection of 35,000 journal articles, we selected a subset of 7,000 cardiology articles from PubMed[1] for training and testing of our categorization system. We used 6,000 articles for training and 1,000 for testing. All the articles indexed in PubMed have meta-data tags available, among them the type of publication.[2] We used this field to automatically label each article. In the training data, 59% of the articles were clinical studies. We took advantage of the preprocessing of articles into an XML format where the different sections are identified, along with their titles, to provide the features used for

categorization. We use simple features such as the length of the document (number of words), the presence of an Abstract section, the presence of sections with title containing the words Methods or Results, as well as the presence of some key terms such as "trial" or "randomized". The categorization achieves 91.8% precision at 97.8% recall for the "Clinical study" category.

6. Re-ranking of Search Results

The re-ranking component receives as input a patient profile and a set of articles that need to be personalized to that patient. The patient profile consists of a set of attribute-value pairs, which are extracted from the various reports and tables in the patient record. The set of articles is typically the result of a distributed search over large collections of online articles. This search is performed with keywords that a physician or patient specifies. Although the particular choice of keywords is naturally influenced by the patient's current condition and prior medical background, the search procedure itself is not informed by the patient record or any other user model. As is the case with most search engines, the search component in PERSIVAL produces the same set of articles for a given query and collections to search; it is the task of the re-ranking module to take into account known information about the patient to produce a modified list of search results that varies from patient to patient for the same query. We have experimented with modifications that reorder the articles originally retrieved from the search so that articles that are more likely to apply to the patient under consideration are ranked near the top.

To achieve this reorganization of the search results, we take advantage of our common representation of medical information and tools for operating on this information (detection of terms, mapping of terms to concepts, semantic categorization of concepts, and primitive matching between concepts). The re-ranking module views the articles and the patient record as sets of attribute-value pairs, where the attributes are the medical terms after they have been disambiguated and mapped to concept identifiers (CUIs), as described in section 4. In addition to the semantic type that is provided by our term disambiguation module using information from the UMLS, the re-ranking module uses several additional features, also extracted during the processing of the articles and patient record when our common representation is constructed:

- *Negation* of terms, which can be explicitly signaled by words such as "no", "none", "without", etc. as in "patients without myocardial infarction were sampled ..." and "no atrial fibrillation was observed", or implicitly specified when the term occurs in an exclusion context, such as "we did not include patients who ...".

---

[1]PubMed is a search engine for medical publications provided by the National Library of Medicine. It is available at http://www.ncbi.nlm.nih.gov/PubMed/.

[2]Note that PERSIVAL uses a distributed search engine that is not limited to PubMed alone. Thus, the hand labeled categories in PubMed are not sufficient for direct use in PERSIVAL. However, they are helpful to build training data.

We have implemented a set of pattern-based rules that recognize the most common constructs that introduce negative context, and each recognized term is assigned either a positive or negative label. The intent of this feature is to prevent spurious matches where a term occurs in both the article and the patient record, but in a negative context in one and positive context in the other. This is exactly the situation that a typical search engine cannot recognize—it would return an article discussing women who *did not* have peripheral vascular disease or a prior heart attack for Patient A. Negation does not occur frequently (less than 0.5% of the cases we detect are negated), but changes meaning when it does.

- *Section information* provides clues as to the relative importance of terms in articles. Certain sections (e.g., Introduction) are more likely to provide general background information that may not apply to the patients in a clinical study, while sections such as Methods more often specify the characteristics of the population under study. We take advantage of the relatively rigid structure of journal papers in medicine to segment the articles into sections, and give priority to primitive matches involving terms in more privileged sections of each article.

- *Values* for recognized terms (such as "blood pressure over 100mm Hg") help to further assess the compatibility of terms that appear both in the patient record and an article. Certain demographic and medical attributes such as age, heart rate, or ejection fraction will appear in many articles in the cardiology domain; however, the fact that both the patient record and an article mention "age" should not influence our assessment of the match between them. It is the compatibility between the values associated with these attributes that determines whether they should contribute to the match in a positive or negative direction. We extract values using our finite-state grammar to recognize modification relationships, as illustrated in Section 4. Presently, our strategy for determining the compatibility of values is rather naïve: values are compatible if identical, partially compatible if they are numeric depending on how close they are, and incompatible otherwise. However, even this simple tactic offers a small improvement over not using the value information at all—solving the hard and interesting issues in comparing values (such as comparing a numeric value to a qualitative expression such as "high") remains a high-priority direction of our future research.

- *Inverse document frequency* (IDF) for each term (the negative of the logarithm of the ratio of the number of articles in our entire collection that contain this term versus the total number of articles (35,000) in that collection) helps locate the rarer terms, which are presumably more informative when they do occur. Primitive matches are weighted so that those involving terms of high IDF influence the overall match more.

Once terms have been extracted and annotated with the above features, they are collected into one vector representing the patient record and a similar vector for each article in the set supplied by the search module. The re-ranking module uses this information to calculate a numeric value for the compatibility of any two such vectors (in practice, we are only interested in the compatibility of each article with the fixed patient record). We base this compatibility value on a modified cosine measure, which takes into account frequency information (to weigh more the concepts that appear more often in either the patient record or the article) as well as the modifying factors expressed by our features. We first construct TF*IDF vectors of the terms in the article and patient record, and start with a simple cosine formula that measures their similarity [15]:

$$\frac{\sum_i a_i \cdot p_i \cdot \log^2(\frac{N}{DF(i)})}{\sqrt{\sum_i (a_i \cdot \log(\frac{N}{DF(i)}))^2} \cdot \sqrt{\sum_i (p_i \cdot \log(\frac{N}{DF(i)}))^2}} \quad (1)$$

where a_i is the number of occurrences of term i in the article, p_i the number of occurrences of the term in the patient record, $DF(i)$ is the number of articles in our collection that contain term i, and N is the total number of articles in the collection from which document frequency is calculated. This basic matching formula utilizes as a basic building block the primitive matching between single instances of terms, which links terms that are expressed differently in the text but all correspond to the same concept (see Section 4).

Given the formula (1), we can modify this basic matching function to take account of the factors modifying a term's importance. First, we account for the influence of section information by replacing term frequency over the entire article by the sum of term frequencies for each section and weighting each such frequency by a weight representing the importance of that section. This results in the normalized frequency of a term according to section information, accomplished by replacing a_i (the term frequency) in the formula above with A_i:

$$A_i = \sum_{j \text{ over all section types}} (a_{ij} \cdot s_j)$$

where s_j is the weight for section type j and a_{ij} is the number of occurrences of term i in section j ($\sum_j s_j = 1$, and $\sum_j a_{ij} = a_i$). Our evaluation of re-ranking alone shows that section weights have a small positive influence on overall results [5].

We further modify the contribution of each term by weights representing the following factors:

- a weight capturing the relative importance of term's i semantic type, represented as t_i in the formula.

- a weight capturing negations when present. For terms occurring once in the patient record and article, this is either $+1$ or -1 depending on whether the terms have been seen in similar (positive/positive or negative/negative) or different exclusion contexts. For terms with multiple occurrences in the patient record, the article, or both, we consider all combinations of these occurrences and average the $+1$ or -1 values assigned to each pair. This weight is represented by n_i in the formula. For example, if the same term is seen twice in the patient record and three times in the article, one of the latter in a negative context, this yields six pairs of terms. Four of these pairs contain two positive contexts and thus each provides a score of $+1$. In two cases, we have a mismatch, with one positive and one negative context. This gives $(4 + (-2))/6$ to yield the final weight of 1/3.

- a weight which captures the similarity between observed values for term i in the article and the patient record. As in the case of n_i, for terms occurring multiple times in the article or the patient record we assign separately a similarity to the values associated with the terms in each pair, and subsequently average these similarities to obtain v_i. In our current implementation, a pair of values is deemed either fully compatible with a similarity of 1 (if they are identical, or if one or both terms have no values assigned to them), incompatible with a similarity of -1 (if both values are present, they are not identical, and at least one of them is non-numeric), or partially compatible (if both of them are present and numeric). In the latter case, the similarity for the pair is based on how much apart the two numbers V_1 and V_2 are, namely,

$$\frac{\min(V_1, V_2)}{\max(V_1, V_2)}$$

This is represented by v_i in the final formula.

With the modifications detailed above, our final formula for the degree of match between an article and a patient record becomes

$$\frac{\sum_i A_i \cdot p_i \cdot \log^2(\frac{N}{DF(i)}) \cdot t_i \cdot n_i \cdot v_i}{\sqrt{\sum_i (A_i \cdot \log(\frac{N}{DF(i)}))^2} \cdot \sqrt{\sum_i (p_i \cdot \log(\frac{N}{DF(i)}))^2}} \quad (2)$$

This ranges from -1 to $+1$, with $+1$ indicating total agreement, 0 indicating no overlap in terms between the documents, and -1 indicating active disagreement (i.e., the two documents share a lot of terms and disagree on the exclusion contexts or the values for those terms).

The weights s_i and t_i in the above formulas represent the relative significance of different sections and different semantic types. Currently, we have empirically determined "good" values for these weights through experimentation on small sets of articles and in consultation with medical experts. We plan to eventually use machine learning techniques to determine optimal values for these weights.

An earlier version of our re-ranking component[3] was evaluated using a set of 93 articles and two patient records [17]. The articles were selected not as a response to a particular query (which would bias the evaluation towards that query type) but by combining articles known to be relevant to each of the three patients (as determined by a medical expert) with articles that randomly matched some of the terms in the patient record. A specialist in cardiology assigned relevance scores for each of these 93 articles and each patient, and we compared the scores assigned to each article by the system to the expert's relevance score. We used different thresholds to convert the relevance scores produced by both the system and the expert to binary judgments ("relevant article for this patient or not"). Our evaluation (see [17] for a full description of experimental setting and results) showed that the re-ranking strategy significantly outperformed our baseline strategy that determined relevant articles by randomly selecting terms from the patient record and submitting them to a standard search engine. Compared to the expert, the re-ranking module achieved as expected lower precision (about 50%) but located many relevant articles that the expert himself did not find using standard queries on PubMed.

More recently, we have collected the data from a large-scale evaluation using the latest version of the re-ranking module. For that evaluation, we expanded the number of patients to three (from two), the number of articles to 939 (from 93), the number of article types to three (prognosis, treatment, and diagnosis from treatment only), and the number of physician evaluators to nine (from one). These results also show that our model outperforms the baseline, and several competitive models for searching medical collections. The full results (available in [5]) will be reported in a future paper.

An example of the effect that re-ranking has can be observed by looking at the results for a sample query that could be asked for our patient A. We provide such a query in Section 8, where we show how re-ranking transforms the results of the query, and how summarization improves

---

[3]Not including the IDF feature and the value matching described above.

```
Parameter(s):
  LVEF [C0428772],
  calcium channel blockers [C0006684],
  hypertension [C0020538],
  diabetes mellitus [C0011849],
  cardiopulmonary bypass time [C0007202]
Relation: not predict
Dependence: independent
Finding: atrial fibrillation [C0004238]
```

Figure 4. Template Example.

```
Parameter(s):
  LVEF [C0428772],
  hypertension [C0020538],
  diabetes mellitus [C0011849],
Relation: not predict
Dependence: independent
Finding: atrial fibrillation [C0004238]
```

Figure 5. Matched Template Example.

when presented with the re-ranked results compared to the originally retrieved articles.

7. Generating Tailored Summaries of Search Results

In the requirements gathering phase of the project, we observed that physicians do not read a study from beginning to end to determine if an article is relevant. Rather, they quickly glance through the *Methods* section describing the patient population, and then focus on the *Results* section. If a clinical study is found to be relevant to the specific patient, then the physician will read the article in more detail. TAS (Technical Article Summarizer) aims to facilitate this process by summarizing the results that are relevant to the patient from the input articles. It also provides links to the original articles, so that the physician can at any time read the whole clinical study.

Given the articles returned by the re-ranking component, we know whether, on the whole, an article is relevant to the patient; this is dependent on the matching weight it was assigned. However, even if a high-ranking article pertains to the input patient, not all the results reported in the article are relevant to the patient. TAS is responsible for finding pieces within the input articles that match with the patient and for including them in the summary in a coherent way.

TAS takes as input the top *k* clinical studies returned by re-ranking, along with the user model and the query passed to the Search component. Information is included in the summary only if it pertains to the patient represented in the user model. In addition, TAS handles repetitions or contradictions across articles by dynamically merging and ordering all the results from the different input articles and generating a coherent, fluent summary.

TAS follows a pipeline architecture.[4] First, results are extracted from the input articles. We analyzed a corpus of clinical studies to formally determine a definition for what constitutes a result. So far, we have focused on result sentences reported in the articles that relate disease, patient

---

[4] The full architecture of TAS is described in [3].

characteristics, or therapies with outcomes. A result is formally defined as a template of the form {*<parameter(s)>*, *<relation>*, *<dependence>*, *<finding>*}, where *finding* is the outcome, *parameter* is typically a condition, or a body part, and *relation* is the type of relation that holds between the two. For instance, the fact that having hypertension and in addition having the habit of smoking increase the risk for heart failure, can be represented as {*(hypertension, smoking), risk, dependent, heart failure*}. This result is encoded as statistically dependent, because the combination of the two *parameters* (hypertension and smoking) represent a risk for the *finding* (heart failure). Based on our corpus, we identified six types of *relations*: risk, association (or statistical correlation), prediction, and their corresponding negations. To extract such templates, we used traditional information extraction technology: sentences are parsed using a shallow syntactic parser, and they are checked against a set of patterns. Since parameters and findings are typically medical terms, we take advantage of the preprocessing of articles which identifies medical terms and tags them with their corresponding UMLS CUI. Given the example sentence "*Atrial fibrillation was not predicted by left ventricular ejection fraction, the use of calcium channel blockers, history of hypertension, diabetes mellitus, or cardiopulmonary bypass time.*", and the pattern "*<finding> was not predicted by <parameters>*", the template shown in Figure 4 is extracted. The result is statistically independent, which means that each parameter, by itself, does not predict atrial fibrillation (as opposed to the combination of them).

Templates constitute a good representation of the information in the input articles. They augment the raw text with semantic information while selecting only the concepts relevant to the summarization task (such as parameters, relations, and findings). Based on the semantic information and the primitive matching operation described in Section 4, we are able to implement complex personalization strategies.

We established two strategies for deciding whether a template matches with a patient record. First, matching should not be performed on the *finding* field of the template representing the article sentence. For instance, in the template {*heart attack, predict, death*}, there is obviously no point in trying to match "*death*" with the patient profile. Only *parameters* are used to determine relevance. This is consistent with our definition of a result: parameters can be considered as the current condition of the patient, while the findings represent current possible outcomes. Second, among the parameters, different matching policies should be applied according to the degree of dependence of the parameters: for each parameter in the template, we check whether it matches the patient record. If the result reports independence on the parameters, we perform a logical *or* of all matching parameters. The matching parameters are kept as input for the next component in the system, while the non-matching parameters are discarded. In contrast, if the parameters are dependent, i.e., their combination relates to the finding, we perform a logical *and* of the matched parameters. If one parameter does not match, the whole template is discarded; if they all match, the whole template is passed as it is to the next component.[5] In our example, the template contains independent results, hence we apply a logical *or*. After matching each parameter with the patient profile using our primitive match operation, we obtain the matched template shown in Figure 5.

This process of matching is made easier by the representation of article and patient records as profiles of medical terms. We can use the same basic matching formula defined above, but we restrict it to parameters of a template only, matching against the full patient record. Merging, described below, also relies on basic matching, but in this case for matching all terms within a template against terms from another template, to see if the two templates represent repetitions in the text.

Matching at the template level is performed for each extracted result, for each input article. The next task is to assemble these independent pieces of information into a coherent set. As a first sub-step we split templates that can be split (that is, the "independent template", such as our example template) without changing its meaning. The template is turned into three separate templates: {*LVEF [C0428772], not predict, independent, atrial fibrillation [C0004238]*}, {*hypertension [C0020538], not predict, independent, atrial fibrillation [C0004238]*}, and {*diabetes mellitus [C0011849], not predict, independent, atrial fibrillation [C0004238]*}. This sub-step seems counterproductive with our goal of assembling templates, but in fact it helps us by simplifying the data whenever possible. The templates are then clustered in a hierarchical fashion. We refer to this step as *Merging*. The similarity function between two templates is computed as a combination of the primitive match between the parameters and the match between the findings, and a manually assigned weight to the type of relation. The clustering achieves two purposes: it identifies strictly identical templates (that is, repetitions across or inside articles) and it dynamically groups together templates that are semantically related to each other.

---

[5] Our ongoing work is investigating cases of partial matches.

Clustering of templates is equivalent to dynamic document paragraph planning, where each cluster represents a paragraph. In the general content planning phase of the summarizer, the last task left is to decide in which order to present the paragraphs. This ordering is also done in a dynamic fashion. Each cluster gets an ordering weight based on several features: the number of templates it contains, the number of repetitions, the number of contradictions, and the number of different input articles that contributed to the cluster. The rationale behind this is based on user studies we conducted in the initial phase of the TAS design: as a general policy, physicians want to see the important pieces of information first. For instance, a paragraph which reports on a contradiction between two results is considered important and therefore its corresponding cluster should have a higher weight. Another feature is whether the cluster contains any template related to the input query. We use again the primitive match function to decide this.

The content planning phase of the summarizer comprises the above three steps: (1) personalized extraction of results, (2) merging, and (3) ordering. The two first steps make heavy use of the semantics associated with medical terms (CUIs) and the primitive for matching two given terms, while ordering uses them to compute the ordering weight. The second phase of the summarizer is the Content Realization. In our current implementation, we generate English text by combining extracted phrases with canned pre-written slotted sentences [8].

An example summary is given in Figure 9. It provides examples of the three main contributions of TAS:

- Personalization — The summary contains only the results relevant to the patient or the question asked. For instance, the second and third sentences are directly tailored to the input patient: she has coronary artery disease, as well as diabetes, hypertension, a low ejection fraction, and a history of smoking. The third and fourth paragraphs report results on amiodarone and sotalol which pertain to what the user asked.

- Merging and cohesion — The summary does not contain repetitions since identical results are merged. For instance, the fact "*a left atrial with diameter > 60 mm predicts atrial fibrillation*" appears in two input articles (articles 6 and 7), but it is mentioned only once in the summary. Merging also allows semantically related results to be presented in a cohesive manner, as in the first sentence of the summary: results such as "*patient age is associated with atrial fibrillation*" and "*hospital stay is associated with atrial fibrillation*" are aggregated into the first sentence of the summary, even though they come from different input articles.

- Ordering and coherence — The dynamic ordering algorithm allows the summary to present the most im-

1. *"Maintenance of sinus rhythm with oral d,l-sotalol therapy in patients with symptomatic atrial fibrillation and/or atrial flutter"*. The American Journal of Cardiology.
2. *"Oral amiodarone reduces incidence of postoperative atrial fibrillation"*. The Annals of Thoracic Surgery.
3. ***"Efficacy and Safety of Sotalol in Patients with Refractory Atrial Fibrillation or Flutter"***. American Heart Journal.
4. *"Low-Dose Amiodarone Versus Sotalol for Suppression of Recurrent Symptomatic Atrial Fibrillation"*. The American Journal of Cardiology.
5. ***"Efficacy of amiodarone for the termination of persistent atrial fibrillation"***. The American Journal of Cardiology.
6. *"Intraoperative amiodarone as prophylaxis against atrial fibrillation after coronary operations"*. The Annals of Thoracic Surgery.
7. *"Efficacy, Safety, and Determinants of Conversion of Atrial Fibrillation and Flutter With Oral Amiodarone"*. The American Journal of Cardiology.
8. *"Amiodarone versus propafenone for conversion of chronic atrial fibrillation: results of a randomized, controlled study"*. Journal of the American College of Cardiology.
9. *"Intravenous amiodarone for the prevention of atrial fibrillation after open heart surgery"*. Journal of the American College of Cardiology.
10. *"Intravenous amiodarone for prevention of atrial fibrillation after coronary artery bypass grafting"*. The Annals of Thoracic Surgery.

Figure 6. The first ten clinical studies returned from the search before re-ranking. Relevant articles are in bold.

1. ***"Prophylactic Oral Amiodarone Compared With Placebo for Prevention of Atrial Fibrillation After Coronary Artery Bypass Surgery"***. American Heart Journal.
2. *"Intravenous amiodarone for prevention of atrial fibrillation after coronary artery bypass grafting"*. The Annals of Thoracic Surgery.
3. *"Intravenous sotalol decreases transthoracic cardioversion energy requirement for chronic atrial fibrillation in humans"*. Journal of the American College of Cardiology.
4. *"Intraoperative amiodarone as prophylaxis against atrial fibrillation after coronary operations"*. The Annals of Thoracic Surgery
5. ***"Oral d,l sotalol reduces the incidence of postoperative atrial fibrillation in coronary artery bypass surgery patients"***. Journal of the American College of Cardiology.
6. ***"Patient Characteristics and Underlying Heart Disease as Predictors of Recurrent Atrial Fibrillation After Internal and External Cardioversion in Patients Treated with Oral Sotalol"***. American Heart Journal.
7. ***"Spontaneous Conversion and Maintenance of Sinus Rhythm by Amiodarone in Patients With Heart Failure and Atrial Fibrillation"***. Circulation.
8. ***"Efficacy and safety of sotalol versus quinidine for the maintenance of sinus rhythm after conversion of atrial fibrillation"***. The American Journal of Cardiology.
9. ***"Efficacy of amiodarone for the termination of persistent atrial fibrillation"***. The American Journal of Cardiology.
10. ***"Prospective Comparison of Flecainide Versus Sotalol for Immediate Cardioversion of Atrial Fibrillation"***. American Journal of Cardiology.

Figure 7. The first ten articles after re-ranking the original search results. Relevant articles are in bold.

portant results first. The first paragraph of the summary is repeated in five articles, and therefore, is considered highly important to report to the user, whereas the fact that "*age predict sinus rhythm maintenance*" is reported in only one article, so it can be included at the end of the summary.

8. The Combined Effect of Personalization

In this section we present a full example and show how personalization can be relevant both at the Re-ranking and Summarization levels.

In our scenario with Patient A, we bypassed the stages of Context Selection and the Query Formulation phases of PERSIVAL, assuming the physician was looking at a patient record and wanted to ask a question about atrial fibrillation and possible treatments. Bypassing these stages allowed us to test just the re-ranking and summarization components alone. Since the physician wants to know about treatment of atrial fibrillation, we performed a search on a collection of technical documents with the following boolean query: get the documents whose titles contain atrial fibrillation AND (sotalol OR amiodarone). The search returned 34 articles.[6] Following the PERSIVAL architecture,

---

[6] The number of hits is small considering that the collection contains more than 35,000 documents. However, this makes sense given that the

Left atrial diameter and arrhythmia duration predict conversion [5,7]. Left atrial size and atrial fibrillation duration are associated with conversion to sinus rhythm [7,8]. However, sex, gender, age, left ventricular ejection fraction, and heart rate were not found to be associated with conversion [5,8].

In a multivariate analysis, age and ejection fraction predict sotalol efficacy [3,4].

Amiodarone and left atrial size and are associated with conversion rate [5,7].

Atrial fibrillation is associated with hospital stay and increased cost [9,10].

Figure 8. Summary I, for the top 10 search results without re-ranking. The numbers in parenthesis refer to articles from Figure 6.

the Categorization module was invoked first, which filtered out documents that are not clinical studies. In this scenario, this resulted in 27 clinical studies. Figure 6 shows the first ten clinical studies retrieved by the search engine, while Figure 7 shows the first ten clinical studies after re-ranking was performed on the 27 articles.

Looking at the two sets of articles, we observe that the top 10 re-ranked articles constitute a better match with the patient record than the top 10 search articles. Manual examination reveals that only two of the top 10 search results (Figure 6) are relevant to patient A (articles 3 and 5). In contrast, the top 10 re-ranked results (Figure 7) contain seven fully relevant articles for Patient A. By providing personalization at the article level, the physician can get to the relevant articles faster by looking at the re-ranked results, than by looking at the search results alone.

In order to compare the combined effect of personalization at both levels, we produced two summaries. In our input to summarization, we used the same patient record and question from the physician (as described above), but we varied the set of articles being summarized. The first one (summary I, shown in Figure 8) was generated using the first ten clinical studies returned by the search engine, without any re-ranking involved (that is, the articles in Figure 6). The second summary (summary II, shown in Figure 9) was generated using the first ten clinical studies returned by the re-ranking component (that is, the articles in Figure 7).

Summarization answers the physicians' needs better than a list of articles. It is easier and quicker for the physician to read Summary I or II than to access all the articles in Figure 6 or Figure 7 and read them to determine which parts are relevant to the patient. In other words, summarization

---

search looks only at the titles of the documents, and the query terms are drug names, and therefore, fairly specific.

Atrial fibrillation is associated with patient age, hospital stay, increased cost, and mortality rate [1,2,6,7,9].

Multivariate analysis identified coronary artery disease to predict atrial fibrillation [6,7]. Left ventricular ejection fraction, hypertension, diabetes mellitus, smoking were not found to predict atrial fibrillation [1].

Left atrial diameter < 4.0 cm is a predictor for conversion [8,9]. Left atrial size > 60mm predicts atrial fibrillation [6,7].

Amiodarone and conversion to sinus rhythm are associated [7]. Sex, age, and baseline heart rate are not associated with conversion [9]. Heart failure does not predict conversion to sinus rhythm [7].

Sotalol was associated with decreasing the incidence of atrial fibrillation, and tolerated recurrences [5,8]. There were no differences of mortality between sotalol and placebo [5].

In a univariate analysis, coronary artery disease and age predict recurrence [6,7].

Age and atrial fibrillation predict sinus rhythm maintenance [8].

In a multivariate analysis, there were no differences of relapsing into atrial fibrillation between the modes of treatment [6,7].

Figure 9. Summary II, for the top 10 re-ranked search results. The numbers in parenthesis refer to articles from Figure 7.

provides a more fine-grained tailoring of the information, complementary to that offered by the re-ranking.

Finally, combining re-ranking with summarization strongly boosts performance: re-ranking provides a "better" input to summarization than search alone. Summary II was generated using globally relevant articles, and therefore, more relevant results were selected to be presented to the user: In Summary I, while the summarizer extracted 40 findings from the ten input articles, only 26 were considered matching with the input patient and ended up in the generated summary (yielding a matching rate of 65%). In contrast, for the re-ranked set of articles, the summarizer extracted 39 findings, and considered 35 of them to be relevant to the patient (matching rate of 89%). This trend was verified when manually going through the intermediate results of the summarizer. In addition, the summarizer was able to pick up many repetitions in articles from the re-ranked results, but not from the unmodified search results. The summarizer detected only 4 pairs of repetitive results when extracting information from the former set of articles, while it detected 8 pairs of repetitive results in the latter set. Thus, more of the information in Summary II is based on multiple sources, thus increasing its reliability. Presence of repetitive results across the input articles confirms the validity of the article selection process as well.

9. Conclusions and Future Work

Our research demonstrates how information about the patient, available in the online patient record, can be used to provide a personalized response to a physician's search query. Re-ranking and summarization leverage a common representation of articles and patient record to make their tasks easier. Through construction of article and patient profiles consisting of extracted medical terms, we enable the use of a relatively straightforward matching procedure based on comparison of term CUIs to determine relevance. Information from our primitive matching function is used as a common building block and combined in a variety of ways to improve determination of document relevance for re-ranking or sentence relevance for summarization. Taken together, re-ranking and summarization provide an increase in personalization that would not be possible with either one alone.

There are many directions that we are currently exploring. Feedback from our evaluation with re-ranking indicates that we could improve relevance if we could find better measures to weight importance of terms. Physicians in our group indicate that the more specific terms of any given type (e.g., diseases such as *atrial fibrillation*) are better indicators of a match. In looking at the profiles that were built for an article and a patient record, it is clear that the specific terms are not distinguished from the more general (e.g., age, heart rate). We are exploring methods to exploit depth in the UMLS hierarchy to help us make this determination.

For both re-ranking and summarization, better handling of value matching would also increase personalization. Currently, we only handle matches between numeric values—yet, often a numeric value (e.g., "ejection fraction of 35%") can be matched to a qualitative description (e.g., "low ejection fraction") if we have medical knowledge about what "low" means for "ejection fraction" in the current clinical context. We will investigate text mining techniques for automatically learning ranges of values for common medical attributes, which will allow us to map qualitative descriptions to a part of the range of possible values.

Acknowledgments

This paper is based upon work supported by the National Science Foundation under Digital Library Initiative Phase II Grant No. IIS-98-17434. Any opinions, findings, and conclusions or recommendations expressed in this paper are those of the authors and do not necessarily reflect the views of the National Science Foundation.

References

[1] P. Clayton, R. Sideli, and S. Sengupta. Open architecture and integrated information at Columbia-Presbyterian Medical Center. *M.D. Computing*, 9(5):297–303, 1992.

[2] S. Ebadollahi, S.-F. Chang, H. Wu, and S. Takoma. Indexing and summarization of echocardiogram videos. In *American College of Cardiology*, 2001.

[3] N. Elhadad and K. McKeown. Towards generating patient specific summaries of medical articles. In *Proc. of NAACL Workshop on Automatic Summarization*, 2001.

[4] N. Green, P. Ipeirotis, and L. Gravano. SDLIP + STARTS = SDARTS: A protocol and toolkit for metasearching. In *Proc. of JCDL*, 2001.

[5] V. Hatzivassiloglou, S. Teufel, K. McKeown, D. Jordan, and S. Sigelman. Personalized search of the medical literature: An evaluation. Technical Report CUCS-003-03, Columbia University, 2003.

[6] G. Hripcsak, J. Cimino, and S. Sengupta. WebCIS: Large scale deployment of a web-based clinical information system. In *Proc. of the AMIA Symposium*, 1999.

[7] B. Humphreys, D. Lindberg, H. Schoolman, and G. Barnett. The Unified Medical Language System: an informatics research collaboration. *JAMIA*, 5:1–11, 1998.

[8] P. Jacobs. PHRED: A generator for natural language interfaces. *Computational Linguistics*, 11(4):219–242, 1985.

[9] R. Kass and T. Finin. Modeling the user in natural language systems. *Computation Linguistics*, 14(3):5–22, 1988.

[10] S. Lok and S. Feiner. The AIL automated interface layout system. In *Proc. of Intelligent User Interfaces*, 2002.

[11] K. McKeown, S.-F. Chang, J. Cimino, S. Feiner, C. Friedman, L. Gravano, V. Hatzivassiloglou, S. Johnson, D. Jordan, J. Klavans, A. Kushniruk, V. Patel, and S. Teufel. PERSIVAL, a system for personalized search and summarization over multimedia healtcare information. In *Proc. of the Joint Conf. on Digital Libraries*, 2001.

[12] K. McKeown, D. Jordan, and V. Hatzivassiloglou. Generating patient-specific summaries of online literature. In *Proc. of Intelligent Text Summarization, AAAI Spring Symposium*, 1998.

[13] E. Mendonca, J. Cimino, S. Johnson, and Y. Seol. Accessing heterogeneous sources of evidence to answer clinical questions. *Journal of Biomedical Informatics*, 34, 2001.

[14] D. L. Sackett, R. B. Haynes, G. H. Guyatt, and P. Tugwell. *Clinical Epidemiology: A Basic Science for Clinical Medicine*. Little, Brown and Company, Boston and Toronto, second edition, 1991.

[15] G. Salton and C. Buckley. Term weighting approaches in automatic text retrieval. *Information Processing and Management*, 25(5):513–523, 1988.

[16] A. Spink, S. Milchak, M. Sollenberger, and A. Hurson. Elicitation queries to the Excite web search engine. In *Proc. of CIKM*, 2000.

[17] S. Teufel, V. Hatzivassiloglou, K. McKeown, K. Dunn, D. Jordan, S. Sigelman, and A. Kushniruk. Personalized medical article selection using patient record information. In *Proc. of AMIA*, 2001.

Session 6B: User Interaction

Session Chair: Ed Fox, Virginia Tech

Visualizing and Exploring Picasso's World

Carlos Monroy, Richard Furuta
*TEES Center for the Study of the Digital
Libraries
and Department of Computer Science
Texas A&M University
College Station, TX 77843-3112, USA
(979) 845-3839
{cmonroy,furuta}@csdl.tamu.edu*

Enrique Mallen
*Department of Hispanic Studies
Texas A&M University
2716 Brookway Drive,
College Station, TX 77845 USA
(979) 696-9921
e-mallen@tamu.edu*

Abstract

*We discuss the preliminary use of a visualization tool
called Interactive Timeline Viewer (ItLv) in visualizing
and exploring a collection of art works by Pablo Ruiz
Picasso. Our data set is composed of a subset of the Online Picasso Project, a significantly-sized on-line art
repository of the renowned Spanish artist. We also
include a brief discussion about how this visualization
tool can help art scholars to study and analyze an artist's
life and works.*

1. Introduction

The On-line Picasso Project [3] is a Web-based
collection hosted at the Department of Hispanic Studies at
Texas A&M University. The collection can be divided
into the following categories: a) A collection of more than
5000 photographs of Picasso's artworks, each with
information such as title, date, location where it was
painted, medium, location where it can be currently
found, and dimensions. b) A detailed biography of Pablo
Picasso, including maps of the most important places
related to his artistic life. c) A list of bibliographical
references about Picasso's works and life, and d) a
collection of news and articles from newspapers and
magazines related to Picasso. The on-line repository
allows users to browse and visualize the items in the
collection, which in turn helps them to explore and
analyze in further detail its contents.

2. The On-line Picasso Digital Library

The current On-line Picasso Project provides a
browsing interface, which has the following basic
functionality: a) browse through a description of Picasso's

relevant events in his artistic life, b) browse through
Picasso's artworks, and c) view a list of museums and
collections owning Picasso's artworks. Entries in a) and
b) are grouped by year, and each year is then divided into
quarters. In the case of events in Picasso's life,
photographs of relevant people or places also are
included. Places are presented within a labeled map
indicating where he lived or worked. Images of the
artwork collection are presented as thumbnails. Clicking
on any thumbnail pops up a new window, displaying
more detailed information about the artwork.

The browsing mechanism works fine for navigating
through the artworks collection, but does not provide
manipulations that can help users deepen their analysis.
We are currently experimenting with ItLv [4], a Timeline-
based visualization tool, to interactively explore and
visualize the collection and prototype analyses of use to
the art scholar.

2.1 Data transformation

Since the collection contains more than 5000 items, a
subset of it was chosen for initial prototyping. The subset
is composed of artworks created in the years 1907, 1908,
and 1909.

An initial task in visualizing the collection was to
regularize the sometimes idiosyncratic coding of dates. In
the original descriptions, dates vary in format, for
example "January/1907", "Fall/1907", "Early/1907", and
"Late Winter/1907". Since the information was not
uniformly stored and formatted, we applied a data-
transformation algorithm that converted the dates into a
numeric range representing the number of months
beginning with January 1907. For example, January 1907
was assigned a value of 1, December 1907 a value of 12,
and February 1908 a value of 14. Seasons were converted
into month ranges, as shown in Table 1. Note that
"Winter" spans two years. In most cases the encoding was
unambiguous as to year(s), but when there was ambiguity

Table 1. Values assigned by the normalizing algorithm to the seasons of the years

Season	Months	1907's values
Summer	Jun, Jul, Aug	6, 7, 8
Spring	Mar, Apr, May	3, 4, 5
Fall	Sep, Oct, Nov	9, 10, 11
Winter	Dec, Jan, Feb	12, 1, 2

Table 2. Input data and its transformation.

Input data	Meaning	Normalized value
June~July/1907	Started in June and completed in July	[6-7]
Early/1907	Started early in 1907	[1-1]
Spring~Summer/1907	Started in Spring 1907 and completed in Summer 1907	[3-8]

we chose the beginning, rather than the end of the year (e.g., "Winter 1908" maps to months 12-14). Table 2 shows three additional transformation examples.

2.2 Using ItLv

Once the data was transformed, we began our first visualization experiments using our ItLv application. Shneiderman, et al. [5], show the use of a 2D visualization tool to explore a highly saturated space. They apply hieraxes to depict categories in further detail (represented as rectangles of the same size). Christel [1] uses timelines as part of an interface to a digital video library. Harris, et al. [2], describe the use of Lifelines to visualize legal information. In our ItLv representation, we represent the duration of the artwork's creation by the length of the rectangle and depict additional detail in adjacent windows. This can be seen in Figure 1, which depicts the artworks made by Picasso in 1907 at three levels of detail. The main window (A) depicts the first level; an overview of the year 1907. The Y-axis corresponds to a selected category; in this case the attribute chosen was the medium in which the work was expressed. However, the user can select any defined

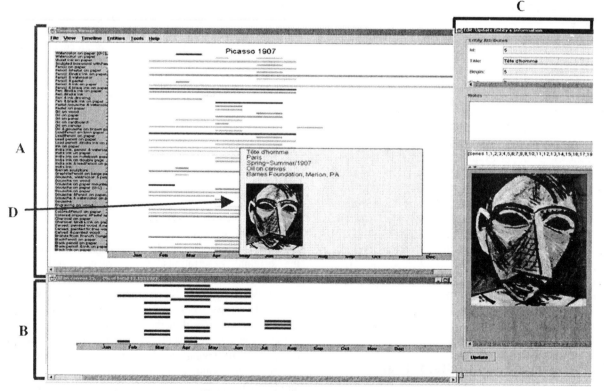

Figure 1. Overview and three levels of detail depicting artworks by Picasso in 1907 using ItLv

174

attribute to be depicted in this axis. The X-axis corresponds to the months of 1907. Mousing over any of the categories in the main window will depict all the elements of that category in the bottom window (B); this corresponds to the second level of detail, and incorporates an algorithm that separates out the elements to avoid the overlapping that is necessary in window A because of the limited available display space.

Mousing over any of the rectangles in the bottom window will depict all the information for that entry in the window on the right (C). This information can be edited and updated. The last level of detail is provided by a pop-up window (D). The user can personalize this window by selecting only those attributes he/she is interested in analyze at any given time.

Note that a degree of uncertainty is expressed in some of the example dates. For example, "Spring-Summer/1907" does not tell us precisely which months are involved. In particular, the records are not as accurate for Picasso's early artistic life, and hence the date ranges for some works are not known with certainty. In other cases, scholars believe, but do not know with certainty, that an artwork was painted in a certain city. We are currently experimenting with a color-fading scheme to depict uncertainty in date specifications, i.e., if one of the dates—start or completion—is not certain, it is depicted with a fading color, whereas if it is certain, a solid color is used.

3. Conclusion and Future Work

We believe that ItLv's functionality can help art scholars in exploring and analyzing an artist's information in further detail, e.g., identifying patterns, discovering correlations, comparing series, or identifying trends in different years or decades. In fact, many Picasso scholars have pointed out the importance of seeing the correlation of Picasso's series in the period from 1907 through 1914 in order to fully understand Picasso's intentions. We believe that our visualization tool will demonstrate the correctness of their assumptions.

We expect to use ItLv to answer questions such as: What kind of artworks did an artist create during any given decade? Was there any trend in which he painted in two different decades? What kind of techniques did he/she use the most in any given year or season? Was he/she more productive during a particular season: summer, fall, spring, or winter? We continue to explore the usefulness of ItLv in providing insight on these questions and seek to discover what functionality can be added to the tool in order to broaden the range of questions it can help the scholar answer.

4. Acknowledgements

Support for this work was provided by the Humanities Informatics Initiative funded by the Office of the Vice President for Research through a Telecommunications and Informatics Task Force grant, with additional support from the College of Engineering, the College of Liberal Arts, the Glasscock Center, and the Texas A&M University Libraries.

5. References

[1] Christel, M., "Accessing News Video Libraries through Dynamic Information Extraction, Summarization, and Visualization", Visual Interfaces to Digital Libraries. Springer-Verlag Berlin Heidelberg 2002, pp. 98-115.

[2] Harris, C., Allen, R. B., Plaisant, C., and Shneiderman, B. "Temporal Visualization for Legal Case Histories", Proceedings of the 62nd Annual Meeting of the American Society for Information Sciences, June 1999, Vol. 36, pp. 271-279.

[3] Mallen, E. The On-line Picasso Project, http://www.tamu.edu/mocl/picasso/. (Viewed on 5 February 2003).

[4] Monroy, C., Kochumman, R., Furuta, R., and Urbina E. "Interactive Timeline Viewer (ItLv): A Tool to Visualize Variants among Documents", Visual Interfaces to Digital Libraries, Springer-Verlag, Berlin Heidelberg 2002, pp. 39-49.

[5] Shneiderman, B., Feldman, D., Rose, A., and Grau, F. "Visualizing Digital Library Search Results with Categorical and Hierarchical Axes", Proceedings of ACM conference on Digital Libraries, San Antonio TX, 2000, pp. 57-66.

Graded Access to Sensitive Materials at the Archive of the Indigenous Languages of Latin America

Heidi Johnson

The University of Texas at Austin
Dept. of Anthropology
Austin, Texas 78712
+1 512-495-4604

ailla@ailla.org

Abstract

The Archive of the Indigenous Languages of Latin America (AILLA) is a web-accessible repository of multi-media resources in and about the indigenous languages of Latin America. In this paper, I describe the Graded Access System developed at AILLA to protect sensitive materials by allowing resource producers - academics and indigenous people - finely-grained control over the resources they house in the archive.

1. Introduction

The Archive of the Indigenous Languages of Latin America (AILLA) was founded at the University of Texas at Austin in 2000. It is a collaborative effort among Anthropology (Dr. Joel Sherzer), Linguistics (Dr. Anthony C. Woodbury) and the Digital Library Services Division of the UT General Libraries (Mark McFarland). Its mission is the preservation and dissemination of resources in and about the indigenous languages of Latin America, which is one of the most linguistically diverse regions of the world [4]. These resources are eclectic in both format and content: audio and video recordings, texts ranging from out-of-print books to word processor documents to handwritten field notes, databases, photographs, drawings, etc. All materials are digitized, archived in standard formats and made available on the Web through parallel interfaces in English and Spanish.

Resources are catalogued using the metadata schema developed for the International Standards for Language Engineering Metadata Initiative (IMDI) by the Max-Planck Institute for Psycholinguistics, Nijmegen, Netherlands [3]. AILLA's resources are also locatable through the

Electronic Metastructures for Endangered Language Data (EMELD; [1]) portal using a standard mapping to the metadata elements employed by the Open Language Archive Community (OLAC; [5]). The IMDI schema forms the basis for the relational database (MySQL) that houses information about AILLA's resources.

2. The Collection

AILLA's resources come from its community of users: the linguists, anthropologists, and indigenous people who have been investigating the indigenous languages of Latin America for more than half a century. Language documentation requires the collection of vast amounts of data, especially recordings of naturally-occurring discourse in a wide range of genres, including narratives, oratory, ceremonial chants, songs, and conversations. These recordings are usually accompanied by textual annotations such as transcriptions and translations, and by analytical materials such as datasets, word lists, elicited forms, ethnographic and grammatical sketches.

Researchers and their indigenous consultants have been creating such multi-media corpora since at least the 1950's. Until the advent of digital archives, there was no place to publish primary data, so these valuable materials have remained in the care of the individual researchers. AILLA is now actively acquiring and archiving these privately-held corpora, in order to make them available to the international community of researchers and more importantly, to the indigenous people themselves.

3. The Graded Access System

As long as these corpora remained in the hands of their original producers, intellectual property rights were not an issue. Now, however, the ability to disseminate recordings of indigenous people's cultural and personal expressions to a global audience is provoking a major re-evaluation of the ways in which these works should be treated.

AILLA has the responsibility of ensuring that the intellectual property rights of the creators of resources in the archive are preserved and that the wishes of the indigenous people whose languages are recorded in the archive are respected. The legal and ethical situation is extremely complex due to the diversity of the region that we serve. There are over 500 indigenous languages spoken in Latin America, in communities which are far from homogenous. The laws of the countries in which the recordings were made vary and in many cases are now undergoing revision in response to indigenous concerns about protecting their cultural heritages.

Some materials are inherently sensitive and must be narrowly restricted. Religious or other cultural practices may require that only certain people be allowed to hear certain works, that have been recorded for fear of losing them [2], but which must be closely guarded. Identification of the narrators of accounts of historical events could in some cases lead to reprisals against the speakers. But AILLA also serves as a medium for collaboration between researchers, educators, and artists, both indigenous and non-indigenous, across the region. Depositors may want to restrict access to some materials to a group of collaborators for some period of time to develop a work in progress.

3.1. The Solution

Given the diversity of the resources and their producers, we determined that no single access restriction mechanism could adequately serve the needs of AILLA's community. We have devised a graded protocol that offers depositors a variety of means for controlling access to their sensitive materials.

All users are required to register with the archive in order to access any resource. Registration is free, but users must agree to abide by the conditions of responsible use in order to establish their accounts, which keep track of which resources they have deposited and which restricted resources they have access to. The Graded Access System provides four levels of access:

1. **Free public access.**
2. **Automatic control.** Three automatic protocols:
   a. Passwords offer fine or coarse control. For example, a secret word disseminated individually finely distinguishes authorized users. For coarse control, a password such as the word for 'friend' in an indigenous language, which only speakers and a few researchers would be likely to know, would let in all appropriate users, with little risk of an inappropriate user gaining access.
   b. Time limits would typically be the lifetime of a speaker, or some generally agreed upon limit for a researcher's exclusive use of data (e.g., 3 years).
   c. Conditions that the user must agree to, such as always crediting speakers by name, can be specified by depositors This control would not prevent a dishonest person from accessing a resource, but would provide electronic evidence that the user had agreed to the conditions, should a dispute arise.
3. **Depositor control.** Users contact the depositor directly to ask for permission to access the resource. The depositor contacts AILLA, and archive staff adjust the user's access list. This allows depositors to know who is interested in using their materials. Most depositors will be reachable by email, so that the communication cycle can be automatically facilitated by archive software.
4. **Indigenous control.** Users contact AILLA and we request permission on their behalf from the indigenous person or group that controls the resource. This allows indigenous people to know who is interested in their materials. Note that this cycle could take months, since communication with the indigenous community would most likely take place by surface mail.

4. Conclusions

The Graded Access System has only recently been implemented, so it is too soon to know how well it will fulfill its intended functions. The technological implementation is simple, but the sociological implications are complex and will take time to develop. We have plans to conduct evaluation workshops at sites in the U.S. and Latin America over the next 5 years, and fully expect it to take that long to determine whether our system is both sensitive enough and complete enough to serve our users' needs. We will adjust the system in response to user feedback as the evaluation period progresses.

The two most problematical areas will certainly be levels 3 and 4, which require communication with external parties. How well will we be able to keep track of depositors over time? What will we do for indigenous people who don't receive mail, like the hunter-gatherer tribes of Amazonia? It may also be possible to devise additional automatic (level 2) protocols, which will probably be the easiest for everyone to use. We hope, however, that we have now at least laid a foundation for supporting finely-grained control over access to sensitive archive resources, and thereby protecting the intellectual property rights of the indigenous people who have created them.

Acknowledgements

AILLA was started with seed money from the Dean of the College of Liberal Arts at UT Austin. It is currently supported by grants from the National Endowment for the Humanties (#PA-23817) and the National Science Foundation (#BCS-0113962).

Our thanks to ACM SIGCHI for allowing us to modify templates they had developed.

References

[1] Aristar, Anthony and Helen Dry. (2001). "The EMELD Project." *Proceedings of the IRCS Workshop on Linguistic Databases*, Philadelphia, 11-13 December 2001. pp. 11-16.

[2] Gnerre, Maurizio. (1986). *The decline of dialogue: Ceremonial and mythological discourse among the Shuar and Achuar of Eastern Ecuador.* In Joel Sherzer and Greg Urban Eds., Native South American discourse. Berlin: Mouton de Gruyter. pp. 307-341.

[3] ISLE Group. (2001)."Metadata Elements for Session Descriptions." *ISLE Metadata Initiative*, Draft proposal version 2.4 (7), May, 2001. http://www.mpi.nl/ISLE/documents/docs_frame.html

[4] Nichols, Johanna. (1990). "Linguistic diversity and the first settlement of the New World." *Language* 66(3).

[5] Simons, Gary and Steven Bird. (2001). *OLAC Metadata Set.* Draft, Open Language Archive Consortium.

Learning Digital Library Technology Across Borders

Sílvia Barcellos Southwick
Instituto Brasileiro de Informação em
Ciência e Tecnologia - IBICT
SAS Q. 5 Bloco H Lote 6
70.070-914 Brasília, DF Brazil
silvia@ibict.br

Richard Southwick
Syracuse University
School of Information Studies
4-116 Center for Science & Technology
Syracuse, New York 13244-5040
rmsouthw@syr.edu

Abstract

This paper describes the background context and initial findings from an ongoing case study of an electronic theses and dissertations (ETD) digital library (DL) project in Brazil. The specific focus of the case study centers on the activities of a Brazilian government agency acting as a mediator between software developers - primarily academic institutions in the United States - and university clients in Brazil. The authors highlight the loosely integrated nature of the DL technology, and the uncertain relationship between developers and users in terms of support. These circumstances reinforce a view of technology transfer as a process of organizational learning. As a consequence, the mediating institution in the study is viewed as assuming multiple roles in advancing the project.

1. Introduction

In recent years, dramatic innovations in information and communication technology (ICT) have created a truly global environment for information exchange. One important area is in developing digital libraries (DLs) for the dissemination of scholarly publications. As these systems grow and become interconnected in global networks, it will be critical for information providers in developing countries to not only adopt these systems to maintain a presence in the scholarly community, but to also be active participants in shaping their development. However, this will also be enormously challenging. In addition to the financial challenges of staying current with state-of-the-art hardware and DL software in the user communities, there is the added challenge for technologists (developers and implementers) of maintaining currency in terms of their *knowledge* of these systems. Here the problem extends beyond the fact of merely remaining aware of changes in the current state of technologies to the problems of participation in design decisions that cross geopolitical boundaries. As is frequently the case for ICTs, control over development of these emerging DL technologies - i.e., regarding: hardware, software, standards and protocols - is often 'located' within the communities of system designers and policy-makers of more economically advanced countries. This scenario raises a major question for researchers in global DL technology: *How do developing countries participate in the development and use of globally networked digital libraries?*

2. Background

In order to begin to answer this broad question, we (the authors) have initiated an exploratory case study of an electronic theses and dissertations (ETD) digital library project in Brazil. The project is led by a Brazilian government information agency (BGIA). BGIA's mission is centered around research and development (R&D) in building infrastructures for disseminating scholarly information. The ETD project is one of several ongoing digital library projects sponsored by the Brazilian government and coordinated by BGIA.

The goal of the ETD digital library project is to promote an integrated system for universal access to distributed electronic collections of scholarly literature in Brazil. Toward that end, BGIA has promoted an ETD system design following the model of the international initiative, Networked Digital Library of Theses and Dissertations (NDLTD) developed by Virginia Tech. It has also promoted the use of the Open Archive Initiative Protocol for Metadata Harvesting (OAI-PMH) in order to ensure interoperability among the various ETD repositories, along with customized national metadata standards for describing theses and dissertations. Within this distributed model Brazilian universities and research centers act as *data providers*. Data providers develop and administer systems to expose metadata to the OAI-PMH. BGIA acts as a *national service provider*, maintaining a centralized repository of metadata harvested from the data providers. An initial objective of the BGIA in developing the ETD project is to create a community of university data providers to allow testing of the networked DL architecture.

3. Discussion

As a beginning step, we have focused the case study around the activities of the BGIA in implementing the ETD digital library project. BGIA has been, and presumably will continue to be, a central player in the effort to build the scholarly digital library community in Brazil. The decision was also practical because of the active participation of one of the researchers in the development of the ETD project from initial conception through the present. This has provided valuable access to project participants within the BGIA as well as key individuals from external stakeholder organizations. Data collection has consisted of unstructured and semi-structured interviews. The participative involvement of one of the researchers also provides an opportunity for sustained observation over the course of the project. Archived project documentation and communications among project participants (developers and user institutions) have also contributed to our analysis thus far.

An initial task in the research has been in identifying and categorizing the set of roles adopted by BGIA in promoting the project. We view this as valuable in understanding the emerging *identity* of the BGIA as the project unfolds. Contributing perspectives on this identity are elicited, first, from the aggregated inputs of key participants within the organization, whose formal and informal work roles may be subject to change through project involvement. Perceptions of the role of BGIA have also been elicited from external developers and clients. The researchers assume that the articulation of perceived project roles will serve as links to understanding the underlying issues and challenges encountered in fulfilling these roles. Three major roles have been identified. (1) *ICT Knowledge Mediator*. This involves acquisition of knowledge about DL technologies, and diffusion of this knowledge among data providers. (2) *Standard Development Promoter*. BGIA coordinates the committee responsible for developing a national metadata standard for describing ETDs. This standard expands the international metadata standard (ETD-MS) in order to include national community needs. (3) *Project Manager*. The BGIA coordinates the project activities and manages resources. In this paper we focus most particularly on the challenges of the first of these roles: ICT Knowledge Mediator as represented in Figure 1.

As is often the case for contemporary ICT, the features of the underlying components of ETD digital library technologies are characterized by rapid innovation and continuous change. For the human beings developing and using the technology, this raises the challenge of maintaining a flexible technical knowledge to adapt to these changes. At a broad, macro level, this phenomenon can be portrayed by researchers as a "diffusion" of ICT innovation, where the demands of the user population creates a *flow* of knowledge, forming networks of communication [1]. We see this communication network

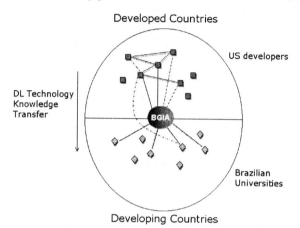

Figure 1: Research scope

perspective on knowledge transfer as relevant and potentially valuable for representing the global DL environment. Initial observations based on practice reveal that the dissemination and exchange of global DL is very much reliant on Internet-based channels, such as listservs and interpersonal email exchanges. An elicitation of these formal and informal communication networks through methods such as social network analysis (SNA) will undoubtedly lend valuable insight in developing research in this area.

While we see potential value in the diffusion perspective as a way of identifying central players in the global network [2], we have taken an alternative view in the present study. Based on our initial observations, we are led to conceptualize the phenomenon as a *process* of knowledge creation and re-creation within BGIA and among participating institutions within the ETD project. That is, we view it as essentially a process of *learning* by individuals, or *organizational learning* in the aggregate. Our perspective in this vein is informed by the observations of other researchers, most notably, Attewell [3], who emphasizes an organizational learning perspective in the context of adopting advanced information technologies. Contemporary ICTs are often works-in-progress. They may not take the form of a finished product (i.e., a 'package'), often require in-house customization, and may require ongoing assistance by external experts in order for the in-house technologists to maintain and adapt the system over time [4]. Attewell portrays this as a process of ongoing, *in situ* learning by user organizations, following notions of "learning by doing" [5] and "learning by using" [6]. We find that this scenario is an appropriate fit with the circumstance encountered by the BGIA in implementing the ETD technology. In effect, this institution must "re-invent" the technology through a process of trial and error. Attwell points out that user organizations must often rely on "mediating institutions" in situations where the complexity and pace of change in the technology may exceed the capacity of the organization to learn. In the present case, BGIA fulfills such a role.

This perspective has led to the emergence of the guiding research question for our present stage of inquiry: *How do service providers and data providers in developing countries become adaptive learning organizations in the context of networked ETD digital library development?* The concept of learning is pervasive, crossing multiple fields of study. This is true for the concept of organizational learning as well [7]. In our analysis we identify two general dimensions of organizational learning. The first is structural. This concerns the *capacity* of the (BGIA) organization to adapt itself to the changes required to be a learning organization. This is interpretable, for example, in terms of internal economic resources and "people" resources (e.g., "champions" and boundary-spanners") in relation to the wider environment [8]. This aspect is addressed in "what" questions: *What are the factors enabling or constraining BGIA's participation as a national service provider and a mediator of the transfer of the ETD digital library technology to system users?* The second dimension of our analysis is cultural. Organizational researchers such as Schein [9] have emphasized this cultural dimension of organizational learning. Along these lines, we see the value of representing the phenomenon of digital library ETD development in terms of a community of practice. However, it is a community crossing organizational, social, and geopolitical borders, raising challenges of the "participation" [10] of developing constituencies.

4. Conclusion

We highlight three general observations: (1) Project participants must become flexible learners in order to adapt to the ongoing uncertainty inherent in the underlying technology. BGIA has attempted to base the system on open source technologies. It is common for digital library technologies to be developed in academic environments (e.g., OAI). The development process is a collaborative dissemination of an intellectual product rather than a packaging and distribution of a fully-formed ICT. Thus, ICT knowledge transfer occurs through more informal channels, such as discussion lists. These channels reveal a weak connection between developers and users in resolving technical problems. Therefore, while open source systems implementing DL and harvesting protocols are made available for free on the Internet, offering developing countries a relatively inexpensive means for bridging the

gap in DL technologies, early adopters face a real challenge in acquiring technical knowledge.

(2) The uncertainty in learning the ETD digital library technology is reflected in uncertainty in project roles. Because learning the technology is largely a process of "situated learning" [10], BGIA must adopt the multiple roles of user, developer (or, user/developer), and mediator. BGIA is a system user in the sense that it must learn the technology in order to act as a national service provider. At the same time, it must act as a mediator in transferring the technology to the university user constituency. In doing so, BGIA must also work in developing the product to conform to the needs of the specific Brazilian context.

(3) While the goal of BGIA generally conforms to the model of a learning facilitator, there are indications that the perceptions of people within some of the user institutions may not support this role. These institutions, while hoping to be beneficiaries of the new ETD digital library technology, are less eager to commit resources. In short, they appear to view BGIA as a provider, rather than a collaborator, in implementing the technology. Interestingly, this scenario conveys the possibility of BGIA having to mediate between the "mythology" generated by developers, and the resulting expectations for the technology in the minds of user institutions. Future research will center on how, or whether, BGIA will be successful in acting as agents of positive change as the universities adopt the ETD digital library technology.

5. References

[1] Rogers, E., *The Diffusion of Innovation.* 3rd ed. 1983, New York: Free Press.

[2] Freeman, L.C., *Centrality in Social Networks: Conceptual Clarification.* Social Networks, 1979. **1**: p. 215-239.

[3] Attewell, P., *Technology Diffusion and Organizational Learning: The Case of Business Computing.* Organization Science, 1992. **3**(1).

[4] Eveland, J.D. and L.G. Tornatzky, *The Deployment of Technology*, in *The Processes of Technological Innovation*, M. Fleischer, Editor. 1990, Lexington Books: Lexington, MA, USA.

[5] Arrow, K., *The Economic Implications of Learning By Doing.* Review of Economic Studies, 1962. **29**: p. 166-170.

[6] Rosenberg, N., *Perspectives on Technology.* 1976, Cambridge: Cambridge University Press.

[7] Dodgson, M., *Organizational Learning: A Review of Some Literatures.* Organization Studies, 1993. **14**(3): p. 375-394.

[8] Cohen, W. and D. Levinthal, *Innovation and Learning: The Two Faces of R&D.* The Economic Journal, 1989. **99**: p. 569-596.

[9] Schein, E.H., *Organizational Culture and Leadership.* 2nd ed. 1985, San Francisco: Jossey-Bass.

[10] Lave, J. and E. Wenger, *Situated Learning: Legitimate Peripheral Participation.* 1991, Cambridge: Cambridge University Press. 138.

Personal Spaces in the Context of OAI

Natalia Reyes-Farfán, J. Alfredo Sánchez
Libraries Division and Center for Research in Information and Automation Technologies
Universidad de las Américas-Puebla
{is101971, alfredo}@mail.udlap.mx

Abstract

We describe MiBiblio 2.0, a highly personalizable user interface for a federation of digital libraries under the OAI Protocol for Metadata Harvesting. (OAI-PMH). MiBiblio 2.0 allows users to personalize their personal space by choosing the resources and services they need, as well as to organize, classify and manage their workspaces including resources from any of the federated libraries. Results can be kept in personal spaces and organized into categories using a drag-and-drop interface.

1. Introduction

The vast repositories comprised by digital libraries pose challenges for user access due to their complexity and dynamism. It is highly desirable to have personalizable interfaces for organizing and classifying digital resources. As part of our digital libraries program, we have proposed the notion of *personal spaces*, which are digital library areas defined by users to organize information that is required to perform information-intensive activities or that is relevant to their individual preferences and needs. They may include information units that are used frequently, tasks performed regularly, personal agents and different maps of the library generated as a result of navigating through collection. We introduced this notion and reported on a couple of prototypical implementations in [1, 2]. In this paper we report on the evolution of our personalized interfaces in the context of a federation of digital libraries.

2. Federated personal spaces

Access to multiple digital collections should be simple and transparent to the user. By making personal spaces aware of the availability of federated resources, the user does not need to explicitly visit each of the underlying repositories. Instead, this is accomplished by a cooperative interface that presents all available resources in a uniform fashion.

The conventional approach to interoperability is for a number of organizations to agree that their services will be built according to certain specifications (which are often selected from formal standards). Organizations that build systems to this specifications form a federation. We have been exploring our notion of federated personal spaces in the context of a federation of digital libraries that operate under OAI-PMH. Three cooperating institutions participate

in our project but the approach is extensible to all OAI-PMH collections. We briefly refer next to each of the participating collections:

U-DL-A: Our digital library program has produced a system architecture that integrates a wide range of collections and services for a highly distributed community of users [3]. "University Digital Libraries for All" (U-DL-A) is the term we use to refer to our overall program. Our digital theses repository, one of our main collections, is publicly available through an OAI-PMH server.

Marian and ENVISION: Virginia-Tech has been building the MARIAN digital library infrastructure. MARIAN is a distributed multi-task system. ENVISION is a system that provides support for visualization of the results produced by MARIAN. Digital theses and other documents are available through an OAI-compliant service [4].

Phronesis: The Monterrey Institute of Technology (Mexico) has produced Phronesis, a software system that functions as a tool for the creation of distributed digital collections [5]. Some of the collections, comprising technical reports in various areas, have also been made accessible via an OAI server.

3. MiBiblio 2.0

MiBiblio2.0 is a component that was developed as a part of the U-DL-A program. This personalizable interface allows for accessing different services provided by the digital library and makes it possible to search information elements in the federation of digital collections comprised by U-DL-A, Phronesis and MARIAN. Users personalize their interface by choosing from a list of icons that represent the various services provided by the digital library. Services include, for instance, book recommendations, annotations, access to digitized materials, and the theses collection.

Figure 1 illustrates the main interface of MiBiblio 2.0. In the figure, the user has selected the services mentioned previously plus "books on loan", which shows books borrowed from the physical library and their due dates, as well as the RDU service, which provides access to the digital reserve section of the library.

One of the main services MiBiblio 2.0 offers is an *organizer*, which is a tool that allows for the representation of categories defined by the user and represented as folders, as illustrated in Figure 2. Documents coming from any of the federated collections can be included in the organizer using a drag-and-drop interface and accessed at any time. Other available services include a personal calendar and library news, which keep the user up to date on new library resources. A personal space thus assists the user in handling the complexity of the federated digital libraries and becomes an area where users feel at ease to manage resources that are relevant to their individual tasks.

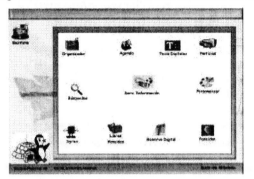

Figure 1. The interface of MiBiblio 2.0.

Figure 2. The *organizer* of resources.

In MiBiblio 2.0, access to federated collections is accomplished by relying on a distributed search platform we refer to as MAIDL. This platform implements distributed information retrieval through mobile agents that travel around the nodes in the federation seeking information that may be relevant for user queries [6].

The interface look and feel was created using Flash. As a development tool, Flash allows for great flexibility in the handling of animation, interaction and navigation. Given the constant interaction of the user with the various services, it is necessary to continuously access information residing on the server of MiBiblio2.0 to obtain documents in XML format.

5. Results

In order to evaluate the functionality of MiBiblio2.0, we selected a representative sample of students, faculty and library staff users. The interface has been well accepted and most of the users have been eager to have it as their main access for digital libraries in the future. The most attractive tool of MiBiblio2.0 for the users has been the *organizer*, as they think it is very useful to keep information organized according to personal criteria regardless of the location of the resources in the federation and to have a graphical representation of this organization. MiBiblio 2.0 is being released during the Spring Semester for general use.

6. Ongoing Work

Digital libraries in our federation continue to add new services and collections. We are currently working on mechanisms to automate the incorporation of new services into personal spaces. We also are integrating information retrieval services based on XML so access to metadata is standardized in future applications.

Acknowledgments

The authors wish to express their appreciation to Conacyt for supporting this project (No. G33309-A).

References

[1] Fernández, L., Sánchez, J. A., García, A. 2000. MiBiblio: Personal Spaces in a Digital Library Universe. *Proc. Fifth International ACM Conference on Digital Libraries*. 232-233

[2] Sánchez, J. A., Proal, C., Carballo, A., Pérez, D. 2001. Personal and group spaces: Integrating resources for users of digital libraries. *Proc. 4th Workshop on Human Factors in Computer Systems* (IHC 2001, Florianópolis, Brazil, Oct. 15-17)

[3] Ayala, G., Sánchez, J. A., Sol, D. 2001. Improving the quality of digital services and collections for large communities: Research issues. *Proc. International Conference on Knowledge-Based Intelligent Information Engineering Systems & Allied Technologies* (KES'2001, Sept. 6-8, Osaka, Japan.), IOS Press, 743-747.

[4] Gonçalves, M., France, R., Fox., E. 2001. MARIAN: Flexible Interoperability for Federated Digital Libraries. *Proc. 5th European Conference on Digital Libraries*. 173-186.

[5] Garza, D., Sordia, M. 1999. Phronesis Project: Technology for the creation of Digital Libraries on the Internet. Technical Report. ITESM-Campus Monterrey.

[6] Sánchez, J. A., Nava Muñoz, S., Fernández, L., Chevalier, G. 2002. Distributed information retrieval from web-accessible digital libraries using mobile agents. *Upgrade 3*, 2 (April).

PoPS: Mobile Access to Digital Library Resources

Nohema Castellanos
Universidad de las Américas, Puebla
Cholula, Puebla 72820 México
sp089077@mail.udlap.mx

J. Alfredo Sánchez
Universidad de las Américas, Puebla
Cholula, Puebla 72820 México
alfredo@mail.udlap.mx

Abstract

Mobile devices represent new opportunities for accessing digital libraries (DLs) but also pose a number of challenges given the diversity of their hardware and software features. We describe a framework aimed at facilitating the generation of interfaces for access to DL resources from a wide range of mobile devices.

1. Introduction

In recent years there has been a widespread use of wireless devices. Analysts forecast that there will be more than a billion mobile phones in use within the next two years, and that over half of Internet accesses will be through non-PC devices. The main appeal of these appliances is *mobility:* the ability to access information and services anytime, anywhere [1].

Internet-enabled personal digital assistants (PDAs), cellular phones and a wide range of mobile devices represent a novel and promising facet to exploit digital library (DL) resources. However, wireless devices exhibit hardware and software features that are different from those in conventional computers. This makes it difficult to access DLs using the existing user interfaces and would make it necessary to redesign user interfaces for each kind of device.

We have designed a framework aimed to produce "generic" user interfaces for accessing DL resources from PDAs and cellular phones via personalizable Web environments. Our framework provides an efficient management of device resources as well as dynamic interfaces for appropriate deployment on small screens.

2. Related work

Several solutions have been proposed to generate Web pages that are well-suited to the limited screen and input capabilities of mobile devices. Methods to summarize and browse Web pages are presented in [3]. WAP (Wireless Access Protocol) includes tools to convert HTML into WML (Wireless Markup Language, the language used by WAP phones) [1]. An approach proposes XML-based markup languages to create *generic interfaces*: interfaces whose aspect may vary in different devices while their functionality remains the same in any of them [7]. Languages and tools that can be used to build generic interfaces include UIML (User Interface Markup Language) [4] and XUL (eXtensible User interface Language) [8]. These languages promote the separation of the interface description from the application as well as a scalable interface design.

An efficient management of device resources—such as CPU, memory, storage and bandwidth capabilities—is also crucial in mobile access. SS/CD (Small Screen/Composite Device) [9] and MOCA [2] are frameworks to provide mobile information services while efficiently managing device resources.

3. Portable Personal Spaces (PoPS)

As part of our digital libraries program, we have proposed the notion of *personal spaces* [10], which refers to virtual areas in a digital library through which users can manage DL resources and services, select contents relevant to their interests and organize them according to their individual needs and preferences. The concept of personal space has been instantiated successfully for use with conventional workstations. However, we would like to make our DL resources accessible to users from portable, wireless devices. Thus, we have designed a framework that provides developers with mechanisms for specifying interfaces for applications accessing DL resources to be rendered in various platforms, including portable and mobile devices. We have focused specifically on instantiating the concept of personal spaces using these facilities, hence we refer to our framework as "Portable Personal Spaces" (PoPS).

PoPS includes the notion of a unique personal space specification, which we name *generic personal space*. This specification is used to build interfaces for personal spaces that are suitable for each of the target devices in an automated fashion.

The framework consists of three major components: the generic personal space, a converter and an interface generator. The generic personal space contains interface descriptions written in a device-independent manner using an XML-syntax, which also enables the separation of content, logic and style. The converter transforms the interface descriptions into code written in the language used by the target device (taking device limitations into account). The interface generator builds the interfaces adapting the produced code to the preferences of the user.

4. Implementation

We have produced an implementation of PoPS that demonstrates our approach. So far, we have produced basic framework functionality and prototypical versions of personal spaces for PDAs and cellular phones.

The personal space version for PDAs was developed using the PersonalJava™ Runtime Environment for Windows CE Version 1.1 [6]. This prototype runs on an iPaq H3870 Pocket PC and accesses our DL via Internet. Figure 1 shows the interface of the main menu.

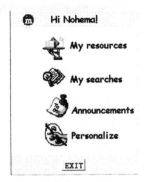

Figure 1. Interface of the main menu for PDAs

The PoPS specification to be rendered on cellular phones was developed in the Java™ 2 Platform, Micro Edition (J2ME™) Wireless Toolkit 2.0 Beta 2 [5]. Our main testing environment has been an emulator that runs on a PC and accesses our DL via an intranet. The interface of the main menu is illustrated in Figure 2.

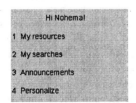

Figure 2. Interface of the main menu for cellular phones

5. Preliminary results

Our prototypical implementations have undergone usability tests with encouraging results. In general, test participants have adapted quickly to this kind of mouseless interaction and have been able to perform the tasks they intended or were asked to do. Most of them have found the interfaces attractive and have shown a great enthusiasm about the use of a mobile device to access our DL.

6. Ongoing work

Based on our usability test results, we are currently working on a formal specification of the generic personal space. After that, our work will focus on these stages: the development of the full-fledged interface generator, the implementation of the corresponding converter and the enhancement of the device resources manager.

7. Acknowledgments

This research is partly supported by the Mexican National Council of Science and Technology (CONACyT Projects 35804-A and G33009-A).

8. References

[1] Arehart, C., *Professional Wap*, Wrox Press, Birmingham UK, 2000.

[2] J. Beck, A. Gefflaut, and N. Islam, "MOCA: A Service Framework for Mobile Computing Devices", *Proceedings of the ACM International Workshop on Data Engineering for Wireless and Mobile Access (MobiDE)*, Seattle USA, August 1999, pp. 62-68.

[3] O. Buyukkokten, H. Garcia-Molina, and A. Paepcke, "Seeing the Whole in Parts: Text Summarization for Web Browsing on Handheld Devices", *Proceedings of the Tenth International Conference on World Wide Web (WWW10)*, Hong Kong, May 2001, pp. 652-662.

[4] Harmonia. *Introduction to UIML*. http://www.uiml.org.

[5] Java. http://java.sun.com/products/j2mewtoolkit.

[6] Java. http://java.sun.com/products/personaljava.

[7] O. Mayora-Ibarra, "Generation of Device Independent User Interfaces", *Proceedings of International Workshop on Research & Development of Human Communication Technologies for Conversational Interaction and Learning*, Puebla México, 2002, pp. 1-3.

[8] Mozilla Org. *Introduction to a XUL Document*. http://www.mozilla.org/xpfe/xptoolkit/xulintro.html.

[9] T. Pham, G. Schneider, and G. Stuart, "A Situated Computing Framework for Mobile and Ubiquitous Multimedia Access using Small Screen and Composite Devices", *Proceedings of the Eighth ACM International Conference on Multimedia*, Marina del Rey CA, 2000, pp. 323-331.

[10] J.A. Sánchez, C. Proal, D. Pérez, and A. Carballo, "Personal and Group Spaces: Integrating Resources for Users of Digital Libraries", *Proceedings of the 4th Workshop on Human Factors in Computer Systems (IHC)*, Florianópolis Brazil, October 2001, pp. 15-17.

How to Turn the Page

Yi-Chun Chu,[*] Ian H. Witten[*], Richard Lobb[†] and David Bainbridge[*]
[*]*Department of Computer Science*
University of Waikato
Hamilton, New Zealand
{ycc1, ihw, davidb}@cs.waikato.ac.nz

[†]*Department of Computer Science*
University of Auckland
Auckland, New Zealand
richard@cs.auckland.ac.nz

Abstract

Can digital libraries provide a reading experience that more closely resembles a real book than a scrolled or paginated electronic display? This paper describes a prototype page-turning system that realistically animates full three-dimensional page-turns. The dynamic behavior is generated by a mass-spring model defined on a rectangular grid of particles. The prototype takes a PDF or E-book file, renders it into a sequence of PNG images representing individual pages, and animates the page-turns under user control. The simulation behaves fairly naturally, although more computer graphics work is required to perfect it.

1. Introduction

Digital libraries invariably present their documents in a manner that is rather bland. Most collections show electronic text, frequently formatted for the screen in a way that is crude compared with typeset book pages. Designers of electronic books [1] pay more attention to the look and feel of the pages, with crisp text, clearly formatted and attractively laid out. Many digital library collections offer page images rather than electronic text, and although these are occasionally rather beautiful they are presented in a flat, two-dimensional manner.

Bibliophiles love books as much for the statements they make as objects as for the statements they contain as text. Indeed, early books were true works of art—beautifully-calligraphed poems inscribed into monumental stone steles in China; ancient scriptures etched onto palm leaves bound with string threaded through holes in India; and Western art treasures such as the *Book of Kells*, produced by Irish monks at the scriptorium of Iona 1200 years ago.

Beautiful books have always been prized for their splendid illustrations, for colored impressions, for decorated illuminated letters, for being printed on special paper, or uncommon materials, for unusual bindings, for their rarity and historic significance. And beauty is functional: these books give their readers an experience that is richer, more enlightening, more memorable, than the prosaic, utilitarian—often plain ugly—web pages offered by today's digital libraries.

The British National Library's "Turning the pages" project (see www.bl.uk/information/ttp.html) is a rare attempt to provide a reading experience that more closely resembles a real book. Readers sit at a touch screen showing a double-page spread of what appears to be a physical rather than an electronic book. Users wipe a finger across a touch-sensitive screen to metaphorically pick up a page and turn it. Pages look three-dimensional; the book's binding moves slightly in sympathy as a page is turned; page edges to right and left indicate how far through the book you are.

To accomplish this, photographs have been taken at (about ten) intermediate points during each page turn—so that what is displayed is a stored photo, not an artifact computed from a model of the book. There are many images—for example, one version of the system consumes 304 Mb for only twenty book pages (this includes zoomed-in versions of each page, and accompanying audio). The system is constructed using Macromedia Director.

The simulation is compelling, and users rapidly become absorbed in the book itself, turning pages unthinkingly—in Coleridge's words, they "willingly suspend disbelief" in these "shadows of imagination."[1] But the main drawback is that a slow animation of every page-turn must be painstakingly photographed in advance, for each book. This note describes an extension of the idea that dynamically texture-maps the current page's content onto a full three-dimensional model of the page-turn, making it easy to turn the pages of any book served up by a digital library.

---

[1] In his Biographie Literaria Samuel Taylor Coleridge (1772-1834) hoped his work would exhibit "a semblence of truth sufficient to procure for these shadows of imagination that willing suspension of disbelief for the moment, [...] which constitutes poetic faith."

186

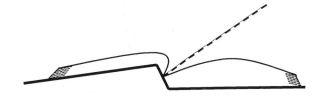

Figure 1 Java/OpenGL page turning prototype

Figure 2 An open book

2. Modeling page-turns

We generate the dynamic behavior of individual page-turns using a model based on a mass-spring structure defined on a rectangular grid of particles. These are connected with primary mesh springs, diagonal bracing, and four-way flexural rigidity springs. Many of the springs are very stiff, leading to a stiff system of differential equations. The shape or "pose" of the page is computed as it is turned by a virtual hand, which holds the page at a given point and moves along a specified trajectory.

A Runge-Kutta method is used to solve for the dynamic behaviour of the page after each small movement of the virtual hand. The largish mesh (18 × 16) takes some time to settle, and the stiffness of the system necessitates small time steps. Consequently, the current implementation takes from minutes to hours for a single page-turn, precluding real-time operation. Though smaller less-stiff meshes can operate in near real time, their appearance is significantly less realistic. It may be possible to achieve a plausible simulation in real time with a faster differential equation solver, smaller mesh, and careful tuning.

For reasons of efficiency we decided to pre-compute a page-turn and save it on disk. Internally the mesh is a series of strips ultimately rendered as triangles. Each page turn comprises a sequence of frames, stored as mesh files. At run-time, these files are read in during the initialization stage. Our prototype implementation is written in Java and uses OpenGL to perform the rendering through the *GL4Java* API. OpenGL is rather quick at putting out textured triangle meshes, provided there is plenty of texture memory.

Different page-turns can be generated by manipulating parameters of the dynamic simulation. For example, one can set the virtual hand to grasp the page anywhere along its edge, alter the angle of its thumb and forefinger, and change its trajectory.

Numerous parameters control the properties of the paper itself. Pre-computing the turn removes the opportunity to vary these parameters, but risks giving an overly mechanical perceptual experience by repeating precisely the same movement. It would be possible to pre-compute several different variants, but this requires a significant amount of storage space. As a compromise, we achieve variety by pre-computing three different page-turns and interpolating between them in different, randomly-chosen, proportions.

3. Modeling the book

The pre-computed page-turn is superimposed on a model of the book's spine and covers that takes account of the page's position in the book. Figure 2 shows a cross-section. The dashed line represents an idealized version of the page in question partway through the page-turn. Its initial and final rest positions are shown: they are basically the same as the following and preceding pages' positions, respectively. The geometric configurations of these pages depend on how far through the book we are—and this also affects the angle of the spine.

Before the turn begins, the page in question rests on the book's next (right-hand) page. The influence of this initial position decays as the turn progresses until it dies out completely at what we call the "midpoint," whereupon the resting position of the previous (left-hand) page begins to have a gradually increasing influence, until at last the page rests on the preceding (left-hand) one. Throughout the turn, the page twists and bends according to the precomputed page model discussed in the preceding section.

The configuration of the cover is calculated from the thickness of the book relative to the page width, and the distance of the current page through the book. Given this information, the positions of the previous and next pages are modeled as spline functions whose parameters are determined by simple heuristics.

4. Putting it together

To operationalize a page-turn, the page is represented in terms of its divergence from the idealized flat-page model whose projection is shown dashed in Figure 2. The rotation angle increases from 0 to 180 degrees as the turn progresses. The page is a mesh, each mesh point being expressed as an offset from its corresponding position on the flat-page model. The value of the offset is formed by weighting and summing three things: (1) the effect of the initial position, whose weight decays as the turn proceeds until it disappears at the midpoint, (2) the effect of the final position, which gradually increases from the midpoint onwards, and (3) the effect of the pre-computed page-turn, which is a function of the angle of the idealized flat-page position.

Many practical problems arise. One is the need to respect the obvious physical constraint that a page may not penetrate its predecessor or successor. We accomplish this by performing the calculation for each mesh point in a radial coordinate system whose origin is the corresponding mesh position on the flat-page model and whose principal axis is normal to that surface. Then, interpenetration can be avoided by performing a min or max operation on each calculated coordinate position with respect to the corresponding mesh point on the page's predecessor and successor. Another problem is to determine the above-mentioned "midpoint" at which the page's initial position ceases to have any influence at all and its final position begins to take effect. Another is to divide the splines corresponding to the initial and final positions accurately into the appropriate number of equal parts. Finally there is a basic difficulty in mapping the 0 to 180 degree pre-computed page-turn into the more restricted angle through which the page must actually turn. We are continuing to investigate these problems. The reader's "willing suspension of disbelief" in the page's ethereal nature immediately breaks down with any distortion of the paper as it turns, and it is surprisingly difficult to preserve the model's integrity.

5. Conclusions

The page-turner exists in prototype form. Pages behave fairly naturally, although more work is required to perfect the computer graphics simulation—for example, saddle-shaped curvature gives the impression of a cloth-like material that is more flexible than paper. The prototype takes a PDF or E-book file, renders it into a sequence of PNG images representing individual pages, and animates the page-turns under user control. Ultimately we plan to integrate this functionality into the Greenstone digital library software [2].

As most users of Apple's System X will testify, well-designed, smoothly-animated screen effects (such as the "genie" put-away animation), in conjunction with touch-pad control, make computer-based activity a more relaxed, richer, higher quality experience than we are accustomed to. The British Library's work brings the same kind of quality to certain prized books. This project explores a generalization that will allow the contents of any digital library to be perused realistically.

Acknowledgements

We are grateful to Brian Wyvill of Calgary University for help and advice in the graphics area.

References

[1] Henke, H. (2001) *Electronic books and ePublishing: a practical guide for authors* Springer Verlag, New York.

[2] Witten, I.H. and Bainbridge, D. (2003) *How to build a digital library.* Morgan Kaufmann, San Francisco.

Session 7A: OAI in Action

Session Chair: Ghalleb Abdulla, Lawrence Livermore National Lab

Repository Synchronization in the OAI Framework

Xiaoming Liu*
Research Library
Los Alamos Research Laboratory
Los Alamos, NM, 87545 USA
liu_x@lanl.gov

Kurt Maly   Mohammad Zubair   Michael L. Nelson
Computer Science Department
Old Dominion University
Norfolk, VA, 23529 USA
{maly,zubair,mln}@cs.odu.edu

Abstract

The Open Archives Initiative Protocol for Metadata Harvesting (OAI-PMH) began as an alternative to distributed searching of scholarly eprint repositories. The model embraced by the OAI-PMH is that of metadata harvesting, where value-added services (by a "service provider") are constructed on cached copies of the metadata extracted from the repositories of the harvester's choosing. While this model dispenses with the well known problems of distributed searching, it introduces the problem of synchronization. Stated simply, this problem arises when the service provider's copy of the metadata does not match the metadata currently at the constituent repositories. We define some metrics for describing the synchronization problem in the OAI-PMH. Based on these metrics, we study the synchronization problem of the OAI-PMH framework and propose several approaches for harvesters to implement better synchronization. In particular, if a repository knows its update frequency, it can publish it in an OAI-PMH Identify response using an optional About container that borrows from RDF Site Syndication (RSS) Format.

1. Introduction

Although now falling out of favor for the architecture of most digital libraries because of its well known limitations [6, 7] , distributed searching does have one strong advantage: the results are always an accurate assessment of the repository contents at the time of the search. Distributed searching has been eclipsed by the metadata harvesting model, as described by the Open Archives Initiative Protocol for Metadata Harvesting (OAI-PMH) [10].

The synchronization problem – how to keep the metadata records of data providers and service providers consistent –

---

*This research was performed while the author was a doctoral student at Old Dominion University

is a problem that can distort the results a user obtains from a search and is a result of the metadata harvesting model. Frequent harvesting has to be done to synchronize the repositories and harvesters, but it is inefficient if data providers seldom change during a harvest interval. On the other hand, without frequent crawling, service providers may become inconsistent with data providers: not only can new records be missed, but deletions and modifications as well. While always undesirable, some applications (e.g. news feeds) are more sensitive to this situation than others (e.g. scholarly publications). The user must trust that the service provider has an accurate assessment of the contents of the repositories that it harvests. The OAI-PMH supports selective, incremental harvests, and the synchronization is maintained by periodic re-harvesting. Service providers are expected to exploit these properties in order to limit the load imposed on the repositories while still maintaining fresh data for their services.

To study this problem, it is imperative to understand the requirement of the application. For example, maintaining freshness in seconds for the market value of a stock could be critical; a news aggregator needs to maintain hourly freshness for a satisfactory service; a web search engine may re-harvest its indexed pages over a span of several months. We define the *acceptable latency* is the interval at which a service provider considers acceptable when it is synchronized with repositories. It is worth noting that originally, OAI-PMH 1.x only supported day granularity, but now OAI-PMH 2.0 supports the option of second granularity. However, the granularity of the protocol is not likely change the nature of the update frequency of a repository.

The metadata harvesting model is built on service providers "pulling" metadata from a set of repositories. After studying the harvest logs of Arc [14, 13], we conclude that most repositories have a steady change rate, but different repositories present significantly different rates. For the traditional publishing medium, the OAI-PMH harvesting model works well. However, freshness can be further improved if the harvester can dynamically adjust the "pulling"

191

rate based on the change rate of repositories. Several possible approaches may be used to determine the change of a repository:

Best Estimation The harvester estimates the record update frequency by learning the harvest history.

Syndication A data provider may describe its update frequency explicitly. Motivated by the work in RSS (RDF Site Syndication Format) [1] and other applications such as news syndication, we define an optional container in which a data provider can describe its update rate.

Subscribe/Notify Best estimation and syndication are compliant with the OAI-PMH framework, but it relies on a constant update rate of data providers, which may not be true in some applications. A data provider may notify a service provider whenever its content is changed. This model is an extension of OAI-PMH.

Push Model Data providers may directly push updates to service provider side.

The remainder of this paper is organized as follows: Section 2 summarizes the previous and related work in synchronizing updates and measuring the freshness of web pages and digital libraries. We formally study the repository synchronization problem in Section 3. We study the update frequency of OAI-PMH compliant repositories in Section 4. Section 5 presents two algorithms to implement repository synchronization in the OAI-PMH framework. Section 6 presents approaches for determining repositories' update frequency.

2. Previous and Related Work

The original Harvest system from the University of Colorado [2] utilized a complex system of gathers and brokers to reduce the redundancy of typical web robot operation. Although no longer in use, portions of the Harvest system did evolve into a number of commercial products and it did provide the first working demonstration of incremental updates in a web environment.

Cho and Garcia-Molina [4, 5] gathered data from 270 web sites over a four month period and analyzed it by defining age and freshness metrics and by modeling the individual elements of a database as well as the database in its entirety. They then looked at the synchronization frequency and compared synchronization order and resource allocation policies. However, they were dealing with uncoordinated changes of web pages, which are different from the incremental harvesting model of the OAI-PMH.

Labrinidis [8] studied update scheduling problem in web materialization, where dynamic pages are cached at the web server and constantly updated in the background, resulting in fresh data accesses on cache hits. A Quality of Data (QoD) metrics was defined to evaluate how fresh the data served to the users is. An update scheduling algorithm was designed to maximize overall QoD by allocating more resources to frequently used pages. This study also focuses on individual web pages.

The RSS syndication module provides hints to aggregators and others picking up this RSS feed regarding how often it is updated [1]. The RSS is widely used in news aggregation services. RSS is roughly the converse of the OAI-PMH model: RSS provides a single URL that is guaranteed to always have the most recent contents, and the OAI-PMH provides a single URL through which a harvester can dynamically discover the contents of a repository during different points in time.

The proposed "HTTP Distribution and Replication Protocol" (DRP) [17] creates an index page based on content digests to avoid unnecessary data transmission in deliberate replication over HTTP. After the initial download, a client can keep the data up-to-date using the DRP protocol. Using DRP the client can download only the data that has changed since the last time it checked. DRP is based on the Message Digest algorithm, such as MD5 [16], to identify the changes of content.

In the Open Citation Project, Brody [3] studied how often papers are changed and updated after initial submission and how extensive the changes are in arXiv.org eprint archive. It explained in more detail about the update pattern in an individual digital library.

3. Metrics for Update Frequency and Freshness

The OAI-PMH is based on a coordinated model in which a harvester can issue a request to get all updated records in a repository after a specific date. This model is superior to the model of web crawlers, which have to discover the update time of each record individually. For smaller web sites (100s of pages), the difference between the OAI-PMH model and that of standard web crawlers is negligible. The power of the OAI-PMH model is realized for large digital library web sites (several 1000s of pages or more).

We formally define several metrics to measure the update frequency of data providers. Let $\{r_1, ..., r_M\}$ be the M repositories we are going to monitor. We assume that n observations are made of each repository, the observations being made at regular intervals. The choice of interval, Δt, will be made appropriate to the latency of the repositories involved and is largely irrelevant to the metrics that follow. We will therefore denote the observation times as $\{t_1, ..., t_n\}$, where $t_{j+1} = t_j + \Delta t$. For any t_j, let t_c denote the nearest update time before t_j.

Repository Update Status: The update status of a repository r_i at time t_j:

$$S(r_i; t_j) = \begin{cases} 1 & if \ r_i \ is \ updated \\ 0 & otherwise \end{cases}$$

Record Update Rate: Let $R(r_i; t_j)$ denote the number of updated records of a repository r_i observed at time t_j.

Repository Update Interval: We define the update interval at time t_j:

$$I(r_i; t_j) = \begin{cases} 0 & if \ S(r_i; t_j) == 0 \\ j - c & if \ S(r_i; t_j) == 1 \end{cases} \quad (1)$$

Average Repository Update Interval: In the period of observance $\{t_1, ..., t_n\}$, the average update interval of a repository r_i is:

$$U(r_i) = \frac{\sum\limits_{j=1}^{n} I(r_i; t_j)}{\sum\limits_{j=1}^{n} S(r_i; t_j)} \quad (2)$$

Average Repository Update Frequency: The average update frequency of a repository r_i is:

$$FRQ(r_i) = \frac{1}{U(r_i)} \quad (3)$$

Average Record Update Rate: The average records update rate of repository r_i is:

$$AVG(r_i) = \frac{\sum\limits_{j=1}^{n} R(r_i; t_j)}{\sum\limits_{j=1}^{n} S(r_i; t_j)} \quad (4)$$

Freshness of a Harvested Data Provider: The freshness of a harvested data provider r_i in harvester side at time t_j is:

$$F(r_i; t_j) = \begin{cases} 1 & if \ r_i \ is \ up-to-date \ at \ time \ t_j \\ 0 & otherwise \end{cases} \quad (5)$$

Freshness of Service Provider: The freshness of the service provider H at time t_j is:

$$F(H; t_j) = 1/M \sum_{i=1}^{M} F(r_i; t_j) \quad (6)$$

Using these metrics we are able to measure the freshness of service providers.

Update Cost for Data Provider: Let C_d denote the update cost for a data provider.

Update Cost for Harvester: Let C_s denote the update cost for harvester.

In the observance period of T, the harvester issues requests to each data provider in an interval of l, and l is the acceptable latency at which the harvester should be synchronized with repositories. This latency could range from several seconds to several months, depending on different applications.

Based on how synchronization resources are allocated to repositories, we can classify synchronization policies as uniform model and adaptive model.

In the uniform model, the harvester issues requests every l interval to each data provider:

$$C_d(r_i) = \frac{T}{l} \quad (7)$$

$$C_s = \frac{TM}{l} \quad (8)$$

In the adaptive model, we assume that the harvester knows when the data provider is updated in advance, and it issues requests right after the data provider is updated.

$$C_d(r_i) = \frac{T}{U(r_i)} = T * FRQ(r_i) \quad (9)$$

$$C_s = \sum_{i=1}^{M} \frac{T}{U(r_i)} = \sum_{i=1}^{M} T * FRQ(r_i) \quad (10)$$

From formula (8) and (10), we can derive that the acceptable latency, number of data providers, and repository update frequency play important roles in calculating the update cost. We illustrate these metrics by two examples.

Example 3.1 In a typical digital library application (i.e., scholarly publications), a daily latency should satisfy most requirements, if the observance period of T equals one day, from formula (8) we can derive $C_s = M$.

Example 3.2 In a news aggregator, the acceptable interval is at the minute level; each participating news agency updates its site every hour. If the observation period is one day, in the uniform model, $C_s = 1440 * M$, the uniform model will not scale. In contrast, in the adaptive model, $C_s = 24 * M$, it promises better efficiency.

The algorithms for both models are described in Section 5. In the adaptive model, the harvester essentially allocates more resources to active repositories; the prerequisite is that harvester must know the update interval of the repositories. The approaches to decide update interval are discussed in Section 6.

4. Study of Update Frequency

The frequency of new or modified records available through the data provider plays a major role in determining the balance between harvesting too often and not enough. The nature of the data provider can influence how often records are modified or updated. E-print type repositories are likely to have a small but steady stream of ongoing daily or weekly updates. Museum or historically oriented archives will have an initial burst period of accession (perhaps all at once), but then are likely to trickle down to just infrequent error corrections or edits. Although not currently implemented by any repositories, if a data provider allowed the metadata to change based on usage, annotations, or reviews as specified in the NSDL project [9], the required harvesting would likely become significant.

In this Section, we present our experimental results that show how OAI-PMH-compliant repositories change. We address the following questions:

- Does the data provider change at a constant rate?

- How often does a data provider change?

We run the Arc harvester once a day to harvest approximately 100 OAI-PMH-compliant repositories. The datestamps of harvested records are kept in a database. The change rate covers new data, modified data, and deleted data.

Table 1 lists the monthly average update rate of records in selected e-print archives. They are randomly selected from production OAI-PMH-compliant e-print services (we consider production services demonstrate a more realistic trend), the complete table is available at [11]. This table shows that in long term many e-print services have steady records update rate. This can be explained that e-print services have a relatively stable user base.

Based on the data we collected, we can analyze how long it takes for a data provider to change. For example, if a data provider changes 5 times in 5 months, we may estimate that the average update interval of the data provider is 5 months/5 =1 month. Note that the granularity of the estimated change interval is one day, because OAI-PMH 1.x uses day as the datestamp granularity. In Table 2, we list the daily average update interval, average update rate, standard deviation of update interval, and Coefficient of Variation (C.O.V.). The complete table is in [11]. It shows that most of them have a relatively small C.O.V. In Figure 1, we summarize the result of this analysis. In the figure, the horizontal axis represents the average update interval of repositories, and the vertical axis shows the fraction of repositories changed at the given average interval. We can observe that less than 10% of the repositories change daily, while about 70% of the repositories change monthly or longer.

In summary, OAI-PMH repositories (especially E-print archives) change at a steady rate overall, and the rates vary dramatically from site to site.

Because the OAI-PMH supports the features of incremental harvesting, with current number of OAI-PMH compliant repositories (about 100), the implementation of a harvester with good freshness is not very difficult. For example, in the current configuration, Arc, a single thread-based harvester, takes less than one day to complete a fresh harvesting cycle over all participating repositories.

5. Synchronization Algorithm for Harvesters

In Section 4, we conclude that the OAI-PMH model of synchronization works well for current OAI-PMH repositories (out of about 100 repositories, most of them are e-prints archives or other digital library applications). However, there are some scenarios that require better synchronization:

- If the OAI-PMH becomes more popular and there are a large number of repositories available.

- If the annotation or review services are widely used, such as in the NSDL project .

- If the OAI-PMH is used in some applications which require rapid updates (granularity of an hour or less), such as news or mailing lists.

In Section 3, we define two synchronization models: uniform and adaptive. The uniform model is implemented in the Arc harvester. The adaptive model is based on the features that most repositories change at a constant but different rate. The change rate can be observed by the harvester, or it can be defined by the data provider, in the optimal case, the harvester can be notified whenever a data provider changes.

5.1. Uniform Model

In the uniform model, we repeatedly synchronize the repositories in the same order. We describe the uniform model more formally in Figure 2. Here, each archive is historically harvested first, and a fresh harvest is repeated forever. Note that the last harvested time is fetched from the response of repositories in order to avoid clock skew. To contain any updates that happen during the harvesting period, the last harvested time is recorded before each harvest.

5.2. Adaptive Model

In this model, the harvester changes its synchronization rate based on the average repository update interval (Figure 3). Here, the harvester adjusts its harvesting frequency

Table 1. Monthly records update rate ($R(r_i; t_j), \Delta t = 1\ month$) of E-Prints archives (from 2002-01 to 2002-09), the complete table is available at [11]

archive	02/01	02/02	02/03	02/04	02/05	02/06	02/07	02/08	02/09
CPS	28	10	9	2	11	15	2	1	6
VTETD	16	25	10	84	115	52	51	78	45
arXiv	7744	3198	3874	3089	3605	3672	4462	4181	4505
bmc	50	20	5	11	68	3	0	0	5
cogprints	13	19	10	11	8	40	15	41	11
in2p3	180	140	276	57	90	110	108	52	141
ltrs.larc.nasa	12	40	31	22	42	35	71	31	24
mathpreprints	5	6	3	3	20	40	12	7	12
mit.etheses	46	86	142	119	189	63	75	124	82

Table 2. Repository update interval (09/30/2001-09/30/2002)

archive	$AVG(r_i)$	$U(r_i)$	$stdv(I(r_i))$	$C.O.V.(I(r_i))$
arxiv.org	145.32	1	0	0
bmc	3.19	3.25	11.93	3.67
cogprints	20.07	3.8	4.13	1.09
CPS	1.58	3.7	7.15	1.93
in2p3	7.89	1.71	2.92	1.71
LTRS	2.36	2.81	7.12	2.53
mit.etheses	7.33	2.03	3.3	1.62
VTETD	3.5	2.11	56.5	26.77

$$\Delta t = 1\ day$$
$AVG(r_i)$: Average Update Rate
$U(r_i)$: Average Update Interval
$stdv(I(r_i))$: Standard Deviation of Update Interval
$C.O.V.(I(r_i))$: Coefficient of Variation of Update Interval

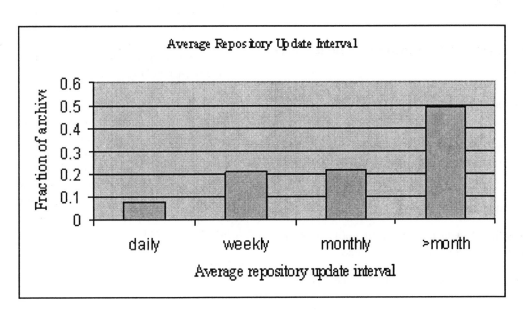

Figure 1. Average repository update interval of OAI-PMH repositories

Algorithm 1 $UniformModel\ Synchronization$
$Input: ArchiveList = \{a_1, a_2, ..., a_n\}$
$LastHarvestTime = \{t_1, t_2, ..., t_n\} = null$
$Procedure$
$for(i = 1; i \leq n; i++)\{$
        $t_i = getresponsetime(a_i);$
        $historical\_harvest(a_i);$
$\}$
$while(true)\{$
    $for(i = 1; i \leq n; i++)\{$
        $responsetime = getresponsetime(a_i);$
        $fresh\_harvest(a_i, t_i);$
        $t_i = responsetime;$
    $\}$
    $sleep(pre\_defined\_interval);$
$\}$

Figure 2. Algorithm for the Uniform Model

based on updated frequency of individual data providers, a more frequently updated data provider is allocated more resources.

The average repository update interval can be learned from the previous harvest, or be defined by an optional container in the data provider as we describe in the next section. Furthermore, beyond the framework of OAI-PMH, a data provider can notify the service provider about its update, or directly push updated metadata to service provider side.

6. Approaches For Determining Update Frequency

There are four approaches to decide update frequency of a data provider.

Best Estimation The harvester estimates the record update frequency by learning the harvest history.

Syndication A data provider may describe its update frequency explicitly.

Subscribe/Notify A data provider may notify a service provider whenever its content is changed.

Push Model Data providers may directly push updates to service provider side.

In the above approaches, best estimation and syndication can be integrated into current OAI-PMH model seamlessly;

Algorithm 2 $AdaptiveModel\ Harvesting$
$Input: ArchiveList = \{a_1, a_2, ..., a_n\}$
$AverageUpdateInterval = \{u_1, u_2, ..., u_n\}$
$(such\ as\ 1\ day, etc.)$
$LastHarvestTime = \{t_1, t_2, ..., t_n\} = null$
$Procedure$
$for(i = 1; i \leq n; i++)\{$
    $t_i = getresponsetime(a_i);$
    $historical\_harvest(a_i);$
$\}$
$while(true)\{$
    $for(i = 1; i \leq n; i++)\{$
        $if(currenttime - t_i \geq u_i)\{$
            $responsetime = getresponsetime(a_i);$
            $fresh\_harvest(a_i, t_i);$
            $t_i = responsetime;$
        $\}$
    $\}$
    $sleep(pre\_defined\_interval);$
$\}$

Figure 3. Algorithm for the Adaptive Model

subscribe/notify and push models extend or modify OAI-PMH model, but they are useful in special cases such as the Kepler service [12, 11].

6.1. Best Estimation

The harvester estimates the record update frequency by learning the harvest history. However, this requires the data provider must present a constant update frequency. After studying the harvest logs of Arc, we conclude in Section 4 that many current OAI-PMH compliant repositories present a constant update rate, and the rates vary dramatically from site to site.

It is difficult to precisely predict update time of one specific repository. However, a harvester may not necessarily provide 100% freshness at any time, for example, a harvester may harvest repositories with higher average update frequency more frequently, and harvest all other repositories once a week, it will still save a significant percentage of the update cost. Typically, the freshness requirement is decided by the application.

6.2. Syndication

In OAI-PMH, the response to an *Identify* request may contain locally defined description containers that can be used

```xml
<?xml version="1.0" encoding="UTF-8"?>
<schema targetNamespace="http://purl.org/rss/1.0/modules/syndication/"
  xmlns="http://www.w3.org/2001/XMLSchema"
  xmlns:syndication="http://purl.org/rss/1.0/modules/syndication/"
  elementFormDefault="qualified" attributeFormDefault="unqualified">
  <element name="syndication">
    <complexType>
      <sequence>
        <element name="updatePeriod" minOccurs="0" maxOccurs="1"
                 type="syndication:updatePeriodType"/>
        <element name="updateFrequency" minOccurs="0" maxOccurs="1"
                 type="integer"/>
        <element name="updateBase" minOccurs="0" maxOccurs="1"
                 type="dateTime"/>
      </sequence>
    </complexType>
  </element>
  <simpleType name="updatePeriodType">
    <restriction base="string">
      <enumeration value="hourly"/>
      <enumeration value="daily"/>
      <enumeration value="weekly"/>
      <enumeration value="monthly"/>
      <enumeration value="yearly"/>
    </restriction>
  </simpleType>
</schema>
```

Figure 4. XML schema for syndication

to express properties of the repository. We define an optional container that identifies the update frequency of a data provider. The information provides an alternate way to build the algorithm in Figure 3.

The RSS (Rich Site Summary) syndication module provides syndication hints to aggregators and others picking up RSS feeds regarding how often it is updated. The RSS defines three parameters to define update frequency of a data source: UpdatePeriod (Describes the period over which the data provider is updated), UpdateFrequency (Describe the frequency of updates in relation to the update period), and UpdateBase (Defines a base date to be used in concert with updatePeriod and updateFrequency to calculate the publishing schedule) [1]. These parameters provide syndication hints to aggregators and others picking up RSS feeds regarding how often it is updated. For example, if a file was updated twice an hour, the update Period would be "hourly" and the updateFrequency would be "2."

According to the RSS specification, we define an optional XML schema (Figure 4), which can be used by a data provider to describe its update rate. We do not address how a repository comes to know its update rate (it is beyond the scope of the OAI-PMH discussion), nor do we address inaccurate or deceitful repositories (cf. [15]).

Similar to best estimation, a syndication container may not be accurate, or a data provider is not able to provide a reasonable syndication container at all. However, a har-

vester can still improve freshness by allocating more resources to frequently changed repositories.

6.3. Subscribe/Notify

Best estimation and syndication are compliant with the OAI-PMH framework, but it relies on a constant update rate of data providers, which may not be true in some applications. A data provider may notify a service provider whenever its content is changed.

The subscribe/notify promises optimal results. It is useful in a repository with low and irregular update rate, such as archivelets in Kepler framework. However, this model requires that a service provider actively listen for the notification, which adds implementation complexity to the service provider. It also requires that a data provider keeps a record of subscribed service providers, and harvester issues OAI-PMH requests in an asynchronous fashion.

We extend the OAI-PMH with one additional "Notify" verbs on the service provider side as a way to optimize the functioning of the OAI-PMH. The repository issues a Notify request to inform the service provider that some new data is available. The harvester issue asynchronous OAI-PMH requests based on its status.

197

6.4. Push Model

Repositories may directly push updates to service providers. In this case, however, repositories decide when and what to push. That would require a data provider to keep the harvesting status. In implementation, the service provider supports a new "PushMetadata" verb, the metadata is attached in a HTTP POST request.

The push model provides additional benefits of bypassing firewalls and/or NAT (Network Address Translation) proxies. Similar to subscribe/notify model, it promises a nearly optimal synchronization. However, in the push model, the repository has additional complexity of saving the status of how it is harvested; in the subscribe/notify model, the communication is asynchronous, the status information is saved in harvester side.

7. Conclusions

The synchronization of harvesters and repositories is the key issue the OAI-PMH resolves. Compared to the general web crawlers, OAI-PMH optimizes the repository synchronization by supporting the incremental and selective harvesting. With more OAI-PMH repositories and an intention to support a wide range of applications, it is imperative to study the efficiency of a harvester and freshness of a service provider. We define some metrics for describing the synchronization problem in the OAI-PMH. Current update frequency of OAI-PMH compliant repositories is studied and several new methods are introduced to improve the efficiency of a service provider staying synchronized with large numbers of data providers. We introduce an optional *About* container (adopted from the RSS) for the OAI-PMH *Identify* response that allows a repository to advertise its update frequency.

References

[1] G. Beged-Dov, D. Brickley, R. Dornfest, I. Davis, L. Dodds, J. Eisenzopf, D. Galbraith, R. Guha, K. MacLeod, E. Miller, A. Swartz, and E. van der Vlist. RDF Site Summary 1.0 Modules: Syndication, 2000. http://purl.org/rss/1.0/modules/syndication/.

[2] C. M. Bowman, P. B. Danzig, D. R. Hardy, U. Manber, and M. F. Schwartz. The Harvest information discovery and access system. *Computer Networks and ISDN Systems*, 28(1-2):119–125, 1995. http://citeseer.nj.nec.com/article/bowman95harvest.html.

[3] T. Brody. Mining the social life of an eprint archive. http://opcit.eprints.org/tdb198/opcit/.

[4] J. Cho. *Crawling the Web: Discovery and maintenance of large-scale web data*. PhD thesis, Department of Computer Science, Stanford University, 2001.

[5] J. Cho and H. Garcia-Molina. Synchronizing a database to improve freshness. In *Proceedings of the ACM SIGMOD International Conference on Management of Data*, pages 117–128, 2000.

[6] J. Davis and C. Lagoze. NCSTRL: Design and deployment of a globally distributed digital library. *Journal of the American Society of Information Science*, 51(3):273–280, 2000.

[7] L. Gravano, K. Chang, H. Garcia-Molina, C. Lagoze, and A. Paepcke. STARTS:stanford proposal for Internet metasearching. In *Proceedings of the ACM SIGMOD International Conference on Management of Data*, pages 207–218, 1997.

[8] A. Labrinidis and N. Roussopoulos. "Update Propagation Strategies for Improving the Quality of Data on the Web". In *Proceedings of the 27th International Conference on Very Large Data Bases (VLDB'01)*, Rome, Italy, Sept. 2001.

[9] C. Lagoze, W. Hoehn, D. Millman, W. Arms, S. Gan, D. Hillmann, C. Ingram, D. Krafft, R. Marisa, J. Phipps, J. Saylor, C. Terrizzi, J. Allan, S. Guzman-Lara, and T. Kalt. Core services in the architecture of the National Science Digital Library (NSDL). In *Proceedings of the Second ACM/IEEE Joint Conference on Digital Libraries*, pages 201–209, Portland OR, July 14-18 2002.

[10] C. Lagoze, H. Van de Sompel, M. Nelson, and S. Warner. The Open Archives Initiative Protocol for Metadata Harvesting, version 2.0. http://www.openarchives.org/OAI/openarchivesprotocol.html.

[11] X. Liu. *Federating Heterogeneous Digital Libraries by Metadata Harvesting*. PhD thesis, Department of Computer Science, Old Dominion University, 2002.

[12] X. Liu, K. Maly, and M. Zubair. Enhanced Kepler framework for self archiving. In *Workshop on Distributed Computing Architectures for Digital Libraries. ICPP 2002*, pages 455–461, Vancouver Canada, August 18-21 2002.

[13] X. Liu, K. Maly, M. Zubair, and M. L. Nelson. Arc - an OAI service provider for digital library federation. *D-Lib Magazine*, 7(4), 2001. http://www.dlib.org/dlib/april01/liu/04liu.html.

[14] X. Liu, K. Maly, M. Zubair, and M. L. Nelson. Arc: An OAI service provider for cross archive searching. In *Proceedings of the ACM/IEEE Joint Conference on Digtial Libraries*, pages 65–66, Roanoke VA, June 24-28 2001.

[15] C. Lynch. When documents deceive: Trust and provenance as new factors for information retrieval in a tangled web. *Journal of the American Society for Information Science and Technology*, 52(1):12–17, 2001.

[16] R. Rivest. The MD5 message-digest algorithm. Technical Report Internet RFC-1321, IETF, 1992. http://www.ietf.org/rfc/rfc1321.txt.

[17] A. Van Hoff, J. Giannandrea, M. Hapner, S. Carter, and M. M. The HTTP distribution and replication protocol. Technical Report NOTE-DRP, World Wide Web Consortium, 1997. http://www.w3.org/TR/NOTE-drp.

eBizSearch: An OAI-Compliant Digital Library for eBusiness

Yves Petinot[1], Pradeep B. Teregowda[2], Hui Han[1], C. Lee Giles[1,2,3], Steve Lawrence[4], Arvind Rangaswamy[2] and Nirmal Pal[2]

[1]Department of Computer Science and Engineering
The Pennsylvania State University
213 Pond Lab.
University Park, PA 16802
{petinot, hhan}
@cse.psu.edu

[2]eBusiness Research Center
The Pennsylvania State University
401 Business Administration Building
University Park, PA 16802
{pbt105, arvindr}
@psu.edu

[3]School of Information Sciences and Technology
The Pennsylvania State University
001 Thomas Bldg.
University Park, PA 16802
{giles}
@ist.psu.edu

[4]Google Inc.
2400 Bayshore Parkway
Mountain View, CA 94043
{lawrence}
@google.com

Abstract

Niche Search Engines offer an efficient alternative to traditional search engines when the results returned by general-purpose search engines do not provide a sufficient degree of relevance and when nontraditional search features are required. Niche search engines can take advantage of their domain of concentration to achieve higher relevance and offer enhanced features. We discuss a new digital library niche search engine, eBizSearch, dedicated to e-business and e-business documents. The ground technology for eBizSearch is CiteSeer, a special-purpose automatic indexing document digital library and search engine developed at NEC Research Institute. We present here the integration of CiteSeer in the framework of eBizSearch and the process necessary to tune the whole system towards the specific area of e-business. We show how using machine learning algorithms we generate metadata to make eBizSearch Open Archives compliant. eBizSearch is a publicly available service and can be reached at [13].

1. Introduction

E-business is concerned with e-zation (digitization) of business processes and encompasses areas as dissimilar as auctions, marketing and customer relationship management (CRM). Here we discuss eBizSearch, a digital library niche search engine for e-business based upon the technology of CiteSeer [5,17,22]. eBizSearch is an ongoing research project at the Pennsylvania State University and is supported by the Smeal School of Business through its eBusiness Research Center.

eBizSearch is an experimental niche search engine that searches the web and catalogs academic articles as well as commercially produced articles and reports that address various business and technology aspects of e-Business. The search engine crawls websites of universities, commercial organizations, research institutes and government departments to retrieve academic articles, working papers, white papers, consulting reports, magazine articles, and published statistics and facts. It performs a citation analysis of all the articles collected, maintains an internal graph based on the citations these articles make and finally provides a web-interface allowing users to explore this graph through various ranking schemes, just as in CiteSeer [5,8,17,22,23]. Articles available through eBizSearch can be downloaded (for fair use) without any charge and in various electronic formats. To date more than 20000 documents are available from eBizSearch.

In section 2 we present the motivations that led to the creation of eBizSearch and what the intended audience for this search engine is. In section 3 we describe the architecture of the system and how it successfully integrates CiteSeer for information-extraction tasks. The issue of OAI compatibility is addressed in section 4. Section 5 is dedicated to our current efforts to extend the applicability of CiteSeer-like digital library niche search engines to various academic fields. Finally in section 6 we reference related projects and present future developments around eBizSearch.

2. Motivations for a Niche Digital Library for e-Business

Many disciplines find that their own focused resources are better sources than general-purpose resources. The current trend is hence in the development of specialized digital libraries [1,10,11,26,29,30] and their aggregators [9]. As CiteSeer [8] would be a search engine for the computer science literature, eBizSearch would be to the e-business literature. Our goals for eBizSearch are:

1. To build a digital library of relevant academic publications in the field of e-business, and, in terms of the relevance of query results, to outperform general-purpose search engines such as Google, AltaVista, Lycos, etc.

2. To make it possible for users to browse through the digital library's papers database using the specificities of academic publications (e.g. citations between papers), as opposed to the traditional, HTML-based, hypertext navigation on which general-purpose search engines rely. This constitutes the navigation model introduced by CiteSeer.

Table 1: Availability of documents at their original URL (11608 URLs considered – HTTP Status of each URL established by requesting the resource header (HTTP HEAD))

HTTP Code	Semantics	Most probable cause	%
HTTP 200	OK	Document still available at original URL	88.23
HTTP 404	Not Found	Document no longer available at original URL	4.71
HTTP 500	Server Error	Server down or no longer exists	4.63
HTTP 400	Bad Request		1.2
HTTP 302	Moved Temporarily		0.59
HTTP 403	Forbidden		0.38
Other			0.26

3. To provide a resilient and durable source of publications. The ever changing topology of the web must be acknowledged: resource locations change from one day to another or simply disappear hence making the simple knowledge of an URL insufficient to guarantee the long term access to an electronic resource. In this perspective our system is independent from the documents authors/hosts and ensures long-term availability since documents are downloaded, processed, converted to multiple formats and hosted on our servers. We recently checked the availability, at their original source, of the documents available (i.e. referenced and downloadable) from eBizSearch

(collection began in 1999); the results are listed in Table 1 and confirm the trend aforementioned.

4. To add features to document search that are appropriate to the e-business community such as automatic document filtering

5. To make eBizSearch compliant with the Open Archives Initiative [31].

CiteSeer [8] has been probably the most successful digital library niche search engine for Computer Science. The high popularity that it benefits from, together with the desire for a permanent archive, enables the documents referenced in its database to be highly ranked among the URLs listed by a general-purpose search engine such as Google. We expect eBizSearch, and the CiteSeer-like niche search engines that will follow, to perform as well, if not better. The intended audience of eBizSearch is researchers in the field of e-business as well as any individual having an interest in this field.

3. Anatomy of eBizSearch

3.1. System Overview

The internal organization of eBizSearch is presented in Figure 1. As can be seen the architecture of eBizSearch essentially exploits that of CiteSeer and uses much of that technology.

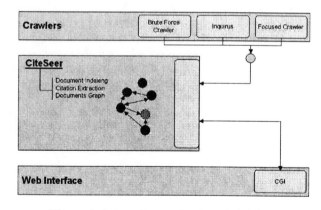

Figure 1: Internal organization of eBizSearch

A set of crawlers, independent from each other, provides the CiteSeer module with the URLs of sources of potential papers. The CiteSeer module takes care of the download phase, converting and parsing each document. If a document falls into the paper category according to CiteSeer (i.e. satisfies various requirements, among which the existence of a "Reference" section, the minimum paper length, etc.), then it is added to the database and made available for user querying. Users can query the system through the dedicated web interface.

In the following sections we go into more details on the role of each component.

3.2. Crawlers

New documents can be submitted to the system in two ways: through manual submission of a given document (URL), or automatically as a result of a crawling phase. The web interface features a submission page allowing users to manually submit paper locations (humanly reviewed before actual addition to the system). We present here the crawling strategies experimented in eBizSearch.

The crawling phase consists into discovering new potential paper sources (URLs) by guided, focused or extensive exploration of the web or subsections of it. The input for a crawler is one or many seed URLs from which to start exploring the web. The crawler follows hypertext links from one page to another in a more or less biased fashion (focused as opposed to brute force). Source pages, that is, pages containing links to potential papers (e.g. links to file with PDF/PS extension), are logged. Periodically the collected URLs are submitted to CiteSeer for processing, and upon adequacy with paper features, the document/paper is added to the database (refer to overview of extraction process). Note also that known source pages of e-business papers are periodically revisited in order to collect new publications.

Three independent crawlers currently provide eBizSearch in potential publication sources:

- Brute force crawler: when a new repository of interest in the field of e-business is brought to our attention we explore the corresponding sub-network in an extensive fashion to locate most, if not all, of the relevant publications sources available on this site. Brute force crawl is the most efficient on sites that feature a publication section, in which case we can take advantage of this explicit organization to optimize the crawl time (e.g. eCommerce Research Forum at MIT [16]).

- Inquirus based crawler: Inquirus is a meta-search engine described in [23]. By querying Inquirus adequately (i.e. by including one or many keywords referring to publications (e.g. "publication" and/or "journal" and/or "preprint" and/or "ps", etc.) we take advantage of the wide coverage of the web of many general-purpose search engines such as Google or Lycos. The concentration domain of the niche search engine, in this case e-business, defines the queries submitted to Inquirus. Our system systematically generates all possible query strings out of a glossary of

words relevant to e-business. The URLs returned by Inquirus are submitted to the CiteSeer module.

- Focused crawler: at an experimental level we work on the development of focused crawlers [6] that would follow only relevant links during their exploration of the web to maximize the eventual discovery of relevant documents. Various crawlers are being tried out for the suitability for this purpose; this includes rule-based crawlers and context-based focus crawlers [7].

As shown in Figure 1, URLs output by all crawlers are pushed in a common queue and batch-submitted to CiteSeer. Batch-submission is made necessary due to CiteSeer's internal organization in which document processing and querying are mutually exclusive operations: the document processing being quite time consuming (the average processing time, including download, is approximately 15 minutes), it is desirable to batch-submit documents to limit the amount of time the service is not reachable.

The crawlers described in this section strongly concentrate on localizing e-business publications originating from academic institutions (Business Schools essentially). We provide in Table 2 the list of US Business Schools for which the crawling of their web domain yielded the largest number of relevant publications in the field of e-Business (publications freely available from the web servers of these institutions). For comparison we mention the ranking of these institutions in the US News ranking of Business School (2003).

Table 2: US Business Schools accounting for the most documents in eBizSearch

School Name (US News Business School ranking)	Percentage of Total Documents.
Massachusetts Institute of Technology (4)	1.55 %
University of Pennsylvania (3)	1.53 %
Northwestern University (5)	0.95 %
University of Chicago (6)	0.53 %
Columbia University (8)	0.47 %
Duke University (6)	0.47 %
University of Virginia (10)	0.14 %
Cornell University (16)	0.13 %

For completeness we also list in Table 3 the general ranking of top sources for documents indexed by eBizSearch.

On completion of the crawling phase it is assumed that the collected URLs are indeed relevant in the domain of concentration of the niche search engine, i.e. e-business.

Source	Percentage of Total Documents.
International Institute for Applied System Analysis	3.32 %
Santa Fe Institute	2.89 %
AT&T	1.56 %
Massachusetts Institute of Technology	1.55 %
University of New Castle upon Tyne	1.54 %
University of Pennsylvania	1.53 %
University of Maryland (CS department)	1.48 %
Federal Reserve Bank of Boston	1.35 %

3.3. CiteSeer

CiteSeer maintains the database of documents and citations, but has no intrinsic knowledge on the field of concentration of the documents. Starting from resource locations, it handles the download of the documents. These are then parsed, their citations information extracted, and if the documents follow the pattern of academic publications, they are eventually indexed and added to the database. The internal organization of CiteSeer is beyond the scope of this paper and can be found in [5] and [17]. We give a brief overview for each of the tasks carried on by CiteSeer.

3.3.1. Document Retrieval. Documents are submitted to the system by their location on the web (URL). For efficiency CiteSeer supports concurrent download of multiple documents. The system is resilient to unavoidable availability and connection issues.

3.3.2. Information Extraction. The information extraction (IE) tasks consist into the parsing of citation information following the typical patterns of academic publications. The document is first converted to plain text, the IE tasks being performed independently from the original electronic format. Among other criteria, CiteSeer will reject a document that cannot be converted to plain text, that is too short, or that is not referring to other documents. The specific problem of citation information extraction is addressed in [22].

3.3.3. Document / Citation Querying. CiteSeer provides a support for full-text querying of both documents and citations (documents and citations are indexed into two independent indexes). After a first query, citation-oriented exploration of the document graph is available to the user. Note that for efficiency in real-time query handling CiteSeer maintains various caches (index cache and query response cache).

3.3.4. Distributed Error Correction. CiteSeer provides functionalities allowing authors to provide correction regarding those of their publications that are available from CiteSeer. The correction functionalities are available from the back-end interface only. Correction requests can be made from the web-interface. Support of distributed error correction by CiteSeer is extensively discussed in [24].

3.4. Web-Interface

The last essential component to eBizSearch is its web-interface. A screenshot of the main form of the web-application is shown in Figure 2. The main form allows full text querying of both documents and citations.

Figure 2: Main form of eBizSearch

The presentation of search results is based on the same model as CiteSeer [8] and is covered in details in [17]. Figure 3 shows typical results presentation when querying the document database for "Malone".

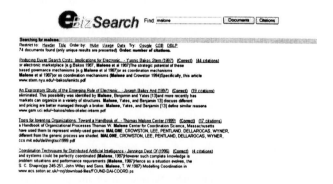

Figure 3: Results for document search

Figure 4 shows a document page for a paper hosted by eBizSearch.

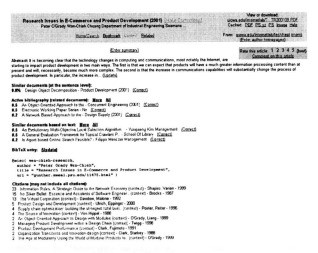

Figure 4: Document page.

Finally, Figure 5 shows typical result display when querying the citation database.

Figure 5: Results for citation search.

Originally the main interface of CiteSeer was to be adopted for eBizSearch. However due to the fact that simple interfaces encourage people to be at ease about using the search engine, a simpler interface was developed, that strongly draws from the search engine Google. The navigation by expected citations (along with the listing of the expected citations) was disabled, as it appears to confuse the user. Note also that the main form page, originally dynamic, was replaced by a static web page in order to reduce loads and ensure place holding in case the server (CiteSeer module) becomes temporarily unavailable. Finally the help pages were updated to make them simpler to understand.

The web-interface is currently CGI-based (Perl) and consists of a single script that provides the presentation layer to our system. CiteSeer runs as a server process

accessible locally only and the communication between the presentation layer and CiteSeer is TCP/IP based.

4. Interoperability and the Open Archives Initiative (OAI)

As part of a larger scale effort, eBizSearch, as well as CiteSeer, intend to integrate with the Open Archives Initiative project and to comply with the associated communication protocol defined in [31]. In this section we discuss the issues arising from OAI metadata and protocol requirements and draw the roadmap towards a fully integrated OAI support of our system.

Table 4: OAI compatibility (*: automated metadata extraction)

Metadata item	Available in CiteSeer database	Required from OAI compliant library (Dublin Core metadata standard)
Title	Yes*	Yes
Creator	Yes*	Yes
Subject – keywords	No	Yes
Abstract	Yes*	Yes
Contributor	No	Yes
Publisher	No	Yes
Date (archived)	Yes	Yes
Type	Yes	Yes
Format	Yes* – multiple formats available via conversion	Yes
Identifier	Yes*	Yes
Source	Yes*	Yes
References	Yes*	Yes
Referenced by	Yes*	Yes
Language	No – English only	Yes
Full-text document querying	Yes	Not required
Full-text citation querying	Yes	Not required

4.1. OAI Metadata and Protocol Requirements

OAI defines an XML-based access and exploration protocol aiming at standardizing the access to digital libraries on the web [2,25]. The National Science Digital Library [28] program promotes this usage and Citidel is an example of metadata information aggregator [9]. Historically the metadata set of CiteSeer has been proprietary as well as the protocol to access it: CiteSeer defines its own metadata requirements and communication with clients is HTML based (i.e. web browsers). On the contrary the OAI project is based upon the XML-based Dublin Core metadata standard [12] and the OAI protocol can potentially be used by a wider variety of clients. Our effort in this context consists into enabling OAI-based access to CiteSeer/eBizSearch and, as suggested in Table 4, to extend the information extraction capabilities of CiteSeer as its original set of metadata for each document (and their citations) does not fully cover the set of metadata required by the Dublin Core metadata standard.

4.2. Architectural and Organizational Issues

Enabling OAI access to CiteSeer intrinsically means upgrading the presentation layer (CGI implementation) such that, provided certain flags are passed in the HTTP query string, the output is OAI-Compliant instead of HTML. This represents an easy aspect of the migration to OAI compliancy and will not be further detailed in this document.

A more delicate and contrived task toward compliance is to provide support for additional metadata items and the possibility to query on them. Some metadata items required by the Dublin Core standard are simply not available from the database of CiteSeer, for instance keywords are not currently extracted. Beyond the issue of the availability of a single metadata item, we must also enable queries based on this item (e.g. keyword-based or date-based queries). Here we need to address an organizational limitation of CiteSeer, which only enables full text querying of both the document texts and citation texts, its metadata collection being available only for internal operations by the system (e.g. ranking, linking) but not directly queriable. The two query modes are enabled through two dedicated indices (inverted files). In order to provide good performance, OAI compliance implies that we index on all the metadata items that can potentially be queried on, that is, all the metadata items required by the OAI specification: we need to provide an index linking keywords to documents, dates to documents and so forth. An item such as publication date is originally available from CiteSeer, but the database organization, even internally to the system, does not provide the capabilities of a standard DBMS, and thus does not allow direct querying on the date. Currently the date information can only be used on the web-interface to sort the set of documents/citations retrieved in response to a query.

Three approaches have been considered to provide OAI support to eBizSearch.

- The first approach is static, in the sense that the Dublin Core XML records are generated (periodically or on demand) and persistently stored (files, DBMS, etc.).

This approach is mentioned for completeness only, but was not given further attention due to the strongly dynamic and interrelated nature of metadata in CiteSeer: for efficiency, CiteSeer maintains for a given document D, not only the set of documents X_i (i in $1...N_i$) cited by D, but also the set of documents Y_j (j in $1...N_j$) citing D. This is how the document graph is internally maintained. The citation information is contained in the Dublin Core record for a document, and therefore a static approach seems inappropriate since citation information is prone to automated modifications. Finally the presentation layer is inherently dynamic and therefore handling generation of XML records at this level, on-the-fly, provides much more flexibility and consistency without affecting performance: the two remaining approaches derive from these observations.

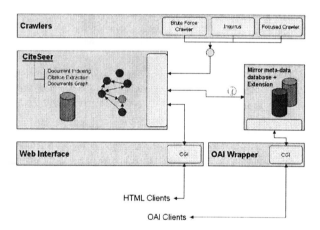

Figure 6: Organization of eBizSearch with non-integrated OAI support

- The second approach, the one currently adopted by eBizSearch, is represented in Figure 6. The level of dynamicity is higher in that XML records generation is performed on the fly. As can be seen, the integration remains poor since the metadata database of CiteSeer is mirrored (external database) and extended in order to address the different requirements induced by OAI compliance. The external database is periodically synchronized with the master database; further metadata extraction is then performed using this mirror. Physically, mostly for isolation purposes during the test phase, we set up an adjunct server to hold the mirror database, this server also supporting an HTTP server dedicated to servicing OAI requests. The URIs that are provided in the XML records are nonetheless pointers to the main server, where documents can be downloaded from. We chose to implement this solution first in order to provide support for OAI as early as possible; this serves as a transient solution which will be superceded by the third approach upon completion of its implementation.

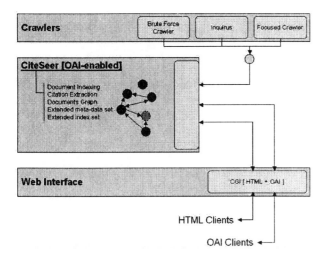

- In a third approach we intend to extend the set of metadata maintained by CiteSeer itself (see section 5.2), increase the number of indexes in order to extend the queriability of metadata (i.e. date-based queries, keywords-based queries, abstract-restricted queries) and finally upgrade the presentation layer to support the OAI protocol. Ultimately the CiteSeer software package is intended to be shipped in this OAI-enabled form. As can be seen from Figure 7, this approach is an improvement over the second approach wherein all redundancies would have been removed. We are currently improving the CiteSeer to follow this approach.

4.3. OAI Access to eBizSearch

The eBizSearch repository is reachable using the OAI protocols at [14].

5. Extending CiteSeer Capabilities

CiteSeer has been originally developed to meet the needs of the Computer Science research community. As a consequence it makes various assumptions based on the peculiarities of this field and takes advantage of these assumptions to collect, parse and extract information. In this section we present enhancements aiming at improving the reliability of eBizSearch, improving the quality of the metadata extraction and ultimately making CiteSeer-like search engines more portable to other research fields. We

provide our most recent experimental results to support the validity of our strategy.

5.1. Extending Document Conversion Capabilities

Document conversion is the corner stone to CiteSeer-like niche digital library: the system must provide support for the conversion of various electronic formats to address the needs of various research communities. As mentioned earlier, CiteSeer performs information extraction using the plain text version of documents. For any electronic format to be supported by CiteSeer, there must exist a converter for documents in that format to plain text. Conversion to plain text of a given electronic format is generally a complex task and is therefore handled by third-parties software libraries. This raises several issues, first the availability of such a software library/service for a given format (this may include platform concerns); second, conversion libraries might fail in converting valid documents (for us, not an uncommon experience). This section presents our setup to combine multiple conversion software libraries to improve the conversion reliability for a single format. We also briefly discuss the adjunction of new conversion software libraries to support additional electronic formats.

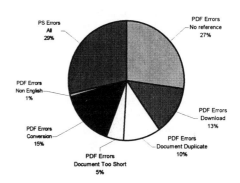

Figure 8: Original breakdown of processing errors

5.1.1. Increasing Conversion Reliability. CiteSeer relies on a single application, *pstotext*, to perform all the conversions needed. Yet, the test phase of eBizSearch revealed that some perfectly valid PDF documents would fail to be converted. Figure 8 shows a breakdown of processing errors of eBizSearch in its original configuration: the failure rate in the conversion of PDF documents is unacceptably high. To improve on the success rate, we conducted an experiment using three freely available tools [27] for conversion of PDF files to text/ASCII files: *pstotext*, *ps2ascii* and *pdftotext*. The applications were called from within a Perl script simulating the working of the applications in the actual eBizSearch/CiteSeer conversion environment. The same set of valid documents in PDF format was submitted to each application for conversion. The converted documents were then examined as to whether information could be extracted from them after conversion.

Table 5: Distribution of documents across the years and failure count for each application

Publication Year (Number of documents)	Failure Count		
	pstotext	*pdftotext*	*ps2acii*
1999 (10)	2	8	1
2000 (15)	2	2	4
2001 (12)	0	0	2
2002 (21)	3	2	7
Total Failure Count (out of 58)	7	12	14

We were primarily interested in documents from a business source and for this we considered all 58 PDF files of the research documents available from the web site of PennState University's eBusiness Research Center [15] which originated from various institutions and authors. We used the following versions of the applications: *pstotext* (DEC - modified version), *ps2ascii* (Ghostscript, version 7.05), *pdftotext* (xpdf, version 1.01). To emulate the real conversion environment, we limited the time taken for the conversion of each document (a maximum of 4 minutes, otherwise the conversion is considered to have failed): even so, all conversions completed before the deadline and therefore the experiment was not affected by this constraint. The conversion was considered successful when the output text file was human-readable and the conversion of the document was complete (entire text content of the original document excluding any figure or table). Note finally that the option q was used with *pdftotext* to ensure suppression of error messages. The counts of conversion failures for each application are listed in Table 5.

Figure 9 allows a more intuitive visualization of the problem: while it is clear that none of the applications converts all the documents successfully, we can nevertheless increase the number of documents successfully converted by combining several conversion applications.

The justification of conversion failures is not quite obvious, and apparently the causes are diverse. Our experience shows that *pdftotext* has problems with version 1.3 of Adobe PDF files. This is reflected in the high failure rate for documents created in 1999 (mostly created using version 1.3, while only two were created using version 1.4). It is also to be noted that some of the documents were image scans and contributed significantly to the failure of all applications. Finally some failures from *ps2ascii* were due to the fact that the words in the resulting text documents were joined together, making information

extraction almost impossible. For further discussion on the suitability of each of these applications for extraction, the reader is referred to [32].

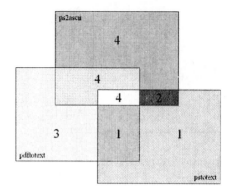

Figure 9: Superposition of conversion failures

Considering these results, a conversion system was adopted for eBizSearch: on completion of the download phase, a document is passed on to a default application for conversion to text, upon failure of the default converter it is passed to an alternative application (if any) and so on until successful conversion, eventually reducing the failure rate conversions (Figure 10). Note also that, since our document conversion system is being constantly upgraded, there is a need to track the efficiency of conversion after each upgrade.

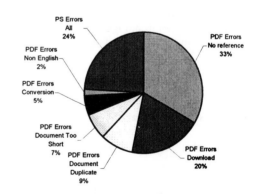

Figure 10: Breakdown of processing errors with conversion enhancement

5.1.2. Supporting Additional Electronic Formats. The large majority of research publications in Computer Science are made available in either PostScript or Portable Document Format formats (or their variants, e.g. compressed PostScript). As a consequence CiteSeer has always been shipped with built-in support for PDF and PS documents only. However the publication of documents using alternative formats, for instance Microsoft Word, has

206

become non negligible in some fields and it is desirable that a support for a wide variety of electronic formats be added to the CiteSeer package in order to facilitate portability to other domains. In this perspective, we extended CiteSeer with a Word to text converter. Accordingly our crawlers now seek candidate URLs of publications in Microsoft Word format.

5.2. Extending Metadata Extraction Capabilities

We saw in section 4 that OAI requires more metadata items than those currently available from CiteSeer. Moreover, due to the strong focus of CiteSeer on Computer Science publications, metadata extraction has been efficiently achieved by using customized regular expressions. Still the performance of CiteSeer in extracting some metadata items (esp. author(s) and date) turns out to be poor and often requires manual correction. To extend the set of metadata items extracted, and improve the extraction quality, we propose a machine-learning-oriented model where the metadata extraction algorithm results from training.

The metadata extraction algorithm used is a Support Vector Machine (SVM), a supervised learning and classification method. This algorithm is extensively covered in [18]. For more details about support vector machines, please see [3,21].

This metadata extraction algorithm extracts the 13 metadata items defined in [34] (Title, Authors, Authors' address, Authors' affiliation, Authors' email, Authors' URL, Authors' phone number, Publication Date, Degree of the thesis, Keywords, Abstract, Publication Number and Note) from the header of the research papers. (Title, Author, Keywords, Abstract and Publication Date) are mapped to their Dublin Core metadata equivalent, i.e. (Title, Creator, Subject, Description and Publication Date respectively).

We use the following manually tagged header [34] to illustrate the working of the extraction algorithm.

```
1:<note>  Computational  Intelligence,
Volume 12, Number 3, 1996 +L+ </note>
2:<title> LOCALIZED TEMPORAL REASONING
USING SUBGOALS +L+
3:AND ABSTRACT EVENTS +L+ </title>
4:<author> Shieu-Hong Lin, Thomas Dean 1
+L+ </author>
5:<affiliation> Department of Computer
Science,      Brown      University,
</affiliation> <address> Providence, RI
02912 +L+ </address>
6:<abstract>  We  are  concerned  with
temporal reasoning problems where there
is uncertainty about the order +L+
```

```
7:in  which  events  occur.  The  task  of
temporal reasoning is to derive an event
sequence consistent with +L+ </abstract>
```

Note: +L+ is the new-line marker

The actual metadata output by our algorithm is given below.

```
1:  chunk(1) - <note> - Computational
Intelligence, Volume 12, Number 3, 1996
2:  chunk(1)  -  <title>  -  LOCALIZED
TEMPORAL REASONING USING SUBGOALS
3:  chunk(1)  -  <title>  -  AND  ABSTRACT
EVENTS
4: chunk(1) - <author> - Shieu-Hong Lin
chunk(2) - <author> - Thomas Dean 1
5: chunk(1) - <affiliation> - Department
of Computer Science
chunk(2) - <address> - Brown University,
Providence, RI 02912
6:  chunk(1)  -  <abstract>  -  We  are
concerned  with  temporal  reasoning
problems  where  there  is  uncertainty
about the order
7:  chunk(1)  -  <abstract>  -  in  which
events  occur.  The  task  of  temporal
reasoning is to derive an event sequence
consistent with
```

Except for line 5, which is a multi-class line, all the lines are single-class lines. The job of the SVM wrapper is to classify each natural line of the research paper header into one or more classes and then seek the best chunk boundaries of the multi-class lines. The identified chunks are the metadata actually extracted. For example, line 5 contains chunks of affiliation and address that have been successfully identified. We also identify each of the authors in the lines with multiple authors (line 4).

We tested our SVM wrapper on the dataset provided by [34]. This dataset contains 935 headers of computer science papers, with 500 training header and 435 test headers. Our method using the SVM yields a slightly better overall accuracy (92.9) than the Hidden Markov Model (HMM) of [34] (90.1). It is also to be noticed that [34] used additional data, namely 5,000 unlabeled headers (287,770 word tokens) and 176 BibTeX files (2,463,834 word tokens) for training.

We list in Table 6 the class-specific classification accuracy, precision and recall achieved by SVM, and the class-specific classification accuracy achieved by HMM (as reported by [34]). The performance is evaluated based on words. These results supports the fact our SVM metadata extraction algorithm could achieve better performance than HMM for metadata extraction with less training data.

Table 6: Comparison of SVM and HMM performance

	SVM Accuracy	SVM Precision	SVM Recall	HMM multi-state L+D Accuracy
Title	98.9	94.1	99.1	98.3
Author	99.3	96.1	98.4	93.2
Affiliation	98.1	92.2	95.4	89.4
Address	99.1	94.9	94.5	84.1
Note	95.5	88.9	75.5	84.6
Email	99.6	90.8	92.7	86.9
Date	99.7	84.0	97.5	93.0
Abstract	97.5	91.1	96.6	98.4
Phone	99.9	93.8	91.0	94.9
Keyword	99.2	96.9	81.5	98.5
Web	99.9	79.5	96.9	41.7
Degree	99.5	80.5	62.2	81.2
PubNum	99.9	92.2	86.3	64.2

6. Related and Future Work

To our knowledge eBizSearch is currently the only automated digital library niche search engine in the field of e-business that focuses on academic publications indexing. Other free, yet manually maintained, similar services exist such as IDEAS [20] in the closely related field of economy. A couple of paying or subscription-based portals exist, among which Bitpipe.com [4]. Bitpipe.com provides and sells a common interface to access papers from various analysts group in the field of IT/e-business. From a broader perspective there exist various general-purpose search engines and portals gathering resources on e-business. We can mention searchCIO.com [33] and IBM's e-business homepage [19]. Like most of the e-business resources on the web, they loosely compile materials from various sources. Most of these materials originate from corporations and do not follow the standards of academic publications. As such a major goal of our work is expand the number of documents indexed by eBizSearch and to increase its functionality. As an example, we wish to automatically generate glossaries categories such as documents which are primarily technical versus those that are primarily business.

The portability of eBizSearch/CiteSeer-like search engines will be a key to their success. The limitation to the portability of eBizSearch is the portability of CiteSeer itself: CiteSeer was originally developed to take advantage of its underlying platform in order to optimize the runtime performance, thus the code is very specialized towards its running platform, i.e. Linux. CiteSeer makes extensive use of the UNIX semantics (e.g. system calls, file operations, POSIX) as well as of software packages that are traditionally shipped with Unix/Linux platforms (e.g.

conversion software such as *pstotext*). If these considerations do not fundamentally prevent porting the eBizSearch/CiteSeer package to commercial platforms (essentially Windows platform) they nevertheless require an additional effort to unify access to OS-managed resources (conversion libraries, file system, network, etc.). Finally the web-interface (CGI engine) is not handled directly by our system but is instead delegated to an Apache HTTP server, which requires specific configuration of its mod-rewrite module. All in all the setting-up of the application is for now fastidious and requires a good level of expertise from the operator. We currently work toward improving the portability and setting-up of CiteSeer (and thus eBizSearch) while still preserving good runtime performance.

Beyond the platform portability we seek to extend the applicability of our model to other fields of academic research. As outlined in section 5.2, a learning-based approach for metadata extraction should allow us to reach this goal. Ultimately, providing configuration towards a specific area of concentration (in the form of sample publications) will be sufficient to deploy our niche search engine technology in various academic fields.

7. Conclusion

We described a new digital library, eBizSearch, which is a digital library niche search engine based upon CiteSeer technology that has found and indexed over 20,000 documents in e-business. The internal organization of eBizSearch, organized around CiteSeer, was presented, along with a discussion on the migration to a fully-integrated OAI-compliant system. Finally the limitations of CiteSeer in terms of metadata availability, reliability and portability led us to propose a Support Vector Machine machine learning approach for the extraction of metadata. Our initial results show that this method accurately automatically extracts and tags untagged text and has the potential for extending the domain of tagged metadata.

8. Acknowledgements

We acknowledge partial support from NSF NSDL 0121679 and useful comments from Josef Behling, Lillian Cassel, Sandip Debnath, Ed Fox, Aaron Krowne, and Eren Manavoglu.

9. References

[1]: H. Anan, X. Liu, K. Maly, M.L. Nelson, M. Zubair, J.C. French, E.A. Fox, P. Shivakumar, "Preservation and transition of NCSTRL using an OAI-based architecture", In *Proceedings of the ACM/IEEE Joint Conference on Digital Libraries (JCDL 2002)*, pp 181-182, 2002.

[2]: M. Baldonado, C.K. Chang, L. Gravano, A. Paepcke, "Metadata for Digital Libraries: Architecture and Design Rationale", In *Proceedings of the 4th Annual Conference on the Theory and Practice of Digital Libraries*, pp 47-56, 1997.

[3]: K.P. Bennett, C. Campbell, "Support vector machines: Hype or Hallelujah", *ACM Special Interest Group on Knowledge Discovery and Data Mining (SIGKDD)*, Explorations 2(2):1-13, 2000.

[4]: Bitpipe.com, http://www.bitpipe.com/.

[5]: K. Bollacker, S. Lawrence, C.L. Giles, "CiteSeer: An Autonomous Web Agent for Automatic Retrieval and Identification of Interesting Publications", In *Proceedings of the Second International ACM Conference on Autonomous Agents (Agents'98)*, pp 116-123, 1998.

[6]: S. Chakrabarti, M. Van den Berg, B. Dom, "Focused crawling: a new approach to topic-specific Web resource discovery", In *Proceedings of the 8th International World Wide Web Conference*, pp 1623-1640, Amsterdam, Netherlands, 1999.

[7]: M. Diligenti, F. Coetzee, S. Lawrence, C.L. Giles, M. Gori, "Focused Crawling Using Context Graphs", In *Proceedings of the 26th International Conference on Very Large Databases (VLDB 2000)*, pp 527-534, 2000.

[8]: CiteSeer homepage, http://www.citeseer.com.

[9]: CITIDEL project homepage, http://www.citidel.org.

[10]: Crane G., "Building a Digital Library: The Perseus Project as a Case Study in the Humanities", In *Proceedings of the 1st ACM International Conference on Digital Libraries*, pp 3-10, 1996.

[11]: Digital Libraries Initiative Phase 2, http://www.dli2.nsf.gov/projects.html.

[12]: "Dublin Core Metadata Element Set, Version 1.1: Reference Description", http://dublincore.org/documents/1999/07/02/dces/.

[13]: eBizSearch homepage, http://www.ebizsearch.org.

[14]: eBizSearch OAI base URL, http://www.ebizsearch.org/oai.

[15]: eBusiness Research Center (eBRC) homepage, the Pennsylvania State University, http://www.ebrc.org.

[16]: eCommerce Research Forum at MIT, http://ecommerce.mit.edu/.

[17]: C.L. Giles, K. Bollacker, S. Lawrence, "CiteSeer: An Automatic Citation Indexing System", In *Proceedings of the 3rd ACM Conference on Digital Libraries (DL'98)*, pp 89-98, 1998.

[18]: H. Han, C.L. Giles, E. Manavoglu, H. Zha, Z. Zhang and E.A. Fox, "Automatic Document Metadata Extraction using Support Vector Machines", In *Proceeding of the ACM/IEEE Joint Conference on Digital Libraries (JCDL 2003)*, In this proceeding, 2003.

[19]: e-Business homepage at IBM, http://www.ibm.com/ebusiness/.

[20]: IDEAS homepage, http://ideas.repec.org/.

[21]: T. Joachims, "Text categorization with support vector machines: learning with many relevant features", In *Proceedings of the 10th European Conference on Machine Learning (ECML-98)*, pp 137-142, 1998.

[22]: S. Lawrence, C.L. Giles, K. Bollacker, "Autonomous Citation Matching", In *Proceedings of the 3rd ACM Annual Conference on Autonomous Agents*, pp 392-393, 1999.

[23]: S. Lawrence, C.L. Giles, "The Inquirus Meta Search Engine", In *Proceedings of the 7th International World Wide Web Conference*, pp 95-105, 1998.

[24]: S. Lawrence, K. Bollacker, C.L. Giles, "Distributed Error Correction", In *proceedings of the 4th ACM Conference on Digital Libraries*, p. 232, 1999.

[25]: C. Lagoze and H. Van de Sompel, "The open archives initiative: building a low-barrier interoperability framework", In *Proceedings of the ACM/IEEE Joint Conference on Digital Libraries (JCDL 2001)*, pp 54-62, 2001.

[26]: C. Lagoze, W.Y. Arms, S. Gan, D. Hillmann, C. Ingram, D.B. Krafft, R.J. Marisa, J. Phipps, J. Saylor, C. Terrizzi, W. Hoehn, D. Millman, J. Allan, S. Guzman-Lara, T. Kalt, "Core services in the architecture of the national science digital library (NSDL)", In *Proceedings of the ACM/IEEE Joint Conference on Digital Libraries (JCDL 2002)*, pp 201-209, 2002.

[27]: C.G. Nevill-Manning, Reed T. and Witten I.H., "Extracting Text from PostScript", In *Software Practice and Experience (SPE) 28(5)*, pp 481-491, 1998.

[28]: The National Science Digital Library community homepage, http://comm.nsdlib.org.

[29]: H. Suleman, A. Atkins, M.A. Gonçalves, R.K. France, E.A. Fox, V. Chachra, M. Crowder, J. Young, "Networked Digital Library of Theses and Dissertations: Bridging the Gaps for Global Access - Part 1: Mission and Progress", *D-Lib Magazine 7(9)*, 2001, http://www.dlib.org/dlib/september01/suleman/09suleman-pt1.html.

[30]: H. Suleman, A. Atkins, M.A. Gonçalves, R.K. France, E.A. Fox, V. Chachra, M. Crowder, J. Young, "Networked Digital Library of Theses and Dissertations: Bridging the Gaps for Global Access - Part 2: Services and Research", *D-Lib Magazine 7(9)*, 2001, http://www.dlib.org/dlib/september01/suleman/09suleman-pt2.html.

[31]: "The Open Archives Initiative Protocol for Metadata Harvesting", http://www.openarchives.org/OAI/openarchivesprotocol.htm.

[32]: N. Robinson, "A Comparison of Utilities for converting from Postscript or Portable Document Format to Text", *CERN-OPEN-2001-065*, 2001.

[33]: searchCIO.com, http://searchcio.techtarget.com/.

[34]: K. Seymore, A. McCallum, R. Rosenfeld, "Learning hidden Markov model structure for information extraction", In Proceedings of the *AAAI-99 Workshop on Machine Learning for Information Extraction*, pp 37-42, 1999.

The OAI-PMH Static Repository and Static Repository Gateway

Patrick Hochstenbach
Los Alamos National Laboratory
Research Library, Prototyping Team
Los Alamos, NM 87545-1362
1 (505) 6674448

hochsten@lanl.gov

Henry Jerez
Los Alamos National Laboratory
Research Library, Prototyping Team
Los Alamos, NM 87545-1362
1 (505) 6674448

hjerez@lanl.gov

Herbert Van de Sompel
Los Alamos National Laboratory
Research Library, Prototyping Team
Los Alamos, NM 87545-1362
1 (505) 6674448

herbertv@lanl.gov

Abstract

Although the OAI-PMH specification is focused on making it straightforward for data providers to expose metadata, practice shows that in certain significant situations deployment of OAI-PMH conformant repository software remains problematic. In this paper, we report on research aimed at devising solutions to further lower the barrier to make metadata collections harvestable. We provide an in depth description of an approach in which a data provider makes a metadata collection available as an XML file with a specific format – an OAI Static Repository – which is made OAI-PMH harvestable through the intermediation of software – an OAI Static Repository Gateway - operated by a third party. We describe the properties of both components, and provide insights in our experience with an experimental implementation of a Gateway.

Categories and Subject Descriptors

H.3.7 [**Digital Libraries**]: Standards; System issues

General Terms

Design, Experimentation, Standardization

Keywords

OAI-PMH, metadata harvesting

1. Introduction

Throughout the different stages that led to the release of version 2 of the Open Archives Protocol for Metadata Harvesting (OAI-PMH) [3, 4, 7, 13, 14, 15], a strong emphasis has been put on devising a specification for metadata harvesting that is straightforward to implement. It is fair to state that, whenever a choice had to be made, the consecutive specifications have favored making it easy for data providers to expose their metadata collections through the protocol instead of for service providers that harvest the exposed metadata. The origin of that bias lies with the Santa Fe Convention of the Open Archives Initiative [7] that aimed at achieving a level of interoperability across repositories of electronic preprints through metadata harvesting.

Recognizing that existing preprint repositories were grass root initiatives operating with quite limited resources, and that new initiatives in that realm would probably operate under similar modest circumstances for some time to come, those involved in the discussions leading to the Santa Fe Convention [13] decided in favor of ease of implementation at the end of the preprint repositories. This strategy was expected to make the barrier to actually exposing metadata through the protocol as low as possible, and eventually increases the impact of preprint-based communication on the scholarly communication system [2].

Nevertheless, for some data providers holding interesting metadata collections, implementation of the protocol has remained problematic. This was first recognized after the release of version 1 of the OAI-PMH, in the context of the Open Language Archives Community (OLAC) project [10]. Several participants in that project wanted to contribute – sometimes small but nevertheless important – metadata collections to the OLAC environment but were unable to do so because OLAC's strategy for federating distributed repositories was fully based on the OAI-PMH. Implementation of the OAI-PMH was not feasible for several OLAC participants, and the reasons ranged from lack of technical expertise, to system administrators having security concerns about operating an OAI-PMH gateway against an enterprise database, to the cost of implementing the protocol being disproportional to the size of the metadata collection to be exposed.

Practice has shown that these problems exist beyond the OLAC Community. In many cases, union catalog projects include participants that are not in a position to operate elaborate software environments, and therefore currently rely on tools such as ftp to add their collection to the central catalog. Also, ideas have been brought forward to trigger duplication of new content in the LoCKSS framework [9] by exposing metadata about that content through the OAI-PMH, i.e. addition of metadata to an OAI-PMH conformant repository operated by publisher would trigger the process of gathering the full-content described by the added metadata. It is anticipated that some smaller publishers contributing to the LoCKSS environment will not be able to collaborate in such an OAI-PMH triggered scheme because the technical barrier is too high for them. And, some organizations that are well known in the digital library community make use of web-servers provided by ISPs that do not allow the installation of third party software. Therefore, these organizations cannot share the metadata of their publications through the OAI-PMH.

So, it seems that – irrespective of the bias in the OAI-PMH that favors ease of implementation for data providers – the barrier to expose metadata through the OAI-PMH remains too high in certain, non-marginal circumstances. Therefore, we have conducted research to devise an approach that further lowers the barrier to sharing metadata collections through the OAI-PMH.

2. Directions Explored

The focus of our research was on delivering an OAI-PMH solution for data providers that are not in a position to operate special software in order to share their metadata collections with harvesters. This focus immediately led to devising solutions by which metadata collections are made accessible as flat files, not databases. And, given that all responses in the OAI-PMH are XML files, this focus narrowed to finding a solution in which a data provider uses an XML file as the container of its metadata collection. Our research led into two quite distinct directions:

- The autonomous data provider approach: In this approach, data providers make an XML file that adheres to an XML Schema created for this purpose available on a Web server, and place an XSL style sheet on that Web server to handle the responses to incoming OAI-PMH requests. Because data providers operating in this mode all use the same format for their XML file, they share a single XSL style sheet. This work led to the insight that, in order to be easily deployable, native support of XSLT in the data provider's Web servers is required. Such support is currently not available by default. Also, experimentation revealed that an implementation of this approach that solely relies on XSLT processing to respond to OAI-PMH requests requires features that are only available in XSL version 2. That specification is currently in a W3C Working Draft status, and

conformant tools must be considered experimental. Both insights led us to conclude that, while definitely promising, this track was not mature for actual deployment to our low-barrier target group.

- The dependent data provider approach: In this approach, data providers make an XML file that adheres to an XML Schema created for this purpose available on a Web server, and rely on external, third-party gateway software to make the data from that file harvestable through the OAI-PMH. This track was inspired by the ViDa [8] – Virtual Data Provider – approach introduced by the OLAC Community to remedy the problems described in the Introduction. While the ViDa approach has properties that are specific to the OLAC Community, and was created for version 1 of the OAI-PMH, our research looked for a generic approach to work in conjunction with version 2 of the OAI-PMH. Our work also paid considerable attention to ensuring the accuracy of responses delivered through a gateway to a harvester. Research on this track led to a collaboration with Carl Lagoze, Michael Nelson and Simeon Warner to specify an Implementation Guideline for version 2 of the OAI-PMH. At the time of writing, that Guideline is in its alpha version. When testing of the specification is completed, it will be officially released by the OAI under the name "The OAI Static Repository and Static Repository Gateway" [16]. Research on this track also led to the creation of an experimental gateway. The remainder of this paper reports on both.

3. The OAI Static Repository Model

The OAI Static Repository model provides a simple approach for exposing relatively static and small collections of metadata records through the OAI-PMH. The Static Repository approach is targeted at data providers that have metadata collections ranging in size between 1 and 5000 records and that are not in a position to host OAI-PMH-compliant repository software. However, the model assumes that these data providers do have access to the file services of a standard, network-accessible Web server.

The OAI Static Repository model builds on two types of components:

- The Static Repository - An XML file that is made accessible by a data provider at a persistent network-location. The XML file has a well-defined structure and it contains information similar to that in OAI-PMH responses. This includes metadata records and supporting information required for the purpose of harvesting via the OAI-PMH.

- The Static Repository Gateway – A network accessible server, operated by a third party, that makes one or more Static Repositories harvestable through the OAI-PMH. Due to the fact that a Static Repository Gateway assigns a unique base URL to each such Static Repository, harvesters can harvest Static Repository information in exactly the same manner as they harvest any other OAI-PMH Repository.

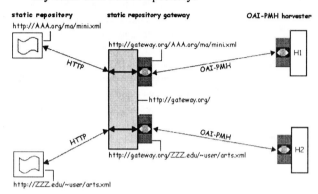

Figure 1. OAI Static Repository Model

Both the Static Repository and the Static Repository Gateway are described in the remainder of this Section. They are further clarified through Figure 1 and through the example in the Appendix. The full details are available in the OAI Implementation Guideline on OAI Static Repositories and Static Repository Gateways [16].

3.1 The Static Repository

A Static Repository is an XML file that validates against a W3C XML Schema [17] that uses XML elements from the OAI-PMH XML Namespace [18]. The data provider makes the XML file available at a persistent HTTP address. It is anticipated that the data provider will create and update the Static Repository by using an XML editor, or by regularly exporting the status of a metadata collection from a database as a Static Repository XML file. That XML file has sections that contain the responses to the Identify and the ListMetadataFormats OAI-PMH verbs. It also contains one ListRecords section per Metadata Format supported by the Static Repository.

Taking into account the nature of the environments in which Static Repositories will be created and updated, and aiming for ease of implementation of Static Repository Gateway software, it was decided that Static Repositories can not use optional notions of the OAI-PMH such as "sets", "deleted records" and "seconds-level datestamps".

3.2 The Static Repository Gateway

A Static Repository Gateway (henceforth referred to as Gateway) is a network-accessible server that makes a Static Repository harvestable as an autonomous OAI-PMH repository. In order to achieve this, the Gateway assigns a unique base URL to each Static Repository that it makes harvestable. That base URL is a specific concatenation of the network-location of the Gateway itself, and the HTTP address of the Static Repository. Knowing the specific concatenation rules, data providers can construct the base URL at which a given Gateway will make their Static Repository harvestable. Data providers make their Static Repository known to a Gateway by issuing an OAI-PMH Identify request against the base URL resulting from the concatenation exercise. A Gateway keeps track of all Static Repositories that have "registered" in this manner, and communicates the base URLs of those Static Repositories to harvesters in a Friends [5] container embedded in every Identify response it generates. This allows for dynamic discovery of Static Repositories through a Gateway.

In order to guarantee that harvesters receive adequate information when accessing a Static Repository through a Gateway, the behavior of a Gateway is quite strictly defined. The core rule guiding this behavior is that a Gateway must always use the most recent version of a Static Repository. In theory, this means that a Gateway should fetch a Static Repository from its network-location for every single harvesting request. However, a Gateway can optimize its performance by caching Static Repositories. When caching, a Gateway must perform a freshness-test on the cached Static Repository by comparing it with the version at the Static Repository network-location before responding to harvesting requests. It can do so by using a HTTP HEAD with an If-Modified-Since header that contains the date of the cached version of a Static Repository. Given the above freshness requirements, the following three scenarios can occur:

(1) If the Static Repository is not accessible at its Static Repository network-location when a Gateway performs this freshness-test, it must respond to the harvesting request with a HTTP status-code 504 (Gateway Timeout).

(2) If the Static Repository is accessible at its Static Repository network-location when a Gateway performs this freshness-test, and the freshness-test indicates that the cached version is out-of-date, then it must fetch the Static Repository from its Static Repository network-location:

- If delaying the response until this fetch from the Static Repository is complete and it is processed, the Gateway can respond to the harvesting request with a HTTP status-code 503 (Service Unavailable). This specifies a Retry-After period covering the estimated time of fetching the Static Repository from its Static Repository network-location, and validating it against the Static Repository XML Schema.

- If the fetched version of the Static Repository does not validate against the Static Repository XML Schema, then the Gateway must respond to the harvesting request with a HTTP status-code 502 (Bad Gateway). It must not respond to the harvesting request using the cached version of the Static Repository.

- If the fetched version of the Static Repository does validate against the Static Repository XML Schema, then the Gateway must respond to the harvesting request using the fetched version.

(3) If the Static Repository is accessible at its Static Repository network-location when a Gateway performs this freshness-test, and the result of the freshness-test indicates that the cached version is the same as the version at the Static Repository network-location, then the Gateway may respond to the harvesting request by using the cached version of the Static Repository.

4. A Gateway Implementation

As described in the Introduction, the aim of the Static Repository specification is to make participation in an OAI-PMH harvesting environment easier for data providers. This is achieved by allowing data providers to put metadata collections out as XML files that adhere to a well-defined format. Data providers then rely on the services of a Gateway to make the information in such XML files harvestable through the OAI-PMH. Especially due to the strictly defined behavior of Gateways imposed to ensure accuracy of harvested data, the implementation of conformant Gateway software seems not trivial. We set out to create experimental Gateway software, to check the feasibility of the OAI Static Repository specification, and – by sharing our experiences in doing so through this paper – to motivate third parties to create robust Gateway implementations.

Our Gateway approach builds on four components:

- The OAI-PMH Interface – A CGI program that accepts OAI-PMH requests targeted at Static Repositories; performs the freshness-test of Cached Static Repositories for incoming OAI-PMH requests; delivers OAI-PMH responses in case a Cached Static Repository was determined to be fresh; generates the appropriate HTTP status-codes when the freshness-test failed; and communicates the necessity of updating a Cached version to the Daemon through the Lock Zone.

- The Cache – A file-system based storage space in which Cached versions of individual Static Repositories are held as separate GDBM databases [1].

- The Lock Zone - A file-system based storage space that acts as a serving-hatch between the OAI-PMH Interface and the Daemon. It holds Lock Files, each of which contain information on a Static Repository that needs to be fetched as a result of a failed freshness-test, as well as on the actual status of the fetching process.

- The Daemon – A daemon that continuously monitors the Lock Zone; fetches Static Repositories when the Lock Zone indicates that doing so is required; updates

the status of the fetching process in the Lock Files; updates the Cache.

The remainder of this Section describes these components and their interaction in more detail. That description is further supported by Figure 2.

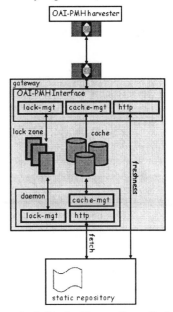

Figure 2. A Static Repository Gateway Implementation

4.1 The OAI-PMH Interface

The OAI-PMH Interface consists of a front-end that ingests OAI-PMH requests, checks those for syntactic validity and responds with appropriate error messages in case requests are invalid. It also passes on responses delivered to it by the back-end of the OAI-PMH Interface, which in itself consists of three components that are called in the listed order:

- The Lock Management Component – Writes information on Static Repositories for which the Cached version is out-of-date to the Lock Zone.

- The Cache Management Component - Interacts with the Cached Static Repositories.

- The HTTP Component – Performs the freshness-test of Cached Static Repositories.

Valid incoming OAI-PMH requests targeted at a specific Static Repository are initially handed over to the Lock Management Component that checks whether a process of caching the Static Repository is currently ongoing, and if so what the status of that process is.

- In case such a process is indeed ongoing, the front-end of the OAI-PMH Interface responds to the harvesting request with an HTTP status-code of 503 (Service Unavailable) specifying a Retry-After period. The

Lock Management Component can derive such status information from the appropriate Lock File in the Lock Zone.

- If no such process is ongoing, control is handed over to the Cache Management Component of the OAI-PMH Interface.

Using a unique key derived from the HTTP address of the targeted Static Repository as the entry into the Cache, the Cache Management Component checks for the existence of a Cached version of the Static Repository. The following two scenarios can occur:

(1) If such a Cached version exists, then the Cache Management Component checks the date/time of the Cached version of that Static Repository. Next, the HTTP Component issues an If-Modified-Since HTTP HEAD request using the obtained date/time against the HTTP address of the Static Repository.

- If doing so reveals that the Cache is fresh, the Cache Management Component reads the appropriate information from the Cached GDBM database for the Static Repository, and hands that information over to the front-end of the OAI-PMH Interface, which can then respond to OAI-PMH request. Depending on whether the Cache indicates that Static Repository is a valid or invalid, the response will be a regular OAI-PMH response containing data, or an HTTP status-code 502 (Bad Gateway).

- If doing so reveals that the Cached version is out-of-date, the Lock Management Component writes a Lock File in the Lock Zone specifying the HTTP address of the Static Repository that needs updating as well as the current status of this fetch, which at this point is "unprocessed". Also, the front-end responds with an HTTP status-code 503 (Service Unavailable), specifying a Retry-After period that is a best guess of the amount of time it may take to update the Cached version. At this point, from the perspective of the Gateway, the OAI-PMH request has been processed. The harvester will need to re-issue the request after the Retry-After period, in order to receive an OAI-PMH response that contains actual data.

- If doing so is unsuccessful in that there is no response to the If-Modified-Since HTTP HEAD request, then the front-end responds with an HTTP status-code 504 (Gateway Timeout).

(2) If such a Cached version does not yet exist, the Lock Management Component writes a Lock File, and the front-end responds with an HTTP status-code of 503 (Service Unavailable) specifying a Retry-After period.

4.2 The Cache

The Cache consists of individual GDBM databases, one per Cached Static Repository. The filename of each GDBM database is a unique key derived from the HTTP address of the Static Repository. Its content consists of administrative information such as date/time of first and most recent caching of the Static Repository, and a processed version of the Static Repository that makes responding to OAI-PMH requests a matter of simply joining appropriate portions of stored XML data obtained by deconstructing the Static Repository XML file.

4.3 The Lock Zone

The Lock Zone is read/write accessible by both the Lock Management Component of the OAI-PMH Interface and the Daemon. When the freshness-test of a Cached version of a Static Repository reveals that the Cached version is out-of-date or not yet existing, the Lock Management Component writes a Lock File in the Lock Zone stating the HTTP address of that Static Repository, its name in the Cache, as well as the "unprocessed" status of the process of updating the Cached version. The Lock Zone is monitored by the Daemon, which interprets a Lock File as an instruction to fetch a Static Repository from its HTTP address. As will be explained in the following Section, the Daemon updates the status of a file in the Lock Zone as it acts upon the fetching instruction; it eventually removes the Lock File from the Lock Zone.

4.4 The Daemon

The Daemon continuously monitors the Lock Zone and acts upon the Lock Files deposited there by the Lock Management Component of the OAI-PMH Interface. The Daemon itself consists of three components that are called in the listed order:

- The Lock Management Component – Reads Lock Files with "unprocessed" status; updates status information of Lock Files as the process of updating/writing the Cached version of the corresponding Static Repository is ongoing; eventually removes Lock Files from the Lock Zone.

- The HTTP Component – Fetches Static Repositories from their network-location.

- The Cache Management Component – Replaces the out-of-date Cached version of a Static Repository by the newly fetched version or creates a Cached version if no Cached version exists; writes a flag if the newly fetched version is not a valid Static Repository.

The Daemon interprets each individual Lock File with a status of "unprocessed" as an instruction to cache a fresh version of the associated Static Repository. The refreshing process starts with the Daemon attempting to fetch the Static Repository from its HTTP address.

- If fetching fails, the Daemon deletes the Lock File. The Cached version will remain out-of-date, and as a result the freshness-test will fail again when the harvester re-issues the OAI-PMH request after the Retry-After period. The process described in Section 4.1 will start from scratch. Eventually, the harvester may decide to give up, or the Static Repository may become accessible. It can be anticipated that the Gateway would maintain the fetching history of Static Repositories, and decide to remove some from its Cache and Friends list based on a history that reveals an unacceptable level of inaccessibility.

- If fetching is successful, the Daemon proceeds to validating the fetched Static Repository. During the validation process, the Daemon updates the status of the Lock File at several points. If the fetched file is a valid Static Repository, its content is used to replace the existing Cached version. The date/time of most recent caching is updated. If no Cached version exists yet, it is created, and the date/time of first and most recent caching is recorded. After doing so, the Daemon removes the Lock File from the Lock Zone. When the harvester returns after the Retry-After period, it is most likely that a response can be generated from the Cache, since chances are high that the freshness-test to be performed for the re-issued request will reveal that the Cached version is still up-to-date. If the fetched file turns out not to be a valid Static Repository, a flag is set in the GDBM database for that Static Repository. Again, the date/time of most recent caching is updated. If no Cached version exists for the fetched invalid Static Repository, it is created. Its only content will be the "invalid" flag, and the date/time of first and most recent caching. Once the "invalid" flag is recorded, the Daemon removes the Lock File from the Lock Zone. When the harvester returns after the Retry-After period, a HTTP status-code 502 (Bad Gateway) response can most likely be generated based on the existing invalid flag in the Cache, since chances are high that the freshness-test to be performed for the re-issued request will reveal that the invalid Cached version is still the up-to-date version of the Static Repository.

5. Discussion

Static Repositories made available through our Gateway pass the validation tests of both the OAI Repository Explorer [11, 12] and the OAI Registry [6].

The current implementation takes some basic precautions inspired by the security considerations listed in the Static Repository specification [16]. For example, an upper limit is imposed on the total amount of Static Repositories that can be Cached and processed at a given point in time, on the size of Cached Static Repositories, as well as on the size of responses sent to harvesters.

In order to guarantee accuracy of responses to harvesting requests our implementation has paid special attention to the actual implementation of the freshness-test. Web servers on which Static Repositories are made available may operate in other time zones than the Gateway, and are not necessarily synchronized to an Internet time-server. Therefore, using the Gateway's time when issuing an If-Modified-Since HTTP HEAD request may lead to significant inaccuracy of the freshness-test. In order to resolve this problem, our implementation stores the content of the Web server's Last-Modified header field in the GDBM database of the Static Repository, and uses that information in a subsequent freshness-test. As such, the freshness-test is always performed according to the Web server's time.

Our Gateway implementation was written in C and tested on a 500 Mhz Redhat Linux 7.3. Processing and Caching fetched Static Repositories takes less than 1 second for small XML files, 2 seconds for 2 Mb files, and 20 seconds for Static Repositories that reach our upper limit of 20 Mb. All operations performed on a fetched Static Repository occur in a reserved address space of 2 Mb of RAM. Therefore, 2 Mb is also the upper limit to the size of an individual metadata record that can be processed by our current implementation. Little robust information can be given on the time required to fetch Static Repositories, as those are dependent on the size of the XML file, and are subject to network conditions. In our testing environment, performing freshness-tests has typically taken between one and two seconds. The time to perform a freshness-test is relevant in that it is good indication of the maximum amount of time a harvester must wait for a response to an OAI-PMH request:

- If a freshness-test reveals that the Cache is still up-to-date, generating a response from Cache requires a little extra time due to the deconstructed manner in which Static Repositories are Cached.

- If a freshness-test reveals that the Cache is out-of-date the HTTP status-code of 503 (Service Unavailable) can be sent immediately.

The only occasion at which responding to a harvester takes longer is when the Web server on which the Static Repository is available fails to respond. Our implementation generates an HTTP status-code of 504 (Gateway Timeout) after having waited for 30 seconds.

6. Conclusions

Our research into devising an approach to further lower the barrier for data providers to share metadata collections in an OAI-PMH environment led us into two directions. Both directions are based on the data provider making its metadata collection available on a Web server as an XML file of a specific format.

In the "dependent data provider approach" detailed in this paper, data providers rely on the services of a gateway operated by a third party to make metadata collections harvestable. The barrier for sharing data via the OAI-PMH is lowered significantly in that the task of data providers consists of creating and updating an XML file containing their metadata records, placing the file on a Web server and "registering" it with a Static Repository Gateway. This approach depends on the actual deployment of such Gateways. In order to guarantee accuracy of the data harvested through a Gateway the specification of its behavior is quite strict, and therefore adequate care must be taken when creating an actual Gateway implementation. Nevertheless, our experiment revealed that no significant hurdles are involved in an actual implementation that could keep parties from stepping forward to create and deploy robust Gateway software.

At the time of writing, both the OAI Implementation Guideline on Static Repositories and our Gateway implementation are in alpha phase, with feedback on both being gathered from selected parties. Based on the attention our work has attracted so far, it is anticipated that parties that are likely to start exposing metadata via a Static Repository approach will emerge in a variety of communities. The OLAC Community has indicated interest in migrating to the generic Static Repository approach; union catalog projects in Belgium, Brazil, and the United States are considering adoption; and institutions collaborating with the Digital Library Federation and the National Science Digital Library project are exploring the use of this low-barrier approach as a means to significantly increase the amount of metadata records they make harvestable at limited expense.

In the "autonomous data provider approach" on which this paper only briefly touches, data providers use an XSL style sheet – which could be provided by the OAI – to respond to OAI-PMH requests. Their task consists of creating and updating an XML file containing their metadata records, and placing both the XML file and the XSL style sheet on their Web server. Not only does this approach significantly lower the barrier for sharing metadata collections through the OAI-PMH, it also turns the target group of low-barrier data providers into autonomous operators of OAI repositories. While truly promising, we decided that this approach was not ready for deployment to our target group due to the status of technologies required in the solution. Deployment may however become feasible and attractive in the near future.

7. Acknowledgments

The authors wish to thank Carl Lagoze, Michael Nelson, and Simeon Warner for invaluable input in the process of specifying the OAI Static Repository Implementation Guideline. The authors are grateful for the most inspiring ViDa work of Steven Bird and Gary Simons on behalf of the OLAC Community. Thanks to Beth Goldsmith, Rick Luce, and Thorsten Schwander for feedback.

8. References

[1] Free Software Foundation. GDBM. http://www.gnu.org/software/gdbm/gdbm.html

[2] Ginsparg, P., Luce, R., and Van de Sompel, H. The Open Archives Initiative aimed at the further promotion of author self-archived solutions, 1999. http://www.openarchives.org/meetings/SantaFe1999/ups-invitation-ori.htm

[3] Lagoze, C. and Van de Sompel, H. The Open Archives Initiative: Building a low-barrier interoperability framework… in Proceedings on ACM/IEEE Joint Conference on Digital Libraries (Roanoke VA, June 2001), ACM Press, 54-62. http://doi.acm.org/10.1145/379437.379449

[4] Lagoze, C., Van de Sompel, H., Nelson, M., and Warner, S. The Open Archives Initiative Protocol for Metadata Harvesting - Version 2.0, 2002 http://www.openarchives.org/OAI_protocol/openarchivesprotocol.html

[5] Lagoze, C., Van de Sompel, H., Nelson, M., and Warner, S. Implementation Guildelines for the Open Archvies Initiative for Metadata Harvesting: XML Schema for repositories to list confederate repositories, 2002 http://www.openarchives.org/OAI/2.0/guidelines-friends.htm

[6] The Open Archives Initiative. Registering as a Data Provider. http://www.openarchives.org/data/registerasprovider.html

[7] The Open Archives Initiative. The Santa Fe Convention, 2001. http://www.openarchives.org/sfc/sfc_entry.htm

[8] The Open Language Archives Community. How to become an OLAC data provider. http://www.language-archives.org/docs/implement.html

[9] Reich, V. and Rosenthal D. LOCKSS: A Permanent Web Publishing and Access System. D-Lib Magazine, 7 (6), 2001. http://www.dlib.org/dlib/june01/reich/06reich.html

[10] Simons, G. and Bird, S. Building an Open Language Archives Community on the OAI Foundation, 2003. Library Hi Tech, 21(2). To appear.

[11] Suleman H. Enforcing interoperability with the open archives initiative repository explorer… in Proceedings on ACM/IEEE Joint Conference on Digital Libraries (Roanoke VA, June 2001), ACM Press, 63-64. http://doi.acm.org/10.1145/379437.379450

[12] Suleman H. The OAI-PMH Repository Explorer. http://www.purl.org/NET/oai_explorer

[13] Van de Sompel, H. and Lagoze, C. The Santa Fe Convention of the Open Archives Initiative. D-Lib Magazine, 6 (2), 2000. http://www.dlib.org/dlib/february00/vandesompel-oai/02vandesompel-oai.html

[14] Van de Sompel, H. and Lagoze, C. The Open Archives Initiative Protocol for Metadata Harvesting - Version 1.0, 2001. http://www.openarchives.org/OAI/1.0/openarchivesprotocol.htm

[15] Van de Sompel, H. and Lagoze, C. Notes from the Interoperability Front: A Progress Report from the Open Archives Initiative. Lecture Notes in Computer Science, 2458: Proceedings of ECDL 2002 (Rome Italy, September 2002), Springer Verlag, 144-157

[16] Van de Sompel, H., Lagoze, C., Nelson, M., and Warner, S. Implementation Guidelines for the Open Archives Initiative for Metadata Harvesting: The OAI Static Repository and Static Repository Gateway, 2002 http://www.openarchives.org/OAI/2.0/guidelines-static-repository.htm

[17] Van de Sompel, H. and Jerez, H. XML Schema defining the OAI Static Repository format, 2002 http://www.openarchives.org/OAI/2.0/static-repository.xsd

[18] Van de Sompel, H. XML Schema for validating responses to OAI-PMH requests, 2002 http://www.openarchives.org/OAI/2.0/OAI-PMH.xsd

9. Appendix

Table 1 shows an OAI Static Repository, which supports two Metadata Formats (oai_dc and oai_rfc1807). It contains metadata about a single resource. That metadata is provided in both Metadata Formats. Note the metadataPrefix attribute that extends the ListRecords element from the OAI-PMH XML Namespace [18]. To improve readability, XML Namespace declarations are not shown in the sample Static Repository.

Table 1: An OAI Static Repository

```
<?xml version="1.0" encoding="UTF-8"?>
<Repository>
 <Identify>
 <oai:repositoryName>Demo</oai:repositoryName>
 <oai:baseURL>http://an.oai.org/ma/mini.xml</oai:baseURL>
 <oai:protocolVersion>2.0</oai:protocolVersion>
 <oai:adminEmail>jondoe@oai.org</oai:adminEmail>
 <oai:earliestDatestamp>2002-09-19</oai:earliestDatestamp>
 <oai:deletedRecord>no</oai:deletedRecord>
 <oai:granularity>YYYY-MM-DD</oai:granularity>
 </Identify>
 <ListMetadataFormats>
 <oai:metadataFormat>
  <oai:metadataPrefix>oai_dc</oai:metadataPrefix>
  <oai:schema>
    http://www.openarchives.org/OAI/2.0/oai_dc.xsd
  </oai:schema>
```

```
  <oai:metadataNamespace>
    http://www.openarchives.org/OAI/2.0/oai_dc/
  </oai:metadataNamespace>
 </oai:metadataFormat>
<oai:metadataFormat>
 <oai:metadataPrefix>oai_rfc1807</oai:metadataPrefix>
 <oai:schema>
   http://www.openarchives.org/OAI/1.1/rfc1807.xsd
 </oai:schema>
 <oai:metadataNamespace>
    http://info.internet.isi.edu:80/in-notes/rfc/files/rfc1807.txt
 </oai:metadataNamespace>
 </oai:metadataFormat>
</ListMetadataFormats>
<ListRecords metadataPrefix="oai_dc">
 <oai:record>
 <oai:header>
  <oai:identifier>oai:an.oai.org:0112017</oai:identifier>
    <oai:datestamp>2003-01-17</oai:datestamp>
 </oai:header>
 <oai:metadata>
  <oai_dc:dc>
    <dc:title>Structural Metadata</dc:title>
    <dc:creator>Smith, Hector</dc:creator>
    <dc:subject>Digital Libraries</dc:subject>
    <dc:date>2001-12-14</dc:date>
   </oai_dc:dc>
   </oai:metadata>
 </oai:record>
</ListRecords>
<ListRecords metadataPrefix="oai_rfc1807">
 <oai:record>
 <oai:header>
  <oai:identifier>oai:an.oai.org:0112017</oai:identifier>
    <oai:datestamp>2002-01-15</oai:datestamp>
 </oai:header>
 <oai:metadata>
  <oai_rfc1897:rfc1807>
    <rfc1807:bib-version>v2</rfc1807:bib-version>
    <rfc1807:id>0112017</rfc1807:id>
    <rfc1807:entry>January 15, 2002</rfc1807:entry>
    <rfc1807:title>Structural Metadata</ rfc1807:title>
    <rfc1807:author>Hector Smith</rfc1807:author>
    <rfc1807:date>December 14, 2001</rfc1807:date>
   </oai_rfc1897:rfc1807>
 </oai:metadata>
 </oai:record>
</ListRecords>
</Repository>
```

Session 8A: Multimedia Issues in Digital Libraries

Session Chair: Mike Christel, Carnegie Mellon University

How Fast Is Too Fast?
Evaluating Fast Forward Surrogates for Digital Video

Barbara M. Wildemuth, Gary Marchionini, Meng Yang, Gary Geisler,
Todd Wilkens, Anthony Hughes, & Richard Gruss
Interaction Design Laboratory
University of North Carolina at Chapel Hill
Chapel Hill, NC 27599
+1 919 9663611
[wildem, march, yangm, geisg]@ils.unc.edu; [tpodd, hughes, gruss]@email.unc.edu

Abstract

To support effective browsing, interfaces to digital video libraries should include video surrogates (i.e., smaller objects that can stand in for the videos in the collection, analogous to abstracts standing in for documents). The current study investigated four variations (i.e., speeds) of one form of video surrogate: a fast forward created by selecting every Nth frame from the full video. In addition, it tested the validity of six measures of user performance when interacting with video surrogates. Forty-five study participants interacted with all four versions of the fast forward surrogate, and completed all six performance tasks with each. Surrogate speed affected performance on four of the measures: object recognition (graphical), action recognition, linguistic gist comprehension (full text), and visual gist comprehension. Based on these results, we recommend a fast forward default speed of 1:64 of the original video keyframes. In addition, users should control the choice of fast forward speed to adjust for content characteristics and personal preferences.

1. Introduction

The ability to create sophisticated digital video productions is now within the reach of anyone with a home computer, since technologies that support the capture, storage, and transmission of digitized video files are common marketplace items. Digital video cameras and cheap webcams are becoming household appliances. Inexpensive disk space allows consumers to store vast amounts of original or commercially produced video, and increasing bandwidth facilitates sharing these files over the internet. These hardware advances are in turn

supported by basic software packages that aid in capturing, editing, and compressing the final digital video production. These technical developments stimulate traditional video enterprises—such as video rental or purchasing, stock footage clearinghouses and distance education purveyors—to move towards on-demand, asynchronous delivery of digital video via the internet. More importantly, they stimulate the incorporation of digital video materials into digital library collections. We believe that there is a crucial need for interfaces that will improve library users' access to digital video collections, and so are focusing our research on a combination of interfaces and surrogates that will support retrieval from digital video libraries.

The design of such interfaces should be rooted in a blend of (1) empirical evidence about how people interact with and understand video and (2) imaginative approaches to leveraging the digital medium. The Open Video Project aims to develop and maintain an open source digital video repository that serves as a testbed for video research, including user studies and evaluations of interface prototypes for digital video applications.

Our current emphasis is on user studies of specific surrogates that help people browse and select materials from libraries of digital videos. Video surrogates stand in for the videos in the collection, just as abstracts are surrogates that stand in for documents in a text-based library. We believe that these interfaces will be more effective if they leverage the digital video medium rather than simply mimic the analog interfaces of television and VCRs or the text-based interfaces of document collections. Thus, we are experimenting with a variety of surrogates using digital video materials, and evaluating them based on their ability to help users of digital libraries make rapid, accurate decisions about the relevance of video materials.

This paper reports on a study of the use of fast forwards as one type of surrogate for digital video. This type of surrogate is worth investigating for two reasons. First, people are familiar with the concept of fast forward movement through a video because of their experience with their VCR's. This familiarity should increase the ease with which people interact with fast forward surrogates. Second, participants in our initial studies expressed the desire to see motion in the video surrogates. Other surrogates, such as poster frames or storyboards, use the images/frames present in the video, but the user loses any sense of movement. The primary question related to design of fast forward surrogates is the tradeoff between speed (i.e., faster speed will shorten the necessary viewing time) and understanding (i.e., if the surrogate is too "fast", it will not be useful in supporting accurate relevance judgments). This question is addressed by the study reported here. The results have import for designers of digital libraries that include digital video.

The current study also makes a methodological contribution. It presents a set of measures useful for evaluating the effectiveness of any type of video surrogate. These measures have been developed, revised, and extended in studies over several years and illustrate a multifaceted approach to assessing human understanding of complex media when using different surrogates.

2. Related work

In digital video libraries, the size of files and time to download and view each video make it particularly important to have meaningful metadata and surrogates that allow people to recognize or assess the pertinence of the full object. Titles, keywords, and other bibliographic metadata have traditionally been used in video retrieval, along with short textual descriptions that act as surrogates to help people assess relevance. In addition to these linguistic representations, the medium of video suggests that image-based surrogates may provide additional cues for people trying to assess the relevance of a particular video for a particular purpose.

Keyframes [15] have been adopted by many digital video researchers as a basis for non-linguistic representations of the information content of a video object. There is a substantial body of work related to finding ways to segment video, extract keyframes or other features, and create indexes for the purposes of retrieval. There is less attention to creating user interfaces that support interactive search and browse capabilities. The Informedia project (www.informedia.cs.cmu.edu/) is perhaps the most comprehensive digital video effort that

includes novel user interfaces and usability testing [1,2,24]. Their video skims are surrogates created from several kinds of features (transcripts, keyframes extracted with color and texture features, superimpositions, and other features such as face recognition). The Físchlár Project (www.cdvp.dcu.ie/) stores and provides access to video programming from broadcast TV. They have developed user interfaces that integrate several different types of surrogates to help users find video [10,23]. The ECHO project (pc-erato2.iei.pi.cnr.it/echo/) aims to provide access to large volumes of historical video in Europe. Their interfaces will support multilingual access. The CueVideo system (www.almaden.ibm.com/cs/ cuevideo/) [19] extracts a variety of features as the basis for indexing (e.g., using speech to text analysis, image analysis, event analysis) and has been the basis for more specific user interface techniques, such as movieDNA [20], that provide visual patterns for where query images occur in lists of video segments. The SmartSkip interface [5] is one of the few interfaces that provide innovative fast forwards beyond the digital TV fast forwards. Their user study compared a standard skip interface and a fast forward interface with a user-controllable SmartSkip interface. They found that, although people found the SmartSkip interface more 'fun' to use, they performed better with the standard skip interface than with the other two interfaces on commercial skipping and weather finding tasks. These results parallel studies of slide shows and story boards [22] that demonstrate that, although people are able to perform effectively on retrieval tasks with very rapid slide shows, they strongly prefer the story board interfaces that give them more control but take more time to use.

The Open Video Project (www.open-video.org) began with efforts to provide digital video from sources like the Discovery Channel and the US Archives to middle school science and social studies teachers [12,21] and has been expanded to serve as an open source test bed for the research and educational communities. The repository points to about 2000 video segments (more than a half terabyte) and draws upon documentaries from many US government agencies, the Prelinger Collection in the Internet Archive, digitized films in the Library of Congress' American Memory collection, and videos from CMU's Informedia Project and the University of Maryland's Human Computer Interaction Laboratory. The MySQL metadata database is accessible from an interface that provides overviews and previews [6] and serves as the testbed for the surrogates developed and tested in the Interaction Design Laboratory at UNC-Chapel Hill.

Because different people may understand the same object differently, we aim to design a variety of surrogates and access mechanisms to support this variability in human sense making. In addition, for any given surrogate or view, there will be variations in human abilities and experience that affect performance with those surrogates. Therefore, we also aim to establish effective ranges of use for those surrogates such as what speed ranges to provide on a slider bar mechanism for slide show surrogates. For example, in previous work [4] we investigated the relationship between speed of keyframe slide shows and performance on object identification and gist determination tasks. Slide shows allowed people to comprehend the video's gist at very high rates of speed (from 4kf/second to 16kf/second) with a predicted fall off in performance as speed increased. These performance effects were strongly moderated by an inverse relationship in user satisfaction—although participants' performance was relatively good at high rates, their preferences decreased at higher rates and they strongly preferred story board surrogates that require more time to view but give them control [9].

Additional studies have demonstrated the importance of linguistic cues in supporting understanding [4], the tradeoff between high performance possibilities and users' comfort levels, and the many influences that individual human characteristics (such as experience) and video content characteristics (such as genre, visual style, pace, and subject matter) have in determining overall user performance and satisfaction. Given the current early stage of mass popularization of digital video, it is important that researchers continue to devote attention to designing and testing interfaces to multimedia libraries that are both user-centered and take advantage of the particular characteristics of digital video.

To this end, the work reported here isolated and examined fast forward surrogates that go far beyond the capabilities of analog video. Home VCRs can support one or two fast forward capabilities but at very low speeds (2-4 times real-time speed) [8]. By contrast, fast forwards of digital video can be simulated at any rate by selecting/displaying each Nth frame. This type of fast forward surrogate[1] is created by sampling from the video frames (rather than speeding up the display of the frames), but the result for the person viewing the surrogate is the ability to speed through the video much faster while still being able to perceive the images. In pilot studies and in a previous study that compared slide show, storyboard, and fast forward surrogates [25], fast forwards constructed in this Nth frame fashion were judged to be effective and realistic by users. Thus, the fast forward surrogates used in this study are an approximation of what may be both technically possible and also useful from the human perceptual system point of view.

The goal of the study was to identify the fastest speed at which people could still gain an understanding of the video represented by the fast forward surrogate. While it was presumed that users should maintain the ability to change the speed of the fast forward surrogate, based on the characteristics of the situation or on their own preferences, we hoped to identify the speed that could be used as a "default" setting for video retrieval applications.

3. Methodology: assessing video browsing success

Because this paper aims to present an approach to assessing people's success in using surrogates to browse a digital video library, as well as the results of a study of one important class of surrogate, the methods section is presented in two parts. In this first part, the six measures of surrogate use are described; in the next section, we provide an overview of the study procedures.

Figure 1 (next page) depicts the general framework within which this study is situated. Our overall goal is to understand (and predict) various performance and preference outcomes. Four main classes of variables influence these outcomes: the user task/need, individual user characteristics, video characteristics, and characteristics of the surrogates that represent the full videos (some examples of each class are shown in Figure 1). Our focus in this paper is on the speed of the fast forward surrogate within the context of all the different types of tasks. The study also took into account the video's genre (documentary vs. narrative) and visual style (black and white vs. color), and the users' video experience and basic demographics (e.g., gender, age). These variables are boldfaced in the figure.

In contrast to text documents, interacting with video relies on multiple informational channels, e.g., sound and moving images. Therefore, in addition to the usual linguistic/ textual measures used to assess the success of people's interactions with textual objects, visually oriented measures were designed for use in our studies of video browsing. Our perspective is that people's interactions with video have multiple facets on multiple dimensions. One dimension is perceptual and includes facets such as text superimposed on the images (visual channel, linguistic encoding), aural representations (audio channel,

---

[1] Rather than using the awkward phase, 'Nth frame fast forward', we simply call these surrogates 'fast forwards'.

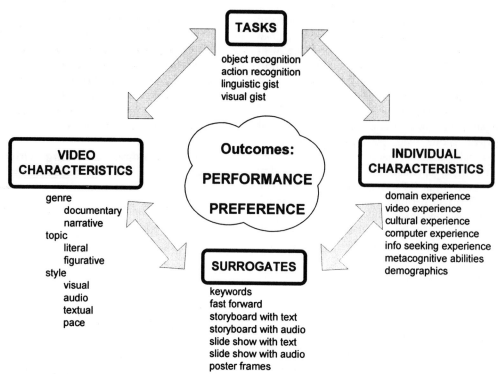

Figure 1. Video browsing assessment framework

linguistic encoding), non-verbal sound representation (audio channel, aural encoding), image representation (visual channel, graphical encoding), and motion representation (visual channel, temporal-graphical encoding). Another dimension is conceptual and includes facets such as the objects represented in video; the juxtapositions, actions, and interactions of these objects; and what these objects and actions, taken together, 'mean' to a viewer. Another dimension is pragmatic and includes facets related to the user's context such as current motivation, temporal and physical resources (e.g., how much time and what kinds of equipment, software, and authority they have), setting (e.g., work, home), and content facets such as the socio/cultural features inherent in the content[2]. Clearly, there are other dimensions and facets at play (e.g., Grodal's [7] theory of film strongly defines an emotional dimension of understanding), and many theories of how people process visual data (see Palmer [17] for a comprehensive treatment of vision science) and other sensory data.

In this and other studies, our aim is to instantiate some of these elements in well-defined tasks executable in studies of video browsing. For the present study, six tasks were defined:

---

[2] The socio/cultural 'meanings' parallel Panofsky's [18] iconographic level in his triarchic theory of of image understanding.

- Object recognition (textual): Select objects seen in the surrogate from a list of nouns.
- Object recognition (graphical): Select objects seen in the surrogate from a set of still images.
- Action recognition: Select clips seen in the surrogate from a set of brief (2-3 second) clips.
- Linguistic gist comprehension (full text). Write a brief summary of the video represented by the surrogate.
- Linguistic gist comprehension (multiple choice): Select the best summary of the video from a set of five statements.
- Visual gist comprehension: Select objects that "belong" in the video represented by the surrogate, from a set of still images.

These tasks were selected for development because they closely relate to the tasks in which users engage when interacting with a library of digital videos [25]. The object recognition tasks are most closely related to the user goal of selecting particular frames from a video, just as the action recognition task is most closely related to the user goal of selecting a particular clip. For example, an elementary school teacher may be trying to locate an image or short clip illustrating the force of a hurricane; an effective surrogate will allow the teacher to recognize that such an image appears in the full video. The linguistic gist comprehension measures are most closely related to the users' ability to make relevance judgments concerning the video represented by the surrogate. If the user can accurately comprehend the gist of the full video by viewing only the surrogate, then we can conclude that the surrogate is useful in helping the user to select videos that are relevant to his or her current information need. The visual gist comprehension task is also related to making relevance judgments, but additionally incorporates stylistic considerations and so is most closely related to the users' desire to evaluate the movement or style in a video. For example, the user's information need may be for a modern-looking overview of the U.S. space program; an effective surrogate supports user judgments about these multiple facets of his or her information need. In summary, each of these measures is grounded in the real-world goals of users of digital video libraries.

Because these measures interact as people complete them, their sequencing is important. In the current study, participants were asked to write brief summaries (*linguistic gist comprehension, full text*) immediately after viewing each surrogate. Graphical and textual object recognition were the second and third tasks respectively. *Graphical object recognition* presented a set of 12 video frames with yes/no radio buttons. Half of the frames were from the stimulus video (i.e., they had been send in the surrogates) and half were not. Half the distractors (i.e., the incorrect frames) were selected from a portion of the video not included in the surrogate and half were selected from other videos. *Textual object recognition* presented a set of 12 words with yes/no radio buttons. Half the words were for objects included in the stimulus video and half were not. A mix of concrete objects (e.g., car) and abstract concepts (e.g., joy) were included among both the correct and distractor words. After the two object recognition tasks, the *action recognition* task was presented. The idea behind the action recognition task was to probe the roles that motion plays in video browsing. Here, participants were given six short clips (2-3 seconds each) and asked whether they had seen those clips in the surrogate (yes/no radio buttons). Participants could replay the clips if they wished (however, the original surrogate shown at the beginning of the tasks was not available for replay at any time in the session). Of the six clips, two were selected from the target video, two were from a video of a similar style, and two were from a video of a different style. Because none of the surrogates incorporated clips from the stimulus video, the participants would not have seen these clips before; however, they would have been exposed to individual frames from the two clips representing the target video. Next, the *visual gist comprehension* task was administered. Participants were given a set of twelve video frames with yes/no radio buttons. This time, they were asked to indicate whether the frames 'belonged' to

the video represented by the surrogate they had seen at the beginning of the session. None of the frames had yet been seen by the study participants. Half the frames were selected from the same video but a different segment and half were selected from other videos. Finally, the *multiple choice linguistic comprehension* measure was administered. Subjects were given a set of five summary statements and asked to select the best. This measure was administered last so that the video summaries provided would not influence performance on the other measures.

4. The fast forward study methods

4.1. Participants

Study participants were recruited through the distribution of flyers on campus and especially in several classes related to video production, with the intention of recruiting study participants who would be interested in using a library of digital videos. The 45 subjects who participated in this study included 19 undergraduate students, 19 graduate students, 2 faculty members and 5 others. They came from a wide variety of departments, included 31 females and 14 males, and had a mean age of 26.1 (s.d.=7.9, ranging from 17 to 51 years old). Forty-four of the 45 subjects reported using computers on a daily basis and 32 of the 45 reported watching videos or films at least weekly; only 12 reported searching for videos or films on at least a weekly basis. The most common way to search for videos was online (32) followed by newspapers or magazines (10). Each subject spent about one hour in the study and received $10 for participation.

4.2. The videos

Four video segments were selected from the Open Video Project repository (www.open-video.org):
- '*Coney Island*' (1940, 9:19), a black & white documentary showing scenes of the amusement park;
- '*How Much Affection*' (1958, 19:48), a black & white educational film (narrative in style) exploring the boundaries of personal relationships;
- '*Iran*' (1954, 14:00), a color documentary on Iran in 1953; and
- '*On the Run*' (1956, 14:09), a color narrative about teenagers competing in the Mobilgas 'Safety Economy Run' in San Francisco.

A surrogate of a fifth video was used as a training example. The video was 'A Ride for Cinderella' (1937, 10:50), a cartoon advertising Chevrolets.

4.3. The fast forward surrogates

For each video segment, the four fast forward surrogates were created from the full video (MPEG-1 format). As noted above, fast forward surrogates for digital videos, created by sampling every Nth frame, could be produced at any speed by varying the value of N. The research team created and reviewed surrogates over a wide range of speeds, eventually selecting 32, 64, 128, and 256 as values for N in the current investigation. Thus, a full video of 18,000 frames would take approximately 10 minutes to view at the standard speed of 30 fps. A surrogate for it, created with N=32, would display 562 frames (every 32nd frame), taking about 19 seconds to view; whereas a surrogate for the same video at N=256 would take about 2 seconds to view. Thus the speeds of these four surrogates, compared to their original video speed, were 1:32, 1:64, 1:128 and 1:256. The surrogate for the training video was at 1:32 only.

4.4. Procedure

The study was conducted in the Interaction Design Lab (IDL) at the University of North Carolina at Chapel Hill. Each individual session was videotaped and the transcripts analyzed. Subjects first signed the consent form and filled out questionnaires about their experience and background. The session included five trials (including one practice trial with a surrogate at N=32) and in each trial the subjects were asked to watch one fast-forward surrogate and complete six tasks/measures. The four videos and four fast forward rates were counter-balanced so that each video/surrogate speed combination was approximately equally represented. After completing the six tasks/measures described above, each subject was debriefed with questions such as: What would you say are two strengths of this video surrogate? Did this surrogate have any strengths related to any of the tasks you had to perform? What would you say are two weaknesses of this video surrogate? Did this surrogate have any weaknesses related to any of the tasks you had to perform? Do you have any suggestions for improving this surrogate?

4.5. Data analysis

The surrogates and measures were presented through a web front end that piped all responses to a MySQL database. The responses were then analyzed through correlation analysis, analysis of variance, or Fisher's exact test. For the full-text linguistic gist comprehension task, an 8-point scoring scheme was devised and two team members scored the 180 responses independently. There was a .76 correlation (Pearson's r) between the raters' scores, and the mean of the two scores was used in further statistical analyses.

5. Results

In general, study participants were able to perform the tasks successfully with these four surrogates (see Table 1), scoring at above the midpoint on all tasks except the two linguistic gist comprehension tasks.

Table 1. Summary of performance

	Max. possible score	Mean	s.d.	Actual Min/Max
Object recognition (textual)	12	8.6	1.35	5/11
Object recognition (graphical)	12	9.7	1.65	5/12
Action recognition	6	4.5	0.93	2/6
Linguistic gist comprehension (full text)	8	2.9	1.72	0/8
Linguistic gist comprehension (multiple choice)	100%	46%		
Visual gist comprehension	12	8.4	1.41	5/12

The speed of the surrogate had a statistically significant effect on four of the tasks (see Figure 2, next page): object recognition (graphical) (F=3.81 with 3df, p=0.0112), action recognition (F=3.62 with 3df, p=0.0143), linguistic gist comprehension (full text) (F=10.77 with 3df, p<0.0001), and visual gist comprehension (F=3.88 with 3df, p=0.0102). Across all these tasks, as the "speed" of the surrogate increased, performance decreased. However, the point at which the performance difference became statistically significant was tested with Duncan's multiple range test and was found to vary from task to task, as noted in Figure 2.

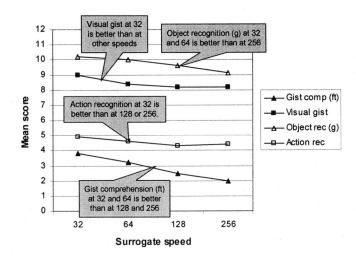

Figure 2. Effects of surrogate speed on performance

Performance on some tasks was also affected by the video with which the participant was interacting (see Table 2). Specifically, video characteristics affected object recognition (textual) (F=11.94 with 3 df, p<0.0001), object recognition (graphical) (F=36.56 with 3df, p<0.0001), gist comprehension (full text) (F=3.15 with 3df, p=0.0263), gist comprehension (multiple choice) (Fisher's exact test, p<0.0001), and visual gist comprehension (F=3.64 with 3df, p=0.0139). Duncan's multiple range test was used to investigate these differences further. Performance on object recognition (textual) was higher on 'Coney Island' and 'On the Run' than on the other two videos. Performance on object recognition (graphical) was highest on 'How Much Affection', followed by 'Iran', followed by the other two segments. Linguistic gist comprehension (full text) was higher on 'How Much Affection' than on 'Coney Island' or 'On the Run'. While no post hoc tests could be run, it would appear that linguistic gist comprehension (multiple choice) was highest on 'Iran', followed by 'Coney Island', followed by the other two videos. Visual gist performance was higher on 'On the Run' than on 'How Much Affection' and 'Iran'. In addition to the main effects of surrogate speed and video, the interactions between these two variables were investigated. They were significant only for action recognition.

Effects of participant characteristics on performance were also investigated. Sex of participant was not related to performance. Age effects were investigated by comparing the performance of those over 25 (n=96 observations) with those under 25 (n=84 observations), splitting the sample at the median age. There were no age effects except for action recognition (t=2.32 with 178 df, p=0.0214), where the older participants performed better (mean score of 4.7 versus 4.4). A parallel finding was

associated with participant status (F=4.54 with 2 df, p=0.0119); undergraduate students (mean score = 4.3) did not perform as well on the action recognition task as the graduate students and faculty/other participants (mean scores = 4.7 and 4.8, respectively). In addition, the frequency with which participants searched for videos was weakly related to linguistic gist comprehension (full text) (Spearman's rho = 0.16, p=0.0275), and object recognition (textual) (Spearman's rho = 0.15, p=0.0430).

Table 2. Mean performance scores, by video

	Iran	Coney Island	On the Run	How Much Affection
*Gist comprehension (full text) (max=8)	3.2	2.5	2.5	3.3
*Gist comprehension (multiple choice)	89%	49%	24%	22%
*Visual gist (max=12)	8.0	8.4	9.0	8.3
*Object recognition (textual) (max=12)	7.9	9.2	9.1	8.3
*Object recognition (graphical) (max=12)	10.1	8.9	8.6	11.2
Action recognition (max=6)	4.8	4.5	4.6	4.3

Asterisk indicates statistically significant differences, by video

6. Discussion

We began with the question, how fast is too fast? Participants in this study were able to perform well on a variety of tasks, regardless of speed. Increased surrogate speed had negative effects on performance on four measures: object recognition (graphical), action recognition, full text linguistic gist comprehension, and visual gist comprehension. For these four measures, participants performed better at the two slowest surrogate speeds. From these results, we conclude that designers should create fast forward surrogates that include at least 1/64th of the video frames, to be sure that user performance is adequate. In similar studies (e.g., Ding's [4] study of the use of slide show video surrogates and Öquist's [16] study of the rapid serial visual presentation of text such as), it has been found that, even when study participants performed relatively well, they were not pleased with the experience. Therefore, the selection of 1:64 as a recommended speed for the fast forward surrogate was intended to be conservative, supporting good performance and user satisfaction with the experience of using the surrogate.

On two of the measures, object recognition (textual) and multiple choice linguistic gist comprehension, performance was not affected by the speed of the surrogate. On these two measures, mean performance was adequate: 8.6 out of 12 correct on object recognition and 46% correct on this measure of gist comprehension. Therefore, we can conclude that performance is adequate, even at the highest speeds tested in this study. If designers set a default speed of 1:64, users should be able to perform these tasks well.

In a previous study [25], participants raised the notion that an important component of video materials is the motion perceived in viewing them. Thus, surrogates that simulate this motion (even in high speed) can help people comprehend the video's gist more completely. A variation of the 'how fast?' question for this implementation of fast forward surrogate is how many frames can be removed before reaching the point at which the surrogate is perceived as a slide show of discrete images, a single image, or none at all? From this point of view, selecting an N in the 50-100 range works well for many genres of video. Picking every 60th frame, for example, means that the user sees a frame from each 2 seconds of real-time video (playing at 30 fps) and this is enough to give a sense of motion for many videos without too many jarring visual disconnects between frames. For high-action video, N may need to be adjusted downward and for low-action video N could be adjusted upward.

Thus, we recommend a default speed of 1/64 of the video's frames based upon our empirical results but also strongly suggest that mechanisms for user control of display speed be included in a video browsing interface. Users may want to adjust the rate depending on video genre, the kind of task at hand, or personal preferences. For a number of tasks, study participants were able to obtain high performance when viewing as few as 1/256 of the video's frames, and there was certainly individual variation in the speed at which people could perform adequately. This variation in optimal speed will likely be influenced by the task the user brings to the browsing

session, the past experience and knowledge of the user, and the setting of the browsing session. It may also be affected by the augmentation of the fast forward with other metadata or representations of the video. For example, the surrogate may be augmented with audio keywords, or the viewing of the surrogate may be preceded by the viewing of metadata describing the video. The current study eliminated any augmentation of the fast forward surrogate in order to isolate the effects of speed on performance, but any real-world digital library would not be constrained in this way and would likely include audio keywords or other metadata in representing the videos in the collection. The addition of these other sources of information will most likely improve user performance with the fast forward surrogate.

Performance on several of the measures was affected by the video used as a stimulus. Differences in the videos were related to the participants' ability to recognize objects from the surrogate (both graphical and textual) and to identify frames that "belonged" in the stimulus video (i.e., the visual gist measure). In addition, the effects of differences in the videos interacted with surrogate speed in relation to action recognition performance. It is unclear which characteristics of the stimulus videos are the sources of these effects. The videos were selected to represent both narrative and documentary styles (two of each) and both color and black-and-white (two of each); the observed effects were not related to these video characteristics. Other possibilities identified as relevant video characteristics in our research framework (see Figure 1) include the rate of scene change, homogeneity of content [25] or other topical or stylistic features. These video characteristics should be investigated through additional analyses of data from the current study, as well as through additional studies.

Reliable, valid measures of user performance in video browsing are needed in order to make progress in this line of research. The six measures employed in this study are a good starting point for such efforts. They represent multiple facets of video browsing behavior: some more conceptual (gist comprehension and visual gist), some more perceptual (object and action recognition); some text-based (object recognition (textual), linguistic gist comprehension) and some image-based (object recognition (graphical), action recognition, visual gist). Further analyses of the measures' reliability are currently being conducted. While they already have some face validity, further analyses of their measurement validity will need to be based on a stronger theoretical understanding of video browsing behaviors. In particular, their applicability in studies of interactions with videos of additional genres, e.g., news broadcasts, should be investigated. We encourage other researchers to employ these measures in their studies and test their psychometric qualities within a variety of video browsing contexts.

In addition, studies of users' interactions with interfaces that provide access to digital video libraries should incorporate measures of user satisfaction. While no such measure was incorporated in the current study, user comments concerning their reactions to the surrogates were systematically collected. These comments will form the foundation on which a valid measure of user satisfaction with video browsing interfaces can (and will) be developed for use in future studies.

7. Conclusion

As one of the early studies on people's use of fast forward surrogates, the results of this study must be evaluated in terms of the necessary limitations of the study design. The design was intended to isolate the effects of surrogate speed, and so could not take into account the effects of potential interactions with other surrogate features if implemented in context. For example, no audio was provided with the fast forward surrogates investigated here; yet, it is likely that a fully-functioning digital library interface would incorporate audio (such as the audio keywords investigated in a previous study [25]). Similarly, these surrogates were viewed in isolation; in a fully-functioning interface, it is likely that users would have viewed additional metadata (e.g., video title or poster frame) before accessing the fast forward surrogates. As such, the fast forward surrogate speed of 1:64 is probably a conservative estimate of the speed at which people can perform well with such surrogates augmented with audio or other metadata.

Nonetheless, for Nth frame fast forwards, we plan to adopt 64 for N as the default setting for fast forward surrogates implemented on the Open Video site.[3] In addition, we will provide control mechanisms that will give users control over the speed of the fast forward display. We are particularly interested in seeing the effects of this design decision as this class of surrogate is implemented within the context of a fully-functioning system (incorporating alternative surrogates and control mechanisms).

We are also interested in the relationship between users' ability to perform with high-speed fast forward surrogates and their satisfaction with that interaction. We are convinced that there is a performance-satisfaction tradeoff—although people may be able to perform accurately at high speeds, they seem willing to exchange

some performance benefits for surrogates that are comfortable and satisfying. While the discrepancies between users' performance and their satisfaction have long been an issue in relation to usability [13], there is recent renewed interest in the affective dimensions of people's interactions with computer-based tools [3,14]. Our future studies will incorporate a measure of user satisfaction, thus explicitly taking into account the "user experience" as people interact with digital video surrogates and the mechanisms that control them.

What is clear from this work is that creating effective digital library interfaces that support video browsing and retrieval will demand a range of user control mechanisms and underlying representations for video. Making sense of video content is a complex cognitive act, depending on multiple facets and cues. Interfaces that aid people in making sense of video based on surrogates must aim to provide a rich mix of these facets and cues and to place them under user control. Designers of digital library interfaces are advised to consider providing such a mix in their implementations.

8. Acknowledgments

We thank the participants in the study. This work is supported by National Science Foundation (NSF) Grant IIS 0099638.

9. References

[1] M. Christel, A. Hauptmann, A. Warmack, and S. Crosby, "Adjustable filmstrips and skims as abstractions for a digital video library", *IEEE Advances in Digital Libraries Conference, (Baltimore, MD, May, 1999)*, pp. 19-21.

[2] M. Christel, M. Smith, C. R. Taylor, and D. Winkler, "Evolving video skims into useful multimedia abstractions", *Proceedings of CHI '98: Human Factors in Computing Systems (Los Angeles, April 18-23, 1998)*, pp. 171-178.

[3] A. Dillon, "Beyond usability: process, outcome and affect in human computer interactions", paper presented as the Lazerow Lecture, Faculty of Information Studies, University of Toronto, 2001.

[4] W. Ding, G. Marchionini, and D. Soergel, "Multimodal surrogates for video browsing". *Proceedings of Digital Libraries '99. the Fourth Annual ACM Conference on Digital Libraries (Berkeley, CA, August 11-14, 1999)*, pp. 85-93.

[5] S. Drucker, A. Glatzer, S. DeMar, and C. Wong, "SmartSkip: Consumer level browsing and skipping of

---

[3] For videos less than 10 minutes in duration, an N of 64 does not produce enough frames to create a fast forward surrogate of useful length. We plan to use an N of 32 for shorter videos.

digital video content", *Proceedings of CHI '02: Human Factors in Computing Systems (Minneapolis, April 20-25, 2002)*, pp. 219-226.

[6] G. Geisler, G. Marchionini, M. Nelson, R. Spinks, and M. Yang, "Interface concepts for the Open Video Project", *ASIST 2001: Proceedings of the 64th ASIST Annual Meeting (Washington, DC, Nov. 3-8, 2001), Volume 38*, pp. 58-75.

[7] T. Grodal, *Moving Pictures --- A New Theory of Film Genres, Feelings, and Cognition.* Oxford: Clarendon Press, 1997.

[8] P. Hoff, *Consumer Electronics for Engineers.* Cambridge: Cambridge University Press, 1998.

[9] A. Komlodi and G. Marchionini, "Key frame preview techniques for video browsing", *Proceedings of ACM Digital Libraries '98 (Pittsburgh, PA, June 24-27,1998)*, pp. 118-125.

[10] H. Lee and A. Smeaton, A. "Designing the user interface for the Físchlár digital video library", *Journal of Digital Information, 2(4)*, 2002. http://jodi.ecs.soton.ac.uk/Articles/v02/i04/Lee/

[11] R. Lienhart, S. Pfeiffer, and W. Effelsberg, „Video abstracting", *Communications of the ACM, 40*(12), 1997, pp. 54-62.

[12] G. Marchionini, V. Nolet, H. Williams, W. Ding, J. Beale, A. Rose, A. Gordon, E. Enomoto, and L. Harbinson, "Content + connectivity => community: digital resources for a learning community", *Proceedings of ACM Digital Libraries '97 (Philadelphia, PA: July 23-26, 1997)*, pp. 212-220.

[13] J. Nielsen, and J. Levy, "Measuring usability: preference vs. performance", *Communications of the ACM, 37*(4), 1994, pp. 66-75.

[14] D. A. Norman, "Emotion & design: attractive things work better", *ACM Interactions, 9*(4), 2002, pp. 36-42.

[15] B. O'Connor, "Access to moving image documents: background concepts and proposals for surrogates for film and video works", *Journal of Documentation, 41*(4), 1985, pp. 209-220.

[16] G. Öquist, Adaptive rapid serial visual presentation, Masters' thesis, Dept. of Linguistics, Uppsala University, 2001. http://stp.ling.uu.se/~matsd/thesis/arch/2001-009.pdf.

[17] S. Palmer, *Vision Science: Photons to Phenomenology.* Cambridge, MA: MIT Press, 1999.

[18] E. Panofsky, *Meaning in the Visual Arts: Papers In and On Art History.* Garden City, NY: Doubleday, 1955.

[19] D. Ponceleon, A. Amir, S. Srinivasan, T. Syeda-Mahmood, and D. Petkovic, "CueVideo: Automated multimedia indexing and retrieval", *ACM Multimedia '99 (Orlando, FL, Oct. 1999)*, p. 199.

[20] D. Ponceleon, and A. Dieberger, "Hierarchical brushing in a collection of video data", *HICSS'34 (Hawaii International Conference on Systems Science), MiniTrack on Video in the office, Maui, HI, January 2001.*

[21] A. Rose, W. Ding, G. Marchionini, J. Beale, Jr., and V. Nolet, "Building an electronic learning community: from design to implementation", *CHI Conference Proceedings (Los Angeles, April 18-23, 1998)*, pp. 203-210.

[22] T. Tse, G. Marchionini, W. Ding, L. Slaughter, and A. Komlodi, A., "Dynamic keyframe presentation techniques for augmenting video browsing", *Proceedings of AVI '98: Advanced Visual Interfaces (L' Aquila, Italy, May 25-27, 1998)*, pp. 185-194.

[23] The user-interface development of Físchlár digital video system, 1999. http://www.computing.dcu.ie/~hlee/ProgressHtml/Progress.html

[24] H. Wactlar, S. Stevens, M. Smith, and T. Kanade, "Intelligent access to digital video: the InforMedia Project", *IEEE Computer, 29*(5), 1996, pp. 46-52.

[25] B. Wildemuth, G.. Marchionini, T. Wilkens, M. Yang, G. Geisler, B. Fowler, A. Hughes, and X. Mu, "Alternative surrogates for video objects in a digital library: users' perspectives on their relative usability", *Proceedings of the European Conference on Digital Libraries (Rome, September 16-18, 2002)*, in press.

Event-Based Retrieval from a Digital Library containing Medical Streams

Mohamed Kholief
*California University of
Pennsylvania
California, PA 15419
1-724-938-4131
Kholief@cup.edu*

Kurt Maly
*Old Dominion University
Norfolk, VA 23529
1-757-683-4817
Maly@cs.odu.edu*

Stewart Shen
*Old Dominion University
Norfolk, VA 23529
1-757-683-4680
Shen@cs.odu.edu*

Abstract

We describe a digital library that contains streams and supports event-based retrieval. Streams used in the digital library are CT scan, medical text, and audio streams. Events, such as 'tumor appeared', were generated and represented in the user interface to enable doctors to retrieve and playback segments of the streams. This paper concentrates on describing the data organization and the user interface.

1. Introduction

A major advantage of using digital libraries over conventional libraries is the ability to store unconventional types of data and use new methods to retrieve these data. In this application, data streams are stored in a digital library and events occurring during these streams are used to retrieve and playback segments of them. The architecture of such a library was introduced in [1]. In this short paper, we present an application that contains streams of medical content. Actual CT scan streams were stored in the repository along with text and audio streams that relate to the subject of the CT scan data. This paper concentrates on two aspects of the digital library: the data organization and the user interface. The data organization in both the file system and the database server is discussed in section 2. The search, the stream display, and the playback interfaces are discussed in section 3.

2. Data organization

2.1. File system organization

A stream object contains its stream data and corresponding metadata. It is implemented in a file system directory, or folder, that contains two main folders: data and metadata. The data folder contains all the data files of the particular stream, e.g. all the image files of a CT scan stream, or all the audio clips of a stream of audio clips. The metadata folder contains the corresponding metadata files: temporal, standard bibliographic, and specific. The temporal metadata file contains a listing of the timing of all the stream frames. The frame could be an image, an audio clip, or a text string depending on the stream type. The standard bibliographic metadata file contains general bibliographic metadata about the stream. The metadata fields in this file are standard for all stream types. These fields are: the stream id, the entry date, the title, the creator, the start date, the end date, the stream type, the stream format, the stream source, and the description. The specific bib metadata file is used to save particular metadata fields that are specific to certain types. This makes the system heterogeneous with regard to the type of the streams that could be saved in the digital library.

2.2. Database server organization

A database system is used to facilitate the retrieval from the digital library. The standard and specific bibliographic metadata information, the events information, and the information about related streams are kept in the database. They include: the stream bib metadata, the event metadata, the stream events, the stream–related streams, the event-related streams, and the stream types. The search engine uses the database to retrieve any stream object based on its bibliographic information or based on the events that occur during this stream. Playback scripts use the database to decide on the related streams that will be played back simultaneous to the retrieved stream, and to decide on the playback start time based on the time of any event instance.

3. The user interface

The user interface is described in figures 1 through 5. This interface and the underlying search engine are based on Arc [2]. The user can choose a simple, an event-based, or a browsing search interface. Figure 1 shows part of the

231

event-based form. Users can select an event and a time range then click the search button. Figure 2 shows part of the search results interface. The left frame shows the archives where the hits are stored and the right frame shows a listing of the hits in the selected archive. Selected metadata information is displayed for each hit. Upon clicking the stream title for any of the hits, the stream display interface shown in figure 3 is displayed. This interface is divided into sections. The upper section shows the standard and specific bib metadata information of the stream and the lower section shows a playback form. In the playback form, the user can select a specific event and a specific time instance of that event from which to start the playback. The user can also select related streams to playback simultaneous with the original stream.

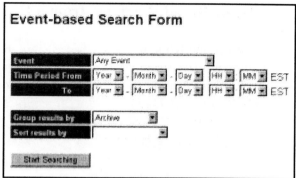

Figure 1. Event-based search interface

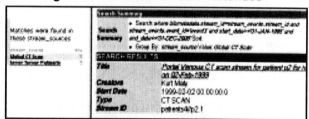

Figure 2. Search results interface

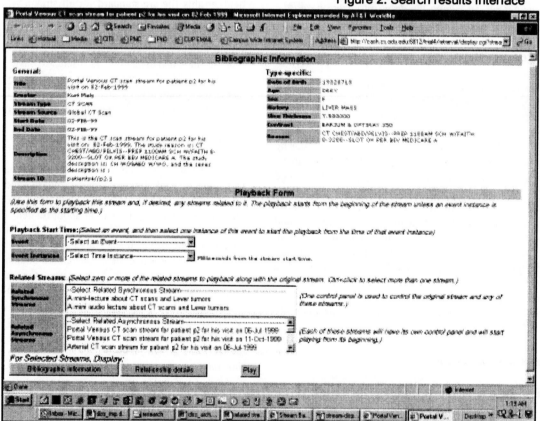

Figure 3. The stream display interface

A sample playback interface is shown in figure 4. It consists of two sections: the upper section contains the players of the related synchronous streams and one control panel to control these players and the lower section contains the players of the related asynchronous streams with one control panel for each. The leftmost stream player in the upper section is the player of the original stream. The control panel, shown in figure 5, controls the behavior of the player applets. The stream player interface consists of three panels. The top panel contains a button "Bib Info", which displays a bib information window for the stream being played. The middle panel shows the stream being played if it is visual as in CT scan and text streams. The bottom panel shows the current status, which is mostly the time of the next frame to be played.

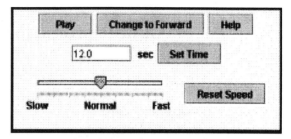

Figure 4. The control panel applet

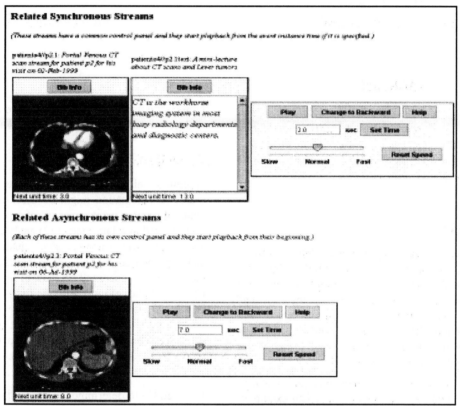

Figure 5. The playback interface

4. Conclusion

The implementation and use of this system demonstrates that it is feasible to create a digital library that contains data streams and supports event-based retrieval. We were able to represent events such that they could be used to retrieve and playback stream segments in as few as 3 mouse clicks. Streams can be displayed such that users can decide whether to playback a stream or not and to set playback options using few menu choices. The playback interface itself was organized to allow playback of both synchronous and asynchronous streams. The ease of use of this library was informally confirmed by a group of radiologists and is yet to be documented. Key to the

specification of events and what metadata to use were the domain experts (radiologists).

5. References

[1] M. Kholief, S. Shen, K. Maly, "Architecture for Event-Based Retrieval from Data Streams in Digital Libraries", *Proceedings of ECDL'2001*, Darmstadt, Germany, September 2001, Springer, pp. 300-311.

[2] X. Liu, K. Maly, M. Zubair, "Arc", http://sourceforge.net/projects/oai

Music Representation in a Digital Music Library

Donald Byrd

School of Music
Indiana University
Bloomington, IN 47401
812-856-0129

donbyrd@indiana.edu

Eric Isaacson

School of Music
Indiana University
Bloomington, IN 47401
812-855-0296

isaacso@indiana.edu

Abstract

The Variations2 digital music library currently supports music in audio and score-image formats. In a future version, we plan to add music in a symbolic form. This paper describes our work defining a music representation suitable for the needs of our users.

1. Introduction

Variations2 is a large-scale digital music library project under development at Indiana University [10]. Version 1 of the software for *Variations2* is now complete. For that version, the digital library contains music in audio and score-image (i.e., scanned) forms. A future version will also support symbolically represented music. Music in symbolic form will be useful to a wide range of people for a wide range of applications, including:

1. music faculty creating assignments and teaching classes (for showing and playing musical examples, plus analyses of those examples);
2. students enrolled in classes with these faculty (for assignments involving tasks such as re-composition or model composition);
3. faculty and student music researchers doing content-based analytical or historical research;
4. music library patrons who for some reason are not content with scanned (or printed!) scores.

Because a large number of symbolic music representations already exist, it makes sense to use one of these rather than to develop a new representation from scratch. But on what basis can we determine which of these representations are satisfactory, and how can we choose which of them is best suited to our needs? While the published literature on music representation is substantial—a few relevant works are [4], [5], [6], and [8]—we know of nothing like a formal description of the requirements for a music representation in any situation. This paper gives an overview of our work to develop such a description for a digital music library.

2. Design Basis

Wiggins et al. [11] discuss three sorts of tasks a symbolic music representation might be used for: (1) recording, in which "the user wants a record of some musical object, to be retrieved at a later date"; (2) analysis, in which the user "wants to retrieve not the 'raw' musical object, but some analyzed version"; and (3) generation/composition. Of these, we are concerned (in view of our expected users and uses listed above) most with the first, less with the second, and least with the third. Declarative representations—by far the more familiar type to most people—rather than procedural ones are much more appropriate for the first type of task and usually for the second, so we consider only declarative representations.

We used [3] to determine the required extent of support for certain types of features, such as the highest, lowest, longest, and shortest notes; the largest numbers of voices and of staves in a score; and so on.

3. Domains of Music Information

The groundbreaking Mockingbird music editor [6] pioneered the approach of storing independently information about the *logical, performance* (also called *gestural*), and *graphic* aspects of music. Logical information about a note might include that it is a quarter note; performance information, that it lasts for 600 milliseconds; and graphic information, that it has a diamond-shaped notehead. Several programs, e.g., [1], adopted Mockingbird's approach; SMDL [9] added a fourth "domain," for *analytic* information, which might include information on the underlying harmony or phrase structure, for example.

234

For a digital music library project, the independent-domain model has a number of advantages. The need for independent logical and performance information is not hard to see. Even if a program can generally play "musically" on its own, it may not be able to handle cadenzas or other passages involving rubato, and it certainly will not be able to reproduce Heifetz's interpretation as distinct from Salerno-Sonnenberg's. The need for graphic information independent of logical is less obvious, but Byrd [2] cites many "counterexamples." To name just two, instances exist in Debussy of clefs in mid-air below the staff, and in Chopin of single noteheads that simultaneously represent normal 16th notes in one voice but triplet 16ths in another voice. Finally, there is little chance a program will be able to produce a high-quality harmonic analysis in the near future, to name just one of many forms of music analysis used in an academic setting; hence the need to be able to store analytic information. Therefore, we strongly advocate SMDL's version of this independent-domain model.

Given likely uses of a music representation in a digital music library, there is no need to represent publishable scores, only serviceable renderings of notation. Therefore the graphic domain is less important than it otherwise would be. But rendering complex music in even a serviceable way is difficult (see [2]; [7] describes limitations of well-known programs in some detail). So representing graphic "tweaking" is still important.

4. Specification Overview

Reflecting its target use at the Indiana University School of Music, the music-representation requirements specification we developed is heavily oriented towards "classical" (western art) music, though we believe it is comprehensive enough to be useful for other styles, e.g., jazz and popular music. We require some sort of schema (including XML DTDs): among several advantages of schemas is the automatic validation of data.

There are some 230 items in 24 categories:

0. Global Information
1. Voices, Staves, and Parts
2. MIDI Channels, Cables, and Patches
3. Musical Symbols in General
4-5. Notes and Chords; Grace Notes and Grace Chords
6 Rests
7. Barlines, Measure Numbers, and Rehearsal Marks
8 Clefs
9. Key Signatures
10. Time Signatures
11-13. Groups: Tuplets; Beams; Octave Signs
14. Tempo Markings
15. Text Strings and Lyrics
16. Dynamics
17. Slurs, Ties, and Horizontal Brackets
18. Staves and Staff Brackets
19. Notation for Chords
20. Endings
21-22. Miscellaneous Graphic Elements, Performance Elements
23. Requirements for Schenkerian Notation

We distinguish three levels of importance: Required, Very Desirable, Desirable. Table 1, extracted from Category 4, gives an idea of the level of detail provided in the document.

5. Conclusions

We sent version 1.0 of "Music Representation Requirement Specification for *Variations2*" to a number of music-representation developers in mid-2002, asking them how well their representations fit our requirements. We received detailed responses from two, and interest from a number of others. Version 1.1 is now on our web site [10]; we have continued to work on the specification since then, and we plan to make further improvements public.

Table 1. An excerpt from the requirements specification.

No.	LPGA	Level	Description
4.8	L	Required	Supports accidentals double-flat thru double-sharp, plus none.
		Desirable	Supports triple-flats and -sharps. (While very rare, these have appeared in published music and could be useful in pedagogy or music-theory work.)
4.9	L	Very Des.	Supports microtonal accidentals, especially quarter-tones.
4.10	G	Required	Supports normal and small-sized accidentals.
		Very Des.	Also supports natural/flat and natural/sharp.

6. Acknowledgments

Thanks to Gerd Castan, Tim Crawford, Jon Dunn, Michael Good, Jim Halliday, John Howard, Douglas McKenna, and Perry Roland for their comments on this work.

7. References

[1] AMNS Nightingale. http://www.ngale.com.

[2] Byrd, D. 1984. *Music Notation by Computer* (doctoral dissertation, Indiana University). UMI, Ann Arbor, Michigan (order no. 8506091).

[3] Byrd, D. 2003. Extremes of Conventional Music Notation. http://mypage.iu.edu/~donbyrd/CMNExtremes.htm.

[4] Dannenberg, R. 1993. Music Representation Issues, Techniques, and Systems. *Computer Music Journal* 17(3): 20–30.

[5] Hewlett, W., & Selfridge-Field, E., eds. 2001. *The Virtual Score: Representation, Retrieval, Restoration (Computing in Musicology* 12). Cambridge, Mass.: MIT Press.

[6] Maxwell, John Turner, III & Ornstein, Severo M. 1984. "Mockingbird: A Composer's Amanuensis." *Byte* 9(1): 384-401.

[7] Powell, S. 2002. *Music Engraving Today: The Art and Practice of Digital Notesetting.* New York: Brichtmark.

[8] Read, G. 1969. *Music Notation.* 2nd ed. Boston: Crescendo.

[9] Sloan, D. 1997. HyTime and Standard Music Description Language: A Document-Description Approach. In Selfridge-Field, E., ed. 1997. *Beyond MIDI: The Handbook of Musical Codes.* Cambridge, Mass.: MIT Press, 469–490.

[10] Variations2: IU Digital Music Library Project. http://variations2.indiana.edu/.

[11] Wiggins, G., Miranda, E., Smaill, A., and Harris, M. 1993. A Framework for the Evaluation of Music Representation Systems. *Computer Music Journal* 17,3, 31–42.

A Quantified Fidelity Criterion for Parameter-Embedded Watermarking of Audio Archives*

A.R. Gurijala

Michigan State University
Dept. Elec. & Comp. Engr.
E. Lansing, MI 48824 USA
+1 517 353-1859
gurijala@egr.msu.edu

J.R. Deller, Jr.

Michigan State University
Dept. Elec. & Comp. Engr.
E.Lansing, MI 48824 USA
+1 517 353-8840
deller@egr.msu.edu

Abstract

A novel algorithm for speech watermarking through parametric modeling is enhanced by inclusion of a quantified fidelity criterion. Watermarking is effected through solution of a set-membership filtering (SMF) problem, subject to an l_∞ fidelity criterion in the signal space. The SMF approach provides flexibility in obtaining watermark solutions that trade-off watermark robustness and stegosignal fidelity.

1. Introduction

Parameter embedded speech watermarking is being developed for the National Gallery of the Spoken Word (NGSW), a Digital Libraries Initiative II project [1], whose goal is the creation of a carefully organized on-line repository of spoken word collections. Development of watermarking techniques to secure the copyright of the on-line material is a key engineering aspect of the project. Digital watermarking is the process of embedding a signal (watermark) imperceptibly into a host signal (coversignal). When copyright questions arise, the watermark is unambiguously recovered from the watermarked signal (stegosignal) to resolve rightful ownership issues. The main requirements of a watermarking technique are robustness, imperceptibility and security. Robustness is the ability of a watermark to survive intentional and inadvertent distortion. The watermarking process must not affect the fidelity of the content. For this reason, the embedded watermark must be imperceptible. Further, the watermarking must be secure to prevent unauthorized detection, embedding or removal.

The parameter-embedded speech watermarking technique described in [4] indirectly alters the linear prediction (LP) coefficients of speech, by modifying the signal's autocorrelation values. The method is briefly described in Section 2. This paper presents a novel algorithm for parameter-based speech watermarking that treats the watermarking process as a set-membership filtering (SMF) [5] problem. The SMF implementation returns a set of solutions (LP coefficients), satisfying an l_∞ fidelity measure in the signal space. A particular model can be selected from the resulting solution set in order to maximize the robustness. Section 3 describes the SMF-based digital speech watermarking algorithm.

The watermarking technique described in this paper involves informed embedding, meaning that the original speech is required during the watermark embedding and recovery processes. Any unauthorized embedding will treat the stegosignal as the original and, hence, will include the watermark. Some of the factors that can contribute to increased security of the new algorithm include use of LP models of different orders, random selection of the speech samples to be watermarked (in accordance with a pseudo random key), and use of coversignal segments of differing lengths. Robustness is a result of the watermark's being concentrated during the embedding and recovery processes, while distributed across the coversignal otherwise. This ensures that the effect of any distortion is localized and its impact on the watermark is minimized.

2. Speech watermarking through parametric modeling

Parametric watermarking is based on linear prediction (LP) modeling in which the speech signal (coversignal), say $x[n]$, is assumed to follow the difference equation (1),

$$x[n] = \sum_{i=1}^{M} \hat{a}_i x[n-i] + e[n] \qquad (1)$$

in which the $\hat{a}_i$ are the LP coefficients of the coversignal, M is the order of the LP model, and $e[n]$ is the prediction residual. In speech coding applications, the goal is to find a set of LP coefficients that optimally model quasi-stationary regions of the speech. In the present application, the LP model is used as a device to parameterize long intervals of nonstationary speech without the intention of properly parameterizing any particular dynamics in the waveform. Rather, the parameters are derived according to the usual optimization criterion -- to minimize the total energy in the residual [3] -- with the understanding the aggregate dynamics will be "distributed" between the parametric code and the residual sequence.

Information is embedded in the parameter domain by modifying the LP coefficients of the coversignal. This embedding alters speech properties that are not linearly related to the signal samples. The stegosignal is reconstructed using the exact residual according to

$$\widetilde{x}[n] = \sum_{i=1}^{M} \widetilde{a}_i x[n-i] + e[n] \qquad (2)$$

where the $\widetilde{a}_i$ are the modified LP coefficients. In [4] the modified LP coefficients were obtained indirectly using Levinson-Durbin (LD) [5] recursion, after adding a watermark sequence to the autocorrelation values of the difference signal ($x[n]-e[n]$).

3. l_∞ fidelity criterion for parametric watermarking

The present watermarking process involves the specification of an l_∞ fidelity criterion between the cover- and stegosignals. That is, the sample-wise discrepancy between the cover- and stegosignals is subject to the bound

$$\delta = \max_{n \in \Gamma} \left| x[n] - \widetilde{x}[n] \right| \qquad (3)$$

in which Γ ⬚represents the time interval over which the watermark is embedded. To obtain the stegosignal and hence the embedded watermark, a SMF algorithm is applied [5], returning a hyperellipsoidal set of parameter vectors, each element of which produces a stegosignal satisfying the fidelity criterion.

$$x[n] - e[n] = z[n] \le \sum_{i=1}^{M} \widetilde{a}_i x[n-i] + \delta \qquad (4)$$

The stegosignal is reconstructed as in (2) using a particular solution, i.e., an $\widetilde{a}$ vector chosen to maximize the watermark robustness. Ongoing research is focused on determining optimally robust solutions under specific attack conditions. By default in the present work, the center of the hyperellipsoid is taken to be the modified LP coefficients. Using LD recursion, the autocorrelation

values of $z[n]$ are determined. The watermark is the difference between the autocorrelation values associated with $z[n]$ and those associated with $(\widetilde{x}[n] - e[n])$.

To recover the watermark, the prediction residual $e[n]$ is subtracted from the stegosignal. Estimation of the $\widetilde{a}_i$ filter coefficients is treated as a least-squares problem [4], for a given input $x[n]$ and desired output $z[n]$. By applying the reverse LD recursion on the estimated LP coefficients, the corresponding autocorrelation values are obtained. The watermark is then recovered as the difference between these autocorrelation values and those of $z[n]$.

4. MSE vs. l_∞ norm as a measure of fidelity

The watermarking process must not affect the fidelity of the stegosignal beyond an acceptable standard. One common measure of fidelity in the watermarking literature is mean square error (MSE),

$$MSE = \frac{1}{N} \sum_{i=1}^{N} \left(x[n] - \widetilde{x}[n] \right)^2 \qquad (5)$$

MSE either overestimates or underestimates the stegosignal fidelity [2] depending on the frequency content of the watermark. By ensuring that the sample difference between the cover- and stegosignals does not exceed the preset δ, the l_∞ fidelity measure does not significantly over- or underestimate the stegosignal fidelity considerably.

A simple experiment illustrates advantage of using the l_∞ norm over MSE as the fidelity measure. In the upper plot below, noise, uniformly distributed in the range [0, 0.2], was added to 400 samples of the vowel /A/, sampled at 10 kHz. For the lower plot, noise uniformly distributed in the range [0, 0.0725] was added to every sample of the vowel /A/. The l_∞ values were 0.1999 and 0.0724 respectively. In both cases, MSE was 0.0014, even though the noise in the former cases, MSE was 0.0014, even though the noise in the first case (upper plot) is apparently more detrimental.

5. Conclusions

By treating parameter-embedded watermarking as an SMF problem, we obtain a set of potential watermarks, subject to an l_∞ fidelity constraint. Preliminary experiments have shown that for watermarks of similar energy, the SMF approach results in more imperceptible watermarks, than if the watermarks were embedded directly without the l_∞ constraint

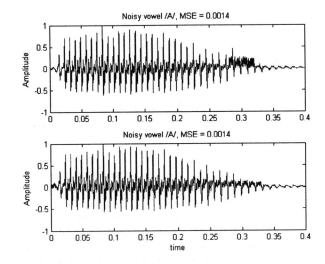

Figure 1. MSE vs. l_∞ norm

6. References

[1] NGSW website. http://www.ngsw.org

[2] I.J. Cox, M.L. Miller, and A.B. Jeffrey, *Digital Watermarking*, Academic Press, 2002.

[3] J.R. Deller, Jr., J.H.L. Hansen, and J.G. Proakis, *Discrete Time Processing of Speech Signals* (2d ed.), New York: IEEE Press, 2000.

[4] A. Gurijala, J.R. Deller, Jr., M. Seadle and J.H.L. Hansen, " Speech watermarking through parametric modeling," Proc. *Int. Conf. on Spoken Language Processing*, Denver, September 2002, on CD ROM.

[5] J.R. Deller, Jr., and Y.F. Huang, "Set-membership identification and filtering for signal processing applications," *Circuits, Systems and Signal Processing*, vol. 21, pp. 69-82, February 2002.

[*] **Acknowledgement.**

This material is based upon work supported by the National Science Foundation under cooperative Agreement IIS-9817485. Conclusions and recommendations expressed in this material are those of the authors and not necessarily those of the NSF.

Fourth-Phase Digital Libraries: Pacing, Linking, Annotating and Citing in Multimedia Collections

J. Alfredo Sánchez

Libraries Division and CENTIA

Universidad de las Américas, Puebla, México

alfredo@mail.udlap.mx

J. Aníbal Arias

ICT - CENTIA

Universidad de las Américas, Puebla, México

anibal@ieee.org

Abstract

We discuss the implications of the use of current multimedia collections and posit that it is possible to build what we term fourth-phase digital libraries (4PDLs). In 4PDLs users can take advantage of both the powerful audiovisual channels and the proven practices developed for media such as text. We demonstrate how various technologies can be integrated to produce a 4PDL.

1. Introduction

The printed word has proven to be an effective means for supporting the generation and dissemination of new knowledge. We posit that multimedia digital libraries can be designed and built as integrative environments in which diverse media are interwoven to overcome their limitations and provide even more effective support for knowledge-intensive tasks. We refer to this sort of digital libraries as fourth-phase digital libraries (4PDLs).

2. The third phase

Simone [4] compares and contrasts the cognitive processes underlying the activities of *reading* and *viewing* documents to conclude that humankind has entered a "third phase" in the history of knowledge: The First Phase would have coincided with the invention of writing, which made it possible to persistently record the individual or collective human memory. A Second Phase started twenty centuries later with the invention of printing, which made books and knowledge accessible to a vast public, changing social and cultural life in profound ways. During the last twenty years, we moved into a Third Phase, in which the we have learned from reading much less than in the past and well-established learning practices and ways of knowing are being lost. Whereas writing allowed for more refined and complex forms of expression, knowledge expressed or acquired from audiovisual media tends to be less articulate and less subtle.

Seven traits of printed and audiovisual documents that impact the way they are used in knowledge access and generation are also discussed in [4]: (1) *Pace:* The pace of reading is determined by the reader, video authors "push" images at will towards the viewer. (2) *Corrigibility*: A reader may stop at any point in time to reflect on the text just read;

a viewer cannot do this easily. (3) *Encyclopedic references:* Reading allows users to stop and use complementary sources; doing that would disrupt the intended rhythm of video. (4) *Citability*: A text can be easily cited or even quoted; video segments do not exhibit this property. (5) *Conviviality*: Reading usually is a quiet, isolated, intent activity; viewing requires less attention and can be done collectively. (6) *Multi-sensoriality*: Reading is mono-sensorial, audiovisual materials reach the user through both sight and hearing. Finally, (7) *iconicity*: Images carry meaning even for the uninitiated; characters and sounds that represent words have zero iconicity.

3. Towards a fourth phase

If the Third Phase is characterized by the prevalence of an audiovisual culture, a Fourth Phase should integrate media, beyond just building multimedia collections, and make it possible for people to take advantage of the best of each of them. The digital substrate is rich and malleable enough to actually recreate existing media and give rise to improved interaction mechanisms. In order to continue to build on the ways of learning and knowing that have been developed for centuries, it is necessary and possible to reshape media such as audio and video so they acquire desirable features. Digital libraries of the fourth phase (4PDLs) should integrate technologies to produce knowledge centers in which reading and viewing occur seamlessly for all available media.

4. The VUDLA 4PDL

In order to explore the notion of a 4PDL we designed and prototyped VUDLA, a multimedia digital library that integrates image and speech processing, video streaming, information retrieval and multimedia databases. In VUDLA, users may create and explore digital video collections. More importantly, as illustrated in Figure 1, they can determine the pace of viewing, search for specific scenes based on their contents, add textual or graphical annotations or specify web links that will be attached to materials at specific points in time. Every time a video document is added, speech and image processing systems generate metadata (terms, color and texture indexes) that will be used to support video querying and viewing. VUDLA relies on information retrieval, video streaming and speech processing components that have been developed by various groups in our research center. We are interested in developing video collections in Spanish and exploring mechanisms for retrieval that are particularly appropriate for them. A complete description of VUDLA is available at [3]. Relevant related projects are [1] and [5].

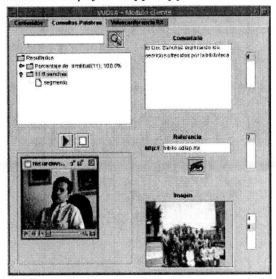

Figure 1. Main user interface of VUDLA.

5. Preliminary results

The VUDLA prototype has been undergoing tests in two major areas: functionality and usability. In the first area, we have successfully integrated diverse technologies. In the second area, we are demonstrating that VUDLA enables the use of digital video in such a way that users are able to perform tasks involving multimedia resources and overcoming the limitations referred to in Section 2. Our video collection is academic, in Spanish, and it includes interviews with researchers from various areas, lectures and software We have been able to observe users interact with the new multimedia collections and we report here results with respect to relevant media traits introduced in Section 2, which guided our design:

Pace: In VUDLA, the interaction with resources in all available media is completely under the user's control. The user determines the pace at which temporal media are "played". *Corrigibility:* Users of VUDLA may stop at any point in time to reflect on resources being examined, regardless of their type. *Encyclopedic references:* Not only can complementary sources be used while examining multimedia resources in VUDLA, but those resources may be associated directly with a section of a document and available immediately for perusal. *Citability.* Content-based

search over digital video using text or images, as well as the possibility to point to any instant within a video segment make multimedia collections in VUDLA citable and quotable. *Conviviality, multi-sensoriality and iconicity:* A 4PDL such as VUDLA redefines the concepts of reading and viewing. In the digital library, reading may be an isolated activity, but the reader may also choose to be aware of the presence of other readers and decide to interact with them by taking advantage of the library's collaboration facilities. In addition to videoconferencing, other communication and awareness facilities are available in the overarching digital library [2]. Reading may involve video illustrations just like viewing may lead to textual annotations. In a way, the multi-sensorial and iconic properties of multimedia are imparted to text.

There is ample room for improving VUDLA. We plan to provide formatting and personalization options for textual annotations as well as *frame hotspots*, which should map specific frame regions to annotations or web links.

6. Conclusions

One of the concerns regarding the prevalence of video and the abandonment of reading is that video appears as a regression from the structured, analytical, sequential reasoning promoted by reading to more primitive, sensorial forms of intelligence. In a 4PDL, multimedia resources are experienced by the user's senses but associative thinking is also promoted. While still some of the mind-structuring properties of knowledge construction based primarily on reading may be at risk, there sure are new, more powerful cognitive processes triggered by 4PDLs.

Acknowledgments

This work is supported by Conacyt (Projects No. 35804-A and G33009-A). Thanks are also due to our colleagues at ICT and the Tlatoa and Videoconferencing Groups.

References

[1] Lyu, M., Yau, E., Sze, S. 2002. A multilingual, multimodal digital video library system. Proceedings of JCDL 2002. 145-153.

[2] Reyes-Farfán, N., Sánchez, J. A. 2003. Personal spaces in the context of OAI. *Proceedings of JCDL 2003* (this volume).

[3] Sánchez, J. A., Arias, J. A. 2003. VUDLA: A fourth-phase digital library. Tech. Report ICT-2003-2. Laboratory of Interactive and Cooperative Technologies, Universidad de las Américas, Puebla, México. http://ict.udlap.mx.

[4] Simone, R. *La Terza Fase.* Laterza. Rome, Italy. 2000

[5] Wactlar, H. D., Kanade, T., Smith, M. A. Stevens, S. M. Intelligent access to digital video: Informedia Project. *IEEE Computer 29*, 3 (May). 1996. 46-52.

Session 8B: Designing and Accessing Scientific Digital Libraries

Session Chair: Sally Howe, Nat'l Coordination Office for Information Technology R & D

On Querying Geospatial and Georeferenced Metadata Resources in G-Portal

Zehua Liu, Ee-Peng Lim, Wee-Keong Ng
Centre for Advanced Information Systems
School of Computer Engineering
Nanyang Technological University
Singapore, 639798
{aseplim, awkng, aszhliu}@ntu.edu.sg

Dion H. Goh
Division of Information Studies
School of Communication and Information
Nanyang Technological University
Singapore, 639798
ashlgoh@ntu.edu.sg

Abstract

G-Portal is a web portal system providing a range of digital library services to access geospatial and georeferenced resources on the Web. Among them are the storage and query subsystems that provide a central repository of metadata resources organized under different projects. In G-Portal, all metadata resources are represented in XML (Extensible Markup Language) and they are compliant to some resource schemas defined by their creators. The resource schemas are extended versions of a basic resource schema making it easy to accommodate all kinds of metadata resources while maintaining the portability of resource data. To support queries over the geospatial and georeferenced metadata resources, a XQuery-like query language known as $\mathcal{RQL}$ (Resource Query Language) has been designed. In this paper, we present the $\mathcal{RQL}$ language features and provide some experimental findings about the storage design and query evaluation strategies for $\mathcal{RQL}$ queries.

1. Introduction

1.1. Overview of G-Portal

Integrated access to geospatial and georeferenced resources on the Web and making them available for both classroom learning and extramural research are important challenges in digital libraries. G-Portal, a research project at the Nanyang Technological University, attempts to address these challenges by providing a web portal system that offers a flexible approach to manage and access collections of metadata resources constructed for geospatial and georeferenced web resources [7].

There are several digital library projects focusing on geospatial and georeferenced information available on the Web. Among them are Alexandria Digital Library (ADL), Alexandria Digital Earth ProtoType (ADEPT) [11, 12], Digital Library for Earth System Education (DLESE) [13], Geospatial Knowledge Representation System (GKRS) [17] and GEOREP [10]. G-Portal is quite distinct compared to these systems due to the following novel features:

- It supports a storage subsystem for metadata resources represented in XML. The resources are organized into projects and they are compliant with some resource schemas. The adoption of XML and schemas ensures that G-Portal can support a wide variety of metadata resources.

- G-Portal provides both map-based and classification-based user interfaces to access the metadata resources. The former are suitable for geospatial resources with location information while the latter caters for all kinds of resources with or without location information. The two interfaces coexist and are synchronized. That is, resources selected using the map-based interface will also be highlighted in the classification-based interface, and vice versa.

- G-Portal allows different classification hierarchies to be defined for metadata resources according to the needs of different digital library user communities. This is a stark contrast to traditional digital libraries adopting only a single classification hierarchy for cataloging data.

- G-Portal provides user annotation facilities on the metadata resources to support better knowledge sharing. By treating annotations as a type of metadata resource, the annotations can be accessed in the same way as other metadata resources [8].

As a digital library system, G-Portal has to provide efficient query processing services to its users. Compared to ADL [11] and ADEPT [12] which assume a distributed digital library architecture consisting of multiple collection

245

servers, G-Portal currently has a centralised storage subsystem for its metadata resources represented in XML. To query these resources, an XML-based query language is required. Furthermore, there is a need to design a suitable query subsystem to support such queries. In GEOREP [10] and DLESE [16], resources are also maintained in centralized storage systems. The two systems however use standard structured database systems (relational or object-oriented) to manage their resources. In other words, the kind of resources that can be handled by GEOREP and DLESE are highly structured and they must comply to some pre-determined database schema. Lastly, the GKRS project focuses on knowledge representation of text and multimedia information instead of metadata resources [17].

XML has been well accepted as a more flexible way to represent semistructured information. Due to its self-describing nature, XML is ideal for representing metadata resources. In G-Portal, all metadata resources are represented in XML and each resource must comply to some resource schema defined using the XML Schema language [15]. To ensure that all resources contain some essential elements required for identification and classification purposes, all resource schemas must share some common elements defined in a basic resource schema [7].

Several query languages have been proposed for XML. Among them, XQuery offers very powerful query capabilities and has been selected by the W3 Consortium XML Query Working Group for further design and standardization [2]. XQuery, nevertheless, does not provide much support for querying spatial elements in resources. It simply treats spatial elements as numerical values and not all spatial search criteria can be expressed as query predicates on these individual spatial elements. Furthermore, the existing XML database systems are not able to process spatial queries efficiently as will be shown in our experiments (see Section 6).

1.2. Objectives and Contributions

In this paper, we will examine the query facilities provided by G-Portal. To this end, we examine the unique way G-Portal represents and organizes its metadata resources, derive the user query requirements, and design a XQuery-based query language to query G-Portal resources. The new query language known as $\mathcal{RQL}$ is small and easy-to-use. While $\mathcal{RQL}$ has a strong XQuery flavor, it also introduces features that cater to integrated queries on XML and spatial information of metadata resources, project-centric organization of resources, and resource schema-compliant resources.

We will also describe some experiments conducted on integrated XML and spatial query processing on a real dataset. In the experiments, we evaluate different XML-

spatial query processing strategies and determine their strengths and shortcomings. The experience in these experiments will guide us in the final design of the G-Portal storage and query processing subsystems.

In the following, we summarize the specific contributions of this paper:

- A new query language, $\mathcal{RQL}$, has been developed for G-Portal resources. This new query language incorporates the concepts of projects and schemas into the query syntax. It also supports geometry object representation and spatial query predicates required for querying geospatial information.

- We have designed the system architecture for G-Portal's storage and query subsystems. We chose the Tamino XML database system to store resources, and the Informix database system to store the spatial information of these resources. Several query evaluation strategies have been developed, some appropriate for queries involving non-spatial predicates only and others are for queries involving both spatial and non-spatial predicates.

- Experiments have been conducted to compare the storage alternatives for G-Portal resources, and their query processing strategies. The experiments show that for queries that involve spatial predicates returning small number of resources, it is better to explore the spatial indexing method provided by Informix to first obtain the resources qualifying the spatial predicates before evaluating the non-spatial predicates on the resources in the Tamino database. Otherwise, we should query both Tamino and Informix separately and obtain the query results by finding the common resources returned by the two queries.

1.3. Outline of Paper

The remaining sections of this paper are structured as follows. Section 2 gives an overview of the related research. Section 3 briefly describes the definition of resources in G-Portal. Our proposed query language $\mathcal{RQL}$ is described in Section 4. Section 5 presents some considerations of processing $\mathcal{RQL}$ queries and the architecture of the G-Portal storage and query subsystems. The experiments and results are given in Section 6. Finally, we give our conclusion in Section 7.

2. Related Work

Both XML and spatial information co-exist in G-Portal resources. We therefore require an integrated approach to formulate queries on resources. We first examine the extensions of the relational query language, SQL, to handle spatial queries. As traditional relational databases only support simple data types, Open GIS Consortium has defined an extension of SQL data model to represent and query geometry data [9]. This extension includes a set of spatial data types and spatial predicate functions to simplify queries on spatial columns. We borrow this idea in our query language design.

The evaluation of spatial queries on relational databases has been a very active area of research. Most research focus on designing specialized indexing methods such as R-tree and its variants to support efficient spatial searches [5, 3]. R-tree and other indexing methods are now supported by several relational database products including the Informix database system used in our G-Portal implementation. However, due to the very flexible structure in XML data, spatial indexing methods are generally not available in XML database systems. Other than spatial indexing, there have been also much research work on spatial join optimization [4]. Since G-Portal only provides direct queries on resources however, spatial joins are not involved.

Our XML and spatial query processing research is also related to the SDSC and UCSD's research on representing remote spatial data sources in XML and employing XML-based query languages to integrate them [1]. In the above project, a query language XMAS was defined and the mapping from XMAS to relational queries is performed to retrieve XML-formatted results from the remote data sources. XMAS is based on XML-Query, not XQuery. Unlike G-Portal, there is no physical repository of metadata resources in XML.

3. Definition of Resources

In G-Portal, metadata resources (or simply resources) are descriptors about geospatial and georeference information on the Web. Represented in XML, they serve as searchable and browsable items in G-Portal as well as pointers to the original sources. To give the flexibility to accommodate different kinds of metadata resources, G-Portal requires every metadata resource to be an instance of some *resource schema*. Resource schemas define the internal structure of resources and are used by G-Portal to interpret the content of resources.

Consider the sample resource schema in Figure 1. It defines the resource schema for County Census resources extracted from the U.S. Census Bureau [14]. Written in the XML Schema language [15], the resource schema derives its resource elements from the *basic resource schema*, *Resource.xsd*, and defines additional elements and attributes relevant to county census resources.

The basic resource schema includes 6 basic resource el-

```
<?xml version="1.0" encoding="UTF-8"?>
<xsd:schema xmlns:xsd="http://www.w3.org/2001/XMLSchema"
    elementFormDefault="qualified">
  <xsd:redefine schemaLocation="Resource.xsd"/>
  <xsd:complexType name="ContentType">
    <xsd:sequence>
      <xsd:element name="GeneralQuickFacts" type="GeneralQuickFactsType"/>
      <xsd:element name="PeopleQuickFacts" type="PeopleQuickFactsType"/>
      <xsd:element name="BusinessQuickFacts" type="BusinessQuickFactsType"/>
      <xsd:element name="GeographyQuickFacts" type="GeographyQuickFactsType"/>
    </xsd:sequence>
  </xsd:complexType>
  <xsd:complexType name="GeneralQuickFactsType">
    <xsd:sequence>
      <xsd:element name="State" type="xsd:string"/>
    </xsd:sequence>
  </xsd:complexType>
  <xsd:complexType name="PeopleQuickFactsType">
    <xsd:sequence>
      <xsd:element name="Population" type="PopulationType"/>
      <xsd:element name="HouseHold" type="HouseHoldType"/>
    </xsd:sequence>
  </xsd:complexType>
  <xsd:complexType name="PopulationType">
    <xsd:sequence>
      <xsd:element name="Year2001Estimate" type="xsd:int"/>
      <xsd:element name="Year2000" type="xsd:int"/>
      ... ...
      <xsd:element name="Distribution" type="DistributionType"/>
    </xsd:sequence>
  </xsd:complexType>
  <xsd:complexType name="DistributionType">
    <xsd:sequence>
      ... ...
      <xsd:element name="ByRace" type="ByRaceType"/>
    </xsd:sequence>
    <xsd:attribute name="Year" type="xsd:short" use="required"/>
  </xsd:complexType>
  <xsd:complexType name="ByRaceType">
    <xsd:sequence>
      <xsd:element name="Category" type="CategoryType" maxOccurs="unbounded"/>
    </xsd:sequence>
  </xsd:complexType>
  ... ...
</xsd:schema>
```

Figure 1. QuickFacts County Census Resource Schema

ements common to all resources in G-Portal. They are *resource id*, *name*, *location*, *creator*, *source*, and *content*. Briefly, the *resource id* is used to uniquely identify a resource in G-Portal. Each resource is also given a *name*, *location* (indicating the spatial information of the resource), and *creator* information. The *location* information is represented by a 2-D geometry object. The *source* element refers to the external link to the original web resource. The *content* element refers to the remaining bulk of the resource information and can be customized for different types of metadata resources. In this example, the content element has been extended to capture the county census information. The extended content element consists of the general, people, business and geography components identified by the *GeneralQuickFacts*, *PeopleQuickFacts*, *BusinessQuickFacts*, and *GeographyQuickFacts* respectively.

Based on the above sample resource schema, resources can be created accordingly. Figure 2 depicts a sample census resource about the Harris County in Georgia.

In G-Portal, resources are further organized into different projects which define a logical set of resources pertinent to a specific task and digital library application. While resources with different schemas can be grouped into a single project, the grouping is logical since the same resource may be shared among different projects. This sharing mecha-

```
<?xml version="1.0" encoding="UTF-8"?>
<Resource xmlns:xsi="http://www.w3.org/2000/10/XMLSchema-instance"
          xsi:noNamespaceSchemaLocation="CountyQuickFacts.xsd"
          ShapeID="1">
  <ID>CountyQuickFacts_1</ID>
  <ResourceName><Name>Harris County</Name></ResourceName>
  <Location Type="Geometry">
    <Geometry>
      <NumberOfParts>1</NumberOfParts>
      <Part Type="Point">
        <NumberOfPoints>1</NumberOfPoints>
        <Point><X>-84.9060</X><Y>32.7407</Y></Point>
      </Part>
    </Geometry>
  </Location>
  <Creator> ... ... </Creator>
  <Source><Link Type="External">
      http://quickfacts.census.gov/qfd/states/13/13145.html
  </Link></Source>
  <Content>
    <GeneralQuickFacts><State>Georgia</State></GeneralQuickFacts>
    <PeopleQuickFacts>
      <Population>
        <Year2001Estimate>24548</Year2001Estimate>
        <Year2000>23695</Year2000>
        ... ...
        <Distribution Year="2000">
          ... ...
          <ByRace>
            <Category Desc="White">78.4</Category>
            <Category Desc="Black or African American"> 19.5 </Category>
            <Category Desc="American Indian and Alaska Native"> 0.4 </Category>
            <Category Desc="Asian">0.5</Category>
            <Category Desc="Native Hawaiian and Other Pacific Islander">
              0</Category>
            <Category Desc="Others">0.3</Category>
          </ByRace>
        </Distribution>
      </Population>
      ... ...
    </PeopleQuickFacts>
    ... ...
    <GeographyQuickFacts>
      ... ...
      <MetropolitanArea>Columbus, GA-AL MSA</MetropolitanArea>
    </GeographyQuickFacts>
  </Content>
</Resource>
```

Figure 2. QuickFacts County Census Resource

nism is provided to prevent replication of resources in G-Portal and to promote reusability among different projects.

4. ($\mathcal{RQL}$) - A Resource Query Language

As XML quickly becomes the choice language for representing and exchanging information on the Web, there is ongoing work to standardize the languages for querying, transforming, exchanging, and publishing XML data. Among the query languages for XML, XQuery has gained acceptance by the W3 Consortium as the XML query language standard [2]. While still evolving, XQuery has been implemented in several database systems, e.g., Tamino, Oracle, etc.. As XQuery is a powerful query language designed to query and transform XML data which are semistructured and nested, the optimized evaluation of queries in XQuery remains a research topic. Moreover, there is little support for spatial access and indexing in XQuery.

G-Portal essentially adopts an XQuery approach to querying its metadata resources represented in XML format. Although XQuery is ideal for generic XML queries, it has to be further customized due to the following salient features of the query model used in G-Portal:

- *Project and schema groupings of resources*: As G-Portal resources are grouped by both projects and resource schemas, it is important to be able to query resources under some specified project and resource schema(s).

- *Selection-based retrieval queries*: XQuery is an highly expressive language that supports selection of XML elements in an XML document, and transforming the XML document into another representation. The transformation aspect of XQuery primarily caters for information exchange. Since information exchange is not the target usage of G-Portal's resources, the XQuery syntax can be further simplified for use.

- *Designated spatial attributes in resource schemas*: Spatial location is a core element in the basic resource schema. This schema element allows us to display resources on the map-based interface and to specify queries with *spatial predicates* describing the selection criteria based on the spatial location of resources. Instead of a verbose specification of such spatial query predicates using XQuery syntax, we have chosen to augment XQuery with spatial object representation and a set of spatial predicates for specifying different kinds of spatial conditions easily.

4.1. $\mathcal{RQL}$ Query Syntax

The $\mathcal{RQL}$ query model follows the XQuery syntax closely. A query can be expressed as follows:

```
select <project>
for $<res_var> in schema((<res_sch>)+)/*/Resource
(<for_expression>|<let_expression>)*
where <filter_expression>
return $<res_var>
```

In the above query expression, the *select* clause indicates the G-Portal project to be queried. The ⟨res_sch⟩ token refers to a resource schema of the project. By specifying the project and resource schema, the resources to be queried can thus be identified. The expression $⟨res_var⟩ schema((⟨res_sch⟩)+)/*/Resource iterates the resources with the specified schema under the project, and binding the resources to $⟨res_var⟩ one at a time. The zero or more ⟨for_expression⟩ and ⟨let_expression⟩ allows further iteration over the child (or descendant) elements of $⟨res_var⟩ and binding some specific child element (or descendant) of $⟨res_var⟩ with other variables. In both the *for* and *let* expressions, additional variables could be defined to bind different portions of the resource elements. Once this is done, the *where* clause filters the unwanted resources by specifying the filtering expression on the binding variables. Finally, the *return* clause generates the resources for each of these bindings fulfilling the filtering expression.

Compared to the original XQuery syntax, the above query expression is restricted to the FLWR (pronounced as "FLO-WER") expression using the *for* expression to iterate the resources in the XML resource file. Unlike XQuery, we introduce the *select* clause to identify the project used in the query. We also do not assume that all resources are stored within a XML file (an assumption made in XQuery's syntax). Instead, we use the project and schema(s) to identify the collection of resources to be queried. Only resources associated with the project and schema will be returned by the query. We further simplify the return clause to include the different bindings of resource variables satisfying the filter expression.

4.2. Queries on Non-Spatial Elements Only

Using the example Census resource schema and assuming that CountyProj is a project that includes some county census resources, we formulate the following query examples using the modified XQuery language.

Q1: Find the census resources that are from the state of Georgia.

```
select CountyProj
for $i in schema(censusDB)/*/Resource
where $i/Content/GeneralQuickfacts/State = "Georgia"
return $i
```

The expression *$i/Content/GeneralQuickfacts/State* in the above query refers to the path leading to the state element of each resource in the XML file using the slash ('/') as the separator between a parent element and its child. Since there is only one state element within a resource, the above query can be simplified further using the double-slash symbol ('//') which indicates stepping through multiple levels of a hierarchy in each resource:

```
select CountyProj
for $i in schema(censusDB)/*/Resource
where $i//State = "Georgia"
return $i
```

Both existential and universal quantifiers are supported by our query language. In the following query Q2, we use an universal quantifier that is specified using the "every" keyword.

Q2: Assuming that all non-white race categories are considered minorities, find the census resources from Georgia that has all minority race categories exceeding 0.1%.

```
select CountyProj
for $i in schema(censusDB)/*/Resource
where every $i//ByRace/Category[@Desc!="White"]>0.1
      and $i//State = "Georgia"
return $i
```

In a census resource, the race distribution is found in the *ByRace* element and the race categories are captured by the *Desc* attribute of the *Category* elements nested within the *ByRace* elements. The predicate expression *[@Desc!="White"]* evaluates to a true value if the "White" is not found in the *Desc* attribute of the *Category* element.

Q3: Find the census resources from Georgia that contain at least one minority race category equal 0%.

```
select CountyProj
for $i in schema(censusDB)/*/Resource
where some $i//ByRace/Category[@Desc!="White"] = 0
      and $i//State = "Georgia"
return $i
```

4.3. Queries on Resources with Spatial Information

Although not every G-Portal resource carries spatial location information, the resource schema includes a *location* element should the information be available. The location element can be as simple as a point to as complex as a set of polygons. G-Portal includes a map-based user interface to both display resources on a map, and to use the map to define spatial search criteria for querying the resources.

To facilitate queries involving the *location* element, the $\mathcal{RQL}$ query syntax includes the following spatial predicates to be used within the where clause.

- equal(): The predicate returns true when the resource has a location identical to a given geometry object.

- cover(): The predicate returns true when the resource has a location containing a given geometry object, false otherwise.

- coveredby(): The predicate returns true when the resource has a location completely enclosed by a given geometry object, false otherwise.

- overlap(): The predicate returns true when the resource has a location overlapping a given geometry object, false otherwise.

- meet(): The predicate returns true when the resource has a location adjacent to a given geometry object, false otherwise.

- disjoint(): The predicate returns true when the resource has a location disjoint with a given geometry object, false otherwise.

Similar to the location element, each geometry object used in the spatial predicates can range from a point to a set of polygons. Due to space constraints, we will not elaborate how all types of location elements (or geometry objects) can be represented in our XML-based resources. Instead, we will use the point and rectangle data throughout our examples.

Q4: Find the census resources that are within a given bounding rectangle with (-95, 30) and (-70, 50) representing the latitude and longitude values of the left-bottom and right-upper corners of the rectangle respectively.

```
select CountyProj
for $i in schema(censusDB)/*/Resource
where coveredby($i,
    Polygon((-95,30),(-95,50),(-70,50),(-70,30)))
return $i
```

Q4 uses the *Polygon* keyword to define a rectangle object using the four corner points given (in latitude and longitude). Other keywords including *Point, Linestring, Multipoint, Multilinestring, Multipolygon*, etc., are used to construct other types of geometry objects. To ease the specification of complex geometry objects in a query, it is necessary to allow end users to draw the objects using a user-friendly query client. Q4 can be further extended with other non-spatial query conditions as shown in Q5 (using the overlap spatial predicate instead).

Q5: Find the census resources that overlap the above given bounding rectangle and are from the state of "Georgia".

```
select CountyProj
for $i in schema(censusDB)/*/Resource
where overlap($i,
    Polygon((-95,30),(-95,50),(-70,50),(-70,30)))
    and $i//State = "Georgia"
return $i
```

4.4. Mixed Schema Queries

So far, our query examples have only involved a single resource schema. As a project may include resources using different resource schemas, it is possible to formulate queries on resources that are associated with different resource schemas. However, due to the schema discrepancies, it is only possible for such queries to involve the common elements in these resources.

Q6: Assume that the project CountyProj also consists of another set of business pattern resources with another resource schema known as "BusPattern". Find the census and business pattern resources that are from the state of "Georgia".

```
select CountyProj
for $i in schema(censusDB,busPatternDB)/*/Resource
where $i//State = "Georgia"
return $i
```

The above query can be treated as two separate queries each involving a single resource schema, and the final result is the union of the two subquery results. In other words, each resource must fulfill the where condition in order to be included in the query result. This is illustrated by the following equivalent query expression.

```
select CountyProj
for $i in schema(censusDB)/*/Resource
where $i//State = "Georgia"
return $i
union
select CountyProj
for $i in schema(busPatternDB)/*/Resource
where $i//State = "Georgia"
return $i
```

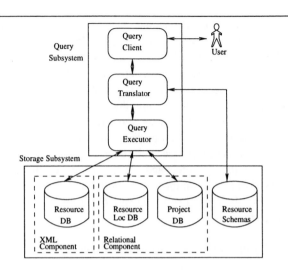

Figure 3. Architecture of the Data Storage and Query Processing Subsystems

5. $\mathcal{RQL}$ Query Processing

5.1. Storage and Query Subsystems

$\mathcal{RQL}$ allows queries on both XML and spatial elements in G-Portal resources. It therefore cannot be directly implemented on existing XML database systems that usually do not support spatial objects and spatial query predicates. Instead of implementing a new XML database system from scratch, we use the Tamino and Informix database systems as our database backends to support both XML and spatial data storage and query processing as shown in Figure 3.

As shown in the figure, G-Portal's storage subsystem consists of a relational component, an XML component, and a collection of *resource schema files*. The relational and XML components are implemented using Informix and Tamino database systems respectively. The relational storage component includes a *resource location database* and a *project database*. The resource location database stores the spatial elements of all resources together with the resource ids. The spatial elements are indexed using R-tree to support efficient evaluation of spatial query predicates. The project database stores the ids of resources belonging to each project. As mentioned in Section 3, projects are logical groupings of resources and the same resource can be shared among different projects. By maintaining the project database, any updates on the project membership of resources can be easily done. The XML storage component of G-Portal consists of a large *resource database* storing all resources (including their spatial elements). Although the spatial elements are also stored in the resource location database, keeping the spatial elements in the resource database makes it much simpler to retrieve resources. Otherwise, we will have to obtain the spatial elements from the resource location database and merge them into the resources from the resource database.

G-Portal's query subsystem consists of a *query client* for users to easily formulate their $\mathcal{RQL}$ queries. Each $\mathcal{RQL}$ query is first translated by the *query translator* into sub-queries on the various databases. In the query translation process, a query evaluation strategy is adopted to ensure that the sub-queries can be efficiently performed on the Tamino and Informix database systems. The actual evaluation of sub-queries is handled by the *query executor* which is also responsible for combining the results from sub-queries (if necessary).

5.2. Evaluation of $\mathcal{RQL}$ Queries

In this section, we explore some query evaluation strategies that can be implemented for $\mathcal{RQL}$ queries. For simplicity, we ignore the project grouping of resources specified by the $\mathcal{RQL}$ queries and focus on the query predicates found in the *where* clause. We first broadly divide $\mathcal{RQL}$ queries into the following 3 categories:

- *Type 1- Non-spatial queries*: They involve only the non-spatial elements of resources.

- *Type 2- Spatial only queries*: They involve only the spatial elements of resources.

- *Type 3- XML and spatial queries*: They involve both the non-spatial and spatial elements of resources.

For Type-1 queries, it is quite clear that the resource location database is not required since the query predicates only apply to the elements found in the resource database. The spatial index provided by the former is also irrelevant to such queries. In this case, the **Tamino-Only** query evaluation strategy is most appropriate where the non-spatial queries are evaluated only on the resource database.

For Type-2 queries, we can apply the **Tamino-Only** strategy or the **Informix-First** strategy depending on the kind of spatial query predicates and the location data of resources involved. The former is applicable only when the spatial query predicates and location information involved are simple and can be translated into simple comparison predicates on individual parts of the location information , e.g. latitude and longitude values of points, connected by AND's and OR's. This is however not always possible for complex spatial query predicates and location which involve complex geometry objects, for example, checking if a polygon overlaps with another polygon. The key feature of the **Tamino-Only** strategy is that it uses only the XML storage component. The **Informix-First** strategy uses the spatial access methods provided by the Informix database

system to first retrieve the ids of resources meeting the spatial query predicates. The ids are later used to construct a disjunction of id comparison predicates in the another query against the resource database.

For Type-3 queries, we can use the **Tamino-First** and **Naive** strategies other than the **Tamino-Only** (only for queries using simple spatial predicates) and the **Informix-First** strategies. The Tamino-First strategy allows the non-spatial query predicates to be first evaluated against the resource database. The ids of resources retrieved are later incorporated into the spatial sub-query sent to the resource location database.

The Naive strategy simply divides a Type 3 query into two sub-queries, one for the resource database and another for the resource location database. The two sub-queries are evaluated by both the Tamino and Informix database systems. Their resultant resource ids are later intersected before the final query result is obtained.

While the Tamino-Only strategy can be used in some situations, we note that this strategy is quite restrictive for Types 2 and 3 queries. In general cases, we need to employ the Informix-First or Naive strategies to handle Types 2 and 3 queries.

6. Experimental Results

We have conducted experiments in order to evaluate the storage alternatives and query evaluation strategies. There are two distinct objectives for the experiments:

- To determine which of the two resource storage alternatives is better; and

- To determine the most suitable query evaluation strategies.

The two resource storage alternatives are:
- **DB1**: storing resources only in an XML database

- **DB2**: storing resources in an XML database and resource location information in a database which supports efficient spatial access method

As described in previous sections, G-Portal adopts the Tamino database as the repository of XML resources and the Informix database for storing spatial attributes of these resources. For both **DB1** and **DB2**, the Tamino database stores the complete resource information, including the location element. The Informix database is used in **DB2** to store the resources' spatial attributes (indexed by R-Tree) together with the resource ids.

The four query evaluation strategies are: **Tamino-Only** (TO), **Informix-First** (IF), **Tamino-First** (TF), and **Naive** (NA). They have been elaborated in detail in Section 5.2. We, nevertheless, want to re-emphasize that the **Tamino-Only** strategy is only suitable for queries with simple spatial predicates. For spatial queries involving complex polygons, the evaluation of the spatial predicates have to be performed at the application level, which is very inefficient.

6.1. Dataset

The dataset in our experiments is constructed using actual data from the U.S. Census Bureau [14]. The original Website contains figures of population, business and geometry information of all counties in the United States. The latitude and longitude of the center of each county is also provided. To convert the data from HTML Webpages into an XML format, we first derived a schema for these resources, which is partially shown in Figure 1. The Webpages containing the data were then downloaded from the Website and the relevant figures were extracted from the pages and stored in XML according to the schema. The latitude and longitude of each county were also extracted and stored in both the location element of the resources in the resource (Tamino) database and in the resource location (Informix) database.

After removing some counties with incomplete information, there were a total of 3138 resources in the dataset. Each resource contained 90 XML elements and 50 XML attributes. The maximum nesting level was 7. The values of most of the elements were numbers (integer or double); whereas attribute values were mostly short text strings. Since we only had the latitude and longitude of the center of each county, the spatial attribute of each resource was of the type Point. To allow numerical predicates (e.g., greater than, less than, etc..) to be evaluated efficiently on the XML location element, indexes on the elements of latitude and longitude were created using Tamino's internal index.

6.2. Experiments

Although we have two different objectives in our experiments, they can actually be achieved with a single set of experiments. This is because the **DB1** storage alternative can only be queried with the **Tamino-Only** strategy. Comparing the efficiency of the **Tamino-Only** strategy against the other three allows us to compare the two storage alternatives.

As discussed in Section 5.2, there are three categories of queries. For Type-1 (non-spatial) queries, all four query evaluation strategies are reduced to **Tamino-Only**. It is thus not necessary to compare strategies for Type-1 queries. In addition, for Type-2 (spatial only) queries, both **Tamino-First** and **Naive** strategies will return all resources in the XML database, due to the absence of XML constraints. Obviously, the **Tamino-Only** approach will be faster than these two. Therefore, in our experiments, we test Type-2 queries only with the **Tamino-Only** and **Informix-First**

strategies and test Type-3 queries with all four strategies.

To ensure a fair comparison, we used only rectangles in our spatial predicates to allow these predicates be easily transformed into XML queries on the location elements so that no application level processing is required for the **Tamino-Only** strategy.

Five queries were used in the experiments. The first (query spatial) is a Type-2 spatial only query with the coveredby() predicate. The other four are Type-3 queries with coveredby() as the spatial predicate. coveredby() is the only meaningful spatial predicate in this case because we only have points in the resources and we had decided to use only rectangles in the queries. The first two Type-3 queries are **Q2** and **Q3** in Section 4.2 coupled with a coveredby() spatial predicate, called query every and query some respectively. These two are more restrictive and return fewer than 100 resources even if the query rectangle covers all counties. The last two queries are less restrictive and can return a much larger amount of resources. The third query, query business, has five conjunctions about the figures concerning the business quickfacts of the counties in the where clause and will return 785 resources without considering the spatial constraints. The last query, query population, also contains two conjunctions of XML predicates but can return up to 1458 resources.

Q7:(Query business)

```
select CountyProj
for $i in schema(censusDB)/*/Resource
where coveredby($i, Polygon((x1, y1),(x1,y2),
     (x2, y2),(x2,y1)))
  and $i//RetailSales > 100000
  and $i//RetailSalesPerCapita > 4000
  and $i//FederalFundsAndGrants > 60000
  and $i//WomenOwnedFirms > 5
  and $i//MetropolitanArea ~= "*A*"
return $i
```

Q8:(Query population)

```
select CountyProj
for $i in schema(censusDB)/*/Resource
where coveredby($i, Polygon((x1, y1),(x1,y2),
     (x2, y2),(x2,y1)))
  and $i//Population/Year2000 > 10000
  and $i/ByAge/Category[@Desc="65 and Above"] > 10
return $i
```

For each query, four types of spatial query rectangles were generated: large area, median area, small area, and random area (random side length). The first three were of around 25%, 5% and 0.5% of the size of minimum bounding box of all counties respectively. The positions of the rectangles were randomly generated. For random area, both the size and the position of the rectangle were randomized. For each area size, we generated 120 rectangles at different positions and the resulting queries were evaluated based on the four strategies. The average time for performing each query and the average number of resources returned by the 120 queries were recorded. In order to obtain a statistical support for our comparisons, the time taken for different strategies were compared using t-test statistics for testing matched pairs' mean difference [6] at 5% significance level.

The results are shown in Tables 1 to 4. Due to space constraints, only the details of the spatial query, query every and query population are shown and only the comparison of **Informix-First** against the other three strategies are presented. The column headers L, M, S, and R represent large area, median area, small area, and random area respectively. In Tables 1 to 3, the columns with (t) is the time in seconds and those with (n) are the number of resources returned. In Table 4, for each X *vs* Y entry, there is a null hypothesis of "X is as good as Y", and two alternate hypotheses of "X is better than Y" (positive) and "X is worse than Y" (negative). A Z indicates that we cannot reject the null hypothesis, while an A means the null hypothesis is rejected and the positive alternative hypothesis is accepted, whereas R means the negative one is accepted.

Table 1. Results of Spatial Only Queries

	L (t)/(n)	M (t)/(n)	S (t)/(n)	R (t)/(n)
TO	10.78/891.35	3.26/174.14	0.78/14.95	3.44/431.65
IF	8.76/891.35	1.26/174.14	0.15/14.95	2.16/431.65

Table 2. Results of query every

	L (t)/(n)	M (t)/(n)	S (t)/(n)	R (t)/(n)
TO	4.42/1.47	1.85/0.38	0.73/0.00	2.18/0.61
IF	3.55/1.47	0.56/0.38	0.11/0.00	2.00/0.61
NA	5.20/1.47	2.97/0.38	1.27/0.00	3.95/0.61
TF	5.16/1.47	5.00/0.38	4.99/0.00	5.80/0.61

Table 3. Results of query population

	L (t)/(n)	M (t)/(n)	S (t)/(n)	R (t)/(n)
TO	11.66/385.43	2.25/85.30	0.71/8.36	2.64/198.12
IF	15.98/385.43	1.50/85.30	0.11/8.36	5.50/198.12
NA	10.45/385.43	4.50/85.30	1.65/8.36	5.37/198.12
TF	15.80/385.43	13.69/85.30	12.73/8.36	13.70/198.12

6.3. Discussion

The results in Table 1 indicate that for spatial only queries, the average query processing time for **Informix-First** is consistently shorter than that of **Tamino-Only**. The advantage of **Informix-First** is reaffirmed by the statistical test results in Table 4 (third row), where the positive alternate hypothesis is always accepted. The reason for the better performance of **Informix-First** is largely due to the use of the efficient spatial access method (R-Tree) provided by Informix database. Since we can only use numerical comparisons to evaluate spatial predicates on the Tamino database, **Tamino-Only** is much slower than the dedicated spatial access method like R-Tree. From Table 1, we can see that evaluating a disjunction of around 900 resource ids in

Table 4. Comparison of Storage Alternatives and Evaluation Strategies

	L (t)	M (t)	S (t)	R (t)
IF vs TO				
spatial	A	A	A	A
every	A	A	A	Z
some	Z	A	A	Z
business	R	A	A	R
population	R	A	A	R
IF vs NA				
every	A	A	A	A
some	Z	A	A	A
business	R	A	A	Z
population	R	A	A	Z
IF vs TF				
every	A	A	A	A
some	Z	A	A	A
business	Z	A	A	A
population	Z	A	A	A

an XML query is still faster than the numerical comparisons for the coveredby() predicate.

In some extreme cases where the sub-query to Informix returns 0 records, there is not even a need to query the Tamino database. This happened quite frequently when the queries involved small areas, making **Informix-First** an order of magnitude faster than **Tamino-Only** when querying with small areas. However, we did observe that when the number of resources returned exceeds 1500, **Tamino-Only** started to outperform **Informix-First**. Nevertheless, with 3138 resources in the entire dataset, it is unlikely that there will be many queries returning more than half of the dataset.

Table 2 shows the results of different strategies for query every. Due to the very restrictive XML query conditions, the number of resources returned by this query is very small (at most 7 for large areas). This means that when a small number of resources are returned, ids disjunctions (averaged 891 for large areas) plus the non-spatial conditions will be evaluated faster than the evaluation of numerical comparisons (in place of spatial predicates) and the non-spatial predicates on the Tamino database.

For query population (Table 3), we can see that in the case of large and random area spatial queries, **Tamino-Only** and **Naive** are faster than **Informix-First**. The statistical test results in Table 4 also ascertains that **Informix-First** performance worse in the two cases. However, for smaller size query rectangles, **Informix-First** is still better than the other three. The performance of **Informix-First** for query some and query business (not shown here) are somewhere between that of query every and query population. We noted that the number of results returned increased from query every to query population. This suggests that the smaller the size of the result, the faster **Informix-First** is compared with the rest.

It can be seen from the Table 4 that most of the time we are confident that the **Informix-First** strategy performs better than the **Tamino-Only** strategy. In other words, we are quite confident that the **DB2** alternative is more efficient than **DB1**, if the **Informix-First** strategy is used to evaluate queries with **DB2**. Since points are the simplest forms of geometry objects, it is obvious that when lines and polygons are involved in the spatial predicates, **DB1** will be slower or even not applicable. Therefore, we conclude that **DB2** is the most suitable choice for implementing the storage subsystem.

When comparing **Informix-First** with **Tamino-First**, Table 4 shows that in most cases **Informix-First** performs statistically better, with only two draws. Therefore, we can also conclude that we should always prefer **Informix-First** to **Tamino-First**.

However, when comparing **Informix-First** with **Tamino-Only** and **Naive**, such conclusions cannot be drawn so easily. We notice that **Tamino-Only** and **Naive** outperformed **Informix-First** in some queries involving large areas. This happened when the number of resources returned by the non-spatial sub-query is large. In particular, we observed that **Informix-First** is more sensitive to this number than the other strategies. When the non-spatial sub-query to Tamino returns more than 700 resources, **Informix-First** starts to slow down. This occurred for queries involving large and random areas which return more than 25% of the records. The reason remains to be investigated mainly due to insufficient knowledge about the internal query processing methods used by Tamino.

Another observation of slower performance of **Informix-First** occurs when the spatial sub-query returns large numbers of records. This causes the sub-query to Tamino to contain a large number of disjunctions of ids to be tested. The reason is also not clear since it is not known to us how disjunctions are evaluated in Tamino. One possible explanation is that such long disjunctions forces the internal query processing engine of Tamino to perform a large number of random database accesses, which is relatively slower than accessing by range index (**Tamino-Only**) or simple non-spatial query (**Naive**).

Nevertheless, we anticipate that most queries will unlikely cover large areas, thus only returning resources fewer than those returned by queries with median areas. The queries would also be relatively restrictive as compared with the ones in query population and query business. For queries with small to median areas, **Informix-First** consistently performs better than the other three strategies. Therefore, we consider it reasonable to adopt the **DB2** alternative and the **Informix-First** strategy.

7. Conclusion

In this paper, we describe the storage design and query features of G-Portal, a digital library system. As G-Portal maintains metadata resources about geospatial and georeferenced information on the Web, it uses different resource schemas for interpreting different types of metadata resources, and supports queries on resources carrying both spatial and non-spatial elements. To handle the geometry object representation of location elements of resources, we have proposed a new resource query language $\mathcal{RQL}$, a variant of XQuery language adapted to G-Portal's resource model and spatial query requirements.

This paper also describes the design of G-Portal's storage and query subsystems and presents our experiments on several proposed query evaluation strategies for $\mathcal{RQL}$ queries. The experiment results suggest that other than spatial-only queries, the Informix-First strategy works well for queries that consist of predicates that are more restrictive. Note that the results were obtained for relatively simple types of spatial predicates. For queries involving complex spatial predicates, the Informix-First and Naive strategies will be more appropriate.

At this point in time, we have implemented the G-Portal storage subsystem. A preliminary version of the query subsystem including the query client has also been implemented in Java. Users are given a query window to formulate the spatial and non-spatial query predicates. So far, only bounding rectangle objects can be specified using the map interface as part of the spatial predicates. The query results are displayed both on the map-based and classification-based interfaces.

As part of our future work, we plan to conduct further experiments on the storage and query subsystems for larger datasets and more complex queries. A hybrid query evaluation strategy could be explored to evaluate query predicates of different selectivities. For sophisticated users, the current $\mathcal{RQL}$ syntax may be too restrictive. For example, it is currently not possible to relate resources from different schemas in a $\mathcal{RQL}$ query. Such queries however may be useful when detailed analysis is to be conducted on the resources within a project. We will look into extending $\mathcal{RQL}$ to support such queries and develop new query evaluation strategies for them.

8. Acknowledgments

This work is funded by the SingAREN Project M48020004.

We would also like to thank Linda Hill for her advice during this research.

References

[1] C. Baru, V. Chu, A. Gupta, B. Ludaescher, R. Marciano, Y. Papakonstantinou, and P. Velikhov. Xml-based information mediation for digital libraries. In *Proceedings of the Fourth ACM conference on Digital Libraries (ACMDL 1999)*, pages 214–215, Berkeley, CA, USA, August 1999.

[2] D. Chamberlin. XQuery: An XML Query Language. *IBM Systems Journal*, 41(4):597–615, 2002.

[3] V. Gaede and O. Gunther. Multidimensional Access Methods. *ACM Computing Surveys*, 30(2):170–231, 1998.

[4] O. Gunther. Efficient computation of spatial joins. In *Proceedings of the International Conference on Data Engineering (ICDE)*, pages 50–59, Vienna, Austria, April 1993.

[5] A. Guttman. R-trees: A dynamic index structure for spatial searching. In *Proceedings of the ACM SIGMOD Conference*, pages 47–57, Boston, MA, June 1984.

[6] G. Keller, B. Warrack, and H. Bartel. *Statistics for Management and Economics*, pages 353–358. Duxbury Press, 1994.

[7] E.-P. Lim, D. H.-L. Goh, Z. Liu, W.-K. Ng, C. S.-G. Khoo, and S. E. Higgins. G-portal: A map-based digital library for distributed geospatial and georeferenced resources. In *Proceedings of the Second ACM+IEEE Joint Conference on Digital Libraries (JCDL 2002)*, Portland, Oregon, USA, July 14-18 2002.

[8] Z. Liu, E.-P. Lim, and D. H.-L. Goh. Resource annotation framework in a georeferenced and geospatial digital library. In *Proceedings of the 5th International Conference On Asian Digital Libraries (ICADL 2002)*, Singapore, December 11-14 2002.

[9] Open GIS Consortium. Open GIS Simple Features Specification for SQL. Revision 1.1. http://www.opengis.org/techno/specs/99-049.pdf.

[10] M.-J. Proulx, Y. Bédard, F. Létourneau, and C. Martel. GEOREP: A WWW customizable georeferenced digital library for spatial data. D-Lib Magazine, December 1996.

[11] T. Smith. A digital library for geographically referenced materials. *IEEE Computer*, 29(5):54–60, 1996.

[12] T. Smith, G. Janee, J. Frew, and A. Coleman. The Alexandria Digital Earth ProtoType system. In *Proceedings of the First ACM+IEEE Joint Conference on Digital Libraries (JCDL 2001)*, pages 118–119, Roanoke, VA, USA, June 2001.

[13] T. Sumner and M. Dawe. Looking at digital library usability from a reuse perspective. In *Proceedings of the First ACM+IEEE Joint Conference on Digital Libraries (JCDL 2001)*, pages 416–425, Roanoke, VA, USA, June 2001.

[14] U.S. Census Bureau. State and County QuickFacts. http://quickfacts.census.gov/qfd/index.html.

[15] W3 Consortium. XML Schema. http://www.w3.org/xml/schema.

[16] J. Weatherley and T. Weingart. Designing a simple resource search user interface for DLESE. http://www.dlese.org/documents/bibliographies/ discovery_sys_final.pdf, March 25 2002.

[17] B. Zhu, M. Ramsey, H. Chen, R. Hauck, T. Ng, and B. Schatz. Create a large-scale digital library for georeferenced information. In *Proceedings of the Fourth ACM Conference on Digital Libraries (DL 1999)*, Berkeley, California, USA, Auguest 1999.

A Scientific Digital Library in Context:

An Earth Radiation Budget Experiment Collection
in the Atmospheric Sciences Data Center Digital Library

Michelle Ferebee,
Gregory Boeshaar
Atmospheric Sciences Data Center
NASA Langley Research Center
Hampton, VA 23681

{m.t.ferebee,g.o.boeshaar}
@larc.nasa.gov

Kathryn Bush
Science Applications International
Corp.
One Enterprise Parkway, Suite 300
Hampton, VA 23666

k.a.bush@larc.nasa.gov

Judy Hertz
Riotsystems
Alexandria, VA 22308

judy@riotsystems.com

ABSTRACT

At the NASA Langley Research Center, the Earth Radiation Budget Experiment (ERBE) Data Management Team and the Atmospheric Sciences Data Center are developing a digital collection for the ERBE project. The main goal is long-term preservation of a comprehensive information environment. The secondary goal is to provide a context for these data products by centralizing the 25-year research project's scattered information elements. The development approach incorporates elements of rapid prototyping and user-centered design in a standards-based implementation. A working prototype is in testing with a small number of users.

Categories and Subject Descriptors

H.3.7 [Digital Libraries]

General Terms

Digital library, Design

Keywords

ERBE, narrative materials, rapid prototyping, long-term data preservation, user-centered design, permanent access, atmospheric science.

1. INTRODUCTION

At the NASA Langley Research Center, the Earth Radiation Budget Experiment (ERBE) Data Management Team and the Atmospheric Sciences Data Center (ASDC) are jointly developing a scientific digital collection for the ERBE project.

The main goal is long-term preservation of a comprehensive information environment. A primary objective is to centralize and document scattered information elements (narrative materials) of a 25-year research project, many of which are varied information types (text, binary) and legacy storage

media (paper, microfiche).

The data products stand on their own scientific merit, but the scattered information elements—together known as narrative materials—provide a context for these data products. The context enriches the data by providing insight into the decisions and processes that went into creating, calibrating, and analyzing the data. The data context is created by the interrelated and sometimes interdependent nature of the narrative materials [1,2].

2. ERBE

Earth's climate system is driven by a radiative energy balance of solar or shortwave radiation absorbed by the earth and the thermal infrared or longwave radiation it emits into space [1]. ERBE uses Earth-observing satellites to measure this radiative balance, producing monthly averages of Earth's long- and shortwave radiation parameters at regional to global scales.

ERBE was the first planned and implemented multisatellite Earth radiation budget mission, enabling greater temporal and spatial coverage than did single satellite missions. All six ERBE instruments underwent extensive ground calibration tied to international calibration standards and regular in-flight calibrations. All radiation budget data sets are tied together, making ERBE data a standard for radiation budget measurements.

The ERBE project collects and processes data, and offers data products ranging from instantaneous to monthly averaged regional, zonal, and global estimates of radiation budget parameters. Users obtain products through the ASDC, which archives and distributes ERBE and other NASA earth science data related to clouds, aerosols, and tropospheric chemistry (http://eosweb.larc.nasa.gov).

3. THE ERBE DIGITAL COLLECTION

ERBE's 25 years of radiation budget data is an invaluable resource for long-term climatological studies. As knowledge about ERBE data improves, long-term datasets will allow the new knowledge to be retroactively applied to historical observations. Designed with continuous user involvement, the interface will enhance the ERBE collection's quality and longevity and encourage its use and dissemination.

3.1 Narrative materials

Reference manuals, operations reports, meeting minutes, source code, and other resources that make up the narrative environment complement and describe the data in a way that enhances understanding and makes data products easier to use. ERBE's oral tradition, an important part of the narrative materials, includes personal collections of informal literature, and products not formally associated with the data. Longtime program participants are vital to structuring contextual relationships among narrative materials.

4. DEVELOPMENT APPROACH

The development approach emphasized standards, extensible architecture, cost-effective features, and a viable preservation strategy. Best practices featured schemes to assure long-term availability such as addressing preservation strategies [2], using a core set of metadata and mark-up language standards, and avoiding expensive and proprietary commercial off-the-shelf (COTS) software solutions. Other advice included developing and maintaining usable systems: providing browsing and directed search, knowing content [3], and supporting and encouraging collaboration [4].

4.1 Rapid-prototyping method

We used rapid-prototyping principles—a way to experiment with system design while providing an iterative platform for gathering user requirements—to develop a working prototype of on-hand search-indexing COTS software.

Binary data is included through embedded hypertext links. Because the integrated web interface allows access to all search/indexing engine search features, we included search-and-browse strategies for testing and will include more complex features (e.g., controlled vocabularies) in follow-on testing.

A working prototype allowed us to gather detailed requirements that would not have been immediately available from methods such as wireframing, storyboards, and paper prototypes. These observations gave us a head start in developing requirements for enhanced features.

4.2 Incorporating user-centered design

We want to offer as many resources and services as possible—a data-use environment rather than a bare-bones interface. The literature describes, and we have found, surprising cost and work savings in involving end users early in development. Substantive improvements can even be made to COTS interfaces, which can be designed without the benefit of usability elements but customized to be more usable.

5. IMPLEMENTATION CHALLENGES

5.1 Preservation strategy

To begin, we used migration [2] of derivatives and the concept of a master digital format [3] as an initial preservation strategy. High-quality lossless TIFF images will serve as master copies and a basis for conversion to multiple formats, including PDF, HTML, XML, and others. PDF is the common display format; an optical character reader creates accompanying text files.

For the large volume of legacy materials to be electronically converted, we began by scanning useful information increments. We defined an initial representative set of 10,000 pages to test the prototype and gather requirements.

We use an expanded metadata set based on Dublin Core and expect to experiment with metadata during prototype testing. We will balance the use of non-core metadata with interoperability requirements. To make ERBE data available to a larger audience, we will assess migration to XML and adoption of the Open Archives Initiative's metadata harvesting protocol [4,5] in postprototype development.

5.2 Preserving Context

Narrative materials' contextual relationships must be defined, translated into the digital collection, and introduced to users in a way that allows them to exploit the relationships but not be restricted by them. We are researching strategies that emphasize developments in information retrieval and information-seeking behaviors for scientists [6,7].

6. PRELIMINARY RESULTS

A working prototype is in testing with a small number of users, and we are gathering requirements on system function and features. The prototype helped speed development, improve the quality of user requirements, and help us gauge the utility of interim improvements such as faceted classification and controlled language tools.

7. REFERENCES

[1] Wielicki, B.A., Wong T., Allan R.P., et al. Evidence for large decadal variability in the tropical mean radiative energy budget. Science 295:841-844, 2002.

[2] Williams, R., Bunn, J., Moore, R., Pool, J.C.T., (eds.). Interfaces to Scientific Data Archives. Workshop, California Institute of Technology, Mar 25-27, 1998.

[3] Levy, D.M. Heroic Measures: Reflections on the Possibility and Purpose of Digital Preservation. In: Proceedings of the Third ACM Conference on Digital Libraries, Pittsburgh, PA, 1998.

[4] McCray, A.T., Gallagher, M.E. Principles for digital library development. In: Communications of the ACM, Vol. 44(5), May: 48-54, 2001.

[5] Lagoze, C., Van de Sompel, H. The open archives initiative: Building a low-barrier interoperability framework. In: Proceedings of the first ACM/IEEE-CS joint conference on Digital libraries, Roanoke, VA: 54-62, 2001.

[6] Crabtree, A., Twidale M.B., O'Brien, J., Nichols, D.M. Talking in the library: Implications for the design of digital libraries. In: Proceedings of the second ACM international conference on Digital libraries, Philadelphia, PA: 221-118, 1997.

[7] Bates, M.J. 2002. Toward an Integrated Model of Information Seeking and Searching, Keynote: The Fourth International Conference on Information Needs, Seeking and Use in Different Contexts, Lisbon, Portugal, Sep 11-13, 2002.

Designing a Language for Creating Conceptual Browsing Interfaces for Digital Libraries

Tamara Sumner, Sonal Bhushan, Faisal Ahmad, Qianyi Gu
Department of Computer Science
University of Colorado at Boulder
Campus Box 430
Boulder, Colorado 80309-0430
{sumner, bhushans, fahmad, qianyi.gu} @colorado.edu

Abstract

Conceptual browsing interfaces can help educators and learners to locate and use learning resources in educational digital libraries; in particular, resources that are aligned with nationally-recognized learning goals. Towards this end, we are developing a Strand Map Library Service, based on the maps published by the American Association for the Advancement of Science (AAAS). This service includes two public interfaces: (1) a graphical user interface for use by teachers and learners and (2) a programmatic interface that enables developers to construct conceptual browsing interfaces using dynamically generated components. Here, we describe our iterative, rapid prototyping design methodology, and the initial round of language type components that have been implemented and evaluated.

1. Introduction

For the past decade there have been a series of reform efforts in science education calling for more emphasis on science literacy and inquiry-based pedagogies and on the development of science curriculum that emphasizes the connections between ideas and skills that students develop over time. These ideas and skills can be expressed as statements of learning goals, or benchmarks [1, 3], describing what learners should know, or be able to do, at key stages in their education.

Benchmarks for Science Literacy articulates 854 learning goals in natural science, social science, mathematics, and technology [3]. These benchmarks have been organized into approximately 100 graphical 'strand maps', half of which are published in the *Atlas of Science Literacy* [1]. Each map provides an overview of K-12 learning goals for a topic important to science literacy (e.g., weather and climate, or the conservation of matter). Within a strand map, benchmarks and the relationships between benchmarks are depicted in a node-link diagram. High level descriptions of the benchmarks are provided in the nodes, while the links explicitly depict how benchmarks both support and depend upon each other. Each strand map contains 2-3 vertical "strands" that reflect key ideas within that topic (e.g., heat, water cycle, and atmosphere are strands within the weather and climate map). Each strand is cross-referenced by grade levels to illustrate how student understanding develops over time.

Strand maps are being used in a National Science Digital Library (NSDL) service in order to provide an interactive interface to educational resources in collections across NSDL. This NSDL service is being constructed such that it can be used directly by educators and learners (through a carefully designed and evaluated graphical user interface) and by digital library developers (through a programmatically accessible protocol). The user interface will enable educators and learners to discover educational resources that support the benchmarks, browse the interconnected benchmarks, and explore background information about the benchmarks, such as common learner misconceptions and strategies for checking learners' comprehension.

2. Service Architecture

Rather than building static presentations of existing maps, we are creating a service middleware capable of generating visualizations of strand maps and map components from a benchmark database. When complete, this service middleware will interoperate with NSDL discovery systems to locate resources aligned with specific benchmarks or learning goals.

Two public interfaces onto this service middleware are being constructed. One is a service protocol that can be used by other library developers to construct tailored interfaces and services that make use of benchmarks and strand maps. This protocol will enable library developers to request rich descriptions of one or more benchmarks, to request visualizations of groups of benchmarks or strands, and to request resources that are aligned to a particular benchmark.

The second public interface is a graphical user interface that enables educators and learners to locate resources aligned to the benchmarks, to browse learning goals through a strand map interface, and to enhance their understanding with relevant background information. This interface is being constructed using the service protocol.

3. Design Methodology

The core of this effort is to identify, implement and evaluate a number of language type components that can be interconnected to create useful and usable conceptual browsing interfaces. Digital library developers, using the service protocol, will be able to create a graphical user interface by linking a subset of these components into their own particular systems.

We are using an iterative task-centered design methodology [2] in order to identify and develop reusable components that lend themselves to computer visualizations and provide useful forms of interactivity. We began by interviewing science educators and library designers in order to identify concrete user needs. These needs were then distilled into a series of task statements describing actual activities users would perform with the service. These task statements were used to generate interface design alternatives. These design alternatives were compared using analytical techniques (i.e., cognitive walkthroughs) and usability testing techniques (i.e. think aloud protocols) [2].

To date, we have developed and evaluated four interfaces comprised of a suite of interconnected components. In doing so, we have identified a number of promising components, such as the Cluster Navigator , the Map Tree Navigator, and the Benchmark Extended Information Viewer. These are illustrated in Figures 1 and 2.

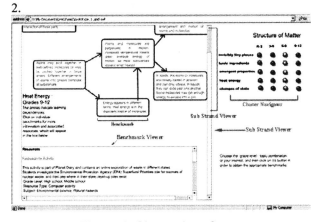

Figure 1. Cluster interface

In Figure 1, the Cluster Navigator navigates through clusters of related strands, and displays relevant sub-sections of these strands using the Sub Strand Viewer, on the left of the screen. Clicking on an individual Benchmark in the Sub Strand Viewer brings up a Benchmark Extended Information Viewer, which displays background information about the benchmark, and associated resources. In Figure 2, the Map Tree Navigator is a component that navigates through the whole Strand Map hierarchical structure via a Windows Explorer like interface. As can be seen, it reuses the Sub Strand Viewer, and the Benchmark Extended Information Viewer components.

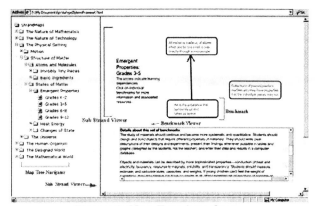

Figure 2. Map Tree interface

4. Related Work

When dealing with such a rich information space, it is important to combine data manipulation strategies with visual query formulations and visual display of results. Our work is similar in spirit to that of Shneiderman et. al. [4], who developed dynamic queries, starfield displays, treemaps, and a wide variety of widgets in order to present, search, browse, filter, and compare rich information spaces.

5. Current Work & Future Plans

We are currently revisiting the components we have visualized in our prototypes in order to articulate inter-component communication. We are also developing an XML schema-based metadata framework for modeling rich descriptions of benchmarks. Using this schema, we propose to model 137 benchmarks (15% of the total number of benchmarks). These will populate a "benchmark database" containing information on learning goals for biology, chemistry, and physics, and Earth System science.

6. References

[1] Project 2061, *Atlas of Science Literacy*, American Association for the Advancement of Science and the National Science Teachers Association, Washington, DC, 2001.

[2] Lewis, C. and J. Rieman, Task-centered Design, Available at: http://hcibib.org/tcuid/ , 1993.

[3] Project 2061, *Benchmarks for Science Literacy*, Oxford University Press, Oxford, UK, 1993.

[4] Shneiderman, B., *Designing the User Interface: Strategies for Effective Human-Computer Interaction: Third edition*, Addison-Wesley, Reading, MA, 1997.

Content Access Characterization in Digital Libraries

Greg Janée
Dept. of Computer Science
U. of Calif., Santa Barbara
gjanee@alexandria.ucsb.edu

James Frew
School of Environmental
Science and Management
U. of Calif., Santa Barbara
frew@bren.ucsb.edu

David Valentine
Davidson Library
U. of Calif., Santa Barbara
valentine@library.ucsb.edu

Abstract

*To support non-trivial clients, such as data exploration and analysis environments, digital libraries must be able to describe the access modes that their contents support. We present a simple scheme that distinguishes four content accessibility classes: **download** (byte-stream retrieval), **service** (API), **web interface** (interactive), and **offline**. These access modes may recursively nest in alternative (semantically equivalent) or multipart (component) hierarchies. This scheme is simple enough to be easily supported by DL content providers, yet rich enough to allow programmatic clients to automatically identify appropriate access point(s).*

1. Background

The Alexandria Digital Library (ADL) Project has created a distributed DL architecture [1] that allows data providers to publish geospatial and other types of highly structured, metadata-rich data. A key feature of this architecture is a middleware layer that allows clients to perform federated collection- and item-level searches over multiple libraries. The middleware uses XML-based communication, and supports HTTP, Java and Java RMI interfaces that make all library functionality available to programmatic clients.

Our first ADL clients focused on discovery of library content – access to and use of library content were only superficially addressed. Users wishing to access a DL item were presented with a "click here to download" hyperlink and left to their own devices. A better approach is to exploit the programmatic nature of ADL's library services by embedding ADL in several data exploration environments, and making discovery and use of library content seamless within those environments.

This effort has brought up several access-related issues. First, any data exploration environment inevitably has constraints on the content formats and protocols it understands. If a corresponding DL doesn't support format- and/or protocol-related query constraints, then it must at least be possible to filter query results by these kinds of criteria.

Second, a data exploration environment needs to understand the structure of an item and its available access options. This is particularly necessary for geospatial data, which is often multipart and typically accessed via multiple formats, protocols, and interfaces. For example, a georeferenced image is often distributed as a pair of files: an image array and a file containing the georeferencing information. A client may have to independently access one or both of these files to successfully use the item. Geospatial data is also often accessible via programmatic services such as WMS, ArcIMS, and DODS.

Note that the issue here is not so much describing the content as it is describing *access* to the content. We wish to semi-formally characterize the methods by which DL items may be accessed. We're particularly trying to capture basic distinctions like: is the item online or offline? If online, can it be directly downloaded? If so, what is the expected format and size? Are there programmatic services associated with the item? If so, how does one interact with them? Is the item decomposable into constituent parts? Are there alternative representations? All this information must be usable by programmatic clients, as well as by human users deciding how to best access the item.

2. Related Work

Metadata standards generally focus on descriptive metadata such as author and title, not structural metadata. The FGDC Content Standard for Digital Geospatial Metadata [2] allows an item to have alternative typed "distributions", but there is no support for describing a multipart item's structure or item-related services. Dublin Core [3] provides essentially no means of describing structure or access. A DC "best practice" is to use URLs as identifiers, but DC has no standard way to describe what such a URL actually refers to.

The Metadata Encoding and Transmission Standard (METS) [4] allows elaborate descriptions of the structure of scanned or transcribed written works. However, support for other content types is limited; more significantly, METS has no simple way to distinguish between components and alternative representations.

Fedora [5] provides an object-oriented framework for describing and invoking item-related services, but its structural metadata is very limited. The Fedora project is exploring integrating Fedora access into METS.

3. The ADL Content Access Model

We describe a DL item's accessibility via zero or more **access points**. Each access point describes how to access a single, independent representation of the DL item. Different types of access points reflect fundamentally different modes of accessing content.

A **download** access point simply returns a byte-stream representation of an entire DL item. A typical download access point is a static file made accessible via HTTP. A download access point's attributes include a URL and (optionally) a high-level format description, a MIME type and encoding(s), and an approximate length. (All access points have optional, human-readable title and description attributes.)

A **service** access point allows a DL item to be accessed by interacting with a programmatic service. A typical service access point is an OpenGIS Web Map Service (WMS) [7] returning selected portions of a map. A service access point's attributes include the service's URL and (optionally) the name of the service's protocol and a pointer to a formal (e.g., WSDL) or informal (e.g., English) description of the service.

A **web interface** access point is a URL that may require additional human interaction before access is granted. (Or, more information about the access point may simply be unknown.) A typical web access point is a license agreement that in turn points to the actual content. The only attribute of a web interface access point is a URL.

An **offline** access point refers to an offline representation (digital or physical) of the DL item. A typical offline access point is a library call number.

Access points may be recursively grouped into hierarchies. An **alternatives** access point describes two or more equivalent representations (for example, HTML and PDF versions of the same document). A **multipart** access point describes constituent parts (e.g., a TIFF image and its accompanying "world" file). A multipart access point's optional format attribute describes the format of the access point as a whole (e.g., a "zip" archive).

From a programmatic client's perspective, the most useful access points are download and service. The web interface access point exists to cover those situations where an item is online but cannot be accessed programmatically, either because human intervention is required, or because the interface is not well specified.

Thus a web interface access point represents a kind of fallback with respect to the other types of access points.

The ADL content access model is formally described (and documented with examples) by an XML DTD [6].

4. Conclusion

We have presented a simple yet effective way to characterize and describe DL content access. Programmatic DL clients can automatically access recognized content formats and protocols, while human readers can make informed choices between alternative download and interactive service options. We are using this model to interface two programmatic clients – the ESRI ArcGIS geographic information system and a Distributed Oceanographic Data System (DODS) data viewer – to the ADL library. Our access model is a good match for these environments.

One outstanding issue is the interaction, if any, between content access and authorization and rights schemes. A DL item whose access points are all hidden behind authorization pages or license agreements is currently forced to describe those access points as web interfaces, not as more programmatically useful downloads and/or services. An improvement might allow authorization to be an attribute of an access point.

We would also like to extend our scheme to describe and automatically invoke conversion services. This would allow a client to access content outside its natively supported domain.

5. References

[1] Janée, G. and Frew, J. The ADEPT digital library architecture. Second ACM/IEEE-CS Joint Conference on Digital Libraries (Portland OR, June 2002). ACM Press, 342-350.

[2] Federal Geographic Data Committee. FGDC-STD-001-1998. Content standard for digital geospatial metadata (revised June 1998). Federal Geographic Data Committee. Washington, D.C. http://www.fgdc.gov/metadata/csdgm/

[3] Weibel, S., Kunze, J., and Lagoze, C. Dublin Core Metadata for Resource Discovery. RFC 2413 (September 1998), Internet Engineering Task Force. http://www.ietf.org/rfc/rfc2413.txt

[4] Library of Congress. Metadata Encoding and Transmission Standard (METS). http://www.loc.gov/standards/mets/

[5] Fedora Project. Mellon Fedora Technical Specification Version 1.1 (December 2002) http://www.fedora.info/documents/master-spec.rtf

[6] http://www.alexandria.ucsb.edu/middleware/dtds/ADL-access-report.dtd

[7] de La Beaujardière, J. (ed.) Web Map Service Implementation Specification. OpenGIS Implementation Specification OGC 01-068r3. Open GIS Consortium Inc. http://www.opengis.org/techno/specs/01-068r3.pdf

SCENS: a System for the Mediated Sharing of Sensitive Data

Song Ye, Fillia Makedon, Tilmann Steinberg, Li Shen,
James Ford, Yuhang Wang and Yan Zhao
DEVLAB, Computer Science Department, Dartmouth College
{yesong, makedon, tilmann, li, jford, wyh, yanzhao}
@ cs.dartmouth.edu

Sarantos Kapidakis
*Department of Archive and
Library Sciences,
Ionian University, Greece*
sarantos@ionio.gr

Abstract

This paper introduces SCENS, a Secure Content Exchange Negotiation System suitable for the exchange of private digital data that reside in distributed digital repositories. SCENS is an open negotiation system with flexibility, security and scalability. SCENS is currently being designed to support data sharing in scientific research, by providing incentives and goals specific to a research community. However, it can easily be extended to apply to other communities, such as government, commercial and other types of exchanges. It is a trusted third party software infrastructure enabling independent entities to interact and conduct multiple forms of negotiation.

1.   Introduction

The aim of SCENS (Secure Content Exchange Negotiation System) is to facilitate data sharing through negotiation on metadata information derived from data of interest ("primary data"). Primary data exchange is done between two parties once they have reached agreement, and, until then, primary data remain in the control of data owners. Applications of this model include banks, scientific repositories and film archives. For convenience, we will use the term *digital libraries* to encompass these and other potential applications.

SCENS was originally designed and implemented to support data sharing in neuroscience research, where sharing is important in promoting discovery and collaboration. Neuroscience data are not only private but also of high value due to production costs. Traditionally, researchers have resisted sharing primary data in this field. Our efforts are synergistic with ongoing efforts (e.g. BIRN [1]) because we provide a flexible, user-centered alternative to large, trans-national archiving of published-only results that provide limited access control to the data

owner once he has given the data. SCENS negotiation services provide a secure mechanism of reaching agreements on conditions for primary data sharing. In this respect, our system offers a novel way for digital libraries composed of sensitive data to grow while enhancing collaboration of users and providing data usage tracking facilities.

2.   Related work

Several Web-based negotiation support systems are currently in use. SmartSettle [2] uses a central server to arrive at agreements without exposing confidential data. WebNS [3] is a prototype Web-based Negotiation System, designed to facilitate remote negotiations on the Internet. INSPIRE [4] is a Web-based negotiation support system containing facilities for specification and assessment of preferences.

However, most existing negotiation support systems do not have enough flexibility to support negotiation agents and automated negotiation. They also do not focus on security and scalability issues.

3.   The Characteristics of SCENS

3.1.   Flexible

SCENS has a flexible 3-layer service structure that provides different levels of negotiation services for different type of users.

Layer 1 behaves as a traditional web-based negotiation support system for human beings. It also provides some negotiation agents, which are actually user customizable utility functions. Users can customize the negotiation agents provided by Layer 1 through multiple parameters, such as the weights assigned to different negotiation conditions. However, the agents provided by Layer 1 are not fully customizable; if the negotiation strategy is very complex, it simply cannot be expressed by these parameters.

This work has been supported by NSF IDM 0083423 and Department of Justice contract 2000-DT-CX-K001.

Layer 2 supports complete negotiation strategy customization by users. In Layer 2, users are allowed to have their own negotiation agents to implement any negotiation strategies. The negotiation agents, which are treated as web service consumers and run on the client side, conduct negotiation with other negotiation agents or human beings through web services. Figure 1 shows the interactivity between Layer 1 and Layer 2.

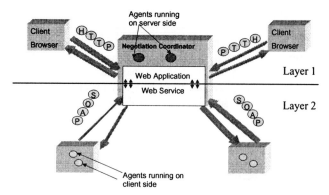

Figure 1. Layer 1 provides web-based negotiation services for human beings; Layer 2 interacts with negotiation agents through web services

Layer 3 is designed to provide an open and automated negotiation environment. DAML+OIL [5][6], a language for creating ontologies and marking up information, is used in Layer 3 to define a negotiation ontology, which allows agents to acquire knowledge about how to conduct negotiations. This knowledge includes negotiation protocols, negotiation proposals and conditions, etc. Agents communicating with Layer 3 can be used in any negotiation activities given the proper negotiation ontology. In Layer 2, in contrast, the knowledge about negotiation rules is actually hard-coded into the agents.

3.2. Secure

Security issues in SCENS involve a trade-off between access and access control. In addition to the traditional triad of confidentiality, integrity, and availability, SCENS introduces the desire to control data rights when one gives the data to another and the need to analyze and compose policies under which data may be shared.

Even though SCENS handles metadata only, privacy issues still must be addressed–for example, aggregation attacks. SCENS can provide tracking of data usage, analysis of the statistical security of data, and traffic analysis to prevent this kind of attacks.

Availability is more difficult to handle. A denial of service attack could easily disrupt negotiations, especially in SCENS, where users are allowed to provide their own negotiation agents running on clients. The negotiation protocol has been constructed to minimize the ability of denial of service attacks to disrupt the negotiations. However, SCENS is still vulnerable under denial of service attacks against the protocols underlying the negotiation protocol (such as TCP and IP).

3.3. Scalable

The deployment of SCENS supports a hierarchical structure. When inter-domain (the notion of domain is very flexible, and can be departments, labs or groups) negotiation is desired, a negotiation party in one domain cannot directly negotiate with a party in another domain; it can only communicate through the SCENS server in its own domain. A SCENS server in a domain only trusts other servers or users in its own domain. Figure 2 shows an example.

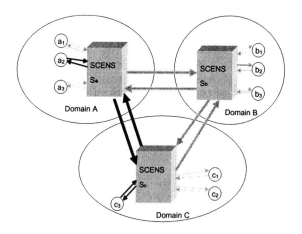

Figure 2. a_2 and c_3 are negotiating

4. How SCENS Works

In [8], an application of SCENS, the Data Broker Framework (DBF), is introduced to automate object acquisition, as well as support decision-making in obtaining the best "data collection deal". DBF tracks collection needs, past transactions, "bargain" for the best conditions, and promotes a common standard for computer-mediated negotiation involving diverse parties.

Based on SCENS, DBF helps any type of collector such as scientific databases, digital libraries, business records, and film archives, to collect content they need.

Figure 3 shows the use of SCENS. As noted earlier, SCENS is responsible for supporting and authenticating negotiations on data exchanges. After agreement is reached, any data exchange is beyond the control of SCENS. However, feedback on the data shared is reported back to SCENS, thus enabling the system to perform user and data tracking.

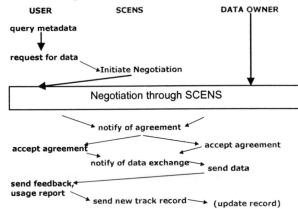

Figure 3. How SCENS works

5.   System Implementation

In our implementation of SCENS, we used AXIS (version 1.0rc2), a SOAP implementation from Apache Software Foundation, to provide negotiation web services (Layer 2). Our web-based negotiation service (Layer 1) is implemented using JSP 1.2. For Layer 3, we are building ontologies for brain tumor research using DAML+OIL and developing agents which interact with Layer 3.

The system is still under development. The services implemented include *user authentication, data quality assessment, web-based negotiation* (Layer 1), *web service based negotiation* (Layer 2), *usage tracking, user evaluation* and other services. We have also developed synthetic tools to simulate the negotiation activities and help evaluate the whole system. Figure 4 shows a partial list of implemented web services; Figure 5 shows a portion of the web-based interface supporting multi-user negotiations.

Figure 4. SCENS web services for Layer 2

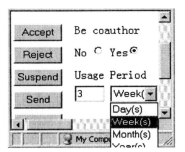

Figure 5. The SCENS interface for Layer 1

6.   Conclusion and future work

Our work builds on earlier work on MetaDLs [7, 9]. SCENS not only can be used to support negotiation activities, but also serves as a testbed for testing different negotiation strategies (Layer 2) and automated negotiation (Layer 3). Our next work is primarily in Layer 3. We are currently building applicable negotiation ontologies for information sharing and will extend these to a general-purpose approach. The long term goal of SCENS is to support fully automated negotiation for sensitive data sharing.

References

[1]   http://www.nbirn.net/ Visited 3/30/2003

[2]   http://www.oneaccordinc.com/ Visited 3/30/2003

[3]   http://webns.mcmaster.ca/   Visited 3/30/2003

[4]   Kersten G., Noronha S., Supporting International Negotiation with a WWW-based System. Internet Research Report INR05/97, 1997

[5]   Hendler J., McGuinness D.L., The DARPA Agent Markup Language, IEEE Intelligent Systems, vol. 16, no. 6, Jan./Feb., 2000, pp. 67-73

[6]   http://www.daml.org/2001/03/daml+oil-index Visited 3/30/2003

[7]   Makedon F., Ford J., et al., MetaDL: A Digital Library of Metadata for Sensitive or Complex Research Data, ECDL'02 , Sept. 2002, Rome, Italy.

[8]   Makedon, F., Kapidakis, S., et al., Data Brokers: Building Collections Through Automated Negotiation, Dartmouth College Computer Science Department, Hanover, NH, Technical Report DEVLAB-SCENS-03-02, March 2003.

[9]   Ford, J., Makedon, F., et al., Evaluation Metrics for User-centered Ranking of Content in MetaDL, Fourth DELOS Workshop on Evaluation of Digital Libraries: Testbeds, Measurements, and Metrics, Budapest, Hungary, May 6-7, 2002

Session 9A: Digital Libraries in the Classroom

Session Chair: Beth Davis-Brown, Library of Congress

Understanding Educator Perceptions of "Quality" in Digital Libraries

Tamara Sumner[1], Michael Khoo[2]
[1]Dept. of Computer Science
[2]Dept. of Communication
University of Colorado at Boulder
1-303-492-2233
sumner@colorado.edu
michael.khoo@colorado.edu

Mimi Recker
Utah State University
2830 Old Main Hill
Logan UT 84322-2830, USA
1-435-797-2688
mimi.recker@usu.edu

Mary Marlino
DLESE Program Center
University Corporation for
Atmospheric Research
1-303-497-8350
marlino@ucar.edu

Abstract

The purpose of the study was to identify educators' expectations and requirements for the design of educational digital collections for classroom use. A series of five focus groups was conducted with practicing teachers, pre-service teachers, and science librarians, drawn from different educational contexts (i.e., K-5, 6-12, College). Participants' expect that the added value of educational digital collections is the provision of: (1) 'high quality' teaching and learning resources, and (2) additional contextual information beyond that in the resource. Key factors that influence educators' perceptions of quality were identified: scientific accuracy, bias, advertising, design and usability, and the potential for student distraction. The data showed that participants judged these criteria along a continuum of tolerance, combining consideration of several factors in their final judgements. Implications for collections accessioning policies, peer review, and digital library service design are discussed.

1. Introduction

Over the past decade, there has been vocal and visible public demand for improved science education across the national, state, and local levels, and a call for greater access to quality science education for all citizens [14, 15]. In part, this call is being answered by the emergence of diverse operational digital libraries devoted to science education across a range of science, mathematics, engineering and technology disciplines. Two such examples are the National Science Digital Library (www.NSDL.org) and the Digital Library for Earth System Education (www.DLESE.org), which provided the context for the research presented in this article. The stated aim of both libraries is to encourage and sustain continual improvements in science education, at all educational levels, through the provision of collections of digital educational resources and associated library services [13, 20].

Given the recent implementation of such initiatives, the process of widespread digital library adoption and uptake in classroom settings is an emerging research area. To date, a few studies have examined the relationship between library service design and library use in classroom settings. For instance, Borgman et al observed the use of the Alexandria Digital Library Prototype in college-level geography classrooms and labs by both teaching faculty and students [2]. The Alexandria Digital Library provides an innovative resource discovery service enabling users to retrieve geo-referenced maps and images based on geographic location [10]. At the K-12 level, Abbas et al examined the use of the Artemis Digital Library by middle school students in 32 schools [1]. A key service of Artemis is the provision of scaffolding, in the form of 'Driving Questions,' that are intended to help students effectively manage their interactions with the library's search function. Recker et al investigated how the Instructional Architect, which provides a web-based portal for combining existing educational resources, was used by teachers in lesson planning activities [5, 16].

In this article, we take a complementary approach and examine the relationships between digital library collection design and accessioning strategies and library adoption and use in classroom settings. This approach is motivated by the belief that the overall value of any digital library results from a combination of the perceived quality of its collections and the usability and usefulness of the provided services. In particular, we are interested in understanding what factors and design affordances, of both individual resources and the collection as a whole, lead teachers to use a digital collection on a regular basis for lesson planning and lesson implementation. That is, what factors lead them to use it themselves for planning and preparing lessons and to ask their students to use the library or library resources as part of explicit instructional activities.

Towards this end, we report on a series of five focus groups conducted with practicing teachers, pre-service teachers, and science librarians, across different learning contexts (i.e., K-5, 6-12, undergraduate education). In the focus groups, each participant was asked to evaluate a range of digital educational resources for classroom use. These resources were deliberately chosen to represent a spectrum of potentially positive and negative design qualities based, in part, on the results of a large-scale quantitative study of factors influencing web site credibility [7]. The results of this individual activity were used to seed group discussions on digital collection design, where participants were asked to articulate their ideal collection design qualities in terms of three levels of importance rankings.

Two significant findings emerge from the research. Overall, there was remarkable consistency across the groups in their recommendations for the design of digital collections for classroom use, and the factors that led them to positively or negatively evaluate a particular resource. This consistency is perhaps surprising when considering the potential differences in classroom use between primary school, secondary school and undergraduate courses. Analyses also revealed that potentially negative design factors, such as political bias or advertising, are judged along a continuum of tolerance, and in some cases, viewed as useful in certain pedagogical contexts. These findings have significant implications for the design of library collections accessioning policies, peer review systems, and digital library services.

2. Related Work

Several recent studies have used quantitative research methods to attempt to identify the design elements, content characteristics, and other factors that lead web sites to be highly rated by users. Ivory et al used statistical methods to try to correlate low-level design issues, such as the amount and positioning of text, or the overall portion of a page devoted to graphics, with expert judgements of overall site quality [9]. Similarly, the outcomes of our focus groups also suggest that these types of design issues can affect users perceptions of site quality. However, in addition to users' perceptions, we are also interested in examining the relationship between low-level design issues and potential site use in instructional settings.

Fogg et al conducted a large-scale online survey, with over 1400 participants, to identify what factors affect perceptions of web site credibility [7]. Participants responded to a survey consisting of 51 general statements about potential web site design or content, such as "The site is difficult to navigate" or "The site makes it hard to distinguish ads from content." For each statement, participants selected a response on a 7 point Likert scale as to whether this aspect made web sites much more believable (+3) or much less believable (-3). Using statistical analysis techniques, seven factors were identified: five that boost web site credibility (real-world

feel, ease-of-use, expertise, trustworthiness, and tailoring) and two that hurt credibility (commercial implications and amateurism). These factors informed the selection of sites used in our focus groups. However, a key difference between our approach and this survey is the context of site evaluation. Fogg et al examined participants' judgements generically, i.e., they were not examining or thinking about real sites, or particular types of use. We, however, looked at the factors that influenced the evaluation of particular resources within a very specific context of use: lesson planning and lesson implementation in instructional settings.

Several educational professional societies and other groups have created guidelines for evaluating web sites for use by teachers and students [4, 6], or guidelines for school district adoption of web-based curricular materials [3, 19]. These guidelines typically offer a series of checklists for evaluating the information and the creators of a particular site, i.e., who is the author, are citations to other references provided, etc. These guidelines are also intended to help teachers and students learn robust web site evaluation skills. The research reported here combines these recommended guidelines, with the generic factors identified by Fogg, and uses qualitative research methods to probe the reasoning behind educators' evaluations of particular sites.

3. Methodology

The data for this study were derived from a series of five focus groups held with science educators in summer and Fall of 2002. Each of the five groups was drawn from a particular learning context: K-5 (one inservice group), 6-12 (two groups, one inservice and one preservice), and undergraduate faculty (two inservice groups). Each group consisted of 7 to 9 science educators: the 6-12 group also included two science librarians. Inservice groups consisted of practicing, experienced educators; the preservice group consisted of education students training to become middle and high school science teachers. All of the focus groups were held in purpose built computer laboratories, equipped with high-speed Internet connections. Sessions were conducted in Boulder, Colorado, and Logan, Utah, with two of the authors (Sumner and Recker) serving as facilitators.

Each focus group commenced with an introduction from the group facilitator, who explained that the goal of the session was to provide advice to two digital libraries - the Digital Library for Earth System Education and the National Science Digital Library - on establishing policies, priorities, and best practices for building useful digital collections for classroom use. Policies, priorities and practices represent three levels of importance, with policies encompassing criteria deemed to be most important, and practices encompassing criteria deemed least important. Specifically, participants were instructed that:

- Policies are rules that govern what items can be included in a digital collection.

- Priorities are directives for how collection-building efforts should spend their time and money.

- Practices are recommendations for action but are not mandated or enforced.

Each focus group lasted between 70 and 90 minutes and was scheduled as follows:

1. The group was briefed on the context of DLESE and NSDL. Participants were instructed to focus on the evaluation criteria important to collection gathering processes; i.e., selecting resources for inclusion in a digital collection.

2. The group was shown a demonstration of the DLESE collection.

3. The group was briefed on the definitions of policies, priorities, and practices to enable them to categorize levels of importance for evaluation criteria.

4. Each group member was then directed to an individual computer and given 30 minutes to evaluate 4 educational web sites. This short time period was selected to reflect the typical time an educator may reasonably devote to analyzing a particular site returned by a search engine. For each site, participants completed a short evaluation rubric (Figure 1).

5. After this review period, group members reconvened for a group discussion, and were asked to contribute the positive and negative criteria by which they had judged the sites. Their comments were recorded on a white board at the front of the room.

6. After enumerating these criteria, the group developed their recommended policies, priorities, and practices, which reflected the group's consensus.

Overall, 38 focus group participants, in five separate groups, reviewed a total of 18 web sites. Considerable thought was given to selecting sites for evaluation. All were selected by a DLESE content expert to be age-appropriate and to reflect criteria that may influence resource evaluation. Some sites were already in the DLESE collection and some were not. Based on the research of Fogg et al [7], and our own prior work [11, 18, 19], we selected sites to reflect four criteria that we hypothesized were potentially relevant to classroom use of web resources: quality content, advertising, scientific bias, and design and usability issues.

With respect to selecting sites with 'quality content,' we did not define what quality meant but merely instructed the content expert to select sites she believed to

have good educational value. With respect to 'usability issues,' the content expert was instructed to select resources that she believed to have educational value but might be perceived to have design or granularity mismatch problems. Prior usability studies conducted with DLESE indicate that 'granularity mismatches' are a type of usability problem specific to educational digital libraries [18]. Mismatches can occur when the educational resources returned by a library's search function are either overly general (e.g., a large portal site) or overly specific compared to the type of resource the user had in mind. Each focus group received one resource illustrative of each of the four categories. It is important to note that none of these initial categories were revealed to participants at any time during the focus group session.

Data from these sessions was collected in three formats – worksheets, whiteboards, and audio tape of group discussions. Each participant was given a worksheet where the first page collected basic demographic information (age, gender), as well as the classroom and computer experience of each participant. Subsequent pages of the worksheet were devoted to the evaluation rubric shown in Figure 1. This rubric asked participants to rate the overall quality of a particular site using a Likert scale ranging from -3 (very low quality) to +3 (very high quality). The worksheet also provided space for participants to record open-ended comments on the 'negative' and 'positive' aspects of each site.

Following completion of the worksheet, there was a group discussion where the facilitator used a whiteboard to summarize and record group discussion across a number of categories, including the perceived negative and positive characteristics of sites, and suggestions for policies, priorities, and practices for developing online collections for educational use. The group discussion was recorded, and the audio transcribed, resulting in approximately 60 pages of transcripts.

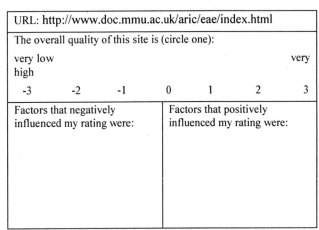

Figure 1. Rubric for evaluating educational resources used in the focus groups.

3.1 Demographic Data

Sixteen respondents were female, 21 were male, and one no response. For the inservice teachers, the length of teaching experience varied from 1 to 30 years, with the average being approximately 14.5 years. Six respondents taught grades K-4, 3 taught grades 5-8, 7 taught 9-12, 16 taught undergraduate, 10 taught graduate, and 4 were pre-service (a number of respondents indicated they taught a range of grade levels). On a Likert scale of -3 ('very low') to +3 ('very high'), participants' mean comfort with information technologies was 2.2. On a Likert scale of -3 ('never') to +3 ('all the time'), participants' mean use of information technology in the classroom was 1.9. They indicated that their students' mean use of information technology in the classroom was 1.6, suggesting that, on average, this group of teachers used information technology slightly more often to support their own classroom activities, in comparison to having their students use technology.

4. Results

The data can be reported in terms of a two-by-two matrix that has as its dimensions 'decision' and 'supporting discussion' at both individual and group levels. At an individual level, the Likert scale recorded how participants ultimately ranked resources, while the open-ended questions recorded their views as to why they made this ranking. At a group level, the facilitator summarized and recorded the group's opinions regarding the positive and negative aspects of the resources being reviewed, while the audio recording provided a precise record of the groups' decision-making process. The data matrix thus looks as follows:

Table 1. Data Collected

	Decision	Supporting Discussion
Individual	Likert scale	Worksheets
Group	Whiteboard comments	Audio recording

4.1 Individual Level

Individually, participants rated the overall quality of 18 different web-based educational resources using a Likert scale. The minimum number of scores a resource received was 3, and the maximum was 17 (see Table 2). Weighted scores for each resource were calculated to produce a summary statistic that pools the independently produced quality ratings. This was done by taking the Likert scores for each resource, multiplying these by the number of times that score was chosen, summing these scores, and then dividing this sum by the overall number of scores. This procedure generated a summary score between -3 and +3. Each resource's overall score was thus:

$$\sum(\text{Likert score x number of scores}) / \text{Total number of scores}$$

Following this procedure, resources were grouped into three categories: high scoring resources (with a weighted score greater or equal to 1), mid range (weighted score greater than 0 but less than 1), and low scoring resources (weighted score less than 0) (see Table 2). Note that different resources received varying numbers of scores because (a) focus groups were of different sizes, (b) each group reviewed different combinations of resources, (c) some resources were reviewed by more than one group and (d) some participants did not review all the resources they were assigned.

The last column in Table 2 shows the initial selection category the resource was chosen to illustrate. For the pool of resources used in these groups, resources chosen by the content expert to illustrate 'quality content' all appear in the high scoring category. With two exceptions, resources deemed to have scientific bias or the presence of advertising have lower quality rankings (low scoring or bottom half of mid range). Four of the six resources with potential usability issues have neutral rankings. Looking at the standard deviations for individual resource quality ratings, there tends to be more agreement about what constitutes a good resource (i.e., smaller standard deviations) and less agreement about what constitutes lower quality resources (i.e., higher standard deviations).

We then examined the worksheet comments accompanying the Likert scores to better understand the factors that influenced the overall quality ratings. Participants made a total of 526 statements about factors influencing their Likert scores, of which 252 were positive and 274 were negative.

Examples of positive statements are:
- Good science
- Nicely laid out introductory page
- Detailed, comprehensive information on various components of the atmosphere
- Teacher resource for lesson plans

Examples of negative statements include:
- Takes you to "ads"
- Kids will need a great deal of direction to use the site
- The text is dry and technical
- Too much text for a 3rd grader to weed through

All the resources reviewed received a mixture of both positive and negative comments. This applied not only to the resources that received 'middle' Likert scores, but also to the resources that were ranked either 'high' or 'low.' Thus, the highest ranked resource was praised for its content, but also received a number of negative comments about its navigation features; while another highly ranked resource was criticized for design, architecture, content, and the presence of advertisements. Conversely, one of the low scoring resources that was seen as scientifically biased, was also consistently described as having good content (although note that some of these positive comments referred to being able to use the bias of the resource as a pedagogical device).

Further content analysis of the positive and negative comments in the worksheet data indicate that while criteria of content quality, advertising, bias and design were widely identified by individual participants as important factors influencing their perceptions, the ways in which participants interpreted these factors and were prepared to make trade offs between them were complex. Specifically, participants made trade-offs between potentially positive and negative factors, and they applied, and even defined, criteria differently when analyzing particular resource features in terms of different users (teachers versus students). As an example of making trade-offs between criteria, a K-5 participant reviewing the high scoring atozteacherstuff.com noted the presence of advertising as a negative feature, but rated the resource more in terms of its positive features: the presence of activities and lessons that were appropriate to younger children and which integrated literacy and numeracy with science instruction. As an example of considering the impact of a feature on different user roles, the presence of links to a variety of related sites is a positive feature when analyzing a resource in terms of a comprehensive resource for teachers. However, this same feature can be interpreted negatively when considered in the context of student classroom use, where educators are concerned that students may become distracted or sidetracked by numerous options.

Table 2. Weighted Likert Scores for Individual Resources' Overall Quality Rating

URL	Reviews	Score	S. Dev	Selection Category
High Scoring Sites				
http://see.gsfc.nasa.gov/education/SEES/strat/strat.htm	8	2.13	0.83	Quality content
http://ww2010.atmos.uiuc.edu/(Gh)/guides/mtr/hyd/home.rxml	6	2.00	0.63	Quality content
http://www.letus.nwu.edu/projects/gw/index.html	5	1.80	0.84	Quality content
http://atozteacherstuff.com/themes/space.shtml	7	1.71	0.95	Advertising
http://btc.montana.edu/ceres/default.htm	8	1.63	1.19	Usability - granularity
http://www.nationalgeo.com/xpeditions/lessons/07/gk2/	8	1.63	1.30	Quality content
Mid Range Scoring Sites				
http://www.usd.edu/esci/exams/atmosph.html	9	0.78	1.27	Usability - granularity
http://www.coaleducation.org/issues/issues1.htm	13	0.62	1.20	Scientific bias
http://vortex.plymouth.edu/sun/sun1.html	9	0.56	1.51	Usability - design
http://www.doc.mmu.ac.uk/aric/eae/index.html	3	0.33	1.53	Usability - granularity
http://geology.about.com/mbody.htm	6	0.33	1.03	Advertising
http://www.homestead.com/desertfootprints/index.html	7	0.14	1.77	Usability - design
http://weather.about.com/	7	0.14	1.21	Advertising
http://www.howstuffworks.com/lightning.htm	7	0.14	1.68	Advertising
http://www.coaleducation.org/lessons/primary.htm	8	0.00	1.19	Scientific bias
Low Scoring Sites				
http://www.usd.edu/esci/exams/masswast.html	6	-0.50	2.26	Usability - granularity
http://www.globalwarming.org/index.htm	17	-0.94	2.11	Scientific bias
http://www.howstuffworks.com/tornado.htm	9	-1.78	0.97	Advertising

4.2 Group Level

In the group discussions, focus group participants identified and defined the evaluative criteria they deemed most important to educational digital library collection quality. They ranked the importance of these identified criteria by making recommendations for digital library collections accessioning policies, priorities, and practices. In addition to tabulating the outcomes of each of the focus groups, we also analyzed the transcripts from the group discussions to understand the ways in which each of these criteria were defined and applied by participants, and to look at participants' assumptions and expectations for educational collection design.

As shown in Table 3, there was considerable consistency across the five groups, in terms of the evaluative criteria deemed to be most significant - quality, bias, advertising, design and usability, and distractions - and the implications of these criteria for collection building.

Quality. Four of the five groups felt that library accessioning policy should emphasize resource quality. All groups except the K-5 group identified scientific accuracy as a critical element of resource quality; the K-5 group defined quality in terms of age appropriate and engaging activities, favoring resources that encouraged active learning, rather than heavily textual resources. Negative comments regarding scientific accuracy included 'superfluous information,' 'factual errors,' 'incorrect scientific content,' 'dated citations,' and 'out of date material'; while positive comments included 'good details,' 'overall good science,' 'directly address student misconceptions,' 'quality of science,' and 'correct content.' For instance a middle/high school participant said:

"I mean like the whole thing is like we are trying to decide what to include in the library, and what not to include, and I think that science is the top thing...That should be the main thing, if it doesn't have that, it doesn't get in."

Bias. 'Bias' for the participants referred to the presence of perceived political or commercial agendas in a resource that may distort its scientific and/or educational qualities. Participants expressed anxiety over the possibility of students finding biased resources on their own and the group discussions on this point were emotionally charged. Overall, four of the five groups viewed bias as undesirable. However, in the discussion, a significant proportion of participants also saw such resources as useful for teaching critical thinking and scientific habits of mind.

Two related issues emerged as salient when considering bias: labeling and pedagogical use. All groups, except for the K-5 group, felt that educational digital libraries should clearly label sites as being biased in the item-level metadata. These labels should ideally: (1) identify the author's point-of-view and (2) suggest possible classroom uses such as seeding debates. For instance, a university faculty member arguing for the inclusion of labeled biased sites said,

"I think it has to have some...meta information, some description like you showed with each web site, saying this is a blatantly political, anti-global warming site, but you might want to use it for your classes anyway."

Related to the issue of bias was the issue of references for cited data (an issue that might be seen as 'objectivity'). Here, the main concern was the provenance of the information presented on the site, provenance that could be indicated by the clear labeling of authors and creators. Bias and objectivity can be seen as being situated at opposite ends of a continuum of trust. For instance a participant in the middle/high school focus group, asked:

"And when we wrote quality affordable sites, are we clear that means quality science?...Like clearly, what's the word I'm looking for, clearly referenced information. Isn't that what we meant?"
Another added,
"Yeah, that's fine, I mean just knowing that it's you know data that 6th graders collected, versus you know this is data from the National Hurricane Center Miami."

Advertising. All groups strongly felt that libraries should limit the accessioning of resources with advertising. This was expressed by participants as recommended library policies or collection building priorities. However, as with opinions on bias, there was a range of tolerance for advertising, varying from none at all to limited. Opinion in all focus groups seemed to converge on permitting resources containing discrete advertising (that is, no pop-ups or animations) that does not detract from learning; for instance, advertising related to scientific products was thought to be permissible, as were resources with static banner advertisements.

For many participants, it was not the commercialism of advertisements that was viewed as negative, it was the distracting implementations of the advertisements that caused concern. Specifically, advertising was frequently viewed as a distraction that would lead students off task. Three K-5 participants, for instance, debated advertising in terms of student distractions:

P: I say no advertising.
P: That's kinda strong. Are you sure there might not be some companies that were gonna have some really good information but yet their
P: [interrupting] Well, you're looking at it for kids. I mean, I guess you could see teachers getting it,

but you want kids to be going to Barnes and Noble when they're in the computer lab to buy a book?

P: And they're not sophisticated enough to know when it says "click here, click here, click here," to not click there...I tell them whenever it says "click here" that means don't click here. But you know, that really is kinda a hard thing in terms of management of kids in labs."

While it might be expected that this type of distraction would be of concern to teachers of younger children, identical concerns were expressed by both middle/high school and undergraduate educators. For instance, the middle/high school participants worried about linked ads sidetracking students off task:

P: Is this what it's going to come to? Is that, are you guys using advertised sites? I mean, that is a real negative because it's constant pop-ups, mostly for interruptions...

P: You can deal with the headers across the top it's the one that leave the data up...

P: I got annoyed with that site

P: Especially with advertising that is linked. In other words, where you can actually click on a link and it will take you from where you are to somewhere else.

P: Yes that's right they did do that.

P: Cause kids will get totally sidetracked.

Table 3. Summary of policies, priorities, and practices developed in each session

Group	Policies	Priorities	Practices
Undergraduate	Reject resources with ads that distract from learning or are unrelated to science	Metadata should include a bias warning Collections should represent a balance [across different opinions and perspectives]	[None]
Undergraduate	Include resources that are: - Relevant to scientific topic - With only limited commercialism - Good science; are correct Metadata should include a bias warning	[None]	[None]
Grades 6-12 (inservice)	Include resources that are: - Quality science - Clearly referenced, citable information Metadata should include a bias warning	Can include resources with discrete advertising with good science and graphics	Metadata should identify the technical requirements needed to use a resource Avoid sites with broken links
Grades 6-12 (preservice)	Include resources that are: - Credible sites with relevant and important information - Sites with good organization - Have no advertising Metadata should include a bias warning	Emphasize resources with: - Content for different audiences - Good classroom activities - Professional look - Offer enhancements and extensions to basic instructional materials	Prefer resources with: - Good use of graphics - Language appropriate to audience
Grades K-5	Include resources that are: - High quality activities: interactive, engaging, supports creativity - No advertising or limited advertising Metadata should: - Accurately characterize grade level; at least a narrow window level, not K-8, but K-1, 2-3, 4-5, etc. - Provide alternative content descriptors, e.g. reading level.	Emphasize resources with: - Fast download times and note which resources have longer download times - That are really age appropriate; too many resources assume advanced readers	Prefer resources: - Ease of organisation - User friendly for audience - That clearly add value; something that you can't do with existing resources or classroom activities

Design and usability. All groups expressed frustration with the current state of web resource design, but also expressed praise for well-designed sites or site features. Particular design issues singled out for criticism included: confusing navigation; broken and/or irrelevant links; slow download times; small, strangely colored, or otherwise unreadable text; and distracting backgrounds. Design elements that were considered favorably included: printable versions of web pages; clear graphics; and advance organizers (such as the clear labeling of the content and purpose of a site at the start of the site). Many of the middle scoring resources in these groups had reasonable scientific content but also had design elements that hindered use, as two university professors found:

P: *Yeah, it was hard to read.*
P: *I couldn't even read it...*
P: *And surprisingly the site was actually pretty good*
... if it wasn't for that stupid background.

Distractions. Analysis of the transcripts revealed that 'distraction' is a significant issue related to design and usability that inhibits use. All participants were particularly concerned that poor web design would negatively affect the attention that students were able to direct to their learning task. Factors such as animated or flashing advertisements, irrelevant content within the site, and links to other web pages that were 'off topic' for the pedagogical task at hand, were all seen as distracting students from their learning. Elements promoting distraction extended to links and other content elements that were deemed to be scientifically accurate but not directly relevant to the immediate topic.

Assumptions and expectations. Content analysis of the transcripts for phrases related to the participants' perceptions suggested that educators in all the groups had similar assumptions and expectations with respect to the 'added value' provided by digital library collections, compared to search engines and the web in general. This added value is frequently characterized in terms of filtering and related labeling. Specifically, many participants stated that educational digital libraries should save them time and effort compared to using web search engines, by engaging in quality filtering and peer reviewing. In turn, some of these expectations about educational digital library collections appear to be based on participants' prior experiences with publicly funded school libraries and subscription educational content services. Two university faculty spoke of searching the web as follows:

P: *Surfing the web is very painful.*
P: *It's tiring*
P: *It is, it is, it's like a sponge*
P: *Well it's also, like when you've got a time limit, and you're trying to get through it...*

On a number of occasions, DLESE was described as providing a superior, peer-review based alternative to search engines. According to a university faculty member:

P: *My, my students can go to Google and find as much as they want, so if they go to DLESE, I would want it to have some sort of, of filter, that you put on it, so to sort of certify that this is valuable to spend your time looking at.*

Similar sentiments regarding the unfiltered nature of search engine results were expressed by a middle school librarian:

P: *I'll tell you why. Kids can find it, I can, anybody, you can spend twenty minutes; I can find you tons of stuff. You just need to go to the right search engines and stuff and you can use the right keywords, you're done. But quality stuff..., there's an issue.*

Related to the issue of added value is the issue of labeling. Overall, these participants viewed collection quality as a product of the quality of the individual resources in the collections and the provision of additional contextual information by digital libraries. Participants identified numerous ways in which they felt digital libraries should provide additional information beyond that in the resource itself. This issue of labeling cropped up in the discussion of bias, as well as in discussions of creator attribution and whether or not resources are age-appropriate. For instance, the middle/high school participants noted that creator attribution in the item-level metadata would be extremely useful for helping students to learn to cite electronic resources. The K-5 participants felt that the age-levels of many resources were incorrect with respect to the reading skills required to use them; they wanted item-level metadata to note the actual reading level required separately from the learning context given by the resource creator.

5. Discussion

Overall, the results indicate that there is a high degree of consensus among middle school, high school, and university educators about what constitutes quality in digital collections, namely scientific accuracy. The focus groups in each of these educational contexts recommended that digital libaries include scientific accuracy as a requirement for collections accessioning policies.

What constituted poor quality was less clearly articulated. Reporting bias and the presence of advertising were recognized by all groups as important negative evaluation criteria. However, four of the five groups did not elect to apply these criteria in a binary fashion; i.e., to ban all sites with advertising or bias. The data showed that participants judged these criteria along a continuum of tolerance, combining consideration of several factors in their final judgements, including the intended audience of the site (teachers versus students), the perceived tastefulness and relevance of the advertising, and the degree to which the bias is called out in the library's item-level metadata.

These findings suggest that library policies in these areas will need to be more nuanced than simple presence or absence filters, especially for libraries that serve multiple audiences. They also highlight the value of metadata for resource comprehension and the influence of metadata on how the quality of collections is perceived as a whole. Educators will tolerate, and in some cases even value, biased sites in educational collections, as long as they are labeled as such. Conversely, finding an unlabeled biased site in a digital collection may irreparably erode the user's confidence in the collection's overall educational value.

In these groups, participants expected library metadata to provide additional context on how an educational resource could be fruitfully used in the classroom, as opposed to merely providing descriptive summaries of resource content. This suggests, that despite promising advances in automatically generated metadata [12], there may always be a role for some human-generated metadata involving informed judgements with respect to the potential range of learning activities for particular educational resources. Such judgments could be stored within item-level annotation metadata frameworks (e.g., [8]).

The issue of course, is who determines the labeling. One approach might be to use a recommender-style system where library users can annotate resources with their experiences and points of view. It is not clear that this approach would address the educational needs since the educator or student would still need to be sufficiently informed and energetic to sort out all the biases of the recommenders. An alternative approach would be to extend existing peer review systems to include controversial sites as opposed to simply reviewing sites submitted by resource creators. This would be one way that peer review systems embedded in educational digital libraries might differ from those in traditional academic journals. In this case, the essence of the peer review process would be to generate this contextual information that would help an instructor determine the appropriateness of a learning resource for instructional activities (e.g., [17]).

As noted by participants, the ultimate educational goal is to create informed citizens who can recognize and analyze alternative points of view. As one participant stated:

P: Well, what, you know, we're, the bigger picture is we're trying to create people who become functional in society. And they have to be able to assess whether what someone else is saying is truthful or not. There's a lot of opinionated stuff going on in the media, and so, our students have to learn how to critique these things. And excluding them from their education is perhaps worse than including them and not telling them that it's biased.

As science and technology increasingly pervade our everyday lives, and the issues become more complex and global, it is critical that science education embraces strategies that develop these critical thinking skills. Digital libraries can contribute to this goal through the careful design of collections and services that not only vet, but also provide additional contextual information.

These data also suggest that usability issues are important considerations when evaluating sites for classroom use. Participants identified a range of usability barriers for every site, including all of those in the highly rated category. Interestingly participants identified a range of design elements that may contribute to student distractions from the learning task at hand. The pervasiveness of distraction as a key design concept in the worksheet comments and transcripts suggests that this might be a particularly salient issue when evaluating sites for classroom use.

6. Limitations of the Study and Directions for Future Work

This study can be critiqued for displaying a number of limitations common to focus group studies in general, including: (a) self selection; (b) the use of zero-history groups studying hypothetical cases; and (c) facilitator influence. In this section we briefly outline and address these critiques.

First, our focus group participants can be criticized for being self-selecting, particularly with regard to participant familiarity with Internet use, and participant comfort with using web-based resources in the classroom (see demographic data, above). Our demographic might thus be thought of as skewed towards an 'early adopter' population characterized by a better understanding of technology and by more nuanced critical stances towards poorly designed web sites. However, as we have also argued, large-scale operational digital libraries for classroom use are nascent technologies, and as of the time of writing, they often are used by teachers who are more comfortable with computer technologies. Such early adopters of web-based resources can thus be seen as representative of a significant group of early users, and the study of their reactions to educational digital library collections thus becomes useful in the ongoing design and rollout of these technologies to wider and wider audiences.

Second, our study can be critiqued for using zero-history groups studying hypothetical cases. A zero-history group is one that is constituted by the researchers for the purpose of observation, out of the social and historical contexts in which the members of the group normally act. In this case, the task of resource evaluation would normally take place 'in the wild' in complex contexts of constraint and opportunity that include wider curricula; local, state and national educational standards; the availability of classroom resources; the amount of time available to the teacher; and so on. Unlike our focus groups, teachers would not normally evaluate randomly selected resources just for the sake of it; and if they are evaluating resources, it is probably because they are already looking for resources to fit a particular purpose. However, as is the case with the 'early adopter' criticism, this criticism can be at least partly addressed by pointing out that at this time, the widespread, longitudinal use of new digital libraries such as DLESE and NSDL is rare, and that 'artificial' focus groups are thus one useful way of surfacing this phenomena within financial and temporal constraints.

Finally, repeat focus groups can be problematic when the facilitator becomes familiar with the sorts of comments that they think participants may make, and so might start to prompt the participants to supply the 'correct' answers. We tried to avoid this by adhering as far as possible to a standard focus group outline and script. These standard procedures also have the advantage that they provide a measure of control for when different facilitators run the group in different places.

In terms of future work, these focus groups concentrated on understanding the educator perspective. Subsequent studies will concentrate on the learner perspective; i.e., understanding the factors and decision-making processes that students use when considering resources for educational use. In the long term, this focus group data needs to be augmented with field studies that examine the actual practices of educators and students in naturalistic settings.

7. Conclusion

In this article, we have reported on an analysis of qualitative data collected from focus groups designed to elucidate the dimensions of educator perceptions of quality in web-based educational resources and digital library collections for classroom use. We believe that this research has generated two important and related outcomes. First, it has provided insight into the value of including qualitative methodologies in digital library evaluative research studies; and second, it has provided additional support for research suggesting that educational digital libraries can provide significant added value over other services (e.g., conventional portals, search engines, etc.) for the teachers who are using them to locate web-based resources.

In attempting to identify predictors of criteria of usefulness, we suggest that a combination of quantitative and qualitative approaches demonstrates some distinct advantages. In our case, our qualitative analysis of the recorded and transcribed focus group discussions illuminated the reasoning behind some of the decisions recorded in the Likert scores and on the whiteboard, and in the process, the complex trade-offs that educators make while evaluating online educational resources. These findings point towards the need for future design work to support educators in this process.

Most importantly, the findings presented here imply a shift in requirements analysis that supplements the identification of basic digital library 'magic bullet' requirements (the library must be fast rather than slow; contain good rather than bad resources; must be easy rather than hard to use; etc.) with qualitative data drawn from user populations. This shift is important to the design of future library services, which should be able to identify the good resources that users expect to find in the library, but also help users to understand, contextualize, and internally negotiate their own continuum of tolerance when they encounter resources that they believe to be inappropriate.

We therefore suggest that digital library credibility can be supported both by the provision of 'good' resources, but also by the provision of contextual explanations - such as the labeling of political and economic agendas - for the inclusion of the 'not bad' resources. The evidence of and demand for such contextualization by educational digital library users in our study also suggests that digital libraries should exist not just as collections of resources, but also as sensemaking tools that help bring those resources to life. The national educational digital library agenda is being developed, in part, as a response to the societal needs for scientific literacy, critical thinking skills, and an informed citizenry in an era of increasing global connectivity and change. The capacity of digital library technologies to provide frameworks and infrastructure to support users in contextualizing information about resource quality, beyond 'basic' metadata and numerical ratings of quality is a key capacity. Building such annotations services may help support users to engage in sense-making and critical thinking skills, and in so doing, come another step closer to meeting the potential of digital libraries for educational use.

8. Acknowledgements

We are grateful to Karon Kelly and Holly Devaul at the DLESE Program Center for their assistance with the focus groups and numerous insightful discussions on these issues. The research is funded in part by the National Science Foundation under a Cooperative Agreement #ATM-9732665 between the NSF and UCAR, and by NSF Grant #0085600.

9. References

[1] Abbas, J., Norris, C. and Soloway, E., Middle School Children's Use of ARTEMIS Digital Library. in *ACM/IEEE Joint Conference on Digital Libraries (JCDL '02)*, (Portland, Oregon (July 14-18), 2002), ACM Press, 98-105.

[2] Borgman, C.L., Gilliland-Swetland, A.J., Leazer, G.H., Mayer, R., Gwynn, D. and Gazan, R. Evaluating Digital Libraries for Teaching and Learning in Undergraduate Education: A Case Study of the Alexandria Digital Earth Prototype (ADEPT). *Library Trends, 49* (2). 228-250.

[3] Brundin, E. Portal Evaluation Rubric, Long Beach Unified School District, Long Beach, CA, 2000.

[4] Descy, D. Evaluating Internet Resources. *Tech Trends, 41* (4). 3-5.

[5] Dorward, J., Reinke, D. and Recker, M., An Evaluation Model for a Digital Library. in *ACM/IEEE Joint Conference on Digital Libraries (JCDL '02)*, (Portland, OR (July 14-18), 2002), ACM, 322-323.

[6] Environmental Education and Training Partnership (EETAP) *Evaluating the Content of Web Sites*. Ohio State University Extension, Columbus, Ohio, 1999.

[7] Fogg, B., Marshall, J., Laraki, O., Osipovich, A., Varma, C., Fang, N., Paul, J., Rangnekar, A., Shon, J., Swani, P. and Treinen, M., What Makes Web Sites Credible? A Report on a Large Quantitative Study. in *Human Factors in Computing Systems (CHI 2001)*, (Seattle, Washington (March 31 - April 5), 2001), ACM Press, 61-68.

[8] Hillmann, D. Annotations, NSDL, 2002. http://annotations.comm.nsdlib.org/

[9] Ivory, M., Sinha, R. and Hearst, M., Empirically Validated Web Page Design Metrics. in *Human Factors in Computing Systems (CHI '01)*, (Seattle, WA (March 31 - April 4), 2001), ACM Press, 53-60.

[10] Janée, G. and Frew, J., The ADEPT Digital Library Architecture. in *ACM/IEEE Joint Conference on Digital Libraries (JCDL '02)*, (Portland, Oregon (July 14-18), 2002), ACM Press, 342-349.

[11] Khoo, M., Community Design of DLESE's Collections Review Policy: A Technological Frames Analysis. in *ACM/IEEE Joint Conference on Digital Libraries (JCDL '01)*, (Roanoke, VA (June 24-28), 2001), 157-164.

[12] Liddy, E., Sutton, S., Paik, W., Allen, E., Harwell, S., Monsour, M., Turner, A. and Liddy, J., Breaking the Metadata Generation Bottleneck: Preliminary Findings. in *ACM/IEEE Joint Conference on Digital Libraries (JCDL '01)*, (Roanoke, Virginia (June 24 -28), 2001), ACM Press, 464.

[13] Marlino, M., Sumner, T.R., Fulker, D., Manduca, C. and Mogk, D. The Digital Library for Earth System Education: Building Community, Building the Library. *Communications of the ACM, Special Issue on Digital Libraries (May)*. 80-81.

[14] NRC. Transforming Undergraduate Education in Science, Mathematics, Engineering, and Technology Education, National Research Council, National Academy Press, Washington DC, 1999, 113.

[15] NSF. Shaping the Future: New Expectations for Undergraduate Education in Science, Mathematics, Engineering, and Technology, National Science Foundation, Arlington, VA, 1996.

[16] Recker, M., Dorward, J. and Nelson, L. Discovery and Use of Digital Library Learning Resources: Case Study Findings. *Submitted for publication*.

[17] Sumner, T., Buckingham Shum, S., Wright, M., Bonnardel, N., Chevalier, A. and Piolat, A. Redesigning the Peer Review Process: A Developmental Theory-in-Action. in Dieng, R., Giboin, A., Karsenty, L. and De Michelis, G. eds. *Designing Cooperative Systems: The Use of Theories and Models*, IOS Press, Amsterdam, 2000, 19-34.

[18] Sumner, T.R. and Dawe, M., Looking at Digital Library Usability from a Reuse Perspective. in *ACM/IEEE Joint Conference on Digital Libraries (JCDL '01)*, (Roanoke, Virginia (June 24 -28), 2001), ACM Press, 416-425.

[19] Sumner, T.R., Dawe, M. and Devaul, H. Creating Reusable Educational Components: Lessons from DLESE. *Journal of Geoscience Education, 50* (1 (January)). 25-30.

[20] Zia, L.L. The NSF National Science, Technology, Engineering, and Mathematics Education Digital Library (NSDL) program: New projects and a progress report. *D-Lib Magazine, 7* (11).

Integrating Digital Libraries into Learning Environments: The *LEBONED* Approach

Frank Oldenettel, Michael Malachinski, Dennis Reil
Oldenburger Forschungs- und Entwicklungsinstitut für
Informatik-Werkzeuge und -Systeme (OFFIS)
Escherweg 2, 26121 Oldenburg, Germany
{frank.oldenettel, michael.malachinski, dennis.reil}@offis.de

Abstract

This paper presents the project LEBONED that focuses on the integration of digital libraries and their contents into web-based learning environments. We describe in general how the architecture of a standard learning management system has to be modified to enable the integration of digital libraries. An important part of this modification is the LEBONED Metadata Architecture which depicts the handling of metadata and documents imported from digital libraries. The main components of this architecture and their interrelation are presented in detail. Afterwards we show a practical application of the concepts described before: The integration of the digital library eVerlage into the learning management system Blackboard.

1 Introduction

With the permanently growing expansion of the internet, more and more people get access to world wide information resources and realise the internet as a medium which can be used for learning. Temporal and local independence of students during their learning process are considered as the most important benefits of web-based learning. Schools and universities in Europe and the USA are already creating and offering study courses via the internet for a few years [25, 27]. [9] predicts that until 2005 virtual universities will influence the area of e-learning significantly. This initiated the development of numerous web-based learning environments. In these web portals, students can work with electronic teaching materials, join online courses, pass tests, and communicate with other students or instructors. These services are provided by a so-called *Learning Management System (LMS)*. It consists of several components representing different services to be used within a learning environment, like presentation and admin-

istration of online courses or testing and assessment functionalities. Detailed descriptions of functionality and architecture of LMS can be found in [8, 25]. One of these web-based LMS is, for example, the *Blackboard Learning System* (http://www.blackboard.com) by Blackboard Inc., which besides the described components especially provides a so-called *Building Blocks*-framework for customisation and interoperability (see 3.1).

An important requirement described by [25] is the integration of external knowledge management resources into LMS. It seems obvious that *digital libraries* are predestinated for this purpose because materials of many digital libraries are valuable for learning. For example, the contents of the digital libraries of the *Association for Computing Machinery* (ACM, http://www.acm.org/dl) and the *IEEE Computer Society* (http://www.computer.org/publications/dlib) can be used for higher education and scientific research. The digital repository of the *Massachusetts Institute of Technology* (MIT), called *DSpace* (http://www.dspace.org), stores the intellectual output of MIT's faculty and researchers and therefore is an important source of knowledge for other researchers and students. The collections of the *New Zealand Digital Library* (NZDL, http://www.nzdl.org) contain a large number of documents addressing numerous themes and include many multimedia materials like audio and video clips. A digital library we especially are taking into consideration is *eVerlage* [20]. This digital library mainly contains high quality literature for higher education and as shown in [19] it is well suited for usage within a learning environment.

A look at the very detailed overview of the state of the art of LMS given by [5] shows that unfortunately none of today's existing LMS is able to fulfil the demand of external knowledge resource integration.

We believe that integrating digital libraries into an LMS will provide benefits for both LMS and digital libraries. On the one hand the availability of teaching materials provided by an LMS could be enlarged by reverting to existing materials. On the other hand, contents of digital libraries could be used in new contexts.

To perform such an integration of digital libraries into LMS, some special problems have to be considered.

One major problem is the nonexistence of appropriate interface components to access heterogenous digital libraries. In particular, most existing digital libraries offer a web interface for search and retrieval of documents only. This is suitable for a human user, but it makes automatic access to the digital library from an LMS difficult.

Another important problem is that adequate descriptions by domain specific metadata are needed to store and manage *learning objects* (document or document component associated with metadata) in the content repository of the LMS. Since most digital libraries are originally not designed to be part of an LMS, they are only able to provide bibliographic metadata for the contained documents. But in this context, e-learning specific metadata like learning topics or difficulty level is needed and therefore has to be added before an imported document can be used.

At last, file formats and structures of the documents contained in digital libraries have been chosen appropriate to publication aspects rather than learning aspects. As a result, most documents delivered from digital libraries are monolithic with poor physical structuring, i. e. they consist only of a single file (e. g. in PDF format) even if they feature a complex logical structure (e. g. chapters, sections, images, etc.). For learning purposes, it would be more appropriate to directly access separate subparts of a document as single learning objects. This would also support the reuse of existing document components in new contexts, which enables the efficient creation of new and specific learning materials. For this reason, it is suitable to fragment such monolithic documents physically into several smaller components. This is, in fact, a hard technical problem that is ignored by most common LMS, too.

To enable the integration of digital libraries into LMS and solve the described problems, we initiated the project *LEBONED* (*Learning Environment Based on Non Educational Digital Libraries*), which is completely funded by the *DFG* (*Deutsche Forschungsgemeinschaft*), the German Research Council, and runs from April 2002 until March 2004. Our main goal is the development of a methodology to integrate digital libraries into LMS. Additionally, we are developing an infrastructure and some essential tools in order to support this task. Because integration of digital libraries will influence several aspects of a conventional LMS in a significant manner, one of our most important sub goals is the refinement and extension of an LMS reference architecture for the integration of digital libraries. For this aim we rely on existing technologies and if necessary we will adapt them to our needs. The main scientific question for us is to find an holistic solution for the integration task. In this context we concentrate on technical aspects. Legal issues (e. g. copyright) are also important, but beyond the scope of this project.

The resulting architecture is the main aspect of this contribution. An overview of this architecture is presented in the next section, while Sect. 2.2 takes a closer look at the process of document and metadata import and their further processing. Sect. 3 describes an application of the metadata architecture where we present the integration of the digital library *eVerlage* into the LMS *Blackboard*. The fourth section shows the relation of our work to other activities in the areas of digital libraries, e-learning and metadata research and the last section closes this contribution with an outlook.

2 Architecture of an integrative LMS

2.1 Generalised view

The integration of digital libraries into LMS requires some modifications and extensions of existing standard LMS components (Fig. 1, patterned) as well as the addition of components (Fig. 1, white).

At first, modifications have to be made to the *content repository*. This central component is responsible for the management of the electronic teaching materials, i. e. learning objects are stored and administrated here. Since different digital libraries may provide very heterogenous kinds of documents, the *content repository* (see also 2.2.4) must be able to handle all relevant document types (e. g. text, graphics, hypermedia, audio, video, etc.) and data formats (e. g. PDF, JPG, HTML, WAVE, MPEG etc.).

Another component which also belongs to a conventional LMS architecture but differs in an integrative LMS is the *search and retrieval component*. It has to provide search and retrieval functionalities for both the local content repository and external resources like digital libraries. The *search and retrieval component* has to encapsulate both kinds of information resources in order to enable unitary access to them.

The additional *wrapper* components are used to connect the digital libraries to the LMS. Since each of these external systems provides its own interface for access, one specific wrapper is needed for each library. The wrappers get search queries (initiated by the user) from the *search and retrieval component* and pass them to the digital libraries. If documents from the query results shall be used within the learning environment, the *document import component* initiates the wrapper of the respective digital library to access these documents. At the same time, the *metadata import and conversion component* requests metadata so that documents together with corresponding meta information can be gathered into the *content repository*. This procedure and the

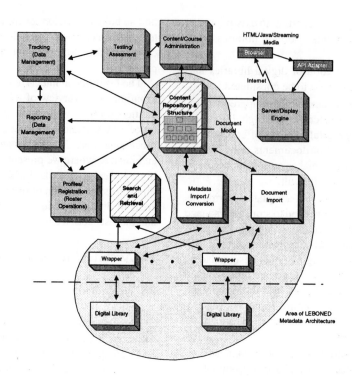

Figure 1. Abstract architecture of an LMS with additional integrative components

interaction of the components mentioned here is described in detail in the LEBONED Metadata Architecture.

2.2 LEBONED metadata architecture

Our LEBONED Metadata Architecture represents just a specific part within a whole integrative LMS architecture and is indicated through the grey area in Figure 1. The *search and retrieval component* was held apart from this area because the processing described by our Metadata Architecture starts at the point where concrete documents shall be imported into the *content repository* of the LMS. At this point the search procedure is already done and the desired documents were already chosen from the query results. Figure 2 shows an illustration of the architecture that will be described in the following.

2.2.1 Wrapper components

The import procedure starts with the wrappers that get the desired documents as well as the corresponding metadata from the digital libraries. The documents are directly forwarded to the *document import component* of the LMS. The corresponding metadata usually is in a format specific for each digital library, but the wrappers have to ensure that they provide imported metadata in a unitary form to the LMS. The wrappers convert the metadata into a simple in-

termediate format that supports generic bibliographic metadata but not e-learning aspects.

This intermediate metadata format is a XML representation conform to the *Metadata Encoding and Transmission Standard* (*METS*, http://www.loc.gov/mets). METS is an initiative of the *Digital Library Federation* (*DLF*, http://www.diglib.org) and is promoted by the *Library of Congress (LOC)*. We decided to use METS because it is a well structured and very simple format. Since it defines no own metadata descriptors, it is very flexible to use with other standards like Dublin Core, MARC or EAD [10]. This means metadata descriptors of these standards can be encoded directly within a METS document. Short and simple meta descriptions with Dublin Core descriptors are as well possible as large and complex encodings with MARC descriptors. Because EAD is as complex as MARC but can be encoded in XML very easily, we decided to use EAD descriptors within the METS format.

As a result, the wrappers could be kept light-weighted and could also be used to connect digital libraries to other applications than LMS.

2.2.2 Document and metadata import components

The next level above the wrappers is built by the *metadata import and conversion component* and the *document import component*. These components load the metadata descriptions delivered by the wrappers and the corresponding doc-

282

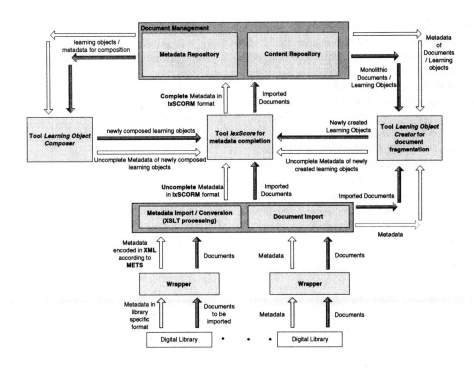

Figure 2. Abstract architecture for metadata and document import

uments respectively. The *metadata import and conversion component* performs another conversion on the metadata and translates it from the intermediate XML format into the final metadata format that is more suitable for learning needs. This final metadata format corresponds to the *document model* on which the *document management* (see Sect. 2.2.4) is based. A document model is a fine-grained data model which describes metadata and structural information (e. g. chapters, sections, images etc.) about documents and facilitates the access to separate document components. Therefore the final metadata format is a very important part of the presented architecture and will be described in more detail in the following.

In general, the metadata format has to be flexible and extensive enough to describe the numerous heterogenous document types and data formats which may be delivered by arbitrary digital libraries. Furthermore, when using documents from digital libraries for learning purposes some special features have to be considered to enable the appropriate description and use of these documents.

On the one hand, bibliographic aspects have to be considered. This requirement is fulfilled by the mentioned bibliographic standards in different ways depending on the intended field of application. A minimalist amount of bibliographic metadata elements is given by Dublin Core (see [14]) while MARC ([12]) or EAD ([2]) provide very extensive descriptions. Because of the complexity of the latter

ones, they are predestinated to fulfil bibliographic requirements.

On the other hand, for learning aspects more meta information is needed. The existence of metadata elements which describe e. g. the *difficulty level* of a document or the estimated *learning time* are very important. Such elements (and many more) are part of the e-learning metadata standards *Learning Object Metadata* (*LOM*, http://ltsc.ieee.org/wg12) [16], *Instructional Management Systems Project* (*IMS*, http://www.imsproject.org), *ARIADNE* (http://www.ariadne-eu.org) and *Sharable Content Object Reference Model* (*SCORM* , http://www.adlnet.org) [8]. These metadata standards even support minimalist bibliographic aspects. We decided to use SCORM as a basis for the final metadata format, because all these standards are very similar and SCORM was built upon the results of a cooperation between the institutions behind these standards and others. Therefore we believe that SCORM is the most well-engineered one of the standards.

Normally, authoring of teaching materials is done from scratch. In this case, learning objects are created and combined with each other in order to define the physical and logical structures of these teaching materials. For the corresponding metadata descriptions SCORM builds a very comprehensive standard which covers all relevant aspects. It classifies descriptors in nine categories (*General*, *Lifecycle*, *Meta-metadata*, *Technical*, *Educational*, *Rights*, *Rela-*

tion, Annotation, Classification). But the creation of learning objects from monolithic documents delivered by digital libraries is different from this normal way of authoring because, as mentioned in Sect. 1, these documents are originally not designed to be used within LMS. A standard for the corresponding metadata description has to meet some strong requirements that are not fulfilled by SCORM. So we developed *lxSCORM (leboned extended SCORM)* that contains some extensions of SCORM which are indispensable in order to satisfy these demands (original specification see [7]). All extensions are declared as additional descriptor elements. None of the existing elements was modified in order to keep lxSCORM downwards compatible to the original standard. In the following we give some short examples of lxSCORM elements.

- *lxType (Category General):* Because it is helpful to know whether a certain learning object is autonomous or part of an originally more complex document, this descriptor indicates that the described learning object has emanated from the fragmentation of an originally monolithic document.

- *Begin, End (Technical):* For instance, it may be that a monolithic document cannot or shall not be fragmented physically (separated into several files) according to its complete logical structure (chapter, section, image etc.). If a file representing a document component is logically structured, it should be possible to describe the logical structure with metadata by defining several learning objects. With SCORM attribute *Location* it is possible to relate several learning objects to one physical resource, but it is difficult to declare which learning object is assigned to which part of the internal structure of the resource. Therefore lxSCORM defines two additional elements *Begin* and *End* which can be used to declare where the described subpart begins and where it ends. This is useful e. g. if several sections of a book shall be described by several learning objects.

- *Origin (Technical):* It is often useful for further searches to know the source from which a certain learning object was received. Therefore, this container indicates from which digital library the described learning objects was delivered. The subelement *Locator* stores a locator to the origin. Normally this would be an URL. The subelement *Query* stores the query that was used to get the document from which the described learning object was created.

- *Technical Quality (Technical):* For several purposes, the technical quality of the content presentation is important, e. g. content which shall be printed has to be presented in a higher resolution than content that

shall be displayed on a screen. This element contains several items in order to describe the technical quality of the resource. The subelement *Level* stores an abstract description (low, medium, high) of the technical quality level. Since quality is described differently depending on the document type, the subelement *Type* describes the quality by a specific keyword (resolution, sample rate, frame rate). It depends on the media type. The third subelement *Value* is a concrete value depending on the *type* element.

- *Extended Learning Resource Type (Educational):* For learners it is very important to distinguish e. g. between books, articles, proceedings, journals, newspapers, audio sequences, or video films in order to be able to choose the appropriate one for a specific learning task. This descriptor provides a more detailed vocabulary than the original SCORM element (*Learning Resource Type*) and thus enables a more concrete specification of the document type.

- *Original document (Relation):* If element *lxType (General)* indicates that the described learning object emanates from an originally monolithic document, this element stores a reference to this document. It has to be used alternatively to the original SCORM element *Kind (Relation)*

2.2.3 lexSCORE

The metadata converted into the final format lxSCORM by the *metadata import and conversion component* must be considered as incomplete, because, as already mentioned in Sect. 1, digital libraries are only able to deliver bibliographic information. E-learning-specific information must be added in order to complete the metadata descriptions. The tool *lexSCORE* supports a human user to add this missing metadata. *lexSCORE* loads the incomplete metadata description as well as entire documents or even single learning objects. By presenting the content of the documents or learning objects and the corresponding metadata fields, it enables comfortable and efficient input of lacking information. An example screenshot of this process is presented in figure 3.

Afterwards, *lexSCORE* exports complete metadata descriptions presented in the lxSCORM metadata format and initiates the storage in the *metadata repository*.

2.2.4 Document management

The *document management* component represents the functionality which was described in Sect. 2 generally as *content repository*. Considered in more detail, the *document management* consists of a *content repository* as well as a

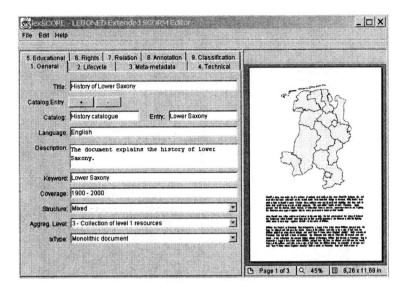

Figure 3. Prototype of *lexSCORE*

metadata repository. Within the *content repository* all documents are stored physically. This may be implemented in the form of a database or a file system where the files of the documents are stored. The management of the documents is mainly based on the *metadata repository*. Here all relevant information about the documents is stored and administrated on basis of a document model which is described according to the lxSCORM metadata format. The *metadata repository* is the most important component for search and retrieval of teaching materials and therefore frequently consulted by the *search and retrieval component*.

After a complete metadata description in lxSCORM format has been created with the tool *lexSCORE*, the *content repository* stores the imported document and the corresponding metadata description in the *metadata repository*. At this point, the import process of documents and metadata from a digital library is completed. The documents are available for further processing and may be fragmented into several document components from which new learning objects can be created. Fragmentation is done with copies of the original versions only and the resulted document components will be stored additionally.

2.2.5 Further document processing

Figure 2 contains further paths leading to the two software tools *Learning Object Creator* and *Learning Object Composer*. These paths represent further processing of imported documents and learning objects.

As mentioned in Sect. 1, most documents imported from digital libraries consist only of a single file, independent of their logical structure. Fragmentation of such monolithic documents into several smaller components would enable

more appropriate and flexible use and reuse of a document's content for learning tasks. Imagine, for example, the common case of a digital book published as a single PDF file. The book consists of several chapters spread over several pages. It may also contain some images or even multimedia supplements like audio or video clips. In a common LMS, the entire PDF file may be used as one learning object. But what if only a certain chapter of the book is of interest? Or even an image within that chapter? And what if these components should be reused in another context, e. g. by combining them with components from another book?

To satisfy these demands, we are developing the graphical software tool *LEBONED Learning Object Creator* whose main task is to support the extraction of smaller components from monolithic documents in order to create separate learning objects for these. The tool provides functionality to semi-automatically identify contained components and document structures within a document as a first step. Proceeding from a computer-based analysis of the original document's internal structure, the *LEBONED Learning Object Creator* enables the user as second step to extract the desired pieces from a document in a common file format and to use these as new learning objects. The tool supports different document types and the corresponding common file formats like print and web publishing formats (HTML, PDF, PostScript, RTF), audio formats (Wave, MP3) and video formats (MPEG, Quicktime, AVI Video). Figure 4 shows a screenshot of the *LEBONED Learning Object Creator*-prototype with an automatically analysed example PDF document. Its separate pages and the contained images can be extracted for further use as new learning objects.

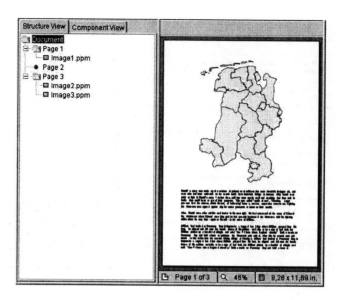

Figure 4. Example PDF document with automatically identified components

The second tool *LEBONED Learning Object Composer*, which hasn't been developed yet, will provide functionality to compile single learning objects to more complex ones. This enables the creation of new learning materials by reusing existing document components from different contexts. The user can select the desired sheet layout for the new learning object from a set of predefined layouts. These layouts determine the basic look of a sheet by defining a spatial division into separate blocks. Each block can be filled with content by selecting the desired component from the pool of existing materials in the *content repository*. It shall be possible to use components of different document types and file formats together on the same sheet and thereby create complex learning materials.

For any learning object created with the *LEBONED Learning Object Creator* and the *LEBONED Learning Object Composer*, a complete lxSCORM metadata description has to be produced before it can be stored in the *document management*. For this purpose, a basic metadata description is generated automatically based on the input metadata of the processed learning objects and documents. This basic description and the new learning objects are passed to *lexSCORE* for manual correction and addition of metadata and will be stored in the *document management* afterwards.

3 Application of the LEBONED metadata architecture

The LEBONED architecture for metadata and document processing, as described in the previous sections, was applied as an example of use to the digital library eVerlage and the widely spread learning management system Black-

board. The architecture and services of eVerlage were introduced in serveral papers like [19, 20].

eVerlage was augmented by a web services interface in [24]. This extension was done by a new component, a so-called *user agent*, which provides several web services.

These digital library services based on web services technology were used for the integration into the Blackboard-system. [24] also describes how to use the web services interface for integrating other digital libraries. As figure 2 shows, there has to be a wrapper for every integrated digital library. In the special case of the eVerlage-integration into Blackboard, this wrapper is built in the form of some web services exposing the necessary functionality. In the following, we give a short introduction of Blackboard and the so called Building Blocks programming interface.

3.1 Blackboard learning management system and Building Blocks

Blackboard is a widely dispersed learning management system. As mentioned before, figure 1 shows the adopted generalized architecture of such a system. Most of the shown components can also be found in the architecture of Blackboard, so it follows the general LMS architecture and can be mapped to it. The core application is provided by perl-files or perl-modules. These modules divide the system into several smaller components similar to the basic architecture. As an addition to the perl-core, there is an application server for system extensions.

Such an extension is possible by so called *Building Blocks*. A Building Block is a special web application and similar to an ordinary Java web application. It uses the

Building Blocks API for accessing the data and services of Blackboard. In addition to a conventional web application with Java Server Pages (JSP), a Building Block consists of a XML description for Blackboard-specific configuration options, especially the entry point of the Building Block. An entry point is the starting point where the extension is shown in the learning management system, e.g. the course control panel, the system administration panel, the communication area. Another option is the description whether the extension is a tool or a content handler. There are also two types of possible Building Blocks regarding the use of external servers:

- plug-in:
  A plug-in Building Block only uses the Blackboard system without connecting to any external server.

- bridge:
  Building Blocks are called bridges when they provide functionality which relies on external servers, e.g. like in our example of use, a digital library.

3.2 Integration of eVerlage into Blackboard

The integration of eVerlage into Blackboard was conceptualized by a bridge Building Block. This bridge uses web services technology to connect to the digital library eVerlage. It will easily be possible to integrate several other digital library systems.

[24] describes a concept for doing a transparent integration of these systems. The user of such services will not know which systems were integrated into Blackboard. It is completely transparent to the user and therefore the usage and especially the user interface is the same for any integrated digital library.

Figure 5 shows an example of our prototype. A basic search form was integrated with the result of such a search below it. Users can then choose a document from the result list and download it from eVerlage. The integration of eVerlage into the Blackboard LMS according to the Metadata Architecture (Sect. 2.2) is shown in figure 6. A Building Block acts as wrapper and connects eVerlage to the *document and metadata import components*.

Another Building Block plug-in provides an user interface to the bridge Building Block. This is not shown in figure 6, because as mentioned before, the metadata architecture starts at the point where concrete documents shall be imported into the content repository of the LMS.

On the left side of figure 6 two main components were added. The digital library eVerlage is on the bottom. It consists of the main system and an additional web services interface (see [24] for a detailed description) called *eVerlageWS*. *eVerlageWS* provides several digital library services like a search service or a document delivery service.

This interface can also be seen as a kind of wrapper as it hides the native API of eVerlage by exposing XML methods. Such a wrapper has to be written for any other digital library system which shall be integrated into Blackboard.

This web services interface is used by the bridge integrated into the Blackboard system. The Building Block uses a protocol from the web services stack (see [15]) to communicate with *eVerlageWS*. The metadata transmitted between these two components is in an *eVerlageWS*-specific XML-based metadata format and will be converted into METS conforming data using XSLT.

Both the converted metadata and the corresponding document are forwarded to the *document and metadata import component* as shown in figure 6. The further processing was already described in Sect. 2.2.

4 Related work

One of the major activities to be named first is the *ARIADNE* project which is funded by the European Union Commission. This project also deals with interconnected knowledge pools. But the integration of existing digital libraries is considered not as detailed as our project does, therefore our work will be an adequate addition to this.

Furthermore, several existing LMS have to be mentioned. [5] gives a comprehensive overview of the state of the art. As shown in Sect. 3 special attention was paid to the LMS *Blackboard*.

Because major activities of our work are dealing with metadata, works about the different standards have to be considered. [11] for instance describes the adaptive hypermedia system *Multibook* used to teach multimedia technology. This application uses metadata to create course sequences semi-automatically. What especially has to be mentioned in the context of document models is the work of the UC Berkeley that has developed the *Multivalent Document Model (MVD)*. The aim of this document model is to support annotations and cooperative work on documents [29]. The goal of the *CUBER* project is to develop a system that supports learners in searching higher education materials from European universities. In this project, metadata also plays an important role and the work also led to modifications of the original LOM schema [22]. Another work described in [26] considers the reusability and adaptability aspects of interactive multimedia content in web-based learning systems. Here dynamic metadata has to be managed which also made extensions of the LOM schema necessary.

Besides metadata standards there is also a standard provided by *IMS* dealing with distributed information resources. This standard is called *IMS Digital Repository Interoperability* and specifies how to access to distributed learning object repositories. Since this specification de-

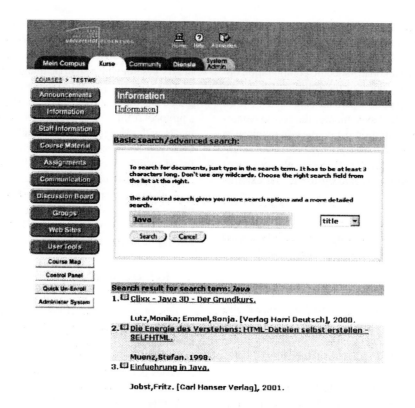

Figure 5. Integrated eVerlage in Blackboard

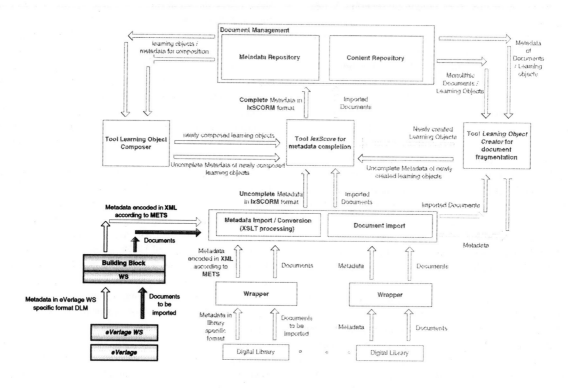

Figure 6. Adapted metadata architecture for the integration of eVerlage into Blackboard

clares concrete technologies like Z39.50, XQUERY and SOAP, which are not supported by many digital libraries yet and assumes that the repositories already contain well defined learning objects [6], it is not applicable for our purpose.

In the area of digital library research (see e. g. [3]) we are touching the aspect of distributed digital libraries. The *New Zealand Digital Library* (*NZDL*, http://www.nzdl.org) project of the university of Waikato, New Zealand, has developed the software suite *Greenstone*. It enables users to create own distributed digital library collections [4]. Another digital library distributed over all campuses of the University of California is the *California Digital Library* (*CDL*, http://www.cdlib.org). One goal of this project is the seamless integration of distributed resources and providing access to them [17]. Very closely related to the CDL is the *Stanford Digital Library Technologies Project* (http://www-diglib.stanford.edu) which created the *InfoBus* technology. InfoBus is a CORBA based infrastructure that enables the integration of distributed heterogeneous digital library collections [21]. Because of the high flexibility of the InfoBus technology, it is taken into special consideration for our work. This applies for the *DAFFODIL* project, too. DAFFODIL is an initiative of the university of Dortmund, Germany. The main goal is to develop an agent-based infrastructure for federated digital libraries [13]. Futhermore several digital libraries providing content valuable for learning purposes have to be considered. These are for instance the systems mentioned here and which were already named in Sect. 1. But there is much larger number of digital libraries available via internet, which provide content that can be used for learning tasks. Generally spoken, all of these digital libraries are potential candidates for closer consideration in order to connect them to an integrative LMS.

A project dealing with infrastructures and tools for the reuse of learning objects is *Teachware on Demand* (http://www.teachware-on-demand.de). Goal of this project is the automatic composition of user-specific learning materials from existing fragments (like text, images or videos). The aim of the *Connexions Project* (http://cnx.rice.edu) is to facilitate the development of educational content. The main technology developed by this initiative is *CNXML* which is a 'lightweight XML markup language' for storing educational content [23]. Unlike our project, these projects assume that learning units are created from scratch and do not consider the fragmentation of existing monolithic documents.

Much work has been done in the field of document analysis. In contrast to our approach, most of these solutions are based on the analysis of document images. An overview of such algorithms for layout detection is given in [18], a work dealing with the recognition of logical structures in document images is [28]. An approach for document analysis based on page description languages is AIDAS that deals with the identification of the logical structure of PDF documents [1].

5 Conclusions and further work

In this contribution we presented some results of the project LEBONED. The main goal of this project is to find a general solution for the integration of digital libraries into LMS. We briefly described how an original LMS architecture has to be modified to enable the integration task. The developed LEBONED Metadata Architecture is an important part of such a modification. It provides a solution for the handling of metadata and documents during the document import and further processing. Here, one important step is the development of lxSCORM. It takes the special requirements into consideration that occur when working with documents imported from digital libraries.

In the same context, the fragmentation of monolithic documents into several learning objects and the composition of them to new learning objects is a basic prerequisite for the appropriate use and reuse of learning materials. The tools *lexSCORE*, *Learning Object Creator*, and *Learning Object Composer* provide solutions for this problem and enables the efficient and flexible creation of new learning materials based on existing documents.

With the integration of the *eVerlage* digital library into the LMS *Blackboard* we presented a concrete application of our concepts we described before. At this time this integration is not much more than a prototype, because work on several aspects is still in progress.

Currently the metadata format lxSCORM is implemented almost completely, but we are still researching wether there are any further requirements which only could be fulfilled by additional elements. Furthermore the described concepts and solutions to identify and physically extract components from monolithic documents are almost completely implemented. All this is most important preparatory work for the development of *lexSCORE* and the *Learning Object Creator* which are currently implemented as prototypes. The *Learning Object Composer* is not implemented yet.

Furthermore, we are working on other aspects of the metadata architecture that were not considered in detail here. For the wrappers we are currently developing a generic framework which will reduce the effort of implementation of further wrappers to a minimum. The LEBONED Metadata Architecture is only one part of the entire integrative LMS architecture that will be implemented in the near future.

At last, we will note down all our experience of the LEBONED project into a process model which will describe the whole integration process. This shall give advise for future intentions of digital library integration into LMS.

References

[1] A. Anjewierden. AIDAS: Incremental logical structure discovery in PDF documents. In *6th International Conference on Document Analysis and Recognition (ICDAR)*, pages 374–378, Seattle, September 2001.

[2] S. o. A. Archivists. Application Guidelines for Version 1.0 - Encoded Archival Description (EAD) - Document Type Definition (DTD), Version 1.0 - Technical Document No. 3. http://lcweb.loc.gov/ead/ag/aghome.html, Society of American Archivists, 1999.

[3] W. Y. Arms. *Digital Libraries*. MIT Press, 2000.

[4] D. Bainbridge, D. McKay, and I. H. Witten. Greenstone Digital Library - Developer's Guide. Manual, University of Waikato, New Zealand, Okt. 2001 2001.

[5] P. Baumgartner, H. Häferle, and K. Maier-Häferle. *E-Learning Praxishandbuch - Auswahl von Lernplattformen*. StudienVerlag, 2002.

[6] I. G. L. Consortium. IMS Digital Repositories Interoperability - Core Functions Information Model. Specification, IMS Global Learning Consortium, Inc., 16 July 2002 2002.

[7] P. Dodds. Sharable Content Object Reference Model (SCORM) - Version 1.2 - The SCORM Content Aggregation Model. Specification, Advanced Distributed Learning (ADL), 1st Oct. 2001 2001.

[8] P. Dodds. Sharable Content Object Reference Model (SCORM) - Version 1.2 - The SCORM Overview. Specification, Advanced Distributed Learning (ADL), 1st Oct. 2001 2001.

[9] J. Encarnaçao, W. Leidhold, and A. Reuter. Szenario: Die Universität im Jahre 2005. In B. Stiftung and H. N. Stiftung, editors, *Studium online: Hochschulentwicklung durch neue Medien*. 1999.

[10] D. L. Federation. METS: An Overview and Tutorial. http://www.loc.gov/standards/mets/metsoverview.html, Digital Library Federation, 2002.

[11] S. Fischer. Course and exercise sequencing using metadata in adaptive hypermedia learning systems. *Journal of Educational Resources in Computing (JERIC)*, 1(1es):5, 2001.

[12] B. Furrie. *Understanding Marc Bibliographic: Machine-Readable Cataloging*. Library of Congress, 6th edition (january 2001) edition, 2001.

[13] N. Gövert, N. Fuhr, and C.-P. Klas. Daffodil: Distributed Agents for User-Friendly Access of Digital Libraries. In *European Conference on Digital Libraries (ECDL)*, pages 352–355, 2000.

[14] D. C. M. Initiative. Dublin Core Metadata Element Set, Version 1.1: Reference Description. http://dublincore.org/documents/1999/07/02/dces/, Dublin Core Metadata Initiative, 1999.

[15] H. Kreger. Web Services Conceptual Architecture (WSCA 1.0). 2001. Access: 13.12.2002.

[16] I. Learning Technology Standardization Committee. Draft Standard for Learning Object Metadata. Draft Standard IEEE P1484.12/D6.1, Institute of Electrical and Electronics Engineers, Inc., 18.April 2001.

[17] J. Ober. The California Digital Library. *D-Lib Magazine*, 5(3), 1999.

[18] O. Okun, D. Doermann, and M. Pietikäinen. Page segmentation and zone classification: a brief analysis of algorithms. In *Information Science Innovations (ISI'2001)*, Proc. of the International Workshop on Document Image Analysis and Understanding, pages 98–104, American University in Dubai, March 2001. UAE.

[19] F. Oldenettel. Eine digitale Bibliothek für den virtuellen Campus - Das eVerlage-System. In E. Wagner and M. Kindt, editors, *Virtueller Campus Szenarien - Strategien - Studium*, pages 345 – 354, Hildesheim, 2001. Waxmann Verlag.

[20] F. Oldenettel. Das eVerlage-System: Eine digitale Bibliothek für kostenpflichtige wissenschaftliche Verlagsprodukte. In K. P. Jantke, W. S. Wittig, and J. Herrmann, editors, *Leipziger Informatik Tage (LIT) 2002*, pages 246 – 257, Leipzig, 2002. infix Verlag.

[21] A. Paepke, M. Baldonado, C.-C. K. Chang, S. Cousins, and H. Garcia-Molina. Building the InfoBus: A Review of Technical Choices in the Stanford Digital Library Project. Working paper, Stanford University, 18. Jan. 2000.

[22] P. Pöyry, K. Pelto-Aho, and J. Puustjärvi. The role of metadata in the CUBER system. In *Proceedings of the 2002 annual research conference of the South African institute of computer scientists and information technologists on Enablement through technology*, ACM International Conference Proceeding Series, pages 172–178, Port Elizabeth, South Africa, 2002. South African Institute for Computer Scientists and Information Technologists.

[23] R. Radaelli-Sanchez. The Basic CNXML. Tutorial, The Connexions Project, 2002.

[24] D. Reil. Konzeption Digitaler Bibliotheksdienste auf Basis von Web Services. Master's thesis, Universitaet Oldenburg, 2002. (in german).

[25] M. J. Rosenberg. *e-Learning - Strategies for Delivering Knowledge in the Digital Age*. McGraw-Hill, 2001.

[26] A. E. Saddik, S. Fischer, and R. Steinmetz. Reusability and adaptability of interactive resources in Web-based educational systems. *Journal of Educational Resources in Computing (JERIC)*, 1(1es):4, 2001.

[27] R. Schulmeister. *Virtuelle Universität, Virtuelles Lernen*. Oldenbourg Verlag, 2001.

[28] K. Summers. *Automatic Discovery of Logical Document Structure*. PhD thesis, Cornell Computer Science Department, 1998. Technical Report TR98-1698.

[29] R. Wilensky and T. A. Phelps. Multivalent Documents: A New Model for Digital Documents. Tech. Report CSD-98-999, University of California, Berkeley, 1998.

The Interactive Shared Educational Environment: User Interface, System Architecture and Field Study

Xiangming Mu, Gary Marchionini, and Amy Pattee
School of Information and Library Science
University of North Carolina at Chapel Hill
{mux, march}@ils.unc.edu, patta@email.unc.edu

Abstract

The user interface and system architecture of a novel Interactive Shared Educational Environment (ISEE) are presented. Based on a lightweight infrastructure, ISEE enables relatively low bandwidth network users to share videos as well as text messages. Smartlink is a new concept introduced in this paper. Individual information presentation components, like the video player and text chat room, are "smartly" linked together through video timestamps and hyperlinks. A field study related to children book selections using ISEE was conducted. The results indicated that the combination of three information presentation components, including video player with storyboard, shared browser, and text chat room, provided an effective and more comfortable collaboration and learning environment for the given tasks than text reviews or text chat alone or in combination. The video player was the most preferred information component. Text comments in the chat room that did not synchronize with the video content distracted some participants due to limited cognitive capacity. Using smartlink to synchronize various information components or "channels" is our attempt to reduce the user's working memory load in information enriched distance learning environments made possible by digital libraries.

1. Introduction

Distance learning separates learners from instructors in space and/or time. Various web-based communication technologies have been adopted in distance learning to connect instructors and learners. Email, hypertext web pages, online forums, email-lists, and Bulletin Board Systems (BBS) are examples of some widely used technologies in current distance learning systems, like the Blackboard system [24]. The increase network bandwidth and computer technology also makes multimedia content such as video and real-time communication and interactive TV, to be incorporated into distance learning. Digital libraries are especially helpful in providing rich content for distance education.

Video digital libraries provide especially good potential for distance learning. Video is able to vividly present complex, abstract concepts and microscopic intricacies; to stimulate thought and emotions through evocative drama or documentary; and to capture and replay events [3,10]. The advance of digital libraries and "open" video projects such as the Internet Archive project (http://www.archive.org) and the Open-video project (www.open-video.org), provide an increasing collection of videos that can be directly accessed through the web by remote learners. With these advances, how to take advantage of video to enhance distance learning becomes a new challenge.

Even with the adoption of advanced compression and encoding technology, like Moving Picture Expert Group (MPEG), video is still an expensive medium with respect to the amount of information transferred over the Internet. Thus another challenge in the distance-learning domain is how to enable low bandwidth network users to get benefits from the new multimedia distance learning tools.

As a tradeoff, decreasing the video quality is routinely utilized to guarantee video continuity for low bandwidth connections. However, this approach constrains the applications of the video and limits the benefits provided by high quality videos. Instruction that focuses on details and requires high resolution images will fail under such a environment.

Streaming, a video delivery format using "push" technology that is similar to sending TV programs, is often adopted to broadcast real-time videos over the Internet. Various qualities of the same video are usually provided as different channels for users to select in accordance with their particular network connection speeds. However, the drawback is that streaming is a one-way technology and few interaction functions are supported. For example, users are not allowed to freely roll back the video player to re-view the past content or forward the video to preview.

Based on a new text-based communication protocol, the Interactive Shared Educational Environment (ISEE) is a novel multimedia distance learning and collaboration tool that is specifically designed for low bandwidth network users. Real-time video sharing among learners and instructors, as well as video navigation functions is supported in the ISEE. By seamlessly integrating four information presentation components, including a high quality pre-packaged digital video player, a video storyboard, a shared web browser for video scripts and web pages, and a real-time text chat room, ISEE provides a rich collaborative learning environment for distributed users. Timestamps of the video are utilized to "synchronize" the contents of each individual information component, a concept we refer to as "smartlink". Immense web information is also accessible and sharable with the help of the built-in web browser enabled component.

This paper is organized as follows: after a brief introduction to the related research, the ISEE user interface and its functionalities are introduced. In the following system architecture section, the concept of "smartlink" is proposed and discussed. Finally the results of a field study using ISEE are presented.

2. Related work

Two temporal modes of distance learning are synchronous and asynchronous. In terms of the direction of delivering instruction, distance learning also can be classified into one-way "push" instruction and two-way interactive instruction. Online chat, instant messaging, audio/video conferencing, shared real-time applications, computer supported cooperative work (CSCW) tools, and interactive television (ITV) are examples of two-way synchronized distance learning (Table 1).

New tools have been developed using more than one medium to provide a more effective or customized learning environment. MediaSite Live [15] from Sonic Foundary is a web-based application built on ASP technology that supports one-way video streaming, which is synchronized with associated PowerPoint™ slides. Windows Media Player™ is used in MediaSite Live to present the streaming video. A minimum bandwidth is required for the video playback (240 * 180 with 15fps). No interaction or collaboration functions are supported.

Stanford University's Stanford Online program [19] adopts a similar approach. In addition to asynchronous streaming video, a synchronous videoconference system is also supported for the purpose of two-way interaction.

The Just-In-Time Lecture Project (JIT) developed at Carnegie Mellon University embedded high resolution slides directly into the video to guarantee "synchronization" between slides and video. E-mail is used to link instructors and learners [12].

The BMRC Lecture Browser [2], developed at the UC Berkeley Multimedia Research Center also uses streaming technology. A visual segmented-video bar is added to facilitate video browsing.

Table 1: Media Used in Distance Learning

Modes	One-way	Two-way
Asyn	Hypertext Webpage, Video streaming, Video on demand, CD-R, Video tapes, etc.	Mail, Email, BBS, Fax online Forum, Email list, etc.
Syn	Radio/TV broadcasting, Real-time Streaming, etc.	Instant messaging, Text Chat, Telephone, MUD/MOO*, Audioconferening, Videoconference, Interactive TV, etc.

*Multi-User Domains/ MUD, Object Oriented

eClass [8] from Georgia Tech (formerly called Class 2000) captures class activities using a video camera and an electronic whiteboard, which are integrated together along a timeline. Slides generated from the electronic whiteboard are linked to the timeline for quick reference. One unique contribution of eClass involves creation and use of hyperlinks attached to each slide to connect to the related video segments. HTML and JavaScript are utilized to implement the eClass environment.

Studies [9,17,18,20] have indicated that students who collaboratively watched video outperformed students who attended live lectures in the traditional classroom as well as students who watched live streaming lectures individually in both situations with or without tutors (mediators). The success in these studies is attributed to the encouragement of collaboration. However, most of the distance-learning systems fail to integrate direct supports for collaboration. External communication tools, such as email or online forums, are usually used for information exchanging or sharing.

Videoconferencing systems were chosen by some education systems to facilitate collaboration across users [6, 7, 13, 16, 22] due to their direct support for two-way interaction. Research demonstrated, however, that little benefit is gained from including talking-head video or videoconferencing [4, 5] for communication in the educational domain. Special requirements for video capture and video encoding/decoding equipment limited the range of their applications. In addition, high speed network connectivity is usually necessary for smooth video presentation.

Realizing the importance of two-way communication between the instructor and remote learners, TELEP, developed by Microsoft, added a dialog chat to the one-way video/slide system [11]. Remote users are able to send questions to the presenter directly, and other users can also join the discussion by replying to the question or issuing comments. However, real-time multicast technology used in the TELEP for the video/audio streaming means users not only cannot rollback or navigate the video while watching, but also had to have a multicast enabled network connection, which is not common for most dialup network users.

ISEE is a real-time collaborative multimedia distance learning tool suitable for heterogeneous network connections. ISEE is distinguished by the following characteristics:

- ISEE supports real-time text chat, video playback, video navigation with a storyboard, video synchronization across users, hypertext browsing, web information access, and web site URL sharing. All these functions are integrated together to form a cohesive learning environment.
- Text chat messages, video scripts and video are linked "smartly". With a single click on the timestamp associated with the message presented in the chat window, a user can automatically synchronize or "align" his/her video to the point in the video playing when the sender wrote the message.
- ISEE can be applied to heterogeneous network connections, including slow dialup networks when video content is stored locally.
- ISEE is operating system independent.

3. User interface

A desktop Graphic User Interface (GUI) was designed in ISEE to accommodate various learning and collaboration components. (Fig.1). One of the benefits of this style is that users can customize their learning environment by re-arranging the number, positions, and size of each component in accordance with their personal learning styles. This is particularly useful when multiple communication and learning components are used simultaneously. Another advantage is that it can take full advantage of screen real estate when the users' screen resolutions are high. For example, students can enlarge the relative size of a video player in a high-resolution (1600*1248) monitor to get a better video display rather than using the default size, which is designed for a screen resolution of 1024*768.

Figure 1 presents a sample screenshot of the ISEE user interface. On the top of the interface is a menu bar that contains a series of buttons that can open corresponding sub-panels in the desktop panel beneath: an Interactive Chat Room (ICR) sub-panel, a user profile sub-panel, a video player sub-panel, a storyboard sub-panel, and a Shared Web Browser (SWB) sub-panel. Buttons for selecting a video, logging in, marking time stamps, and other functions are also available.

In Figure 1, the top right of the desktop panel displays the user profile sub-panel, which lists users currently logged in. Beneath it is the Interactive Chat Room (ICR)

sub-panel that allows users to share text chat. The sender's name, timestamp of the video, and the message are displayed. The SWB is located on the left side of the desktop panel to display hypertext documents, which can be shared among users. The video player and storyboard sub-panels are in the middle of the ISEE interface in default mode. Thumbnails of the video frames are displayed on the storyboard for video content navigation. Thumbnails are generated using our procedures developed for the Open Video Digital Library. There is a slider bar just beneath the video player. Users are able to drag the bar to change the current playback point or use it to preview the content of the video quickly.

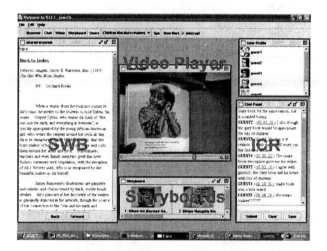

Figure 1: ISEE User Interface

The four learning and communication components are not only juxtaposed together in appearance, but also coherently connected with each other through a mechanism called "smartlink".

4. Smartlinks

Each of the learning and communication components in the ISEE, including ICR, SWB, video player, and storyboards, are "smartly" linked through the video timestamps or hypertext URLs. We refer to this feature as "smartlink". Table 2 lists the current available smartlinks.

In ISEE, the Interactive Chat Room (ICR) is different from the generic online text chat tools in terms of supporting interaction between users via messages. Each message sent by a user contains not only the sender's username and the message content, but also the sender's video timestamp representing the point when the message was sent (Fig. 2). A single click on the timestamp by a particular user immediately updates that user's local video player to the point in the video corresponding to the timestamp. Thus any user who is interested in a particular message is able to share both the text message and the video context associated with the message. Such a mechanism brings convenience to users who want to discuss topics that are tightly associated with the video context. For example, when discussing a video picture book, a message such as "look at the little thing sitting on the nose of the bear, is it a mouse?" makes no sense to another user if he/she cannot share the same scene.

Table 2: Smartlinks Between ISEE Components

	ICR	SWB	Storyboard	Video Player
ICR		yes	no	yes
SWB	yes		no	yes
Storyboard	no	no		yes
Video Player	yes	yes	yes	

ICR also supports hypertext links just like a generic web browser. The hyperlink is formed automatically when the message contains "http", "HTTP", "www" or "WWW". A single left click on such links immediately updates the display content in the SWB with the corresponding web page. With the help of this feature, users are able to take advantage of the immense information resources available in the Internet and share directly within the ISEE environment (Fig.2).

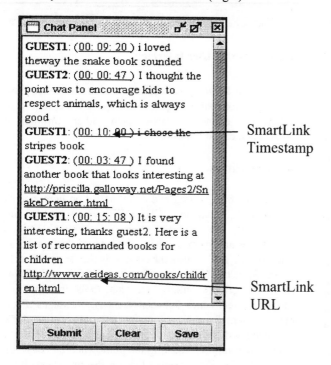

SmartLink Timestamp

SmartLink URL

Figure 2: Chat Room with Smartlink Support

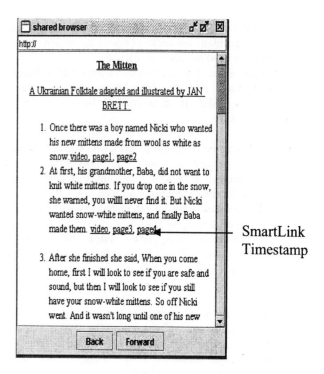

SmartLink Timestamp

Figure 3: Shared Web Browser with Smartlink Support

The Shared Web Browser (SWB) is a built-in web browser we developed using Java. The SWB enables users to share hypertext documentation without leaving the ISEE. One way we have used the SWB in classroom demonstrations is to display session notes and assignments. There are three parts in the SWB panel: On the top is a text field that enables users to provide a URL. Beneath it is the hypertext area used for displaying the content of the URL. On the bottom there are two web page caching buttons that enable users to view the history of browsing. Individual users are able to use SWB to share hypertext documents. When a return key is pressed after a URL is given, not only that user's SWB is updated, other users logged in to the same session are also updated with the same web page referred to by the URL.

Smartlinking between the SWB and the video player is supported in the ISEE. Figure 3 illustrates a sample screenshot of the SWB component in which a transcript of the video generated from the children's book "The Mitten" is presented. Underlined texts in blue are smartlinks that contains the timestamps of the video player. A single left click on the text will immediately update the local video player to begin to playback from the corresponding segment.

5. ISEE System

5.1 Overview

Our practical goal is to design a new multimedia distance-learning environment based on the current computer and network technologies that enables distributed learners with typically modest network connections to get benefits from multimedia resources in digital libraries. Such an environment will allow instructors to develop instruction that takes advantage of video content. Thus, interactions with the video, such as pausing, stopping, and navigating, must be available. Instead of streaming video, we used pre-packaged video (either downloaded outside of class or collaborative study time, or provided on CDs mailed to remote students) to reduce delay and pre-caching time. Of course, a small number of users on an Internet-2 network could use ISEE with distributed video but such situations will remain the exception rather than the rule for some time for distance learning.

The environment itself will enable us to attack our larger goals of understanding how people make sense of video and more specifically how people manage multiple information channels while learning and working. Toward these ends, session logging is built into the ISEE to allow interactions at various levels of granularity to be captured for analysis.

Java was chosen as the development language to achieve interoperability across commonly used platforms. Java Shared Data Toolkits (JSDT) APIs were utilized for information sharing and group communication functions. Java Media Frame (JMF) APIs were used for developing the video related components, including the video player and video storyboards.

5.2 System architecture

Figure 4 illustrates the framework for the ISEE system. The Session Managing Service (SMS) is a daemon service that manages user interactions. Each user registers in the SMS by logging in. Text messages are shared across each registered user via SMS. A database that maps the user names with the Java objects is built in the SMS. Java sockets are used as the communication protocol across each client.

The logging module is a special "user" that logs selected activities within the session. Actions issued by users automatically trigger the "WriteLog" method built into each client. A message that contains the information about the action is sent by the "WriteLog" method to the Logging module, which records the received messages in the backend MySQL database

The MySQL database provides support for both the Login Check Module and the Logging Module. Only authorized users can join the session and share information. Actions and messages captured by the Logging Module are stored in the database for further analysis or system maintenance.

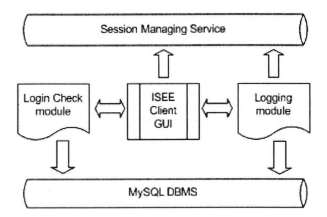

Figure 4: Framework for ISEE Architecture

5.3 Flexibility

A lightweight multimedia communication protocol has been developed for the ISEE to provide flexibility on heterogeneous network connections (Table 3).

Table 3: Communication Protocol in ISEE

Tags	Functions
<Message>… </Message>	Text message from users
<TextColor>…</TextColor>	Text color from users
<Status>…</Status>	Status information from users
<SynVideo> …</SynVideo>	Timestamp from users
<URL>…</URL>	URL from users
<VideoID>…</VideoID>	Video ID from users

In this protocol, text messages and video metadata, such as the timestamps of the video, are transmitted across clients for information sharing. The heavyweight video, in contrast, is pre-cached in each member user's local storage and is not transmitted. The collaboration is achieved through parsing the coded lightweight text metadata instead of the heavyweight video itself. In other words, the video metadata is shared instead of the video. To synchronize the video playback between two users, for an example, one user sends his/her local video timestamp to another user, instead of sending the video stream itself. As a result, even users with slow dialup connections are able to take advantage of the real-time multimedia collaborative environment.

6. Field study

6.1 Instruction

In order to evaluate the design and performance of the ISEE, user and field studies are needed. The initial version of ISEE was demonstrated at the Internet2 2002 Spring meeting in Virginia. At that demo, two users (one at the conference site and one in North Carolina) were logged in to mimic the real-time distance instruction between the instructor and a remote learner. Early in the Fall 2002 semester, the ISEE was used by one of the authors in a class of thirty students where several students participated at remote locations in the building using their laptops via a wireless network. In that case, performance dropped dramatically as more remote students joined the discussion. Also in that version of the ISEE, an additional multicast component beyond the ICR, SWB, and local video functions were used to broadcast the classroom activity. Based on that experience, the system infrastructure was rebuilt to solve the scalability problem and the multicast feature was dropped. The revised version of ISEE was tested in November, 2002 in a classroom field study.

6.2. Participants and procedure

Volunteers were recruited to participate in the field study from a population of students in the Children's Literature & Related Materials course. Twenty-eight students participated in the study. Most were female (only two males) and they ranged in age from 20 to 45. Eighteen participants were graduate students and all claimed that they used computers and the Internet on a daily basis. Two-thirds of the participants (19 of 28) never or occasionally had used interactive online chat. Most of the participants (89%) had no past experience with video conferencing systems and about one-third (10 of 28) of the participants had taken an online class.

Participants were asked to assume that they were librarians and should order three children books for their library from five available selections. They were asked to read reviews of each book and to use ISEE to get peer opinions to help them make their decisions. The study was conducted in the computer lab with 10Mb fast Ethernet connected to each computer and ISEE pre-installed on each workstation along with the video files. Each participant was assigned a random user name from a pool ("user1" to "user31"). Although the decision-making class session was conducted in a single computer laboratory, each student worked at an individual workstation and wore headphones in phase three when the video was available. No talking was allowed during the entire study. Thus, the test session was a reasonable simulation of a distance learning setting.

There were three phases in the study: review, review + chat, and review + chat + video:

- Phase I: The SWB was used to browse text reviews of each book;
- Phase II: The ICR was used to share text messages with other group members; the SWB was still accessible in this phase.
- Phase III: Participants were asked to watch brief video readings for each book. Each page was shown as it was read. Storyboards were available for quick shifting between books. The SWB and ICR were available in this phase

Before the study, a brief tutorial (a few minutes) was given to let participants become familiar with the interface and functions of the ISEE system. After each phase, participants made or revised their book selections. Finally, a questionnaire with Likert scales assessing each of the components and various preferences and binary choices for preference and satisfaction, was provided to elicit reactions from participants on their experience using ISEE. The entire field test lasted about one hour.

6.3. Results

Results for basic performance and for specific features are discussed.

6.3.1. ISEE. The tested subjects found the ISEE easy to learn. Although the field test marked the first time any participant had used ISEE and only a brief tutorial was given, only three participants asked for help on how to use ISEE or its functions during the entire study. As user24 commented after the study, "It was amazingly easy to use". Additionally, ISEE was fairly stable and robust during the study. Only two participants re-started their ISEE environments.

6.3.2. Video, chat discussion, and text reviews. In this study, video was reported to be the most effective information channel in helping the participants make their final book selections. Only 3.6% of the participants selected the online chat and 7.1% selected the text review as most useful informant of their decision-making. The other 89% reported that the video was the most effective information resource. Participants felt more comfortable (t=4.42, df=27,p<0.001) using the preview + chat + video setting and found that this setting was more effective than the preview + chat setting (t = 10.5 , df = 27 , p<0.001). Most of the participants gave positive comments about the video. For examples: "The video was extremely helpful" (user12). "The videos were excellent! Great resources! This is a wonderful idea" (user17). "To see books with reviews helped immensely. (Video) changed my mind" (user19). In addition, even though we did not formally introduce the navigation functions associated with the video player, some participants tried them and indicated that they were helpful and convenient.

6.3.3. Smartlinks.
As this was the first time for participants to use the ISEE user interface, the smartlink feature was not emphasized in the tutorial. However, most of the participants still used the storyboards for video navigation. Figure 5 shows the distribution of the 73 clicks on the video storyboards. The mean number of clicks per participant was 2.54 and the figure shows how usage was heavy early in phase 3 while participants explored the videos and then trailed off as they moved toward finalizing their selection decisions.

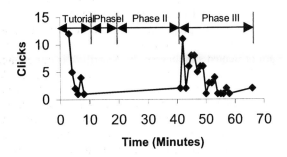

Figure 5. Storyboard Click Distribution Over Session

Five participants used the smartlink between the ICR and the video player. There were a total of twenty-five clicks on the linked timestamps. Table 4 lists the number of clicks on the ICR timestamps by each of the five users who used the smartlinks.

Table 4: ICR Timestamp Clicks

User ID	User01	User10	User15	User19	User24
Clicks	7	3	3	1	11

User24 was the most active user in terms of using smartlinks. This suggests that she was very serious about the comments from others and used smartlinks in the ICR to share the same video context with the message sender. However, she remarked negatively on her chat room experience ("the chat rooms conversation got pretty silly") and she ranked the chat room as the least effective module in order of helpfulness. User10 gave a relatively positive remark about the smartlink: "I liked being able to chat while watching the videos and linking straight to the spot where another user was at when commenting". It is interesting to note that user25, who did not use the timestamp smartlink in the study but tried it in the tutorial gave a very positive comment. When asked for one positive comment on ISEE, user25 indicated her preference for "the timestamp on the chat".

6.3.4. Online chat.
There were 323 messages sent to the chat room in the entire study. Figure 6 depicts the distribution of messages over the session. The most active user contributed 30 messages and each user sent at least one message. The average number of messages each user sent was 11.5. The number of messages sent to the chat room dropped nearly 50% in phase III (111 messages) compared to phase II (212). This is natural because the video channel added in phase III would divide part of the cognition time from the devoted text chat.

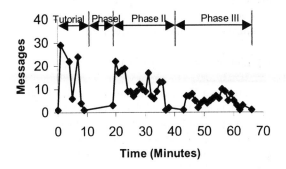

Figure 6. Message Distribution Over Session

When the participants were asked to give one negative comment about the ISEE, to our surprise, the chat room received the most criticism. Some participants (25%) indicated that too many users in one chat room made the ICR "crowded". As a result, "it was hard to read everything" (user6); "It was difficult to keep up with the chat" (user17); and it was "hard to really isolate a comment I found pertinent" (user27). Only 3.6% participants think they relied completely on the opinions from the online chat. In addition, two participants believed that there was bias in the text chat contents and one participant (user29) indicated that the anonymity made the comments from others untrustworthy.

From another perspective, many criticisms and comments from the users also suggest the critical role that the text chat played in this experience. As mentioned by one participant in the study, "Through the chat I was able to see other perspectives and able to re-evaluate my opinion of the books" (user1), and "I really liked reading the peer comments. They were very helpful"(user3). More than half (53.6%) of the participants changed their book selection decisions in terms of choosing different books or re-ranking the same selections over the course of the three phases.

7. Discussion

In ISEE information components, such as text chat, video, and the shared browser, provide an enriched collaborative learning environment. A comment from user14 illustrates this: "The combination of reviews, chat, and video is helpful to make educated choices." However, cognitive theories suggest that there is a limit to the capacity of an individual's working memory, measured in terms of information chunks. Instructions needed to be carefully designed to reduce the learners' cognitive load [1,21]. With multiple information presentation and communication components being juxtaposed together, it is natural to ask the questions: Will users feel comfortable using ISEE and not feel "overloaded"? How can the system and user interface be optimized to minimize cognitive load?

7.1. Cognitive load in ISEE

In the two Yes/No questions on the questionnaire, all the participants indicated that ISEE provided an effective platform to help them complete their tasks and that they had a comfortable experience in using the ISEE system. As one participant (user2) commented: "This is a wonderful learning tool...I have not spotted a fault yet. It's cool stuff".

In phase III, when all the information channels were available, including reviews, video and text chat, some participants (14.3.%) felt distracted, especially when the chat comments were not synchronized with the video they currently watched (user10, user12, user15, user23). Some exemplary comments include, "It was difficult to see two windows--say video and chat-- at the same time"(user10); "It is distracting to try reading the chat comments while listening to the video"(user12); "comments don't necessarily match up with timed point in video"(user15). This "distractedness" may explain the drop in chat usage during phase III. As the participants sought to minimize cognitive overload, they focused their attentions on only one information channel. Iignoring other channels in favor of the channel most users deemed the most helpful and informative (video) may be a strategy employed by users to reduce cognitive load. Thus, we can see that overall, subjects were positive about ISEE but that issues of overload and coordination among information channels bear consideration. Clearly, instructors who use such environments should take this into consideration in designing activities for students and should discuss strategies to balance cognitive load as students become familiar with the environment. Likewise, digital libraries that provide client-side tools for users should take these results into account in developing such services.

7.2. Managing cognitive load

A desktop user interface provides a flexible environment for people to manage cognitive load by selecting and moving the information components. Even though some participants just accepted the default user interface during the entire session, most of the participants (82.1%) rearranged the layout of the user interface to meet their specific needs as they worked. For example, students were observed enlarging the video player, minimizing the SWB, enlarging the ICR, and putting the ICR in the center of the user interface. One user even enlarged the video player to occupy all the available display estate, thus filtering out other information components (Figure 7) for part of the work session. Most students liked having this flexibility. User3 commented, "Having all three items available at once was great; you could select when you needed".

Mayer [14] proposed that students learn better when corresponding information, such as words and pictures, are presented simultaneously. Smartlink is our attempt in ISEE to build quick and direct links between related individual information components. User10 noted: "I liked being able to chat while watching the videos and linking straight to the spot where another user was at when commenting.". This field study demonstrates that such links facilitate the management of multiple information channels and possibly helps people to better manage the cognitive load associated with multiple information channels.

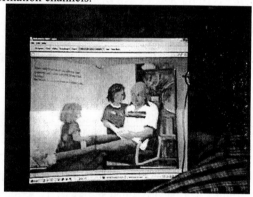

Figure 7: Screenshot of One User's ISEE User Interface

7.3. Future work

The ISEE is an evolving distance learning environment and improvements are needed before it can be widely applied in practice. The ICR with smartlink support is a novel feature and was liked by participants in this study. In this version of ISEE, both the instructors and the students viewed the same user interface. A function for the instructor to broadcast a question to the entire class is also available but was not used in any of our tests so far.

New features are planned that distinguish the user interface of the instructor from the students. The instructor will be able to survey the students with instant messages. Further, control over the students' video players will be added to the instructor's interface. A multicast video/audio streaming module will be added back in future versions as an option so that fast network users are able to take full advantage of their bandwidth. Audio communication was mentioned as an important communication channel by participants and may be added to the next generation of ISEE. New field studies with heterogeneous network connection speeds are planned to explore the relationship between smartlinks and cognitive load.

8. Conclusions

The increasing volume of videos in digital libraries provides an immense resource for distance learning and education. Collaboration and cooperation activities are encouraged by modern learning theories [23]. This study showed how ISEE might be used in a "real life" collaborative setting. The students were engaged in a simulation activity, mimicking the kind of interaction that could support and enhance a common professional task: the selection of materials for a library's collection. Data in the form of student comments shows that the participants actively considered information from multiple sources. An integrated multimedia environment, like that provided by ISEE, discourages passive information use. In a digital library environment, various interactions offered by a rich environment such as ISEE can enhance both the information seeking and information assimilation tasks.

It is a challenge to develop a real-time multimedia collaborative distance-learning environment that coherently integrates video, text chat, and text documents without overloading users' working memory. Based on lightweight communication architectures, ISEE supports synchronizations across four information components: a shared web browser, a interactive chat room, video storyboards, and a video player. Videos can be pre-packaged for quick access and navigation functions. Users are able to connect with each other using slower dialup connections.

This classroom field study indicated that the combination of video and text chat is an effective and helpful setting for some decision-making tasks. Smartlinks that are able to quickly present related information from various information channels were introduced in ISEE to minimize the cognitive load in the information-enriched environment. Participants felt comfortable in using the ISEE environment to select children's literature for a library. They reported that video was highly useful in helping them to make their comparisons and selections and although video and chat together increased cognitive load, they were able to use smartlinks to help manage some of this load. These results are promising and will guide continued development and evaluation of ISEE.

9. Acknowledgements

Our thanks go to Dr. Barbara Wildurmth for her support in the IRB preparation and to the students who participated in the field study. This work was supported by NSF Grant #0099638 and the Open Video Project.

10. References

[1] Anderson, J. (1983). The Architecture of Cognition. Cambridge, MA: Harvard University Press.

[2] BMRC Lecture Browser: http://bmrc.berkeley.edu/frame/projects/

[3] Brown, B. & Fortosky,D. (1986). Use of television. In I. Mugridge & D. Kaufman(Eds.), Distance education in Canada(pp. 260-282). London, England: Croom Helm.

[4] Cadiz, J., Balachandran, A., Sanocki, E., Gupta, A., Grudin, J. and Jancke, G. Distance learning through distributed collaborative video viewing. Proc. CSCW 2000, 135-144.

[5] Chapanis, A., Ochsman, R. B., Parrish, R.N., and Weeks, G.D. (1972). Studies in interactive communication: The effects of four communication modes on the behavior of teams during a co-operative problem solving. Human Factors, 14,487-509.

[6] Chen, M. 2001, Design of a Virtual Auditorium. Proceedings of ACM Multimedia 2001,19-28

[7] Deshpande, S.G., and Hwang, J.,2001, A real-time interactive virtual classroom multimedia distance learning system, IEEE Transactions on Multimedia, Vol.3, No. 4, 2001. 432-443

[8] eClass: http://www.cc.gatech.edu/fce/eclass/

[9] Gibbons, J. F., Kincheloe, W.R., and Down, K.S.(1977). Tutored videotape instruction: a new use of electronics media in education. Science. 195:1139-1146.

[10] Heinich, R., Molenda, M. & Russell, J. D. (1989). Instructional media and the new technologies of instruction (3rd ed.) New York: Macmillan Publishing Company.

[11] Jancke, G., Grudin, J., and Gupta, A., 2000. Presenting to Local and Remote Audiences: Design and Use of the TELEP System. Proc. CHI 2000, 384-391.

[12] Just-In-Time Lecture (JIT): http://www.jitl.cs.cmu.edu/

[13] Maly, K., Abdel-wahab, H., Wild, C., Overstreet, C.M., Gupta, A., Abdel-hamid, A., Ghanem, S., Gonzalez, A., and Zhu, X., 2001, IRI-h, A Java-Based distance education system: architecture and performance. ACM Journal of Educational Resources in Computing, Vol.1, No.1, Spring 2001, Article #6, 15 pages

[14] Mayer, R. E. 2001, Multimedia Learning. Cambridge University Press.

[15] MediaSite Live: currently available at http://sonicfoundry.com/systems/mslive.asp

[16] Shirmohammadi, S. 2001, Web-based multimedia tools for sharing educational resources, ACM Journal of Educational Resources in Computing, Vol.1, No.1, Spring 2001, Article #7, 13 pages.

[17] Sipusic, M., Pannoni, R., Smith, R., Dutra, J., Gibbons., J., and Sutherland, W.(1999). Virtual Collaborative learning: A Comparison between Face-to-Face tutored Video Instruction and Distributed Tutored Video Instruction (DTVI). Sun Microsystems Laboratories, Inc. TR-99-72.

[18] Smith, R., Sipusic, M., and Pannoni, R. (1999). Experiments Comparing Face-to-Face with Virtual Collaborative Learning. Sun Microsystems Laboratories, Inc. TR-99-0285.

[19] Stanford University's Stanford Online program: http://scpd.stanford.edu/scpd/about/delivery/stanford Online.htm

[20] Stone, H. R.(1990). Economic development and technology transfer: Implications for video-based distance education. In M.G.Moore(Ed.), Contemporary issues in American distance education(pp231-242). Oxford, England: Pergamon.

[21] Sweller, J., Cognitive load during problem solving: Effects on learning, Cognitive Science, 12, 257-285 (1988).

[22] White Pine's CU-SEEME: http://www.cuseeme.com

[23] Vygotsky, L.S. (1978). Mind in Society. Cambridge, MA: Harvard University Press.

[24] Yaskin, D. & Gilfus, S. Introducing the Blackboard 5: learning system. Available online at http://company.blackboard.com/docs/cp/orientation/E nterpriseLearningWhitePaper.pdf

Session 9B: Standards, Mark-Up, and Metadata

Session Chair: Herbert Van de Sompel, Los Alamos National Laboratory

XML Semantics and Digital Libraries

Allen Renear and David Dubin
Graduate School of Library and Information Science
University of Illinois at Urbana-Champaign
{renear, ddubin}@uiuc.edu

C. M. Sperberg-McQueen
World Wide Web Consortium
MIT Laboratory for Computer Science
cmsmcq@acm.org

Claus Huitfeldt
Department for Culture, Language, and Information Technology
Bergen University Research Foundation
Claus.Huitfeldt@hit.uib.no

Abstract

The lack of a standard formalism for expressing the semantics of an XML vocabulary is a major obstacle to the development of high-function interoperable digital libraries. XML document type definitions (DTDs) provide a mechanism for specifying the syntax of an XML vocabulary, but there is no comparable mechanism for specifying the semantics of that vocabulary — where semantics simply means the basic facts and relationships represented by the occurrence of XML constructs. A substantial loss of functionality and interoperability in digital libraries results from not having a common machine-readable formalism for expressing these relationships for the XML vocabularies currently being used to encode content. Recently a number of projects and standards have begun taking up related topics. We describe the problem and our own project.

1 Introduction

Much textual content in digital libraries is encoded with XML document markup. XML provides a rigorous machine-readable technique for defining descriptive markup languages — languages usually designed to explicitly identify the underlying meaningful structure of document, apart from any intended processing. The superiority of descriptive markup over earlier strategies has been well-confirmed [1], and XML metalanguage supports the development of interoperable domain-specific descriptive markup vocabularies. However it has always been clear that XML and descriptive markup alone cannot deliver the level of functionality and interoperability originally anticipated.

The problem is that even though XML markup identifies a document's meaningful structure, XML itself does not explicitly represent fundamental semantic relationships among document components and features. XML supports the specification of a machine readable "grammar," but because it has no mechanism for providing a semantics for that grammar what an XML vocabulary *means* still cannot be formally specified. Even very simple fundamental semantic facts about a document markup system — facts that are routinely intended by markup language designers, and relied on by both markup language users and software designers — cannot be expressed. Prose documentation of markup vocabularies provides some assistance of course, but even when established principles of documentation are followed, prose documentation is not a machine-readable formalism — and that is what is required to address current problems with digital libraries.

2 Related Work

The lack for a machine-readable semantic description of SGML/XML constructs was noted in the 1980s. [3, 4] Recently a number of other technologies, standards, and research projects have recognized and responded to this challenge. For particularly promising research projects see [7, 8, 13, 14]. In addition, standards such as W3C Schema, ISO Topic Maps, RDF, and HyTime architectural forms address some of the problems mentioned here, but do not provide complete or systematic solutions. The W3C's "Semantic Web" activity is certainly producing important relevant results, but its overall agenda is to develop XML-based techniques for knowledge representation in general, while our project focuses on identifying and processing actual document markup semantics, as found in existing document markup languages, and not on developing a new markup language for representing semantics in general.

3 XML Semantics: What it is

XML semantics in our sense refers simply to the facts and relationships expressed by XML markup. It does not refer to processing behavior, machine states, linguistic meaning, business logic, or any of the other things that are sometimes meant by "semantics". Consider for example the markup <p lang="english">. The semantics of this expression might be informally expressed by saying that the markup attributes to its content the property of being a paragraph and being in the English language. This example suggests that a semantics for XML markup vocabulary might be given by providing rules for a translation into predicate logic (or an equivalent formalism), perhaps along with appropriate axioms — and this is indeed our approach. It also suggests that the translation will be trivial, which turns out not to be the case, as the following examples of some specific problems show.

Propagation: Often the properties expressed by markup are understood to be propagated, according to certain rules, to child elements. For instance, if an element has the attribute specification lang="de", indicating that the text is in German, then all child elements have the property of being in German, unless the attribution is defeated by an intervening reassignment. Language designers, content developers, and software designers all depend upon a common understanding of such rules. But XML DTDs provide no formal notation for specifying which attributes are propagated or what the rules for propagation are. The property of being a paragraph, for example, is not propagated at all (the child elements of a paragraph aren't necessarily paragraphs), the property of being in German is propagated until defeated, and the property of being rendered in Helvetica will be defeated by a subsequent rendition assignment of, say, TIMES, but *not* by a subsequent rendition assignment of BOLD. In addition some properties are distributed to their textual content, and others apply only at the element level. Although there is no way to specify in a DTD which properties propagate, and what the logic of that propagation is, such relationships are intended by markup language designers, routinely assumed by content developers, and routinely inferred by software designers — and reflected in tools and applications [11].

Class Relationships and Synonymy: XML itself contains no general constructs for expressing class membership or hierarchies among elements, attributes, or attribute values — one of the most fundamental relationships in contemporary information modeling. Full and partial synonymy, within and across markup languages, is also an important semantic relationship, and the lack of characterizing mechanisms is an obstacle to dealing with heterogeneity.

Ontological variation in reference: XML markup might appear to indicate that the same thing, is-a-noun, is-a-

French-citizen, is-illegible, has-been-copyedited. But obviously either these predicates really refer to different things, or must be given non-standard interpretations. While humans readers are not confused by such familiar ambiguities, they are an obstacle to automatic processing.

Arity and Deixis: Some properties expressed by markup appear to be monadic, some polyadic — a title that is the immediate first child of a section is probably the title *of* that section. But property arity is not evident from the markup itself, and it is necessary to provide "deictic" mechanisms to locate and identify arguments.

Parent/Child overloading: The parent/child relations of the XML tree data structure support a variety of implicit substantive relationships. A paragraph might have page break, sentence, and footnote as child elements, but in each case the parent/child relation represents a different substantive relationship: the parent/child relationship indicates that the sentence is *part of* the paragraph, but means something else for the page break and footnote [2].

These examples demonstrate several things: what XML semantics is, that it would be valuable to have a system for expressing XML semantics, and that it would be neither trivial nor excessively ambitious to develop such a system — we are not attempting to formalize common sense reasoning in general, but only the inferences that are routinely intended by markup designers, assumed by content developers, and inferred by software designers.

(Parts of this section were adapted from Renear et al 2003 [5]; much of the original analysis is from Sperberg-McQueen et al 2000 [11].)

4 Consequences for Digital Libraries

Much current digital library research is focused on three closely related problems: efficiency in the creation and management of high-performance content, functionality of software tools, and interoperability of both tools and content. A persistent problem in all three areas is the efficient exploitation of diverse systems for representing information. A standard metalanguage, such as XML, is an essential part of the solution, but by itself a metalanguage for specifying syntax does not provide the needed semantic information. Wide adoption within a domain of specific well-designed XML vocabularies, such as the TEI [9] does make important semantic information available, but only through prose documentation and shared practice — and information in this form is not sufficiently systematic, uniform, complete, or exploitable to achieve high levels of functionality and interoperability.

On the other hand a common standard for providing machine-readable semantics for XML vocabularies would go directly to the heart of the problem. Without a machine-readable semantics computational access to even the simplest facts — that a word is in German, that a sentence is "part of" a paragraph, that a title is the title of a section — requires explicit human inference and intervention. This is because, as indicated above, the data structure provided by an XML document depends on a semantic interpretation in order to actually deliver the information it represents. Markup language designers, content developers, software engineers, and stylesheet developers easily carry out this interpretation. But they do so only opportunistically and there is no way for them to formally express their decisions and inferences, either to each other or to software. The resulting scenarios of content development and exploitation are idiosyncratic, error-prone, incomplete, and involve a massive duplication of effort. This lack of interoperability results in systems that are low function. Digital libraries will not reach their full potential until the semantic information, which is easily and routinely inferred, is made computationally available in a standard format.

It is easy to see how a common standard for XML application would support functionality and interoperability in areas such as information retrieval, presentation, browsing, federation, inferencing, and conversion. [2,5,12] In addition it is likely that a formalism for XML semantics can help in other areas of digital library research as well. For instance, XML semantics could support digital preservation and authentication by providing a representation of content at a higher level of abstraction than character streams, canonical serializations, or even data structures [6]. This suggests that beyond improving the functionality and interoperability of tools and content, the research in XML semantics may also result in important theoretical contributions to the digital library research agenda.

5   The BECHAMEL Project

The BECHAMEL Markup Semantics Project, led by Sperberg-McQueen (W3C/MIT), grew out of research initiated by in the late 1990s [11] and is a partnership with the research staff and faculty at Bergen University (Norway) and the Electronic Publishing Research Group at the University of Illinois. The project explores representation and inference issues in document markup semantics, surveys properties of popular markup languages, and is developing a formal, machine-readable declarative representation scheme in which the semantics of a markup language can be expressed. This scheme is applied to research on information retrieval, document understanding, conversion, preservation, and document authentication. An early Prolog inferencing system [11] has been developed into a prototype knowledge representation workbench for representing facts and rules of inference about structured documents [2]. Preliminary findings have been reported elsewhere [2, 5, 10–12].

References

[1] J. H. Coombs, A. H. Renear, and S. J. DeRose. Markup systems and the future of scholarly text processing. *Communications of the Association for Computing Machinery*, 30(11):933–947, 1987.

[2] D. Dubin, C. M. Sperberg-McQueen, A. Renear, and C. Huitfeldt. A logic programming environment for document semantics and inference. *Journal of Literary and Linguistic Computing*, Forthcoming in 2003.

[3] D. R. Raymond and F. W. Tompa. Markup reconsidered. Technical Report 356, Department of Computer Science, The University of Western Ontario, 1993. An earlier version was circulated privately as "Markup Considered Harmful" in the late 1980s.

[4] D. R. Raymond, F. W. Tompa, and D. Wood. From data representation to data model: Meta-semantic issues in the evolution of SGML. *Computer Standards and Interfaces*, 18(1):25–36, January 1996.

[5] A. Renear, D. Dubin, C. M. Sperberg-McQueen, and C. Huitfeldt. Towards a semantics for XML markup. In R. Furuta, J. I. Maletic, and E. Munson, editors, *Proceedings of the 2002 ACM Symposium on Document Engineering*, pages 119–126, McLean, VA, November 2002. Association for Computing Machinery.

[6] A. Renear, D. Dubin, C. M. Sperberg-McQueen, and C. Huitfeldt. Towards identity conditions for digital documents. Technical Report UIUCLIS–2003/2+EPRG, Graduate School of Library and Information Science, University of Illinois at Urbana-Champaign, Champaign, IL, 2003.

[7] G. F. Simons. Conceptual modeling versus visual modeling: A technological key to building consensus. *Computers and the Humanities*, 30(4):303–319, 1997.

[8] G. F. Simons. Using architectural forms to map TEI data into an object-oriented database. *Computers and the Humanities*, 33(1-2):85–101, 1999.

[9] C. M. Sperberg-McQueen and L. Burnard, editors. *Guidelines for Electronic Text Encoding and Interchange (TEI P4)*. TEI Consortium, Oxford, 2002.

[10] C. M. Sperberg-McQueen, D. Dubin, C. Huitfeldt, and A. Renear. Drawing inferences on the basis of markup. In B. T. Usdin and S. R. Newcomb, editors, *Proceedings of Extreme Markup Languages 2002*, Montreal, August 2002.

[11] C. M. Sperberg-McQueen, C. Huitfeldt, and A. Renear. Meaning and interpretation of markup. *Markup Languages: Theory and Practice*, 2(3):215–234, 2000.

[12] C. M. Sperberg-McQueen, A. Renear, C. Huitfeldt, and D. Dubin. Skeletons in the closet: Saying what markup means. Presented at ALLC/ACH, Tübingen, July 2002.

[13] C. Welty and N. Ide. Using the right tools: Enhancing retrieval from marked-up documents. *Computers and the Humanities*, 33(1-2):59–84, 1999. Originally delivered in 1997 at the TEI 10 conference in Providence, RI.

[14] V. Wuwongse, C. Anutariya, K. Akama, and E. Nantajeewarawat. XML declarative description: A language for the semantic web. *IEEE Intelligence Systems*, 16(3):54–65, May/June 2001.

Utility of an OAI Service Provider Search Portal

Sarah L. Shreeves, Christine Kirkham, Joanne Kaczmarek, Timothy W. Cole
University of Illinois Library at Urbana-Champaign
{sshreeve, ckirkham, jkaczmar, t-cole3}@uiuc.edu

Abstract

The Open Archives Initiative (OAI) Protocol for Metadata Harvesting (PMH) facilitates efficient interoperability between digital collections, in particular by enabling service providers to construct, with relatively modest effort, search portals that present aggregated metadata to specific communities. This paper describes the experiences of the University of Illinois at Urbana-Champaign Library as an OAI service provider. We discuss the creation of a search portal to an aggregation of metadata describing cultural heritage resources. We examine several key challenges posed by the aggregated metadata and present preliminary findings of a pilot study of the utility of the portal for a specific community (student teachers). We also comment briefly on the potential for using text analysis tools to uncover themes and relationships within the aggregated metadata.

1. Background

The Open Archives Initiative (OAI) Protocol for Metadata Harvesting (PMH) is now established as an important tool for interoperability between digital collections. It was designed as a technically low-barrier means to share metadata, particularly metadata describing XML documents, digital images, content in other non-HTML formats, or resources contained in databases i.e. formats and locations not readily available to current Web search engines. [1] Based on a harvesting model, the OAI-PMH relies on both *data providers*, who expose their metadata through the protocol, and *service providers*, who harvest and aggregate metadata from one or more providers. [3]

OAI-PMH service providers can facilitate efficient interoperability among data providers by constructing, for example, search portals that present aggregated metadata to specific communities. The OAI-PMH project based at the University of Illinois at Urbana-Champaign tested the efficacy of the OAI-PMH model for search and discovery of metadata describing content in the domain of cultural heritage. The Illinois OAI-PMH project began in June 2001 and ends in May 2003.

2. Building a portal to aggregated metadata

The Illinois project built a repository which can be accessed through a search portal called the UIUC Digital Gateway to Cultural Heritage Materials (http://oai.grainger.uiuc.edu/search). The repository contains approximately 1.1 million original metadata records. The web portal uses the XPAT indexing and search tools developed by the Digital Library Extension Service (DLXS) at the University of Michigan. As of December 2002, we had collected metadata from 39 providers, including museums, archives, academic and public libraries, historical societies, consortiums, and digital libraries. The aggregated metadata describes an array of cultural heritage resources held by more that 500 institutions worldwide. Some resources exist in digital formats, such as .JPG images. Other resources exist only in analog format and are represented digitally through the metadata.

The common schema used for metadata stored in the repository is Dublin Core (DC). Approximately half of the participating institutions are registered OAI data providers, whose records are harvested directly from their own servers. The non–OAI-registered providers delivered "data dumps" of metadata, which are used as sources for surrogate metadata provider sites implemented at Illinois (only for harvest by this project). Included in the repository are item-level metadata records derived from more than 8,000 Encoded Archival Description (EAD) finding aids. Using an algorithm developed as part of this project [4], these 8,000 EAD files generated more than 1.5 item level DC records (describing mostly analog resources) bringing the total number of item-level DC records to approximately 2.5 million.

Analysis of a subset of approximately 600,000 records provided natively in DC revealed wide variations in the interpretation and application of DC elements by different communities. [5] For example, 93% of records from museums used the *subject* element versus only 15% of records from academic libraries. Such disparities, coupled with the variety of controlled vocabularies in use, present specific problems for anyone attempting to build an effective search service for aggregated metadata. We developed a variety of strategies to minimize these disparities, including indexing and organizing metadata by type of material (image, text, physical object, etc.) and applying a normalization vocabulary to the *date*, *coverage*, and *type* elements. [2]

3. Testing utility of search portal

A goal of the Illinois project was to evaluate the utility of a search portal to aggregated metadata. We examined how one group of users interacted with the portal. Our user population was comprised of 23 college students training to become K-12 social studies teachers in an honors-level curriculum and instruction course. They were asked to use the site to find primary sources for use in preparing a lesson plan on a specific social sciences topic, write short papers about their experience, and participate in one focus group interview. Prior to their searches, users were introduced to the concept of *metadata aggregation* and were informed that the search portal would provide pointers to digital content held elsewhere and would include analog resources. Preliminary results from this pilot study highlight three key issues.

First, despite their prior introduction to the nature of the portal, in practice the test group expected all records to point directly to corresponding digital objects. They reported feelings of frustration in finding analog resources when they expected digital resources. This was exacerbated by the large number of item-level records derived from EAD files that described analog resources. Thus, a user who selected a result for "letters from a WWI soldier" might find that the record referred to the holding institution's finding aid instead of to the letters themselves. Likewise, they reported a significant slowing of their efforts when the pointers (the URLs within the record) went to a top-level or intermediate page, where they might have to resubmit their request using the institution's own search engine.

Second and not unexpectedly, the lack of a ranking facility in our portal resulted in the test group feeling overwhelmed by the quantity of unsorted results. Because of the lack of consistent metadata caused by variations in controlled vocabularies and disparities in the use of DC, the Illinois team had decided to enable greater recall by designing the default search screen as a keyword search on all elements. This exacerbated the lack of a ranking facility. In an attempt to address these known limitations we provided an advanced search screen, which included standard methods for refining a search, such as restricting searches to specific groups of fields and setting limits. However, the test group seldom used the advanced search tools, and the few users who

did attempt to refine their searches were unfamiliar with the types of entries required by metadata fields like "Format." This suggests that a robust ranking facility is of great importance.

Third, users accorded equal credibility to all contributing collections. They reported that they made no decisions about which items to examine based on the name of the holding institutions. Feelings of frustration around failed searches were directed at the search portal rather than at individual institutions. Thus, users held the portal responsible for the usability of its aggregated metadata, even when that metadata originated elsewhere and remained outside the control of the Illinois project.

4. Conclusions and future work

A clear and perhaps obvious finding of our work is that, while the OAI-PMH itself is readily implemented, the challenges posed by large amounts of heterogeneous metadata are significant. Certainly the application of more sophisticated pre-processing tools as well as robust, scalable search tools would aid in making the search portal a more effective tool for users. Other options include the development of thematic exhibits (based on human and/or machine analysis of metadata) that would offer glimpses into the range and type of materials available through the search portal, as well as the ability for users to annotate individual records, thus highlighting particularly useful resources.

While normalizing scripts for elements such as *type* and *date* are feasible because of the limited range of variations in those elements, manual normalizing of more complex free text elements such as *subject* and *description* would require time-consuming and cost-prohibitive efforts. We are exploring the use of an automated text analysis tool to learn whether such a tool can ferret out shared concepts or themes hidden in many thousands of *subject/description* fields. ThemeWeaver is a data mining tool developed by the automated learning group at the National Center for Supercomputer Applications (NCSA). Although this tool was designed to analyze large sets of documents with large amounts of text per document, we are testing whether it can provide natural groupings of metadata within the search portal. Thus far, we have found that the content of the metadata fields tested was too sparse and/or inconsistent to enable this text-analysis application to uncover useful clusters. The Illinois team continues to work with the developers of ThemeWeaver to test upcoming versions.

Although the Illinois OAI-PMH project ends in May 2003, members from the project team are continuing investigations into ways OAI-PMH–based services can be built and sustained. These include (1) an IMLS-funded project to create an item-level metadata repository of digital content created under the auspices of the IMLS National Leadership Grant program; (2) a project to create a state-wide repository of Illinois government and library information; and (3) a NSF-funded project to allow harvesting of a mathematics digital library. With the support of Grainger Engineering Library, the UIUC Gateway to Cultural Heritage Materials will be continued as a search portal to cultural heritage resources available from registered OAI data providers.

5. Acknowledgments

This material is based upon work supported by a grant from the Andrew W. Mellon Foundation.

6. References

[1] M.K. Bergman. "The Deep Web: Surfacing Hidden Value," *Journal of Electronic Publishing*, vol. 17, Aug. 2001, http://www.press.umich.edu/jep/07-01/bergman.html.

[2] T.W. Cole, et al, "Now That We've Found the 'Hidden Web' What Can We Do With It? The Illinois Open Archives Initiative Metadata Harvesting Experience", *Museums and the Web 2002: Selected Papers from an Int'l Conf.* (MW 2002), Archives & Museum Informatics, Toronto, 2002, pp. 63-72.

[3] C. Lagoze and H.V. de Sompel, "The Open Archives Initiative: Building a Low-Barrier Interoperability Framework", *Proc. 1st ACM-IEEE Joint Conf. on Digital Libraries.* (JCDL 2001), ACM Press, New York, NY, 2001, pp 54-62.

[4] C.J. Prom, "Reengineering Archival Access Through the OAI Protocols", to be published in *Library Hi Tech.* vol. 21, no.2, Jun.2003.

[5] S. L. Shreeves, J. Kaczmarek, and T.W. Cole. "Harvesting Cultural Heritage Metadata Using the OAI Protocol," to be published in *Library Hi Tech.* vol. 21, no.2, Jun. 2003.

The Dienst-OAI Gateway

Terry L. Harrison, Michael L. Nelson, Mohammad Zubair

Old Dominion University, Norfolk, Virginia

{tharriso,mln,zubair}@cs.odu.edu

Abstract

Though the Open Archive Initiative Protocol for Metadata Harvesting (OAI-PMH) is becoming the de facto standard for digital libraries, some of its predecessors are still in use. Although a limited number of Dienst repositories continue to be populated, others are precariously unsupported. The Dienst Open Archive Gateway (DOG) is a gateway between the OAI-PMH and the Dienst (version 4.1) protocol. DOG allows OAI-PMH harvesters to extract metadata records (in RFC-1807 or Dublin Core) from Dienst servers.

1. Introduction

Dienst was once a popular, rich digital library (DL) protocol, comprised of over 30 verbs [1]. The Open Archive Initiative Protocol for Metadata Harvesting (OAI-PMH) [2] represents some of the lessons learned during the deployment of Dienst, including a significantly decreased scope. As such, the OAI-PMH has only 6 verbs and introduces the division of responsibility for harvesters and repositories.

While many of the 100+ institutions that once used Dienst to participate in the Networked Computer Science Technical Reference Library (NCSTRL) have transitioned to the OAI-PMH [3], not all have. Some Dienst repositories continue to be populated and supported, while others are no longer being updated, and in the worst case, no longer being maintained. The Dienst OAI-PMH Gateway (DOG) was created to allow OAI-PMH harvesters to extract data from existing and at-risk Dienst 4.1.x repositories. Dienst 4.1 is the canonical version of the protocol and is not backward compatible with older versions. We are unaware of any existing DL(s) using earlier versions of the Dienst protocol.

DOG was initially created to allow for the harvesting of the ICASE Dienst repository for the OAI-PMH enabled NASA Technical Report Server [4], but the general nature of DOG allows it to be used for any Dienst repository, including those current DL projects based on Dienst, such as OpenDLib [5].

2. OAI-PMH Verb Implementation

DOG is a Java servlet and is available both as a demonstration service at ODU and as a tar file for local implementation (http://dlib.cs.odu.edu). DOG allows a specified Dienst repository to appear as a normal "baseURL" to a harvester:

http://128.82.7.113:5187/dog/servlet/dataprovider/ (DOG)
dienst.iei.pi.cnr.itSLASHDienstSLASH/ (Dienst)
?verb=ListRecords&metadataPrefix=oai_dc (OAI-PMH)

The Dienst server URL is imbedded the request URL. DOG parses out this URL and issues the appropriate Dienst verbs to the Dienst repository (Table 1 has the OAI-PMH to Dienst mapping), parsing the RFC-1807 plain text results and returning an OAI-PMH formatted response. Metadata can be returned as either RFC-1807 or Dublin Core (DC) The mapping from RFC-1807 to DC is shown in Table 2 and is described further in [6]. The mapping is modifiable if a local installation is chosen.

Table 1. OAI-PMH to Dienst Mapping

OAI-PMH Verb	Dienst Service/Verb
Identify	Repository/2.0/List-Contents
ListIdentifiers	Index/2.0/List-Contents
ListRecords	Index/2.0/List-Contents
GetRecord	Index/2.0/Bibliography/*handle*
ListSets	hard-coded response
ListMetadataFormats	hard-coded response or: Index/2.0/Bibliography/handle if identifier provided

2.1 Identify

The Identify verb extracts much of its required content from hard-coded variables or parsing of the request URL, with the exceptions of "earliestDatestamp" and "sampleIdentifier". The earliestDatestamp element guarantees harvesters a lower bound on record "datestamps". To discover the earliest date is an expensive operation and requires the parsing of all records for a given Dienst repository. To reduce this overhead, the resulting value is cached so that the operation need only be performed once per repository. As with all datestamps, RFC-1807 format (May 31, 2003) is converted to ISO-8061 format (2003-05-31). Values for the sampleIdentifier element are intentionally not cached, as the Dienst call needed to extract this from the repository also provides a status check on it, returning an http exception if the archive is no longer available. Some escaped character sequences had to be created to accommodate characters in some Dienst repository identifiers that did not conform with OAI-PMH character restrictions for the sampleIdentifier element content. One such case is the underscore in repository identifiers such as ncstrl.mit_ai. To resolve this, the "_" character is replaced with "UNDERSCORE".

2.2 ListSets

The Dienst collection service [7] was never widely adopted and most Dienst repositories have no equivalent to the OAI-PMH concept of sets. Since none of the active NCSTRL Dienst repositories implemented the collection service, the response to a ListSets request is hard-coded to be the "noSetHierarchy" error. Local implementers are welcome to modify this to suite their requirements.

2.3 ListMetadataFormats

Since Dienst metadata is in RFC-1807 and OAI-PMH requires support of DC, DOG supports both formats. ListMetadataFormats without an identifier argument will show support for both formats. Requests with an identifier argument require issuing a Dienst verb to verify the metadata for the given identifier exists.

Table 2. RFC-1807 to Dublin Core Mapping

Dublin Core	RFC-1807
title	title
creator	author
subject	keyword
description	abstract
contributor	corp-author
publisher	organization
date	date
type	type + id (concatenated)
format	cr-category
identifier	other_access
source	(no mapping)
language	language
relation	(no mapping)
coverage	(no mapping)
rights	copyright

2.4 GetRecord

Getting a single record from the Dienst archive is relatively simple, as the request maps well into Dienst protocol. The OAI-PMH identifier is formatted as a Dienst handle and appended into a Dienst record request. The record is returned in RFC-1807 as plain text, which DOG parses and returns as an XML formatted RFC-1807 or DC record.

2.5 ListRecords & ListIdentifiers

ListIdentifiers and ListRecords utilize the same Dienst calls and only differ in the amount of metadata returned for each record. DOG issues an "Index/2.0/List-Contents" verb that gives it an RFC-1807 metadata dump of all the records. Initially the parameter "file-after" was utilized to implement an OAI-PMH "from" argument, but since many Dienst archives had not implemented this argument, its use threatened to corrupt result sets. Once the metadata dump is received, DOG parses it, extracting any records that meet any given "from" or "until" arguments. Interestingly, by its ability to handle the "until" parameter, DOG adds utility that did not previously exist within the Dienst protocol. DOG does not cache the results of the metadata dump, which permits it to provide real-time harvesting.

3. Issues & Error Handling

OAI-PMH 2.0 adds requirements for handling OAI-PMH errors, which are distinct from http errors. Subsequently, DOG is careful to distinguish the two. An http 404 (File Not Found) error will be returned to DOG (from the Dienst server) if the repository is down, if a non-existent repository name is used, or a request is made for a file that does not exist. DOG explores the error to see if it qualifies as an OAI-PMH error. Invalid syntax issues like a malformed identifier are resolved by pattern matching to OAI-PMH regular expressions provided in its schema. Should the syntax be deemed valid, then it still must be determined if the problem is a communications fault or a non-existent file. To resolve these uncertainties, a subsequent call is made ("Repository/2.0/List-Contents/"). If the Dienst connection is made, an OAI-PMH error "idDoesNotExist" is returned instead of an http 404 error.

A different development issue was the hiding of the Dienst archive URL into the request URL to DOG. Traditionally this might be accomplished through the use of standard escape character ""%2F" for the forward slashes, but a security feature in Tomcat 4.0.4 which does not handle these escape characters before the method call, necessitated the use of the custom "SLASH" chars to escape instances of "/" in the Dienst URL. In anticipation of the resolution of this issue, DOG handles escape characters "%2f", "%2F" and "SLASH".

Another issue was the metadata inconsistency in the use of the RFC-1807 fields "ID::" and "HANDLE::". Since handles are unique permanent identifiers of the form HANDLE:: <repository>/<identifier> they seem the most logical choice for <identifier>. However, because they are optional, they may be missing altogether from an archive (i.e.: dienst.iei.pi.cnr.it). In this case, DOG uses data from the mandatory ID:: field, which is typically the same data. This also works when searching for a record. For example, when a GetRecord request is made and

DOG is comparing Dienst record metadata for a match, should there not be a HANDLE:: field, then the ID:: field is used instead. Due to RFC-1807 syntax, the ID:: field data will contain two forward slashes (ID:: <publisher-id>//<free-text>) instead of one as in the HANDLE:: field. To avoid confusion the DOG response represents the <identifier> using only one slash. DOG can resolve this, should it need to match the ID:: field later. Additionally, DOG will handle requests that mistakenly use two slashes in the identifier.

4. Conclusions

While the previous NCSTRL transition project provided a specific strategy for OAI-PMH conversion, DOG provides on-demand, general OAI-PMH compatibility for any Dienst archive. DOG has been exhaustively tested with the Repository Explorer and has been used to harvest ICASE Dienst repositories. Sadly, ICASE no longer exists at NASA and its Dienst repositories have been shut down. This underscores the importance of providing protocol gateways with an eye toward long-term preservation.

5. References

[1] Davis, J., and Lagoze, C. NCSTRL: design and deployment of a globally distributed digital library. Journal of the American Society for Information Science, 51(3), 2000, 273-280.

[2] Van de Sompel, H., and Lagoze, C. Notes from the interoperability front: A progress report on the Open Archives Initiative. in Proceedings of ECDL 2002 (Rome, Italy, September 2002), 144-157.

[3] Anan, H., Liu, X., Maly, K., Nelson, M., Zubair, M., French, J., Fox, E., and Shivakumar, P. Preservation and transition of NCSTRL using an OAI-based architecture. in Proceedings of JCDL 2002 (Portland OR, July 2002), 181-182.

[4] Nelson, M., Rocker, J., and Harrison, T. OAI and NASA scientific and technical information. Library Hi-Tech, 21(2), 2003.

[5] Castelli, D., and Pagano, P. OpenDLib: A digital library service system. in Proceedings of ECDL 2002 (Rome, Italy, September 2002), 292-308.

[6] Harrison, T., Nelson, M., and Zubair, M. The Dienst-OAI gateway: A preservation gateway for a legacy protocol. ODU CS TR 2003-01, Feb. 2003.

[7] Lagoze, C. and Fielding, D. Defining collections in distributed digital libraries, D-Lib Magazine, 4(11), 1998.

The XML Log Standard for Digital Libraries: Analysis, Evolution, and Deployment

Marcos André Gonçalves, Ganesh Panchanathan,
Unnikrishnan Ravindranathan, Aaron Krowne,
Edward A. Fox
Virginia Polytechnic and State University
Blacksburg, VA, 24061, USA
{mgoncalv, fox}@vt.edu

Filip Jagodzinski, Lillian Cassel
Villanova University
Villanova, PA 19085-1699
+1-610-519-7341
{filip.jagodzinski, lillian.cassel}@villanova.edu

Abstract

We describe current efforts and developments building on our proposal for an XML log standard format for digital library (DL) logging analysis and companion tools. Focus is given to the evolution of formats and tools, based on analysis of deployment in several DL systems and testbeds. Recent development of analysis tools also is discussed.

1. Introduction

In 2002 we proposed an XML log standard for digital libraries (DLs), and companion tools for storage and analysis [1]. The goal was to minimize problems and limitations of web servers, search engines, and DL systems log formats (e.g., incompatibility, incompleteness, ambiguity). Accordingly, our new format and tools allow capturing a rich, detailed set of system and user behaviors supported by current DL systems. In this paper, we report advances based on analysis of experimentation and deployment in several DL systems and testbeds. We hope that discussion of this work will move the community toward agreement on some DL log standard, which is urgently needed to support scientific advance.

2. Evolution of the Tool

The evolution of the log tool is illustrated in Figure 1. The first version had a monolithic architecture, which was strongly coupled within the target system. Whenever DL events needed to be logged, the DL invoked the corresponding methods of the log tool, since specific calls had been inserted within the target system. The first tests were performed with the MARIAN DL system [2]. This implementation revealed two major drawbacks: 1) small changes in the log format required complex changes in the DL logger code and complete recompilation of the tool and target system, therefore preventing extensibility; and 2) the Java-based implementation and close coupling required a deep understanding of the target tool architecture which

would cause problems in connecting the tool with DLs implemented in other languages (e.g., Perl), therefore preventing wide-spread adoption.

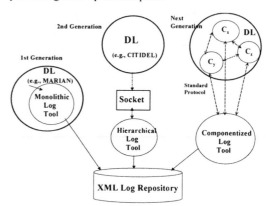

**Figure 1. Evolution of DL Log Tool
(Key: C_i=i_{th} DL component).**

Our second generation implementation solved those problems by: 1) re-implementing the tool with an object-oriented, bottom-up design that mimics the organization of the XML schema of the log format, therefore making internal communications clearer and isolating points of communication and modification; and 2) detaching the tool from the target DL system by using connectionless sockets. For socket communication, we devised a simple, ad-hoc datagram packet format.

Our next generation DL logger will enhance this communication by allowing direct, peer-to-peer communication between DL components and the (componentized) log tool. Following the philosophy of the Open Archives Initiative [3], we intend to use standard (or slightly extended) lightweight protocols, to allow this direct communication, therefore promoting interoperability and reuse. In particular, the extended OAI (XOAI) set of protocols defined by the ODL approach [4], provides specialized OAI protocols for several DL services and can serve as a foundation for such communications.

3. Evolution of the Log Format for DL Services

To be useful, the DL log format has to be reflective of how a generic DL system behaves. Accordingly, we have designed and organized the log structure in accordance with our 5S theory for digital libraries [5]. In 5S, services are composed of scenarios, which describe service behavior through sequences of specific user and system events. Since we are mostly interested in understanding user interactions and the perceived value of responses, we have chosen to record only the initial user input and final service output events along with corresponding parameters (modeled as XML sub-elements of events), and ignore most of the internal system communications (except administrative information).

The Computing and Information Technology Interactive Digital Educational Library (CITIDEL) [6] constituted the first large-scale application of our second-generation tool. From the beginning, it was clear that the log format, which currently models only storage, searching, and browsing services, as well as administrative information, was not able to capture all the CITIDEL interactions, given the rich set of requirements and services offered by CITIDEL. Therefore, extensions of the format were required. According to the 5S philosophy, extensions regarding new service events are to be modeled by analyzing user inputs and system outputs. Table 1 shows the current and in-development services and input events supported by the log format. The table also connects log events with Open Digital Library (ODL) [4] components which: 1) currently or in the near future will implement services in CITIDEL; 2) support the necessary underlying protocols for communication between the DL services and the next generation XML DL logger.

Table 1. DL service, log event, ODL component

Service	XML log event and sub-elements	ODL component
Searching	Search (Collection, SearchBy(Field), QueryString)	IRDB
Browsing	Browse (DocInfo(PathName,DocID, Collection), Category, SortOrder)	ODL-Browse
Storing	Update(AddInfo(DocInfo))	Box
Annotating	Annotate (AnnotateInfo (AnnotationID, DocInfo))	ODL-Annotate
Filtering	Filter (Criteria (expression), UserId)	Filter
Recommending	Currently being modeled	ODL-Recommend
Rating	Currently being modeled	ODL-Rating
Reviewing	Currently being modeled	ODL-Review

4. Log Analysis Tools

Standardization of the logs will ideally lead to a standardization of their processing/analysis. Accordingly, we are developing several analysis modules and tools, designed for easy expansion. The primary component of the log analysis tools is the log line parser that sends the content of each log line to an appropriate module. A module increments appropriate variables, populates files that are intermediate aggregate statistics of key log features, and performs a host of other required actions. The modules that are already developed track browse and search requests for each resource, maintain a record of the number of accesses from each domain; keep statistics on the words used in all the search queries; record the number of hits and logons per day, month, year, etc.; and keep track of the number of times that various tools and DL provided resources have been utilized.

The design of the log analysis tools is highly object oriented, with little or no coupling between modules. The design makes modification and creation of new modules very easy. In the case where a novel statistic is required or in the case that a new XML format feature is added, a new module can be built and connected to the already existing set of modules.

The modular design of the log analysis tools also will allow for more advanced analysis capabilities to be integrated into future versions. The current document search and browse output statistics provide information about the total number of hits for each document as well as a breakdown of hits based on aspects of the server domain. We are extending these output statistics so that we can see the clickstream path of users through the website, which will allow us to identify bottleneck pages and features. We also are developing an analysis query system that will address the large combinatorial possibilities that result from the union of multiple log variables. The query system will mine the intermediate statistics files to get a specific result.

5. Conclusions

As expected with any newly proposed standard, evolution to cope with results of the early stages of experimentation is expected. Accordingly, our formats and tools have evolved to deal with the results of such experiments. With the interest demonstrated by many DLs and institutions (e.g., CiteSeer, MyLibrary, Daffodil) in adopting the format and tools, we expect soon to release stable versions of both. Once this phase is achieved, other research issues will become the focus of future efforts, such as richer analysis and evaluation, and efficient use of distributed storage.

6. Acknowledgments

Thanks are given for the support of NSF through its grants: IIS-9986089, IIS-0002935, IIS-0080748, IIS-0086227, DUE-0121679, DUE0121741, and DUE-0136690. The first author is supported by CAPES, 1702-980.

7. References

[1] M. A. Gonçalves, M. Luo, R. Shen, M. F. Ali, E. A. Fox: An XML Log Standard and Tool for Digital Library Logging Analysis, Proceedings of the 6th European Conference on Research and Advanced Technology for Digital Libraries, ECDL 2002, 129-143, Rome, Italy, September 16-18, 2002.

[2] M. A. Gonçalves, P. Mather, J. Wang, Y. Zhou, M. Luo, R. Richardson, R. Shen, L. Xu, E. A. Fox: Java MARIAN: From an OPAC to a Modern Digital Library System, Proceedings of the 9th International Symposium on String Processing and Information Retrieval, SPIRE 2002, 194-209, Lisbon, Portugal, September, 11-13, 2002.

[3] Open Archives. http://www.openarchives.org

[4] H. Suleman. Open Digital Libraries. Ph.D. dissertation. Virginia Tech, Department of Computer Science. Nov. 2002

[5] M. A. Gonçalves, E. A. Fox, L. T. Watson, N. A. Kipp. Streams, Structures, Spaces, Scenarios, Societies (5S): A Formal Model for Digital Libraries. Virginia Tech, Department of Computer Science, Technical Report: TR-03-04, 2003. http://eprints.cs.vt.edu/archive/00000646/.

[6] CITIDEL. http://www.citidel.org.

A Quantitative Analysis of Unqualified Dublin Core Metadata Element Set Usage within Data Providers Registered with the Open Archives Initiative

Jewel Ward

University of North Carolina at Chapel Hill
School of Information and Library Science
wardj@ils.unc.edu

Abstract

This research describes an empirical study of how the unqualified Dublin Core Metadata Element Set (DC or DCMES) is used by 100 Data Providers (DPs) registered with the Open Archives Initiative (OAI). The research was conducted to determine whether or not the DCMES is used to its full capabilities. Eighty-two of 100 DPs have metadata records available for analysis. DCMES usage varies by type of DP. The average number of Dublin Core elements per record is eight, with an average of 91,785 Dublin Core elements in each DP. Five of the 15 elements of the DCMES are used 71% of the time. The results show the unqualified DCMES is not used to its fullest extent within DPs registered with the OAI.

1. Introduction

The authors of the Open Archives Initiative Protocol for Metadata Harvesting (OAI-PMH) [5] require administrators of digital libraries acting as DPs to expose a set of the repository's metadata using the unqualified DCMES [3], either in addition to or in lieu of a native metadata format. This requirement is intended to facilitate cross-domain resource discovery and digital library interoperability.

Although the DCMES is an accepted standard that provides for interoperability between disparate information communities, it is not without its critics, who would like to see the OAI technical committee mandate use of a metadata format that provides more detail about resources than the unqualified DCMES [4]. The problem facing the OAI technical committee, however, is that a metadata format suitable for cross-domain description that is less complex than the unqualified DCMES does not exist, while a format more complex will not provide for low-barrier cross-domain interoperability.

Lost within the debate over whether or not use of the unqualified DCMES should be mandated by the OAI technical committee is an examination of how the DCMES is currently used within DPs. Is the DCMES used to its fullest extent? An analysis of current usage

patterns is necessary to determine the appropriateness of the unqualified DCMES as a facilitator of interoperability between and resource discovery across OAI-PMH-compliant DPs. This paper presents the results of a larger study [7].

2. Methodology

We harvested metadata between 8 May and 12 October 2002 from the 100 OAI-PMH v. 1.1 DPs that were registered on the OAI web site by 28 July 2002. We used the Perl OAI Harvester v. 1.1 [6] as the Service Provider (SP) with which to harvest the metadata from the DPs, with the exception of arXiv. The harvester software ran on a Dell Precision 530, with dual 1.7 GHz Xeon processors, 2 GB RAM, and a U160 SCSI with 10,000 RPM drives. We harvested arXiv's metadata in November 2002 from an aggregator, Celestial [1], which harvested version 2.0 of the OAI-PMH. We harvested records from 82 of the 100 DPs, but only 76 of the 82 DPs could be harvested consistently.

In order to analyze usage of the DCMES, we wrote a Perl program to count the number of records harvested from each DP, and parsed the individual elements from the content of each record in order to count the number of times a record contained each of the 15 DC elements.

We determined the type of repository either by using a web browser to issue an Identify request or by exploring the DPs web site.

3. Results

3.1. Data Providers

Based on the information we gathered from reviewing the metadata records and/or web sites of the 82 DPs, we divided the DPs into three broad categories: STI (Scientific and Technical Information), Humanities, and Combo (both STI and Humanities). By number of repositories, 33 DPs fell into the Humanities category, 27 into STI, and 22 into Combo (STI-Humanities), not adjusting for duplicate domain names.

3.2. Metadata Records

The total number of records harvested from the 82 DPs was 910,919. The average number of records per DP was 11,109. When we divided the number of records as a percentage among the three types of repositories, Humanities repositories held 43% of the records, STI repositories 31%, and Combo (STI-Humanities), 26%.

3.3. Dublin Core Metadata Elements

As a ratio against the total number of records, there was an average of eight DC elements used per record, with an average of 91,785 DC elements in each DP (Table 1). The top five DC elements used, taken as a proportion of either the total number of DC elements or the total number of records, accounted for 71% of all element usage while the least-used five elements accounted for 6% of usage. The results showed that just over half of the 82 DPs used only the creator and identifier elements for approximately half of their overall usage.

Table 1. Percentage of DC Elements by All DC Elements and All Records

	Records (General Summary)		
DC Element	Number of Elements per Record	Each Element as a % of the Total Number of Elements Used (n/7,526,331)	Each Element as a % of the Total Number of Records Across All DPs (n/910,919)
creator	1,617,910	21.5	177.6
identifier	1,292,707	17.2	141.9
title	860,488	11.4	94.5
date	834,949	11.1	91.7
type	802,538	10.7	88.1
subject	495,414	6.6	54.4
description	463,833	6.2	50.9
rights	312,403	4.2	34.3
publisher	235,759	3.1	25.9
coverage	202,936	2.7	22.3
language	146,579	1.9	16.1
format	136,501	1.8	15.0
relation	47,748	0.6	5.2
contributor	39,743	0.5	4.3
source	36,823	0.5	4.0
Total:	7,526,331	100	826.2

When the 15 DC elements were cross tabulated as a percentage within each DP (Table 2), the top five elements used remained the same, but the order, from most- to least-used, changed. When calculated as a percentage within each DP, almost 99% of DPs used the title element. Calculating the least-used DC elements as a percentage within a DP changed two of the five least-used elements, compared to the previous order.

STI, Humanities, and Combo (STI-Humanities) DPs each used creator, title, identifier, and type as their top four most-used elements. STI and Combo (STI-Humanities) DPs both used date to round out the top five, matching the trend across all DPs, while Humanities DPs used rights as the fifth most-used element. The creator and identifier elements accounted for more than half of the DC elements used by STI DPs, while in Humanities DPs, title, identifier, creator and type accounted for 48% of element usage. The creator, identifier and date elements accounted for almost 60% of the total number of DC elements used by Combo (STI-Humanities) DPs.

Table 2. Percentage of DC Elements by All DPs

DPs (Summary of Crosstabs Results)				
DC Element	Number of DPs That *Never* Used a Particular Element Out of 82 DPs		Number of DPs That Used a Particular Element Out of 82 DPs	
	No.	%	No.	%
title	1	1.2	81	98.8
creator	4	4.9	78	95.1
date	6	7.3	76	92.7
identifier	7	8.5	75	91.5
type	10	12.2	72	87.8
subject	14	17.1	68	82.9
description	23	28.0	59	72.0
language	39	47.6	43	52.4
publisher	41	50.0	41	50.0
format	43	52.4	39	47.6
rights	46	56.1	36	43.9
contributor	50	61.0	32	39.0
source	52	63.4	30	36.6
coverage	66	80.5	16	19.5
relation	66	80.5	16	19.5

We examined univariate statistics for all variables, but other than those reported above these were not particularly informative. The chi-square values test showed no significant difference in the observed versus the expected results for the eight most-used DC elements within a DP, but $p < .05$ for the 7 least-used DC elements. We ran three Independent Samples t-tests, and paired the 3 types of DPs as three sets against each of the 15 DC elements. The results did not produce $p < .05$ in any of the three tests.

4. Discussion

The results show that the unqualified DCMES is not used to the fullest extent possible within OAI-PMH-compliant DPs. We did not expect every author or cataloguer who submits metadata to use each element at least once, but neither did we expect that two elements out of fifteen would make up half the element usage in over half of the DPs. The implication for the OAI is that building relevant cross-resource services based on the unqualified DCMES will be difficult at best, due to its underutilization. As well, the OAI technical committee may need to reconsider mandating the use of the unqualified DCMES.

Burnett, Ng, & Park [2] studied six metadata standards and found that title, author, and identifier are common to all the schemes, and that two others – place and date – are common to five of the six schemes. The top five elements used in OAI-PMH-compliant DPs are: title, creator, date, identifier, and type, whether viewed as a proportion of total elements, total records, or total DPs. Thus, the results correlate with the results of previous studies of metadata elements, but support the results at the system level, rather than the schema level.

The trend we see across all of the results is for a very small number, whether it is DPs or DC elements, to dominate. Out of 82 DPs, five (citebase, arXiv, dlpscoll, lcoa1, and uiLib) hold 85% of the metadata records. Users have a choice of 15 DC elements, but five (creator, identifier, title, date, and type) are used 71% of the time.

The fact that approximately a quarter of the DPs could not be harvested, could not be harvested regularly, or did not provide any records reflects the version 1.1 experimental phase of the OAI-PMH. Many administrators adopted the OAI-PMH early in the protocol development; thus, either the implementation was problematic or the administrators registered their repositories before they had records in place to be harvested.

The high number of Humanities and "Combination" DPs supports the belief in the information community that the OAI has long since extended beyond its e-print roots.

5. Future work and conclusions

One area for future work would be an examination of why the DCMES is so underutilized. Is the source of the underutilization problem with the unqualified DCMES itself or with the users and information professionals who supply the metadata to the DPs, or both? Although some DPs are author self-archiving, others contain metadata prepared by information professionals. Until the source of the underutilization issue is determined and resolved, it will be difficult to build relevant cross-resource services on top of the OAI-PMH using the unqualified DCMES.

In conclusion, the unqualified DCMES is not used to its fullest extent within OAI-PMH-complaint DPs. Five of the 15 elements of the DCMES – creator, identifier, title, date and type – are used 71% of the time. The least-used five elements – language, format, relation, contributor, and source – account for 6% of usage. Just over half of the 82 DPs used only the creator and identifier elements for approximately half of their overall usage. While the reasons for the underutilization of the DCMES need to be determined, the implication of this study is that the unqualified DCMES may not be the most appropriate metadata format for the OAI technical committee to mandate for the OAI-PMH.

6. Acknowledgements

We would like to thank Gregory B. Newby for his advice and editorial feedback. We would also like to thank Michael L. Nelson for suggesting the initial area that evolved into the actual research topic as well as his advice and feedback.

7. References

[1] Brody, T. (2002), "Celestial Open Archives Gateway". Retrieved November 9, 2002 from http://celestial.eprints.org/.

[2] Burnett, K., Ng, K., & Park, S. (1999). A Comparison of the Two Traditions of Metadata Development. Journal of the American Society for Information Science, 50(13), 1209-1217.

[3] Dublin Core Metadata Initiative. (1999). Dublin Core Metadata Element Set, Version 1.1: Reference Description. Retrieved November 24, 2002, from http://www.dublincore.org/documents/dces/.

[4] Lagoze, C. (2001, January). Keeping Dublin Core Simple: Cross-Domain Discovery or Resource Description? D-Lib Magazine, 7(1). Retrieved January 27, 2001 from http://www.dlib.org/dlib/january01/lagoze/01lagoze.html.

[5] Lagoze, C., Van de Sompel, H., Nelson, M., & Warner, S. (2002). The Open Archives Initiative Protocol for Metadata Harvesting. Protocol Version 2.0 of 2002-6-14, document version 2002/09/13T11:34:00Z. Retrieved July 12, 2002, available from http://www.openarchives.org/OAI_protocol/openarchivesprotocol.html.

[6] Suleman, H., & Fox, E. (2001, December). A Framework for Building Open Digital Libraries. D-Lib Magazine, 7(12). Retrieved November 26, 2002, from http://www.dlib.org/dlib/december01/suleman/12suleman.html.

[7] Ward, J. (2002). A Quantitative Analysis of Dublin Core Metadata Element Set (DCMES) Usage in Data Providers Registered with the Open Archives Initiative (OAI). Unpublished master's paper, the University of North Carolina at Chapel Hill.

Extracting Geometry from Digital Models in a Cultural Heritage Digital Library

Thomas L. Milbank
Perseus Project
Tufts University
124 Eaton Hall
Medford MA 02155
tmilbank@perseus.tufts.edu

Abstract

This paper describes research to enhance the integration between digital models and the services provided by the document management systems of digital libraries. Processing techniques designed for XML texts are applied to X3D models, allowing specific geometry to be automatically retrieved and displayed. The research demonstrates that models designed on object-oriented paradigms are most easily exploited by XML document management systems.

1. Introduction

Much like a traditional library, a digital library can operate as a repository of objects that are identified using separate metadata records and subsequently disseminated as is. But more sophisticated digital libraries have evolved that are able to process objects both before and as they are delivered. The processes or "services" customize the document to the user.

Electronic texts are possibly the most frequently and most highly customized of objects disseminated by digital libraries. The Perseus Digital Library, for example, filters SGML- and XML-encoded documents through processes that automatically add links to lexical tools, named-entities, and citations (to name only a few of the customizations offered). Other library objects, too, can be customized. For example, much effort is being expended on new systems that index, search, and extract content from multimedia documents [1, 5, 9]. These systems are not widely available, however, and digital libraries often disseminate multimedia files without customization as a consequence.

2. Models and libraries

Digital models are characteristic of multimedia documents. That is to say, digital libraries typically treat models as immutable objects retrieved in toto on the basis of their cataloged metadata. If one assumes that a single model represents a logical whole, and that users will be interested in that whole, then in toto retrieval is a suitable method for model dissemination. These assumptions are not defensible, however, in the context of a cultural heritage digital library where the models' subjects themselves might not be complete and where user interest might be expected to lie solely in specific parts of a model [9].

The problem with in toto retrieval of digital models can be expressed in a paradigm. Imagine, for example, two digital models: one of a column capital cataloged in a digital library system as "Capital," and one of a peripteral temple cataloged as "Temple" — without additional reference to any component architectural blocks. Imagine, too, that the Temple model includes geometry for every architectural element, from the foundation blocks right up through the column capitals and the roof tiles (but note that this model could be constructed with less detail and only contain geometry for "platform," "columns," "roof," etc.). Now assume a user who is exclusively interested in models of column capitals to evidence research on shape development. This user is likely to retrieve the Capital model but is not likely to retrieve the Temple model, among the sub-objects of which are models of column capitals. Of course, had the creator of the Temple model simplified its geometry, the failure to retrieve it could have less significance to the user. But what might be done to identify undocumented geometry that has been individually modeled and incorporated into a larger construct? And what might be done to extract that sub-object from the larger construct automatically?

3. Models as texts

The paradigm illustrates the need for enhanced integration between digital models and the services provided by the document management systems of digital libraries. One might argue that more detailed cataloging of metadata is all that is necessary. But, while resolving the problem of sub-object identification, more exacting practices will collide with cost-benefit barriers and still not provide a method for sub-object extraction. A superior solution is to develop a way to parse the models and index their component geometry. The method proposed here is to masquerade digital models as XML (Extensible Markup Language) texts and to extend processing techniques that are already used by document management systems to these veiled models [8, 3, 7]. There are additional benefits to this approach; the method provides a basis for the integration of models with automatic linking services and has the potential to improve integration with 3D shape-matching services [5].

The proposed method is appropriate to models that have been stored in an ASCII format. For an object that is preserved in a cultural heritage digital library, the use of ASCII also makes archival sense [2, 6, 8]. Any structured ASCII format (e.g. IGES/STEP and DXF) for which an XML application might be composed is suitable. The research described here focuses on models encoded in X3D (Extensible 3D, ISO/IEC 19775), an XML application of VRML (Virtual Reality Modeling Language, ISO/IEC 14772).

The document management system of the Perseus Digital Library has multiple capabilities [10]. Chief among these are its ability to handle XML documents of any DTD (Document Type Definition), to extract structural and descriptive metadata from XML documents, and to deliver fragments of documents in well-formed XML. The system is based on abstract structures to which elements of one or more DTDs are mapped, and on indices of these mappings. The generation of the indices is automatic and can be configured to include descriptive content; this content is simultaneously extracted and stored in an RDF (Resource Description Framework) database to improve the discovery of resources.

In the extension of the Perseus document management system to X3D models, an abstract structure is proposed for each culturally significant object (be it a sculpture, vase, etc.). The following example illustrates the procedure using objects of Egyptian architecture. For one or more models of the site of Giza, the elements of the X3D Compact DTD are mapped to an abstract structure "Giza." And for one or more models of the Gizan tomb G 2110, the elements of the X3D Compact DTD are mapped to an abstract structure "Tomb G 2110." Although only one DTD is used, the abstract structure mapping is necessary for the document manager to handle instances in which there are multiple versions of a model encoded according to different DTDs (e.g. three models of tomb G 2110 with DTDs for X3D, XML-ized STEP, and XML-ized DXF defining the structure of one model each). The document management system generates for each model

an index that includes the byte offset for `<Group>` elements (those that assemble sub-objects into meaningful hierarchies) and `<Transform>` elements (those that define meaningful hierarchies and describe associated coordinate systems). Additionally, each index includes the content from the `DEF` attributes, which name a model's sub-objects and sub-object groups. Using the indexed information, the document manager is able to open an X3D model, find the extents of a desired group, and read the embedded sub-object(s). The output is merged with additional tags to create a valid X3D document that is passed to an XSL (Extensible Stylesheet Language) transformation utility for styling into VRML; the result is displayed in an HTML page. Ultimately, when presented with a request for "Tomb G 2110," the document manager is not only able to return the geometry of the tomb model, but also that of the tomb sub-object in the Giza model.

4. Implications for model design

The treatment of digital models as electronic texts illuminates the need for well-defined and well-named geometry. Object-oriented modeling, a common paradigm among the tools designed for mechanical engineers and artists, is suited to these requirements natively [4]. Nested and related hierarchies of uniquely named components characterize models constructed with object-oriented tools. Layer-oriented modeling, the most common paradigm for tools targeted to Architecture/Engineering/Construction professionals, is suited to these requirements only with forethought. Since a component is identified by the name of the layer on which it resides, several components grouped on the same layer effectively have identical names. And since layers are not nested, layer-oriented modeling flattens the hierarchies that establish name inheritances crucial to the identification and extraction of geometry. If a layer-oriented paradigm is used, a separate layer with an appropriately specific name should be created for every component of the model. However, this practice contradicts various standard layer naming conventions, which currently do not accommodate the necessary specificity.

5. Conclusions

Research conducted thus far suggests that common XML text processing techniques can be applied to digital models successfully. The techniques facilitate the identification of geometry that has been individually modeled and incorporated into larger constructs. And they enable the extraction of sub-object geometry. Moreover, the application of XML text processing techniques establishes a framework for the integration or improved integration of digital models with additional services, such as automatic linking and 3D shape-matching. The achieved enhancements add value to the models, which are able to be tailored to the needs of specific cultural heritage research.

6. Acknowledgments

A grant from the Digital Libraries Initiative Phase 2 (NSF IIS-9817484) provided support for this work.

7. References

[1] Advanced Research and Development Activity (ARDA): Video Analysis and Content Extraction (VACE) Program. http://www.ic-arda.org/InfoExploit/vace/index.html

[2] Aschenbrenner, A. *Long-Term Preservation of Digital Material*. Thesis. Institut für Softwaretechnik und Interaktive Systeme der Technischen Universität Wien. 2001. http://citeseer.nj.nec.com/aschenbrenner01longterm.html

[3] Chavez, R.F., and T.L. Milbank. London calling: GIS, VR, and the Victorian period. In *Proceedings of the 7th International Conference on Virtual Systems and Multimedia*, pp. 335–344, 2001. http://www.perseus.tufts.edu/Articles/20011025_Chavez_V SMM.pdf

[4] Fishwick, P.A. On Web-Based Models and Repositories. In *Proceedings of SPIE: Enabling Technology for Simulation Science V*, 4367:11–16, 2001. http://citeseer.nj.nec.com/fishwick01webbased.html

[5] Funkhouser, T., P. Min, M. Kazhdan, J. Chen, A. Halderman, D. Dobkin, and D. Jacobs. A search engine for 3D models. *ACM Transactions on Graphics (TOG)*, 22(1):83–105, 2003. http://doi.acm.org/10.1145/588272.588279

[6] Isenburg, M. and J. Snoeyink. Coding with ASCII: compact, yet text-based 3D content. In *Proceedings First International Symposium on 3D Data Processing Visualization and Transmission*, pp. 609–616, 2002. http://citeseer.nj.nec.com/article/isenburg02coding.html

[7] Milbank, T.L. Spacing Out: Web 3D and the Reconstruction of Archaeological Sites. Paper presented at *Ancient Studies -- New Technology: The World Wide Web and Scholarly Research, Communication, and Publication in Ancient, Byzantine, and Medieval Studies*, Newport, Rhode Island, 8–10 December 2000. http://www.perseus.tufts.edu/Articles/20001208_Milbank_ ASNT.pdf

[8] Niccolucci, F. XML and the future of humanities computing. *Applied Computing Review*, 10(1):43–47, 2002. http://doi.acm.org/10.1145/568235.568244

[9] Schurmans, U., A. Razdan, A. Simon, P. McCartney, M. Marzke, D. van Alfen, G. Jones, J. Rowe, G. Farin, D. Collins, M. Zhu, D. Liu, and M. Bae. Advances in Geometric Modeling and Feature Extraction on Pots, Rocks and Bones for Representation and Query via the Internet. *Computer Applications in Archaeology (CAA)*, 2001. http://3dk.asu.edu/archives/publication/g3dk/caa2001.pdf

[10] Smith, D.A., A. Mahoney, and J.A. Rydberg-Cox. Management of XML Documents in an Integrated Digital Library. *Markup Languages: Theory and Practice*, 2(3):205–214, 2000. http://www.perseus.tufts.edu/Articles/hopper.pdf

Assembling and Enriching Digital Library Collections

David Bainbridge, John Thompson and Ian H. Witten
Department of Computer Science
University of Waikato
Hamilton, New Zealand
{davidb, jmt12, ihw}@cs.waikato.ac.nz

Abstract

People who create digital libraries need to gather together the raw material, add metadata as necessary, and design and build new collections. This paper sets out the requirements for these tasks and describes a new tool that supports them interactively, making it easy for users to create their own collections from electronic files of all types. The process involves selecting documents for inclusion, coming up with a suitable metadata set, assigning metadata to each document or group of documents, designing the form of the collection in terms of document formats, searchable indexes, and browsing facilities, building the necessary indexes and data structures, and putting the collection in place for others to use. Moreover, different situations require different workflows, and the system must be flexible enough to cope with these demands. Although the tool is specific to the Greenstone digital library software, the underlying ideas should prove useful in more general contexts.

1. Introduction

One attractive feature of digital libraries is that they make it possible—even easy—to assemble new anthologies of targeted information, organize them, provide worldwide access through the Internet, and distribute them on removable media. Moreover, this can be accomplished by domain specialists who do not necessarily have information science training and who lack the institutional backup of a conventional library catalog room.

These advantages could be more widely realized if appropriate support were available for people who create information collections. Such people, who have been called "corpus editors" [6], need an interactive tool that facilitates the entire process of building digital library collections, and that is what this paper describes. We assume that the source material is available electronically, or has already been scanned into digital form. In practice when building digital library collections it is often

necessary to deal with paper documents and the process of digitization and OCR [10]; however, we cannot address these issues here.

The requirement for such a tool originated in the context of digital libraries for sustainable development [13]. Effective human development blossoms from empowerment rather than gifting: as the Chinese proverb says, "Give a man a fish and he will eat for a day; teach him to fish and he will eat for the rest of his days." Although disseminating information originating in the developed world is certainly a useful activity, a more effective strategy for sustained long-term human development is to disseminate the capability of creating information collections rather than the collections themselves. And if we can help inhabitants of developing countries to assemble their own information collections, surely we can use the same techniques in our own homes and institutions too.

The tool that we describe here, called the "Gatherer," works in consort with the Greenstone digital library software [14, 16], and is GPL-licensed open source software. This makes the work of building it much easier, for other GPL modules can be incorporated verbatim—and we have taken full advantage of this. It is implemented in Java, for portability and efficiency, and uses the Swing user interface system [4].

This paper begins by identifying the requirements for assembling and enriching digital library collections, and then reviews public domain digital library software tools that help with collection creation. We next describe the Gatherer by presenting a detailed illustrated walkthrough of its operation and then expand upon this to describe how it supports different workflows.

2. Requirements

Our conception of digital libraries is captured by the following brief characterization [1]:

A collection of digital objects, including text, video, and audio, along with methods for access and retrieval, and for selection, organization and maintenance of the collection.

Table 1 Implementation summary of sample open source digital library systems

System	URL	Platform	Technology	Supported standards
CDS/ISIS	www.unesco.org/webworld/isis	Windows	Various	
Harvest	harvest.sourceforge.net	Unix	C, PERL, Bison, Flex	
Koha	www.Koha.org	Unix	mySQL, PERL	Z39.50, MARC
EPrints	www.EPrints.org	Unix	mySQL, PERL	Open Archives
DSpace	www.DSpace.org	Java/Unix	postgreSQL, Lucene (indexing)	Open Archives
Greenstone	www.greenstone.org	Unix, Windows, MaxOS X	GDBM, MG (indexing), PERL (building), C++ (runtime)	Z39.50, Open Archives , MARC

It is the last point—selection, organization and maintenance—that is addressed in this paper. Our view is that just as new books acquired by physical libraries are integrated with the existing catalog on the basis of their metadata, so one should easily be able to add material to a digital library without having to edit its content in any way. Once added, such material should immediately become a first-class component of the library, fully integrated with existing search and browsing structures through explicitly-stated metadata. The challenge is to provide an easy-to-use interactive interface to help librarians provide appropriate metadata, and design and build collections.

The first step in putting together a new information collection is to gather the source material from local files, or from the Web, or perhaps from already-existing digital library collections. These files may be in many different formats. Furthermore, they may include metadata, perhaps contained in document files, perhaps in separate metadata files, or perhaps already embedded in an existing digital library collection.

Next, it is necessary to select, define, or modify a metadata set. When importing existing metadata, it may be necessary to convert between different standards, or modify an existing metadata schema to include new elements. Also, it is frequently convenient to be able to specify metadata for each document interactively. Sometimes one wishes to assign the same metadata value to a group of files, or directories, in a single operation. New element values should be stored so that they can be re-used by selecting them, to reduce the risk of introducing errors through retyping.

The next step is to design the collection structure around the available metadata, build the indexes and browsing structures, and move the collection to a place where it can be served to potential users. These operations tend to be specific to a particular digital library system. In our case, we have used Greenstone as the underlying digital library infrastructure.

The extensible nature of open-source software poses its own difficulties. New modules ("plug-ins" and "classifiers" in Greenstone terminology; see below) are self-documenting in that they contain information on the options and switches they support. This needs to be garnered automatically and presented to users where appropriate when they are designing collections.

Building digital library collections inevitably involves some consideration of workflow. Is the collection built on a local computer or a central digital library server? If the latter, do the files originate on the server or the local workstation from which the digital library is being accessed? Or is the material sent to a central collection editor from one or more remote locations? And if so, where is the metadata assigned—remotely, centrally, a combination of both, or produced remotely and checked and edited centrally?

On the whole, existing systems assume a specific workflow model that is motivated by the needs of the intended user base. However, in our work we strive for greater generality. A range of different workflows can be accommodated, and we believe that the design is flexible enough to be used in situations that have not explicitly been envisaged. For example, in the "remote submission/central collection" scenario, our system helps in both roles: preparing metadata that accompanies documents when they are submitted, and reviewing and editing submissions before incorporating them into the collection.

3. Related Work

Recent years have seen a steep rise in the number of digital library solutions available, and it is impractical to review them all here. Instead we concentrate on examining pertinent strategies that have been successfully deployed. Proprietary systems are not discussed because insufficient design information is available.

The designers of the digital library systems described below generally use off-the-shelf technology to implement significant parts of the system. In particular they use a database (typically relational) to store and retrieve metadata, and an indexing tool if full-text searching of document content is to be provided. A web server capable of running CGI scripts is another widely used component, because the most prevalent form of digital library user interface acts through a web browser. These components are bound together by custom software that implements the workflow constituting the digital library system.

Table 1 lists six open source digital library systems, the last being our own, and summarizes the platforms, principal implementation technologies, and component standards.

CDS/ISIS is an information storage and retrieval system that has been under continual development by UNESCO since 1985 and is intended, in particular, to address the requirements of developing countries [3]. It provides a multilingual text database that is widely used for storing bibliographic information and distributing it on CD-ROM, and also for thesaurus management.

Harvest is a system designed to collect information and make it searchable through a web interface [7]. It has a module (also called "Gatherer," but no relation to the system described here) that extracts metadata from source documents using a *flex* parser for pattern matching. Customizing extraction is, in essence, writing a new set of *flex* rules. Extracted metadata is used as a "snippet" to present to the user when displaying search results. However, it is not possible to restrict searches to particular metadata fields.

EPrints is designed for archiving on-line reports, particularly academic research papers [8, 9]. Indexing and a subject hierarchy are based around a relational database of bibliographic metadata that a site administrator can adjust to suit the sort of reports being stored. Source documents are linked to their corresponding bibliographic record so that they can be accessed at runtime as a side-product of record retrieval. Through a network of web pages, end-users (who are often authors of papers in the archive) and the administrator participate in a workflow cycle of submission (article and descriptive metadata), optional editing control, and deposit—thereby accomplishing the developers' stated aim of a "self-archiving" methodology.

Using exactly the same implementation technology, Koha[1] focuses on a different community—public librarians and their users [2]. The services provided are strikingly different to those offered by EPrints, but the underlying techniques are similar. In addition to bibliographic information (expressed in MARC format) in the relational database, recorded items are extended to include membership, reading list, acquisition, and budget information, amongst other things. However, the same basic arrangement of web forms is used to support a workflow of submission and editing (password protected

---

[1] The name is a Maori word meaning gift or donation, chosen to reflect the open source nature of this project.

if required). From the user's perspective, Koha is like the graphical, web-based OPAC systems one has come to associate with public libraries.

DSpace, a combined venture by MIT and Hewlett Packard, targets the digital content needs of institutions [17]. Strongly influenced by the Open Archival Information Systems (OAIS) reference model [5], DSpace supports submission, searching, browsing and retrieval. Searching includes full-text retrieval, which, through the use of Apache's Lucene indexing tool, allows for incremental updates.

Considerable attention is paid to the submission workflow. Users wishing to submit items first log into DSpace, then enter files and associate metadata with them using a modified Dublin Core schema. On receipt of a submission, DSpace notifies the following people:

Reviewer, who accepts or rejects the submission

Approver, who checks for file errors, etc.

Editor, who checks and augments metadata.

Once these steps are complete, the submission is archived into the system, paying particular attention to the data format and level of preservation.

3.1 Greenstone

Based on the study of the requirements, we have designed a new piece of software, the Gatherer, which supports interactive collection building and is closely coupled with Greenstone. The design has benefited greatly from our study of other open source digital library systems, and from our own experience with two existing Greenstone modules, the Collector [15] and the Organizer [12]. We have also learned from the "Metadata Editor," an independent software module created by a separate organization that works with Greenstone. We describe these related systems first before providing an account of the Gatherer in the next section.

Developed over the last five years, the Greenstone open source digital library software from the New Zealand Digital Library project enjoys considerable success and is widely used [14, 16]. It provides a new way of organizing information and making it available over the Internet. A *collection* of information is typically comprised of several thousand or several million *documents*, and a uniform interface is provided to all documents in a collection. A library may include many different collections, each organized differently—though there is a strong family resemblance in how they are presented. Its strengths include international language support, multilingual interfaces, and a flexible document importing process that handles different formats— HTML, Word, PDF, PostScript, and E-mail messages, to name but a few. Images, video and audio require accompanying textual metadata.

For the purposes of the present paper it is necessary to learn a little about three key design features of Greenstone: plug-ins, classifiers, and the collection configuration file. In Greenstone, the structure, organization, and presentation of any particular collection are determined when the collection is set up. This includes such things as the format or formats of the source documents, how they should be displayed on the screen, the sources of metadata, what browsing facilities are to be provided, what full-text search indexes are required, and how the search results should be displayed. Once the collection is in place, it is easy to add new documents to it—so long as they have the same format as the existing documents, and the same metadata is provided, in exactly the same way. The structure, organization, and presentation of the collection is recorded in a text file called the "collection configuration file."

Source material is imported into the system through "plug-ins" that cater for different document formats. Any given collection may have source documents in many different forms. There are plug-ins to handle all the file formats mentioned above, along with some proprietary formats, and for generic tasks such as recursively traversing directory structures containing such documents. Plug-ins can be written to accommodate new document types.

Greenstone builds browsing indexes from metadata. This is done using "classifiers," which are analogous to plug-ins. Classifiers create browsing indexes of various kinds, based on metadata—alphabetically tabbed lists (of titles, for example), date-selected lists, and hierarchical browsing structures. Like plug-ins, new classifiers can be written for special-purpose browsing structures.

3.2 The Collector

Part of Greenstone, the Collector is a utility for collection building with the following basic functions [15]:

- create a new collection with the same structure as an existing one;
- create a new collection with a different structure from existing ones;
- add new material to an existing collection;
- modify the structure of an existing collection;
- delete a collection;
- write an existing collection to a self-contained, self-installing CD-ROM.

It is modeled after popular end-user installation software (such as InstallShield[2]). Frequently called a software "wizard"—a term we deprecate because of its appeal to mysticism and connotations of utter inexplicability—this

---

[2] www.installshield.com

interaction style suits novice users because it simplifies the choices and presents them clearly.

The Collector is implemented as a web-based system. A user goes to a certain web address in any Greenstone installation to find a page that facilitates collection building. The ability to build collections is protected: users must log in first, and only those with appropriate privileges are allowed to build collections. Being web-based imposes certain restrictions. First, there are security issues with letting remote users transfer files to the site running the web server. Second, the user's local file space is only available in a limited way through the file-upload mechanism, meaning that only one file at a time can be specified. Third, web-based interaction was not designed for lengthy processes such as building digital library collections (which can take many hours of processor time for non-trivial collections), and special measures must be taken to ensure that the user receives appropriate feedback, and that the right things happen on moving to another page, or pressing the *Back* button, while the collection is being built.

Greenstone is so easy to install and run that, contrary to the assumptions we made when designing the Collector, users often work on a local copy of the software that runs on their own computer. They quite reasonably expect there to be a convenient mechanism for populating their collections with local files, which the Collector cannot do directly.

3.3 The Organizer

One of Greenstone's early adopters, SimpleWords of Brasov, Romania, uses it to build and distribute collections for humanitarian purposes—collections that share a common collection configuration file but have different content. Librarians must manually assign a substantial amount of metadata to each document in the collection. They do this using a uniform metadata scheme called the Development Library Set (DLS). However, the Collector does not provide any interactive way of specifying metadata to be added to documents. Although Greenstone accommodates different metadata formats, including a simple but flexible XML format, OAI, MARC records, a spreadsheet format, BibTeX, and even Refer, all metadata must be available in advance, stored in files.

SimpleWords implemented a separate utility, the Organizer, to create and edit the material associated with a collection conforming to their humanitarian format [12]. This is a Microsoft Visual C++ application, distributed with Greenstone. It assists in the creation of collections that use DLS.

The Organizer is designed to help manage all aspects of organizing a digital library collection: entering document titles, assigning subjects and other metadata, altering them, etc. It is, however, limited to a particular

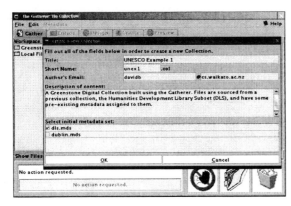

Figure 1. Starting a new collection

Figure 2. Exploring the local file space

document model, and users who wish to add metadata not included in this model would have to make manual modifications to the Organizer's results. Also, because it is restricted to Windows whereas Greenstone runs under Unix and MacOS X too, the Organizer is not fully integrated but works by generating intermediate files that Greenstone uses when building collections. While this loose coupling has some advantages in flexibility, it prevents the full collection-building process from being a single, integrated, task.

3.4 The Metadata Creator

Another organization, the Mercy Corps, centered in Portland Oregon and with operations in about thirty of the world's most unstable countries, uses Greenstone to organize its extensive collection of in-house documents, manuals, forms, and memos. They have made significant enhancements to support a workflow for new acquisitions to the library.

In their organization, field offices submit new documents by filling out metadata using a simple web-based form and attaching the document. This arrives in the in-tray of a central librarian who checks it for correctness and integrity before including it in the appropriate collection. Collections, rebuilt automatically every night, are available on the web for in-house use, and are written at regular intervals to CD-ROM for physical distribution.

Mercy Corps designed and implemented the Metadata Creator, an interactive web-based database system that allows users to enter and edit the metadata associated with a document. This module is used both by people in the field office when initially entering metadata, and by the central librarian who checks it. For the former it incorporates facilities for automatically submitting the document and metadata to the central office, while for the

latter it makes it easy to periodically rebuild the Greenstone collections with the new documents.

Although the Metadata Creator is at present restricted to the Mercy Corps' own in-house metadata standard, they are planning to release a Dublin Core version to the Greenstone community for general usage. Though it will remain useful as a lightweight metadata entry utility, like the Organizer it does not provide a tight coupling with the collection-building process, a serious omission from our requirements analysis.

4. The Gatherer: Functionality

The Gatherer allows users to collect sets of documents, import or assign metadata, and build them into a Greenstone collection. It differs from the Collector in that its default behaviour is to work on the computer running the Greenstone digital library software rather than building collections on a remote machine, and this permits a more flexible interface. It differs from the Organizer and the Metadata Creator in that it deals with unrestricted metadata sets, and can be tightly integrated with the Greenstone collection design and creation process.

The Gatherer is written in the Java language and is platform-independent. It incorporates various open-source packages for such tasks as file browsing, HTML rendering, web mirroring, and efficient table sorting.

The user works with it to build a Greenstone collection. It supports five basic activities, which can be interleaved but are nominally undertaken in this order:

1. Copy documents from the computer's file space, including existing collections, into the new collection. Any existing metadata remains "attached" to these documents. Documents may also be gathered from the web through a built-in mirroring facility.
2. Enrich the documents by adding further metadata to individual documents or groups of documents.

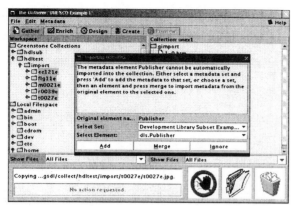

Figure 3. Importing existing metadata

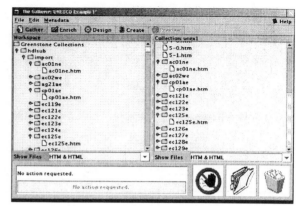

Figure 4. Filtering the file trees

3. Design the collection by determining its appearance and the access facilities that it will support.
4. Build the collection using Greenstone.
5. Preview the newly created collection.

4.1 Assembling the source material

To convey the operation of the Gatherer we work through a simple example. Figures 1 to 12 are screen snapshots at various points during the interaction. This example uses documents in the Humanity Development Library Subset collection, which is distributed with Greenstone. For expository purposes, the walkthrough takes the form of a single pass through the steps listed above. A more realistic pattern of use, however, is for users to switch back and forth through the various stages as the task proceeds.

Since Greenstone is a lightweight system that can easily be installed on small workstations or laptops, we have decided to focus on the situation where the collection editor works interactively on the same computer where collections are built. However, it is possible to use the Gatherer to collect document files and define interaction locally, without a digital library installation, and send them to a central location for building into a collection and serving on the Internet. At the central location a librarian can also use the Gatherer when deciding whether the documents are suitable to be added to the collection, and to check and edit the metadata that has been associated with them. This affords a degree of flexibility for different workflow requirements.

To commence interaction with the panels, the user must either open an existing collection or begin a new one. Figure 1 shows the user in the process of starting a new collection. She has selected *New* from the file menu and begun to fill out general information about the collection—its name, the E-mail address of the person responsible for it, and a brief description of the content— in the popup window. The collection name is a short phrase used throughout the digital library to identify the collection's content: existing collections have names like *Food and Nutrition Library*, *World Environmental Library*, and so on. The E-mail address specifies the first point of contact for any problems encountered with the collection. If the Greenstone software detects a problem, a diagnostic report is sent to this address.

The brief description is a statement describing the principles that govern what is included in the collection. It appears under the heading *About this collection* on the collection's initial page. Lesk [11] recommends that digital libraries articulate both the principles governing what is included and how the collection is organized. *About this collection* is designed to address the first point. Greenstone takes care of the second using help text, which is formed by automatically generating a list of access mechanisms based on the searching and browsing facilities that are included in the collection.

At this point, a metadata set is selected. Dublin Core is pre-supplied, but the user can create new metadata using a popup panel activated through the "metadata" menu. This has already been done for the DLS metadata set mentioned above, and the user has chosen this item for her new collection. Several different metadata sets can be associated with the same collection; the system keeps them distinct (so that, for example, documents can have both a Dublin Core *Title* and a DLS *Title*). Behind the scenes, metadata sets are represented in XML.

After clicking the *OK* button on the "new collection" popup, the remaining parts of the interface, which were grayed out before, become active. The *Gather* panel, selected by the eponymous tab near the top of Figure 1, is displayed initially. This allows the user to explore the local file space and existing collections, gathering up selected documents for the new collection. The panel is divided into two sections, the left for browsing existing

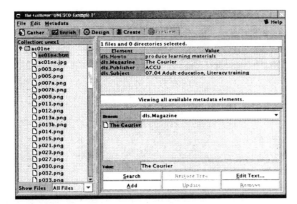

Figure 5. Assigning metadata using the Enrich view

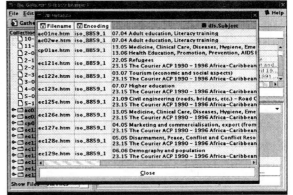

Figure 6. Viewing all metadata assigned to selected files

structures and the right for the documents in the collection.

Operations available at this stage include:

- Navigating the existing file structure hierarchy, and the one being created, in the usual way.
- Dragging and dropping files into the new collection.
- Multiple selection of files.
- Dragging and dropping entire sub-hierarchies.
- Deleting documents from the nascent collection.
- Creating new sub-hierarchies within the collection.
- Filtering the files that are visible, in both the local file system and the collection, based on predetermined groups or on standard file matching terms.
- Invoking the appropriate program to display the contents of a selected file, by double-clicking it.

Care is taken to deal appropriately with name clashes when files of the same name in different parts of the computer's directory structure are copied into the same folder of the collection.

In Figure 2 the user is using the interactive file tree display to explore the local file system. At this stage, the collection on the right is empty; the user populates it by dragging and dropping files of interest from the left to the right panel. Such files are "copied" rather than "moved": so as not to disturb the original file system. The usual techniques for multiple selection, dragging and dropping, structuring the new collection by creating subdirectories ("folders"), and deleting files from it by moving them to a trashcan, are all available. Through an extra panel, which can optionally be activated, the user can browse external Web sites and selectively mirror them; the result of this copying appears as another top-level folder on the left-hand side of the *Gather* panel.

Existing collections are represented by a subdirectory on the left called "Greenstone Collections," which can be opened and explored like any other directory. However, the documents therein differ from ordinary files because they already have metadata attached, which the Gatherer preserves when it moves them into the new collection.

Conflicts may arise because their metadata may have been assigned using a different metadata set from the one in use for the new collection, and the Gatherer helps the user resolve these. In Figure 3 the user has selected some documents from an existing collection and dragged them into the new one. The popup window explains that the metadata element *Publisher* cannot be automatically imported, and asks the user to either select a metadata set and press *Add* to add the metadata element to that set, or choose a metadata set, then an element, and press *Merge* to effectively rename the old metadata element to the new one by merging the two. Metadata in subsequent documents will automatically be handled in the same way.

When large file sets are selected, dragged, and dropped into the new collection, the copying operation may take some time—particularly if metadata conversion is involved. To indicate progress, the Gatherer shows which file is being copied and what percentage of files has been processed. The implementation is multi-threaded: the user can proceed to another stage while copying is still in progress.

Special facilities are needed for dealing with large file sets. For example, the user can choose to filter the file tree to show only certain files, using a dropdown menu of file types displayed underneath the trees. In Figure 4, only the HTM and HTML files are being shown (and only these files will be copied by drag and drop).

Another source of documents is the web itself. The Gatherer has a *Mirror* panel that allows the user to interact with a mini web browser and select certain pages, or sites, for mirroring. There are many options: mirroring depth, automatically download embedded objects like images, only mirror from the same site, etc. The actual download operation is accomplished by *wget*, a widely-used open-source mirroring utility.

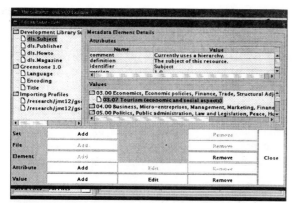

Figure 7. Editing the metadata set

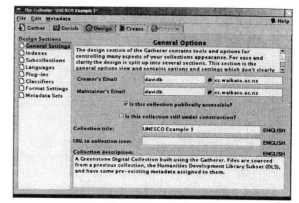

Figure 8. Designing the collection

4.2 Enriching the documents

The next phase in collection building is to enrich the documents by adding metadata. The *Enrich* tab brings up a new panel of information (Figure 5), which shows the document tree representing the collection on the left and on the right allows metadata to be added to individual documents, or groups of documents.

Documents that are copied during the first step come with any applicable metadata attached. If a document is part of a Greenstone collection, previously defined metadata is carried over to the new collection. Of course, this new collection may have a different metadata set, or perhaps just a subset of the defined metadata, and only metadata that pertains to the new collection's set is carried over. Resolution of such conflicts may require user intervention via a supplementary dialog (Figure 3). Any choices made are remembered for subsequent file copies.

The *Enrich* panel allows the metadata set in use for the collection to be edited. For example, new elements can be added, or new values can be added to the set of existing values for an element. If the element's values have a hierarchical structure, the hierarchy can be edited using the same editor that is used when editing the metadata set.

Operations at this stage include:

- Assigning new and existing metadata values to documents.
- Assigning metadata to an individual document or to a directory of documents (including nested documents).
- Assigning hierarchical metadata, whose structure can be dynamically updated if required.
- Editing or updating assigned metadata.
- Reviewing the metadata assigned to a selection of files and directories.

For our walkthrough example, in Figure 5 the user has selected the document *ac01ne.htm* and assigned "The

Courier" as its *Magazine* metadata. The buttons for updating and removing metadata become active depending on what selections have been made.

During the enrichment phase, or indeed at any other time, the user can choose to view all the metadata that has been assigned to documents in the collection. This is done by selecting *Metadata* from the main menu bar, which brings up a popup window like that in Figure 6 that shows the metadata in spreadsheet form. For large collections it is useful to be able to view the metadata associated with certain document types only, and if the user has specified a file filter as mentioned above, only the selected documents are shown in the metadata display.

The panel in Figure 7 allows the user to edit metadata sets. Here, the user is looking at the *Subject* element of the DLS set. The values of this element form a hierarchy, and the user is examining, and perhaps changing, the list of values assigned to it. The same panel also allows you to change the "profile" for mapping elements of one metadata set to another. This profile is created when importing documents from collections that have pre-assigned metadata.

4.3 Designing the collection

The *Design* panel (Figures 9–10) allows one to specify the structure, organization, and presentation of the collection being created. As noted earlier, the result of this process is recorded in a "collection configuration file," which is Greenstone's way of expressing the facilities that a collection requires. This step involves a series of separate interaction screens, each dealing with one aspect of the collection design. In effect, it serves as a graphical equivalent to the usual process of editing the configuration file manually.

Operations include:

- Reviewing and editing collection-level metadata such

as title, author and public availability of the collection.

- Defining what full-text indexes are to be built.
- Creating sub-collections and having indexes built for them.
- Adding or removing support for predefined interface languages.
- Constructing a list of plug-ins to be used, and their arguments.
- Presenting the list to the user for review and modification.
- Configuring individual plug-ins.
- Constructing a list of "classifiers," their arguments, assignment and configuration.
- Assigning formatting strings to various controls within the collection, thus altering its appearance.
- Reviewing the metadata sets, and their elements, used in the collection.

In Figure 8 the user has clicked the *Design* tab and is reviewing the general information about the collection, entered when the new collection was created. On the left are listed the various facets that the user can configure: Indexes, Subcollections, Languages, Plug-ins, Classifiers, Format Settings, and Metadata Sets. Appearance and functionality varies between these. For example, clicking the *Plug-in* button brings up the screen shown in Figure 9, which allows you to add, remove or configure plug-ins, and change the order in which the plug-ins are applied to documents.

Both plug-ins and classifiers have many different arguments or "options" that the user can supply. The dialog box in Figure 10 shows the user specifying arguments to some of the plug-ins. The grayed-out fields become active when the user adds the option by clicking the tick-box beside it. Because Greenstone is a continually growing open-source system, the number of options tends to increase as developers add new facilities. To help cope with this, Greenstone has a "plug-in information" utility program that lists the options available for each plug-in, and the Gatherer automatically invokes this to determine what options to show. This allows the interactive user interface to automatically keep pace with developments in the software.

4.4 Building the collection

The *Build* panel (Figure 11) is to construct a collection based on the documents and assigned metadata. The brunt of this work is borne by the Greenstone code itself (which must be installed for the Gatherer to perform this step). The user controls this external process through a series of separate interaction screens, each dealing with the arguments provided to a certain stage of the creation process.

The user observes the building process though a window that shows not only the text output generated by Greenstone's importing and index-building scripts, but also progress bars that indicate the overall degree of completion of each script.

Figure 11 shows the *Create* view. On the left are shown groups of options that can be applied during the creation process: General, Import, Build, All, Message-Log. The user selects appropriate values for the options.

This figure illustrates a popup "tool tip" that is available throughout the Gatherer to explain the function of each argument. In this case the user is selecting the verbosity level for the collection creation process, and the tool tip advises that this is a number between zero and three that controls how much information about the process is printed to the standard error stream—0 gives a little, 3 gives lots.

When satisfied with the arguments, the user clicks *Build Collection*. Greenstone programs continually print text that indicates progress, and the Gatherer shows these, along with a more informative progress bar.

4.5 Previewing

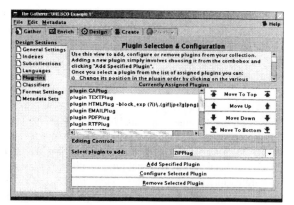

Figure 9. Specifying which plug-ins to use

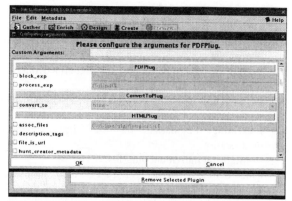

Figure 10. Configuring the arguments to a plug-in

The *Preview* panel (Figure 12) is to view the collection that has been built. The Gatherer provides a preview in a panel that looks just like a web browser. In practice, previewing often shows up deficiencies in the collection design, or in the individual metadata values, and the user frequently returns to earlier stages to correct these. This tab becomes active once the collection has been created.

4.6 Help

The Gatherer incorporates extensive on-line help, which is invoked using the *Help* item at the right of the main menu bar at the top of each of the Figures. This opens up a hierarchically structured file of help text, and account is taken of the user's current context to highlight the section that is appropriate to the present stage of the interaction. Furthermore, as noted above, whenever the mouse is held still over any interactive object a small window pops up to give a textual "tool tip," as illustrated in Figure 11.

5. Configurability

Each system reviewed under "Related work" in Section 3 adopts a particular style of workflow, a natural consequence of the focused application domain that motivated the project. However, our requirements include the more ambitious goal of supporting multiple workflow styles. This is accomplished through a "preferences" screen that allows users to choose which panels appear. Panels can be activated or deactivated according to the desired work flow, which—in combination with importing and exporting options—adjusts the entry and exit points of the interactive process. Here are some examples.

Suppose the Gatherer is configured to show the first two panels (*Gather* and *Enrich*) at remote sites and the

last four (*Enrich, Design, Create, Preview*) at a central server (where Greenstone is also installed), and data exchange is activated using the file-export menu option. This gives the same workflow as that used by Mercy Corps' *Metadata Creator* (Section 3.4). The metadata (*Enrich*) panel occurs in both the remote and central configurations, permitting remote users to enter metadata and a central librarian to make editorial corrections. For maximum flexibility the remote site version could be packaged an applet delivered from the central site that used a certificate to request permission to access the remote user's local file system. EPrints' submission process can be accomplished using the same mechanism. Since the Gatherer supports different metadata sets, it could be used in both of these very different application contexts.

Configuring the Gatherer to include web mirroring support provides comparable abilities to Harvest. Two new panels appear when this option is switched on. The first is used to browse the web. Once a page, set of pages or site of interest has been located, the "mirror" panel is used to control what is downloaded. This naturally flows onto the *Gather* panel, already discussed, where material is selected for inclusion in a collection.

Dispensing with the *Gather* and *Enrich* panels allows catalog-only datasets (produced using, for example, CDS/ISIS) to be incorporated by specifying the appropriate plug-in in the *Design* panel. Alternatively these panels can be switched back in and the file-import menu used instead. This allows individual records within the catalog to be viewed and edited in the *Enrich* panel.

Providing the functionality of a regular library catalog system like Koha is more challenging because additional infrastructure needs to be included in Greenstone. Despite the very different context, this could be accomplished using Greenstone's extensible system of plug-ins and classifiers. Custom plug-ins would be required to manipulate the relevant kind of datasets. Each Koha

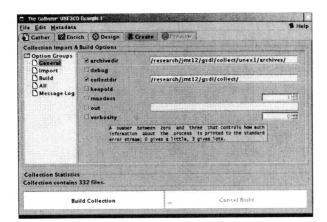

Figure 11. Getting ready to create the new collection

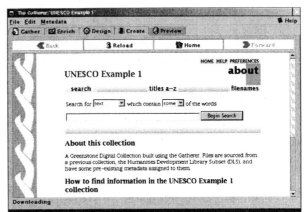

Figure 12. Previewing the newly built collection

database would be viewed as a Greenstone "collection," and each item in it as a document with metadata.

For example, library membership information could be accessed by building a collection whose documents are personal records with metadata that records their name, membership number, and books borrowed. Then the Gatherer can be used to operate and maintain the system. Data is entered and edited through the *Enrich* panel, and users change collection to switch to a different database.

6. Conclusion

The goal of the Gatherer is to provide an interactive environment for collection editors who build digital library collections using Greenstone. We have identified the requirements for such a system. Prominent amongst these are the need to be able to recruit documents into the collection from a variety of sources; the ability to assign metadata sets, modify them if necessary, and assign metadata to documents interactively; and the process of designing, configuring, building, and testing the collection itself. Other requirements include

- creating and editing metadata
- being able to work with different metadata sets
- capability of assimilating new features of Greenstone (plug-ins and classifiers) without the need for specific program modifications.

The Gatherer has been designed to satisfy these requirements. It guides the user step by step through the process of defining and building a digital library collection. Although formal user studies have yet to be undertaken, informal user trials indicate that it provides an environment for collection-building that is superior to anything previously available. We are currently in the process of establishing field trials with several international users. The name "Gatherer" was coined to describe a much earlier version of the design and is somewhat inappropriate now: ultimately this will

probably become known simply as the librarian's interface to Greenstone.

Although the Gatherer is tightly integrated into the Greenstone system, it is possible to run the early stages of document gathering and metadata editing without Greenstone being installed on the user's computer. This allows many different workflow configurations (for example, remote users, central librarian) and also raises the possibility of exporting documents and metadata for other digital library systems. One of the strengths of the Gatherer is its ability to use "Preferences" selections to emulate workflow models built into other systems.

Different users of digital libraries, naturally, have different needs. While access and retrieval is an obvious requirement, and dominates digital library research, we believe that end-user collection creation is another important element that deserves careful attention and further development. Including this capability in digital library systems will help them move away from the large and mostly static entities currently seen, and evolve into more dynamic and responsive environments.

The Gatherer represents a significant enhancement to Greenstone. Although it is specific to this particular digital library software, we hope that the ideas show how such an interface can be applied more widely to provide interactive collection-building facilities in other digital library systems.

Acknowledgements

Greenstone is the work of a great many people and we gratefully acknowledge the contributions of them all, and in particular the stimulating research environment in the Digital Library Lab at Waikato. We are also grateful to the anonymous reviewers for helping us to focus our message.

References

[1] Akscyn, R.M. and Witten, I.H. (1998) "Report on First Summit on International Cooperation on Digital Libraries." ks.com/idla-wp-oct98.

[2] Blake, R. and Hamilton-Williams, R. (2000) "The Koha story." http://koha.org/about/story.html.

[3] Buxton, A. and Hopkinson, A. (2001) *The CDS/ISIS for Windows Handbook*. UNESCO, Paris, September.

[4] Cole, H., Eckstein, R., Elliott, J., Loy, M. and Wood, D. (2002) *Java Swing*. O'Reilly and Associates.

[5] Consultative Committee for Space Data Systems (CCSDS) (2002) *Reference model for an Open Archival Information System (OAIS)*. CCSDS 650.0-B-1 Blue Book, Washington, DC.

[6] Crane, G. and Rydberg-Cox, J.A. (2000) "New technology and new roles: the need for 'corpus editors'." *Proc Digital Libraries 2000*, San Antonio, Texas, pp. 252–253.

[7] Hardy, D.R., Schwartz, M.F. and Wessels, D. (1996) Harvest 1.4 User's Manual. Technical Report CU-CS-743-94, University of Colorado. Revised by K.-J. Lee in 2002 for Harvest version 1.8.

[8] Harnad, S. & Carr, L. (2000) "Integrating, navigating, and analysing open Eprint archives through open citation linking (the OpCit project)" *Current Science*, Vol. 79, No.5, pp. 629-638.

[9] Hitchcock, S., Carr, L., Jiao, Z., Hall, W. and Harnad, S. "Developing Services for Open E-Print Archives: Globalisation, Integration and the Impact of Links." *Proc. ACM Digital Libraries Conference*, San Antonio, Texas, 2000, ACM Press: New York.

[10] Kenney, A.R. and Rieger, O.Y. (2000) *Moving theory into practice: digital imaging for libraries and archives*. Research Libraries Group, Mountain View, CA.

[11] Lesk, M. (1997) *Practical digital libraries*. San Francisco, CA: Morgan Kaufmann.

[12] Loots, M., Carmazan, D. and Witten, I.H. (2002) "From paper to collection." Greenstone Digital Library software manual, available at greenstone.org.

[13] Witten, I.H., Loots, M., Trujillo, M.F. and Bainbridge, D. (2002) "The promise of digital libraries in developing countries." *The Electronic Library*, Vol. 20, No. 1, pp. 7-13.

[14] Witten, I.H., McNab, R.J., Boddie, S.J. and Bainbridge, D. (2000) "Greenstone: A comprehensive open-source digital library software system." *Proc Digital Libraries 2000*, San Antonio, Texas, pp. 113–121.

[15] Witten, I.H., Bainbridge, D. and Boddie, S.J. (2001) "Power to the people: end-user building of digital library collections." *Proc Joint Conference on Digital Libraries*, Roanoke, VA, 94-103; June.

[16] Witten, I.H. and Bainbridge, D. (2003) *How to build a digital library*. Morgan Kaufmann, San Francisco.

[17] Wolpert, A.J. (2002) "The future of electronic data." *Nature* Vol. 420, pp. 17-18.

A System for Building Expandable Digital Libraries

Donatella Castelli, Pasquale Pagano
ISTI-CNR
Area di Ricerca
Via G. Moruzzi, 1
Pisa (Italy)
castelli,pagano@iei.pi.cnr.it

Abstract

Expandability is one of the main requirements of future digital libraries. This paper introduces a digital library service system, OpenDLib, that has been designed to be highly expandable in terms of content, services and usage. The paper illustrates the mechanisms that enable expandability and discusses their impact on the development of the system architecture.

1. Introduction

Recent advances in technology have stimulated new expectations about digital libraries (DLs). The DLs of the future will be ever-expanding systems, i.e. the content, the services and the usage modalities will evolve to meet new requirements and opportunities.

The content will grow not only because new documents are published by the DL, but also because new information providers will join the DL making their content available. New services, enabled by the advent of new technologies, will be added to satisfy and stimulate new usages of the system. New modalities interaction will be integrated in the system to satisfy the requirements of previously unenvisaged user communities.

Many of the DLs of the future will be networked systems hosted by servers belonging to supporting institutions. Services can be distributed or replicated on more than one server. Communication among the different service instances allocated on different servers will be dynamic since it will depend on the free source availability of the hosting institutions and on the status of the connection.

This new vision of DLs is encouraging the research community to design systems able to support these forms of evolution. In order to provide service expansion, these systems must be based on open architectures. An open architecture is an architecture in which the total functionality is partitioned into a set of well-defined services that conform to a number of established rules. An open architecture makes it possible to expand the system functionality by adding a new service component instead of re-building the whole system. The new systems must also provide expandable and scalable services able to support the handling and processing of new content

and capable of satisfying the needs of new user communities. Combining expandability and scalability is not simple and requires a re-thinking of DL architectures and a successive exhaustive experimentation.

This paper presents a DL system, OpenDLib, with a new architecture, explicitly designed to support plug-and-play expansions. We started building OpenDLib almost four years ago, as a response to a pressing request for software that could enable different user communities to create their own DLs. We decided to design a general-purpose software that could be customized to meet the needs of the different application frameworks. We called this software a Digital Library Service System, to stress that it is a system that manages digital library services and makes them publicly available [1]. The role of OpenDLib is analogous to the role of a database management system for a database, i.e. it supports the creation and maintenance of distributed DLs. A DL can be created by instantiating OpenDLib and then either loading or harvesting the content to be managed.

Our initial aim was to design a software that could provide a number of core DL functions on general content and that could be easily expandable. By exploiting expandability, the core functionality can be enhanced with other services that can cover the needs of specific application areas. In order to achieve this goal, we began to investigate open architectures. Our starting reference point was the Dienst system and the notion of open architecture as described in [2]. As our experience with the design of OpenDLib grew, however, we realized that the expandability that was required by our vision was wider than initially envisaged. A DL is a very expensive resource that must be maintained over time. During its lifetime, new technologies may be developed that enable new functionality, new institutions may decide to join the DL by offering their content and their computers to host the system, new kinds of usage may be proposed. To be able to satisfy this dynamic scenario, the DL must grow over time along several dimensions, e.g. services, metadata formats supported, host servers, user communities, etc. OpenDLib was designed to support this powerful notion of evolution.

The overall functionality of OpenDLib is partitioned into a set of well-defined interacting services that provide functions for coordination of tasks (e.g. mutual reconfiguration, distribution and replication handling, work-load distribution), basic utility functions, (e.g. users handling, rights management, information space mediators) and application functions (e.g. acquisition, storage and preservation of documents, search, browse and retrieval, dissemination). OpenDLib supports the addition of new content drawn from unforeseen information sources, it can include new services that implement additional functions, and can be customized to serve new communities of users. All these expansions are done on-the-fly, i.e. without switching off the DL. OpenDLib supports these dynamic expansions through the following key mechanisms:

- *Configurable services.* These offer a dynamically customizable behavior. This behavior is specified by a number of service-specific parameters. These parameters are selected when the DL is installed and can be changed dynamically over the DL lifetime to extend the service behavior for new content and new usages.

- *Open architectural infrastructure.* This supports the dynamic and consistent expansion of the DL architecture, both in term of services and host servers. It also provides the basis for the automatic re-configuration of the DL services and their communication paths.

- *Basic utility services.* These are services which implement general utility functions that can be usefully employed by the application services. Examples of these services are information space mediators and user registries.

The rest of the paper is organized as follows. Section 2 introduces OpenDLib. Section 3 describes what we mean by dynamic configurable services; this notion is exemplified by presenting the Repository Service. Section 4 presents the OpenDLib architectural infrastructure focusing in particular on the Manager Service that co-ordinates the entire set of service instances. Section 5 introduces the notion of basic utility service and presents the Collection Service as an example of this kind of service. Section 6 surveys some of the most recent proposals for expandable DL systems and compares them with OpenDLib. Finally, Section 7 presents conclusions, lessons learned, and planned enhancements.

2. An Overview of OpenDLib

The OpenDLib system consists of an open and networked federation of services. These services co-operate in order to implement OpenDLib functionality. This co-operation is more complex than a simple client-server application. A service can act both as a provider and as a consumer, and sharing relationships can exist a priori among any subset of the services. Services, in fact,

may be combined to support different functionality, and the same services may be used in different ways, depending on the restrictions placed on sharing and the goal of sharing.

OpenDLib services can be centralized, distributed or replicated on different hosting servers. A DL system running OpenDLib thus usually comprises multiple instances of the same service type hosted on remote servers of different organizations. Each service may require functionality from other services in order to carry out its task. The OpenDLib Protocol (OLP) regulates communication among services [3]. OLP is an open protocol, i.e. it can be expanded by adding additional service requests. OLP requests are expressed as URLs embedded in HTTP requests. All structured requests and responses are XML-based.

There are three classes of OpenDLib services. The first two, that we have named OpenDLib architectural infrastructure services and basic utility service, implement the core functionality which is needed to support the third class of services: the application services. In particular, the infrastructure services manage the DL (see Section 4); whereas the utility services provide basic general functionality, such as users and rights handling (see Section 5). In the first release of OpenDLib we have chosen to support a number of application services that implement the functionality of a conventional digital library (see below). Given the expandability of OpenDLib this set of services can be enhanced by adding more advanced services or services that serve the need of specific communities.

All the OpenDLib services of the first release are configurable. This provides a great flexibility that permits to uses the system for a variety of different DL application frameworks.

Figure 1 illustrates an OpenDLib networked federation of service instances. The infrastructure instances are colored in light gray, the utility service instances in dark gray and the application service instances are white. The arrows show the flow of service requests among the instances.

The application services implemented by the current OpenDLib release are:

- *Repository Service*

This service stores and disseminates documents that conform to a powerful document model, named DoMDL [4], able to represent structured, multilingual and multimedia documents. This service is described in detail in the next Section.

- *Multimedia Storage Service*

This service supports the storage, the (real-time) streaming and the download delivery of the stored video manifestations of a document (according to the DoMDL document model). Furthermore, it supports their dissemination either as whole documents or as aggregations of scenes, shots and frames.

- *Library Management Service*

This service supports the submission, withdrawal, and replacement of documents. It is configurable with respect to the metadata formats. Each of its instances can manage multiple metadata formats, helping the users to compile and submit them to the Repository.

- *Index Service*

This service accepts queries and returns documents matching those queries. The Index Service is parametric with respect to the metadata formats, to the set of indexed fields, to the set of result formats and to the language of the terms.

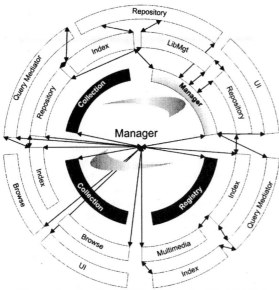

Figure 1 – An OpenDLib networked federation

- *Query Mediator Service*

This service dispatches queries to appropriate Index Service instances. It adapts its behavior by taking into account the available Index Service instances, and therefore exploits the potentiality of the Index Service to the full.

- *Browse Service*

This service supports the construction of indexes for browsing and the actual browsing of these indexes on library contents. It is parametric with respect to the metadata formats, to the set of browsable fields, and to the set of formats for result sets.

- *User Interface Service*

This service mediates human interaction with the application services and their protocols.

Each of the above services can be centralized, distributed or replicated. The configuration of the architecture, i.e. which are the replicated services, how many are replicated, where they are hosted, etc, is decided when the DL is installed but can also be modified over the DL lifetime. The selection of the best architectural configuration is driven by contextual requirements, such as scalability, availability, privacy, etc. For example, in the experimental OpenDLib DL now operational at our Institute, the Repository Service has been distributed. We made this choice as publishing institutions usually want to maintain control over their documents. When a new publishing institution joins the DL consortium, it can either decide to maintain its documents on the Repository handled by another organization, or can set up its own new Repository on its local server. In the same experimental DL, the Index Service has been both distributed and replicated. It has been distributed in order to better support scalability. The distribution is by publisher, i.e. each instance indexes documents published by a subset of the DL registered institutions. It has been replicated because it is a critical component in serving user requests and can likely become a bottleneck in the whole architecture. Figure 2 illustrates a possible configuration of Repository and Index instances. Repository 1 maintains the documents published by the institutions A1 and A2, and Repository 2 those published by A3 and A4. When a registered user submits a document into an OpenDLib DL, this document is transparently stored in the Repository instance associated with his institution. The documents maintained in the two Repositories are indexed by three different instances of the Index Service that are both distributed and replicated. Note that replication does not necessarily mean that the content of two or more instance is the same, but rather that the same information is maintained on more that one instance. In the figure, for example, documents published by authority A3 are indexed by both Index 1 and Index 2, and those published by A1 are indexed by Index 1 and Index 3.

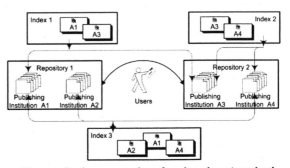

Figure 2- An example of a legal networked federation of Repository and Index instances.

As services may be distributed and replicated, an OpenDLib DL architecture usually contains multiple instances of the same service hosted on different networked servers. These instances co-operate in order to process the user requests. A service may use other services in order to implement its functionality. When there are several instances of the "used" service, then each "using" instance must decide where to address its requests. As we will explain in Section 5, in OpenDLib this communication flow is not established statically, but can change over time depending on the set of services instances registered and on the availability and workload of the hosting servers.

3. Configurable Services

The services that have been included in Release 1 of OpenDLib can adapt their behavior to a new context on-the-fly, i.e. without any explicit re-programming. The behavior of these services is customizable according to a number of service-specific configuration parameters. For example, the Index is configurable with respect to the indexed fields and to the language of the documents in the collections, the Browse with respect to the browsable fields, the Repository with respect to the metadata formats stored, etc. These configuration parameters are initially set on creation of the DL and their value can be modified over the DL lifetime. For example, an instance of the Repository Service can be updated to accept other metadata formats; the corresponding Index Service instances, in turn, can automatically extend the set of metadata indexed to include the new format; and the Query Mediator instances can be configured to accept queries on the fields of the new formats. Figure 3 illustrates the above chain of changes. In the initial situation Repository 1 maintains MARC and Dublin Core metadata records. The Dublin Core format is indexed by Index 1 and the MARC format by Index 2. The Query Mediator supports two query languages based on the fields extracted by the two formats. When Repository 1 is reconfigured to maintain the RFC-1806 format as well, Index 2 is automatically modified to index this new format and the Query Mediator is enhanced to provide a new query language based on the new format.

These changes in the configuration of the service instances can be made dynamically, without switching the system off. In many cases, they are automatically triggered by the service itself in reaction to other changes in the DL service federation. However, changes are constrained by rules that establish the consistency of the global configuration. For example, there must always be at least an Index instance that indexes the metadata disseminated by a Repository instance, and a Query Mediator cannot support a search on a language that is

not indexed by any Index Service instance. Note that different instances of the same service may have different configurations, unless this is not explicitly forbidden by the consistency rules. For example, there may be two different instances of a Query Mediator: one that supports a free-of-charge accessible simple search and another that provides a set of more complex search operations, such as cross-language, upon the payment of a certain fee.

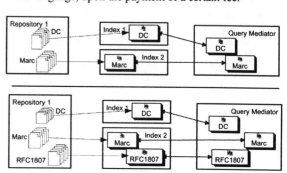

Figure 3.- A chain of dynamic service re-configurations

All the OpenDLib services can describe themselves and disseminate their configuration parameters through a standard protocol response. By periodically invoking the appropriate protocol requests, each service instance can become aware of the current state of instances used. Depending on the response, the instance can decide, for example, to re-adjust its behavior automatically or to use alternative instances.

Certainly, the development of dynamic (re-) configurable services is more complex than the development of services with an established constant behavior. It needs a careful design and longer implementation phase. It also requires an appropriate infrastructure to support the chain of automatic re-configurations that may be implied by the change of a single instance. Despite this, we decided to pay this extra price since one of our main objectives was to have extensible services able to adapt to new content and to new usages.

The next section will exemplify the notion of dynamically configurable services by presenting one of the most relevant services of the infrastructure: the Repository Service. The variety of configurable scenarios of this service, the role they play in the customization of the service behavior, and how they contribute to the expandability of the DL are described.

3.1. The Repository Service

The structure of the documents that can be handled by a DL can vary considerably. For example, a digital library can contain conference proceedings that are aggregates of other documents (the preface and the articles). Each article, can be disseminated in different ways, for example it can be disseminated both as a text in postscript format (the readable content of the article) and as an audio in MPEG3 format (the speaker presentation). The same digital library can also contain project deliverables. These are likely to have a completely different structure. For example, they may be textual reports, structured into sections, and demos of the project prototypes. A digital library can also support different metadata formats. For example, it can have both a MARC format, used by library professionals, and a RFC-1807 format used by the general public. In order to support this variability in DL content, we built a Repository Service which stores and disseminates documents that conform to a powerful document model, the Document Model for Digital Libraries (DoMDL) [4]. This model can represent a wide range of document structures and associate any number of different metadata formats with them. Given its flexibility, this model represents the first mechanism implemented by the Repository Service to support the expandability of the DL content.

The Repository Service is often distributed in order to better support scalability. In the OpenDLib DL created at our institute it has been distributed by the publishing institutions, i.e. each instance maintains the documents published by one or more publishing institutions. Each instance has been set up as "locally configured". This is one of the two configuration modalities that can be chosen for a distributed service. The configuration of a locally configured instance is selected by its local administrator. The other modality is "centrally configured". In this case, the configuration is decided by the DL administrator and is prescribed for all the distributed instances. When the local configuration is chosen, the behavior of each Repository instance may be different both at system start up and over the DL lifetime. In particular, each instance may be extended independently of the others, according to local needs.

The Repository Service is dynamically configurable along several dimensions. Below we list some of these.

- *Publishing institutions.* These are the publishing institutions that are entitled to store their documents in the Repository instance.
- *Basic collections.* A collection is a set of documents that satisfy some commonly established set of criteria. The documents stored in a Repository instance may be organized into basic collections. For example, the documents in a repository managed by a group of Computer Science institutions might be organized into basic collections that reflect the ACM subject schema classes. The basic collection is a cross-repository instance notion, i.e. documents belonging to the same collection can be distributed

over several Repository instances. This storage policy assumes agreement among the publishing institutions on the semantics of the collections and of their hierarchical structure.

- *Metadata formats.* The Repository is capable of storing multiple metadata formats. The simplest way to specify these formats is to describe them as simple XML configuration files that maintain (for each metadata format) the name and description, plus references to its DTD and to the list of used namespaces.
- *Derived metadata formats.* The Repository service can automatically derive metadata records from other existing metadata formats. For example, it can be configured to generate a Dublin Core record each time a MARC record is submitted. This automatic generation is executed by a generic procedure whose input is a tuple indicating the source metadata format name, the target name, and a reference to an XML file that maintains the corresponding mapping. This configuration file, called the mapping table, is very easy to define because it maintains the relation between source and target attributes plus a function, or a reference to it, to map source values into target ones.
- *Manifestation type.* Any view of a document can have several different manifestations, i.e. formats in which the document can be disseminated. For example, a conference paper can be disseminated both as a Postscript file and as a PDF file, the video of its presentation at the conference can be disseminated as MPEG and as AVI files. Manifestations can be physically stored within the Repository, or be handled by other specialized services. The Repository maintains these as dummy manifestations that report, as one of their attributes, the URL of the real manifestation.
- *Derived manifestation type.* The Repository service can automatically derive manifestation types from others. For example, it can be configured to generate a PDF manifestation each time a Postscript is submitted. This automatic generation is executed by using appropriate procedures pre-loaded by the service. Other derivations can easily be added by specifying the source and target manifestation type, plus a reference to an internal procedure or to an external program.

The Repository service can be customized by specifying the value of a number of configuration parameters. Some of these correspond to the content configuration dimensions listed above. Others specify the values for variation features, such as the security and the preservation policies, that allow additional customization of the document and metadata handling functions.

The values assigned to the parameters are constrained by consistency rules that establish both the legal configurations of each single instance, (e.g. derived metadata formats must belong to the set of metadata formats supported), and the legal configurations of the whole group of instances, (e.g. a publishing institution cannot be associated with more than one instance). The Repository and Manager Services, which will be described in the next section, check these rules both at the DL start-up and each time the configuration is modified.

By changing the value of the above parameters and by exploiting the flexibility of the document model, the Repository Service can adapt its behavior to many different situations. Below we give some examples.

Example 1. A new publishing institution joins the DL. The DL must be updated in order to accept the documents published by the new institution. Two solutions are possible in an OpenDLib DL: i) a new Repository instance is set up on a new host server or ii) a Repository instance, managed by another institution, is reconfigured so that it also accepts documents published by the new participating institution. If the second solution is selected, it could be that the chosen Repository instance does not completely support the set of metadata and manifestation types disseminated by the new publishing institution. Therefore, the addition of a new publishing institution can also imply changes to the set of handled metadata and manifestation formats.

Example 2. A group of institutions change the organization of their documents. The institutions can, for example, add a new basic collection or split an existing one. This alteration in the organization of the DL content can be automatically supported by modifying the set of basic collections in every Repository instance that hosts the institutions that have agreed on the change.

Example 3. A new service is added to the DL to accommodate a new kind of usage. This service needs metadata in a given format. It could be that not all the Repository instances disseminate the metadata format required by the new service. This problem can be overcome by preparing a table to map from the existing metadata formats to the required format, and by including it in all the Repository instances that do not already support the required format.

Example 4. The content of the DL is expanded with digital documents harvested by a non-OpenDLib-compliant repository. This could occur when a publisher organization that joins the DL wants to import into the DL all its documents published in the past. These documents are usually stored in proprietary repositories and have their own structure. This expansion of the DL content requires the creation of mechanisms to ingest the documents and to transform the original document structure into a DoMDL structure. This can be done by assigning appropriate values to handling function parameters and by providing a specification of how to obtain the final document structure.

As the above examples illustrate, a Repository instance exhibits a behavior that depends on the values given to its parameters. The knowledge of these values is important for all the other services that use the Repository instance since, through them, they can know how it behaves. The service parameters are thus also important descriptive properties of each instance. Other properties are, for example, the service requests implemented, the usage rights, etc.

4. The Infrastructure

Our decision to design and implement an architectural infrastructure has grown out of a progressive understanding of the needs of ever-expanding DL service systems. We have found that certain evolutionary dimensions require specific supporting services, like controllers, registries, security and authentication handlers, etc. In the current release of OpenDLib, we have introduced a number of these specific services. Together with some standard technology, the services collectively form the OpenDLib Infrastructure.

Like any other service, the architectural services assume a communication protocol. Any service that wants to use the functionality of the architectural infrastructure must implement this protocol.

In the next subsection, we will present the key service of the infrastructure: the Manager Service. This service maintains a continuously updated status of the networked federation of services, checks its consistency and controls the flow of the communication.

4.1. The Manager Service

OpenDLib supports three kinds of dynamic service expansions:
1. new services can be added;
2. new instances of a replicated or distributed service can be mounted on either an existing or a new hosting server;
3. the configurations of the services can be modified so that they can handle new document types, new metadata formats and support new usages.

Most of these expansions, even when they regard a specific service instance, also require a change in the configuration of other instances. For example, when a Repository instance is modified to accept a new metadata format, at least one Index instance must be updated to index the new format; when a new Query Mediator instance is set up to reduce the workload on the existing Query Mediators, then a certain number of User

Interfaces must change their communication flow and address their service requests to the new instance.

The new or modified service instances are included in the networked federation "on-the-fly", i.e. they are able to be invoked and operate without switching off the DL. The objective of the Manager Service is to provide the functionality required to support this dynamic service expansion. The complexity of this functionality varies according to the kind of service expansions provided.

The Manager Service is partially configured by the DL administrator at the start-up of the DL. Its configuration parameters contain the minimum information required to specify the DL architecture: e.g. the address of the hosting servers; the list of the services and whether they are centralized, replicated or distributed; the number of instances for each service; their allocation to the servers, etc[1]. The configuration parameters also include those parameters required to set up the "centrally configured" services, i.e. those services whose instances have the same configuration. Finally, the configuration parameters contain a number of consistency rules that specify the legal configurations of the service instances in the federation. These rules strictly depend on the type of service chosen and on the "use" relation that links them. For example, the language of the terms in a query that is processed by the Query Mediator must be one of the languages indexed by the Index service, the document and metadata descriptions submitted to a Library Management Service must conform to those managed by the corresponding Repository.

By exploiting the information about the DL architecture acquired at start-up time, the Manager begins to collect more detailed information about the service instances by periodically sending them appropriate protocol requests. It then processes the information gathered, controls its consistency, and takes decisions about the organization of the federation, such as, for example, the communication paths between the instances. These decisions can change over time according to the value of different parameters, such as the set of running service instances, the workload of a server and the status of the connection.

All service instances notify the Manager of any changes in the architectural configuration by sending it an appropriate service request. The Manager updates the architectural map and executes the necessary steps to collect information about any new instance.

The service instances periodically harvest information about the federation from the Manager. For example, each service that uses another replicated service asks for the address of the instances that can serve its requests, a "centrally configured" replicated service asks for the value of the configuration parameters chosen for that service, etc. The instances of the federation can configure themselves either by directly exploiting the information received from the Manager, or by sending appropriate service requests to the instances whose addresses have been obtained through the Manager. Once configured, the various instances can start the co-operation required to process the DL user requests. Note that the Manager service is never involved in the processing of a user request. It only plays the role of an intelligent, continuously updated dynamic registry that controls the consistency of the federation and selects the best communication paths between the service instances.

The OpenDLib architecture infrastructure can also accept services that are anarchic to a certain extent, i.e. services that participate in the federation with different levels of engagement. Such services can implement the established protocol only partially or not at all. Their implementation is simpler, but the possibilities they offer for the expansion of the DL are certainly more restricted since they cannot exploit the mechanisms provided by the architectural infrastructure. Let us analyze the extreme case of completely anarchic services, i.e. services that never invoke the Manager nor provide co-ordination requests. For these services the Manager only operates as a registry of services. Anarchic services are never informed about changes in the configuration of the other services nor do they have any support for dynamically publishing their changes unless they implement such functions themselves. For example, they can only communicate with an established already existing set of instances. Moreover, their replicated and distributed instances can only appear as new services. If one of these instances crashes, there is no way of re-directing requests to alternative instances; etc.

We can thus repeat the same remark that we made in Section 3: there is certainly a trade-off between the cost of service development and DL expandability. In designing OpenDLib, we have tried to reduce this cost by introducing an architectural infrastructure. The infrastructure, however, it is not sufficient by itself, the services must participate by implementing the protocol for coordination.

In an attempt to limit this unavoidable cost, OpenDLib makes publicly available a set of Perl packages that can be used when implementing this part of the protocol. This set includes packages that prepare the service requests according to the syntax required by the OLP protocol, and packages that implement the protocol common to all the services[2] and the service-specific protocol, i.e. according

---

[1] Configuration information must also be given for the Manager Service. For example, it is possible to specify that the Manager Service is a replicated service, where the replicas are located, etc.

[2] The common protocol comprises requests for acquiring a description of the service, such as the value of its parameters, the rights required for accessing it, the list of service requests that can be served, etc.

to whether it is centralized, distributed, or replicated. These packages can be used in developing any new service whose programming environment permits the inclusion of Perl packages.

5. Basic Utility Services

While designing OpenDLib we realized that, in addition to the application and the infrastructure services, there was also the need for services able to provide a number of DL support functions. These services use the infrastructure services and may be used by the application services. They thus provide a sort of intermediate functionality level in the DL architecture. In the current release of OpenDLib we have implemented only two such services: the User Registry, which stores and maintains information about the registered users and interest groups, and the Collections Service, which provides a virtual view of the organization of the DL content space. We plan to include other basic services such as a Rights Manager Service and an Accounting Service in the near future. Of course, given the specificity of the rules that can govern distinct application contexts, all these services will be highly configurable.

In the next subsection, we present the Collection Service as an example of a basic utility service. It represents a first attempt to develop a more general information space mediator able to take into account the different variables of a DL content space. We will return to this point at the end of the next section.

5.1. The Collection Service

An ever-expandable DL may well contain an extremely large and heterogeneous content. The growth of the content space does not necessarily result in a benefit for the DL users. The heterogeneity forces them to use generic services such as, for example, generic query languages. Thus a large content may result in a loss of precision with respect to retrieval and in a degradation of performance. The solution that is usually proposed to this problem is to build a number of specialized portals that provide different views of the DL [5,10]. These portals may offer partial views of both the content space and the set of services. In a highly expandable DL this solution presents a number of drawbacks if it is not appropriately implemented. In particular, the portals are the expression of the needs of the user communities, thus any time a new community is added, or a community changes its requirements, a new portal must also be developed.

In order to overcome these drawbacks, we decided to design a more general solution that could provide the basis for building a dynamic set of virtual views of both the content space and the available services. This solution is based on the use of content space mediator services.

The Collection Service is the first of these general utility services that we have developed.

The Collection is a service that mediates between the virtual dynamic organization of the content space, built according to the requirements of the DL community of users[3], and the concrete organization into basic collections of documents held by publishing institutions. The virtual organization consists in a number of hierarchically structured subsets of the DL documents that we call "collections". Each collection is characterized by a set of criteria, the membership condition, that must be satisfied by all its members. Examples of membership conditions are: "all the documents published by a certain institution", and "all the documents on a certain subject published after a certain date". Each community of users has the possibility to define dynamically its own virtual collections by specifying the name of the collection, and providing a textual description and its membership condition.

The Collection Service accepts collection creation requests and processes them. In particular, it generates a set of collection descriptive metadata from information gathered by sending requests to the Manager. For example, it derives the Repository instances that maintain the documents of the collection and the conditions (termed filtering conditions) that select documents for a collection within each Repository. Moreover, it can derive the common metadata formats for the documents in a given collection. These collection metadata are periodically refreshed in order to allow for the addition of new Repository instances and the updating of the existing ones.

The Collection Service disseminates the list of existing collections and their metadata, on demand. All the application services can exploit this information when implementing customized views of their functionality. For example, the Query Mediator can make a particular search operation available on the collection "Recent Italian Computer Science" that accept queries with fields extracted from the RFC1810 schema, and terms selected from an official Italian translation of the ACM schema vocabulary. The User Interface service can exploit the same information to show a menu that lists the available collections to the users. The User Interface can then visualize the services available on a selected collection.

The application service can use the collection metadata not only to provide a community with a customized view of their functionality but also to improve their efficacy. Let us illustrate this point by considering again the

---

[3] Here, the expression "user community" stands for any group of users that share a common interest. There are no constraints on the number of community members. A community can also have only one member; in this case the collection defined is actually a personal collection.

behavior of the Query Mediator Service. By exploiting the list of publishing institutions that submit documents to the collection, the Query Mediator can derive the subset of the Index instances that index the documents in the collection. It can thus improve query performance by sending requests only to this restricted subset of Index instances. Moreover, it can improve the retrieval precision by appending the filtering condition that characterizes the collection to the user query.

The Collection Service is an example of a basic service tool that operates as a content space mediator. We are currently working on the design of other kinds of content space mediators that cover other dimensions, such as the structure of the documents, the metadata formats, and the controlled vocabularies used to describe the documents. We strongly believe that these utility tools will offer possibilities for new types of usages.

6. Related Work

The DLs designed in the past do not support expansion. They offer their own (more or less advanced) set of services, they operate on established sources of content, and they serve given classes of users. This situation is now changing. A number of projects that aim at defining expandable DL systems are in progress. The most notable of these new projects is certainly the National Digital Library for Science Education (NSDL) [5]. At the present, only the core services of the NSDL have been developed; over time this DL will include heterogeneous users, content and services. The content of this DL comes, or is computationally derived, from contributing external repositories, i.e. repositories that do not belong to the DL itself. The main requirement in designing the architecture of the first release of NSDL was a low cost of adoption. In order to satisfy this requirement, NSDL supports a large spectrum interoperability, i.e. the co-existence of alternative mechanisms that are adaptable to different situations. NSDL consists of a centralized Metadata Repository (MR), and a set of component services accessible through a number of user community specific portals. MR holds the set of all the document metadata. These are collected from heterogeneous source repositories using different modalities. The NSDL architecture is a networked federation of services. Each service implements a specific functionality, possibly relying on the functionality implemented by the other services. These services comprise what we have called application services and basic utility services. Both the MR and the given services are accessible through protocol requests. There is no single protocol, but each service imposes its own. A new source of content can be added provided that it conforms to one of the supported ingesting mechanisms. A new service can be added as a new component to the architecture. It can use the functionality of the other services by sending them requests formulated according to the accepted protocol.

We believe that the large spectrum interoperability is certainly a key aspect for a DL built by incrementally acquiring contributions form different sources. We also believe in the importance of supporting different levels of engagements. At the same time, however, as often repeated in this paper, we believe in the importance of supporting the co-ordination and the mutual consistency of the services. Indeed, both these features require a participation of the services that must implement the established rules. As NSDL services, and the portals that make these services accessible, are currently neither customizable nor can they be distributed or replicated, they have no explicit need for an infrastructure that offers the above features. It will be interesting to see how the design of the NSDL architecture will evolve and, if a solution that satisfies the apparently contrasting requirements mentioned above will be found.

The Open Digital Libraries (ODL) proposal by Suleman and Fox [6] goes in the direction of incrementally building DLs by loosely connecting independent sources of content and services through lightweight protocols, like OAI-PMH or specialized version of it. According to the proponents [7], customized DLs can be developed with little or no programming, by simply interconnecting components, possibly extracted from a pool of generic and reusable components, that implement the required functionality. These DLs are trivially expandable. We have found no mention in these reports of any DL infrastructure. We are not able to say whether this is because the authors are thinking about an alternative solution, or whether this is because they assume centralized and not customizable components.

The Greenstone software [8], developed as part of the New Zealand Digital Library Project, is an open-source system for the construction and presentation of heterogeneous collections of documents. A mechanism is given to create collections by acquiring documents either automatically, from existing heterogeneous sources, or manually, by importing them from selected file directories. The heterogeneity of the documents is handled by translating the given document structure and metadata formats into a common document structure and metadata format. Several "plug-ins" are given to accommodate this translation from standard formats, such as HTML, Microsoft Word, PDF, etc; others can be dynamically added to the system.

The structure of each collection is described at creation time by specifying a collection configuration file that contains the value for a number of collection metadata. These metadata comprise the format of source documents, how they are displayed on the screen, how the search results and target documents are displayed, etc. During the collection building process, indexes for both browsing and searching are constructed on the local server according to the instructions of the collection configuration file. Once a collection has been constructed, new documents can be added as long as they are in the same format as the existing ones and they are described by the same metadata format. Whenever a new document is added, a manually initiated rebuilding process to recreate the searching and browsing indexes must be launched. The Greenstone services are thus customizable, but, since there is no manager, their mutual update has to be done manually.

There is a wide experimentation activity around Greenstone since the system is currently used in several different application contexts. Certainly, this will produce interesting insights on the issues related to the expandability of content and on those related to customizable services.

The Distributed National Electronic Resource (DNER) [10,11] is a managed information environment for accessing quality assured Internet resources from many heterogeneous sources that may vary over the time. This environment supports the discovery of resources of interest to the end user, it enables access to these resources and facilitates their use. In order to provide this functionality, it addresses two main problems. Firstly, the problem of allowing the end user to interact with multiple discovery services in a seamless way, secondly the problem of guiding the use of the most appropriate copy of the resource[4]. The architecture of this environment consists of a number of networked content and co-operating service providers, and a shared infrastructure. The infrastructure comprises a number of services, such as a collection description service, a service description service, one or more resolution services and an institutional profiling services. Other shared services are also planned for the future, such as metadata registries, user preference, thesauri and terminology, ratings and terms and condition supporting services.

Even if DNER assumes a different underlying framework, the design of its architecture shares many features with the design of OpenDLib. In particular, the DNER architecture introduces a notion of infrastructure services, such as collection and service description services, that cover some of the functionality of our Collection and Manager services. It is not clear from the documents we have read, how many of these initial design decisions have been currently implemented and experimented.

We conclude this brief overview of some of the most recent on-going DL project by observing that most of

these proposals do not mention the need of an architectural infrastructure similar to that of OpenDLib, able to co-ordinate the services, drive the communication paths and check the consistency of the service instances. We believe that the reason for this difference is the level of expandability supported. Actually, none of the systems mentioned, have introduced both dynamically configurable services and distribution and replication. These features offer wide expandability but also create a wide variability in the behavior of the DL that needs to be appropriately controlled.

7. Conclusions and Future Plans

This paper has described the mechanisms that have been introduced in OpenDLib in order to support expandable DLs.

We strongly believe that future DLs will be built by first constructing a "core DL" (i.e. a core content accessible through core services able to satisfy the needs of a core set of users) and then expanding this DL to cover emerging needs and to exploit new opportunities. Expandability will be one of the main requirements of these DL systems.

We have seen that the introduction of mechanisms to support expandability implies an unavoidable cost in the realization of the services since these must comply with certain established protocol rules. These rules regulate the co-ordination of the networked federation of services and guide their auto-reconfiguration. However, our experience has shown that this cost can be greatly reduced by designing the service software appropriately.

At the present, there is not much experience on expandable DL systems. Many of the current systems limit their expandability to the addition of new services with a constant and established behavior. They do not have dynamically re-configurable services nor can they add service instances or change the communication paths dynamically. Certainly, much research and experimentation is needed. One of the difficulties of digital library research is that the experimentation is usually very complex and expensive. This is especially true for the experimentation of an architectural infrastructure. This involves the construction of huge amounts of software and the gathering of significant amounts of content. This is one of the reasons why DL infrastructures have not been sufficiently investigated in the past. However, it is also true that many issues become clear only when they are put into practice. In building OpenDLib we have learnt a lot. Many of the initial design choices have been re-thought in the light of the better understanding we achieved. We can certainly affirm that this experience has produced a clearer vision of what a

---

[4] Resource here is used with a broad meaning which includes content, service, collections, etc.

DL infrastructure is and what techniques are required for its development.

The service expandability of OpenDLib has been partially tested in the framework of the EU IST V Framework Project Scholnet [12]. The aim of this project is to construct a DL system that supports communication and collaboration within the scholarly communities. The Scholnet system has been built by customizing some of the OpenDLib application services and by extending them with additional services that support annotation on documents, cross-language search and personalized information dissemination. The experimentation made with Scholnet has validated many of the OpenDLib choices and has allowed us to improve our awareness of the problems involved in its expandability.

Currently, we are continuing our experimentation by building other OpenDLib DLs. In parallel, we intend to refine the three mechanisms for dynamic expandability that we have discussed in this paper. In particular, we want to refine our work on the infrastructure and explore further the idea of information source mediators.

More information about OpenDLib can be found at the address http://www.opendlib.com.

8. References

[1] Donatella Castelli and Pasquale Pagano, OpenDLib: A Digital Service System. in Proceedings of ECDL'02, (Rome, September 2002), LNCS 2458, Springer Verlarg, 292-308.

[2] Carl Lagoze and Sandra Payette, An Infrastructure for Open-Architecture Digital Libraries, Cornell Computer Science Technical Report, TR98-1690.

[3] Donatella Castelli and Pasquale Pagano, OLP: the OpenDLib Protocol. Istituto di Elaborazione dell'Informazione. Technical Report. 2002.

[4] Donatella Castelli and Pasquale Pagano, A Flexible Repository Service: the OpenDLib solution. in Proceedings of Elpub '02 Conference (Karlovy Vary, Czech Republic). 2002.

[5] Carl Lagoze et al. Core Services in the Architecture of the National Digital Library for Science Education (NSDL) In Proceedings of JCDL'02, (Portland, July 2002), ACM Press.

[6] Hussein Suleman and Edward A. Fox. Design Protocols in Support of Digital Libraies Componentization. In Proceedings of ECDL'02, (Rome, September 2002), LNCS 2458, Springer Verlarg, 568-582.

[7] Digital Libraries in a Box - The Project Homepage. http://dlbox.nudl.org/

[8] Ian H. Witten, David Bainbridge, Stefan J. Boddie. Greenstone Open-Source Digital Library Software. D-Lib Magazine 7(10).

[9] Ian H. Witten, David Bainbridge. How to Build a Digital Library. Morgan Kaufmann Publishers,.

[10] Andy Powell and Liz Lyon. The DNER Technical Architecture: scooping the information environment. http://www.ukoln.ac.uk/distributed-systems/jisc-ie/arch/dner-arch.html

[11] Pete Cliff, Pete Dowdell, Andy Powell. Working with the RDN. http://www.rdn.ac.uk/publications/workingwithrdn/

[12] SCHOLNET Project Homepage, http://www.ercim.org/scholnet

The Web-DL Environment for Building Digital Libraries from the Web

Pável P. Calado*   Marcos A. Gonçalves†   Edward A. Fox†   Berthier Ribeiro-Neto*
Alberto H. F. Laender*   Altigran S. da Silva‡   Davi C. Reis*   Pablo A. Roberto*
Monique V. Vieira*   Juliano P. Lage*

*Federal University of
Minas Gerais
Dep. of Computer Science
31270-901, Belo Horizonte,
MG, Brazil
{pavel, alti, berthier, laender,
palmieri, davi, pabloa,
monique}@dcc.ufmg.br

†Virginia Tech
Dep. of Computer Science
Blacksburg, VA 24061, USA
{mgoncalv, fox}@vt.edu

‡Federal University of
Amazonas
Dep. of Computer Science
69077-000, Manaus, AM,
Brazil
alti@dcc.fua.br

Abstract

The Web contains a huge volume of unstructured data, which is difficult to manage. In digital libraries, on the other hand, information is explicitly organized, described, and managed. Community-oriented services are built to attend specific information needs and tasks. In this paper, we describe an environment, Web-DL, that allows the construction of digital libraries from the Web. The Web-DL environment will allow us to collect data from the Web, standardize it, and publish it through a digital library system. It provides support to services and organizational structure normally available in digital libraries, but benefiting from the breadth of the Web contents. We experimented with applying the Web-DL environment to the Networked Digital Library of Theses and Dissertations (NDLTD), thus demonstrating that the rapid construction of DLs from the Web is possible. Also, Web-DL provides an alternative as a large-scale solution for interoperability between independent digital libraries.

1. Introduction

The Web contains a huge volume of information. Almost all of it is stored in the form of unstructured data and is, therefore, difficult to manage. Access to the information is granted through browsing and searching, which normally involves no assumptions about the users' tasks or their specific information needs. On the other hand, we have databases, where data has a rigid structure and services are provided for specialized users. Digital libraries (DLs) stand in the middle. We can say that DL users have broader interests than database users, but more specific interests than regular Web users. Also, within DLs information is explicitly organized, described, and managed—targeted for communities of users with specific information needs and tasks, but without the rigidness of database systems.

In this paper we present Web-DL, an environment that allows the construction of digital libraries from the Web. Web-DL allows us to collect data from Web pages, normalize it to a standard format, and store it for use with digital library systems. By using standard protocols and archival technologies, Web-DL enables open, organized, and structured access to several heterogeneous and distributed digital libraries and the easy incorporation of powerful digital library and data extraction tools. The overall environment thus supports services and organization available in digital libraries, but benefiting from the breadth of the Web contents.

By moving from Web to DL we are providing quality services for communities of users interested in specific domain information. Services like searching over several different DLs, browsing, and recommending are made available with high quality, since we reduce the search space, restricting it to the data related to the users' interest, and structuring and integrating such data through canonical metadata standards.

We demonstrate the feasibility of our approach by implementing the proposed environment for a digital library of electronic theses and dissertations (ETDs), in the context of the Networked Digital Library of Theses and Dissertations (NDLTD). The NDLTD currently has over 160 members

346

among universities and research institutions, providing support for the implementation of DL services using standard protocols, but is deficient in dealing with members that publicize their ETDs only through the Web. Fortunately, our approach matches with the growing tendency among sites that publish ETDs to create a Web page for each ETD, containing all the relevant data (or metadata). Using our proposal, we will be able to add such ETDs to the NDLTD collection with little user effort.

The Web-DL environment builds upon tools and techniques for collecting Web pages, described in [10], extracting semi-structured data, described in [6, 14], and managing digital libraries, described in [12]. In this paper we show how these tools are seamlessly integrated under Web-DL and extended to provide solutions for data normalization problems, usually found when extracting data from the Web. Experiments performed in the context of the NDLTD confirm the quality of the results reported in [4], now obtained with a more general solution and less user effort, since the data extraction process has been further automated.

The rest of this paper is organized as follows. Section 2 discusses some related works. Section 3 presents an overview of the architecture proposed for the Web-DL environment. Sections 4, 5, and 6 describe the main components of Web-DL, and the ASByE, DEByE and MARIAN tools, respectively. Section 7 presents our approach for the Web data normalization problem. Section 8 shows an example digital library built using Web-DL. Finally, in Section 9 we discuss some of the problems found and present our conclusions.

2. Context and related work

Digital libraries involve rich collections of digital objects and community-oriented specialized services such as searching, browsing, and recommending. Many DLs are built as federations of autonomous, possibly heterogeneous DL systems, distributed across the Internet [8, 17]. The objective of such federations is to provide users with a transparent, integrated view of their collections and information services. Challenges faced by federated DLs include interoperability among different digital library systems/protocols, resource discovery (e.g., selection of the best sites to be searched), issues in data fusion (merging of results into a unique ranked list), and aspects of quality of data and services.

One such federated digital library is the Networked Digital Library of Theses and Dissertations (NDLTD) [7], an international federation of universities, libraries, and other supporting institutions focused on efforts related to electronic theses and dissertations (ETDs). Although providing many of the advantages of a federated DL, NDLTD has par-

ticular characteristics that complicate interoperability and transparent resource discovery across its members. For instance, institutions are autonomous, each managing most services independently and not being required to report either collection updates or changes to central coordinators. Also, all NDLTD members do not (yet) support the same standards or protocols. The diversity in terms of natural language, metadata, protocols, repository technologies, character coding, nature of the data (structured, semi-structured, unstructured, multimedia), as well as user characteristics and preferences make them quite heterogeneous. Finally, NDLTD already has many members and eventually will aim at supporting all those that will produce ETDs. New members are constantly added and there is a continuing flow of new data, as theses and dissertations are submitted.

In DL cases like NDLTD, there are basically three approaches for interoperability and transparent resource discovery. They differ in the amount of standardization or effort required by the DL [19], as follows:

- **Federated services**: In this approach to interoperability a group of organizations decide that their services will be built according to a number of agreed upon specifications, normally selected from formal standards. The work of forming a federation is the effort required by each organization to implement and keep current with all the agreements. This normally does not provide a feasible solution in a dynamic environment such as the NDLTD.

- **Harvesting**: A difficulty in creating large federations is increasing motivation. So, some recent efforts aim at creating looser groupings of digital libraries. The underlying concept is that the participants make some small efforts to enable some basic shared services, without specifying a complete set of agreements. The best example is illustrated by the Open Archives Initiative (OAI) [16], which promotes the use of Dublin Core as a standard metadata format and defines a simple standard metadata harvesting protocol. Metadata from DLs implementing the protocol can be harvested to central repositories upon which DL services can be built. Particularly in the case of OAI, there is an initial impedance for its implementation by some archives since it involves small amounts of coding and building of middleware layers, especially for local repositories that sometimes do not match very well the OAI infrastructure, such as, for example, those repositories based on the Z39.50 protocol. Further, very small archives may lack staff resources to install and maintain a server. Moreover, some archives will not take any active steps to open their contents at all, making gathering, the next approach, the only available option.

- **Gathering**: If the various organizations are not prepared to cooperate in any formal manner, a base level of interoperability is still possible by gathering openly accessible information. The best example of gathering is via Web search engines. Because there is minimal staff cost, gathering can provide services that embrace large numbers of digital libraries, but the services are of poorer quality than those that can be achieved by partners who cooperate more fully. This is mainly due to the quality of the data that can be gathered, including aspects of lack of structure and absence of provenance information.

For NDLTD, a combination of federated search (for a small number with Z39.50 support), harvesting (from institutions who agree to use a set of standard protocols), and gathering (from institutions who cannot, or do not want to use such protocols) is the best solution.

Although the problem of quality with Web data is well known, many have collected data from the Web in order to develop collections of suitable size for various DL-like systems. The Harvest system, one of the first systems to apply focused gathering, had simple HTML-aware extraction tools [3]. PhysNet [20], a project to collect Physics information from the Web, still uses Harvest. The New Zealand digital library (http://www.nzdl.org) has been developing collections since 1995 based on content distributed over the Internet. Recent enhancements to the Greenstone system provide additional support, but require the manual construction and programming of wrappers, called plugins and classifiers [21]. On a different approach, the CiteSeer system [18] collects scientific publications from the Web and automatically extracts citation information. The data extraction process, however, is specific for identifying author, title, citations, and other fields common to scientific papers. Similarly, Bergmark [2] proposes the use of clustering techniques to collect pages on scientific topics from the Web, but does not approach the issue of how to extract relevant data from such pages. Nevertheless, these works show that, with sufficient manual intervention, useful services can be built with data from the Web.

In the following, we present the architecture of the Web-DL environment, which (1) combines harvesting and gathering to broaden the scope of interoperability in federated digital libraries, and (2) provides a framework to integrate a number of technologies, such as focused crawling, data extraction, and digital library toolkits. Ultimately Web-DL provides an infrastructure for building high-quality digital libraries from Web contents. We illustrate the usefulness of our approach by using the Web-DL environment to integrate data from OAI and non-OAI compliant members of NDLTD.

3. The Web-DL environment architecture

To build an archive from the Web, data must be collected from Web sites and integrated into a DL system. This operation has three main steps: (1) crawl the Web sites to collect the pages containing the data, (2) parse the collected pages to extract the relevant data, and (3) make the data available through a standard protocol. Figure 1 shows the Web-DL environment and architecture for the integration and building of a digital library from the Web.

Collecting Web pages with the target information is done by using the ASByE tool, described in detail in Section 4. After providing ASByE with a simple navigation example, a Web crawler is created for the site. This crawler collects all the relevant pages, leaving them available for data extraction.

Collected pages then must be parsed to extract the relevant data. This is accomplished by the DEByE tool, described in detail in Section 5. Given one or more example pages, DEByE is able to create a wrapper for the site to be collected. The site pages are then parsed by DEByE generated wrappers and the data is extracted and stored locally in a relational database.

In order to be used by most digital library systems (in our case, the MARIAN system [12]), data must be stored in a structured way, (e.g., MARC or XML), usually using community-oriented semantic standards (e.g., Dublin Core, or FGDC for geospatial data). In the work reported in this paper, we use ETD-MS, a metadata standard for electronic theses and dissertations [1], which builds upon Dublin Core. Nonetheless, since data in Web sites is frequently in non-standard, non-structured formats, we need some normalization procedure. In Section 7, our approach to normalize the extracted data is described. This approach presents a more general solution than the one proposed in [4], allowing Web-DL to be easily used in different domains.

After the data in ETD-MS format is stored, an OAI server set up on top of the local database will make it available to anyone using the OAI protocol for metadata harvesting (OAI-PMH), in our particular case, available to the MARIAN system. The MARIAN system, described in Section 6, uses an OAI harvester to collect the metadata provided by DEByE, extracted from the Web pages. This data is stored in a union archive, using MARIAN's indexing modules. DL regular services are made available to users through the union archive created by MARIAN.

The following sections describe in detail all the mechanisms used to build the architecture proposed here.

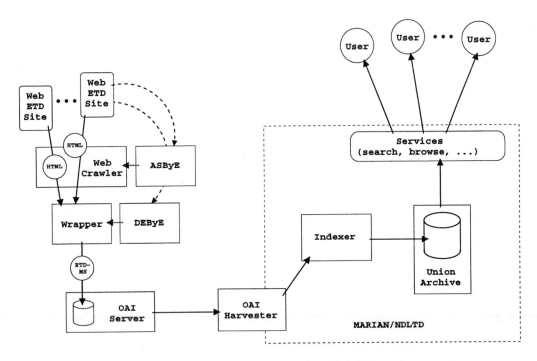

Figure 1. Proposed architecture for the Web-DL environment.

4. Obtaining pages from the ETD sites: the ASByE tool

In this section we describe how we use the ASByE tool for generating the agents that automatically collect pages containing data of interest from the Web. These agents can be seen as specialized crawlers that automatically traverse the publishing sites, exploring hyperlinks, filling forms, and following threads of pages until they find the *target pages*, that is, the pages that contain data of interest. Each target page found is retrieved and can have their data extracted by a wrapper.

ASByE (Agent Specification By Example) is a user driven tool that generates agents for automatically collecting sets of dynamic or static Web pages. The ASByE tool features a visual metaphor for specifying navigation examples, automatic identification of collections of related links, automatic identification of threads of answer pages generated from queries, and dynamically filling of forms from parameters provided for the agents, by the user. In a typical interaction with the tool, the user provides examples of (1) how to reach the target pages, filling any form, if needed, and (2) how to group together related pages. The output of the tool is a parameterized agent that fetches the selected pages. The ASByE tool is fully described in [10].

The graphical interface of the ASByE tool uses a graph-like structure in which nodes displayed in a workspace represent pages (or page sets) and directed arcs represent hy-

perlinks. The user navigates from node to node exploring the hyperlinks according to her interests. The source nodes in the graph (i.e., the ones not pointed to by any other node) are called *Web entry points* and are directly selected by the user by entering the URL of the page used to start the exploration. The tool then fetches the page and builds a node corresponding to it. From this point onward, the user can select, for each node, an operation to perform. The set of operations available depends on the type of node reached. The most common and simple operation allows the user to access a document to explore by selecting one of the hyperlinks.

In Figure 2, we illustrate other features of the ASByE tool showing how to generate an agent for retrieving pages from the Virginia Tech ETD Collection. The user begins by selecting the URL http://scholar.lib.vt.edu/theses/browse/by_author/all.htm as an entry point. The page at this URL contains a list of hyperlinks to each one of the target pages containing the documents available on the Virginia Tech ETD Collection. Using a number of heuristics based on criteria such as hyperlink distribution, hyperlink placement, similarity among URLs, and similarity among hyperlink labels, the tool identifies the list of links to the target pages, i.e., the pages to be collected. The user then can select the *agent generation* operation. The agent resulting from this specification session will first retrieve the entry point URL, extract from it all URLs currently belonging to the link collection, and then retrieve each target page

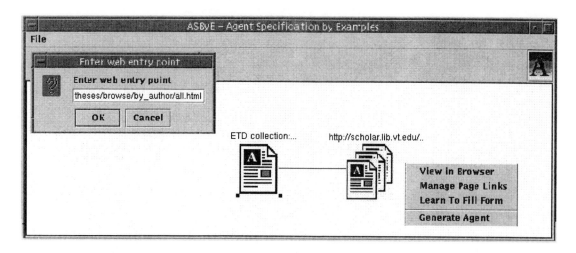

Figure 2. Snapshot of an agent specification session with the ASByE tool.

corresponding to these URLs, giving them as its output.

In some sites, there is no way to browse the whole document collection. The only way of reaching the target pages is by filling an HTML form, submitting it, and then navigating through the answer pages. Although ASByE is capable of generating agents to perform such operations, this feature was not used for the problem presented in this paper. A detailed description of the feature can be found in [10].

5. Wrapping publishing sites: the DEByE tool

We now describe the use of the DEByE tool for generating wrappers that extract data from pages in the collected sites. For a full discussion of the DEByE tool and the DEByE approach, we refer the interested reader to [14].

DEByE (Data Extraction By Example) is a tool that generates wrappers for extracting data from Web pages. It is fully based on a visual paradigm which allows the user to specify a set of examples of the objects to be extracted. These example objects are taken from a sample page of the same Web source from which other objects (data) will be extracted. By examining the structure of the Web page and the HTML text surrounding the example data, the tool derives an *Object Extraction Pattern (OEP)*, a set of regular expressions that includes information on the structure of the objects to be extracted and also on the textual context in which the data appears in the Web pages. The OEP is then passed to a general purpose wrapper that uses it to extract data from new pages in the same Web source, provided that they have structure and content similar to the sample page, by applying the regular expressions and some structuring operations.

DEByE is currently implemented as a system that functions as a Web service, to be used by any application that wishes to provide data extraction functionality to the end users. This allows us to implement any type of interface on top of the DEByE core routines. For instance, for general data extraction solutions, we use a DEByE interface based on the paradigm of nested tables [5], which is simple, intuitive, and yet powerful enough to describe hierarchical structures very common in data available on the Web. For the Web-DL environment, we have built an ETD-MS specific interface, with which the user can extract examples and assign them directly to ETD-MS fields. The DEByE/Web-DL interface was fully implemented in Javascript and can be used via any Web browser that supports the language.

In Figure 3 we show a snapshot of a user's session for specifying an example object on one or more sample pages. The sample pages are displayed in the upper window, also called the *Source* window. In the lower window, also called the *Fields* window, all the ETD-MS fields, such as Identifier, Title, etc., are available. The user can select pieces of data of interest from the source window and "paste" them on the respective cells of the fields window. After giving an example attribute, the user can select the "Test Attribute" button, to verify if DEByE is able to collect the selected attributes from the sample pages, and finally, after specifying all the example objects, the user can click on the "Generate Wrapper" button to generate the corresponding OEP, which encompasses structural and textual information on the objects present in the sample pages. Once generated, this OEP is used by an Extractor module that, when receiving a page similar to the sample page, will perform the actual data extraction of new objects and then will output them using an XML-based representation.

Since we are using ETD-MS, all the extracted objects are plain, i.e., they do not have a hierarchical or nested structure. In practice, the ETD-MS field thesis.degree contains four nested fields: name, level, discipline, and grantor. However, to simplify the interface, we chose to represent

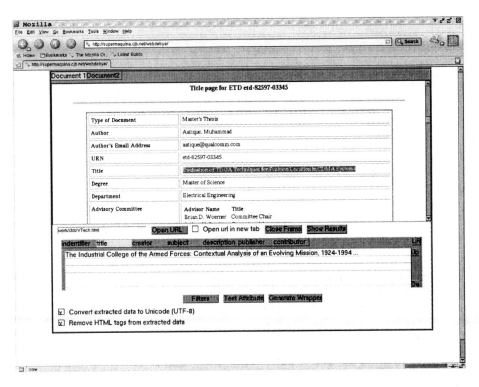

Figure 3. Snapshot of an example specification session with the DEByE/Web-DL interface.

them as independent fields. It is interesting to note that DE-ByE also is capable of dealing with more complex objects, by using a so-called *bottom-up* assembly strategy, explained in [14].

6. Providing DL services: the MARIAN system

MARIAN is a digital library system designed and built to store, search over, retrieve, and browse large numbers of diverse objects in a network of relationships [12] (See also about Java MARIAN at http://www.dlib.vt.edu/projects/MarianJava/index.html). MARIAN is built upon four basic principles: unified representation based on semantic networks, weighting schemes, a class system and class managers, and extensive use of lazy evaluation.

In MARIAN, semantic networks, which are labeled directed graphs, are promoted to first-class objects and used to represent any kind of digital library structure including internal structures of digital objects and metadata and different types of relationships among objects and concepts (e.g., as in thesauri and classification hierarchies). In order to support information retrieval services, nodes and links in MARIAN's semantic networks can be weighted. The fundamental concept is that of weighted object set: a set of objects whose relationship to some external proposition is encoded in their decreasing weight within the set. Nodes and links are further organized in hierarchies of object-oriented

classes. Each class in a particular digital library collection is the responsibility of a class manager. Among their other functions, each MARIAN class manager implements one or more search methods. All MARIAN searchers are designed to operate "lazily". During result presentation, only a small subset of results is presented until the user explicitly requests the remaining answers. The number of instances requested, and thus the transmission costs across the network, are severely limited relative to the size of the sets they manage.

In the context of the Web-DL environment, MARIAN provides searching and browsing services for the DL built from the Web. Data from OAI providers and from non-OAI-compliant members coming from the Web-DL environment are integrated into a Union Catalog. MARIAN is equipped with OAI harvesters able to collect data periodically from the Union Catalog.

MARIAN is completely reconfigurable for different DL collections; it uses digital library generators and a special DL declarative language called 5SL [11] for this purpose. Using these, specific loaders for different metadata formats (e.g., ETD-MS) can be generated. Once a new sub-collection is harvested, the loading process is applied. For every OAI record in the new sub-collection, a new part of the semantic network for the metadata record is created, representing its internal structure according to a metadata standard and the connections among text terms and text parts. The new part of the semantic network for the record is then integrated into the MARIAN knowledge base. At the end of the loading process weights for the resulting collection network are recomputed to consider global statistics.

Structured searches are supported by processing classes, class managers, and specific user interfaces also created during the DL generation process. Results of structured queries are displayed as ranked lists for browsing with entries and links created by specific XSL stylesheets. Presentations of full documents, also generated with special stylesheets, contain links that allow navigation to the originally collected Web page.

7. Converting the extracted data

For our particular problem, to store the data extracted by DEByE wrappers, we chose to use the ETD-MS format, to comply with the OAI-PMH. Web sites, however, are far from containing standardized data, and some normalizing operations need to be performed. Four main problems were found, when converting data to standard format: (1) mandatory data is not present in the page; (2) data is present, but only implicitly; (3) data is not in a required format; and (4) the extracted data is not in the appropriate encoding.

Regarding the first problem, when data is not present in the page, some replacement must be found. The solution for most mandatory fields is to use a default value, like "none". For other fields, like "identifier", a unique value must be generated, for instance by using sequential values or timestamps. The second problem happens when some piece of information is known, but the data is not explicitly represented in the page. For instance, for the *dc.publisher* field, we may know we are collecting from the Virginia Tech site, but this information appears nowhere in the page. The third problem occurred mainly for the *dc.date* field. As required by the ETD-MS, the date should be in ISO 8601 format. Therefore, dates collected from the Web pages must be converted before being stored. Finally, in many ETD pages, many formatting HTML tags and HTML entities are found within the text fields extracted. Also, non-English sites use many different character encodings to represent foreign characters. Some cleaning routines are needed to eliminate spurious tags and to convert between character encoding systems.

A general solution to this data cleaning and conversion problem is very hard to find. In Web-DL, we chose to use an intermediate solution between fully automating the process and manual user intervention. A set of predefined modules for processing the data is available and the user can select which ones to apply to the data being extracted. This process is fully implemented in the DEByE/Web-DL interface, providing a seamless integration to the Web-DL environ-

ment. For instance, as shown in Figure 4, for the date field, the user can apply a filter that converts the collected date to ISO 8061 format. A filter to insert a default value also can be applied to all fields. Filters to convert the character encoding and to strip HTML tags can be selected using the checkboxes on the bottom of the window, since these will be applied to all objects collected, independently of their value or type. When extracting the data from a Web page, the DEByE generated parser applies the selected modules to the objects. As a result all data will be in the desired standard format and can be stored using ETD-MS.

The data cleaning and conversion modules are simply string processing routines. They take a string as input, process it, and return the resulting string as output. This provides great flexibility for the construction of such modules. Thus, users can implement data cleaning modules according to their own specific needs, using any available programming language. More complex modules can be built making use of an API provided by DEByE, which allows, for instance, the passage of parameters other than the string to be processed. Of course, a set of predefined modules is already included in DEByE, to provide users with no programming experience with as much data cleaning functionality as possible. These are fully reusable and appropriate for any project. This approach solves the problems found on our preliminary experiments with Web-DL [4], while maintaining the modularity of the environment and minimizing user intervention in the process of building a digital library from the Web.

Once all the normalizing problems are solved, data can be stored in a relational database, later to be rendered using ETD-MS. The database is then made accessible through an OAI server. Using the OAI-PMH, the data extracted from the Web can be shared with any DL acting as an OAI service provider. In our environment, the extracted data is harvested, and integrated with data harvested from other NDLTD members within MARIAN.

8. An example Web ETD digital library

For this work, we collected pages containing ETDs from the sites of 21 different institutions selected from the list of NDLTD members, available at http://www.theses.org. These experiments were performed in the same context as reported in [4], but using the new integrated data cleaning and conversion modules. The ETD sites contained a total of 9595 ETDs. It was not possible to collect information from the sites of 7 institutions, since these were off-line or available only through a search interface.

Of the 6 mandatory ETD-MS fields, an average of 29.5% were missing in the collected pages, and were therefore filled with a default value. This value was inserted by the DL builder through the "default value filter" of the

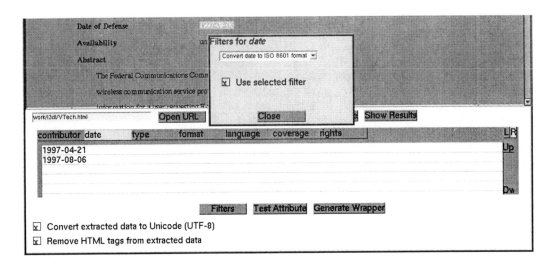

Figure 4. Data cleaning and conversion in the DEByE/Web-DL interface.

DEByE/Web-DL interface, thus requiring only one simple operation per field. The default value filter also allowed for the creation of unique identifiers by appending a serial number to the *dc.identifier* field. This was one of the major problems found in our previous experiments [4], which had required the manual implementation of data insertion routines. Here, it was solved by simply selecting options from the user interface. Table 1 shows the number of ETDs in which mandatory fields were missing.

Field name	ETDs missing
dc.title	43 (0.4%)
dc.creator	23 (0.2%)
dc.subject	2349 (24%)
dc.date	283 (3%)
dc.type	703 (7%)
dc.identifier	4800 (50%)

Table 1. Mandatory fields missing from the collected ETDs.

Table 2 shows the numbers for each site collected. It can be seen that, although not all, most of the information was collected and extracted. It is interesting to note that fields like *dc.publisher* or *dc.type*, which are often implicit in the collected site entry pages, but not available as extractable examples, could be easily inserted as a default value for the whole site. This means that the user needed only to type one value for each site, whereas in our previous experiments each site required the implementation of a separate routine.

The work required to include a site in the digital library consisted of providing sets of examples to the ASByE and DEByE tools. For each collected site only one example was needed to create the crawling agents. To generate parsers for data extraction, an average of 2–3 examples per field were required. This represented an average of 9 minutes of work per site, by a specialized user, much less than previously reported in [4]. The reduction in time was greatly due to the new automated process of converting data to a standard format. An interesting example is that of the *dc.date* field, which previously required that the user extracted each part of the date (day, month, year) individually or implemented a conversion routine for the ISO 8061 format.

For the 21 institutions in our example, the total effort of the user summed up to approximately 3 hours and 15 minutes. Notice that most of this is due to processing time, which can be improved by further optimizing the system code or using faster hardware. Since we do not expect Web sites to be massively submitted to the system, this is a reasonable human effort to collect the data of interest. In the future, we expect to further automate this process, to reduce the time required, as more sites are harvested.

To illustrate, Figure 5 shows an ETD published by Uppsala University. Once collected and extracted, all the metadata is stored and made available by the MARIAN system. Figure 6 shows the results of a query over the ETDs collected from the Web, using the MARIAN system. By using Web-DL, not only searching, but any number of DL services, such as browsing and filtering, among others, can be performed over the data extracted from the Web.

9. Summary and conclusions

We proposed the Web-DL environment for the construction of digital libraries from the Web. Our demonstration environment integrates standard protocols, data extraction, and digital library tools to build a digital library of electronic theses and dissertations. The proposed environment

ETD Site	Number of ETDs	Fields per ETD	Mandatory fields missing	Optional fields inserted
Adelaide U.	19	4	3	5
Australia N.U.	39	5	3	4
Concordia U.	3	9	0	2
Curtin U.T.	57	10	0	2
Griffith U.	40	5	3	4
H-U. Berlin	439	7	1	2
N.S.Y.U. Taiwan	1786	9	1	3
OhioLINK	932	6	2	4
Queensland U.T.	53	5	3	4
Rhodes U.	134	5	3	5
U. Kentucky	30	9	1	2
U. New South Wales	89	5	3	4
U. Tennessee	10	8	1	3
U. Virginia	619	8	0	2
U. Waterloo	105	5	3	5
U. Wollongong	6	5	3	4
U.P. Valencia	264	6	1	3
Uppsala U.	1567	3	3	5
Victoria U.T.	3	5	3	4
Virginia Tech	3278	9	0	2
Worcester P.I.	122	10	0	2

Table 2. Statistics for the data collected from the ETD sites.

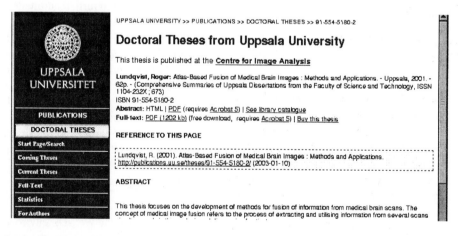

Figure 5. Metadata for an ETD, available at the Uppsala University Web site.

member sites. A need resulting from this integration is that of *deduping*: e.g., recognizing two instances of the same object, coming from different sources, or combining search results coming from internal repositories and external sources. Approaches to these problems are currently being studied and will be implemented in the future. MARIAN also allows for the use of probability estimates for the quality of the extracted data and their utilization in retrieval operations [12]. We are currently studying a coherent way of computing these probabilities directly from the DEByE tool.

In the current stage of our work, the generation of wrappers for each Web source was accomplished by using the DEByE tool by selecting example objects (i.e., bibliography entries) from sample pages from each of the sources. As we expect the number of sources to increase rapidly, we intend to deploy the automatic example generation method described in [9]. Such a method allows using data available on a pre-existing repository (e.g., titles, author names, keywords, subject areas, etc.) to automatically identify similar data in sample pages of new sources and to assemble example objects. By using it, we expect to automate the generation of wrappers, at least for a considerable number of cases.

We also will be extending the current Web-DL environment to consider classification of data extracted from the Web using a number of classification schemes, such as the ACM or the Library of Congress classification schemes and domain-specific ontologies. Finally, the current work on the Web-DL environment is largely concentrated on improving quality of data. In the near future we will extend and incorporate new kinds of networks (e.g., belief networks) into MARIAN to improve the quality of current and future DL services.

10. Aknoweledgments

Thanks are given for the support of NSF through its grants IIS-0086227 and DUE-0121679. The first author is supported by MCT/FCT scholarship SFRH/BD/4662/2001. The second author is supported by AOL and by CAPES, 1702-980. Work on MARIAN also has been supported by the National Library of Medicine. Work at UFMG has been supported by CNPq project I3DL, process 680154/01-9.

References

[1] A. Atkins, E. A. Fox, R. K. France, and H. Suleman. ETD-MS: an interoperability metadata standard for electronic theses and dissertations. http://www.ndltd.org/standards/metadata/, 2001.

[2] D. Bergmark. Collection synthesis. In *Proceedings of the 2nd ACM/IEEE-CS Joint Conference on Digital Libraries, JCDL'02*, pages 46–56, Portland, Oregon, USA, June 2002.

[3] C. M. Bowman, P. B. Danzig, D. R. Hardy, U. Manber, and M. F. Schwartz. The Harvest information discovery and access system. *Computer Networks and ISDN Systems*, 28(1-2):119–125, December 1995.

[4] P. Calado, A. S. da Silva, B. A. Ribeiro-Neto, A. H. F. Laender, J. P. Lage, D. de Castro Reis, P. A. Roberto, M. V. Vieira, M. A. Gonçalves, and E. A. Fox. Web-DL: an experience in building digital libraries from the Web. In *Proceedings of the 2002 ACM CIKM International Conference on Information and Knowledge Management*, pages 675–677, McLean, Virginia, USA, November 2002. Poster session.

[5] A. S. da Silva, I. M. R. E. Filha, A. H. F. Laender, and D. W. Embley. Representing and querying semistructured web data using nested tables with structural variants. In *Proceedings of the 21st International Conference on Conceptual Modeling ER 2002*, pages 135–151, October 2002.

[6] D. de Castro Reis, R. B. Araújo, A. S. da Silva, and B. Ribeiro-Neto. A framework for generating attribute extractors for web data sources. In *Proceedings of the 9th Symposium on String Processing and Information Retrieval (SPIRE'02)*, pages 210–226, Lisboa, Portugal, September 2002.

[7] E. A. Fox, M. A. Gonçalves, G. McMillan, J. Eaton, A. Atkins, and N. Kipp. The Networked Digital Library of Theses and Dissertations: Changes in the university community. *Journal of Computing in Higher Education*, 13(2):102–124, Spring 2002.

[8] N. Fuhr. Networked information retrieval. In *Proceedings of the 19th Annual International ACM SIGIR Conference on Research and Development in Information Retrieval*, page 344, August 1996.

[9] P. B. Golgher, A. S. da Silva, A. H. F. Laender, and B. A. Ribeiro-Neto. Bootstrapping for example-based data extraction. In *Proceedings of the 2001 ACM CIKM International Conference on Information and Knowledge Management*, pages 371–378, Atlanta, Georgia, USA, November 2001.

[10] P. B. Golgher, A. H. F. Laender, A. S. da Silva, and B. Ribeiro-Neto. An example-based environment for wrapper generation. In *Proceedings of the 2nd International Workshop on The World Wide Web and Conceptual Modeling*, pages 152–164, October 2000.

[11] M. A. Gonçalves and E. A. Fox. 5SL: A language for declarative generation of digital libraries. In *Proceedings of the 2nd ACM/IEEE-CS Joint Conference on Digital Libraries, JCDL'02*, pages 263–272, Portland, Oregon, USA, June 2002.

[12] M. A. Gonçalves, P. Mather, J. Wang, Y. Zhou, M. Luo, R. Richardson, R. Shen, L. Xu, and E. A. Fox. Java MARIAN: From an OPAC to a modern digital library system. *Lecture Notes in Computer Science*, Springer, 2476:194–209, September 2002.

[13] P. G. Ipeirotis, L. Gravano, and M. Sahami. Probe, count, and classify: categorizing hidden Web databases. *SIGMOD Record*, 30(2):67–78, June 2001.

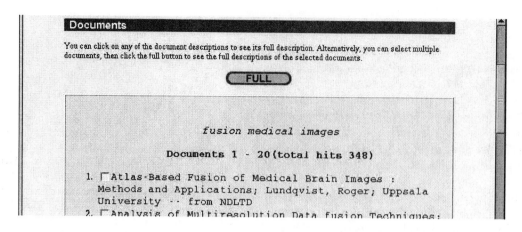

Figure 6. Search results for query "fusion medical images" over the ETDs collected from the Web.

provides an important first step towards the rapid construction of large DLs from the Web, as well as a large-scale solution for interoperability between independent digital libraries.

In this paper, Web-DL was applied to the Networked Digital Library of Theses and Dissertations, where we were able to collect data from more than 9000 electronic theses and dissertations. Due to the flexibility of the tools that compose Web-DL, we expect it to be easily applicable to any other domain, requiring, at most, changes in the user interface. Different interfaces are easily implementable for specific areas. Alternatively, a general interface like nested tables can be used for the majority of data available on the Web.

9.1. Lessons learned

Moving from the Web to a digital library is not a trivial task. Besides page collecting, we are faced with the difficult problem of transforming semi-structured data into structured data. Since there may not be a general solution for this problem, it is important to summarize the problems found and solutions applied when building the digital library of ETDs from the Web.

One of the main problems found was that some of the ETD sites to be collected provide access to their data only through search interfaces, resulting in the *hidden web* problem [13]. Although we did not approach this problem in our experiments, it can be partially solved by the use of the AS-ByE tool, which allows filling forms and submitting queries to reach the hidden pages. Thus, although it is impossible to guarantee that all data will be collected, the Web-DL environment is able to minimize the hidden Web problem, allowing us to obtain information otherwise unavailable by common Web crawlers.

Although there are many approaches for data extraction, as discussed in [15], cases will always be found where

wrappers must be built manually. For instance, Web pages within a site can be very different from each other, making it very hard to build a generic wrapper for the whole site. In our experiments, the use of the DEByE tool avoided all such problems and all wrappers were built with minimum effort. This may be due to the fact that most ETD sites were quite regular, but other experimental results [14] have shown that our approach for Web data extraction might be equally effective in more general and complex environments.

Finally, we face the problem of making the unstructured Web data fit a standard pattern. In Web-DL, we adopted a compromise solution, where a set of predefined data cleaning and conversion modules is available and can be selected by the user collecting data. To keep the solution as general as possible, we allow users to implement their own extra modules, according to their specific needs. This solution still requires some user intervention, but it is very general, and user effort is reduced to a minimum.

In sum, each of the tasks for extracting information from the Web into a DL environment presents its own set of problems. A general solution for building digital libraries from the Web depends on general solutions for each of these tasks and on an efficient integration of such solutions. The Web-DL environment provides such an integration and, through experiments, has shown itself to be a fast and efficient DL colection building tool. Further, using Web-DL to achieve interoperability between independent digital libraries requires as little effort as a gathering solution but provides the quality of data and services usually obtained only by harvesting or federated solutions.

9.2. Future work

The MARIAN system allows for harvesting data from NDLTD member sites using a variety of standard protocols. Therefore, an immediate first step is to integrate the data extracted from the Web with data collected from other

[14] A. H. F. Laender, B. Ribeiro-Neto, and A. S. da Silva. DE-ByE – data extraction by example. *Data and Knowledge Engineering*, 40(2):121–154, February 2002.

[15] A. H. F. Laender, B. Ribeiro-Neto, A. S. da Silva, and J. S. Teixeira. A brief survey of Web data extraction tools. *SIGMOD Record*, 2(31):84–93, June 2002.

[16] C. Lagoze and H. V. de Sompel. The Open Archives Initiative: Building a low-barrier interoperability framework. In *Proceedings of the 1st ACM/IEEE-CS Joint Conference on Digital Libraries, JCDL'01*, pages 54–62, June 2001.

[17] C. Lagoze, D. Fielding, and S. Payette. Making global digital libraries work: Collection services, connectivity regions, and collection views. In *Proceedings of the 3rd ACM International Conference on Digital Libraries, DL'98*, pages 134–143, Pittsburgh, Pennsylvania, USA, June 1998.

[18] S. Lawrence, C. L. Giles, and K. Bollacker. Digital libraries and Autonomous Citation Indexing. *IEEE Computer*, 32(6):67–71, June 1999.

[19] K. Maly, M. Zubair, and X. Liu. Kepler - an OAI data/service provider for the individual. *D-Lib Magazine*, 7(4), April 2001.

[20] PhysNet. http://physnet.uni-oldenburg.de/PhysNet/, 2002.

[21] I. H. Witten, S. J. Boddie, D. Bainbridge, and R. J. McNab. Greenstone: A comprehensive open-source digital library software system. In *Proceedings of the 5th ACM International Conference on Digital Libraries*, pages 113–121, San Antonio, Texas, USA, June 2000.

Session Chair: Ee-Peng Lim, Nanyang Tech. University, Singapore

Distributed Proofreading

Dr. Gregory B. Newby
Arctic Region Supercomputing Center
newby@arsc.edu

Charles Franks
Project Gutenberg Literary Archive Foundation
charlz@lvcablemodem.com

Abstract

Distributed proofreading allows many people working individually across the Internet to contribute to the proofreading of a new electronic book. This paper describes Project Gutenberg's Distributed Proofreading project, along with our general procedures for creating an electronic book from a physical book. Distributed proofreading has promise for the future of Project Gutenberg, and is likely to be a useful strategy for other digital library projects.

1. Introduction

According to the Internet Public Library (http://www.ipl.org), there are more than 20,000 publicly-accessible electronic books or eBooks on the Internet. About 30% of those originated with Project Gutenberg™ (http://www.gutenberg.net), one of the oldest all-electronic producers of content on the Internet.

Rather than emphasize particular authors, genres, languages or time periods, Project Gutenberg's content is very much determined by volunteer eBook producers' interests. All of the content comes from volunteers, rather than from a central collection development policy or work paid-for-hire. For a small number of eBooks, content was born digital – this occurs most frequently when a contemporary author donates his or her work for distribution by Project Gutenberg.

For well over 95% of the content, however, items were originally in print form and needed to be digitized for distribution. Creating and freely distributing eBooks is the mission of Project Gutenberg. General steps for digitization of Project Gutenberg eBooks are to:

1. Identify a printed copy of a book of interest
2. Assess whether this item is in the public domain in the United States, usually by seeking a copyright clearance from Project Gutenberg's copyright clearance coordinators
3. Scan the book
4. Perform optical character recognition (OCR) on the book
5. Proofread the OCR output
6. Confirm the formatting meets guidelines and submit the eBook for distribution

Over 2400 new Project Gutenberg eBooks were created in 2002 using this process. For 2003, we are striving to release our 10,000th eBook by completing an average of 75 new eBooks per week.

In order to accomplish this goal, we have embraced a new and innovative method for the most labor-intensive and time-consuming activity in eBook production: proofreading OCR output against actual page images. We call this method Distributed Proofreading.

In this paper, we will present a description of the Distributed Proofreading project, procedures, outcomes and plans. Future plans, as well as the possible role of DP for other digital libraries, follow.

2. Distributed Proofreading

Distributed Proofreaders (DP) is by far the easiest way for people to get involved with producing a Project Gutenberg eBook. We believe it can offer a useful training ground for many digital libraries. DP makes the process more efficient at every step in the eBook production phase. During 2002 DP contributed about 75% of Project Gutenberg's new eBooks.

The basis of DP is centralization. By centralizing copyright, scanning, proofreading and submission, economies of scale result, with enhanced qaulity. For proofreading, the main bottleneck in eBook production, DP means that thousands of individuals with only a few minutes to donate can help to make a difference.

The general steps for DP are the same as for any other eBook, but modified to follow the centralized model. First is the identification of candidate books. At this phase, several volunteers are engaged in book-hunting activities. They seek book auctions, library sales, and auction opportunities, purchasing books by the box.

For items suitable for scanning, the title and verso pages are scanned and sent to the copyright team. The copyright team is a small number of experts who can confirm whether the book is in the public domain in the United States. They perform "due diligence" (as defined by copyright law) to insure no copyright violations are made. Scans are kept centrally in case of a copyright question in the future.

Once a book is copyright-cleared, it is sent to one of two locations where volunteers run page-fed scanners. These volunteers chop the spine from the book and are then able to scan a complete book in only a few minutes. The scans are run through OCR, and the OCR'd text and images are uploaded to the DP server. DP uses ABBYY FineReader version 6.

On the server, page scans and information about the book are input to the DP database system. When all is ready, the book is released for proofreading. The Project Manager (PM) for the book monitors its progress through the DP site.

The proofreading phase is where the greatest increase in performance is seen. Previously, one person would typically perform all of the steps, often taking months to complete the scanning, OCR and proofreading of an eBook. With DP, many individuals complete proofreading much more quickly.

Proofreading is accomplished using a Web interface (Figure 1). Proofreaders may take as long as they need to compare the OCR output to the page images, making necessary changes and updating formatting. Each page image is viewed by two different DP proofreaders. The first proofreader sees the original page scan and the raw OCR output. The second proofreader sees the original page scan and the output from the first proofreader. Proofreaders may complete as many pages as they would like in either phase of any of the available eBook projects. At any given time, there are usually forty or more eBook projects to choose from with different topics and in different languages. Some easier books (such as English fiction) are geared towards novices.

Once all pages have been proofread, the PM or a Post Processor (PP) performs final assembly of the eBook (making sure that page breaks, headings, and other structural items are properly formatted). Various off-the-shelf and in-house developed programs are used to assist in error checking and formatting.

Figure 1: Distributed Proofreading Web Interface

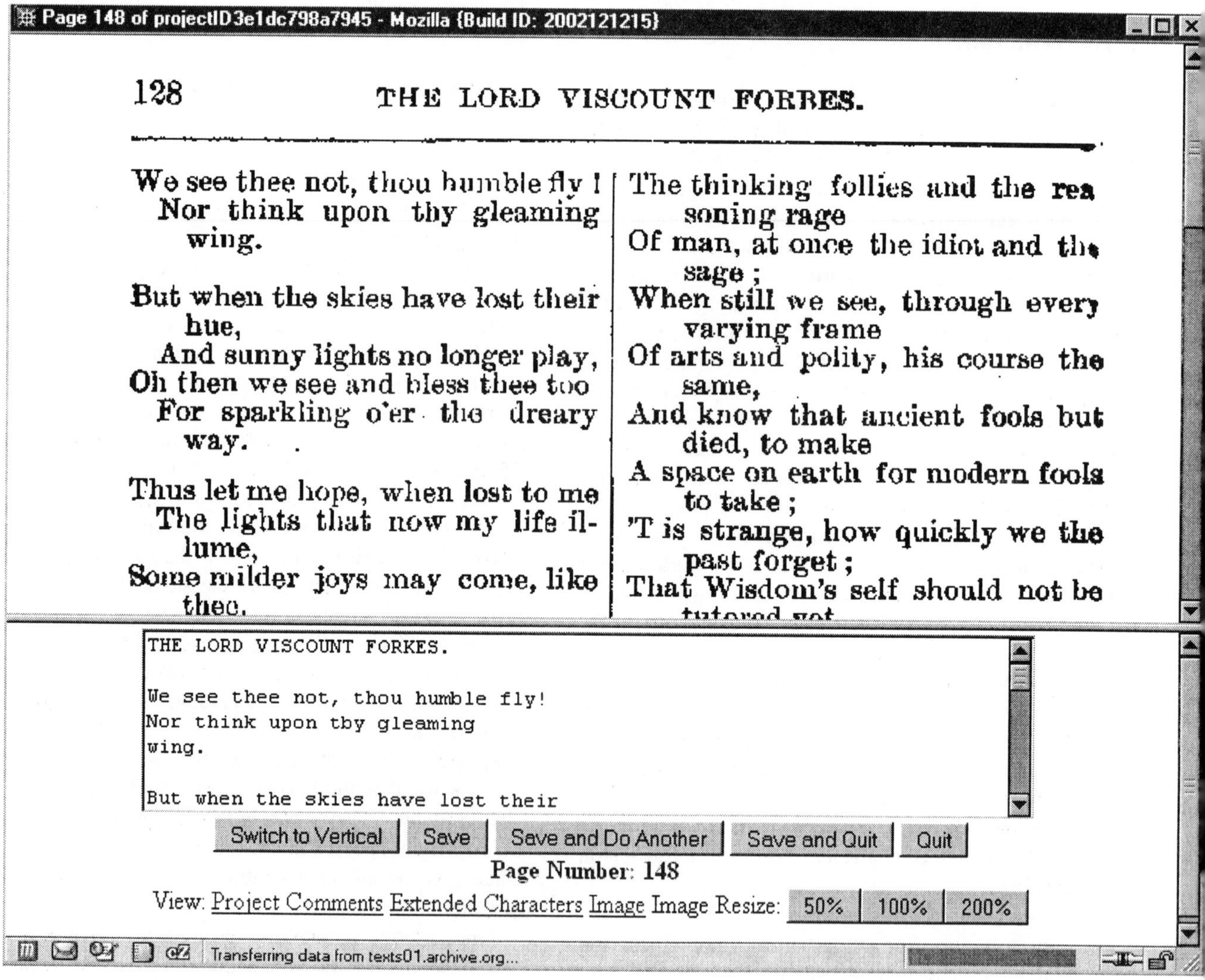

The PM/PP submits the eBook file(s) plus any additional information about the book to the posting team, who performs a final check, assigns a unique eBook number, generates metadata, uploads the files, and announces them.

The success of DP is evident in its numbers. In 2002, over 250,000 unique pages were proofread at DP, with each being examined twice. Over 6000 individuals performed proofreading ranging from a single page of work to many thousands. The page rate has gone up consistently, with a large spike thanks to Slashdot coverage in November (http://slashdot.org). DP is seeking to maintain or exceed December 2002's rate of over 110,000 pages per month throughout 2003.

3. The Future of Distributed Proofreading

Apart from an ongoing desire for growth, the biggest immediate goal for DP is to add facility for text markup. The first step towards this goal has been to enable tagging for italics and other text emphasis with <i> and </i>. DP volunteers are able to add such markup easily.

Other aspects of markup that are easily and automatically generated are paragraph and chapter breaks. For the future, though, we desire to add more complete XML markup (based on TEI LITE) to eBooks. This will enable conversion "on the fly" to different electronic formats, and will retain more of the information in printed texts. In the future, DP will markup and reformat all existing Project Gutenberg eBooks as XML documents.

DP is also seeking new volunteers and new opportunities. By coordinating with real-world organizations, we hope to have special projects – for example, for an entire class could spend an hour or so to complete a whole eBook.

4. Utility of Distributed Proofreading for Other Digital Libraries

Nearly all digital libraries are engaged in creating electronic content from physical artifacts such as books, catalogs, pamphlets, and so forth. While some have relatively deep pockets to pay for this digitization, and others might have rare or fragile materials that cannot be easily handled by volunteers, we believe that many digital library projects could benefit from the type of procedures that DP has developed.

For the casual volunteer, DP provides a very low barrier to getting involved with eBook creation. Using a standard Web browser, the process of signing up as a DP volunteer and viewing the first page for proofreading takes only a minute or two. Compared to the time, training and expense of setting up a scanning and OCR station to create an eBook from scratch, DP is extremely cost effective for volunteers.

For digital library projects engaged in work for hire or volunteers with more time or expertise, DP has created an infrastructure that scales well to make the creation of eBooks a routine task with high quality control. The author's experience with digitization and markup in a (non-Gutenberg) rare books project was that creating a single eBook cost about $1000. Similarly, the first eBooks produced with DP also took about $1000 worth of time and equipment. The difference is that the incremental cost with DP is very small – essentially, the cost of purchasing and shipping books. For professionally completed eBook generation the author was engaged in, *each* eBook cost $1000.

Project Gutenberg has a small number of key volunteers who contribute many hours per week, a larger number of volunteers who work somewhat less, and a very large number of volunteers who might only spend an hour or two per month working on eBook creation. This experience seems very typical for volunteer-driven organizations. Our goal, which is common to many digital libraries, is to make it easy for new volunteers to get involved – while at the same time having a scalable and efficient infrastructure to bring these new volunteers aboard. It is our contention that Distributed Proofreading represents the state-of-the-art in eBook creation for digital libraries in volunteer-driven organizations.

5. Conclusion

At the start of 2003, we expect approximately 1 million pages will be proofread during the year, significantly adding to the total number of eBooks online via Project Gutenberg. Visit the Distributed Proofreading site online at http://text01.archive.org/dp or http://pgdp.org.

5. Acknowledgement

Our thanks to the many Project Gutenberg volunteers for their work in making Distributed Proofreading effective. We are grateful to the Internet Archive for hosting DP and to iBiblio (http://ibiblio.org/gutenberg) as the main distribution point for Project Gutenberg eBooks.

Correcting broken characters in the recognition of historical printed documents

Michael Droettboom

Digital Knowledge Center, Johns Hopkins University
3400 N. Charles St., Baltimore, MD 21218
mdboom@jhu.edu

Abstract

This paper presents a new technique for dealing with broken characters, one of the major challenges in the optical character recognition (OCR) of degraded historical printed documents. A technique based on graph combinatorics is used to rejoin the appropriate connected components. It has been applied to real data with successful results.

1 Introduction

Most commercial optical character recognition (OCR) systems are designed for well-formed, modern business documents. Recognizing older documents with low-quality or degraded printing is more challenging, due to the high occurrence of broken and touching characters. This paper presents an algorithm that rejoins the pieces of broken characters so they can be more robustly identified. The success of this algorithm is then measured using a set of real-world historical documents.

This research is part of the Gamera project [2], which aims to create a tool for building document-specific recognition systems for humanities documents. One of our goals for this project has always been to provide general solutions that will work across multiple languages and printing techniques.

For the purposes of this paper, a *connected component* (CC) is a set of black pixels that are contiguous. By definition, characters are *broken* when they are made up of too many CCs. Broken characters can not be joined simply by the distance of the CCs alone, since two intentionally separate characters can often be closer than the two parts of an accidentally broken character.

The inverse problem of touching characters is solved using another approach where a symbol classifier is trained to split connected components using projection-based heuristics [3]. While the original intent of that approach was for the splitting of musical symbols, it also performs extremely

well on Roman text (93% accuracy on our dataset).

2 Other approaches

Thresholding converts a color or greyscale image to a bi-level image, such that black is used to indicate the presence of ink on the page and white is used to indicate its absence. Improving thresholding by looking for shades of grey in the areas where CCs almost touch, using entropy, can reduce the number of broken characters [7]. However, in many historical documents, the characters are completely broken on the page and intelligent thresholding, since it has no knowledge of the shapes of the target characters, performs poorly.

Active contour models (ACM), or snakes [5], find a vector outline for each symbol using certain constraints on the elasticity of the outline. Unfortunately, ACMs, which were designed for gross shape recognition, perform poorly on the fine details that are required to recognize printed characters.

Post-processing using some kind of language model, including a dictionary or n-grams of a language [4] has also been used to handle broken characters. However, such models are less useful for documents containing ancient languages, mixed-languages or a high occurrence of proper nouns.

Therefore, an ideal solution would include knowledge of the individual symbols without requiring a language-specific model.

3 The algorithm

The goal of the broken character connection (BCC) algorithm is to find an optimal way to join CCs on a given page that maximizes the mean confidence of all characters.

The algorithm begins by building an undirected graph in which each vertex represents a CC in the image. Two vertices are connected by an edge if the border of the bounding boxes are within a certain threshold of distance. Experiments demonstrated that this threshold is best set to $3/4$ of the average distance between all bounding boxes. (CCs

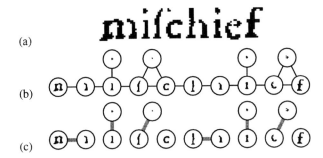

(a)

(b)

(c)

Figure 1. (a) an original image of a word from the testbed; (b) how the connected components are connected to form a graph; (c) the correct solution.

complete characters	81.3%
broken characters	10.7%
legitimately broken characters (**i**, **j**, **;**, **:** etc.)	6.2%
touching characters	1.8%

Table 1. Distribution of character types in the sample data. Note that failure to deal with broken and touching characters gives a maximum possible accuracy of 81.3%.

can also be connected by morphological dilation, though the bounding box method is much faster and produces only slightly less accurate results.) This creates a forest of graphs where each graph is roughly equivalent to a word in the document. Figure 1(b) shows one such graph. A graph representation, rather than a string representation, of connectivity is necessary, since characters can be broken in the x- and/or y-direction and cycles can occur between CCs.

Next, all of the different ways in which the CCs can be joined are evaluated. Every possible connected subgraph is enumerated, by performing a depth-first search from each vertex. To avoid enumerating duplicate possibilities, the vertex v assigned a number N_v, and an edge is traversed from vertex a to b only if $N_b > N_a$. To improve runtimes, the depth of the search is limited to the maximum number of CCs that would typically make up a single broken character. This constant is adjusted automatically based on the amount of degradation in the image and is usually between 3 and 5. Each of these subgraphs is evaluated by merging all of its CCs into a single image and sending it to the symbol classifier. The symbol classifier returns a confidence value that indicates how similar the merged image is to known symbols in the database.

Since we are using a k nearest neighbor (k-NN) classifier [1] for symbol classification, it was most convenient to use a confidence measure based on distance. More elaborate ways of determining confidence, such as analyzing the clustering of symbols within the database, have been suggested, but they do not significantly affect the success of the BCC algorithm.

Once the parts of the subgraph have been evaluated, dynamic programming is used to find an optimal combination of these parts that maximizes the mean confidence of the characters across the entire subgraph (word).

While a full runtime complexity analysis of the algorithm is beyond the scope of this paper, the asymptotic upper bound is $O(n \ln n)$, where n is the number of vertices in

the graph. However, when there are no cycles, the runtime is reduced to roughly $O(kn)$, where k is the maximum size of the subgraphs.

4 Results

To evaualte the BCC algorithm, we used the Statistical Accounts of Scotland [6]. This collection of census-like data was printed in 1799, with reused metal type on wooden blocks. The age of the paper, combined with the low-quality type and press-work, presents challenges for OCR. Table 1 shows the distribution of the types of characters in the collection. The manually-generated groundtruth data also makes this collection valuable for research.

The results below were obtained by training the classifier using five pages, and then testing the algorithm on five additional unseen pages with similar typeface.

If the symbol classifier only has knowledge of the complete characters in the image, BCC correctly finds 71% of the broken characters in our test data. By training the symbol classifier with examples of broken characters that were manually identified, BCC correctly finds 91% of the broken characters.

BCC also performs well with legitimately broken characters, such as **i**, **j**, **;** and **:**. By training the symbol classifier with examples of each of these characters, BCC was able to find and join 93% of the legitimately broken characters. This renders further procedural programming of heuristic rules (such as to attach ı's to dots) unnecessary. Therefore, it easy to support new character sets that have other legitimately broken characters, such as the Greek majuscule xi (Ξ).

5 Conclusion

The technique presented here performs very well on the test dataset, not only for "accidentally" broken characters, but also for those that are legitimately broken. In addition, it seems to satisfy our goal of being relatively independent of document type: it seems to adapt to new kinds of symbols gracefully with a minimum of manual intervention.

References

[1] T. Cover, and P. Hart. 1967. Nearest neighbour pattern classification. *IEEE Trans. on Inform. Theory.* 13(1): 21–7.

[2] M. Droettboom, K. MacMillan, I. Fujinaga, G. S. Choudhury, T. DiLauro, M. Patton, and T. Anderson. 2002. Using the Gamera framework for the recognition of cultural heritage materials. *JCDL.* 11–7.

[3] I. Fujinaga, B. Alphonce, B. Pennycook, and K. Hogan. 1991. Optical music recognition: Progress report. *Int. Comp. Music Conf.* 66–73.

[4] S. M. Harding, W. B. Croft, and C. Weir. 1997. Probabilistic retrieval of OCR degraded text using N-grams. *Europ. Conf. on Dig. Libraries.* 345–59.

[5] M. Kass, A. Witkin and D. Terzopolous. 1987. Snakes: Active contour models. *Int. Conf. on Comp. Vision.* 259–68.

[6] *Statistical Accounts of Scotland.* 1799. http://edina.ac.uk/statacc/

[7] Ø. D. Trier, and A. K. Jain. 1995. Goal-directed evaluation of binarization methods. *IEEE Trans. on Pattern Analysis & Machine Intelligence.* 17(12): 1191–201.

Correcting Common Distortions
in Camera-Imaged Library Materials

Michael S. Brown and Desmond Tsoi
Department of Computer Science
H.K.U.S.T.
Clear Water Bay, Hong Kong

ABSTRACT

We present a technique to correct image distortion that can occur when library materials are imaged by cameras. Our approach provides a general framework to undo a variety of common distortions, including binder curl, fold distortion, and combinations of the two. Our algorithm is described and demonstrated on several examples.

Keywords: Digital collections; distortion removal

1. INTRODUCTION

Camera-based imaging of library materials is becoming increasingly common. This non-contact imaging technique is particularly useful for items such as paintings, rare documents, and other media that are too large or fragile for flatbed scanners. Because these items are not physically pressed flat when imaged, their underlying shape cannot be guaranteed to be flat. This can cause what is perceived as distortion. One well-known example is the curl distortion present near the binding of a book. Other examples include distortion from folded pages (see Figure 1).

Techniques to correct this distortion are desired to make the imagery more visually appealing and to facilitate subsequent post-processing, such as OCR. In this paper, we provide a novel approach to undo common distortions encountered in camera-imaged library materials.

2. RELATED WORK

The term "skew" is used to describe the presence of distortion in an imaged document. Currently, there are two fundamental "de-skewing" algorithms. The first targets mis-aligned documents imaged on a flat-bed scanner. These algorithms compute planar transforms to align the scanned content to the image's raster representation [4]. The second common de-skewing approach corrects the paper curl effect that occurs near a book's binding. Because assumptions can be made about the physical properties that cause this distortion, for example, the page is always curled in a cylindrical fashion, this problem is fairly well defined and commercial solutions exist [5].

While planar and book-binding skew can be corrected, these types of distortions are specific to bound books and loose document collections. Items that warrant camera-imaging often introduce more complex distortions that cannot be corrected by these techniques. For example, the image in Figure 1(b) of a three-page fold-out exhibits distortion from both folding and binder curl. This distortion *cannot* be corrected using current de-skewing algorithms. Distortion after imaging such materials remains a problem.

Some recent approaches have addressed arbitrary distortions. These techniques work by extracting 3D information about the imaged material. Brown et al [1,2] recovered 3D points on a

Figure 1: Examples of image distortion. (a) book binder distortion (b) a more complex example of a three page fold-out.

material's surface and used a physics-based simulation to virtually "flatten" the material back to a plane. Pilu [5] provided a similar solution in which sparse 3D data of a document's surface was captured and used to construct a triangulated 3D mesh. A relaxation algorithm pushed the points to a plane while maintaining equal distance between the points. While these techniques do correct arbitrary distortions, they have two drawbacks. First, additional imaging equipment is needed to acquire 3D information. Second, the algorithms used are computationally slow.

In this paper, we propose a correction algorithm that uses only 2D information. Our approach works by extracting boundary information of the distorted image. Using these boundaries, we can compute a corrective function to map the distorted image to a rectangular image using boundary interpolation. This boundary interpolation approach provides a general solution that can be used to correct many common types of distortion including paper-binding curl, paper folds, and fan-like distortion.

3. OUR APPROACH

3.1 Assumptions

Two assumptions are made: (1) the imaged material was originally planar and recti-linear, and (2) the boundary information can be used to describe the deformation. Our first assumption is valid for the majority of library collections. As we will demonstrate, our second assumption is true for common distortions encountered in imaging, including binder curl and fold distortion. We note that our approach cannot correct for completely arbitrary distortion, such as an image of a crumpled piece of a paper. Currently, only the techniques that utilize 3D information [1,5] have shown promise in correcting this type of distortion. Such severe distortion, however, is found in only a small number of items. We, instead, focus on correcting *common* distortions using 2D information.

3.2 Boundary Representation

Our correction procedure begins by identifying the boundary of the imaged material. Since it is assumed that the item is recti-linear, only four boundaries need to be extracted. Due to the imaged

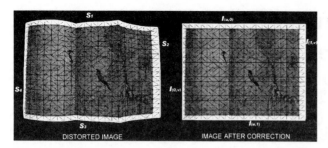

DISTORTED IMAGE   IMAGE AFTER CORRECTION

Figure 2: Four boundaries curves, S1-S4, are identified in the distorted image. These correspond to the edges in the corrected image. A triangulated mesh guides texture-mapping between the distorted image and the corrected image.

material's non-planar shape, these edges will not appear as straight lines, but instead as curves.

Boundary extraction can be done manually, by using a graphical interface, or by using imaging processing tools such as the "magic lasso" in Adobe Photoshop. If the material is imaged with a high-contrast background, automatic extraction routines can be used.

The boundary is represented by four curves: S_1, S_2, S_3, S_4 as shown in Figure 2. Discrete points on the extracted boundary are used to define a natural cubic spline (NCS), denoted as follows:

$$S_i(t) = \begin{cases} S_i x(t) & t \in [0,1] \\ S_i y(t) & t \in [0,1] \end{cases}$$

Mathematically, the NCS is a parametric function, $S_i(t)$, that provides a continuous representation of the boundary curve (see [3] for an overview on splines). With this representation, the (x,y) image coordinates on the boundary curves can be obtained by evaluating the spline function, $S_i(t)$, with a parameter, t, over the interval [0-1].

3.3 Distortion Correction

The boundary curves, S_1-S_4, in the distorted image correspond to the boundary of an undistorted recti-linear image. We have used (x,y) to represent 2D image points in the distorted image; we use (u,v) to represent 2D image points in the restored image, I. For simplicity, the restored image is defined from $u \in [0,1]$ and $v \in [0,1]$. In Figure 2, we can see that the 2D (x,y) image points along the boundary of $S_1(u)$ should map to the restored image axis, defined as $I(u,0)$. This correspondence holds for the other curves, e.g., $S_2(v)$ should map to $I(1,v)$. Thus, the mapping of the distorted boundary curves to their correct locations in the undistorted image, I, is known. What is needed is a 2D function, $S(u,v)$, which returns internal (x,y) points within the distorted image's boundary. Since the only available information is the four boundary curves, the function $S(u,v)$ must be defined as a combination of S_1, S_2, S_3, S_4. This can be realized using a boundary interpolation technique known as Coons patch interpolation [3] as follows:

$$S(u,v) = \begin{bmatrix} 1-u & u \end{bmatrix} \begin{bmatrix} S_4(v) \\ S_2(v) \end{bmatrix} + \begin{bmatrix} S_1(u) & S_3(u) \end{bmatrix} \begin{bmatrix} 1-v \\ v \end{bmatrix} - \begin{bmatrix} 1-u & u \end{bmatrix} \begin{bmatrix} S_1(0) & S_2(0) \\ S_4(1) & S_3(1) \end{bmatrix} \begin{bmatrix} 1-v \\ v \end{bmatrix}$$

Using this function $S(u,v)$, we can compute the (x,y) locations of equally sampled (u,v) points in the restored image. By constructing a triangulated mesh of the sampled points, we can texture-map triangles from the distorted image to the restored image (see Figure 2). This texturing process performs the distortion correction.

4. RESULTS

Figure 3 shows results of our approach on three examples. The first two are the examples shown in Figure 1. These are pages (including a three-page fold-out) from two oversized books. The last image is of a 2.5x1 meter Chinese paper cut. This medium is pasted on a folded tablet. To fit inside the display case, the item cannot be completely unfolded, which is apparent in the image. Our approach is able to correct these different distortions.

Figure 3: Results from three examples. (Top) Correction of two over-sized books imaged by a camera (from Figure 1). The first corrects binder distortion. The second corrects both binder and fold distortion. (Bottom) A Chinese paper-cut on a folded tablet - before and after correction.

5. CONCLUSION

We have presented an image distortion correction algorithm that is suitable for correcting common distortions encountered in imaged library materials. This technique is particularly useful for camera-imaged items that cannot be physically flattened before imaging. Our algorithm requires only the imaged material's 2D boundary information to be extracted. Boundary interpolation is used to provide a general framework that can correct a variety of common distortions.

6. REFERENCES

[1] Brown, M. S. et al. "Document Restoration Using 3D Shape". Int'l Conference on Computer Vision (ICCV'01), Vancouver. July 2001.

[2] Brown, M. S. et al. "Digital Atheneum: New Approaches for Preserving, Restoring, and Analyzing Damaged Manuscripts". JCDL '01, Roanoke, June 2001.

[3] Farin, G. "Curves and Surfaces for Computer-Aided Geometric Design", Academic Press, 4th Edition, 1997.

[4] Gatos, B. et al. "Skew detection in line position determination in digitized documents", In Pattern Recognition, 30(9):1505-1519, 1997.

[5] Pilu, M. "Undoing Paper Curl Distortion Using Applicable Surfaces", Computer Vision and Pattern Recognition (CVPR '01), Hawaii, Dec 2001.

[6] US Patent 5,084,611, "Document Reading Apparatus for Detection of Curvature in Documents", Minolta Camera, Kabushiki Kaisha, Jan 1992.

Link Attachment (Preferential and Otherwise) in Contributor-Run Digital Libraries*

Miles Efron and Donald Sizemore
School of Information and Library Science
University of North Carolina, Chapel Hill, 27599
efrom@ils.unc.edu, don@unc.edu

Abstract

Ibiblio *is a digital library whose materials are submitted and maintained by volunteer contributors. This study analyzes the emergence of hyperlinked structures within the ibiblio collection. In the context of ibiblio, we analyze the suitability of Barabasi's model of preferential attachment to describe the distribution of incoming links. We find that the degree of maintainer activity for a given site (as measured by the voluntary development of descriptive metadata) is a stronger link count predictor for ibiblio than is a site's age, as the standard model predicts. Thus we argue that the efforts of ibiblio's contributors positively affect the popularity of their materials.*

1 Introduction

In [4] Paul Jones describes the notion of contributor-run digital libraries. Under Jones' formulation, these repositories are characterized by low barriers to material contribution and a high degree of end-user involvement in the description and organization of materials. One example of such a project is ibiblio (www.ibiblio.org), a repository of websites that has been in operation since 1992. ibiblio hosts over 1000 projects (called "collections"), totaling over a terabyte of data. The subject matter of these collections runs a wide gamut, from open source software to libraries of fine art images. Despite their diversity, however, these sites share a common interest insofar as they are all maintained by volunteers who upload, update, and describe their own materials.

This study analyzes the outcome of these volunteers' labor. In particular we pursue the question, do increased contributor efforts lead to increased collection popularity? Barabasi's notion of preferential attachment in hyperlinked environments suggests that older collections will, on average, be more popular than younger collections [1]. In a classic "rich-get-richer" scenario, preferential attachment predicts that new sites are more likely to create hyperlinks to well-established sites than they are to link to obscure new sites. In work by Huberman and Adamic, (cf. [3, 2]) the notion of preferential attachment is contextualized in the general tendency of data from hyperlinked environments to display power-law distributions.

Though ibiblio's incoming hyperlinks do display a classic power-law distribution, we argue that this contributor-run digital library environment displays a unique dynamic. While our data show some preferential attachment effect, we argue that its effect is minor, and that the number of links pointing to an individual collection in ibiblio has more to do with the efforts of its maintainers than with its age. Instead of the rich getting richer, then, in ibiblio's contributor-run digital library, the diligent get popular.

2 Data Collection

Ibiblio is a complex repository of information. To make the current study manageable we took a conservative view of what constitutes an individual website. We limited our analysis to documents in ibiblio's main web space. Moreover, we assumed that any top-level directory in this space contained a single and complete collection[1]. This method of counting yielded $n=1123$ collections in total.

Having obtained these data, we measured a variety of characteristics of each collection. First we captured

---

*The authors wish to acknowledge the support of Paul Jones and the Center for the Public Domain.

[1]There are several ways to count the total number of collections, since ibiblio hosts projects in various capacities. However, the described approach constitutes a conservative count.

the number of kilobytes used by the collection (*kbytes*). To approximate the age of the collection we found the site's earliest file modification time (*minMod*). We also found the newest mod time in the collection (*maxMod*). Next we found how many external hyperlinks point to this collection by using link searches on both Google (*gLinks*) and AltaVista (*aLinks*). These counts were fairly different (correlation= 39%), however, and so we averaged them into a single number (*mLinks*), retaining all three measures[2]. Finally, we consulted the ibiblio collection index database to note how often collection maintainers were updating their metadata records. The collection index is a metadata repository to which collection maintainers can submit Dublin Core descriptions of their material. Of the 1123 collections we considered, 525 had submitted a metadata record. These records may be edited over time, and ibiblio tracks how often maintainers of each collection edit its metadata. For each site we measured the number of metadata edits (*cCount*).

While these data are admittedly blunt instruments, we argue that *minMod* gives a sense of a collection's age. On the other hand, a count of in-bound links provides evidence for the size of a collection's audience. Finally, if a site developer creates and maintains descriptive metadata, we argue that this is evidence that he is expending effort on his project.

3 Data Analysis

Figure 1 plots the number of inbound links (according to the averaged *mLinks* measure) against the place of a collection in the list of collections, ranked by *mLink*. The plot is shown on a log-log scale, along with the least-squares fit for the data. This regression yielded $R^2 = 0.88$, suggesting a good fit to the data. The slope of this line, -2.04, is within the range predicted by Barabasi for a hyperlinked environment. A similar power-law distribution appeared for *gLinks* and *aLinks*. Thus our data appear to adhere to Barabasi's model, and as a consequence, we expected preferential attachment to be evident in the system.

To test for preferential attachment's impact on link distribution, we isolated a popular subset of the 1123 collections. We defined the "popular" sites to be those sites with a link count (using *mLink*) above the 95% quantile (i.e. *mLinks*>105). We then conducted a one-sided, two-sample *t*-test for equality of *minMod* between the popular sites and the rest of the sample.

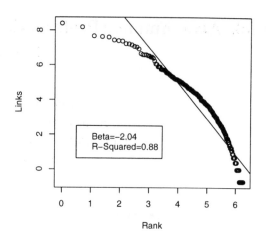

Figure 1. Incoming Link Distribution

	Best	*Rest*
Frequent	12	64
Rare	70	977

Table 1. *cCount* **Contingency Table**

This yielded $p \approx 0$, suggesting that popular sites are, on average, older than the others.

However, preferential attachment appears to be only a weak predictor of link count. The Pearson correlation between *minMod* and *mLinks* was only -0.11, suggesting that site age only accounts for 11% of the variance in link count. On the other hand, *cCount*, the frequency of metadata updates, explained 23% of the variation in link count. We also expected *kbytes* and *maxMod* to be significant factors, but their impact on link count was subtle. For these data, only metadata update frequency is a better predictor of link count than is collection age.

This suspicion was borne out by a χ^2 test on the contingency table shown in Table 1. In this table, the *Best* sites are those defined above as "popular"— sites whose *mLink* count is above the 95th quantile. The rows correspond to metadata activity. "Frequent" updaters have *cCount*>1, while "rare" updaters have *cCount* $\leq$ 1. Thus 17% of the "popular" sites have frequent metadata updates, while only 6% of the non-popular sites are frequent updaters. For the null hypothesis that metadata update frequency and link count are independent, we obtained $p = 0.007$. Thus maintainer activity and collection popularity, as measured here, are statistically related.

---

[2]In the interest of space, the following results only report statistics calculated on *mLinks*. However, results for *aLinks* and *gLinks* were similar.

4 Conclusion

This study is necessarily preliminary. Ibiblio is a complex digital library, and the phenomena we have tried to measure are similarly nuanced. In future research we plan to adopt a more robust model of user activity. In addition, we will supplement our use of link count as a surrogate for audience size with an analysis of actual download statistics. Finally, we hope to develop a more valid model of contributor activity than the simple metadata update count used here.

However, the data reported here do suggest that if a contributor takes an active role in the promotion of his site he is likely to enjoy a wider audience than if he puts little effort into his project. In our sample, preferential attachment accounted for about 11% of the variance in incoming link count. On the other hand the metadata update rate captured 23% of the variance in link count. A χ^2 test formalized these results, suggesting that the role of maintainer activity in link count is significant above the 99% level.

The upshot of this finding is that the work of ibiblio's contributors appears to pay off. The preferential attachment model suggests that link count is predictable as a function of time. In the highly participatory venue of ibiblio, however, it seems that another mechanism—maintainer initiative—is a more significant factor in the emergence of popular resources.

References

[1] A. Barabasi and R. Albert. Emergence of scaling in random networks. *Science*, 286:509–512, October 1999.

[2] B. A. Huberman. *The Laws of the Web: Patterns in the Ecology of Information*. MIT Press, Cambridge, 2001.

[3] B. A. Huberman and L. A. Adamic. Evolutionary dynamics of the world wide web. *Nature*, 401, September 1999.

[4] P. Jones. Open(source)ing the doors for contributor-run digital libraries. *Communications of the ACM*, 44(5):45–46, 2001.

Automatic Disambiguation of Latin Abbreviations in Early Modern Texts for Humanities Digital Libraries

Jeffrey A. Rydberg-Cox

Department of English

University of Missouri at Kansas City

816-235-1305

rydbergcoxj@umkc.edu

ABSTRACT

Early modern books written in Latin contain many abbreviations of common words that are derived from earlier manuscript practice. While these abbreviations are usually easily deciphered by a reader well-versed in Latin, they pose technical problems for full text digitization: they are difficult to OCR or have typed and — if they are not expanded correctly — they limit the effectiveness of information retrieval and reading support tools in the digital library. In this paper, I will describe a method for the automatic expansion and disambiguation of these abbreviations.

Categories and Subject Descriptors

Content, Collection Development, Document Processing

General Terms

Algorithms, Experimentation, Languages

Keywords

Digitization, Tagging Early Modern Texts, History of Science

1. INTRODUCTION

In the past ten years, large digital library projects have made great strides in the scalable techniques for the digitization of texts. The bulk of this research has been focused in two areas. One area focuses on particularly difficult early materials that pose interesting and unique problems such as the Beowulf project, Project Cervantes, Cuneiform Digital Library Initiative, or the Electronic Text Corpus of Sumerian Literature. The other area focuses on scalable cost effective techniques for digitizing nineteenth and twentieth century printed editions, such as the Making of America, Olive Software, and Project Guttenberg. The bulk of this research has, however, largely ignored early printed works and incunabula even though they pose interesting research problems of their own for full text digitization. For example, in early Latin texts, broken words at the ends of lines are not

always hyphenated; space between words is often compressed so that word breaks are difficult to recognize; and common words and word-endings are abbreviated with non-standard typographical symbols. Likewise, early Greek texts are printed using a wide variety of ligatures, abbreviations, and typographical conventions that do not correspond with modern practice. Finally, even works printed primarily in English share some of these typographical problems and replicate others when they include quoted passages of Greek and Latin texts. While all of these ambiguities can be resolved by human editors who are well versed in Greek and Latin, this is a time consuming and expensive process. If these problems can be addressed with automatic processes, it becomes possible to dramatically reduce the costs associated with digitizing these materials, and to make many more of them available in digital form ([1]). In this paper, I will describe an automatic method that we have developed to address one of these problems — the resolution of ambiguous and non-standard abbreviations in early-modern Latin texts — as we digitize a corpus of early texts in the history of science from the Linda Hall Library of Science, Technology, and Engineering located in Kansas City.

2. THE SCOPE OF THE PROBLEM

Early typographers used a wide variety of abbreviations in their works, such as a tilde or a straight line over vowels to indicate the omission of one or more characters from a printed text. This symbol sometimes denotes the omission of a following 'n' or 'm'; at other times, it indicates the omission of both the preceding and following nasal, and it sometimes marks the omission of an almost arbitrary combination of nasals with a vowel. Thus, McKerrow ([2]) points out that the abbreviation î can stand for "in", "im", "ni", "mo", "nim", "min", "mni", and "mnin" in different contexts. McKerrow further points out, "Besides this, abbreviations in this form are used to stand, apparently quite arbitrarily for parts of a large number of common words, thus ê = est, eê = esse, mõ = modo, orõnê = orationem, spûs = siritus, &c." While vertical bars or tildes over vowels are among the most common abbreviations, there are other similarly ambiguous abbreviations formed with "g", "l", "p", "q", "r", "t,", "w", "y" and a small handful of other special forms ([3] and [4] both provide a useful practical guides). While the density of these abbreviations varies, they are by no means uncommon. In sixty early modern texts that have been keyed in for the Archimedes Digital Library, an NSF funded project to create a digital library of early texts in the history of mechanics (http://archimedes.fas.harvard.edu), the average rate of abbreviations is almost three to five per page, while earlier texts have a much higher rate. For example, a single page of the 1525 edition of Ptolemy's *Geography* has more than 50 abbreviations on a single page and almost thirty in the one paragraph shown in figure 1.

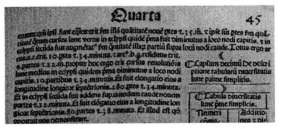

Figure 1: Heavily abbreviated paragraph from the 1525 edition of Ptolemy's *Geography*. Page image courtesy of the Linda Hall Library History of Science collection.

Overall, this error rate is significant enough to hinder the performance of routine digital library applications such as information retrieval and more complex applications such as keyword extraction, named entity recognition, and other types of linguistic analysis. For example, we have tried several keyword extraction algorithms on uncorrected versions of the texts in the Archimedes corpus and discovered that these sorts of abbreviations introduced significant errors into our results.

3. APPROACHING THE PROBLEM

We have adopted a three step algorithm to automatically expand these abbreviations for texts that have been manually entered. The first two steps use different methods to identify all possible valid expansions of an abbreviation while the third attempts to select the best possible expansion for the context in those contexts where more than one expansion is possible. First, we try to parse every possible expansion of an abbreviation with a Latin morphological analyzer (an expansion of the system described in [5]). All forms that return a valid parse are accepted as possible correct expansions.

In the second step, the primary letter of the abbreviation is used as the core of a regular expression (i.e. /.*?i.*?/ in Perl regular expression syntax for the abbreviation î) that is used to search a database of known inflected forms of Latin literature. This database is based on three distinct, large corpora of texts: the Packard Humanities Institute corpus of Latin texts consisting of 362 works and 7.5 million words; the Latin texts contained in the Perseus project, consisting of 63 works and 4.5 million words; and the small but growing corpus of Latin texts in the history of science that we are creating in partnership with the History of Science collection at the Linda Hall Library of Science, Engineering, and Technology with ten texts and 370,000 words of Latin as of January 2003. Any matched query is also added to the list of possible expansions. This step accounts for two possibilities. First, that we have encountered an abbreviation that is not included in one of our standard catalogs. Second, that we are working with a proper noun such as a person or place name that might not be correctly identified by the morphological analysis system.

This first two steps aim for high recall rates rather than high rates of precision; we want to locate every potential possible match. In the second phase, we then attempt to winnow our

list and identify the correct expansion for the context. We use three relatively simple metrics to accomplish this task. First, any expansion that is discovered by the morphological analysis engine is preferred to those that are discovered using regular expressions to search the database of known inflected forms. Second, we consult frequency tables and give more weight to expanded forms that appear more frequently in our corpus. Finally, we look at collocation data to determine whether the current context is similar to other contexts where a possible expansions of the abbreviation occur in our corpus. These three metrics are taken together in order to determine the most appropriate expansion of each abbreviation in the context where it appears.

4. FUTURE WORK

In preliminary tests in a small corpus, this procedure for automatic expansion of Latin abbreviations has provided accurate expansions for most abbreviations, and at least suggested accurate expansions in almost every case. Our next steps involve testing this algorithm on a much larger scale. We also need to test our approach more thoroughly with incunabula and other very early texts because these texts are usually very heavily abbreviated and, therefore, among the most difficult to transcribe and tag. Likewise, the disambiguation algorithm for our third step is overly simple. We need to develop better statistical methods so that we can suggest the proper expansion in more circumstances. Finally, an entirely automatic process will never be able to correctly resolve and expand every abbreviation. Therefore, we need to develop an interface that allows for the integration of our results into an XML editor, so that we can provide subject specialists and editors with a simple easy-to-use interface that will allow them to see the possible expansions for an abbreviation, and select the correct one as they are editing the text. If we can integrate this sort of tool into an editing environment, we should be able to dramatically reduce the cost and streamline the process of editing early modern texts

5. ACKNOWLEDGMENTS

A grant from the National Science Foundation International Digital Libraries Program (IIS-0122491) provided support for this work.

6. REFERENCES

[1].   Crane, G. and J.A. Rydberg-Cox. *New Technology and New Roles: The Need for "Corpus Editors".* in *Proceedings of the 5th Annual ACM Digital Library Conference.* 2000.

[2].   McKerrow, R., *Introduction to Bibliography.* 1927, Oxford: Clarendon Press.

[3].   Johnson, J., *Typographia, or the Printer's Instructor.* 1824, London: Longman.

[4].   Cappelli, A., *Dizionario Di Abbreviature Latine Ed Italiane.* 1990, Rome: SF Vanni.

[5].   Crane, G., *Generating and Parsing Classical Greek.* Literary and Linguistic Computing, 1991. **6**: p. 243-245.

Demonstrations

Educational Tools in Support of the Stanford *MediaServer*

Derek Stevenson
Learning Tech/SUMMIT
Stanford University
251 Campus Dr MSOB x244
Stanford CA 94305
dereks@stanford.edu

Chih-Chien Chao
EE Department
Stanford University
350 Serra Mall x067
Stanford CA 94305
jichien@stanford.edu

Sakti Srivastava
SUMMIT
Stanford University
251 Campus Dr MSOB x230
Stanford CA 94305
sakti.srivastava@stanford.edu

Jeremy C. Durack
Biological and Medical
Informatics
UC San Francisco
San Francisco CA 94143
jcdurack@yahoo.com

Amy Ladd
Stanford University
Medical Center
900 Welch Road #15
Stanford CA 94305
alad@stanford.edu

Kevin Montgomery
National Biocomputation Center
701A Welch Road Suite 1128
Stanford CA 94305

kevin@biocomp.stanford.edu

Jenn Stringer
Learning Tech/SUMMIT
Stanford University
251 Campus Dr MSOB x222
Stanford CA 94305
jenn@stanford.edu

Parvati Dev
Learning Tech/SUMMIT
Stanford University
251 Campus Dr MSOB x226
Stanford CA 94305
parvati@stanford.edu

Abstract

Medical media resources exist in a variety of analog and digital formats. Collections are generally organized and stored by their owners, each of whom utilizes their own method of cataloging and retrieval. As faculty retire, move on, or pass away, institutions risk losing the expertise that enhances the value media. The Stanford MediaServer has previously been deployed to catalog, organize, and centralize management of such media collections via the World Wide Web. Educational tools have been developed on top of existing MediaServer infrastructure to address a range of pedagogical models, and to promote widespread adoption within the Stanford Medical School curriculum and departments. These tools include Slide Show, Export to PowerPoint, Teaching File, and e-Books. With the exception of e-Books, these tools use web-based wizards to lead the user through the steps for creating each component.

Slide Shows consist of an ordered set of images and provide the underpinning data structures for PowerPoint and Teaching File creation. Slide Shows can be assembled from any accessible media in the MediaServer and shared with other users of the system.

Export to PowerPoint is a utility function to address the widespread use of PowerPoint in medical education and multimedia presentation. It allows Slide Shows to be converted to PowerPoint and downloaded to the client system for offline use, easing the process of assembling media and creating a PowerPoint document. This function leverages XML Web Services and the SOAP protocol to achieve the desired outputs.

Teaching Files are used to illustrate a particular educational topic, and consist of a multi-page interface. Each page contains media and annotations specific to the educational topic at hand. Annotations are stored with the Teaching File and not with the collated media. Individual pages are assembled by choosing existing Slide Shows and further annotating the media.

E-Books are web-based books built on a particular design template provided by the MediaServer. Authors can integrate media from the MediaServer into these e-Books, which are assembled through the use of 3rd party tools such as Macromedia Dreamweaver.

MediaServer resources were deployed in a gross anatomy course through the use of these tools and integration with third party applications, including a three-dimensional stereo viewing system. This pilot project was well received by the course participants and evaluation of usage data is ongoing.

These educational media tools must be further evaluated for their teaching efficacy. These tools will be evaluated with volunteer faculty contributing media and creating Slide Shows, PowerPoint documents, Teaching Files, and e-Books. These educational modules will then be used for medical school classes. Feedback will be integrated into further development of new educational tools, providing new views into the large Stanford MediaServer dataset.

Access rights management and security is paramount for the protection of digital media. The existing MediaServer security system will be enhanced to address privacy concerns, while providing faculty the flexibility to appropriately create and share educational units with their students and colleagues. Standard APIs will also be created to allow third-party developers to access the media in the MediaServer and deliver it through their own web-based applications.

This work was partially funded by gifts from the Yamazaki-Yang Family Foundation, the Siminoff Family Foundation, Sun Microsystems, and Silicon Graphics.

References

1. Durack JC, Chao C, Stevenson D, Andriole KP, Dev P, "The Stanford MediaServer Project: Strategies for Building a Flexible Digital Media Platform to Support Biomedical Education and Research", *Proc AMIA Symp.* 2002:225-9.
2. LaPorte RE, Linkov F, Villasenor T, Sauer F, Gamboa C, Lovalekar M, Shubnikov E, Sekikawa A, Sa ER, "Papyrus to PowerPoint (P 2 P): metamorphosis of scientific communication", *BMJ.* 2002 Dec 21;325(7378):1478-81.

Processing and Formatting System for Digital Collections

Frances Webb
Mann Library, Cornell University
fbw4@cornell.edu

Abstract

This system is being used to build structure data for the HEARTH digital collection and to manage the collection under the DLXS system. It allows student workers or unskilled employees to build structure metadata from scanned images for both monographs and serials, and manages the process of delivering the titles under DLXS once prepared. It allows supervisors to manage the work, simplifying tasks like re-assigning the in-progress work of graduated students.

1. Purpose of software

The software system was designed to automate many of the technical steps involved in processing digital titles before they may be included in a digital collection, and to offer an interface that would allow unskilled employees to build structure data.

Several steps are automated, including the importation of MARC records from our electronic catalogue, and the combining of the MARC records, OCR data, and structure data into the TEILite format metadata used by the DLXS system.

The entire system is web-based, allowing our collection management tools to be accessed from any networked computer without the installation of any specialized software. It is designed with the goal of allowing digital collections to be built and maintained, as much as possible, by the staff of Collection Development rather than Information Technology Services.

2. Document structuring

The document structuring and quality review steps are combined in the same process. This is the largest and most important piece of the system. A minimum of a 19" monitor is recommended for this work because it is necessary to work with the structure information and the documents themselves simultaneously.

The interface consists of a web-based form to be used while a staff member reviews full-quality scan images on the same screen. The interface is designed to allow student employees with minimal training to handle any of the structuring or quality control issues that are likely to be encountered.

The web form allows images to be associated with page numbers and important page features (e.g. TOC, title page, index). It allows images to be easily resequenced or removed, and blank images to be inserted into an image sequence. The quality control feature allows a user to review all of the versions of an image that exist in the system and select the one that should be used, or mark the image as a scanning issue if there is no acceptable image available.

The serials portion of the form allows the definition of issue and article units. Articles may be assigned titles, authors, and page sequences. Broken page sequences (e.g. "continued on page 44") are handled seamlessly. By necessity, the issue units are more complex, but they are designed to not require the skills of a serials cataloguer. Issues are assigned image ranges, dates, and enumerations (e.g. volume and issue numbers). A fairly sophisticated date processor forces the date of issue to be very clearly identified - for the purpose of issue sorting - while date display formats are determined more flexibly. The assumption is made that dates and not issue enumerations are the most fool-proof way for any system to automatically sort serials.

The review and structuring work for a title may be saved at any time, and restored from any saved version.

3. User account system

A simple home-grown user account system serves the dual purpose of restricting access to the staff-only interface to users with permission to be there, and of allowing a simple means of keeping track of work progress. Users either have administrator or user privileges. The primary difference is that administrators may maintain system accounts, assign users to review specific titles or un-assign them - which comes in handy when student employees leave.

4. Notes

This system was written under the IMLS grant for the HEARTH digital collection, with Joy Paulson as project lead. The HEARTH collection is available at: http://hearth.library.cornell.edu. The system is coded in C and Perl. It is currently running on Red Hat Linux 7.1, and relies on the Apache web server.

CMedPort: A Cross-regional Chinese Medical Portal

Yilu Zhou, Jialun Qin, Hsinchun Chen, Zan Huang, Yiwen Zhang, Wingyan Chung, Gang Wang

Artificial Intelligence Lab
Department of Management Information Systems
The University of Arizona
Tucson, Arizona 85721, USA
1-520-621-2748
{yilu, qin}@u.arizona.edu, {hchen, zhuang, yiwen, wchung, gang}@eller.arizona.edu

Abstract

CMedPort is a cross-regional Chinese medical Web portal developed in the AI Lab at the University of Arizona. We will demonstrate the major system functionalities.

Introduction

Many Web sites have been developed to provide access to Chinese medical information over the Internet. However, the regional differences among mainland China, Hong Kong and Taiwan result in an information gap. Although people in all three regions speak Chinese, they use different forms of Chinese characters and different encoding standards in computer systems. When searching in systems encoded one way, users are not able to get information in the other encoding. Users who want to find information from other regions have to use different systems. To address these problems, we developed the CMedPort prototype, an integrated web portal aiming to help researchers and the public in mainland China, Hong Kong and Taiwan find online medical information.

CMedPort System Features

We will demonstrate the CMedPort prototype, both the system as a whole and the individual components. The CMedPort has the following features:

Searching components. The searching components take users' queries and return Web pages that match the query. Three regional Web page collections and six meta-search engines were built for users to search. The three regional collections, containing more than 300,000 indexed web pages, were built using the 'SpidersRUs' Digital Library Toolkit developed at the University of Arizona. To alleviate the low coverage of one single search engine [1], it also meta-searches six key Chinese search engines. They are www.baidu.com, www.sina.com.cn, hk.yahoo.com, search2.info.gov.hk, www.yam.com, and www.sina.com.tw.

Encoding converter. Chinese users from different regions use different forms of Chinese (simplified and traditional Chinese). The encoding converter helps users locate information from other regions. After a user types a query in one form of Chinese, the encoding converter will 'translate' the query to the other form and use both forms to search for information. When the results are returned, the encoding converter will convert the results to the form that is familiar to the user.

Summarizer. After results are returned, users can let the system automatically generate a 1-to-5-sentence summary of a Web page. On the summarizer page, summary sentences are displayed on the left-hand side, and the original Web page is displayed on the right-hand side with summary sentences highlighted. This feature is especially useful for browsing long documents [2].

Categorizer. In addition to the traditional result list display, a user could use the Categorizer which extracts key phrases with high occurrences as folder topics. Web pages that contain the folder topic are included in that folder.

Acknowledgement

The project has been supported in part by a grant from the NSF Digital Library Initiative-2, "High-performance Digital Library Systems: From Information Retrieval to Knowledge Management," IIS-9817473, April 1999-March 2002. We would also like to thank Michael Chau, Thian-Huat Ong, Dan McDonald, Byron Marshall, Wai-Ki Sung, Chienting Lin, Mark Chen, Alan Yip, Hui Liu, and Su-Hsien Chang for contributing to the project.

References

[1] Chen, H., Fan, H., Chau, M., and Zeng, D.: MetaSpider: Meta-Searching and Categorization on the Web. Journal of the American Society for Information Science and Technology, 52(13), 1134-1147, 2001.

[2] McDonald, D. and Chen, H.: Using sentence selection heuristics to rank text segments in TXTRACTOR. In Proceedings of JCDL'02, Portland, Oregon. ACM/IEEE-CS, 28-35, 2002.

V2V: A Second Variation on Query-by-Humming

William P. Birmingham, Kevin O'Malley
EECS Department, University of Michigan
1101 Beal Ave., Ann Arbor MI 48109, USA
wpb@eecs.umich.edu, omalley@umich.edu

Jon W. Dunn, Ryan Scherle
Digital Library Program, Indiana University
1320 E. 10th St.,Bloomington IN 47405, USA
jwd@indiana.edu, rscherle@indiana.edu

1. Introduction

Music information retrieval (MIR) systems tend to fall into two camps: that camp developing cataloging and providing advanced access systems for large collections of music and that camp developing specific query or access mechanisms. By and large, the former camp concentrates its efforts on developing large collections and integrating with existing library systems, while the latter experiments with relatively small collections that are stand alone.

We have started to merge these camps by integrating Variations2, which provides access to a digitized portion of Indiana University's vast music library, with Michigan's VocalSearch [1], which provides a query-by-humming (QBH) search engine. The joint system, V2V, demonstrates how QBH can be used in connection with a large number of holdings in a real-world environment.

2. System architecture

The Variations2 digital music library system combines a music-specific bibliographic search facility based on a unique metadata model [2] with a variety of tools for working with music content in its various formats. Version 2.0 of Variations2 adds support for synchronized sound and score playback as well as a Timeliner tool that can be used by music students and instructors to create form diagrams of musical works in combination with audio.

The VocalSearch program works as follows: A user sings a query, assumed to be a theme, into the audio-recording software of the computer. VocalSearch processes the audio query by converting it to an internal format, matching it against a database of musical themes, and then constructing a song list, ranked by similarity. Next, VocalSearch writes the song list to an XML file.

In V2V, VocalSearch sends the XML file to the Variations2 client application (running on the same machine as VocalSearch) for processing. The user is then able to access Variations2 content related to each theme the query matched, taking advantage of the various tools provided, including sound-score synchronization and the Timeliner.

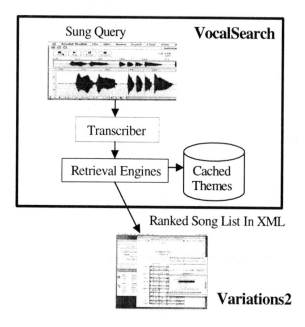

Figure 1. VocalSearch integrated with Variations2

3. Acknowledgments

This work is supported by the National Science Foundation grants IIS-9909068 and IIS-0085945. Any opinions, findings, and conclusions or recommendations expressed here are those of the author(s) and do not necessarily reflect the views of the National Science Foundation.

4. References

[1] W. Birmingham, B. Pardo, C. Meek, and J. Shifrin, "The MusArt Music-Retrieval System: An Overview", *D-Lib Magazine*, February 2002. http://www.dlib.org/

[2] N. Minibayeva and J.W. Dunn. "A Digital Library Data Model for Music", In *Proceedings of the Second ACM/IEEE-CS Joint Conference on Digital Libraries*, Portland, Oregon, 2002, pp. 154-155.

A Digital Collections Management System
Based On Open Source Software

Allison Zhang   Don Gourley

Washington Research Library Consortium
901 Commerce Drive
Upper Marlboro, MD 20774 USA
+1 301 390 2049, +1 301 390 2036
zhang@wrlc.org, gourley@wrlc.org

ABSTRACT

Robust and flexible digital collections management and presentation software is essential for creating and delivering digital collections. But digital library technologies and contents are not static. Continual evolution and investment are required to maintain the digital library. Few commercial digital library products are comprehensive and extensible enough to support this evolution. Many of these systems are in early release and have not been used and tested widely. Some require an initial investment in license fees or staff time that we could not afford. None of the products covered the full range of functionality needed for our digital library.

An alternative for practical, real-world digital libraries is to build the infrastructure from a variety of distinct systems, including commercial products, components constructed with specialized tool kits, open source applications, and homegrown programs. Open source applications in particular allow developers and users to modify the system and tailor it to their own particular needs. Like commercial software, open source software will not be a perfect solution. But open systems at least give developers and users the opportunity to modify functionality and create interfaces for integration with other software. With close collaboration between programmers and digital library staff, many creative features can be identified and added to the system. That is the approach taken by the Digital Collections Production Center at the Washington Research Library Consortium, where we integrated the Greenstone digital library software and DC-dot Dublin Core generator into a powerful and flexible digital collections management system.

Our demonstration presents a comprehensive digital collections management and presentation system built by customizing and integrating freely available open source software. We adapted the DC-dot Dublin Core generator for metadata creation and management, and integrated it with the Greenstone digital library software to present our digital collections on the Web. Additional functions were implemented using freely available scripting tools. The result is a highly extensible system, tailored to our local environment and requirements, with easy-to-use tools for data entry and collections administration and a powerful and attractive user interface.

The features of the metadata creation tool include:

- Digital object identification.
- Local authority control.
- Metadata editing.
- Template creation.
- Digital object access.

The features of the administration tool include:

- Collection configuration.
- Importing Dublin Core records.
- Global changes.
- Nightly rebuilds.

The Greenstone user interface was customized to highlight the unique features of the individual digital collections. The metadata description is presented in a standard library OPAC format with a thumbnail image. The full-size images in the digital object can be viewed with Image Viewer in another browser window. Full-text transcriptions in any formats are linked within the record and can be viewed through appropriate applications.

Extensibility was a key goal for the DCPC digital collection management and presentation system so it can evolve and expand. Currently we are integrating EAD-encoded finding aids into the digital collections. We also plan to implement additional interfaces to the metadata to facilitate the construction of virtual collections.

URL: http://www.aladin.wrlc.org/dl/

Object-Oriented Modeling, Import and Query Processing of Digital Documents

Andre Zeitz
Database Research Group
Computer Science Department
University of Rostock, Germany
zeitz@informatik.uni-rostock.de

Ilvio Bruder
Database Research Group
Computer Science Department
University of Rostock, Germany
ilr@informatik.uni-rostock.de

Introduction

Digital libraries have to manage data structures of bibliographic documents in a more complex way. The requests of librarians and library users are growing. They expect different points of view to the data and different search possibilities. The demonstration described here defines a way to integrate fine granular structures of digital documents in an object-oriented database. A generic data model was specified to provide a simple and flexible way to manage the documents.

Due to the fact that documents can be multifaceted it is quite difficult to manage bibliographic documents in a digital library. We want to provide different search and representation scenarios. The system should be efficient and also flexible managing heterogeneous documents. The building of digital library collections should be as simple as possible.

The demonstration system includes a possibility to create and import document collections, to map document structures to the internal generic model, and finally to search for documents and to present them.

Generic Data Model

The generic data model presented in this demonstration is organized as a tree which consists of two node types: inner nodes and leaf nodes. An inner node contains a set of attributes and a set of further nodes. Attributes describe the node or the data inside that node independent of the metadata. Optionally, an inner node contains a metadata record that can occur in different representations, e.g., in Dublin Core and USMARC. A leaf node is used to store any kind of unstructured data like fulltext, e.g., a book chapter or a chapter of a DVD.

All kinds of nodes are stored inside an object-oriented database. The content of each leaf node is additionally managed outside the database, dependent on the data type of the leaf nodes. For example, fulltexts are indexed using a fulltext indexer.

Import of Documents

Documents have a schema defined during the digitalization or during the authoring. This schema describes the logical and the physical structures of a document.

The import of documents is a two-stage process. During the first stage the schema is manually imported in the database. Then the documents corresponding to the schema are automatically imported during the second stage. Imported documents have often a specified schema, e.g., XML-DTD or XML-Schema. Documents without a schema are imported as one structure unit. Documents have also metadata which are described in other resources.

The first import step implies the definition of a mapping from schema elements onto internal data structures. Thereby, some schema elements are mapped to inner nodes of the generic model, the others are left as fulltext in the leaf nodes. If the schema element is important for search scenarios, or if it specifies a logical structure, or if it is a metadata element, it has to be defined as an inner node. Layout elements and structure elements which are not used in search scenarios are converted into leaf nodes. The result schema of the mapping is an internal data model similar to the generic data model as mentioned before.

The second import step is the document parsing to import the document data into the database. The document parsing is document type dependent. In our test case (a couple of XML-structured books) we use an XML parser for XML documents. The mapping definition of the first import step is used to import automatically the documents corresponding to the schema. The data object of one document is created by traversing the document structure. After creating the data object, its state is changed from transient to persistent.

Searching the Data

Searching in our system is done through search forms which are derived automatically from the schemes. Because of the structuring of data, users can search for parts of objects, e.g., for particular sections of a book. Thus using our implementation you can search for a chapter that is part of a certain book and contains a given word. The result of such a query is not the whole document but the chapter you are looking for.

To search for documents that do not have a corresponding schema you can only search for metadata and fulltext. To search for structure elements a schema is essential.

Stanford Encyclopedia of Philosophy: A Dynamic Reference Work

Colin Allen[†], Uri Nodelman[*], Edward N. Zalta[*]
[*]Stanford University and [†]Texas A&M University
colin-allen@tamu.edu, nodelman@stanford.edu, zalta@stanford.edu

The Stanford Encyclopedia of Philosophy <http://plato.stanford.edu/> is a dynamic reference work that has been rapidly growing over the past 2 years. We have been working towards finanical independence and recently did an extensive user survey of our readership towards that end. Our particular project is to produce an authoritative and comprehensive dynamic reference work devoted to the academic discipline of philosophy that will be kept up to date *dynamically* so as to remain useful to academic *and* general readers.

Our concept of a *dynamic reference work* is defined in a way which distinguishes it from other online publishing projects, namely: (1) it is published in a continuously revisable electronic medium, (2) it offers a comprehensive set of entries on topics in a target discipline, (3) it *provides the authors of the entries with electronic access* to the reference work's central web server, so that they can remotely edit and update private copies of their entries and submit them for publication according to a regular update schedule and at any other time it becomes necessary to revise, (4) it maintains quality by way of a distinguished Board of Editors, the members of which commission the entries and referee both the initial versions of the entries and subsequent substantive modifications, *prior to publication* on the web, and (5) it creates, and makes publicly available, archives of the entries on at least a quarterly basis (i.e., these contain fixed versions of the entries, which can be cited in scholarly publications). A dynamic reference work based on this model constantly evolves and becomes *responsive* to new research.

Thus, a dynamic reference work is not merely a revisable work or one that is published online. Successful implementation of the dynamic aspects of this definition depend upon the ease with which the authors, subject editors, and the principal editor have access to the tools and information that allow entries at all stages of the work flow to be managed asynchronously. In such an environment, each entry has its own deadlines and it is necessary to track electronically the location of every entry in the work flow and provide automated reminders to individuals with work pending.

Over the past two years, the encyclopedia has grown rapidly.

We have been publishing new entries at an average rate of over 10 entries per month. To maintain this growth we have been: (1) working to insure that the asynchronous publication schedule for the entries is met even though there is no pre-determined publication date, (2) working to enable a small support staff on a small budget (compared to traditional reference work publishing) to manage the project in the face of rapid growth, and (3) working to help our users more quickly access and navigate the growing reference work as more entries become available.

As we have grown we have begun to examine ways in which our project can become self-sustaining. In that direction, we have done an extensive user survey to better understand our readers and how they are using the Stanford Encyclopedia of Philosophy. In our demonstration, we will have more detailed analysis of our survey results available.

We will also demonstrate how our web interfaces, back-end processing system, and new front-end features, work together to facilitate the collaborative effort of creating and managing the dynamic reference work. We will highlight the newest parts of the system, including: (1) our new dynamically generated citation and version history information available for each entry to all of our users, that is essential for scholarly purposes, (2) an integrated calendar reminder system that allows the principal editor to track and manage deadlines whether or not associated with any particular entry (such as deadlines for subject editors to suggest new entries in their field), and (3) our new systems supporting efficient delivery of feedback from subject editors to authors.

When compared to other online publishing efforts of similar scale, we face some unique technical challenges. For example, most serial publications do not require re-cross-referencing of their documents as new articles are published. People who want to navigate thematically do so through searches which can return irrelevant results that are easily ignored. Because our documents contain links to the related entries, we must maintain those links properly – lest the irrelevant links become part of the document itself.

A more in-depth discussion of the concept of a dynamic reference work, our implementation of it, and a discussion of the current state and future of our project is available in our recent paper 'The Stanford Encyclopedia of Philosophy: A Developed Dynamic Reference Work', *Metaphilosophy*, **33**/1-2 (January 2002): 210-228 — available at <http://plato.stanford.edu/sep.pdf>. Technical specifications are available at <http://plato.stanford.edu/~editors/NSF/-project-description.pdf>. This research is supported by NSF grant #IIS-9981549.

Digital Library Service Integration

Xin Chen*, Dong-ho Kim**, Nkechi Nnadi*, Himanshu Shah*, Prateek Shrivastava*
Michael Bieber*, Il Im* and Yi-Fang Wu*
http://is.njit.edu/dlsi/

*New Jersey Institute of Technology
University Heights, Newark, NJ 07102, USA

**Rutgers University Grad. School of Mgmt
University Heights, Newark, NJ 07102, USA

The Digital Library Service Integration project (DLSI) automatically generates links to related collections and services. Users see a totally integrated environment, using their system just as before. However, they will see additional link anchors, and when clicking on one, DLSI will present a list of supplemental links. DLSI will filter and rank order this set of generated links to user preferences and tasks.

The DLSI infrastructure provides a systematic approach for integrating systems with Web interfaces. Systems generally require no changes to integrate.

DLSI generates link anchors and links *automatically*. If a collection or service can operate on an element, DLSI will generate a link leading directly to that system's feature. For example, if there were a discussion thread about a course, any time that course's identifier appears in a screen or document, DLSI would automatically detect this and add an anchor over the course identifier.

DLSI typically generates link anchors in two ways. First, "wrappers" parse screens and documents based on an understanding of the structure of the system's displays (i.e., using form templates, XML markup or parsing rules). Most anchors are identified this way.

Second, DLSI parses the screen and document content using lexical analysis to identify additional anchors. DLSI generates links automatically based on relationship rules.

This research's primary contribution is providing a relatively straightforward, sustainable infrastructure for integrating information systems. Other contributions include:

- Developing filtering mechanisms for customizing large sets of links to particular users.
- Combining automatically generated structural links and links found through lexical analysis as a way of achieving integration

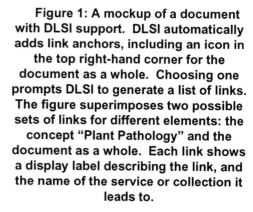

Figure 1: A mockup of a document with DLSI support. DLSI automatically adds link anchors, including an icon in the top right-hand corner for the document as a whole. Choosing one prompts DLSI to generate a list of links. The figure superimposes two possible sets of links for different elements: the concept "Plant Pathology" and the document as a whole. Each link shows a display label describing the link, and the name of the service or collection it leads to.

ACKNOWLEDGMENTS

We gratefully acknowledge support by the NSF under grants EISA-9818309, EIA-0083758, IIS-0135531 and DUE-0226075. The DLSI project is part of the National Science Digital Library project (http://www.nsdl.org).

5SGraph Demo: A Graphical Modeling Tool for Digital Libraries

Qinwei Zhu, Marcos André Gonçalves, Edward A. Fox
Virginia Polytechnic and State University
Blacksburg, VA, 24061, USA
{qzhu, mgoncalv, fox}@vt.edu

Abstract

The current demand from non-experts who wish to build digital libraries is strong worldwide. However, since DLs are complex systems, it usually takes a huge amount of effort and time to create and tailor a digital library to satisfy specific needs and requirements of target communities/societies. What is desired is a simplified modeling process and rapid generation of digital libraries. To enable this, digital libraries should be modeled with descriptive domain-specific languages [1]. In a domain-specific modeling language, the models are made up of elements representing concepts, rules, and terminology that are part of the domain world, as opposed to the code world or generic modeling languages (e.g., UML [2]). A visual modeling tool would be helpful to non-experts so they may model a digital library without knowing the theoretical foundations and the syntactical details of the descriptive language.

In this demonstration, we present a domain-specific visual modeling tool, 5SGraph, aimed at modeling digital libraries. 5SGraph is based on a metamodel that describes DLs using the 5S theory [3]. The output from 5SGraph is a digital library model that is an instance of the metamodel, expressed in the 5S description language (5SL) [4].

5SGraph presents the metamodel in a structured toolbox, and provides a top-down visual building environment for designers (see Figure 1). The visual proximity of the metamodel and instance model facilitates requirements gathering and simplifies the modeling process. Furthermore, 5SGraph maintains semantic constraints specified by the 5S metamodel and enforces these constraints over the instance model to ensure semantic consistency and correctness. 5SGraph enables component reuse to reduce the time and efforts of designers. 5SGraph also is designed to be flexible and extensible, able to accommodate and integrate several other complementary tools (e.g., to model scenarios or complex digital objects), reflecting the interdisciplinary nature of digital libraries. The tool has been tested with real users and several modeling tasks in a usability experiment [5] and its usefulness and learnability have been demonstrated.

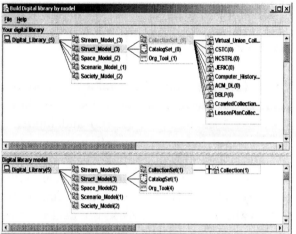

Figure 1. 5SGraph sample interface with structured toolbox (bottom part) and workspace (upper part); figure shows modeling of collections for the Computing and Information Technology Interactive Digital Educational Library (CITIDEL) project [6].

Acknowledgments

Thanks are given for the support of NSF through its grants: IIS-9986089, IIS-0002935, IIS-0080748, IIS-0086227, DUE-0121679, DUE0121741, and DUE-0136690. The second author also is supported by CAPES, process 1702-980.

References

[1] R. B. Kieburtz et al., A Software Engineering Experiment in Software Component Generation, Proc. of 18th Int. Conf. on Software Engineering, Berlin, March, 1996.

[2] G. Booch, J. Rumbaugh, and I. Jacobson. The Unified Modeling Language User Guide, Addison-Wesley, Reading, Massachusetts, USA, 1999.

[3] M. A. Gonçalves, E. A. Fox, L. T. Watson, and N. Kipp, "Streams, Structures, Spaces, Scenarios, Societies (5S): A Formal Model for Digital Libraries," Virginia Tech, 2003. TR-03-04, http://eprints.cs.vt.edu/archive/00000646/.

[4] M. A. Gonçalves, Edward A. Fox: 5SL - a language for declarative specification and generation of digital libraries. JCDL 2002: 263-272, Portland, Oregon.

[5] Zhu. Q. 5SGraph: A Visual Modeling Tool for Digital Libraries. Masters Thesis. Virginia Tech, 2002, http://scholar.lib.vt.edu/theses/available/etd-11272002-210531/.

[6] CITIDEL. http://www.citidel.org

ICON (Innovation Curriculum Online Network):
The National Digital Library for Technological Literacy

Quentin M. Briggs
Eisenhower National Clearinghouse,
The Ohio State University
1929 Kenny Rd., Columbus, Ohio
43210
+1 614 292 3438

qbriggs@enc.org

ABSTRACT

The **International Technology Education (ITEA),** in partnership with the **Eisenhower National Clearinghouse (ENC)** and funded by the **National Science Foundation** has created a comprehensive digital library collection for K-12 technological literacy in an accessible virtual environment. **ICON,** or the **Innovation Curriculum Online Network**, is a central source for information dealing with technology and innovation.

ICON serves as a national electronic roadmap to connect users, such as teachers, professors, students, museum staff, and parents with information about our human built and innovated world. Users may use the digital library to access resources ranked according to technological literacy content and pedagogy, interact with quality instructional resources, and to enhance online search capabilities relevant to the needs of the user population. The focused digital library contains online resources including websites, electronic files, information about professional organizations, government agencies, public and private foundations, and commercial enterprises. Identification and selection of these resources are in alignment with national standards, grade and age level appropriateness, sound instructional and disciplinary content, and current availability of and access to materials.

ENC has built a robust electronic infrastructure to support: the development of relevant and appropriate metadata (in conjunction with other synergistic NSDL projects); the processing of records and abstracts; the development of value-added user interfaces; and the maintenance of computer services for optimum and continuous digital library operations. An advisory board is providing annual input into digital library development and identification of quality digital resources. Formal evaluation of the ICON project is being conducted by Horizon Research.

Field testing of the collection and its services is being undertaken with diverse groups of users to evaluate ease of navigation and discovery of content-rich, pedagogically sound resources.

A variety of methods of sustainability for the collection are being explored including public and/or private sponsorship and subscriber support. ICON was officially launched March 2003 (www.icontechlit.org) and presented in a special interest session on March 13, 2003 at the ITEA Conference in Nashville, Tennessee. Currently, ICON has established tools for simple search, advance search, and browse by technology concepts. The technology concepts are classified and based from the National Standards for Technological Literacy initially driven by the Technology for All Americans Project (http://www.iteawww.org/TAA/Listing.htm).

Continuous user feedback will be monitored through a "contact us" link established to receive not only communications on problems with the digital library but to allow user questions and site evaluations. Users may also "Suggest a Resource" to ICON to be considered for inclusion in the collection.

NanoPort: An Example for Building Knowledge Portals for Scientific Domains

Jialun Qin, Zan Huang, Yilu Zhou, Michael Chau, Chunju Tseng, Alan Yip, T. Gavin Ng,
Fei Guo, Zhi-Kai Chen, Hsinchun Chen
Department of Management Information Systems
The University of Arizona
Tucson, Arizona 85721, USA
qin@u.arizona.edu

Abstract

We describe the NanoPort (www.nanoport.org) system to demonstrate a general framework of building domain-specific knowledge portals. These portals consolidate diverse information resources and provide rich functionalities to support effective information retrieval and knowledge discovery.

Introduction

With increasing academic and research contents available online, the Web has become the largest information repository ever for most scientific domains. However, it has become increasingly difficult to search for high-quality domain-specific information. The resulting information overload problem calls for domain-specific knowledge portals that provide high-quality collection and integrated retrieval and knowledge discovery functionalities for scientific domains. We describe NanoPort, a domain-specific knowledge portal for nanoscale science and engineering (NSSE) field to demonstrate our framework of building such portals.

The NanoPort System

NanoPort integrates and applies several information searching and analysis techniques in the NSSE domain. We describe three major components of the system:

Content Collection Building. We provided both vertical searching and meta-searching features in NanoPort to build a comprehensive NSSE-related information repository: (1) *vertical searching*: we developed a new crawling technique called meta search enhanced global crawling which traverses the Web in a global search manner. The technique keeps expanding starting points by dynamically incorporating relevant meta-search results from other search engines; (2) *meta-searching*: NanoPort also connects to several carefully selected online databases (e.g., MedLine, MatWeb, Molecular Expression, ScienceDirect, and US Patent Database) and journals (e.g. Science, MIT Technology Review, and PNAS).

Retrieval Functionalities. NanoPort integrates several functionalities to support the retrieval process, including: (1) *keyword suggestion*: implemented based on important phrases and relations between them identified by a noun-phrasing tool [2] and a co-occurrence-based automatic thesaurus building tool [1]; (2) *document categorization*: the search results are organized based on key phrases appeared in the documents to provides a content overview of the entire result set; (3) *document summarization*: a summarization tool, AI Summarizer, is embedded into NanoPort to provide document-level sentence-based summarization; and (4) *document visualization*: two self-organizing map-based visualization tools have been employed to generate topic and document maps based on the returned results, a jigsaw-puzzle topic map and a GIS-like document map.

Knowledge Discovery. As a first step of knowledge discovery from text, we analyzed a collection of about 77,000 NSSE-related U.S. patents. Our current efforts include three types of analyses: basic performance evaluation, content map visualization, and citation network analysis. With appropriate text preprocessing, these analyses can also be applied to other types of digital documents.

Acknowledgement

The project is partly supported by the NSF SGER grant "NanoPort: Intelligent Web Searching for Nanoscale Science and Engineering," CTS-0204375, February 2002 - November 2002.

References

[1] Chen, H., and Lynch, K. J. "Automatic construction of networks of concepts characterizing document databases," *IEEE Transactions on Systems, Man and Cybernetics*, 22, 5 (1992), 885-902.

[2] Tolle, K. M., and Chen, H. "Comparing noun phrasing techniques for use with medical digital library tools," *Journal of the American Society of Information Systems*, 51, (2000), 352-370.

EconPort: A Digital Library for Microeconomics Education

Hsinchun Chen, Daniel Zeng, Riyad Kalla, Zan Huang
Department of Management Information Systems
The University of Arizona
Tucson, Arizona 85721, USA
{hchen, zeng, rkalla, zhuang} @bpa.arizona.edu

James C. Cox, J. Todd Swarthout,
Economic Science Laboratory
The University of Arizona
Tucson, Arizona 85721, USA
{jcox, swarthout} @bpa.arizona.edu

Abstract

We present the EconPort system (www.econport.org), a digital library for Microeconomics education that incorporates experimental economics software and automated e-commerce agents

Introduction

Courses on Microeconomics play an important role in economics, social sciences, business, and engineering curricula. Recent research has shown the overall success of integration of experiments into undergraduate microeconomics courses [1, 2]. We are developing a Digital Library-based approach to build an extensible and scalable collection of Microeconomics related contents and an integrated online teaching environment with experimental software support. We present major components of the resulting digital library, called EconPort, and discuss digital library challenges applicable to other applications.

EconPort and Related Technical Challenges

EconPort consists of two major components, a Microeconomics education content collection and an online experimentation environment to support effective Microeconomics teaching and learning.

Microeconomics Education Contents: An integrated Microeconomics curriculum is being created in EconPort. Related online experiment materials including experiment description, instructional manuals, and downloadable experimental software are also included in the collection to form a "live" text for experiment-based Microeconomic education. EconPort currently contains materials on the following topics: auctions, common pool resources, fairness and reciprocity, game theory and industrial organization.

Experimentation Environment: EconPort provides a Web-enabled infrastructure to set up, launch, and run a wide range of experimental software. The instructors can select relevant economics experiments, configure the parameters and treatments, and launch the experimental server through the portal. Students can then start the client-side experiment software through the Web to participate in these experiments. When the experiments end, the instructor can use post-experiment analysis tools to analyze and visualize the experimental data. Experimental software with support for simple execution automation agents have been implemented for English, Dutch, First price and Second price auctions.

Developing EconPort poses significant digital library technical challenges, because a variety of library contents are involved, including standard documents and different "active" objects like experiment software, software agents, and e-commerce services. We propose to leverage recent developments in Web Service Description Language to develop an XML schema to represent these objects in order to support effective retrieval and management. This extension is also potentially applicable to other digital library applications where rich dynamic contents exist.

Acknowledgement

EconPort is supported by the NSF grant, "An Active Object-based Digital Library for Microeconomics Education," DUE-0226344. We would like to thank the EconPort team, consisting of members of the Artificial Intelligence Laboratory and Economic Science Laboratory at the University of Arizona.

References

[1] Cardell, S. N., Fort, R., Joerding, W., Inaba, F., Lamoreaux, D., Rosenman, R., Stromsdorfer, E., and Bartlett, R. Laboratory-based experimental and demonstration initiatives in teaching undergraduate economics. AEA Papers and Proceedings, Teaching Undergraduate Economics, 86, 2 (1996), 454-59..

[2] Dickie, M. Experimenting on classroom experiments: Do they increase learning in introductory microeconomics? Working Paper, Department of Economics, University of Southern Mississippi, (2000).

Posters

Displaying Resources in Context: Using Digital Libraries to Support Changes in Undergraduate Education

Cathryn A. Manduca
Science Education Resource Center
Carleton College
cmanduca@carleton.edu

Sean Fox
Science Education Resource Center
Carleton College
sfox@carleton.edu

Abstract

Education digital libraries strive to foster major improvements in education by supporting adoption of more effective teaching methods. We present initial efforts to assist faculty in changing teaching practice by displaying digital library resources in portals that address a specific educational issue and provide the full spectrum of resources needed to both motivate and implement a change in practice.

We have developed two example sites to date:
Using Data in the Classroom (serc.carleton.edu/research_education/usingdata/; highlighted as an NSDL specialized portal nsdl.org) Designed for use by faculty in all science disciplines, this site presents a discussion of why faculty might be interested in engaging students with data in their courses, examples of current practice, a variety of data access and manipulation tools, links to pedagogic resources, and a discussion forum

Teaching Quantitative Skills in the Geosciences (serc.carleton.edu/quantskills/) Teaching quantitative skills is often challenging. This site, designed for geoscience, provides information on strategies and methods for teaching quantitative skills, teaching materials, and resources for students drawn from geosciences, mathematics, and other science disciplines

Both sites have a steadily increasing user populations with current use at approximately 50 sessions per day. A more extensive evaluation study is under development.

Our initial work exposes three primary challenges in development and management of websites embedding digital library resources in the context of a specific issue:

Location of resources and generation of issue-specific content is time consuming and requires participation by geographically distributed experts.

The number of links to outside resources quickly grows to a scale where managing them becomes a significant issue.

A wide variety of means must be used to draw linkages between content-specific teaching resources and effective pedagogy and methods.

Building on the DLESE Catalog System and the DLESE OAI tool (www.dlese.org/Metadata/tool) we have developed a content management system (CMS) that supports distributed authoring of site content; metadata harvesting to build and share the resource collection; management of resource collections and site content; and dynamic generation of web pages that adhere to web standards and meet web accessibility guidelines.

The CMS enables resource management in three ways. Resources currently cataloged in any of our collections or DLESE can be browsed and inserted into pages; resources can be aggregated into lists and inserted into pages with standard or customized short descriptions; or new resources can be cataloged and inserted simultaneously into the page and the relevant local collection. The metadata are easily harvested by DLESE and NSDL using the OAI protocol. In this way, the resources are managed in a format that allows sharing with other digital library efforts.

The digital library tools and their integration with our CMS automate the tracking and cross-referencing of resource links, drastically simplifying management. We expose these cross-references internally, providing links from content-specific resource descriptions to their referent pedagogic pages. These cross-references can also be made explicit in our web sites to assist users in moving from resources to pedagogic material. Inclusion of this information in the metadata we share with other digital libraries will allow them to provide links from resource records in their library to our pages incorporating the reference. In this way, educators could move directly from a content-specific resource in DLESE or NSDL to the information on our site about how to use that resource in a specific educational context.

Our sites demonstrate how portals can be used to provide context for digital library resources tailored to a particular audience or issue. The use of existing digital library collections, readily available digital library tools, and standards for metadata and interoperability makes development of such sites feasible. While initial use-metrics indicates strong interest on the part of educators, an important next step is a thorough evaluation of site use and its impact on teaching practice.

This work was funded by National Science Foundation grants 0085600, 0127298, 0238104.

A Proposal for Digital Library Protection

Hideyasu Sasaki, Esq.
New York State Bar
Keio University
5322, Endo, Fujisawa, 252-8520 Japan
hsasaki@alumni.uchicago.edu

Yasushi Kiyoki, Ph.D.
Keio University
Faculty of Environmental Information
5322, Endo, Fujisawa, 252-8520 Japan
kiyoki@mdbl.sfc.keio.ac.jp

Abstract

We propose systematic digital library protection by patentable content-based retrieval processes, especially on image digital libraries in specified domains, without any excessively exclusive protection in general domains.

The proposed systematic method assures content-based retrieval processes to uniformly classify candidate images for retrieval into mutually exclusive classes of similar images in a certain specified domain. That specified domain has an identical combination of classes of similar images to which all the possible combinations of those classes converge, as outlined in Fig. 1.

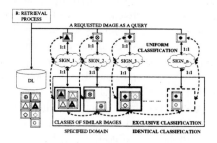

Figure 1. Classification in a specified domain.

By patenting those retrieval processes that satisfy our proposed method in the specified domain, then any other digital library systems could not be implemented without the equivalents to those retrieval processes. Any digital library creation by equivalent digital content collection in the specified domain means direct misappropriation, *i.e.*, infringement of the equivalents to those patented retrieval processes. The retrieval processes contain parameter setting components that define the scope of the equivalents to those retrieval processes with clear boundary [1]. Consequently, the patent enforcement over those retrieval processes restricts any more digital library creation as a sys-

tematic catalyst of protection over the digital contents of their target digital library in the specified domain, without any excessively exclusive protection in general domains, as outlined in Fig. 2.

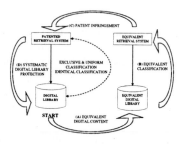

Figure 2. Systematic digital library protection.

We have provided our proposed method with mathematical formulation and its brief proofs. In the course of proving, we have applied topologic formulation to the relations of images, signs and classes of similar images. We have also applied our method for its case study to several medical image retrieval systems on brain and lung tumors, *etc.* that are formed based on domain-specific approach of CBIR.

Our proposed method is based on the technical property of domain-specific approach of content-based retrieval, especially on its parameter setting component. Its potential application grows as expansion of networked digital libraries with domain-specific approach of CBIR. We have a plan to publish a paper on the proposed method with its mathematical reasoning and a number of case studies.

References

[1] H. Sasaki and Y. Kiyoki. Patenting the Processes for Content-based Retrieval in Digital Libraries. In *Digital Libraries: People, Knowledge, & Technology, 5th Int'l Conf. on Asian Digital Libraries, ICADL 2002 Proc.*, LNCS, No. 2555, pages 471–482, Singapore, December 2002. Springer-Verlag.

Content-Based Summarization for Personal Image Library

Joo-Hwee Lim[1], Jun Li[1], Philippe Mulhem[2], Qi Tian[1]
[1]Institute for Infocomm Research   [2]IPAL-CNRS
21 Heng Mui Keng Terrace, Singapore 119613
{joohwee,lijun,mulhem,tian}@i2r.a-star.edu.sg

Abstract

With the accumulation of consumer's personal image library, the problem of managing, browsing, querying and presenting photos effectively and efficiently would become critical. We propose a framework for automatic organization of personal image libraries based on analysis of image creation time stamps and image contents to facilitate browsing and summarization of images.

1. Summarization Framework

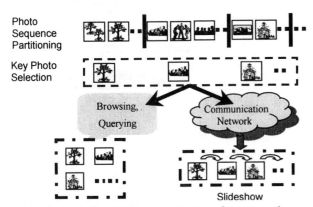

Photo Sequence Partitioning

Key Photo Selection

Browsing, Querying

Communication Network

Slideshow

Figure 1. A photo summarization framework

1.1. Photo Sequence Partitioning

Essentially, photo summarization is a mapping θ of n photos $P = \{p_1, p_2, ..., p_n\}$ to m photos $S = \{s_1, s_2, ..., s_m\}$ ($m < n$),

$$\theta : p_1, p_2, ..., p_n \rightarrow s_1, s_2, ..., s_m \quad (1)$$

Here P is assumed as a sequence of photos ordered by their acquisition time. The two-level partitioning steps are

seen as a mapping Φ to group photos in P into smaller subsequences q_j, and then into finer subsequences r_k

$$\Phi : p_1, p_2, ..., p_n \xrightarrow{} q_1, q_2, ..., q_u \xrightarrow{} r_1, r_2, ..., r_v \quad (2)$$

Time-based   Content-based

The subsets q_j and r_k are respectively formed such that

$$Sim_t(time(last(q_j)), time(first(q_{j+1}))) > \lambda_t \quad (3)$$
$$Sim_c(content(last(r_k)), content(first(r_{k+1}))) > \lambda_c \quad (4)$$

1.2. Key Photo Selection

The key photo selection step maps each subsequence $r_k = \{p_{x+1}, p_{x+2}, ..., p_{x+y}\}$ to one representative photo, called p_k, of r_k,

$$\Psi : p_{x+1}, p_{x+2}, ..., p_{x+y} \rightarrow p_k \quad (5)$$

There are various selection criteria. In our case, we consider Ψ as a function that depends on the following two aspects. First, with the information of the presence of face and the location and size of the detected face in each photo, we decide which photo contains larger and better-positioned frontal faces in the photo and that photo is selected as the key photo for the partition r_k. Next we define the function f_k, from N^+ (going from the time of p_{x+1} to the time of p_{x+y}) to N^+ (image numbers going from 1 to y), as an interpolation of the cumulative function indicating for one time point t_x the number of images taken before (or at) t_x in the current image sequence. Such a function f_k is generated using cubic-spline interpolation. The temporal representative value of one image p is then computed as the absolute value of the derivative $f'_k = df_k/dt$ for the value t_p. The key photo is the one with the maximum temporal representative value. Finally all key photos are concatenated into a sequence as a photo summary.

We have implemented and applied our photo organization and summarization framework to genuine personal photos that demonstrates the effectiveness and usefulness of our approach. We will work on more systematic user studies, automatic algorithm for setting the threshold and more powerful content-based representation for content-based partitioning.

Modularization Framework for Digital Museum Exhibition

Bai-Hsun Chen   Sheng-Hao Hung   Jen-Shin Hong

Department of Computer Science and Information Engineering

National ChiNan University, Taiwan

jshong@ncnu.edu.tw

Abstract

Conventionally, digital museum online exhibitions are constructed using handcrafted HTML pages which require tedious hypermedia composing. This paper proposes a sophisticated modularization framework for exhibition website construction by integrating XML and Flash MX. A typical exhibition page is differentiated into several "layers" containing specific types of "media elements". Several categories of modularized Flash-based "media-handlers" are used to process and present the layers containing media elements. A complete set of media-handlers presenting the content are then integrated together to give the final page presentation. Based on this modularization framework, the workflow for exhibition construction and management are significant improved.

1. Framework

A digital museum exhibition is essentially a large-scale website with interlinked webpages which may contain "content elements" (e.g., content images, texts, audios, etc.) as well as "style elements" (e.g., artistic graphics, Javascript, etc.) providing the page presentation styles. To increase the efficiency and flexibility for the construction of an exhibition website, there are certain issues that we consider central as described below [1].

1. There should be an easy way to produce exhibition pages from the digital archive.
2. Once an exhibition page is produced, there should be an easy way to create different presentation styles.
3. There should be an easy way to re-arrange an existing exhibition site to accommodate different user's need and to make new exhibitions from existing ones.
4. Both the content elements and style elements of an exhibition page should be interoperable, reusable, accessible and adaptable.

To fulfill the above-mentioned requirements, this paper proposes a webpage modularization framework with which the content, style elements, and functionalities of an exhibition page should be able to be decomposed into a set of cohesive and loosely coupled "modules". For example, there could be image-handlers for processing and presenting a sequence of images inside a page. These modules could be essentially used as the "building blocks" that can be re-arranged and assembled into an exhibition.

Based on the proposed framework, we have implemented a system using XML for the exhibition page formatting and FlashMX [2] for media-handler design. The system intends to help the content experts to quickly select, manipulate, and integrate the digital artifacts in the "National Archive of Cultural Heritage" into instructive online exhibitions. The prototype system is available at http://dlm.ncnu.edu.tw.

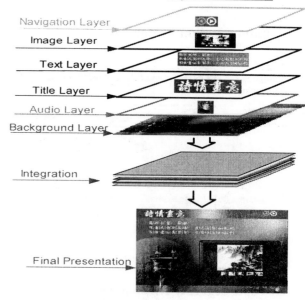

Figure 1: Integrating a set of modularized Flash media-handlers to present an exhibition page.

2. ACKNOWLEDGMENTS

This project is supported by the National Science Council (NSC-91-2422-H-260-322), and National Council of Cultural Affairs.

3. REFERENCES

[1] Jen-Shin Hong, Bai-Hsuen Chen, Jieh Hsiang: XSL-based Content Management for Multi-presentation Digital Museum Exhibitions. ECDL 2001: p.p. 378-389, Damstat, Germany, September 2001.

[2] Flash MX, http://www.macromedia.com/support/flash/

Sustainability Issues and Activities for the NSDL

David J. McArthur

Computer Science Department

University of North Carolina, Wilmington

dmcarthur1@nc.rr.com

Sarah Giersch

Consultant

University of North Carolina, Wilmington

sgiersch@bellsouth.net

Howard Burrows

Senior Researcher

Autonomous Undersea Systems Institute

ghburrows@attbi.com

Abstract

This poster will review the work on sustainability of digital libraries in the context of the NSF-supported National Science Digital Library (NSDL) program. Applied to digital libraries, sustainability is a broad term, referring to everything from technical issues about the digital preservation of materials, to the social questions surrounding the long-term accessibility of resources to the public at large.

INTRODUCTION

The NSDL is a highly distributed and loosely coupled set of digital collections, knit together by a centralized Core Integration (CI) project that provides a common infrastructure for the collections. Sustainability is especially important to the NSDL since its mission is to become one of the premier sources of digital educational materials in the country. To achieve this goal, it will have to tackle issues of growth and long-term stability from many perspectives. Overall, the NSDL faces at least two kinds of sustainability problems: the NSDL as a whole must grow and ensure the availability and preservation of digital materials for users; and, the projects that provide NSDL with content, services and tools must also acquire the financial and social resources they will need to survive beyond their current short-term funding.

ISSUES & ACTIVITIES

This poster will review the work of different NSDL groups that are contributing ideas about sustainability—principally the Sustainability Standing Committee (SSC), the Policy Committee (PC) and the CI—and will discuss their recent plans, activities and results. These include:

- *Investigating traditional business models for the NSDL.* As a result of discussions begun at a workshop with educational publishers [3], the NSDL has considered various partnerships opportunities with the traditional publishing community, which involve providing content or services to generate revenue. The poster will summarize a number of these alternatives, including: selective contributions from publishers to the NSDL; using materials from NSDL collections to provide digital collateral resources for publishers' e-books; and, the role the NSDL in providing an intellectual "commons" through which new tools and services could be developed for publishers and the digital library community.

- *Considering non-traditional business models for NSDL.* Traditional business models for the NSDL roughly equate to ones where end-users pay either directly or indirectly (e.g., through institutional licenses). However, the NSDL is also considering a number of more innovative approaches, such as the possibility of large-scale public investments in the national digital library infrastructure [1] on the ambitious scale of the Land-Grant Colleges Act of the 19th century, as well as open-source and open-access business models.

- *Analyzing the business costs of building and maintaining a large-scale digital library.* Regardless of the revenue streams the NSDL eventually establishes, it will also need a good understanding of its costs, including not only one-time and recurring requirements, but also the timing of these funds, likely sources, and the obligations that may go with support from various funding institutions. Recent NSDL studies have begun to consider these issues.

- *Establishing a Governance and Organization Task Force. Pathways to Progress* [2], established an interim governance structure for the NSDL, and provided an action-plan for the design and implementation of the federated library and its infrastructure. A task force has been formed recently to consider other governance models. The early thinking of this group will be reviewed in the poster, keeping in mind that no authoritative steps to reshape the current governance structure, or establish a legal entity for the NSDL, are likely to be taken for several years.

REFERENCES

[1] Grossman, K. and Minow, N. A Digital Gift to the Nation: Fulfilling the Promise of the Digital and Internet Age. The Century Foundation Press, New York, NY, 2001.

[2] Manduca, C., McMartin, F. and Mogk, D. Pathways to Progress: Vision and Plan for Developing NSDL. (2001), http://www.nsdl.org.

[3] McArthur, D., Giersch, S., Wittenberg, K. and Luby, M. NSDL & Educational Publishers' Workshop Report. (Columbia University, October 2002), http://publishers.comm.nsdlib.org

Poster: Contribution and Collaboration Strategies for the National Science Digital Library (nsdl.org): Investigating Technological Solutions to Facilitate Social Evolution of a Collaborative Infrastructure

Elly Cramer

Cornell Information Science, National Science Digital Library, elly@cs.cornell.edu

Dean Krafft

Cornell Information Science, National Science Digital Library, dean@cs.cornell.edu

Diane Hillmann

Cornell Information Science, National Science Digital Library, dih1@cornell.edu

John Saylor

Cornell Information Science, National Science Digital Library, jms1@cornell.edu

Carol Terrizzi

Cornell Information Science, National Science Digital Library, clt6@cornell.edu

Abstract

The NSDL community consists of large, discipline diverse, and decentralized user groups made up of collaborator communities who create, aggregate, and contribute digital resources to the NSDL. NSDL Core Integration provides "wholesale" services to NSDL collaborator communities who may "retail" those services through their own portals, perhaps packaged with additional content selected to meet their specialized users' needs. NSDL "wholesale" services will support rich representations of complex data relation-ships. NSDL will distribute access to aggregations and annotations stored in the NSDL metadata repository that have been harvested, normalized (based on the scaleable library production model in use at nsdl.org), and exposed for re-harvest. "Retailers" may use the Open Archives Initiative (OAI) for Metadata Harvesting Protocol to harvest these structured data relationships and make them available for use in other library services.

Investigations into establishing an environment where end users can be contributors to encourage the development of communities of practice and knowledge sharing is the focus of the NSDL Core Integration teams' current development cycle. A key factor in "wholesaling information to retailers" is to offer core services that allow other services, agents, and users the opportunity to build on a broad base of information, and to expose characterizations of resources and discipline-specific aggregations to portals and end users. The usefulness of a resource for an individual user will be determined by a number of factors; among them might be access to a collaborative evaluation and selection process both as a consumer and a contributor.

The NSDL Core Integration technical team's prototype annotation, exhibits and news services are all based on a Simple Metadata Based Services (SIMBAS) model designed to provide access to several kinds of relationship links. An experimental SIMBAS service now in early stages of development will provide rapid availability of this functionality. This model may later be subsumed or augmented by more advanced collaborative service models developed through work on "retail" portals.

The NSDL Exhibits service offers a customized view of the library resources by providing timely and/or topically related resources for educational or display purposes. The NSDL prototype Exhibits Service will encourage distributed development and contribution of several types of exhibits based on the following content models:
1. "Current Awareness," News, New and Featured Collections, Featured Services
2. Content assembly associated with one or more collections and resources
3. Exhibits directory service

FLOW: Co-constructing Low Barrier Repository Infrastructure in Support of Heterogeneous Knowledge Collection(s)

Karen S. Baker
Scripps Institution of Oceanography
kbaker@ucsd.edu

Anna K. Gold
UCSD Libraries
agold@ucsd.edu

Frank Sudholt
San Diego Supercomputer Center
fsudholt@sdsc.edu

Abstract:

Institutional repositories are being constructed today to address the needs of scholarly communication in a digital environment [1, 2]. The success of such institutional infrastructures as knowledge collections depends in part on offering low barriers for participation and on supporting heterogeneous knowledge inputs and outputs. The San Diego Supercomputer Center (SDSC) in partnership with CERN (European Center for Nuclear Research), the Scripps Institution of Oceanography (SIO), and the University of California, San Diego (UCSD) Science & Engineering Library, has modified CERN's CDSware software to initiate the process of creating a local low barrier repository.

The SDSC prototype of CDSware is a work in progress, a modified package of CDSware's open source software for managing an institutional repository of references and documents. Such short-term/local approaches are not only compatible with long-term federation strategies but are critical to initiating information flow, contributing to knowledge diversity, and ensuring reflexivity in the design and development processes.

Given the social aspects of documents in particular and artifacts in general, building successful institutional repositories requires exploring how to create new infrastructures that place documents, people, and organizations into unified and expressive relationships [3]. CDSware as implemented at SDSC adapts an OAI-compliant document and citation management system to more fully express the relationships between documents, people, and the organizational resources to which both are related [4]. By starting with a document-oriented view and making the social relations of documents explicit (to individuals, research groups, administrative reports and organizational metrics, sources of funding and research instruments), this project seeks to expand the knowledge management role of a document repository [5]. This work also suggests that personal document collections provide a mechanism to extend informal communications *if* collection-making tools are available [6]. We seek to create a process of learning and informing involving participants by providing mechanisms that enable the work of individuals and organizations. The project name FLOW is a purposeful metaphor calling to mind how rivulets shaped by the local landscape join a river of information, contributing to heterogeneous pools of knowledge.

CDSware encompasses both the referatory concept of collecting citations and links, as well as the repository concept of archiving the digital objects cited along with local classification and relationship information about the objects. Challenges include *technical* hurdles (ongoing resource support, open design, implementation strategies), *social* barriers (the need for a critical mass of participation to supply the activation energy for the system), and *conceptual* difficulties (articulating associations between individuals, materials and organizations in order to capture complex interdependencies). Our design approach is to start with a single research program within the SDSC - with an eye to federation, both across the institution via closely-managed institutional data tables - and across a looser network of affiliated research partners. For coordination at the institution level (SDSC) an ORACLE-based management data pool was linked to CDSware. To extend this to include associates, a second tier was implemented with MySQL, used by the CERN distribution of CDSware. (Project support has included funding from SIO, SDSC (Integrative Computational Sciences), and NSF Grants DBI-01-11544 and OPP-02-17282.)

References:

[1] R. Crow, "The Case for Institutional Repositories," 2002, http://www.arl.org/sparc/IR/ir.html.

[2] C. A. Lynch, "Institutional Repositories: Essential Infrastructure for Scholarship in the Digital Age," February 2003, *ARL Bimonthly Report* 226. http://www.arl.org/newsltr/226/ir.html.

[3] S. J. McMillan, "Exploring Models of Interactivity from Multiple Research Traditions: Users, Documents, and System," *The Handbook of New Media*, L. Lievrouw and S. Livingstone (eds.), p. 163-182, SAGE Publications, London (2002).

[4] A. K. Gold, K. S. Baker, K. K. Baldridge, and J. LeMeur. "Building FLOW: Federating libraries on the Web," *ACM-IEEE Joint Conference on Digital Libraries*, Portland Oregon, July 2002, http://doi.acm.org/10.1145/544220.544286.

[5] A. K. Gold, "The Roles of Documents in Knowledge Management," unpublished paper, December 18, 2002.

[6] K. S. Baker, A. K. Gold, F. Sudholt, "Collection Repository: Personal to Project to Organizational," Technical report http://pal.lternet.edu/projects/semantics (2003).

MetaTest: Evaluation of Metadata from Generation to Use

Elizabeth D. Liddy, Eileen E. Allen, Christina M. Finneran
Center for Natural Language Processing, School of Information Studies, Syracuse University
{liddy,eeallen,cmfinner}@mailbox.syr.edu

Geri Gay, Helene Hembrooke, Laura A. Granka
Human-Computer Interaction Group, Cornell University
{gkg1,hah4,lag24}@cornell.edu

1. Introduction

Syracuse University's Center for Natural Language Processing and Cornell University's Human-Computer Interaction Group are collaborating to evaluate the utility of metadata within the Science, Technology, Engineering, and Mathematics (STEM) education domains. We are studying metadata from its initial generation to its use in accessing desired educational resources. With a testbed of lesson plans and activities, we are comparing the manually and automatically generated metadata for their retrieval effectiveness (i.e. ability to retrieve the most relevant resources); conducting a subjective evaluation of manually and automatically generated metadata as representations of the resource as judged by subject matter experts, and; conducting studies of users' search and navigation behavior when accessing the digital library. These evaluations successfully combine what we believe are necessary foci on how and whether metadata affects the user and system performance.

2. Information Retrieval Experiment

The information retrieval experiment compares the precision and recall of manually generated metadata to automatically generated metadata. The retrieval experiment is conducted on resources which have both manually and automatically assigned metadata elements. Users' queries are run on the two collections and the results are merged before presentation. Users in the STEM education domain judge the relevance of the retrieved lesson plans or educational activities.

3. Qualitative Experiment

We are extending the pilot study from our earlier digital library project that showed minimal differences in users' satisfaction with automatically generated versus manually generated metadata. In the current experiment, pre-service and in-service STEM teachers evaluate how well the automatically generated metadata and manually generated metadata represent the resources. Specifically, there are two conditions: the first measures the user's degree of satisfaction with the metadata after first viewing the resource and the second measures how well the user believes the metadata predict the actual contents of the resource, having viewed the metadata before the resource. Each experiment is a blind test in which users do not know how the metadata they are evaluating were generated – either manually or automatically.

4. User Study

The user study is evaluating the extent to which individuals use metadata to search for relevant resources, and will elucidate which metadata elements are most frequently used. Through a series of experiments involving eye-tracking and information search, we are investigating metadata use under various conditions and as a function of different demographic variables. The eye-tracking technology enables us to explore how the various ocular indices can serve to inform methods of metadata extraction. This technology also allows us to visually represent the entire scan path of individual users as they search documents for relevant information. From this we hope to be able to identify patterns or configurations of successful and unsuccessful searches, and to determine which parts of the metadata and resources are most informative.

5. Conclusion

Overall, our project goal is to assess the relative utility of metadata for retrieval and for helping the user access and browse resources. We will be sharing our preliminary findings on all experiments in our poster.

6. Acknowledgements

This project is funded by the National Science Foundation under the NSDL program (NSF Award Number: 0226312).

Finding and Using Data in Educational Digital Libraries

Rajul Pandya
DLESE Program Center
UCAR, P.O. Box 3000
Boulder, CO 80307-3000
+1 303 497 2650

pandya@ucar.edu

Ben Domenico
Unidata Program Center
UCAR, P.O. Box 3000
Boulder, CO 80307-3000
+1 303 497 2650

domenico@ucar.edu

Mary Marlino
DLESE Program Center
UCAR, P.O. Box 3000
Boulder, CO 80307-3000
+1 303 497 8350

marlino@ucar.edu

ABSTRACT

THREDDS (THematic Real-time Earth Distributed Data Servers) services catalog geophysical data and other data services to support discovery and use by researchers. THREDDS, however, doesn't support data discovery and use by learners and educators (i.e. novices). Educational digital libraries, like DLESE (Digital Library for Earth System Eduation) provide rich metadata descriptions that are effective in helping novices locate and use most types of learning resources. DLESE, however, doesn't provide a way for novices to discover geophysical data in immediately usable forms. The VGEE (Visual Geophysical Exploration Environment) supports novices' discovery and use of geophysical data by linking THREDDS services with educational curricula and learner-centered data tools. The curricula are cataloged in DLESE and so can be discovered in educational settings. These curricula then guide novices to the appropriate tools and illustrate meaningful use of the data. More generally, by coupling data to curricular documents, text-based discovery tools (e.g. search engines) can be extended to data.

Categories and Subject Descriptors

H.4.0 **[Information Systems Applications]**: *General*
E.3.0 **[Data]**: *General*
J.2 **[Computer Applications]**: *Physical Sciences and Engineering: Earth and atmospheric sciences*

General Terms

Human Factors, Design

Keywords

Education, Geoscience, Data

1. INTRODUCTION

Geoscientists have access to a tremendous range of data, using a variety of technology across a number of sub-disciplines. THREDDS (THematic Real-time Earth Distributed Data Servers)[1] uses digital library technology to give researchers

transparent access to these data. The Digital Library for Earth System Education (DLESE) has created a rich metadata framework and catalog to support the needs of geoscience educators and learners, but this framework doesn't support educational use of data. DLESE users have asked for data sets as part of integrated packages that include the tools to use the data and some guidance in the appropriate use of the data [2].

2. VGEE

The Visual Geophysical Exploration Environment [3] addresses the needs of novice data users (e.g. learners and educators) by providing a way to connect data with curricula and tools that facilitate meaningful and appropriate use of the data. The VGEE consists of an inquiry-based curriculum guiding data exploration, a visualization tool designed to support learner use of geophysical data, and connections to THREDDS-delivered data. By linking these three components, learners and educators discover the data in contexts that ensure its comprehensibility and usability.

3. DISCOVERY IN DIGITAL LIBRARIES

Activities within the VGEE curriculum are catalogued as resources within DLESE. These activities, once discovered, include embedded links to the learner-centered visualization tool. The visualization tool itself is configured to link to THREDDS servers, which provide catalogs of distributed data relevant to the curriculum. Further development would allow discovery of data or tools, with connections to the appropriate curricular element.

4. ACKNOWLEDGMENTS

NSF NSF/CCLI #9972491 supports VGEE development. THREDDS is supported by NSF/DUE #0121623. Unidata's IDV is the basis for the VGEE visualization tool. Unidata is funded by NSF/ATM #9218790. DLESE is funded by NSF/EAR #0215640.

5. REFERENCES

[1] THREDDS Catalog.
    http://www.unidata.ucar.edu/projects/THREDDS/

[2] DLESE Data Working Group Report.
    http://www.dlese.org/documents/reports/meeting/Feb_01/dawg20801_outcomes.html.

[3] VGEE curriculum. http://www.dpc.ucar.edu/vgee.

An XQuery Engine for Digital Library Systems

Ji-Hoon Kang
Dept. of Computer Science,
Chungnam National University
220 Gung-Dong, Yuseong-Gu,
Daejeon, 305-764, South Korea
+82-42-821-5447

jhkang@cs.cnu.ac.kr

Chul-Soo Kim
Dept. of Computer Science,
Chungnam National University
220 Gung-Dong, Yuseong-Gu,
Daejeon, 305-764, South Korea
+82-42-821-7447

chulsu1@cs.cnu.ac.kr

Eun-Jeong Ko
Dept. of Computer Science,
Chungnam National University
220 Gung-Dong, Yuseong-Gu,
Daejeon, 305-764, South Korea
+82-42-821-7447

brain08@cs.cnu.ac.kr

Categories and Subject Descriptors

H.3.7 [**Information Systems**]: Digital Libraries

General Terms

Design, Languages

Keywords

Digital Library System, XML, XQuery, Information Retrieval

ABSTRACT

XML is now a standard markup language for web information. Many application areas are producing XML documents on the web. This situation urges digital library systems to deal with not only typical text documents but also XML documents. XML documents are semi-structured. Some queries based on the structures are useful and necessary.

MPEG-7 is a metadata standard for multimedia objects. MPEG-7 metadata can describe some features such as color histogram of image, so that a multimedia digital library system using MPEG-7 for metadata representation can provide content-based search for multimedia objects. MPEG-7 is defined by XML schema. In order to retrieve MPEG-7 metadata, a query language for XML data is required.

A standard query language is very helpful for interoperability among digital library systems over the Internet. XQuery, which has been influenced from most of the previous XML query languages, is a forthcoming standard for querying XML data.

In this paper we propose an XQuery Engine as depicted in the figure that can be used as an XQuery processing module in a digital library system that supports XML documents. We assume generic digital library system architecture. It consists of four modules: a user interface, an XQuery Engine, an Information retrieval Engine, and an XML Repository. The user interface module gives a user an easy way to search XML documents and transforms a given user query to an equivalent XQuery. The XQuery Engine module takes an XQuery as input and provides a query plan for an information retrieval module as output. The information retrieval engine executes a query plan by communicating with the XML repository, which stores XML documents.

The XQuery Engine parses an input XQuery and constructs a syntax tree for the query. Then, it transforms the syntax tree into a query plan, called a Primitive Operation Tree (POT). Each node of a POT represents an atomic operation in terms of the information retrieval engine and can be interpreted and processed by the information retrieval engine. The result set is given back to the XQuery engine, which in turn transforms the result into an XML document of the form being required by the user interface. The final result in XML is returned back to the user interface.

Our approach has the following useful aspects. First, any user interface that generates XQuery is able to access any digital library system including our XQuery Engine. Second, we define a set of primitive operations for POTs so that they can become a standard interface between an XQuery Engine and an Information Retrieval Engine for our generic digital library system that supports XML documents. Third, some query optimizations over POTs can be done in the XQuery Engine so that better searching performance is expected.

Currently we are developing an XQuery Engine prototype. It will be installed inside an MPEG-7 based Digital Library System that supports content-based searching for images. The XQuery Specification is an ongoing working draft and is not completed yet. Since the current version of the XQuery specification does not define full functions for information retrieval, we need to extend XQuery syntax by adding some functions such as *rankby()*.

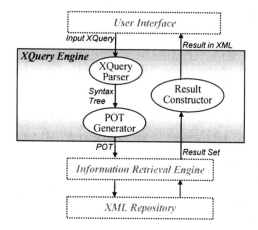

ACKNOWLEDGEMENTS

This research is supported by Software Research Center in Chungnam National University.

CephSchool: a Pedagogic Portal for Teaching Biological Principles with Cephalopod Molluscs

James B. Wood
CephSchool Project Manager
University of Texas Medical Branch
Galveston, TX 77555-1163
001 409 747-2934
jbwood@utmb.edu

Caitlin M.H. Shaw
University of Texas Medical Branch
Galveston, TX 77555-1163
001 409 722-2122
cmshaw@utmb.edu

CephBase is an online, user-friendly database directed towards the scientific community in order to disseminate information about cephalopods (a class of mollusks including octopus, cuttlefish, and nautilus). Although, our initial audience was scientists, we found that the majority of our users were students, educators, and the general public [1].

CephSchool is based on CephBase and will take the information present in CephBase's digital libraries and redirect it towards students and teachers. CephSchool will modernize the way students learn about basic biological processes by giving them a dynamic web page that will be updated as new information is made available. Textbooks are often dated. CephSchool will present very current data[1].

CephSchool will be organized into eight arms (OCTOPUS!)

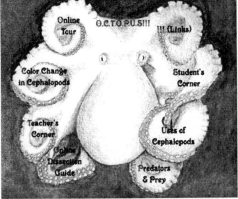

Figure 1: CephSchool index page.

and which will contain information about cephalopods, discussion topics, teacher support, and student assessment techniques. These eight sections will provide an accurate and inquiry base learning environment for students to learn basic biological concepts using cephalopods as the subject organism [2]. The information present in CephSchool will be supplemented with images, video and current scientific data.

Online Tour: This will give students a glimpse into the National Resource Center for Cephalopods (NRCC), a working cephalopod lab which "cultures and rears cephalopods for scientific uses as well as public aquaria" [2].

Cephalopod Behavior and Evolution: Cephalopods' ability to dynamically change shape and color has been a main driving force in their evolution [3]. In this section those color changing abilities will be explained and

explored and the students will be faced with the open ended question: "Do squid have a language?"

Teacher's Corner: This is a password protected portion of CephSchool intended to familiarize the teachers with CephSchool. We will provide potential PowerPoint presentations, test questions, and portfolios. It will also give the teachers a chance to give feedback on CephSchool, and an e-mail focus group to communicate with other teachers utilizing CephSchool.

Online Dissection Guide: This component of CephSchool will provide dissection guides for all four groups of cephalopods available at the NRCC. The dissection guides will contain still images as well as video. Still image and video will enrich this section.

Predators and prey: This section of CephSchool will incorporate the ecology of cephalopods and the role they play in marine environments. Basic ecological concepts will be discussed through this section.

Use of Cephalopods: This section will help students understand the high importance of cephalopod research in the biomedical world due to the large amount of research done on their physiology, reproduction, and genetics just to mention a few.

Students' corner: This section will pose potential project topics and will display select completed projects. It will also include "just for fun" test questions, and a list of free online scientific tools will be accessible.

!Links!: This component will include a list of cephalopod, marine biology, and science links for the students to use.

1. REFERENCES:

[1] Wood, J.B., Envisioning Education. ACM

[2] Shaw, Caitlin, From the Caribbean to the Indo-Pacific to hundreds of meters below: CephSchool Bringing Cephalopods into the Classroom through a Video Digital Library. ACM

[3] Packard A. Visual Tactics and Evolutionary Strategies. In: Cephalopods Present and Past. Wiedmann J. and J. Kullmann, ed. Schweizerbart'sche Verlagsbuchhandlung, Stuttgart, Germany. 1988: pp.89-103

VIVO -A Video Indexing and Visualization Organizer

Meng Yang, Xiangming Mu, & Gary Marchionini

School of Information and Library Science, University of North Carolina at Chapel Hill
CB 3360 100 Manning Hall, Chapel Hill, NC 27599-3360, (+ 1) 919-9663589
[yangm, mux, march]@ils.unc.edu

1. Introduction

Traditional video libraries only catalog and index videos at the piece level. Thus users can only search whole videos, however, they might also want to search specific segments of videos, such as a frame which has a child's face, or a scene of a train getting into a rail station. Digital videos need to be catalogued and indexed both on multiple levels (e.g. video, segment and frame) and through multiple modalities (e.g., textual description and visual surrogate).

2. VIVO system

VIVO (Video Indexing and Visualization Organizer) is such a prototype tool we developed to help digital video librarians to input, edit and manage video metadata elements on different levels. It is also part of the work in NSF-funded Open Video Digital Library [2]. Figure 1 shows the prototype interface for VIVO system. It has the following characteristics:

- Multiple levels

VIVO uses a hierarchical tree to organize the multiple-level (e.g., video, segment and frame) video structure. Each segment or frame can inherit some or all metadata elements such as date and creator from the video level, and also might have their own metadata such as format, description and subject. New video/segment/frames can be added to the tree structure.

- Multiple modality

VIVO supports both visual surrogate and textual metadata for each video level. For instance, each video has visual storyboard and textual metadata such as title and description. Each segment also has its own storyboard and textual metadata such as title and keywords. Each frame also has its own metadata and indexes such as title and color. Previous research [3] demonstrates that using visual surrogates such as storyboard can effectively help people to index videos.

Some additional features of VIVO include saving the xml file of a video metadata, playing the video or segment, and grabbing a frame while watching the video or get the

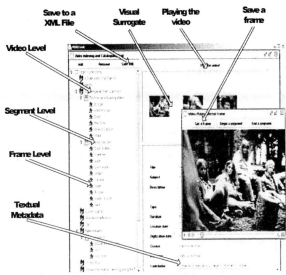

Figure 1. VIVO Interface

starting and end time for each new segment (see Figure 1). A preliminary user test for VIVO demonstrates its viability. The digital librarian for the Open Video Digital Library [2] appreciated the convenient links between video, segment and frame and stated that it would speed the current cataloguing and indexing process. Some users from the education school would also like to use VIVO to catalogue some classroom digital videos made for teacher training.

According to the feedback of preliminary user tests, some additional functions will be added to VIVO, such as controlled vocabulary for indexing and providing dynamic metadata elements for different users. More formal user studies will be conducted to further develop VIVO.

REFERENCES

[1] Open Video Digital Library, www.open-video.org

[2] Stachowicz, C. (2002). *The Effectiveness of Storyboard Surrogates in the Subject Indexing of Digital Video.* A Master's paper at University of North Carolina at Chapel Hill

This work was supported by NSF Grant # IIS 0099

The Roadies Take the Stage: On-going Development and Maintenance of the Legacy Tobacco Documents Library at the University of California San Francisco

Heidi Schmidt

University of California San Francisco Library/Center for Knowledge Management

530 Parnassus Avenue

San Francisco CA 94143

415-514-0186

heidi@library.ucsf.edu

1. INTRODUCTION

The Legacy Tobacco Documents Library (LTDL) was launched January 31, 2002. The launch was the successful completion of an intense one-year project to build a public digital library of approximately 4 million tobacco industry documents released under terms of the Master Settlement Agreement between US tobacco companies and the National Association of Attorneys General.

After being "open" for a year – and expanding the size of the collection by another million documents or so - the LTDL team is faced with several challenges. In this poster presentation, the presenter hopes to engage attendees in discussion of these challenges.

2. QUESTIONS FOR DISCUSSION

2.1 Middleware

We built the LTDL using the University of Michigan's DLXS middleware and the XPAT search engine. Some modifications were made to the software to optimize image displays and other features. The implementation we used – bibliographic class – does not readily accommodate searching text versions of document image files. We are faced with either a major upgrade of DLXS with the entanglements of modified code, or conversion to an entirely new middleware environment.

2.2 Search System Performance

The XPAT search engine we implemented with DLXS was an excellent choice for the initial LTDL deployment. The LTDL now has about 5 million documents comprised of about 38 million pages, however, and we are beginning to stress the search and retrieval capabilities of the system. We are looking at possibilities such as rewriting the middleware to optimize the use of multi-processor computing systems.

2.3 Collection Integration

The LTDL is the largest of several tobacco document digital libraries maintained by UCSF. Other collections were built through support of different agencies and with somewhat different objectives. The collections vary in size, content, metadata, user interface, the availability of text (from optical character recognition) for searching and the underlying databases, search engines and middleware code. Optimizing cross-collection searching would have benefits, but could result in sacrificing some of the value and uniqueness of individual collections. We also have concerns about how to present the collections so users can appreciate their unique characteristics without becoming confused.

2.4 Searchable Text

The LTDL is currently based on searchable metadata and document images. The ability to search the text of documents in the collection is an extremely high priority for researchers. Provided searchable text for the 5 million documents is made available, what consequences will adding text searching have on the middleware, database design, user interface and search functionality?

2.5 Document Formats

The LTDL acquires documents in different formats. At startup, most of the documents were TIF files. The library was designed to offer viewers a choice of TIF, PDF or GIF format for presentation. Format conversions are handled "on the fly." Documents added through harvesting tobacco industry sites are predominantly PDF's, and most users prefer PDF format. We are wondering if we should store documents in their original format in a "dark digital archive," and simplify active file management by using only PDF's.

3. ACKNOWLEDGMENTS

The work described in this poster session was supported by the American Legacy Foundation, the Robert Wood Johnson Foundation, the National Cancer Institute and the American Medical Association.

4. REFERENCES

[1] Legacy Tobacco Documents Library
http://legacy.library.ucsf.edu

BioSci Education Network (BEN) Collaborative

Linda Akli
AAAS
1200 New York Ave, NW
Washington, DC 20005
(202) 326-6671

lakli@aaas.org

Cal T. Collins
e-guana.net, Inc.
56 John F. Kennedy St., 3rd Floor
Cambridge, MA 02138
(617) 868-9669

cal@e-guana.net

Jason Smith
AAAS
1200 New York Ave, NW
Washington, DC 20005
(202) 326-8972

jsmith@aaas.org

Ron Butler
American Society for Microbiology

Amy Chang
American Society for Microbiology

Yolanda George
AAAS

Nancy Gough
AAAS/*Science's* STKE

Melinda Lowy
American Physiological Society

Marsha Matyas
American Physiological Socitey

Brandon Muramatsu
SMETE Open Federation

Susan Musante
American Society for Microbiology

Jason Taylor
Ecological Society of America

The BEN Collaborative, spearheaded by the American Association for the Advancement of Science (AAAS) and composed of professional societies and coalitions for biology education, is developing a revolutionary approach for transforming biology teaching and learning in undergraduate and graduate institutions, as well as professional schools. Through the development of a BEN portal site, the BEN Collaborative is providing users with searchable and seamless access to BEN Collaborators' digital library collections of accurate and reliable biology education resources.

Materials in the digital library are designed primarily for undergraduate biology educators, including ones that prepare K – 12 faculty members. Also, materials are useful for graduate and medical school educators. The materials are collected and maintained by respected professional societies representing a broad spectrum of biological sciences.

Currently there are fourteen BEN collaborators with over 1000 resources catalogued; covering fifty-one biological sciences disciplines and thirty-eight different types of resources ranging from articles and papers to images, animations, and simulations. The BEN Collaborative collection is anticipated to grow to more than 3,000 resources by 2004. Currently, there are 830 registered BEN users.

There are many challenges to collaboratively developing a portal site and digital collection that BEN has been able to meet, including:

1. Creating common resource descriptions using metadata and metadata vocabularies for collections that are in the same broad discipline but were originally developed for substantially different audiences and purposes.

2. Developing technical specifications that support a wide range of technical capabilities and infrastructures, and allow flexibility for adding new partners, collections, and resources.

3. Evaluating the metadata specification and vocabularies against the variety of approaches and vocabularies faculty use to locate resources and updating the specification with minimal impact to current metadata catalogs.

4. Addressing issues such as the implementation of metadata harvesting software on multiple hardware/software platforms, compatibility with a universal character set that represents all languages and symbols, and search engine scalability as the user base increases.

Ms. Imengel Mad
Palau Community College
imengelm@palau.edu

Abstract

*PALAU COMMUNITY COLLEGE-BELAU NATIONAL MUSEUM IMAGE ARCHIVES DIGITIZATION
AND ACCESS PROJECT*

*This poster presentation will describe a collaboration project between the Palau Community College
(PCC) Library and the Belau National Museum (BNM). The project, funded by a two-year U.S. Institute of
Museum and Library Services (IMLS) National Leadership Grant, will enhance access to the BNM Media
Collection. The Media Collection is in great demand, and the pressures of human use exacerbate an
already tenuous situation for the long-term preservation of the images. While digitization is not viewed as
the preservation solution, it will assist the Museum to lessen the impact of human handling. By making the
Media Collection more accessible through integration of the PCC Library's online catalog, a much wider
audience will be reached, and mishandling of the original images will be significantly reduced.*

*The PCC website, currently under final development will link the Library WebCollection Plus which will
contain digitized images selected from the extensive photo archives, as well as digitized images of the
ethnographic and other objects in the Museum's collection, including contemporary art. This poster
session will enable viewers to see the range of images included in the project.*

This poster presentation will enable researchers to learn how this project will support scholarly research.

Steps Towards Establishing Shared Evaluation Goals and Procedures in the National Science Digital Library

Tamara Sumner
*Chair, NSDL Evaluation and
Education Impact
Standing Committee
Department of Computer Science
University of Colorado at Boulder
sumner@colorado.edu*

Sarah Giersch
*Secretary, NSDL Evaluation and
Education Impact
Standing Committee
iLumina Digital Library
CollegisEduprise, Inc.
sgiersch@eduprise.com*

Casey Jones
*Core Integration Liaison, NSDL
Evaluation and Education Impact
Standing Committee
NSDL Central Office, UCAR
Boulder, Colorado
caseyj@ucar.edu*

Abstract

A community-based process was used to develope shared evaluation goals and instruments to begin evaluating the National Science Digital Library (NSDL). Results from a pilot study examining library usage, collections growth, and library governance processes are reported. The methods used in the pilot included web log usage analysis, collections assessment techniques, survey instruments, and semi-structured interviews.

1. Project Overview

The National Science Digital Library (NSDL) is envisioned to be a comprehensive source for resources, research and tools in science, technology, engineering and mathematics education. This NSF-funded program consists of over one hundred projects, led by principal investigators from a variety of institutions across the country. Some are developing collections, others are developing library services, some are engaged in library research, and one large effort is charged with developing core integration services. These core services include a central portal, a metadata repository, and the social and technical infrastructure necessary for integrating distributed libraries, services and collections.

Part of the social infrastructure supporting library integration includes a community governance process. This governance process includes Standing Committees charged with providing formative input into library development in a number of areas including content, sustainability, evaluation, etc. Evaluating NSDL is challenging due to its distributed nature; users are not interacting with a single system or artifact, they arrive into the library network from a variety of entry points that are separately designed and managed. Within this distributed context, the NSDL Evaluation and Educational Impact Standing Committee is developing shared instruments and procedures that work across a variety of libraries and programs to provide individual projects and the NSDL program as a whole with useful formative tools. Through an open, community-based participatory process, the Standing Committee has taken important steps towards creating a shared vision for evaluation as an integral activity within the NSDL. This consensual and participatory approach is crucial for enculturating evaluation activities and concerns within NSDL. A key activity of the committee to date has been to design and conduct a pilot study to examine the following four questions:

1. How are people using the libraries?

2. How are collections growing and changing?

3. How well are the distributed library building and governance processes working?

4. What is the time and effort required, both centrally and at distributed sites, to participate in this evaluation? Do the results justify this effort?

Six digital library projects participated in the pilot study, which ran for 3 months beginning 01 April 2002 and ending 30 June 2002. To examine the questions of library usage and collections growth, a suite of usage metrics and indicators were devised based on analyses of web server logs. Collections growth metrics and indicators examined changes in the amounts and types of metadata records over the period of the pilot. These were completed monthly, that is 3 times, during the pilot. A survey instrument was used to examine the question surrounding library building and governance processes. This survey was administered to project personnel at each participating pilot site. Interviews were conducted with selected respondents to help assess the overall value of the study to participating sites and the NSF.

2. Results

The results of the pilot study indicate that there is already considerable use of library sites within NSDL (millions of user sessions per month), and that library collections grew steadily during the pilot to just over a million objects. Significant amounts of content at participating sites were non-traditional in nature, i.e., discussion forums, newsletters, data archives, etc and as such do not have item-level metadata. A key finding from the survey is that personnel at distributed project sites perceive collaboration to be critical to success, at both the project and program levels, but are frustrated with perceived inadequacies in current communication and collaboration mechanisms. The most important outcomes of the pilot study concerned recommendations for improving the evaluation methodology and instruments, particularly with respect to data reliability and scalability. Study instruments, results, and recommendations are available at the NSDL Communications Portal (http://comm.nsdlib.org) and should be of use to other distributed library projects considering coordinated evaluation activities.

A Comparison of Two Educational Resource Discovery Systems

Tamara Sumner, Sonal Bhushan, Faisal Ahmad
Department of Computer Science
University of Colorado at Boulder
Campus Box 430
Boulder, Colorado 80309-0430
{sumner, sbhushan, fahmad} @colorado.edu

Lynne Davis
DLESE Program Center
University Corporation for Atmospheric Research
4700 Mitchell Road
Boulder, Colorado 80309-0430
lynne@ucar.edu

Abstract

We describe the results from a pilot study that compared two different discovery systems designed and built to operate in the same educational digital library – one based on searching over metadata records and another hybrid system which combined metadata and content-based indexing.

1. Overview

Educational digital libraries employ resource discovery systems that are aimed at providing educators and learners with curriculum materials to support learning in both formal and informal settings. We report here on the design and evaluation of an innovative hybrid educational resource discovery system that merges metadata and content-based information retrieval methods. Metadata-based retrieval methods search over library catalogs; i.e., sets of structured records that describe individual library resources. These records typically include information such as title, subject, description, resource type, URL, etc., and are usually created by skilled personnel. As such it requires human effort, experience, and cost to index and describe resources using this approach. Content-based discovery systems search across the resources themselves. These systems rely on automatic and often opaque methods of information indexing such as inverted indices [1] or complex term-weighting schemes [2]. As such, no human effort is required to describe and index library resources.

Both retrieval methods have their strengths and weaknesses, and our research considers how these methods can be blended to better serve the specific discovery needs of educators and learners. A hybrid discovery system was implemented and evaluated in the context of DLESE – the Digital Library for Earth System Education. In this system, the URL in the metadata record is used as the starting point for guided crawling and content-based indexing, only indexing pages that are within the resource. We do this in an attempt to ensure, to some degree, that the results returned from the content-based search have passed the library selection criteria and been formally accessioned into the library for discovery by users. A key design decision was to use a hierarchical representation in which a resource's list of pages resulting from the content-based search is 'framed' within the related metadata record, preserving the important contextual information provided by the metadata brief description. Within the frame, below the brief description, users are informed as to the number of pages within the resource satisfying their query. The top five pages are shown as embedded links where the HTML title attribute is constructed as a hyperlink to the actual web page.

2. Pilot Study

A pilot study was conducted to compare this hybrid system with an existing metadata-based system currently being used in DLESE, with the aim of finding out if the hybrid system helps educators locate relevant resources with less effort. Users were given two types of tasks, one involving well-specified criteria (find an object for a particular lesson plan) and one that was more open-ended (find a suite of objects as part of a course planning process). Each task was timed; users were given 7 and 20 minutes respectively for these two tasks. They were asked to bookmark resources they believed to be relevant. Their actions were recorded and an activity log was generated. The results were evaluated on the premise that well designed discovery systems reduce the overall amount of actions necessary to locate learning objects, where some of the necessary actions take place in the library and others take place in the resource itself.

The results of the pilot study suggests that the hybrid system helped decrease the variability in finding relevant resources, providing a more consistent and predictable user experience. This could be beneficial for educators preparing a lesson: to make use of digital libraries in this context, they need to be reasonably sure they can find useful resources within their tight time constraints. The results also suggest that the hybrid system was more effective at pointing educators toward individual learning objects. There was also an indication that within the hybrid system, educators spent more time exploring search results, whereas in the metadata system, they spent more time conducting searches. Thus, it can be argued that while the effort to locate relevant resources was similar across the two systems, the hybrid system helped users to spend their time more productively.

3. References

[1] Berger, A. and J. Lafferty (1999). *Information retrieval as statistical translation.* 22nd Int'l ACM/SIGIR Conference on Research and Development in Information Retrieval, Berkeley.

[2] Tomasic, A. and H. Garcia-Molina (1992). Performance of inverted indices in distributed text document retrieval systems. Palo Alto, Technical Report STAN-CS-92-1434, Stanford University Department of Computer Science.

Collections and Access Policies of the Digital Material of Ten National Libraries

Alexandros Koulouris, Sarantos Kapidakis
Ionian University. Department of Archive and Library Sciences
Plateia Eleftherias, Palea Anaktora, Corfu 49100, Greece
akoul@ionio.gr, sarantos@ionio.gr

Abstract

There is an ongoing effort from the National Libraries to provide digital content. We encompass the digital collections of ten National Libraries. We examine and analyze the access policies that the ten National Libraries implement, based on the variation of their digital content and the diversification of their access policies. The National Libraries are the following: Library of Congress, British Library, National Library of Australia, National Library of New Zealand, National Library of Canada, National Library of Wales, National Library of Scotland, National Library of Finland, National Library of Greece and National Library of the Netherlands. Our goal is to discover the differences among the implemented access policies of these National Libraries.

In this poster, we explore the collections and the applied access policies, when the digital material is free or restricted or the reproduction requires written permission or fees.

We classify the implemented access policies according to their characteristics. We examine the differences among the implemented access policies and we generalize the solution approaches combining the varying parameters and other relevant emerging ones.

The implemented access policies differ in various aspects. We generalize them into one unified policy, which can implement the specific policies by varying some of its parameters. We study these parameters and explain their most useful alternative values and their semantics. We also foresee new policy parameters, such as charging for access, the delivery method, the permission for reproduction etc., which will be appropriate to more complex policies that will be needed soon.

The National Libraries provide free access for onsite and offsite users for the metadata and the non-copyrighted digital material. The variations on their policies mostly refer to the way they handle the copyrighted material. Nearly always, the National Libraries give free access to onsite users for copyrighted material, with few exceptions. The access for offsite users is diversified depending on the collection. However, in most cases, onsite and offsite users have unrestrictedly access to the copyrighted digital material. The Libraries trust the users and present it to them directly.

Some National Libraries (e.g. National Library of Wales etc.), plan on charging offsite users for copyrighted digital material but they delay the implementation possibly because of the absence of candidate policies. In some cases, written permission is needed for the reproduction of the digital material usually for non-private use, but not for online access. In addition, the Library or any other copyright owner may require a fee for the reproduction. While, the fee given to the copyright owner is copyright fee the fee given to the Library may refer to reproduction or conservation costs (e.g. National Library of New Zealand etc.).

At this moment, most libraries have only digitized or made digitally available, part of their material, the one that is simpler in accessing restrictions, which was simpler to implement and more appropriate to do first. As this process evolves and matures, the libraries want to make more material available and this will force them to handle material that is more complex in terms of copyright and access. The policies that will be applied for accessing this new material will necessarily be more detailed and complex. Thus, the new policy variations must be predicted and standardized.

In the proposed generalized access policy, we classify the users up to four groups that have non-increasing access abilities, as will be defined by the implemented policy. We also classify new charging and delivery parameters for use or reproduction of the non-free digital material. The delivery method could be online when the permission granting is automatic. When written permission is involved, the Library or other permission granter can also provide the digital material online, mainly through ILL.

In conclusion, the digital content is increasing. However, the selection of the access policies is crucial for the acceptance and maintenance of the digital libraries. The success of any conventional or digital library depends on the usage of its material from the users. The usage of the material depends on the selection of the access policy.

To extend this work, it would be interesting to relate the access and the reproduction policies with the way that the library has acquired the material and examine more Libraries.

Session 11: Closing Keynote

**Tom Moritz, Boeschenstein Director, Library Services,
American Museum of Natural History**

Cross-Cultural Usability for Digital Libraries

Nadia Caidi
Faculty of Information Studies
University of Toronto, Canada
caidi@fis.utoronto.ca

Anita Komlodi
Department of Information Systems
University of Maryland, Baltimore County
komlodi@umbc.edu

Abstract

The scope and reach of digital libraries (DL) is truly global, spanning geographical and cultural boundaries, yet few scholars have investigated the influence of culture as it pertains to the design and use of digital libraries. This workshop will examine cross-cultural issues around the use and development of DLs, especially as they relate to supporting cross-cultural usability of DLs.

1. Aims and Objectives

The advent of information and communication technologies (ICTs) is said to have precipitated the blurring of geographical boundaries and made us into a 'global village.' Yet, few scholars have investigated the ways in which digital libraries have been used across cultures. Previous research on the use of online public access catalogs [1] and Internet search tools [2] have shown differences in how users from different cultural groups searched for information. These differences in behavior have implications for the usable design of DLs.

Like any socio-technical system, a digital library embodies the values, beliefs and practices of its producers along with their broader social and cultural contexts. A user with different sets of beliefs and assumptions about the organization of the content, the categories assigned or the user interface design may find it hard to interact with the system. Lessons learned from cross-cultural usability and international user interface design are thus important for the design of DLs. Equally important is the study of the information-seeking behavior of users from various cultural groups.

The goals of this workshop are: 1) to increase awareness about the area of cross-cultural usability in the digital library community, 2) to identify new tools, techniques and methodologies for cross-cultural study of user behavior in DLs and international user interface design, and 3) to provide a forum for generating new research directions and cross-disciplinary collaboration. The format will be highly interactive. In addition to reviews of actual projects being undertaken, attendees will be asked to contribute real examples of successful (and/or poor) interfaces and website designs. The outcome of the workshop will be the establishment of a road map for this type of research, which includes the identification of key issues/questions around cross-cultural usability (e.g., user interface design guidelines, methodological considerations, etc.). All information will be posted on the workshop's website.

Papers will be reviewed by a panel of experts consisting of: Christine L. Borgman, UCLA, Andrew Dillon, University of Texas, Austin, Elke Duncker, Middlesex University (UK), Elaine Toms, University of Toronto (Canada), Noriko Kando, National Institute of Informatics, Tokyo, (Japan), and Preben Hansen, Swedish Institute of Computer Science, Kista (Sweden).

2. Workshop Organizers

Nadia Caidi is an Assistant Professor at the Faculty of Information Studies, University of Toronto. Her research interests are social and community informatics. She teaches and is involved in cross-cultural and comparative studies, researching the influence of culture on the creation, access and use of information and its technologies.

Anita Komlodi is an Assistant Professor at the Department of Information Systems, UMBC. Her research interests are at the intersections of human-computer interaction and information retrieval (IR). She is especially interested in the design and usability of IR interfaces. She also researches the information-seeking behavior of users from various cultural backgrounds.

References

[1] E. Duncker. Cross-cultural usability of the library metaphor. In *Proceedings of the JCDL*, pages 223–230, 2002.
[2] M. Iivonen and M. D. White. The choice of initial web search strategies: A comparison between finnish and american searchers. *Journal of Documentation*, 57(4):465–491, 2001.

International Workshop on Information Visualization Interfaces for Retrieval and Analysis (IVIRA) at the Joint Conference on Digital Libraries 2003

Javed Mostafa & Katy Börner
1320 E. 10ᵗʰ St. LI025
Indiana University, Bloomington, 47405-3907
{jm,katy}@indiana.edu

Abstract

The IVIRA workshop has been organized to attract cutting-edge efforts that concentrate on improving information retrieval and analysis by applying visualization techniques in interface design.

1. Introduction

Voluminous and complex nature of information in digital libraries demands more powerful means of human-computer interaction than what is currently available. Advances in information visualization point to new possibilities for developing enhanced interfaces for improving retrieval, interaction, and management of data stored in digital libraries. We are planning to merge two successful JCDL workshops held last year (see section 5) and hold a single workshop this year.

2. Workshop scope

The workshop will cover both theoretical and experimental research on the development, usage, and evaluation of effective interfaces to digital libraries. Of particular interest is research that exploits visualization to support improved browsing, retrieval, analysis, and understanding of domains represented in digital libraries. Interfaces for the following types of resources are of special interest to this workshop:

- Textual documents (literature databases)
- Statistical data
- Multimedia or mixed-media data
- Geo-spatial data
- Genomics and proteomics data
- Time-variant or dynamic data

3. Workshop objectives

The main objectives are: 1) to increase awareness of the area of visual interfaces to DLs, 2) to identify new tools, techniques, and design methodologies for visual interfaces to DLs, 3) to learn about design approaches that support rich visualization functions in diverse systems ranging from desktops to mobile devices, 4) to develop frameworks, models, and theories of data access, management, and system evaluation, and 5) to provide a forum for generating new directions in research and development, identify funding sources, and support collaborations.

4. Expected audience

Researchers and practitioners with expertise and interest in information visualization, user interfaces for DLs, search/retrieval, human-computer interaction, interface design methodologies, and evaluation.

5. Related publications

More information on this year's and last year's workshops can be found at:

- http://vw.indiana.edu/ivira03/
- http://vw.indiana.edu/visual02/jcdl.html
- http://xtasy.slis.indiana.edu/jcdlui/uiws.html.

As with last year's visualization workshop, Springer-Verlag will be contacted to produce the workshop proceedings (see: http://www.springer.de/comp/lncs/).

6. Program committee

Katy Börner and Javed Mostafa,
Indiana University, Bloomington, USA (Chairs)
Kevin Boyack, Sandia National Laboratory, USA
Robin Burke, DePaul University, USA
Chaomei Chen, Drexel University, USA
Martin Dodge, University College London, UK
James French, Univ. of Virginia, Charlottesville, USA
Xia Lin, Drexel University, USA
André Skupin, University of New Orleans, USA
Kiduk Yang, Indiana University, Bloomington, USA

Building a Meaningful Web:
From Traditional Knowledge Organization Systems to New Semantic Tools

Gail M. Hodge
IIa, Inc.
gailhodge@aol.com

Marcia Lei Zeng
Kent State Univ.
mzeng@kent.edu

Dagobert Soergel
Univ. of Maryland
ds52@umail.umd.edu

Abstract

This Networked Knowledge Organization Systems/Services (NKOS) workshop focused on the transformation of traditional knowledge organization systems (KOSs) to new forms of knowledge representation that are being developed to support a more semantic-based, meaningful Web environment. The goal of the workshop was to identify principles from more traditional practices that can contribute to the design of new knowledge organization systems and ways to exploit the extensive intellectual capital available in traditional KOSs when developing new KOS tools.

Traditional KOSs include a broad range of system types from term lists to classification systems and complex thesauri. Term lists may be simple authority lists. Classification systems put resources in broad groups or "buckets". Traditional thesauri are built on broader-narrower, synonymous and associative (or related term) relationships. These and other traditional KOSs were developed in a print environment or in the early days of computerized databases to control the vocabulary used when indexing and searching a specific product, such as a bibliographic database, or when organizing a physical collection such as a library.

New forms of knowledge representation include ontologies, topic maps, and other semantic Web components. The relationships between concepts in these tools are richer. In particular, the associative relationships and broader-narrower relationships are defined in more detail. New semantic tools emphasize the ability of the computer to process the KOS against a body of text, rather than support the human indexer or trained searcher. These tools are intended for use in the broader, more uncontrolled context of the Web to support information discovery by a larger community of interest or by Web users in general.

While the traditional KOSs and newer tools are related, the development of the newer forms of KOS tools has, on the whole, not taken advantage of traditional KOSs. There is little understanding of how traditional tools can be transformed for the demands of the Web environment and whether there are lessons that can be learned from the decades of development and maintenance of these traditional systems.

This workshop compared the traditional KOSs and new approaches to improving the semantic capabilities of the Web. Best practices and lessons learned from the development, maintenance and use of traditional KOSs were identified. Descriptions of projects involving the transformation of traditional KOSs to newer forms emphasized the transition process, including the analysis of the traditional KOS, and the characteristics of the KOS that could be carried through to the new tool. The presenters also discussed the degree to which the traditional KOS and the new tool would be used together in the future, whether there would be parallel or separate maintenance activities, etc.

Presenters described the development of specific Web service functionality applicable to KOSs. The benefits of this service-based approach and the possibility of universal or community-based KOS services were explored.

In addition to formal presentations, the workshop participants gave brief updates on their work or interest in this area. A facilitated discussion identified areas where standards, best practices, technologies, or more research are needed to take advantage of the investment in traditional KOSs when developing new tools.

NKOS is an ad hoc group devoted to the discussion of KOSs as networked interactive information services to support the description and retrieval of diverse information resources through the Internet. This is the 6th in a series of NKOS workshops held in conjunction with JCDL. More information about NKOS is available from http://nkos.slis.kent.edu/.

OAI Metadata Harvesting Workshop

Simeon Warner
Computing and Information Science
Cornell University, Ithaca, NY, USA
simeon@cs.cornell.edu

Abstract

This workshop will bring together people with Open Archives Initiative (OAI) [1] metadata harvesting experience to discuss problems, their solutions, and to identify best practices. The focus will be on near- to medium-term practical issues. Participants will have the opportunity to discuss problems or raise issues that they have encountered and will benefit from the shared experience of the other participants. The workshop will combine and distill the OAI harvesting knowledge and experience of the participants to detail 1) best practices and existing solutions to particular harvesting problems; and 2) unresolved problems and issues with current implementations, the specification, or limitations of version 2.0 the OAI protocol for metadata harvesting (OAI-PMH) [2]. The conclusions of the workshop will be disseminated to the wider OAI community.

Topics and format

Workshop participants are invited to present short papers papers on issues of particular concern. Topics may include, but are not limited to:

- scalability issues
- response size, response compression
- XML response validity/parsing/robustness
- response size and number of requests/responses to harvest/re-harvest/update
- automated repository discovery (including the friends schema)
- metadata formats (mandatory unqualified DC, qualified DC)
- use and interpretation of metadata in <about> blocks
- harvester notification mechanisms (is there a need?)
- expected future problems

The morning will be divided into short sessions where participants will use half the time to present a short paper on a particular issue and proposed or possible solutions. The other half of each session will be reserved for moderated discussion. The first part of the afternoon will be reserved for in-depth discussion of the most interesting or difficult issues identified in the morning session. The remainder of the afternoon will be devoted to identification of issues upon which there is consensus and those for which further work is required.

Participation

Participation is open to those who have OAI harvesting experience. Participants will be expected describe their OAI harvesting experience in a brief position statement, and to propose a topic or topics for discussion. Selected participants will be invited to present a short paper to describe and seed discussion on a topic they proposed.

Dissemination

The collected position statements, short papers and conclusions of the workshop will be made available on the workshop web site [3]. The conclusions may also be published elsewhere.

References

[1] Open Archives Initiative web site:
http://www.openarchives.org/

[2] Carl Lagoze, Herbert Van de Sompel, Michael Nelson and Simeon Warner (editors) (2002), *The Open Archives Initiative Protocol for Metadata Harvesting v2.0. http://www.openarchives.org/ OAI/2.0/openarchivesprotocol.htm*

[3] *Workshop web site: http://www.cs.cornell.edu/ people/simeon/workshops/JCDL2003*

Author Index

IEEE Computer Society Publications
The world-renowned IEEE Computer Society publishes, promotes, and distributes a wide variety of authoritative computer science and engineering texts. These books are available from most retail outlets. Visit the CS Store at *http://computer.org* for a list of products.

IEEE Computer Society Proceedings
The IEEE Computer Society also produces and actively promotes the proceedings of more than 160 acclaimed international conferences each year in multimedia formats that include hard and soft-cover books, CD-ROMs, videos, and on-line publications.

For information on the IEEE Computer Society proceedings, please e-mail to csbooks@computer.org or write to Proceedings, IEEE Computer Society, P.O. Box 3014, 10662 Los Vaqueros Circle, Los Alamitos, CA 90720-1314. Telephone +1-714-821-8380. Fax +1-714-761-1784.

Additional information regarding the Computer Society, conferences and proceedings, CD-ROMs, videos, and books can also be accessed from our web site at *http://computer.org/cspress*

Revised 11 March 2002